# Sociology: Windows on Society

## An Anthology

## Seventh Edition

Robert H. Lauer

Jeanette C. Lauer

*Alliant International University*

OXFORD

UNIVERSITY PRESS

D1502239

# OXFORD
UNIVERSITY PRESS

Oxford University Press, Inc., publishes works that further Oxford University's
objective of excellence in research, scholarship, and education.

Oxford  New York
Auckland  Cape Town  Dar es Salaam  Hong Kong  Karachi
Kuala Lumpur  Madrid  Melbourne  Mexico City  Nairobi
New Delhi  Shanghai  Taipei  Toronto

With offices in
Argentina  Austria  Brazil  Chile  Czech Republic  France  Greece
Guatemala  Hungary  Italy  Japan Poland  Portugal  Singapore
South Korea  Switzerland  Thailand  Turkey  Ukraine  Vietnam

First published 2005 by Roxbury Publishing Company
Published by Oxford University Press, Inc.
198 Madison Avenue, New York, New York 10016
http://www.oup.com

Oxford is a registered trademark of Oxford University Press

Library of Congress Cataloging-in-Publication Data available

ISBN 978-0-19-533052-6

*We wish to dedicate this book to those who have taught us the joy of life: Jon, Kathy, Julie, Jeffrey, Kate, Jeff, Krista, Benjamin, David, and John Robert.*

# Contents

## Unit I: The Sociological Enterprise

---

\* Indicates chapters new to this edition.

# Unit II: Culture, Socialization, and Social Interaction

---

\* Indicates chapters new to this edition.

# Unit III: Inequality

---

* Indicates chapters new to this edition.

* Indicates chapters new to this edition.

---

\* Indicates chapters new to this edition.

\* Indicates chapters new to this edition.

# Unit V: Social Processes

---

* Indicates chapters new to this edition.

# Introduction

Any anthology for introductory sociology has two somewhat contradictory obligations: (1) to be interesting, current, and accessible to its readers and (2) to fairly represent what the discipline is all about. We say that these are contradictory requirements because introductory students are not necessarily interested in, or equipped to fully understand, the many sociological studies that are published. Moreover, sociologists are not always concerned with examining issues that are timely or topical nor do they write for student readers. In an attempt to strike a balance between these contradictory ideals, we have tried to emphasize sociological substance without sacrificing interest and readability.

## The Readings

In order to encourage student debate about sociological issues facing society today, this anthology provides a wide variety of articles from contemporary sources as well the classical literature of sociology. Classic selections include readings from the works of Marx, Weber, and Durkheim—all of which are both central to the classic tradition and highly readable.

Contemporary selections in the Seventh Edition have been updated to include topics of current interest and concern, such as egalitarianism in marriage and family life; sexuality; the meaning of masculinity; the sources of poverty; the struggles of women of color in academe; sexism in everyday matters; civil liberties in the face of terrorism; the problem of underemployment; and meeting people through the Internet.

Gender is a major focus of this anthology because it is of central concern to people everywhere and is fundamental to many social and political issues in the United States. Moreover, gender has been at the heart of some of the most exciting sociological research of recent years. In addition, we emphasize the issues of race/ethnicity and inequality because of their significance in American history and in sociological research.

The selections in this anthology also challenge preconceived notions and conventional wisdom by showing the distinctive power of a sociological viewpoint. As the title suggests, the selections in this anthology can be viewed as "windows" on society. They permit you to see everyday activities in a new light—from the familiar (Bernstein's article on ways that students justify not working) to the more exotic (Harris' study on India's worship of the sacred cow).

A few of the articles in *Sociology: Windows on Society* may prove difficult reading. Nevertheless, we have decided to include these selections for two reasons. First, they are important in accurately presenting what the discipline of sociology is all about. Second, they provide an opportunity to master difficult material—an opportunity that can increase your knowledge and hone your academic skills.

## Organization

*Windows* is divided into five units. Unit I introduces the enterprise of sociology, illustrating both the perspectives sociologists take and the kinds of methods they use. Unit II features topics related to culture, socialization, and social interaction. Unit III considers various forms of social inequality based on class, race/ethnicity, gender, and international stratification, while Unit IV focuses primarily on social institutions. Finally, Unit V addresses two broad social processes—deviance and social change.

*Windows* can stand alone or be used as a supplement to a standard introductory text. The chart on page xiv cross-references topic areas that commonly appear in introductory sociology texts to related selections in this anthology. Both the primary and secondary emphases of each chapter are listed. This will facilitate use of *Windows* as a supplement to any major text.

To facilitate understanding, we have highlighted major concepts in the introductions to the units and the selections. Review questions, suggested applications, and related Web sites follow each selection. The applications and Web sites can serve as class or small group projects; they offer an opportunity to experience how the process of sociological research is conducted.

The updated *Instructor's Manual/Testing Program* gives suggestions for classroom use of each selection, lists key points, and provides both essay questions and multiple-choice questions. We hope that these materials will assist instructors in opening the *Windows* on the sociological enterprise to their students.

## In Appreciation

The editors and publisher express appreciation to the following individuals whose feedback and revision suggestions helped us prepare the Seventh Edition: Francis O. Adeola (University of New Orleans), Grace Auyang (University of Cincinnati, Raymond), Janet Bogdan (LeMoyne College), Marisol Clark-Ibáñez (California State University, San Marcos), Linda Jasper (Indiana University Southeast), Catherine Petrissans (Clarion University), Rasby Marlene Powell (University of North Carolina–Pembroke), Kent Sandstrom (University of Northern Iowa), and Jeffrey Sherman (Kirkwood Community College). ◆

# Use of Selections

*Sociology: **Windows on Society,*** Seventh Edition, comfortably stands alone as a single assigned text. However, most instructors use this anthology to supplement another text. These instructors may find the following chart, which groups the selections, helpful. Primary and secondary emphases are listed separately.

| Generic topics for an introductory sociology course: | *Windows* selections in which the topic is a primary emphasis: | *Windows* selections in which the topic is a secondary emphasis: |
|---|---|---|
| Introduction | 1, 4 | 2, 3 |
| Research methods | 2, 3, 4, 5 | 9, 18, 19, 36, 40, 41 |
| Culture | 6, 7, 8 | 11, 19, 26, 30, 34, 37, 43 |
| Socialization | 9, 10 | 32, 33, 34 |
| Social interaction | 5, 12, 13, 37 | 6, 21, 22, 25, 32, 33 |
| Social stratification | 14, 15, 16, 23 | 17, 29, 32, 35, 38, 42, 43 |
| Racial/ethnic groups | 8, 17, 18, 19, 28 | 13, 31, 36 |
| Gender | 5, 9, 10, 11, 12, 20, 21, 22 | 8, 16, 24 |
| Sexuality | 8, 11 | 22, 26, 36, 39 |
| Family | 16, 24, 25, 26 | 5, 9, 13, 21, 34, 41 |
| Government/politics | 27, 28, 44 | 14, 15, 18, 31, 35 |
| Economy | 15, 17, 23, 29, 30, 31 | 6, 14, 27, 34, 40, 42, 43 |
| Religion | 30, 34, 42 | 3, 6 |
| Education | 32, 33 | 2, 9, 17, 34 |
| Health and medicine | 35, 36 | 21, 39 |
| Deviance | 39, 40, 41 | 3 |
| Collective behavior/social movements | 27, 41, 44 | 36 |
| Demography/urbanization | 41, 42 | 18 |
| Technology/social change | 37, 38, 42, 43, 44 | 6, 7, 10, 23 |

# Contributors

**Barbara A. Arrighi** teaches sociology at Northern Kentucky University.

**Philip Aspden** is the executive director of the Center for Research on the Information Society, Pennington, New Jersey.

**Nancy V. Baker** is Associate Professor in the Department of Government at New Mexico State University.

**Joel Best** teaches sociology at Southern Illinois University at Carbondale. He is the author of *Threatened Children* (1990) and the editor of *Images of Issues* and *Troubling Children: Studies of Children and Social Problems.*

**Robert Blendon** is Professor of Health Policy and Management at the Harvard School of Public Health.

**Darcia Harris Bowman** is a staff writer for Education Week.

**Trudy Bush** is an associate editor of Christian Century.

**Dwight Conquergood** teaches in the Performance Studies Department at Northwestern University.

**Rosemarie Dibiase** is Associate Professor of Education and Human Services at Suffolk University, Boston, MA.

**Emile Durkheim** (1858–1917) is considered one of the principle founders of modern sociology. His major works include *The Division of Labor in Society* (1893), *Rules of Sociological Method* (1895), *Suicide* (1897), and *The Elementary Forms of Religious Life* (1912).

**Kathleen J. Ferraro** teaches sociology at Arizona State University.

**Katherine Frank** is an Assistant Professor of Cultural Anthropology at the College of the Atlantic in Bar Harbor, Maine. She is the author of *G-Strings and Sympathy: Strip Club Regulars and Male Desire.*

**Marvin Harris,** a well-known contemporary anthropologist, has published numerous books including *Cows, Pigs, Wars and Witches, Cannibals and Kings, Our Kind,* and *Culture, People and Nature.*

**Dan K. Hibbler** is an Assistant Professor in the Department of Health, Physical Education, and Recreation at Florida International University.

**Thomas A. Hirschl** is Professor of Sociology and Director of the Population and Development Program at Cornell University.

**Gerald T. Horiuchi** teaches sociology at California State University, Fresno.

**Donald W. Huffman** is Professor of Sociology at Cedar Crest College, Allentown, Pennsylvania.

**Martin Sánchez Jankowski** teaches sociology at the University of California, Berkeley, and is chair of the Chicano/Latino Policy Project sponsored by the Institute for the Study of Social Change, also at Berkeley. He is the author of *City Bound: Urban Life and Political Attitudes Among Chicago Youth* and *Islands in the Street: Gangs and American Urban Society.*

**Leif Jensen** is Professor of Rural Sociology and Demography at The Pennsylvania State University.

**John M. Johnson** teaches sociology at Arizona State University.

**James E. Katz** is director of social science research at Bell Communications Research, Morristown, New Jersey.

**Karl Marx** (1818–1883) is best known for *The Communist Manifesto* (published with Friedrich Engels in 1848) and *Das Kapital* (1867, 1885, 1894). His concern with, and analysis of, social issues makes him important to sociology.

**David S. Meyer** is Associate Professor of Sociology and Political Science at the University of California, Irvine. He is the co-editor of *Social Movements: Identity, Culture, and the State.*

**Jeffrey S. McQuillen** is Assistant Professor in the Communications Department of the University of Texas–Pan American.

**C. Wright Mills** (1916–1962) was a leading critic of modern American civilization.

Among his books are *White Collar, The Power Elite, Sociology and Pragmatism, Power, Politics and People,* and with H. H. Gerth, *From Max Weber: Essays in Sociology.*

**Joyce Munsch** is in the Department of Child and Adolescent Development at California State University, Northridge.

**Sumie Okazaki** teaches in the Department of Psychology, University of Illinois at Urbana–Champaign.

**William M. Pinsof** is President of the Family Institute at Northwestern University and Director of the Center for Applied Psychological and Family Studies.

**Mark R. Rank** is Professor of Social Welfare in the George Warren Brown School of Social Work, Washington University, St. Louis. His most recent book is *One Nation, Underprivileged: Why American Poverty Affects Us All.*

**Alan Reifman** teaches in the Department of Human Development and Family Studies at Texas Tech University.

**Barbara J. Risman** teaches sociology at North Carolina State University. Her books include *Gender in Intimate Relationships* (with Pepper Schwartz) and *Gender Vertigo: American Families in Transition.*

**Lillian B. Rubin** is a psychologist and a sociologist. She teaches at CUNY–Queens College. Her books include *Worlds of Pain, Women of a Certain Age, Intimate Strangers, Just Friends,* and *Erotic Wars: What Happened to the Sexual Revolution?*

**Kent L. Sandstrom** teaches sociology at the University of Northern Iowa. He is the coauthor, with Gary Alan Fine, of *Knowing Children: Participant Observation with Minors.* He has also published articles on media conceptions of community planning and parental attitudes toward youth work.

**Robin G. Sawyer** is Associate Professor in the Department of Health Education, University of Maryland.

**Glenn R. Schiraldi** is Instructor in the Department of Health Education, University of Maryland.

**Joshua Sharfstein** is a pediatrician who teaches at the Boston University School of Medicine.

**Kimberly J. Shinew** is Associate Professor of Leisure Studies at the University of Illinois at Urbana–Champaign.

**JoEllen Shively** teaches sociology at the Center for Research on Social Organization at the University of Michigan.

**Gregory Squires** teaches sociology at the University of Wisconsin–Milwaukee.

**Janet K. Swim** is Associate Professor of Psychology at The Pennsylvania State University. She has published extensively in the areas of prejudice, discrimination, and sexism.

**Caroline Sotello Viernes Turner** is Professor of Educational Leadership and Policy Studies at Arizona State University.

**Max Weber** (1864–1920) is another of the founders of modern sociology. His major works include The Protestant Ethic and the Spirit of Capitalism, Theory of Social and Economic Organization, and Methodology of the Social Sciences.

**Susan D. Witt** is Assistant Professor, School of Family and Consumer Sciences, The University of Akron.

**Hong-Sik Yoon** teaches in the Department of Social Welfare, Chonbuk National University, Jeonju, Korea.

---

Biographical information has been provided where available. Some authors do not appear in this list. ✦

# Unit I

## *The Sociological Enterprise*

Why sociology? In simplest terms, the answer is that human behavior cannot be fully understood and explained by such things as personality or genetic makeup. Humans are social creatures, and can only be understood as you take into the account the social context in which they function. Sociologists, then, study social groups and individuals as members of those groups (a group can be anything from a friendship clique to a family to social categories like gender, race, and age). Sociological studies give you a clearer view of human life, a set of windows on society that should enhance your understanding both of society and of yourself.

Every discipline uses a distinctive set of concepts to explain the phenomena studied. The "mass" of physicists, the "behavior modification" of psychologists, the "supply and demand" of economists, the "acculturation" of anthropologists, and the "pluralist model of power" of political scientists are among the concepts used by various disciplines. Sociologists also employ concepts in an effort to be more precise about explanations. In various unit, part, and selection introductions, therefore, we will briefly explain the important concepts that are introduced. Some of these concepts are words that are commonly used. However, they have particular (and sometimes different) meanings in sociology and constitute the distinctive vocabulary of sociological study.

This first unit examines different aspects of the sociological enterprise. The first article discusses the "sociological imagination," a distinctive vision of sociology as a discipline. The following two articles demonstrate the diversity of styles in sociological analysis. The next article is an example of critical thinking, an essential part of sociological analysis. The last article illustrates the important distinction between, and use of, micro and macro factors in sociological research. ✦

# Part One

## *The Sociological Perspective*

Sociology is the scientific study of social life. The founders of sociology wanted to improve the quality of human life and realized that in order to do so they had to understand the workings of society. Their attempt to understand those workings led to the development of the sociological perspective.

The meaning of the sociological perspective is captured in the notion of the **sociological imagination,** a term coined by C. Wright Mills, the author of the first selection. It refers to a way of thinking that enables people to understand the impact of culture, society, and group memberships on their behavior. In contrast to those who try to understand human behavior by studying internal processes in individuals, sociologists explain behavior by examining the social factors that circumscribe the lives of all individuals. ✦

# 1

# The Sociological Imagination

## C. Wright Mills

Sociology has a unique place among the social and behavioral sciences. As a discipline, it studies many of the same phenomena as other social sciences but from a distinct vantage point. For example, both sociologists and economists study unemployment. But while economists are more interested in how the rate of unemployment is associated with other economic indicators, sociologists are more likely to be concerned with the broader social context in which joblessness occurs. They ask, is **unemployment** (the number of people out of work and actively looking for jobs) the result of social policies adopted by the government or by multinational corporations? More important, sociologists may want to learn the social consequences of unemployment. Does the crime rate rise? Does the incidence of family disruption or domestic violence increase?

Like psychology, sociology is concerned with the individual. Rather than studying the individual in isolation, however, sociologists prefer to examine how each person is socially situated and affected by social factors. How has his or her life been shaped by social class, race and ethnicity, gender, age, and so forth? **Social classes** are groups that are unequal with regard to things valued in a society, such as income, power, and prestige. **Ethnicity** refers to shared cultural background that leads people to identify with each other; hispanics, for example, are an ethnic group. **Gender** is the social male and female, as distinct from **sex,** the biological male and female. Considerable debate exists about the extent to which the characteristics and behavior of males and females are rooted in social or biological factors.

Sociologists point out that all such social factors come to bear on people's behavior. We are social creatures, so that even our individual self-expression is related to social circumstances. For instance, a person who is shy by nature is more likely to behave differently when forced to take center stage in a social event, such as a family celebration.

In the following selection, Mills presents his version of the distinctive focus of sociology. In his view, the sociological imagination is reflected by the place of the individual in society and the place of that society in history. Mills looks at social phenomena from the perspective of **conflict theory,** a theory that focuses on contradictory interests, inequalities, and the resulting outcomes. Those outcomes include conflict and **social change** (alterations in social factors at various levels of social life from the individual to the global).

Ironically, in the late 1950s, when this piece was written, Mills did not foresee that a greater consciousness of gender would render obsolete the use of the term "men" for both men and women. Nevertheless, his ideas still serve to this day as an excellent guide to the nature of sociology.

Nowadays men often feel that their private lives are a series of traps. They sense that within their everyday worlds, they cannot overcome their troubles, and in this feeling, they are often quite correct: What ordinary men are directly aware of and what they try to do are bounded by the private orbits in which they live; their visions and their powers are limited to the close-up scenes of job, family, neighborhood; in other milieux, they move vicariously and remain spectators. And the more aware they become, however vaguely, of ambitions and of threats which transcend their immediate locales, the more trapped they seem to feel.

Underlying this sense of being trapped are seemingly impersonal changes in the very structure of continent-wide societies. The facts of contemporary history are also facts about the success and the failure of individual men and women. When a society is industrialized, a peasant becomes a worker; a feudal lord is liquidated or becomes a businessman. When classes rise or fall, a man is employed or unemployed; when the rate of investment goes up or down, a man takes new heart or goes broke. When wars happen, an insurance salesman becomes a rocket launcher, a store clerk, a radar man, a wife lives alone, a child grows up without a father. Neither the life of an individual nor the history of a society can be understood without understanding both.

Yet men do not usually define the troubles they endure in terms of historical change and institutional contradiction. The well-being they enjoy, they do not usually impute to the big ups and downs of the societies in which they live. Seldom aware of the intricate connection between the patterns of their own lives and the course of world history, ordinary men do not usually know what this connection means for the kinds of men they are becoming and for the kinds of history-making in which they might take part. They do not possess the quality of mind essential to grasp the interplay of man and society, of biography and history, of self and world. They cannot cope with their personal troubles in such ways as to control the structural transformations that usually lie behind them.

Surely it is no wonder. In what period have so many men been so totally exposed at so fast a pace to such earthquakes of change? That Americans have not known such catastrophic changes as have the men and women of other societies is due to historical facts that are now quickly becoming "merely history." The history that now affects every man is world history. Within this scene and this period, in the course of a single generation, one sixth of mankind is transformed from all that is feudal and backward into all that is modern, advanced, and fearful. Political colonies are freed, new and less visible forms of imperialism installed. Revolutions occur; men feel the intimate grip of new kinds of authority. Totalitarian societies rise, and are smashed to bits—or succeed fabulously. After two centuries of ascendancy, capitalism is shown up as only one way to make society into an industrial apparatus. After two centuries of hope, even formal democracy is restricted to a quite small portion of mankind. Everywhere in the underdeveloped world, ancient ways of life are broken up and vague expectations become urgent demands. Everywhere in the overdeveloped world, the means of authority and of violence become total in scope and bureaucratic in form. Humanity itself now lies before us, the super-nation at either pole concentrating its most coordinated and massive efforts upon the preparation of World War Three.

The very shaping of history now outpaces the ability of men to orient themselves in accordance with cherished values. And which values? Even when they do not panic, men often sense that older ways of feeling and thinking have collapsed and that newer beginnings are ambiguous to the point of moral stasis. Is it any wonder that ordinary men feel they cannot cope with the larger worlds with which they are so suddenly confronted? That they cannot understand the meaning of their epoch for their own lives? That—in defense of selfhood—they become morally insensible, trying to remain altogether private men? Is it any wonder that they come to be possessed by a sense of the trap?

It is not only information that they need—in this Age of Fact, information often dominates their attention and overwhelms their capacities to assimilate it. It is not only the skills of reason that they need—although their struggles to acquire these often exhaust their limited moral energy.

What they need, and what they feel they need, is a quality of mind that will help them to use information and to develop reason; in order to achieve lucid summations of what is going on in the world and of what may be happening within themselves. It is this quality, I am going to contend, that journalists and scholars, artists and publics, scientists and editors are coming to expect of what may be called the sociological imagination.

The sociological imagination enables its possessor to understand the larger historical scene in terms of its meaning for the inner life and the external career of a variety of individuals. It enables him to take into account how individuals, in the welter of their daily experience, often become falsely conscious of their social positions. Within that welter, the framework of modern society is sought, and within that framework the psychologies of a variety of men and women are formulated. By such means the personal uneasiness of individuals is focused upon explicit troubles and the indifference of publics is transformed into involvement with public issues.

The first fruit of this imagination—and the first lesson of the social science that embodies it—is the idea that the individual can understand his own experience and gauge his own fate only by locating himself within his period, that he can know his own chances in life only by becoming aware of those of all individuals in his circumstances. In many ways it is a terrible lesson; in many ways it is a magnificent one. We do not know the limits of man's capacities for supreme effort or willing degradation, for agony or glee, for pleasurable brutality or the sweetness of reason. But in our time we have come to know that the limits of "human nature" are frighteningly broad. We have come to know that every individual lives, from one generation to the next, in some society; that he lives out a biography, and that he lives it out within some historical sequence. By the fact of his living he contributes, however minutely, to the shaping of this society and to the course of its history, even as he is made by society and by its historical push and shove.

The sociological imagination enables us to grasp history and biography and the relations between the two within society. That is its task and its promise. To recognize this task and this promise is the mark of the classic social analyst. It is characteristic of Herbert Spencer—turgid, polysyllabic, comprehensive; of E. A. Ross—graceful, muckraking, upright; of Auguste Comte and Emile Durkheim; of the intricate and subtle Karl Mannheim. It is the quality of all that is intellectually excellent in Karl Marx; it is the clue to Thorstein Veblen's brilliant and ironic insight, to Joseph Schumpeter's many-sided constructions of reality; it is the basis of the psychological sweep of W. E. H. Lecky no less than of the profundity and clarity of Max Weber. And it is the signal of what is best in contemporary studies of man and society.

No social study that does not come back to the problems of biography, of history and of their intersections within a society has completed its intellectual journey. Whatever the specific problems of the classic social analysts, however limited or however broad the features of social reality they have examined, those who have been imaginatively aware of the promise of their work have consistently asked three sorts of questions:

1. What is the structure of this particular society as a whole? What are its essential components, and how are they related to one another? How does it differ from other varieties of social order? Within it, what is the meaning of any particular feature for its continuance and for its change?

2. Where does this society stand in human history? What are the mechanics by which it is changing? What is its place within and its meaning for the development of humanity as a whole? How does any particular feature we are examining affect, and how is it affected by, the historical period in which it moves? And this period—what are its essential features? How does it differ from other periods? What are its characteristic ways of history-making?

3. What varieties of men and women now prevail in this society and in this period? And what varieties are coming to prevail? In what ways are they selected and formed, liberated and repressed, made sensitive and blunted? What kinds of "human nature" are revealed in the conduct and character we observe in this society in this period? And what is the meaning for "human nature" of each and every feature of the society we are examining?

Whether the point of interest is a great power state or a minor literary mood, a family, a prison, a creed—these are the kind of questions the best social analysts have asked. They are the intellectual pivots of classic studies of man in society—and they are the questions inevitably raised by any mind possessing the sociological imagination. For that imagination is the capacity to shift from one perspective to another—from the political to the psychological; from examination of a single family to comparative assessment of the national budgets of the world; from the theological school to the military establishment; from considerations of an oil industry to studies of contemporary poetry. It is the capacity to range from the most impersonal and remote transformations to the most intimate features of the human self—and to see the relations between the two. Back of its use there is always the urge to know the social and historical meaning of the individual in the society and in the period in which he has his quality and his being.

That, in brief, is why it is by means of the sociological imagination that men now hope to grasp what is going on in the world, and to understand what is happening in themselves as minute points of the intersections of biography and history within society. In large part, contemporary man's self-conscious view of himself as at least an outsider, if not a permanent stranger, rests upon an absorbed realization of social relativity and of the transformative power of history. The sociological imagination is the most fruitful form of this self-consciousness. By its use men whose mentalities have swept only a series of limited orbits often come to feel as if suddenly awakened in a house with which they had only supposed themselves to be familiar. Correctly or incorrectly, they often come to feel that they can now provide themselves with adequate summations, cohesive assessments, comprehensive orientations. Older decisions that once appeared sound now seem to them products of a mind unaccountably dense. Their capacity for astonishment is made lively again. They acquire a new way of thinking, they experience a transvaluation of values: in a word, by their reflection and by their sensibility, they realize the cultural meaning of the social sciences.

Perhaps the most fruitful distinction with which the sociological imagination works is between "the personal troubles of milieu" and "the public issues of social structure." This distinction is an essential tool of the sociological imagination and a feature of all classic work in social science.

*Troubles* occur within the character of the individual and within the range of his immediate relations with others; they have to do with his self and with those limited areas of social life of which he is directly and personally aware. Accordingly, the statement and the resolution of troubles properly lie within the individual as a biographical entity and within the scope of his immediate milieu—the social setting that is directly open to his personal experience and to some extent his willful activity. A trouble is a private matter: values cherished by an individual are felt by him to be threatened.

*Issues* have to do with matters that transcend these local environments of the individual and the range of his inner life. They have to do with the organization of many such milieux into the institutions of an historical society as a whole, with the ways in which various milieux overlap and interpenetrate to form the larger structure of social and historical life. An issue is a public matter: some value cherished by publics is felt to be threatened. Often there is a debate about what that value really is and about what it is that really threatens it. This debate is often without focus if only because it is the very nature of an issue, unlike even widespread trouble, that it cannot very well be defined in terms of the immediate and everyday environments of ordinary men. An issue, in fact, often involves a crisis in institutional arrangements, and often too it involves what Marxists call "contradictions" or "antagonisms."

In these terms, consider unemployment. When, in a city of 100,000, only one man is unemployed, that is his personal trouble, and for its relief we properly look to the character of the man, his skills, and his immediate opportunities. But when in a nation of 50 million employees, 15 million men are unemployed, that is an issue, and we may not hope to find its solution within the range of opportunities open to any one individual. The very structure of opportunities has collapsed. Both the correct statement of the problem and the range of possible solutions require us to consider the economic and political institutions of the society, and not merely the personal situation and character of a scatter of individuals.

Consider war. The personal problem of war, when it occurs, may be how to survive it or how to die in it with honor; how to make money out of it; how to climb into the higher safety of the military apparatus; or how to contribute to the war's termination. In short, according to one's values, to find a set of milieux and within it to survive the war or make one's death in it meaningful. But the structural issues of war have to do with its causes; with what types of men it throws up into command; with its effects upon economic and political, family and religious institutions; with the unorganized irresponsibility of a world of nation-states.

Consider marriage. Inside a marriage a man and a woman may experience personal troubles, but when the divorce rate during the first four years of marriage is 250 out of every 1,000 attempts, this is an indication of a structural issue having to do with the institutions of marriage and the family and other institutions that bear upon them.

Or consider the metropolis—the horrible, beautiful, ugly, magnificent sprawl of the great city. For many upper-class people, the personal solution to "the problem of the city" is to have an apartment with private garage under it in the heart of the city, and forty miles out, a house by Henry Hill, garden by Garrett Eckbo, on a hundred acres of private land. In these two controlled environments—with a small staff at each end and a private helicopter connection—most people could solve many of the problems of personal milieux caused by the facts of the city. But all this, however splendid, does not solve the public issues that the structural fact of the city poses. What should be done with this wonderful monstrosity? Break it all up into scattered units, combining residence and work? Refurbish it as it stands? Or, after evacuation, dynamite it and build new cities according to new plans in new places? What should those plans be? And who is to decide and to accomplish whatever choice is made? These are structural issues; to confront them and to solve them requires us to consider political and economic issues that affect innumerable milieux.

In so far as an economy is so arranged that slumps occur, the problem of unemploy-ment becomes incapable of personal solution. In so far as war is inherent in the nation-state system and in the uneven industrialization of the world, the ordinary individual in his restricted milieu will be powerless—with or without psychiatric aid—to solve the troubles this system or lack of system imposes upon him. In so far as the family as an institution turns women into darling little slaves and men into their chief providers and unweaned dependents, the problem of a satisfactory marriage remains incapable of purely private solution. In so far as the overdeveloped megalopolis and the overdeveloped automobile are built-in features of the overdeveloped society, the issues of urban living will not be solved by personal ingenuity and private wealth.

What we experience in various and specific milieux, I have noted, is often caused by structural changes. Accordingly, to understand the changes of many personal milieux we are required to look beyond them. And the number and variety of such structural changes increase as the institutions within which we live become more embracing and more intricately connected with one another. To be aware of the idea of social structure and to use it with sensibility is to be capable of tracing such linkages among a great variety of milieux. To be able to do that is to possess the sociological imagination.

## Review

1. What does Mills see as the "first fruit" of the sociological imagination?

2. What is the "purpose and task" of the sociological imagination?

3. Why does Mills suggest that the distinction between the "personal troubles of milieu" and the "public issues of social structure" is an essential tool of the sociological imagination?

## Application

Select a social problem such as crime, unemployment, homelessness, or discrimination. Over the course of the term, gather at least 15 to 20 articles from newspapers and magazines on the topic. Toward the end of the term, use your sources to write a paper organized around the themes of the "sociological imagination" (i.e., the historical setting, the social structure, and the personal dimensions) and the relationships among them.

## Related Web Sites

1. *http://www.asanet.org/*. The official site of the American Sociological Associa-

tion has much information on sociologists and their work.

2. *http://www.faculty.rsu.edu/~felwell/Theorists/Mills/*. A site devoted to C. Wright Mills and his sociology.

---

# Part Two

## *Studying Social Phenomena*

How do sociologists get the information necessary to understand social life? From the first, sociologists have striven to make the discipline a science, to base their findings not on speculation or "common sense" but on theory and data. A **theory,** in simplest terms, is simply a coherent explanation of something. It is a way to understand and explain a social phenomenon. Theory can be used to stimulate a particular line of research. It can also be used to interpret data gathered.

We noted conflict theory in the introduction to Mills' article. **Structural-functionalism** is a theory focusing on social systems and how their interdependent parts maintain order. **Symbolic interactionist** theory focuses on the interaction between individuals and the resulting construction of social life (see, e.g., selections 2 and 36).

**Methods** are the ways that sociologists gather their data.

Just as the telescope is used to gather data by astronomers and the particle accelerator gathers data for physicists, sociologists use their own set of tools: questionnaires, interviews, statistical data provided by the government, experiments, etc. In this part, we will look at selections that illustrate the two broad categories of methods sociologists use: qualitative (selection 2) and quantitative (selection 3). The fourth selection illustrates the need for critical thinking. ✦

# 2
# Getting It Done

## Notes on Student Fritters

*Stan Bernstein*

**Social role** *is an important concept in socio-logical analysis. A role is the behavior expected of people who hold a particular position in so-ciety (parent, student, worker, citizen, etc.). Roles vary, however, in the extent to which they give individuals flexibility in behaving. As Bernstein suggests in this article, the role of the student in the educative process is open-ended. For example, you may be given a class assign-ment to write a paper. But how long should the paper be and how much research does it re-quire? How should you structure your time to meet the deadline for completion of the assign-ment? These decisions may be left up to you.*

*When students are given the freedom to or-ganize their own efforts, some will not meet the requirements of their instructors. This can produce feelings of guilt for the student. Bernstein shows the sources of these feelings and describes the ways in which students frit-ter away their time. "Fritters," then, are the strategies students use for coping with the open-ended nature of their work.*

*Bernstein's article exemplifies the interactionist approach to sociology. Sym-bolic interactionists emphasize the need for understanding the meaning of things from the actor's point of view. Bernstein illustrates an interactionist approach in three ways. First, he closely analyzes the role of student in the ed-ucative process. Second, Bernstein's method is a version of **participant observation,** a method in which the researcher takes part in the phenomenon that he or she is observing. Sociologists have used participant observa-tion to study such things as urban gangs, sup-port groups, religious cults, mental hospitals, and various kinds of work settings. Bernstein based his observations on his own experiences*

*as a student. He describes various types of frit-ters based on these observations.*

*Third, the discussion of fritters illustrates the internal dialogue people use in adjusting their actions to the actions of others. In this view, the **self** (the capacity to observe, respond to, and direct one's own behavior) is com-posed of two aspects—the I and the me. The "I" is the acting part of the self, which operates in the present. ("I'm not going to start that term paper until tomorrow.") The "me" evaluates these actions in terms of the expectations of society. ("It will be difficult for me to do a good term paper if I keep on putting it off. My in-structor expects me to show more effort.") Out of this internal dialogue, some kind of accept-able justification for delaying work—a frit-ter—may arise. ("Nobody can expect me to work when it's almost time to eat. I'll start after lunch.")*

**Social roles** vary in the degree to which their constituent tasks are "closed" or "open" in character. At one extreme are roles such as assembly-line worker, where precise defini-tions communicate when the task starts, one's progress in it, and when it ends. At the other extreme are roles such as student, when the tasks are highly open or never-end-ing. The role of student, in particular, in-volves learning to think and learning the "facts" of various fields. The infinite expandability of these tasks places no practi-cally determined restrictions on the amount of time occupants can dedicate to the role. Like politicians, housewives, and entrepre-neurs, students' work is never done. Indeed, students are counseled that people only stop learning when they die. Death is not, stu-dents lament, in sight, but learning demands are.

This paper seeks to explore how people cope with roles that are open or never-ending in their demands. In particular, it focuses upon how students justify not working under the ever-present pressure to work. Fre-quently, when there is work to be done, stu-dents fritter away time. An analysis of strate-gies students adopt in accounting for their time not working will be presented. The objective truth or falsity of the strategies is irrelevant to the purpose of this analysis. What is important is their use in coping with open-ended situations. This analysis treats a student population. The central notion is that of fritter devices or strategies. A fritter is "a justification a student gives to himself for not doing student work in response to felt pressures to work." While the success of a fritter in neutralizing work pressure or guilt is increased by its receiving social support, this consideration is not part of the definition.

The dynamic nature of fritters makes categorizing them difficult. In actual practice, combinations or complex sequences are likely as the student continually reconstitutes his work avoidance as new kinds of justified activity. For ease of presentation, they may be divided into the following four classes: (1) person-based; (2) social relations-based; (3) value-based; and (4) task-based.

## Person-Based Fritters

Person-based fritters involve definitions of biological need and personal history.

### Biological Necessity

Even a student is human. Being human involves, among other things, the satisfaction of biological needs. These practical necessities are just that—necessities. Therefore, they are foolproof justifications for not working. When, for example, nature calls, what is a person to do?

Similarly, hunger can serve as a justification for work avoidance. Not only can an argument be made for biological necessity, but the student can also argue that hunger impairs studying ability. This argument need not be limited, of course, by actual hunger. The great business done by vending machines in dormitories and the concentration of all-night eating places in areas of high student residence attest to the utility of this justification. Some popular student foods (pizza in particular) are not eaten alone. Time must be spent gathering other people. And once you have them, you can do more with them than eat.

Cleanliness is yet another excellent justification. Anything next to godliness surely takes precedence over work. Washing and showering can serve another function. An entire battery of work-avoidance tactics can be justified by their necessity in keeping the student awake. These activities include preparing and drinking cups of coffee, cold showers, long walks in cold weather, running a half-mile, standing on one's head for a few minutes, listening to Sousa marches, Chopin preludes, or acid rock, and eating rich food. A variety of drugs are now routinely used to fight fatigue. The effects of these are frequently not restricted to fatigue reduction. Subtle and not very subtle alterations of consciousness are common. Attending to these changes can become more interesting than studying. Should these activities fail, or even should they succeed, another way of handling "fatigue" is the I'll-get-up-very-early-tomorrow-morning-when-I'll-be-able-to-work-better fritter. Students have to keep healthy, too. Many regimens, physical and medical, may be required. At some times, it may be crucial that the student get "adequate rest."

### Rest on Your Laurels

Focusing on personal history leads to the nostalgia or rest-on-your-laurels fritter. Using this strategy involves employing past accomplishments as justification for present work avoidance. This can take the form of delaying work, since previous history shows (or can be interpreted to suggest) it well within one's capability and therefore not a matter of pressing concern. Or when the present activity proves frustrating to the point of work avoidance, the individual may bolster his esteem by "celebrating" previous successes. A variant on this theme is especially handy for avoiding work when a number of different tasks must be done. Upon completion of one of them, the student may use a you-owe-it-to-yourself justification for work avoidance, the avoidance period being defined as self-payment for a job well done.

## Social Relations-Based Fritters

Fritters based upon social relations directly employ other people in the action of avoiding work. The impact of employing other people, however, is not so much in having an audience before which one gives accounts as simply in having an audience. There are three main patterns of social relations fritters.

### Group Discussion

The group-discussion fritter is also called the commiseration fritter. Commiserating may be done in a large group or in pairs either in person or over the telephone. It involves "getting together" and consoling one another on the unreasonability or irrationality of the assignment. Complaining about the assigned work is an excellent fritter technique. It justifies work avoidance by directly protesting against the work itself. The more intelligent or discriminating the complaints, the clearer it is that the work task is within the student's later capability. Critical ability may be developed in avoiding studying as well as in doing studying. Sometimes discussions of this sort get around to a comparison of actual work done, leading to the social-comparison fritter.

### Social Comparison

Students sometimes compare their progress with one another. When a student discovers he is ahead of others in his work, he can then feel justified in freeing time for work avoidance. This fritter has two aspects. First, there is the time spent gathering comparisons of others. This may involve personal contact or telephoning. Or the comparison others may not be real others working on the same task. Instead, high relative standing earlier in the course may be extrapolated to the present. Because of information from the past, the student may believe he is at present ahead of others. When this is coupled with the perception that relative position is the criterion of final evaluation, it becomes possible, for example, for "curve-breaking" midterm students to free time from final studies and projects. Second, there is the effect of the comparison. The choice of comparison to others is a stra-

tegic choice. For a student to feel justified in his current work avoidance, he must compare his work with someone who is less advanced than he. (Choice of either will vary depending on whether the student wishes to take a break from work or gain incentive to continue it.) The two dangers of this technique for the student are: first, he may choose someone who is, in fact, more advanced in the work; and, second, he may fritter away the time needed for students to catch up and pass him.

### Group Work

The decision to study in a group has a number of work-avoidance functions. On the one hand, it immediately makes possible commiseration and social-comparison fritters. Study groups from the same course can, of course, commiserate easily. Students studying together, but for different courses, are able to have even longer commiseration sessions. Each can complain about his course without redundancy and without risk of contradiction or challenge.

Getting a number of people together functions, on the other hand, to increase enormously the range of alternatives to studying. These activities can be justified using any number of the techniques elsewhere mentioned. Work-avoidance maneuvers with group approval are especially difficult to ignore. There is a "risky shift" in the direction of longer fritters, too. This is because, once you have stopped working, it is difficult to know when to suggest to your partners that you should get back to work. It may be hard to stop frittering without being impolite or pressuring. Responsibility for directing attention back to work becomes diffused through the group.

## Value-Based Fritters

While the above-mentioned fritter techniques are common and successful, they do not have the guilt-binding power of valuative fritters. One way work can be avoided especially, but not exclusively, in the early college years is using time to discuss values. Political, moral, and aesthetic topics are common in these conversations. Finding out who you are, "getting your shit together," and so on is an important task. Mundane work considerations do not look very important measured against this larger activity. Valuative fritters based on already held values place work and work avoidance within a larger framework of values and choices. It is here that considerations of nonstudent activities enter with greatest effect. Three primary types of valuative fritters may be described and ordered in terms of increasing generality and abstraction.

## Higher Good

In the higher-good work-avoidance strategy, the student ranks being a student as less important to him in his scheme of values than other interests and aspects of his identity. Here friendship, love, cultural values (e.g., charity, service), political interests, physical fitness (the sound-mind-in-a-sound-body fritter), and much else can be justified as more worthy of attention for the moment than the study tasks at hand. These other values, of course, vary in strength and, therefore, in their guilt-free binding power in role management. For this reason, the strength of each of the alternative values is enhanced immeasurably if it can be asserted that the opportunity for acting on that value is soon to be gone. Stated another way, *rare events*, or at least infrequent events, have a special ability to bind time from studying, even if the value of the act would otherwise be questionable in relation to the pressure to study. Makes-Jack-a-dull-boy valuative fritters, involving, say, a movie, will be more potent the last day the picture is playing than the first day of an extended run, concerts involving rarely heard performers are able to appease guilt from role violation, and eclipses of the moon draw crowds of guilt-free students as an audience.

## Experience Broadens

The experience-broadens fritter is less specific in the sense of presenting a less clear-cut value conflict. It has, nonetheless, the attraction of serving as a ready backup to a post-facto unjustified valuative fritter (say, the movie was lousy, the instruments out of tune, the friend crabby, the eclipse cloud-rid-den, or what have you). In such an event, or generally in any event, it can be argued somehow that experience qua experience broadens the person, makes him more complete, or wiser, or what have you. This can bind successfully enormous amounts of time on a scale much larger than the mere work requirements for a specific course. Even career decisions (or decision evasions) can be justified under the experience-broadens rubric. The crucial difference from the higher-good fritter is that any experience will do.

## Existential

The most general of valuative fritters is the existential, or the what-the-hell-sort-of-difference-will-it-make, fritter. In this strategy, the decision to work or not work is cast as having no lasting practical or existential effect on the course of one's life. Scholastic failures of prominently successful individuals may be remembered. Einstein's failure of a high school math course can offer solace to the fritterer. If one's activities are ultimately of no consequence anyway, the immediate consequences of work avoidance are not even worthy of consideration. Extreme application of this principle can lead to failure in the student role, in which event one's very studenthood may be justified as an experience-broadens fritter from what one should really be doing.

## Task-Based Fritters

Fritters discussed to this point are based upon the student's history, biology, social relations, and values. We come finally to the task itself. Task-based fritters focus upon the direct handling of study time and the allocation of work resources. Specifically, there appear to be four main clusters of task-based fritters: time-related; preparation-related; creativity-related; and task-involved.

### Time-Related Fritters

*The time symmetry fritter.* Many students appear to find it easier to start studying on the hour, half-hour, or, at the very least, quarter-hour than at any other minute. This may be due to the ease these times make for scheduling fritters discussed belov These times are more generally importar plans and schedules between individuals. A common social use of time shapes action. (On a larger scale, weekends, holidays, or Mondays assume special status in the week.) It is, further, "easier" to compute total study time and pages per hour if you start at some such prominent time division. One of the advantages of this technique is that, with a little effort, a large amount of time can be frittered if the activity one chose to do until, say, the quarter-hour starting time, can be extended just a few minutes beyond this starting point. The student is then, by the same logic, justified in waiting until the next prominent time division. Depending on the individual and on the amount of time already spent in time symmetry fritters, the student can choose to wait for the next hour, half-hour, or quarter-hour. As good a fritter technique as this is, there is a problem in its use. Each time it is used in succession, the student feels less justified in invoking the time symmetry fritter. This is sometimes manifested by the setting of the starting time at progressively shorter prominent intervals: e.g., at 7:00, 8:00, 8:30, and then 8:45. In any event, at some point, this technique loses its efficacy. Fortunately, there is a larger-scale, more successful technique which can then be used.

*The great divide fritter.* At some point, say, in an evening to be devoted to work, it becomes too late to get serious work done (or finish the task, the scheduled amount, or what have you). At this point, the student feels perfectly free to give up for the rest of the night all pretense to studying. It is simply too late to get enough work done to make any work worthwhile. Some other activity is then chosen to occupy the remaining time, but without any need for a higher-good valuative justification. Thus, a particular student might not consider it worthwhile to start studying after 9:00 at night. The time symmetry fritter brought the student up to 8:45, a biological-imperative fritter or a phone-call-for-a-commiseration fritter might be sufficient to add enough time to set up a great divide fritter.

*Scheduling fritters.* Students justify spending enormous amounts of time making up work schedules. These can be done for the day, evening, week, or whatever the rele-

vant work session to be planned. Plans can be made not just for the coming work, but also for coming work breaks. Fritters of the future become bound into a longer series of work intentions and are in that way neutralized. Of course, scheduling may be resorted to whenever the actual progress of the work falls far enough off schedule to warrant the writing of a new one. Schedule-related fritters, then, become a consideration whenever something goes wrong or could go wrong with the schedule. Indeed, the more detailed the schedule, the greater the chance of derailment.

There are two salient forms of scheduling fritters. First, there are anticipated interruption fritters. If one knows in advance that at a certain point in the work period, studying will be interrupted by some other activity, there is set up a situation in which frittering the time until after the interruption is justified. This can be considered the application of a great divide fritter on a smaller scale. Second, there are disruption-of-sequence fritters. These occur whenever the student, for some reason, performs a task out of order from the planned sequence. If this involves successful completion of the different task, conditions are set up for an owe-it-to-yourself fritter as well as a new scheduling fritter. The disruption of sequence can also justify waiting for a new prominent starting point, like a new day, before actually working.

*Deadline change fritters.* On occasion a teacher will change the date that some work is due either for the whole class or, by special arrangement, for single students. When this happens, the student feels free to use a postponed-deadline fritter. Since study time is reckoned backward from a deadline date rather than forward to new work opportunities, when the deadline is postponed, time is freed to avoid working. If, for example, a paper due Friday is postponed for one week on Wednesday, the student can wait for the following Wednesday before working again.

### Preparation-Related Fritters

Preparation fritters involve all activities immediately attendant to preparing to study: getting books, paper, pens, cleaning the desk, and what have you. These are easily justified activities, preparatory as they are to work. These immediate preparations are easily escalated. Thus, a student decides that, in the interest of greater efficiency, he should clean his desk top (no matter what the actual nature of his work habits—tidy or abominable). Having done this, a crucial point is reached. He can now actually start to work. Instead, he says while-I'm-at-it and proceeds to clean out the whole desk, or rearrange all his books, or even move on to cleaning the whole room or apartment. This technique is especially interesting, developing as it does from the preparation fritter, in that it quickly ignores the originally work-related starting point. A good job is worth doing well, as long as it isn't the good job you have to do.

Preparation can be difficult (or made difficult), and work can be delayed. In the spread-resources or shuttle fritter the student does not bring, or chooses work for which he cannot bring, all the needed materials to one place for work. Traveling between work sites becomes necessary. What started as the path to work intersects with other paths (perhaps to other places).

## Creativity Fritters

Once all the material preparations have been completed there are two other factors left to be prepared—the student and, say, the paper. Let us consider these in reverse order. Preparation of the paper itself will offer many opportunities for work avoidance.

(1) *For the-first-step-is-the-hardest.* This can mean working for a long time on an outline, or, commonly, working hard at getting exactly the proper first sentence or first paragraph. The opening of a paper is felt in an important way to constrain the range of alternatives, stylistic and organizational, for the rest of the work. It becomes, therefore, of utmost importance that the opening be precisely correct—no matter how much time it takes.

(2) *In addition, the student must be ready to work.* Every creative endeavor, however, has an incubation period and every endeavor, creative or not, requires motiva-

tion. Both needs can require time, justified time. It is best to wait until you are bursting with ideas or are sufficiently motivated, even if the motivation is guilt due to unsuccessful previous application of fritter techniques. This is therefore the let-it-brew-for-a-while fritter (closely related to this is the I'll-lie-down-and-think-about-it fritter; the possible danger in this tactic is, of course, very clear; listing all things people are designed to do horizontally, studying is one of the lowest on the list).

(3) *Related to these is the I'm-sure-there-is-something-else fritter.* No matter how much advanced preparation there has already been, the conscientious student is justified in allowing some free time to think of something else which should be included (say, in a paper, or when considering how to psych out the teacher's exam questions). This is especially useful when, for example, a paper is on a topic requiring an interdisciplinary approach or a number of different viewpoints for elucidation. The "something else" can then be in an area only vaguely related to the original topic. This justification can thus successfully be used to allow additional time for readings and thinking more and more peripheral to the original topic—i.e., to the work itself. When the task is taking a test, students can spend a great deal of time trying to psych out the teacher. Information on prior exams and teacher's specialization or personal quirks may be important in deciding what significant knowledge is.

## Task-Involved Fritters

Finally, the student, to remain in concept and in fact a student, must occasionally actually work. Once work is started, however, there are still some devices which can be used to slow it or end it quickly without endangering one's view of self as student.

(1) One important consideration, especially to someone who has been using scheduling fritters, is a reliable measure of how quickly the work is going. Time

is thus justifiably spent computing pages, hours, words per minute, or what have you. This is the what's-my-rate fritter.

(2) Every work goal can be divided into subgoals whose individual accomplishments are significant since each contributes to the final completion. This is the principle behind the logical-stopping-point fritter. Small owe-it-to-yourself fritters are justified by the completion of the subgoals. As the time symmetry fritter has prominent dividing points for the time continuum, so the logical-stopping-point fritter divides up the work task itself. Thus, for example, one may set up subgoals such that one is justified in taking a break after completing only a single chapter in an assigned book. This technique, however, like the time symmetry fritter, is conducive to fractionalization. The subgoal can shift from finish the chapter to finish the topic of discussion or, more extremely, the page or the paragraph.

(3) Sometimes the student has more than one project to work on at once. The jack-of-all-trades fritter is a way of avoiding working too hard on any one subject by shifting from task to task before the work gets too taxing in any one of them.

## Recovery Fritters

Sometimes the student does not complete the task when it is due. If he can get an open-ended extension, he is free to postpone additional work for a long time. This is the effect of the you-can't-pick-up-spilled-milk fritter.

## Concluding Remarks

There are features of the student role which facilitate the use of these strategies. Students are granted great liberty in the planning of their use of time. Student time is more often "individual time" than "social time." Time demands are stricter in high schools than in colleges. Required class time and daily evaluated assignments are less characteristic of the college years. The schools frequently cite the increased maturity of the students as the reason for the greater liberty permitted. However, time use in statuses occupied by even more mature adults are frequently more regulated by institutions. Perhaps most important, the student is in a transitional role. The schools and the population as a whole are not favorably disposed to lifetime students. It is an early stage in commitment to professional careers and a late stage in formal education for yet other careers. Widespread use of fritter techniques can ease the difficulties of early commitment for the former and aid the termination of formal education for the latter.

## Review

1. How does Bernstein define fritters?

2. Name and describe each of the four classes of fritters.

3. What are the main differences among the four classes of fritters?

4. What can account for greater use of fritters by college students than high school students or adults not in college?

## Applications

1. For a one-week period, record the number of times you use various fritters, on which days, at what times, and related to what areas of study. Give examples of each. Use the specific types and subtypes discussed by Bernstein. Discuss your use of fritters compared with their use by students in general as brought out by Bernstein.

2. For a one-week period pay close attention to what other students say to you directly or what you overhear being said regarding their use of fritters. Record the numbers and types. Compare your findings with those of Bernstein.

## Related Web Sites

1. *http://sun.soci.niu.edu/~sssi/*. Official Web site of the Society for the Study of Symbolic Interaction, with links to other useful sites.

2. *http://caps.unc.edu/TenTraps.html*. Information on good study habits and ten traps of studying.

Reprinted from: Stan Bernstein, "Getting It Done: Notes on Student Fritters." In *Urban Life and Culture*, Vol. 1, No. 3, October 1972. Copyright © 1972 by Sage Publications. Reprinted by permission. ✦

# 3
# Egoistic Suicide

*Emile Durkheim*

Sociologists make use of existing sources (e.g., census data or crime rates) for research purposes. Organizing this data into an appropriate statistical format is just the beginning of the sociologist's work. Since the facts never speak for themselves, the sociologist must determine how the statistics express underlying social processes. Facts without such interpretation are meaningless to the scientific enterprise.

*The best sociological interpretation is that which is applicable to society at large. In this sense, Durkheim's book on suicide has become the standard model for statistical and quantitative sociology. In the selection that follows, Durkheim takes the observed differences between Catholic and Protestant suicide rates as indicating differing degrees of social integration in these two faiths. In turn, this interpretation affirms a more general theory about the processes of integration in all social groups.*

*Beyond serving as an exemplar for later quantitative research, Durkheim's study can be seen as a critique of commonsense notions about suicide. Self-destruction is most often seen in egoistic terms—an individual acting out of psychological causes such as depression or unhappiness. The premise that the causes of suicide are psychological is actually an expression of individualist beliefs dominant in present-day society. This premise has not always existed. And, as Durkheim shows, the belief in individualism itself has social causes. There is, then, irony in his reference to this social cause of suicide as "egoistic."*

If one casts a glance at the map of European suicide, it is at once clear that in purely Catholic countries like Spain, Portugal, Italy, sui-cide is very little developed, while it is at its maximum in Protestant countries, in Prussia, Saxony, Denmark. The following averages compiled by Morselli confirm this first conclusion:

*Average of Suicides per Million Inhabitants*

| | |
|---|---|
| Protestant states (Protestant and Catholic) | 96 |
| Catholic states | 58 |
| Greek Catholic states | 40 |

The low proportion of the Greek Catholics cannot be surely attributed to religion, for as their civilization is very different from that of the other European nations, this difference of culture may be the cause of their lesser aptitude. But this is not the case with most Catholic or Protestant societies. To be sure, they are not all on the same intellectual and moral level; yet the resemblances are sufficiently essential to make it possible to ascribe to confessional differences the marked contrast they offer in respect to suicide.

The only essential difference between Catholicism and Protestantism is that the second permits free inquiry to a far greater degree than the first. Of course, Catholicism by the very fact that it is an idealistic religion concedes a far greater place to thought and reflection than Greco-Latin polytheism or Hebrew monotheism. It is not restricted to mechanical ceremonies but seeks the control of the conscience.

So it appeals to conscience, and even when demanding blind submission of reason, does so by employing the language of reason. None the less, the Catholic accepts his faith ready made, without scrutiny. He may not even submit it to historical examination since the original texts that serve as its basis are proscribed. A whole hierarchical system of authority is devised, with marvelous ingenuity, to render tradition invariable. All variation is abhorrent to Catholic thought. The Protestant is far more the author of his faith. The Bible is put in his hands and no interpretation is imposed upon him. The very structure of the reformed cult stresses this state of religious individualism. Nowhere but in England is the Protestant clergy a hierarchy; like the worshipers, the priest has no other source but himself and his conscience. He is a more instructed guide than the run of worshipers but with no special authority for fixing dogma. But what best proves that this freedom of inquiry proclaimed by the founders of the Reformation has not remained a Platonic affirmation is the increasing multiplicity of all sorts of sects so strikingly in contrast with the indivisible unity of the Catholic Church.

We thus reach our first conclusion, that the proclivity of Protestantism for suicide must relate to the spirit of free inquiry that animates this religion. Let us understand this relationship correctly. Free inquiry itself is only the effect of another cause. When it appears, when men, after having long received their ready-made faith from tradition, claim the right to shape it for themselves, this is not because of the intrinsic desirability of free inquiry, for the latter involves as much sorrow as happiness. But it is because men henceforth need this liberty. This very need can have only one cause: the overthrow of traditional beliefs. If they still asserted themselves with equal energy, it would never occur to men to criticize them. If they still had the same authority, men would not demand the right to verify the source of this authority. Reflection develops only if its development becomes imperative, that is, if certain ideas and instinctive sentiments which have hitherto adequately guided conduct are found to have lost their efficacy. Then reflection intervenes to fill the gap that has appeared, but which it has not created. Just as reflection disappears to the extent that thought and action take the form of automatic habits, it awakes only when accepted habits become disorganized. It asserts its rights against public opinion only when the latter loses strength, that is, when it is no longer prevalent to the same extent. If these assertions occur not merely occasionally and as passing crises, but become chronic, if individual consciences keep reaffirming their autonomy, it is because they are constantly subject to conflicting impulses, because a new opinion has not been formed to replace the one no longer existing. If a new system of beliefs were constituted which seemed as indisputable to everyone as the old, no one would think of discussing it any longer. Its discussion would no longer even be permitted, for ideas shared by an entire society draw from this consensus an authority that makes them sacrosanct and raises them above dispute. For them to have become more tolerant, they must first already have become the object of less general and complete assent and been weakened by preliminary controversy.

Thus, if it is correct to say that free inquiry once proclaimed multiplies schisms, it must be added that it presupposes them and derives from them, for it is claimed and instituted as a principle only in order to permit latent or half-declared schisms to develop more freely. So if Protestantism concedes a greater freedom to individual thought than Catholicism, it is because it has fewer common beliefs and practices. Now, a religious society cannot exist without a collective *credo* and the more extensive the *credo* the more unified and strong is the society. For it does not unite men by an exchange and reciprocity of services, a temporal bond of union which permits and even presupposes differences, but which a religious society cannot form. It socializes men only by attaching them completely to an identical body of doctrine and socializes them in proportion as this body of doctrine is extensive and firm. The more numerous the manners of action and thought of a religious character are, which are accordingly removed from free inquiry, the more the idea of God presents itself in all details of existence, and makes individual wills converge to one identical goal. Inversely, the greater concessions a confessional group makes to individual judgment, the less it dominates lives, the less its cohesion and vitality. We thus reach the conclusion that the superiority of Protestantism with respect to suicide results from its being a less strongly integrated church than the Catholic Church.

The beneficent influence of religion is not due to the special nature of religious conceptions. If religion protects man against the desire for self-destruction, it is not that it preaches the respect for his own person to him with arguments *sui generis*, but because it is society. What constitutes this society is the existence of a certain number of beliefs and practices common to all the faithful, traditional and thus obligatory. The more numerous and strong these collective states of mind are, the stronger the integration of the religious community and also the greater its preservative value. The details of dogmas and rites are secondary. The essential thing is that they be capable of supporting a sufficiently intense collective life. And because the Protestant church has less consistency than the others it has less moderating effect upon suicide.

So we reach the general conclusion: suicide varies inversely with the degree of integration of the social groups of which the individual forms a part.

But society cannot disintegrate without the individual simultaneously detaching himself from social life, without his own goals becoming preponderant over those of the community, in a word without his personality tending to surmount the collective personality. The more weakened the groups to which he belongs, the less he depends on them, the more he consequently depends only on himself and recognizes no other rules of conduct than what are founded on his private interests. If we agree to call this state egoism, in which the individual ego asserts itself to excess in the face of the social ego and at its expense, we may call egoistic the special type of suicide springing from excessive individualism.

But how can suicide have such an origin?

First of all, it can be said that, as collective force is one of the obstacles best calculated to restrain suicide, its weakening involves a development of suicide. When society is strongly integrated, it holds individuals under its control, considers them at its service and thus forbids them to dispose willfully of themselves. Accordingly it opposes their evading their duties to it through death. But how could society impose its supremacy upon them when they refuse to accept this subordination as legitimate? It no longer then possesses the requisite authority to retain them in their duty if they wish to desert; and conscious of its own weakness, it even recognizes their right to do freely what it can

no longer prevent. So far as they are the admitted masters of their destinies, it is their privilege to end their lives. They, on their part, have no reason to endure life's sufferings patiently. For they cling to life more resolutely when belonging to a group they love, so as not to betray interests they put before their own. The bond that unites them with the common cause attaches them to life and the lofty goal they envisage prevents their feeling personal troubles so deeply. There is, in short, in a cohesive and animated society a constant interchange of ideas and feelings from all to each and each to all, something like a mutual moral support, which instead of throwing the individual on his own resources, leads him to share in the collective energy and supports his own when exhausted.

But these reasons are purely secondary. Excessive individualism not only results in favoring the action of suicidogenic causes, but it is itself such a cause. It not only frees man's inclination to do away with himself from a protective obstacle, but creates this inclination out of whole cloth and thus gives birth to a special suicide which bears its mark. This must be clearly understood for this is what constitutes the special character of the type of suicide just distinguished and justifies the name we have given it. What is there then in individualism that explains this result?

***

A whole range of functions concern only the individual; these are the ones indispensable for physical life. Since they are made for this purpose only, they are perfected by its attainment. In everything concerning them, therefore, man can act reasonably without thought of transcendental purposes. These functions serve by merely serving him. In so far as he has no other needs, he is therefore self-sufficient and can live happily with no other objective than living. This is not the case, however, with the civilized adult. He has many ideas, feelings and practices unrelated to organic needs. The roles of art, morality, religion, political faith, science itself are not to repair organic exhaustion nor to provide sound functioning of the organs. All this supra-physical life is built and expanded not because of the demands of the cosmic environment but because of the demands of the social environment. The influence of society is what has aroused in us the sentiments of sympathy and solidarity drawing us toward others; it is society which, fashioning us in its image, fills us with religious, political and moral beliefs that control our actions. To play our social role we have striven to extend our intelligence and it is still society that has supplied us with tools for this development by transmitting to us its trust fund of knowledge.

Through the very fact that these superior forms of human activity have a collective origin, they have a collective purpose. As they derive from society they have reference to it; rather they are society itself incarnated and individualized in each one of us. But for them to have a *raison d'être* in our eyes, the purpose they envisage must be one not indifferent to us. We can cling to these forms of human activity only to the degree that we cling to society itself. Contrariwise, in the same measure as we feel detached from society we become detached from that life whose source and aim is society. For what purpose do these rules of morality, these precepts of law binding us to all sorts of sacrifices, these restrictive dogmas exist, if there is no being outside us whom they serve and in whom we participate? What is the purpose of science itself? If its only use is to increase our chances for survival, it does not deserve the trouble it entails. Instinct acquits itself better of this role; animals prove this. Why substitute for it a more hesitant and uncertain reflection? What is the end of suffering, above all? If the value of things can only be estimated by their relation to this positive evil for the individual, it is without reward and incomprehensible. This problem does not exist for the believer firm in his faith or the man strongly bound by ties of domestic or political society. Instinctively and unreflectively they ascribe all that they are and do, the one to his Church or his God, the living symbol of the Church, the other to his family, the third to his country or party. Even in their sufferings they see only a means of glorifying the group to which they belong and thus do homage to it. So, the Christian ultimately desires and seeks suffering to testify more fully to his contempt for the flesh and more fully resemble his divine model. But the more the believer doubts, that is, the less he feels himself a real participant in the religious faith to which he belongs, and from which he is freeing himself; the more the family and community become foreign to the individual, so much the more does he become a mystery to himself, unable to escape the exasperating and agonizing question: to what purpose?

If, in other words, as has often been said, man is double, that is because social man superimposes himself upon physical man. Social man necessarily presupposes a society which he expresses and serves. If this dissolves, if we no longer feel it in existence and action about and above us, whatever is social in us is deprived of all objective foundation. All that remains is an artificial combination of illusory images, a phantasmagoria vanishing at the least reflection; that is, nothing which can be a goal for our action. Yet this social man is the essence of civilized man; he is the masterpiece of existence. Thus we are bereft of reasons for existence; for the only life to which we could cling no longer corresponds to anything actual; the only existence still based upon reality no longer meets our needs. Because we have been initiated into a higher existence, the one which satisfies an animal or a child can satisfy us no more and the other itself fades and leaves us helpless. So there is nothing more for our efforts to lay hold of, and we feel them lose themselves in emptiness.

In this sense it is true to say that our activity needs an object transcending it. We do not need it to maintain ourselves in the illusion of an impossible immortality; it is implicit in our moral constitution and cannot be even partially lost without this losing its *raison d'être* in the same degree. No proof is needed that in such a state of confusion the least cause of discouragement may easily give birth to desperate resolutions. If life is not worth the trouble of being lived, everything becomes a pretext to rid ourselves of it.

But this is not all. This detachment occurs not only in single individuals. One of the constitutive elements of every national temperament consists of a certain way of estimating the value of existence. There is a collective as well as an individual humor inclining peoples to sadness or cheerfulness, making them see things in bright or sombre lights. In fact, only society can pass a collective opinion on the value of human life; for this the individual is incompetent. The latter knows nothing but himself and his own little horizon; thus his experience is too limited to serve as a basis for a general appraisal. He may indeed consider his own life to be aimless; he can say nothing applicable to others. On the contrary, without sophistry, society may generalize its own feeling as to itself, its state of health or lack of health. For individuals share too deeply in the life of society for it to be diseased without their suffering infection. What it suffers they necessarily suffer. Because it is the whole, its ills are communicated to its parts. Hence it cannot disintegrate without awareness that the regular conditions of general existence are equally disturbed. Because society is the end on which our better selves depend, it cannot feel us escaping it without a simultaneous realization that our activity is purposeless. Since we are its handiwork, society cannot be conscious of its own decadence without the feeling that henceforth this work is of no value. Thence are formed currents of depression and disillusionment emanating from no particular individual but expressing society's state of disintegration. They reflect the relaxation of social bonds, a sort of collective asthenia, or social malaise, just as individual sadness, when chronic, in its way reflects the poor organic state of the individual. Then metaphysical and religious systems spring up which, by reducing these obscure sentiments to formulae, attempt to prove to men the senselessness of life and that it is self-deception to believe that it has purpose. Then new moralities originate which, by elevating facts to ethics, commend suicide or at least tend in that direction by suggesting a minimal existence. On their appearance they seem to have been created out of whole cloth by their makers who are sometimes blamed for the pessimism of their doctrines. In reality they are an effect rather than a cause; they merely symbolize in abstract language and systematic form the physiological distress of the body social. As these currents are collective, they have, by virtue of their origin, an authority which they impose upon the individual and they drive him more vigorously on the way to which he is already inclined by the state of moral distress directly aroused in him by the disintegration of society. Thus, at the very moment that, with excessive zeal, he frees himself from the social environment, he still submits to its influence. However individualized a man may be, there is always something collective remaining—the very depression and melancholy resulting from this same exaggerated individualism. He effects communion through sadness when he no longer has anything else with which to achieve it.

Hence this type of suicide well deserves the name we have given it. Egoism is not merely a contributing factor in it; it is its generating cause. In this case the bond attaching man to life relaxes because that attaching him to society is itself slack. The incidents of private life which seem the direct inspiration of suicide and are considered its determining causes are in reality only incidental causes. The individual yields to the slightest shock of circumstance because the state of society has made him a ready prey to suicide.

## Review

1. What types of countries, according to Durkheim, are likely to have high suicide rates? Explain why.

2. How does Durkheim define the egoistic type of suicide?

3. What are the origins of egoistic suicide?

4. How does Durkheim differentiate between social man and physical man?

## Applications

1. Compare suicide rates of the different countries mentioned by Durkheim, as well as other countries. Are there differ-

ences in the rate according to whether the society is predominantly Catholic, Protestant, Jewish, Hindu, or nonreligious? Are Durkheim's conclusions relevant today?

2. Interview four people—a Catholic, a Protestant, a Jew, and an atheist. Develop an interview format that addresses

   a. attitudes toward suicide

   b. the group's position on suicide

   c. perceptions of causes and reasons for suicide

   d. perceptions about the importance of religion in causing or preventing suicide

   e. perceptions about societal influences on suicide—both causes and prevention

Summarize your findings, contrasting them with Durkheim's.

## Related Web Sites

1. *http://www.relst.uiuc.edu/durkheim/*. A site devoted to the life and works of Emile Durkheim.

2. *http://www.suicidology.org/*. Home page of the American Association of Suicidology, with information and links to other sites dealing with suicide.

---

# 4

# 'It's Awful! It's Terrible! It's . . . Never Mind'

*Steven A. Holmes*

**H**ow do people know what they know? It's a question posed and extensively discussed by philosophers. It's also a question raised by sociologists, who frequently challenge both the conventional wisdom and the opinions of experts.

*Much of what people know comes from the media. You read in a magazine article, for example, that half of all marriages fail. You tell this to friends, who pass it on to others. Soon, it is a part of the conventional wisdom—everyone knows that half of all marriages fail. The problem is, it isn't true that half of all marriages fail. Half of all marriages have never failed. Among some younger age-groups, half of all marriages would ultimately fail if the divorce rate had remained as high as it was in the late 1970s. But the rate has fallen somewhat, so the proportion of marriages that ultimately fail is uncertain.*

*In this selection, Holmes provides some additional examples of information reported in the media that was either wrong or misleading. Why does it matter? Well, if you go into marriage believing that you have a 50-50 chance of divorcing, you may not be as committed or as willing to work through problems as you would be if you thought that most marriages succeed. If you read that high-tension electrical wires cause cancer, you may avoid living somewhere that would have been an ideal home for you. If you agree that people are poor because they are unwilling to work, you may oppose government programs to help the poor.*

*Information, in other words, affects what people do as well as what they believe. It is im-portant therefore to engage in critical thinking when you sort through the information that comes to you. And as Holmes notes, critical thinking is needed whether the information comes from a popular or professional source. Experts are not infallible.*

*Critical thinking does not mean cynicism—as though you can't believe anyone or anything. It means exercising caution in the face of massive amounts of information, not dismissing all information as tainted or purely a matter of opinion.*

*Critical thinking means the willingness to raise such questions as these: Is this information consistent with my experience (keeping in mind that it may be true even if it isn't consistent)? Is it consistent with other things I know? Is it reasonable? What is the basis for the facts presented? Are the conclusions the only ones that can be drawn from the facts? Is the source a generally reliable one? And so on. Critical thinking, in sum, is the rational road between the extremes of gullibility and cynicism.*

**T**he reports were shocking, even enraging, the type that can make one wonder where American society is headed. In 1995, several research organizations reported that a hefty percentage—in one study, 65 percent—of teen-age mothers had babies by adult men. The image of lecherous men seducing troubled young girls barely past menarche prompted several states to step up enforcement of statutory rape laws, both to protect the girls and to reduce out-of-wedlock births.

There was one problem, though. The image was largely wrong. What many news reports on the studies neglected to mention was that 62 percent of the teen-age mothers were 18 or 19 years old and, therefore, like the fathers of their babies, adults. Also ignored was the fact that the researchers did not differentiate between married and single teenagers. Subsequent studies have determined that of all those age 15 to 17 who gave birth, only 8 percent were unmarried girls made pregnant by men at least five years older.

"It's a sizable minority," said John Hutchins, a spokesman for the National Campaign to Prevent Teen Pregnancy, "a percentage that we should definitely be concerned about. But it is still a small percentage. If all of our attention is placed on that, we're not understanding the full problem."

The tale of the predatory males is just one example of what has become a disquieting trend. Call it the "whoops factor," a phenomenon that starts with shoddy research or the misinterpretation of solid research, moves on quickly to public outcry, segues swiftly into the enactment of new laws or regulations and often ends with news organizations and some public policy mavens sounding like the late Gilda Radner's character, Emily Litella, as they sheepishly chirp, "Never mind!"

## Arson, Rape, Poison

The public has been buffeted by reports suggesting a campaign to torch black churches, a surge in juvenile crime, rampant child abuse in day-care centers, a rape crisis on college campuses and the continued poisoning of the country by cancer-causing chemicals like alar, saccharin or cyclamates or by electromagnetic forces emanating from high-voltage power wires.

Last week a panel of scientists from the National Cancer Institute and some leading hospitals reported after an exhaustive study that there is no evidence that living near power lines causes elevated rates of childhood leukemia. The link had been suggested by a poorly designed 1979 study by researchers at the University of Colorado. After that study was reported, parents of children with cancer sued power companies, and property values near power lines plummeted.

While there tends to be enough truth in many of these claims to warrant serious investigation and remedial action, some of the initial reports are so overblown as to produce panic and then cynicism. "It's what I call the Weather Channel phenomenon," said Robert Thompson, a professor of radio and television at Syracuse University. "Five minutes into watching it, you're convinced that you have to be really concerned about

that front moving in. The next thing you know you've turned off the TV in a state of panic, feeling that you should be sand-bagging your house."

When the brewing problem is exposed as a kind of Comet Kohoutek of social pathology, there is a sense of betrayal, complacency and, finally, attention is drawn away from the true extent of the problem to the methodology that was used to unearth it.

"A brilliant sleight-of-hand gets achieved," Mr. Thompson said. "These are problems that are difficult to solve. And if we divert attention to a debate on how they are covered or how they are measured, then we don't have to make the tough choices on how to actually address them."

Underneath the embarrassing retreats from what in hindsight seems shabby research, superficial journalism or a triumph of politically motivated public relations lies a much deeper problem: Americans' willingness, almost eagerness, to accept a Hobbesian view of man as a brutish thug who if left unchecked would sow chaos and destruction. In this atmosphere, even reports like the one claiming that one quarter of all female college students are raped each year are readily believed.

Moreover, "people are always looking for one single-bullet answer," said Kristin Moore, president of Child Trends Inc., a Washington-based research organization specializing in adolescent sexual issues. "But things are more complicated than people want them to be."

And they are more complicated than many reporters and editors want them to be. Cramped by space and time, and usually not having much knowledge of statistics, journalists are often bamboozled by "experts" bearing impressive numbers or they fail to put the numbers in historical or demographic perspective.

"The media do not have the time, inclination or skill to really dig deeply into reports of research or claims made by political leaders," said Alfred Blumstein, a professor of criminology at Carnegie Mellon University in Pittsburgh. "It merely transmits them, and transmits them in a way to make headlines or sound bites on TV."

Thus, when the Department of Health and Human Services estimated in 1983 that 1.5 million children are reported missing each year, few people questioned the information. With the imprimatur of the Federal Government, a national campaign sprang up that included pictures of missing children on milk cartons and campaigns instructing children how to avoid being kidnapped.

Later, more rigorous studies would find that 3,200 to 4,600 children a year are abducted by strangers. To be sure, that is a large number. But it is dwarfed by the more than 350,000 children who, the Justice Department estimated later, are snatched by a parent in custody disputes, and it is nowhere near 1.5 million.

The definition of a particular group as victims—often with solid historical and contemporary evidence—also helps color the public's receptivity to studies or claims about them.

For example, last year, a spate of fires at African-American churches conjured images of white nightriders running amok or a reprise of the 1963 Birmingham church bombing. President Clinton appointed a task force to look into the problem. Last month, the task force reported that there was no national conspiracy of hate groups; the fires stemmed in part from racism but also from financial profit, burglary and personal revenge. Indeed, about one-third of the 76 people arrested in the church cases between Jan. 1, 1995, and May 27, 1997, were black.

Often, the unwillingness of reporters to ask hard questions or of policy makers to provide a context for data can lead regulators and lawmakers into broad-brush policies that waste resources and political capital.

In May, the House of Representatives, in response to reports of surging juvenile crime and an increase in the number of young killers, voted to offer states $1.5 billion in financial incentives to require that juveniles accused of violent crimes be tried as adults. Even as the House acted, the Bureau of Criminal Justice Statistics reported that while juvenile homicides had risen, they were highly concentrated. The bureau determined that in 1995, one-third took place in just 10 of the counties in the country. It added that 84 percent of the nation's counties had no juvenile homicides at all.

## Review

1. What does Holmes mean by the "whoops" factor?

2. Why do the media sometimes report false or misleading information?

3. What are the consequences of false or misleading information?

## Applications

1. Use the *Readers' Guide to Periodical Literature* to look up articles that pertain to two or more of the cases cited by Holmes. Do any of the articles acknowledge the possibility that the information might be erroneous or incomplete? Practice your critical-thinking skills by making a list of questions that could be raised about the claims in the article, questions that might lead you to look for additional evidence.

   Now look through a recent magazine or newspaper. Find an article that makes a claim about some social or natural phenomenon. Make a list of questions that you would like to have answered before accepting the conclusions of the article.

2. Even though claims are made and later retracted, some people read or hear about the original claim but not the retraction. How many people do you think still accept some of the erroneous claims made in this article? Interview a dozen people. Take each of the claims that Holmes describes, and put them into this kind of format: "A report appeared that 65 percent of teen-age mothers have children by adult men. Have you heard of the report? Do you think it is true? Why or why not?"

   How many people recall the reports? How many believed the reports whether or not they had heard of them? How many knew both of the original reports and the retractions?

## Related Web Sites

1. *http://www.criticalthinking.org/*. Home page of the Critical Thinking Consortium, with information on critical thinking in various areas of life, including education.

2. *http://www.skeptic.com/*. The Skeptic's Society and publications offer many good illustrations of applying critical thinking to information and events.

# Part Three

## *Micro and Macro*

Imagine that you have finished school and secured a well-paying job. Your work is not the passion of your life, but you are pleased with the income you get from it. After five years, you have gotten a number of promotions and your income continues to rise. You don't always get along with your boss—your personalities clash. Even so, you're a good team player and do your job well. Then one day the boss calls you in and tells you that you are going to be laid off. It could be temporary, but more likely it will be permanent. In fact, you are one of a group of people who are being let go and only a small number have any hope of coming back to work for the company.

How can you explain the loss of your job? Actually, there are a number of possibilities. Perhaps there was a downturn in the economy that negatively affected the industry, in which you worked, and led to downsizing. Perhaps new government regulations greatly increased the costs of running the business, forcing the layoff of personnel. Perhaps you were one of those chosen to be laid off because you were not sufficiently enthused about your work. Perhaps you are unlikely to be among the small group rehired because of your often strained relationship with your boss.

The first two explanations are macro, and the last two are micro. In essence, sociologists define micro factors as those at the individual level–such as attitudes and patterns of interaction–and macro factors as those at the level of society–such as inequality, social roles, and institutions like the economy and government. Macro factors may be used to explain other macro factors (government action affects the economy) or micro factors (education tends to foster more liberal attitudes). Similarly, micro factors may be used to explain other micro factors (prejudicial attitudes result in discriminatory behavior toward someone of another race) or macro factors (negative attitudes toward the poor inhibit government action to alleviate poverty in the society).

In practice, as this selection shows, a more realistic and complete understanding requires us to recognize that both micro and macro factors are at work. Social life is a never a simple matter of A causes B, but rather that the more complex A, B, C, D, E, and F together cause G. ✦

# 5
# Who Believes in Equality in Marriage and Family Life?

*Malathi L. Apparala*
*Alan Reifman*
*Joyce Munsch*

*Most of our students, like a majority of Americans surveyed, say that they prefer an egalitarian marriage, one in which husband and wife share equally in both the work and the rewards of family life. Not everyone agrees. There are many people, both in the United States and other nations, who believe that the husband should be the head of the family, the final authority over all marital and family matters. Those who hold to the latter position typically view housework and child-rearing tasks as the responsibility of the wife. How can we explain these differing **attitudes**?*

*The authors of this selection tackle that question by looking at a variety of both micro and macro factors that might affect attitudes about egalitarianism in marriage and family life. Using a number of different theories along with research done by others, they pose a series of **hypotheses**, testable statements about relationships between individual attitudes and other variables. Before you read this selection, think for a moment about your own attitude. Do you believe in equal sharing or in the husband having the final authority? Now try to answer the question of why you have this attitude. Do you think your age, gender, religion, **social class** position, or political beliefs have anything to do with it? How about the American **economy** or **culture**? All of these are among the factors the authors examined in their effort to explain differences in attitudes. Their research clearly demonstrates the importance of both macro and micro factors in explaining any social phenomenon.*

*In addition, the authors draw out the practical applications of their findings. They suggest some actions that can be taken to shape and change attitudes about egalitarianism in marriage and family life, and note that changing the attitudes will also change the behavior. In other words, they show that social scientific research is not merely an "academic" affair, but that it has implications for improving the quality of life.*

Men's and women's roles have experienced a major historical transformation due to changes in family, society, and paid labor. The traditional one career family is slowly diminishing with the increased participation of women in the labor force, with the greatest increase in labor force participation among married women with young children. In the United States at the end of the 1990s, among married couples with children less than 6 years of age, 61% of the mothers were employed (Bureau of Labor Statistics, 1998). One might expect women's increased labor force participation to influence men's and women's participation in household tasks. In fact, recent research in the United States on changes in gender role attitudes has found a general liberal trend of increasing support for egalitarian roles (Iglehart, 1982; Jorgenson & Tanner, 1983; National Election Study, 1999). Household labor, in particular, has been the subject of extensive research in recent years. In his decade review paper for the 1990s, Coltrane (2000) was able to cite more than 200 scholarly papers and books on household labor that were published during that time.

In this study we focused on respondents' attitudes about whether certain household and childcare tasks should be performed primarily by fathers, mothers, or both. Because the data set being used did not include a measure of actual task performance, we could not look specifically at attitude/behavior correlation, but many researchers have found positive associations between husbands' (and wives') egalitarian attitudes and husbands' household and childcare participation (e.g., Baxter, 1997; Bird, Bird, & Scruggs, 1984; Ishii-Kuntz & Coltrane, 1992; for a review, see Coltrane, 2000). Although some researchers (Bittman & Lovejoy, 1993; Lamb, 1986) have found that fathers' amount of actual participation has not kept pace with other societal changes, attitudes remain a reasonably good indicator of participation. This correspondence is enhanced by the fact that the attitudes measured in this study are highly specific to household and childcare tasks (e.g., who should feed the children or take them to the doctor) rather than general gender-role attitudes (e.g., men's and women's roles in society at large). Therefore, they are the kind of attitudes most likely to correlate with actual household behaviors. This argument follows from what social psychologists have referred to as the correspondence or specificity issue, which says that for attitudes and behavior to correlate, they must be measured at the same level of specificity (Ajzen & Fishbein, 1977; Kraus, 1995). The present research, therefore, is based on the belief that it is important in its own right to examine specific attitudes toward fathers' and mothers' performance of household tasks and childcare, but also on the assumption that such attitudes may be predictive of actual behavior.

Another important focus of this study is our examination of both individual- and societal-level influences on individuals' attitudes. Prior studies have concentrated on respondents' attitudes toward and participation in household labor as a function of micro-level factors such as individual resources and time spent on paid work (e.g., Baxter, 1997). Less information has been collected at the societal level. Feminists argue that gender issues operate not only at the micro level but also at the macro level. One might expect that countries that have progressed toward gender equality might also have progressed in terms of domestic division of labor between husbands and wives. Coltrane (2000) noted that cross-national and comparative studies of household labor have become increasingly common, and that this may further our understanding of "links

between household labor and other cultural, institutional, and structural factors" (p. 1218). Accordingly, another contribution of the present study is the use of a multinational data set that allowed variables at both the micro (individual) and macro (country) levels to predict attitudes toward parents' division of household labor and childcare. . . . The theories and empirical findings that ground our hypotheses are discussed next.

## Exchange/Resource Theory

Exchange/resource theory assumes that "the social organization of married couples' family role dynamics is based on the continual exchange of rewards and gratifications" (Lam & Haddad, 1992, p. 69). This theory and similar ones (Ishii-Kuntz & Coltrane, 1992; Sanchez & Kane, 1996) assume that household members use their resources to bargain for lower involvement in household tasks. This theory predicts that the increasing movement of married women into the labor market should lead to an egalitarian division of labor in families and a move in the direction of "equal partner marriages" (Lam & Haddad, 1992). On the basis of Lam and Haddad's resource theory, at the individual level, it could be assumed that when women have more resources (e.g., education, income, occupation), belong to a higher social class, and contribute more to household income, they would have more liberal attitudes toward participation in household tasks (i.e., husbands should share equally in these tasks). Similarly it could be assumed that the more resources men have (e.g., power, income, education), the less liberal their attitudes toward participation in household tasks would be (i.e., women should do most of the work). At the macro level, respondents living in countries in which women are empowered would be expected to have more liberal attitudes. In sum, this theory suggests that the person with more material resources derived from outside the home will have more marital power and hence do less household work.

## Social Role Theory

Eagly and Steffen (1984) proposed that stereotypic beliefs arise from perceivers' observations of women and men in differing social roles. For instance, women are considered to be more communal (selfless and concerned about others) and less agentic (self-assertive and motivated to master) than men (Eagly & Steffen, 1984; Hoffman, 1977). The differences in the distribution of women and men into the roles of homemaker and employee might account for the stereotypic beliefs. The fact that in family settings husbands tend to have an overall power and status advantage over wives also contributes to these perceptions. At the macro level, Eagly's social role theory predicts that in countries where women have a large presence in the paid labor force, this distribution of social roles will lead citizens to perceive men and women on more equal terms and thus to endorse egalitarian attitudes.

## Postmaterialism

Materialism and postmaterialism (Inglehart, 1988) refer to the degree to which people have as their primary concern, respectively, maintaining order and economic growth or giving people a "voice." As used in the present study, materialism/postmaterialism represents a tool for describing individuals and societies, rather than a theory per se. Inglehart argued that individuals in wealthier societies hold more postmaterialistic values. It is expected that individuals with postmaterialist values hold more egalitarian attitudes than do individuals with materialistic values. At the societal level, it is expected that the more postmaterialistic a country is, the more egalitarian are its citizens' attitudes toward the division of household work and childcare. As is apparent from the above discussion, materialism can be seen as a property either of the individual or of the country (aggregating over its citizens). In this study, we took the latter approach and used each country's percentage of postmaterialistic respondents as a measure of national materialism because this seemed most consistent with Inglehart's writings.

## Gender-Role and Household Attitudes

Studies that focus on predicting attitudes toward men's and women's participation in household tasks and childcare per se appear to be rare. Nonetheless, there are at least two bodies of literature that cover areas similar enough to perceptions of the gender division of household labor that they could inform our hypothesis development. One line of research is on fairness evaluations; by examining men's and women's perceptions of the fairness of their own amount of housework, we may be able to draw some inferences as to how respondents (of both genders) would designate tasks as being better performed by the father, mother, or both. The second line of research is on the prediction of more general attitudes toward gender roles.

## Fairness Evaluations

Fairness evaluations must be judged in the context of the fact that women on the whole tend to perform about two thirds of household labor (Coltrane, 2000). In translating fairness evaluations into the kinds of attitudes measured in the present study, we argue that the same factors that lead women to perceive their own amount of housework as unfair should also lead respondents (especially women) to believe that both the father and mother should perform each of the household tasks. We also expect the same pathway from perceiving unfairness to believing that both parents should share housework to hold for men although perhaps more tentatively.

Coltrane (2000) concluded that "Fairness evaluations . . . are influenced by employment, education, and ideology, but 1990s results were mixed" (p. 1224). Some apparent trends, however, include a negative relationship for women between paid work hours and perceived fairness and higher levels of education for both spouses being associated with perceiving less fairness. Gender itself appears to predict fairness evaluations. In one study, Dancer and Gilbert (1993) examined husbands' and wives' perceptions of who was doing their "fair share" of household work and parenting. In self-ratings, wives were more likely than husbands to say that they were doing their fair share. Ratings of the other spouse revealed that husbands thought that their wives were doing their fair share more so than wives thought their husbands were.

## General Gender-Role Attitudes

In the more general domain of gender-role attitudes, husbands' gender-role orientations are more traditional than wives' (Kamo, 1988). When Jorgenson and Tanner (1983) compared husbands' and wives' attitudes on items such as "it is more important for a wife to help her husband's career than to have one herself" and "it is much better for everyone involved if the man is the achiever outside the home and the woman takes care of the home and family," more egalitarian attitudes tended to be endorsed by individuals who were younger, highly educated, and had an employed spouse.

## Hypotheses

Based upon these theories and prior findings in the literature, the following hypotheses were offered (most follow straight from the literature reviewed previously, but hypotheses based on more limited findings or our own surmises are also presented here).

### Individual-Level Hypotheses

1. Attitudes toward the division of household work and childcare will be more egalitarian when respondents are younger.
2. Women will hold more egalitarian attitudes than will men.
3. Unmarried individuals will hold more egalitarian attitudes than will their married counterparts.
4. (a) The more resources (i.e., social class, education, and income) women have, the more egalitarian their attitudes toward domestic labor and childcare will be.
   (b) The more resources (i.e., social class, education, and income) men

have, the less egalitarian their attitudes toward domestic labor and childcare will be.
5. Attitudes toward the division of household work and childcare will be more egalitarian when families live in medium or large towns.
6. Attitudes toward the division of household work and childcare will be less egalitarian when respondents identify themselves as Catholic (derived from Wilcox & Jelen, 1993).

### Family-Level Hypotheses

7. Attitudes toward the division of household work and childcare will be more egalitarian when the family size is large, as both parents' efforts are needed to attend to many children.
8. Attitudes toward the division of household work and childcare will be more egalitarian when child(ren) less than 4 years old is (are) present.
9. (a) Similar to 4(a), when women contribute most to family income, they will have more egalitarian attitudes.
   (b) Similar to 4(b), when men contribute most to family income, they will have less egalitarian attitudes.

### Macro-Level Hypotheses

10. Countries that score high on the United Nations Gender Empowerment Measure (GEM), which measures women's power, will have citizens who hold egalitarian attitudes (derived from Lam and Haddad's exchange/resource theory).
11. Countries with a large presence of women in the paid labor force will have citizens who hold egalitarian attitudes (derived from Eagly's social role theory).
12. The more postmaterialistic the countries are, the more egalitarian will be citizens' attitudes toward the division of household work and childcare (derived from Inglehart's postmaterialism and materialism).

# Method

## Euro-barometer Data Set

We used data from the Euro-barometer surveys, which were conducted in March–April 1993 (Reif & Melich, 1993). Euro-barometer surveys have been conducted for many years. The one used presently included 13 European countries: Belgium, Denmark, France, Germany (we combined the data for West Germany and East Germany, Greece, Ireland, Italy, Luxembourg, the Netherlands, Norway, Portugal, Spain, and the United Kingdom. All are members of the European Union (also known as the European Community) economic cooperation group except Norway, whose voters declined to join (Wright, 1995). Finland also participated in the Euro-barometer, but the crucial parenting items used in this research were not asked in this country. A special focus of this Euro-barometer was family issues. Most of the data were gathered through personal interviews. . . . The target population was individuals at least 15 years of age residing in the 13 nations.

# Measures

## Dependent Variables

Attitudes toward household participation were measured with a set of questions. The investigators introduced the questions as follows: "Here is a list of household tasks which may be completed by the father or the mother, or by both. Please tell for each of them, whether you think they should be carried out mainly by the father (score 1), mainly by the mother (score 2), by both (score 3), or don't know (score 4)." The 12 household and childcare tasks scored included "playing sport with the children, bringing the children to activities such as drama, music, (boy) scouts . . . changing the baby's nappies, dressing the children or choosing their clothes, taking the children to the doctor, helping the children with their schoolwork or going to parent meetings, feeding the children, buying toys for the children, giving pocket-money to the children, punishing the children, putting the children

to bed, and answering important questions raised by the child."

Egalitarianism was measured by counting for each respondent the number of "both parent" (3) answers on the parenting tasks (12 maximum). Percent egalitarianism was then calculated by dividing the number of egalitarian answers by the number of parenting items answered with one of the three main choices (mainly father, mainly mother, and both).

## Independent Variables

The study included the following measures of individual and family/household variables. The respondent's actual age in years was used. For gender, respondents identified themselves as male (1) or female (2).

Education was measured using the question: "How old were you when you stopped full-time education?" We created a four-level variable of education: 1 for still studying, 2 for an early end (by age 16), 3 for a traditional end (ages 17–22), and 4 for a late end (older ages).

Size of household was measured by asking the question: "How many people live in your household, including yourself, all adults and children?"

We found the work hours variable in the Euro-barometer data set to be somewhat ambiguous. We therefore constructed a simple dichotomous variable of heavy work hours (40–100 hr per week; coded as 1) versus all other lesser hours of work or no work (coded as 0).

The marital status variable was originally measured by asking the question: "Here is a list describing possible family circumstances. Could you give me the letter which corresponds best to your own situation?" The list included items such as married and never lived in a couple before; married and lived in a couple before; remarried; unmarried and never having lived with a partner before; unmarried and having lived with a partner before; divorced; separated; and widowed. Marital status was dichotomized into 0 for live alone (single, divorced, separated, and widowed) and 1 for married or living as married.

Social class was measured by asking the question: "If you were asked to choose one of these five names for your social class, which would you say you belong to?" The responses included middle class, lower middle class, working class, upper class, and upper-middle class, plus the option of "other."

Religion was measured by collapsing several categories of religion (such as Roman Catholic, Protestant, Orthodox, Jew, Muslim, Buddhist, Hindu) into a dichotomous variable (coded 1 if the respondent was Catholic and 0 if the respondent was not Catholic). This decision was based on Wilcox and Jelen's finding in the 1987 Euro-barometer survey that Catholic respondents were less supportive of gender equality than non-Catholics (Wilcox & Jelen, 1993).

Presence of young children was measured by asking the question: "In which of these age category(ies) are the children who still live in your household?" The responses included categorical choices such as under 4 years, 4–6 years, and so forth. The original variable was recorded by assigning a score of 1 if the respondent had child(ren) under 4 years, and a 0 if his or her children were exclusively older than 4 years or the person did not have children.

Contribution to family income was measured by asking the question: "In your household [are you] the person who contributes most to the household income?" The responses were coded 1 for "Yes" and 2 for "No."

Political ideology was based on a 10-point scale that ranged from 1 (left) through 10 (right). Respondents who scored toward the left are those who believe in liberal political ideas and views and might affiliate with the Democratic party in the United States or labor or socialist parties in other countries. Respondents who scored toward the right are those who believe in conservative political ideas and views and might affiliate with the Republican party in the United States or conservative parties in other countries.

The following country-level variables were also obtained. Female empowerment was measured using GEM, which includes as its indicators each country's percentage of seats in parliament held by women, percentage of professional and technical workers who are women, and women's share of earned income (United Nations Statistical Report, 1998a). A higher GEM value represents greater empowerment of women.

Women's share of adult labor force is a statistic focused on individuals aged 15 and above who were in the labor force in 1995. It comes from UN labor force statistics (United Nations Statistical Report, 1998b).

The percentage of people in each country who hold postmaterialistic, materialistic, or mixed values was measured in the Euro-barometer by asking respondents to rank the importance of items such as "maintaining order in the nation; giving the people more say in important government decisions; fighting rising prices; and protecting freedom of speech." Respondents were asked to rank their first and second choice. The respondents who selected the first and third items were labeled "materialist," those who selected the second and fourth items were labeled as "postmaterialist," and other combinations were labeled as "mixed."

Per capita Gross National Product (GNP) was measured using the 1991 GNP values given by Oishi, Diener, Lucas, and Suh (1999), converted to U.S. dollars.

Collectivism/individualism ratings for each country were based on a scale reported by Oishi et al. (1999), which ranged from 1 (most collectivist) to 10 (most individualist).

# Results

## Individual-Level (Within-Country)

The individual (level 1) results used to predict egalitarianism within each nation showed that . . . respondents in general seemed to be high in egalitarianism. When we looked at the predictor variables, several patterns emerged. In all of the countries except Luxembourg, age was significantly and negatively related to egalitarianism. Attitudes toward parenting tasks were thus more egalitarian when respondents were younger, which supports Hypothesis 1.

Hypothesis 2 predicted that women would hold more egalitarian attitudes than would men. Results for gender showed that in almost half of the countries, being female was significant and positively related to egalitarianism, which provides partial support for Hypothesis 2. In no country was egalitarianism significantly related to marital status; therefore, Hypothesis 3 did not receive support.

In slightly more than half of the countries, conservative political ideology was significant and negatively related to egalitarianism. The more liberal or left-leaning the respondents were, the more egalitarian were their attitudes.

In most of the countries, egalitarianism was not related to whether or not the respondent was Catholic, worked long hours (40–100 hr per week), or lived in locations of different sizes. Thus, Hypotheses 5 and 6 are not supported. In four countries, social class was significant and positively related to egalitarianism, which indicates that the more resources the respondents had, the more egalitarian their attitudes toward domestic work and childcare.

### Country-Level Analyses

The country-level data . . . found that gender empowerment, per capita GNP, and individualism were significantly and positively related to countries' level of egalitarianism. Thus, Hypothesis 10 (countries that score high on the United Nations GEM of women's political and economic power have citizens who hold egalitarian attitudes) was supported. However, Hypothesis 11 (countries with a large female presence in the paid labor force have citizens who hold egalitarian attitudes) was not supported. Similarly, Hypothesis 12 (the more postmaterialistic the countries are, the more egalitarian are the citizens' attitudes toward the division of household work and childcare) was not supported.

### Analyses Within Gender

Some of the hypotheses predicted that the relationship between resources (social class, education, and income) and egalitarianism would be different in women and men. Hypothesis 4(a) predicted that the more resources women had, the more egalitarian their attitudes toward domestic labor and childcare would be. On the other hand, Hypothesis 4(b) predicted that the more resources men had, the less egalitarian their attitudes toward domestic labor and childcare would be. . . . For men, egalitarianism was predicted from age, marital status, political ideology, and Catholicism. Younger men, those who were married, those who were more liberal, and those who were not Catholic were more egalitarian. Similar findings were observed for women. Age, political ideology (conservatism), and Catholicism were significantly and negatively related to egalitarianism for women. Women who were younger, politically liberal, and not Catholic were more egalitarian. Thus, Hypothesis 6 (attitudes toward the division of household work will be less egalitarian when respondents identify themselves as Catholic) was supported. Social class was significantly and positively related to egalitarianism for women; those who belonged to higher social classes were more egalitarian, which supports Hypothesis 4(a).

## Education Analyses

Early enders stood out as the least egalitarian in their attitudes toward domestic and parenting tasks. It was also revealed that early enders were the oldest respondents (M = 50.63 years, compared to 40.87 for the traditional enders and 43.38 for the late enders). This suggests that the connection between less education and low egalitarianism could be due to age, as people born in the first half of the twentieth century may not have as much education as younger people and may have been socialized to hold more traditional attitudes toward gender roles. However, education was still a significant predictor of egalitarianism with age held constant.

## Discussion

In this study, we used both individual- and macro-level variables to test a series of hypotheses about attitudes toward fathers' and mothers' involvement in household tasks and childcare. The hypotheses were based upon resource theory (Lam & Haddad, 1992), social role theory (Eagly & Steffen,

1984; Eagly & Wood, 1999), and Inglehart's postmaterialism/materialism construct (Inglehart, 1988).

At the individual level, respondents were more likely to hold egalitarian attitudes toward household work and childcare when they were younger, were female, and held liberal political attitudes. At the country level, women's empowerment, GNP, and individualism were positively related to egalitarianism. When individual-level results were examined separately by gender, an additional finding of particular importance to power/resource theories was that social class was positively related to egalitarian attitudes in women, but not in men. It appears that as women gain resources, they expect there to be a more equal division of household and childcare responsibility. It is perhaps not surprising that men (who usually have the greater resources in a relationship) hold similar attitudes toward the division of household labor across socioeconomic statuses.

In all of the countries except Luxembourg, age was significantly and negatively related to egalitarianism, which supports Hypothesis 1. Banaszak and Plutzer (1993) found that irrespective of age, residents of Luxembourg appear to be exceptionally egalitarian in their attitudes. A possible explanation for the negative relationship between age and egalitarian attitudes in most of the countries might be that younger men are more likely to have wives who are younger, work outside the home, and have children under the age of 6 years. This increases demands at home on both the husband and wife and necessitates a more equitable allocation of work at home. Younger women, on the other hand, might be more egalitarian because they are likely to be more educated, to be employed, and may have been socialized to accept more egalitarian family roles than were older women. Other research has supported the idea that younger respondents more closely identify with nontraditional attitudes (Baxter & Kane, 1995; Jorgenson & Tanner, 1983) than do older respondents. Another cross-national study of gender equality and gender attitudes revealed that older respondents held more conservative views than did their younger counterparts (Baxter

& Kane, 1995). Banaszak and Plutzer reported a similar finding that age had a significant negative relation to feminist attitudes.

We also found that in nearly half of the countries, women held significantly more egalitarian attitudes than did men, which partially supports Hypothesis 2. Women who have experienced oppression or discrimination in families or at work, who lack opportunities, and who are relegated to lower positions in society, family, and politics might develop strong feminist values and a willingness to fight against inequality and thus have more egalitarian attitudes toward family roles (Banaszak & Plutzer, 1993). Other researchers have found that although both husbands and wives hold traditional views on family roles, wives are generally less traditional than their husbands (Jorgenson & Tanner, 1983).

Because some of the countries exhibited a significant positive individual-level relationship between gender and egalitarianism and others did not, we looked for a common characteristic that could distinguish these results . . . further work is needed to explain why gender is significantly related to egalitarianism only in certain countries.

The individual-level regressions done separately for men and women showed that non-Catholic men and women were more egalitarian in their household attitudes than were their Catholic counterparts . . . individual Catholics have been found in other research (Wilcox & Jelen, 1993) to be less supportive than non-Catholics of gender equality, which suggests that religious affiliation may influence one's attitudes toward gender equality.

In roughly half of the countries, conservative political ideology was significantly and negatively related to egalitarianism, which partially supports the conclusion of Banaszak and Plutzer (1993) that, for both women and men, affiliation with a leftist party significantly increases feminist attitudes. It appears that people with leftist political affiliations might be more egalitarian in their attitudes toward household tasks and childcare and have more liberal values and beliefs about family roles.

At the macro level, results indicated that countries with high scores on the United Nations GEM, which measures women's power in terms of participation in politics and the work force, have citizens who hold more egalitarian attitudes. Thus, it is likely that women in countries with greater macro-level empowerment of women have more resources that may enable them to have egalitarian attitudes toward household work and childcare. The results also indicated that per capita GNP and individualism were significantly and positively correlated with egalitarianism. Because per capita GNP measures national wealth, countries with higher GNPs have men and women who are educated, working, and earning relatively high incomes, resources that allow them to hold egalitarian attitudes toward family roles. Individualism, on the other hand, may also foster egalitarian attitudes because individualism basically means that people are responsible for their own actions. An individualist recognizes that humans must work to transform their environment to meet their needs in the family and workplace. Therefore, in an individualistic society it is likely that people give importance to each individual, are aware of gender equality, and hence have egalitarian attitudes toward family roles. However, given that countries' individualism and GNP are themselves highly correlated, caution must be exercised in interpreting these results.

Because the macro-level data set we built around the Euro-barometer study included only a small number of economically advantaged countries, replication from other data sets would increase our confidence in the results. Norris and Inglehart (2000) provided a partial replication based on the World Values Surveys, which involve 55 societies that span a wide range of economic well-being. Norris and Inglehart used a single item about male and female political leaders as their indicator of egalitarianism (respondents' answers were averaged within each country to provide country-level data). Two of Norris and Inglehart's findings conceptually replicated our own: Country-level egalitarianism was positively correlated with both per capita GNP and percentage of women in parliament. The GEM used in our study includes a measure of countries' percentages of women in parliament.

The findings of this study also have implications for how men and women enact their roles in the family and workplace. Egalitarian attitudes toward participation in household tasks and childcare may lead to actual greater involvement of fathers and mothers in household tasks and childcare and this, in turn, might lead to greater intimacy in parent-child relationships, which fosters positive development in children (Berry & Rao, 1997). Congruence between men's and women's attitudes toward household tasks and childcare and their actual participation in those tasks are also related to marital satisfaction (Coltrane, 2000; Perry-Jenkins & Crouter, 1990).

An important message from the household-labor literature is that attitudes do matter. We suggest that rather than focusing solely on the importance of role-sharing and equal responsibility in families, researchers must also examine attitudes about roles and how those attitudes predict role behavior. Family scholars and professionals who work with families must understand the relation between attitudes and behaviors and support couples and families when differences arise between the two. Knowledge of attitudes toward participation in household tasks and childcare also informs issues such as gender equality, career choices, and work-related problems.

Programs that promote favorable attitudes toward household tasks and childcare should be undertaken by organizations that work for the welfare of families and children. These programs should be complemented by policies and practices adopted by both government and employers that allow not only for paid maternity leave but also for paid paternity leave so that fathers can spend time with their newborn infants. Such changes are likely to encourage more favorable attitudes toward household tasks and childcare over time. According to a report (National Center for the Workplace, 1993) on the U.S. Family and Medical Leave Act of 1993 (which pertains to unpaid leave), many European countries are already extending generous family and medical leave benefits to their citizens. A review of parental leave policies in 16 European countries showed that these countries mandate an average of 68 weeks of leave, including 33 weeks of paid leave (National Center for the Workplace, 1993). In a recent development, California became the first state in the United States to offer a paid family leave program (USA Today, 2002).

# References

Ajzen, I., & Fishbein, M. (1977). Attitude-behavior relations: A theoretical analysis and review of empirical research. *Psychological Bulletin*, 84, 888–918.

Banaszak, L. A., & Plutzer, E. (1993). Social bases of feminism in Europe. *Public Opinion Quarterly*, 57, 29–53.

Baxter, J. (1997). Gender equality and participation in housework: A cross-national perspective. *Journal of Comparative Family Studies*, 28, 220–247.

Baxter, J., & Kane, E. W. (1995). Dependence and independence: A cross-national analysis of gender inequality and gender attitudes. *Gender and Society*, 9, 193–215.

Berry, J. O., & Rao, J. M. (1997). Balancing employment and fatherhood: A systems perspective. *Journal of Family Issues*, 18, 386–402.

Bird, G. W., Bird, G. A., & Scruggs, M. (1984). Determinants of family task sharing: A study of husbands and wives. *Journal of Marriage and the Family*, 46, 345–355.

Bittman, M., & Lovejoy, E. (1993). Domestic power: Negotiating an unequal division of labor within a framework of equality. *Australian and New Zealand Journal of Sociology*, 29, 302–321.

Bureau of Labor Statistics. (1998, May). Labor force statistics from the Current Population Survey. Washington, DC: Author. Retrieved February 2, 1999, from *http://stats.bls.gov/news.release/famee.t04.htm*.

Coltrane, S. (2000). Research on household labor: Modeling and measuring the social embeddedness of routine family work. *Journal of Marriage and the Family*, 62, 1208–1233.

Dancer, L. S., & Gilbert, L. A. (1993). Spouses' family work participation and its relation to wives' occupational level. *Sex Roles*, 28, 127–145.

Eagly, A. H., & Steffen, V. J. (1984). Gender stereotypes stem from the distribution of women and men into social roles. *Journal of Personality and Social Psychology*, 46, 735–754.

Eagly, A. H., & Wood, W. (1999). The origins of sex differences in human behavior: Evolved dispositions versus social roles. *American Psychologist*, 54, 408–423.

Hoffman, L. W. (1977). Changes in family roles, socialization, and sex differences. *American Psychologist*, 32, 644–657.

Iglehart, A. P. (1982). Wives, husbands, and social change: The role of social work. *Social Service Review*, 56, 27–38.

Inglehart, R. (1988). The renaissance of political culture. *American Political Science Review*, 82, 1203–1231.

Ishii-Kuntz, M., & Coltrane, S. (1992). Predicting the sharing of household labor: Are parenting and housework distinct? *Sociological Perspectives*, 35, 629–647.

Jorgenson, D. E., & Tanner, L. M. (1983). Attitude comparisons toward the wife/mother work-role: A study of husbands and wives. *International Journal of Sociology of the Family*, 13, 103–115.

Kamo, Y. (1988). Determinants of household division of labor—Resources, power and ideology. *Journal of Family Issues*, 9, 177–200.

Kraus, S. J. (1995). Attitudes and the prediction of behavior: A meta-analysis of the empirical literature. *Personality and Social Psychology Bulletin*, 21, 58–75.

Lam, L., & Haddad, T. (1992). Men's participation in family work: A case study. *International Journal of Sociology of the Family*, 22, 67–104.

Lamb, M. E. (1986). The changing roles of fathers. In M. E. Lamb (Ed.), *The father's role: Applied perspectives* (pp. 3–27). New York: Wiley.

National Center for the Workplace. (1993). Introduction: International comparisons. Retrieved September 22, 1999, from *http://violet.berkeley.edu/~iir/ncw/wpapers/scharlach/pagel.html*.

National Election Study. (1999). Equal role for women: The NES guide to public opinion and electoral behavior. Retrieved October 6, 2000, from *http://www.umich.edu/~nes/nesguide/toptable/tab4c_1.htm*.

Norris, P., & Inglehart, R. (2000, August). Cultural barriers to women's leadership: A worldwide comparison. Paper presented at the International Political Science Association World Congress, Quebec City. Retrieved July 26, 2001, from *http://ksghome.harvard.edu/~.pnorris.shorenstein.ksg/acrobat/IPSA2000culture.pdf*.

Oishi, S., Diener, E. F., Lucas, R. E., & Suh, E. M. (1999). Crosscultural variations in predictors of life satisfaction: Perspectives from needs and values. *Personality and Social Psychology Bulletin, 25,* 980–990.

Perry-Jenkins, M., & Crouter, A. C. (1990). Men's provider-role attitudes: Implications for household work and marital satisfaction. *Journal of Family Issues, 11,* 136–156.

Reif, K., & Melich, A. (1993, March–April). Euro-barometer 39.0: European community policies and family life [computer file]. 4th Edition Inter-university Consortium for Political and Social Research, Ann Arbor, MI.

Sanchez, L., & Kane, E. W. (1996). Women's and men's constructions of perceptions of housework fairness. *Journal of Family Issues, 17,* 358–387.

United Nations Statistical Report. (1998a). Human development indicators—Gender Empowerment Measure. New York: Author. Retrieved June 24, 1999, from *http://www.undp.org/hdro/98gem.htm.*

United Nations Statistical Report. (1998b). Human development indicators—Profile of people in work. New York: Author. Retrieved June 24, 1999, from *http://www.undp.org/hdro/iwork.htm.*

USA Today. (2002, September 24). California first state to offer paid family leave. Retrieved November 13, 2002, from *http://careers.usatoday.com/service/wfmy/national/content/news/onthejob/2002-09-24-calif-family-leave.*

Wilcox, C., & Jelen, T. G. (1993). Catholicism and opposition to gender equality in Western Europe. *International Journal of Public Opinion Research, 5,* 40–57.

Wright, J. W. (Ed.). (1995). *The universal almanac 1996.* Kansas City, MO: Andrews and McMeel.

## Review

1. Relate how this selection illustrates the point that theory is not just an intellectual exercise but a guide to research.

2. Briefly describe the factors that influence attitudes about egalitarianism in marriage and family life.

3. What are the implications for social policy of the authors' findings?

4. To what extent did this selection help you understand your own attitudes and those of your family and friends toward egalitarianism?

## Applications

1. Think about the family in which you grew up. How egalitarian was your family life? How egalitarian was the family life of others you knew—close friends or relatives? Which of the variables used in the authors' research helps explain what you have observed?

2. The authors point out that there tends to be congruence between attitudes and behavior, but also note that egalitarianism is not practiced as much as it is affirmed. Ask two or three sets of parents if they believe in an egalitarian division of labor. Then ask them to list which household and child care tasks each of them does. To what extent does their actual division of labor seem consistent with their attitudes?

## Related Web Sites

1. *www.undp.org/eo/documents/Micro Macro_SouthAsia.pdf.* A U.N. article offering a micro-macro analysis of poverty alleviation in Asia.

2. *http://www.unc.edu/~kurzman/iranian_family/.* An article about the attitudes of Iranian women toward marriage and family life.

---

Reprinted from: Malathi L. Apparala, Alan Reifman, and Joyce Munsch, "Cross-national comparison of attitudes toward fathers' and mothers' participation in household tasks and childcare." In *Sex Roles* 48 (March, 2003): 189–203. Copyright © 2003 by Kluwer Publishing. Reprinted with permission. ✦

# Unit II

## *Culture, Socialization, and Social Interaction*

This unit introduces more of the fundamental concepts in contemporary sociology. These concepts are essential to understanding the sociological perspective.

Take the concept of **culture,** for instance. In contrast to the popular use of the term as a synonym for refinement, sociologists and anthropologists define culture as everything that people create, ranging from technology to art to moral codes to customs. Thus, you can think of culture in contrast to nature. It is generally accepted that animals and insects adapt to their environment by instinctive means set by nature. On the other hand, the great variety of human adaptations to the environment depend on culture for their explanation. Since culture is learned rather than genetically transmitted, it is more readily changeable than nature's arrangements.

The first three articles in this unit, 6, 7, and 8, show the impact of norms. Like roles, norms are crucial for maintaining social order. They let you generally know what to expect from people even though you don't know them or know much about them. Norms can lead people in one society to behave in ways that appear odd or irrational to those in other societies. But all societies have norms, and those norms help maintain social order.

Order is also maintained through **socialization,** the fundamental process by which individuals learn about and adjust to their surrounding social world. All human beings are born into a particular social context in which they must learn to function. If the socialization is effective, the individual will internalize the culture, believing that this is the right way of life. Thus, the individual will fit in with the culture, follow its ways, and perpetuate them.

Socialization is a part of learning what it means to be male and female—gender is not a purely biological phenomenon. Selections 9 and 10 illustrate the socialization process by examining aspects of the learning of gender roles: the outcome when children are subjected to contradictory socializing forces and the influence of television. Selection 11 focuses on masculinity, and how patronizing strip clubs reflects some men's views of their masculinity.

Another concept addressed in this section is **interaction.** What kinds of factors affect the way we interact with each other? As selection 12 shows, gender roles and culture interact to affect touching behavior when people interact. Selection 13 highlights the way in which social norms and social background variables like race can affect people's social interaction. ✦

# Part One

## *Culture*

Culture includes everything created by people: their technology, their system of knowledge and beliefs, their art, their morals and laws, their customs, and all other products of human thought and action. By asserting that culture is the creation of human thought and action, sociologists stress that social life is the result of human interaction and human decisions rather than instincts.

In a sense, then, all the selections deal with culture in one way or another. In this part, however, we focus on norms and the way in which particular norms in two different societies—India and the United States—lead to behavior not found in many other societies. ✦

# 6

# India's Sacred Cow

*Marvin Harris*

**Structural-functional** *reasoning in sociology looks at cultural items such as norms, beliefs, institutions, and behavior patterns in terms of their consequences for social groups. When all the consequences are thoroughly assessed, a seemingly irrational belief or practice may appear more reasonable because of the functions it serves for the group. For example, a primitive tribe doing a rain dance to end a drought may seem irrational to an observer. But the collective ritual of the dance may keep tribal morale high until rain does come and, thereby, help preserve the group in the face of a crisis.*

*A cultural practice that strikes many observers as highly irrational is the strong reverence for cattle in India. Westerners (and even some Indians themselves) have long considered cattle worship to be a key element in India's continual flirtation with famine. Indian people go hungry while sacred cows are fed by the government. What could be more irrational? In his analysis of the Indian **ecosystem** (the system of living things, their environment, and their interrelationships), Harris finds these critics to be shortsighted. As a human ecologist, he is concerned with how a population adapts to its environment, given the technology and resources available. He is also interested in the prominent place cattle occupy in India's system of agricultural production. Most Indian farmers have small plots of land, so cattle are useful for fertilizer and for hauling. They also supply the farm family with milk, and their waste products serve as fuel and floor covering material. And cattle supply meat and leather for the larger economy. Most important, since cattle primarily eat what is inedible to humans, the two species are not in competition with each other for food. Devotion to cattle ensures that even when famine threatens, Indians will not slaughter their cattle to prevent starvation. To do so would cause even more severe problems in the long run.*

. . . Hindus venerate cows because cows are the symbol of everything that is alive. As Mary is to Christians the mother of God, the cow to Hindus is the mother of life. So there is no greater sacrilege for a Hindu than killing a cow. Even the taking of human life lacks the symbolic meaning, the unutterable defilement, that is evoked by cow slaughter.

According to many experts, cow worship is the number one cause of India's hunger and poverty. Some Western-trained agronomists say that the taboo against cow slaughter is keeping one hundred million "useless" animals alive. They claim that cow worship lowers the efficiency of agriculture because the useless animals contribute neither milk nor meat while competing for croplands and foodstuff with useful animals and hungry human beings. A study sponsored by the Ford Foundation in 1959 concluded that possibly half of India's cattle could be regarded as surplus in relation to food supply. And an economist from the University of Pennsylvania stated in 1971 that India has thirty million unproductive cows.

It does seem that there are enormous numbers of surplus, useless, and uneconomic animals, and that this situation is a direct result of irrational Hindu doctrines. . . .

Love of cow affects life in many ways. Government agencies maintain old age homes for cows at which owners may board their dry and decrepit animals free of charge. In Madras, the police round up stray cattle that have fallen ill and nurse them back to health by letting them graze on small fields adjacent to the station house. Farmers regard their cows as members of the family, adorn them with garlands and tassels, pray for them when they get sick, and call in their neighbors and a priest to celebrate the birth of a new calf. Throughout India, Hindus hang on their walls calendars that portray beautiful, bejeweled young women who have the bodies of big fat white cows. Milk is shown jetting out of each teat of these half-woman, half-zebu goddesses.

Starting with their beautiful human faces, cow pinups bear little resemblance to the typical cow one sees in the flesh. For most of the year their bones are their most prominent feature. Far from having milk gushing from every teat, the gaunt beasts barely manage to nurse a single calf to maturity. The average yield of whole milk from the typical hump-backed breed of zebu cow in India amounts to less than 500 pounds a year. Ordinary American dairy cattle produce over 5,000 pounds, while for champion milkers, 20,000 pounds is not unusual.But this comparison doesn't tell the whole story. In any given year about half of India's zebu cows give no milk at all—not a drop. . . .

Mohandas K. Gandhi was an ardent advocate of cow love and wanted a total ban on cow slaughter. When the Indian constitution was drawn up, it included a bill of rights for cows which stopped just short of outlawing every form of cow killing. Some states have since banned cow slaughter altogether, but others still permit exceptions. The cow question remains a major cause of rioting and disorders, not only between Hindus and the remnants of the Moslem community, but between the ruling Congress Party and extremist Hindu factions of cow lovers. . . .

· To Western observers familiar with modern industrial techniques of agriculture and stock raising, cow love seems senseless, even suicidal. The efficiency expert yearns to get his hands on all those useless animals and ship them off to a proper fate. And yet one finds certain inconsistencies in the condemnation of cow love. When I began to wonder if there might be a practical explanation for the sacred cow, I came across an intriguing government report. It said that India had too many cows but too few oxen. With so many cows around, how could there be a shortage of oxen? Oxen and male water buffalo are the principal source of traction for plowing India's fields. For each farm of ten acres or less, one pair of oxen or water buffalo is considered adequate. A little arithmetic shows that as far as plowing is concerned, there is indeed a shortage rather than a surplus of animals. India has 60 million farms, but only 80

million traction animals. If each farm had its quota of two oxen or two water buffalo, there ought to be 120 million traction animals—that is, 40 million more than are actually available. . . .

The shortage of draft animals is a terrible threat that hangs over most of India's peasant families. When an ox falls sick a poor farmer is in danger of losing his farm. . . . The Indian farmer who can't replace his sick or deceased ox is in much the same situation as an American farmer who can neither replace nor repair his broken tractor. But there is an important difference: tractors are made by factories, but oxen are made by cows. A farmer who owns a cow owns a factory for making oxen. With or without cow love, this is a good reason for him not to be too anxious to sell his cow to the slaughterhouse. One also begins to see why Indian farmers might be willing to tolerate cows that give only 500 pounds of milk per year. If the main economic function of the zebu cow is to breed male traction animals, then there's no point in comparing her with specialized American dairy animals, whose main function is to produce milk. Still, the milk produced by zebu cows plays an important role in meeting the nutritional needs of many poor families. Even small amounts of milk products can improve the health of people who are forced to subsist on the edge of starvation. . . .

Agriculture is part of a vast system of human and natural relationships. To judge isolated portions of this "ecosystem" in terms that are relevant to the conduct of American agribusiness leads to some very strange impressions. Cattle figure in the Indian ecosystem in ways that are easily overlooked or demeaned by observers from industrialized, high-energy societies. In the United States, chemicals have almost completely replaced animal manure as the principal source of farm fertilizer. American farmers stopped using manure when they began to plow with tractors rather than mules or horses. Since tractors excrete poisons rather than fertilizers, a commitment to large-scale machine farming is almost of necessity a commitment to the use of chemical fertilizers. And around the world today there has in fact grown up a vast integrated petro-chemical-tractor-truck industrial complex that produces farm machinery, motorized transport, oil and gasoline, and chemical fertilizers and pesticides upon which new high-yield production techniques depend.

For better or worse, most of India's farmers cannot participate in this complex, not because they worship their cows, but because they can't afford to buy tractors. Like other underdeveloped nations, India can't build factories that are competitive with the facilities of the industrialized nations nor pay for large quantities of imported industrial products. To convert from animals and manure to tractors and petrochemicals would require the investment of incredible amounts of capital. Moreover, the inevitable effect of substituting costly machines for cheap animals is to reduce the number of people who can earn their living from agriculture and to force a corresponding increase in the size of the average farm. We know that the development of large-scale agribusiness in the United States has meant the virtual destruction of the small family farm. Less than 5 percent of U.S. families now live on farms, as compared with 60 percent about a hundred years ago. If agribusiness were to develop along similar lines in India, jobs and housing would soon have to be found for a quarter of a billion displaced peasants.

Since the suffering caused by unemployment and homelessness in India's cities is already intolerable, an additional massive build-up of the urban population can only lead to unprecedented upheavals and catastrophes.

With this new alternative in view, it becomes easier to understand low-energy, small-scale, animal-based systems. As I have already pointed out, cows and oxen provide low-energy substitutes for tractors and tractor factories. They also should be credited with carrying out the functions of a petrochemical industry. India's cattle annually excrete about 700 million tons of recoverable manure. Approximately half of this total is used as fertilizer, while most of the remainder is burned to provide heat for cooking. The annual quantity of heat liberated by this dung, the Indian housewife's main cooking fuel, is the thermal equivalent of 27 million tons of kerosene, 35 million tons of coal, or 68 million tons of wood. Since India has only small reserves of oil and coal and is already the victim of extensive deforestation, none of these fuels can be considered practical substitutes for cow dung. The thought of dung in the kitchen may not appeal to the average American, but Indian women regard it as a superior cooking fuel because it is finely adjusted to their domestic routines. Most Indian dishes are prepared with clarified butter known as *ghee*, for which cow dung is the preferred source of heat since it burns with a clean, slow, long-lasting flame that doesn't scorch the food. This enables the Indian housewife to start cooking her meals and to leave them unattended for several hours while she takes care of the children, helps out in the fields, or performs other chores. American housewives achieve a similar effect through a complex set of electronic controls that come as expensive options on late-model stoves.

Cow dung has at least one other major function. Mixed with water and made into a paste, it is used as a household flooring material. Smeared over a dirt floor and left to harden into a smooth surface, it keeps the dust down and can be swept clean with a broom.

Because cattle droppings have so many useful properties, every bit of dung is carefully collected. Village small fry are given the task of following the family cow around and of bringing home its daily petrochemical output. In the cities, sweeper castes enjoy a monopoly on the dung deposited by strays and earn their living by selling it to housewives.

From an agribusiness point of view, a dry and barren cow is an economic abomination. But from the viewpoint of the peasant farmer, the same dry and barren cow may be a last desperate defense against the money-lenders. There is always the chance that a favorable monsoon may restore the vigor of even the most decrepit specimen and that she will fatten up, calve, and start giving milk again. This is what the farmer prays for; sometimes his prayers are answered. In the meantime, dung-making goes on. And so one gradually begins to understand why a skinny old hag of a cow still looks beautiful in the eyes of her owner.

Zebu cattle have small bodies, energy-storing humps on their back, and great powers of recuperation. These features are adapted to the specific conditions of Indian agriculture. The native breeds are capable of surviving for long periods with little food or water and are highly resistant to diseases that afflict other breeds in tropical climates. Zebu oxen are worked as long as they continue to breathe. . . .

But sooner or later there must come a time when all hope of an animal's recovery is lost and even dungmaking ceases. . . . By slaughtering or selling his aged and decrepit animals, a farmer might earn a few more rupees or temporarily improve his family's diet. But in the long run, his refusal to sell to the slaughterhouse or kill for his own table may have beneficial consequences. An established principle of ecological analysis states that communities of organisms are adapted not to average but to extreme conditions. The relevant situation in India is the recurrent failure of the monsoon rains. To evaluate the economic significance of the antislaughter and anti-beef-eating taboos, we have to consider what these taboos mean in the context of periodic droughts and famine.

The taboo on slaughter and beef eating may be as much a product of natural selection as the small bodies and fantastic recuperative powers of the zebu breeds. During droughts and famines, farmers are severely tempted to kill or sell their livestock. Those who succumb to this temptation seal their doom, even if they survive the drought, for when the rains come, they will be unable to plow their fields. I want to be even more emphatic. . . . Cow love with its sacred symbols and holy doctrines protects the farmer against calculations that are "rational" only in the short term. To Western experts it looks as if "the Indian farmer would rather starve to death than eat his cow." The same kinds of experts like to talk about the "inscrutable Oriental mind" and think that "life is not so dear to the Asian masses." They don't realize that the farmer would rather eat his cow than starve, but that he will starve if he does eat it. . . .

From a Western agribusiness viewpoint, it seems irrational for India not to have a meat-packing industry. But the actual potential for such an industry in a country like India is very limited. A substantial rise in beef production would strain the entire ecosystem, not because of cow love but because of the laws of thermodynamics. In any food chain, the interposition of additional animal links results in a sharp decrease in the efficiency of food production. The caloric value of what an animal has eaten is always much greater than the caloric value of its body. This means that more calories are available per capita when plant food is eaten directly by a human population than when it is used to feed domesticated animals.

Because of the high level of beef consumption in the United States, three-quarters of all our croplands are used for feeding cattle rather than people. Since the per capita calorie intake in India is already below minimum daily requirements, switching croplands to meat production could only result in higher food prices and a further deterioration in the living standards for poor families. I doubt if more than 10 percent of the Indian people will ever be able to make beef an important part of their diet, regardless of whether they believe in cow love or not.

I also doubt that sending more aged and decrepit animals to existing slaughterhouses would result in nutritional gains for the people who need it most. Most of these animals get eaten anyway, even if they aren't sent to the slaughterhouse, because throughout India there are low-ranking castes whose members have the right to dispose of the bodies of dead cattle. In one way or another, twenty million cattle die every year, and a large portion of their meat is eaten by these carrion-eating "untouchables". . . .

Like everything else I have been discussing, meat eating by untouchables is finely adjusted to practical conditions. The meat-eating castes also tend to be the leather-working castes, since they have the right to dispose of the skin of the fallen cattle. So despite cow love, India manages to have a huge leathercraft industry. Even in death, apparently useless animals continue to be exploited for human purposes.

I could be right about cattle being useful for traction, fuel, fertilizer, milk, floor covering, meat, and leather, and still misjudge the ecological and economic significance of the whole complex. Everything depends on how much all of this costs in natural resources and human labor relative to alternative modes of satisfying the needs of India's huge population. These costs are determined largely by what the cattle eat. Many experts assume that man and cow are locked in a deadly competition for land and food crops. This might be true if India's farmers followed the American agribusiness model and fed their animals on food crops. But the shameless truth about the sacred cow is that she is an indefatigable scavenger. Only an insignificant portion of the food consumed by the average cow comes from pastures and food crops set aside for their use. . . .

The major constituent in the cattle's diet is inedible by-products of human food crops, principally rice straw, wheat bran, and rice husks. . . . Probably less than 20 percent of what the cattle eat consists of humanly edible substances; most of this is fed to working oxen and water buffalo rather than to dry and barren cows. Odend'hal found that in his study area there was no competition between cattle and humans for land or the food supply: "Basically, the cattle convert items of little direct human value into products of immediate utility."

One reason why cow love is so often misunderstood is that it has different implications for the rich and the poor. Poor farmers use it as a license to scavenge while the wealthy farmers resist it as a rip-off. To the poor farmer, the cow is a holy beggar; to the rich farmer, it's a thief. Occasionally the cows invade someone's pastures or planted fields. The landlords complain, but the poor peasants plead ignorance and depend on cow love to get their animals back. If there is competition, it is between man and man or caste and caste, not between man and beast. . . .

Cow-slaughter enthusiasts base their recommendation on an understandable error.

They reason that since the farmers refuse to kill their animals, and since there is a religious taboo against doing so, therefore it is the taboo that is mainly responsible for the high ratio of cows to oxen. Their error is hidden in the observed ratio itself: 70 cows to 100 oxen. If cow love prevents farmers from killing cows that are economically useless, how is it there are 30 percent fewer cows than oxen? Since approximately as many female as male animals are born, something must be causing the death of more females than males. The solution to this puzzle is that while no Hindu farmer deliberately slaughters a female calf or decrepit cow with a club or a knife, he can and does get rid of them when they become truly useless from his point of view. Various methods short of direct slaughter are employed. To "kill" unwanted calves, for example, a triangular wooden yoke is placed about their necks so that when they try to nurse they jab the cow's udder and get kicked to death. Older animals are simply tethered on short ropes and allowed to starve—a process that does not take too long if the animal is already weak and diseased. Finally, unknown numbers of decrepit cows are surreptitiously sold through a chain of Moslem and Christian middlemen and end up in the urban slaughterhouses.

If we want to account for the observed proportions of cows to oxen, we must study rain, wind, water, and land-tenure patterns, not cow love. The proof of this is that the proportion of cows to oxen varies with the relative importance of different components of the agricultural system in different regions of India. The most important variable is the amount of irrigation water available for the cultivation of rice. Wherever there are extensive wet rice paddies, the water buffalo tends to be the preferred traction animal, and the female water buffalo is then substituted for the zebu cow as a source of milk. That is why in the vast plains of northern India, where the melting Himalayan snows and monsoons create the Holy River Ganges, the proportion of cows to oxen drops down to 47 to 100. As the distinguished Indian economist K. N. Raj has pointed out, districts in the Ganges Valley where continuous year-round rice-paddy cultivation is practiced have cow-to-oxen ratios that approach the theoretical optimum. This is all the more remarkable since the region in question—the Gangetic plain—is the heartland of the Hindu religion and contains its most holy shrines. . . .

Do I mean to say that cow love has no effect whatsoever on the cattle sex ratio or on other aspects of the agricultural system? No. What I am saying is that cow love is an active element in a complex, finely articulated material and cultural order. . . .

Since the effective mobilization of all human action depends upon the acceptance of psychologically compelling creeds and doctrines, we have to expect that economic systems will always oscillate under and over their points of optimum efficiency. But the assumption that the whole system can be made to work better simply by attacking its consciousness is naive and dangerous. Major improvements in the present system can be achieved by stabilizing India's human population, and by making more land, water, oxen, and water buffalo available to more people on a more equitable basis. The alternative is to destroy the present system and replace it with a completely new set of demographic, technological, politico-economic, and ideological relationships—a whole new ecosystem. Hinduism is undoubtedly a conservative force, one that makes it more difficult for the "development" experts and "modernizing" agents to destroy the old system and to replace it with a high-energy industrial and agribusiness complex. But if you think that a high-energy industrial and agribusiness complex will necessarily be more "rational" or "efficient" than the system that now exists, forget it.

Contrary to expectations, studies of energy costs and energy yields show that India makes more efficient use of its cattle than the United States does. In Singur district in West Bengal, Dr. Odend'hal discovered that the cattle's gross energetic efficiency, defined as the total of useful calories produced per year divided by the total calories consumed during the same period, was 17 percent. This compares with a gross energetic efficiency of less than 4 percent for American beef cattle raised on Western range land. As Odend'hal says, the relatively high efficiency of the In-dian cattle complex comes about not because the animals are particularly productive, but because of scrupulous product utilization by humans: "The villagers are extremely utilitarian and nothing is wasted."

Wastefulness is more a characteristic of modern agribusiness than of traditional peasant economies. Under the new system of automated feed-lot beef production in the United States, for example, cattle manure not only goes unused, but it is allowed to contaminate ground water over wide areas and contributes to the pollution of nearby lakes and streams.

The higher standard of living enjoyed by the industrial nations is not the result of greater productive efficiency, but of an enormously expanded increase in the amount of energy available per person. In 1970 the United States used up the energy equivalent of twelve tons of coal per inhabitant, while the corresponding figure for India was one-fifth ton per inhabitant. The way this energy was expended involved far more energy being wasted per person in the United States than in India. Automobiles and airplanes are faster than oxcarts, but they do not use energy more efficiently. In fact, more calories go up in useless heat and smoke during a single day of traffic jams in the United States than is wasted by all the cows of India during an entire year. The comparison is even less favorable when we consider the fact that the stalled vehicles are burning up irreplaceable reserves of petroleum that it took the earth tens of millions of years to accumulate. If you want to see a real sacred cow, go out and look at the family car.

## Review

1. What effects does India's love of cows have on life in that country?

2. What are the negative aspects of India's cow love, according to its critics?

3. What actual functions does cow love serve for the Indian people?

## Applications

1. Many Westerners maintain that cow love as practiced in India is irrational,

especially considering India's need for more food for the people in times of famine. Some sociologists might consider such a belief to be ethnocentric, i.e., viewing Western ways as superior to Indian ones. But people in other societies might consider our refusal to eat dog meat as irrational when there are people starving in the United States. Peruse the popular media looking for common practices, beliefs, and values that are part of American culture but that you think could be considered irrational by others (e.g., our not eating dogs). Report your findings.

2. Develop and use an interview questionnaire on the ideas brought out in this article pertaining to cow love. Interview several people, including one or more of Indian ancestry if possible. Summarize your findings.

3. Describe ethnocentric responses you have had while traveling in another country or a different part of the United States. What bothered you and why?

## Related Web Sites

1. *http://www.judypat.com/india/cow.htm.* A site that features a number of articles and links that deal with the sacred cow.

2. *http://www.tamu.edu/anthropology/newscult.html.* An archive of news of topics related to social/cultural anthropology.

# 7

# Cosmetic Surgery

## Beauty as Commodity

*Debra Gimlin*

In *every society, there are norms that deal with physical appearance—how a person should look in order to be attractive. In **preindustrial societies,** the norms involved such things as decorating or altering the body (including scarring, elongation of the neck, shaping the head from infancy, etc.). In our society, some of the norms about appearance vary between groups. Among youth, for example, body piercing is considered attractive, while many older adults find the practice repugnant. Other norms are more pervasive—such as the standards we have about the kind of body an attractive person should have. For a woman, the ideal includes being slender, in contrast to a hundred years ago when the "full-figured" woman was considered the most attractive.*

*In an effort to attain the requisite slimness, some women succumb to eating disorders. Others, including teenage girls, use various surgical procedures to enhance their beauty, including breast augmentation, eyelid surgery, liposuction (to remove fat), reshaping the nose, and the "tummy tuck" to tighten the abdomen.*

*In this article, Gimlin describes how women succumb to the norm of attractiveness by resorting to cosmetic surgery.*

*Ironically, in so doing, they break another norm—that attractiveness should be "natural" or attained by more natural means such as diet and exercise. Gimlin also notes how the women justify breaking one norm in order to satisfy the other one.*

After several unsuccessful attempts to schedule an appointment with her, I finally managed to meet with Jennifer, a 29-year-old grade school teacher who volunteered to talk with me about the cosmetic surgery that she had undergone. On a typically cold November afternoon, I spoke with Jennifer in her apartment on the south shore of Long Island. Jennifer, who is 5' 6" tall and has long, straight blond hair and expressive light blue eyes, was dressed in an oversized gray pullover and black sweat pants. While we talked, she peeled and sliced the crudités that would be her contribution to the "pot luck" engagement party that she would be attending later that evening.

Sitting at her kitchen table for nearly two hours, Jennifer and I discussed her decision to have cosmetic surgery. During our conversation, I noticed that by far the most prominent—and largest—feature in her small studio apartment was the enormous black and chrome stair-climbing machine set slightly off from the center of the living-room/bedroom. I learned that Jennifer spends 40 minutes each day on this machine and works out with weights at a nearby gym three to four times per week. She eats no meat, very little oil or fat, no sweets and drinks very little alcohol. Despite her rigorous body work routine, Jennifer's legs have remained a disappointment to her. Rather than appearing lean and muscular, they look, by her account, thick and shapeless—particularly around her lower thighs and knees. Jennifer says that her decision to have liposuction performed was motivated primarily by her inability to reshape her legs through diet and exercise. During the procedure, the fatty deposits were removed from the insides of Jennifer's knees, making her legs appear slimmer and more toned.

During the time I spent with Jennifer, she discussed her reasons for having liposuction, including her own significant ambivalence about taking surgical steps to alter her body. Jennifer argued that, if possible, she would have preferred to shape her body through aerobics, weight training and dieting, and that liposuction was, for her, a last, desperate option. By her account, plastic surgery was an attempt to alter physical attributes that Jennifer referred to as "genetic flaws," attributes that she could change through no other available means. Expressing some shame, as she says, "for taking the easy way out," Jennifer's feelings of guilt are not so great that she regrets having surgery. Indeed, quite the opposite is true; Jennifer plans to have a second liposuction in the near future, this time to remove the fatty tissue from her upper and inner thighs.

Cosmetic surgery stands, for many theorists and social critics, as the ultimate symbol of invasion of the human body for the sake of physical beauty. It has epitomized for many—including myself—the astounding lengths to which contemporary women will go in order to obtain bodies that meet current ideals of attractiveness. Moreover, plastic surgery is perceived by its critics as an activity that is somehow *qualitatively* different from other efforts at altering the body (including aerobics, hairstyling, or even dieting) in that it is an activity so extreme, so invasive, that it leaves no space for interpretation as anything but subjugation. Even more than women who may participate in other types of body-shaping activities, those who undergo cosmetic surgery appear to many observers—both casual and academic—to be so obsessed with physical appearance that they are willing to risk their very existence in order to become more attractive.

While cosmetic surgery has been dealt powerful (and some would say well-deserved) blows from the score of feminist writers who criticize body work generally (Dally 1991; Kaw 1994), the cosmetic surgery industry is nonetheless rapidly expanding (Wolf 1991). Three hundred million dollars are spent every year on cosmetic surgery and the amount is increasing annually by 10 percent (Davis 1995, p. 21). In 1988, more than two million Americans underwent some form of cosmetic surgery. Between 1984 and 1986 alone, the number of cosmetic operations in the U.S. tripled (Wolf 1991, p. 251). Ninety percent of these operations are performed on women: virtually all breast augmentations and reductions, 90 percent of face-lifts, 86 percent of eyelid reconstructions, and 61 percent of rhinoplasties (better known as "nose jobs"). In 1987, American women had 94,000 breast reconstructions, 85,000 eyelid surgeries,

82,000 nose jobs, 73,230 liposuctions, and 67,000 face-lifts. . . . At the end of World War II, there were only about one hundred plastic surgeons in the United States; today there are approximately four thousand along with an unknown number of additional specialists, mostly dermatologists, also performing face-lifts, eyelid surgeries and other "minor" procedures (Davis 1995, p. 21).

Criticisms of surgical alteration of the female body multiply nearly as rapidly as the procedures themselves. One of the main critiques of cosmetic surgery derives from the dangers involved in many of the procedures. Cosmetic surgery is undeniably painful and risky and each operation involves its own potential complications. For instance, pain, numbness, bruising, discoloration and depigmentation frequently follow a liposuction, often lingering up to six months after the operation. Similarly, face-lifts can damage nerves, leaving the patient's face permanently numb. More serious disabilities include fat embolisms, blood clots, fluid depletion, and in some cases, death. Indeed, health experts estimate that the chance of serious side effects from breast augmentation are between 30 percent and 50 percent. The least dramatic and most common of these include decreased sensitivity in the nipples, painful swelling or congestion of the breasts, and hardening of the breasts that makes it difficult to lie down comfortably or to raise the arms without the implants shifting (Goldwyn 1980). More serious is the problem of encapsulation, where the body reacts to foreign materials by forming a capsule of fibrous tissue around the implants. This covering can sometimes be broken down manually by the surgeon, but even when successful, this procedure is extremely painful. When it is unsuccessful, the implants must be removed; in some cases, the surgeon is actually forced to chisel the hardened substance from the patient's chest wall.

Clearly, the recipient of cosmetic surgery may very well emerge from the operation in worse shape than when she went in. Unsuccessful breast augmentations are often disfiguring, leaving the recipient with unsightly scars and deformation. An overly tight face-lift produces a "zombie" look, in which the countenance seems devoid of expression. Following a liposuction, the skin can develop a corrugated, uneven texture so that the recipient looks worse than she did before the surgery.

Finally, some criticisms of cosmetic surgery focus on the implications of such procedures for contemporary conceptualizations of the body and identity. In particular, cosmetic surgery has expanded in conjunction with such developments in medical equipment as magnifying lenses, air drills for severing bone and leveling skin, and perfected suturing materials, all enabling surgical interventions to be performed with better results and less trauma for the patient (Meredith 1988). According to some critics, these developments, and the increasing flexibility in body altering that they permit, are inextricably linked to cultural discourses likening the body to what Susan Bordo (1990) has called "cultural plastic." The body is now understood as having a potential for limitless change, "undetermined by history, social location or even individual biography" (p. 657). Not only has the body come to stand as a primary symbol of identity, but it is a symbol whose capacity for alteration and modification is understood to be unlimited. The body, instead of a dysfunctional object requiring medical intervention, becomes a commodity, not unlike "a car, a refrigerator, a house, which can be continuously upgraded and modified in accordance with new interests and greater resources" (Finkelstein 1991, p. 87). The body is a symbol of selfhood, but its relation to its inhabitant is shaped primarily by the individual's capacity for material consumption. . . .

## Research and Methods

The research for this chapter involves field work in a Long Island plastic surgery clinic and interviews with the clinic's surgeon [Dr. John Norris] and 20 of his female patients. . . . The women I interviewed ranged in age from 24 to 50. The procedures they underwent include breast augmentations, nose jobs, face-lifts, eye reshaping, tummy tucks, and liposuctions. The women are Asian American or European American; among the latter, the group members' geographical heritage varies in terms of Eastern and Western, Northern and Southern Europe. Three of the women are of Semitic ancestry. All but one (a full-time mother) held salaried jobs or were students at the time of the interviews. They were employed as opticians, medical technicians, receptionists, insurance agents, teachers, office administrators, hairstylists, and secretaries.

## Stories of a Face-Lift: Ann Marie

Ann Marie, a slender, soft-spoken 50-year-old medical technician with upswept blonde hair, was one of the first surgery patients I interviewed for this research. Married for nearly 30 years, Ann Marie carried herself with a careful gentility. The type of woman my mother would refer to as a "lady," Ann Marie's daintiness and obvious concern for her appearance made me self-conscious of the bulky sweater and combat boots I was wearing. Dressed in snug-fitting woolen pants, low-heeled brown pumps, and a fuzzy light mauve sweater, Ann Marie invited me into her small, tidy home and asked demurely if I would like coffee. Anxious to begin my first interview with someone who had had a face-lift, I refused her offer. Ann Marie brought her own drink back from the kitchen in a tiny, flower-painted china cup and saucer and began telling me about her experiences with plastic surgery.

Somewhat to my surprise, Ann Marie was not at all shy about discussing her face-lift. In fact, she actually seemed eager to tell me the reasons for her decision. By her account—and, as anyone with even the most limited understanding of physiology would expect—Anne Marie's appearance began to change in her late thirties and forties. She developed "puffiness underneath the eyes," and "drooping upper eyelids." Most unattractive by Ann Marie's account, "the skin of my throat started getting creepy." In her words, "You get to an age" when "you look in the mirror and see lines that were not there before." Because her physical appearance had begun to reflect the aging process, she explained, "All of a sudden the need [for cosmetic surgery] was there."

While Ann Marie described her need for a face-lift as "sudden," she actually planned to have the procedure long before she believed that she needed it. Ann Marie recalled that "about ten years ago," she spoke with several close friends about having a face-lift at some point in the distant future. She explained,

> We talked about it a long time ago. I guess I have never accepted the axiom of growing old gracefully. I have always sworn I would never picture myself as a chubby old lady.

Ann Marie and her friends "talked and decided that when the time was just right, we would definitely do it." Even so, Ann Marie was the only member of the group who actually went through with the surgery.

Despite her seemingly firm decision, Ann Marie did not enter into cosmetic surgery lightly. Instead, she considered having the procedure over several years, during which she "thought about it from time to time. There was a lot to be considered." In her estimation, "Having plastic surgery is not something to undertake lightly." Among the issues she contemplated were the physical dangers involved in the operation, the potential for looking worse after the surgery than before and the importance of choosing a well-qualified doctor with an excellent reputation. She explained,

> You are putting your face in the hands of a surgeon; there is the possibility of absolute disaster, very possibly permanently. You have to choose the surgeon very carefully.

Ann Marie chose John to perform the face-lift. Largely because he had performed an emergency procedure for her just over one year earlier, Ann Marie claimed that she felt completely comfortable with her selection of a surgeon. She explained,

> John was recommended to me by my dermatologist. I had an infection on my face; it was quite serious. The dermatologist told me I had to go to a plastic surgeon and John was the only one he would recommend.

Because of the dermatologist's recommendation and her satisfaction with John's ear-lier work, Ann Marie returned to him when she decided to have the face-lift. She visited his office in Long Island for a consultation and, not long after her appointment, decided to have the procedure.

During their first meeting, Ann Marie learned what she refers to as two "surprises." She learned the price of the operation and that she would have to stop smoking, due to the health risks associated with nicotine intake. According to Ann Marie, John explained that she must stop smoking because "you will not heal as well if you continue to smoke. Because it impedes circulation, smoking decreases your ability to heal properly." She said, "The most difficult part was to stop smoking. I was puffing away a pack and a half a day for over 20 years." John told Ann Marie that she would not be able to smoke for three months in advance of the surgery. She said, "I thought, 'What? I will never be able to do this.' But I did, I stopped cold. That was the real sacrifice for me."

While giving up cigarettes may have been the greatest sacrifice for Ann Marie, there were clearly many others. For a full year, Ann Marie had to work "one day job, one night job, occasionally a third job" in order to afford the surgery. She had to "bank" four weeks of overtime at her primary job so that she could take time off to recover from the procedure. She also postponed repairs on her home because she could not afford to pay for both the repairs and the operation. She explained, "There were things my house needed but my feeling was, I needed a face-lift more than my house did." Like many of John's patients, having cosmetic surgery was a priority for Ann Marie.

Ann Marie spent most of our interview explaining her reasons for having the face-lift. By providing me with a long and detailed account of her need for the procedure, she hints at an awareness that her behavior is somehow subject to criticism, that it might, for example, be construed by others as superficial or shallow. With a hint of defensiveness in her tone, Anne Marie explained that she "needed" the face-lift—despite its financial costs and physical risks—not merely because she is concerned with her appearance, but instead, because of pressures in "the work field." She says,

> Despite the fact we have laws against age discrimination, employers do find ways of getting around it. I know women my age who do not get jobs or are relieved of jobs because of age. This [the face-lift] will ensure my work ability.

Ann Marie, by her account, decided to have a face-lift not out of narcissism but out of concerns for her professional well-being. Justifying her behavior as a career decision, she implies that she is sensitive to the social disapproval of plastic surgery, that she knows that the behavior requires some justification.

And yet, even though Ann Marie believes that looking younger would help her professionally, she also admitted that she had "not seen anything that has really changed in that area [her career]." Instead, the procedure had affected her primarily "on a personal basis, a social basis." Explaining these effects in more detail, she said,

> I meet people I haven't seen for two or three years who will say, "There is something different about you, but I don't know what it is." I met a sister of a very good friend of mine in June, which is five months after my surgery. She looked at me and said, "I don't know you." I said, "Of course you do. I've known you nearly all of my life." She realized who I was and was astounded at my appearance.

Plastic surgery, then, in Ann Marie's telling, provides an account of herself as a younger woman that has, in turn, improved her self-image. By attributing a series of positive experiences—and the resulting improvement in her self-perception—to her face-lift, Ann Marie justifies her decision to have cosmetic surgery. . . .

## 'A Deep Dark Secret': Having Liposuction

John arranged for me to speak with a woman named Bonnie, who was planning, but had not yet had, cosmetic surgery. In sharp contrast to the other women John suggested I interview, Bonnie was hesitant to speak with me about the procedure, because, as she later acknowledged, she considered it to be "a deep dark secret" which she had discussed with no one but her husband of five months. Bonnie worked out at the same gym that both John and I frequented. Because she and I were previously acquainted, John suggested that Bonnie speak with me about the procedure she was considering and she agreed. Over the next six months, Bonnie and I met several times to discuss cosmetic surgery; during that period, she decided to have liposuction, underwent the procedure, and recovered from it.

Having recently completed a masters degree in a New England university, Bonnie moved to the east end of Long Island to take a position as a chemist in a large biomedical research firm. She explained to me that she had, over the years, spoken casually to various women about cosmetic surgery, and had "fantasized about" having liposuction herself, though she had never considered it seriously. Prior to having the operation, Bonnie told me why she had been reluctant, even though the procedure had always been, as she described, a "fantasy" of hers. She explained her hesitation as follows:

> It's always seemed to me to be one step too far. I have dieted and exercised my whole life, find sometimes I've gone over the edge and done some things that probably weren't very healthy, but I could always stop myself before I became totally obsessed. I guess I have always thought that I would never get so obsessed that I would allow my body to be cut into just so I could look better. At least that's what I had always hoped. I couldn't imagine myself as one of "them," as one of those weak women who would go that far.

Despite her stated objections to cosmetic surgery and her characterization of its patients as "weak," Bonnie considered, and, after extensive deliberation, underwent, liposuction on the outside of her upper thighs. Bonnie described this area of her body as

> . . . flabby, no matter what I do. I've always had these lumps that I couldn't get rid of. My friends used to tease me because whenever I'd look at myself in the mirror, I'd always push that part of my leg in, so

you couldn't see the lumps. I wanted to imagine how I'd look without them. I exercise five or six times a week; I cycle with my husband. I do all the weightlifting that is supposed to tone up the muscles in those areas. Nothing works!

Despite her frustrations, Bonnie had never seriously investigated the procedure until, at age 26, she finished graduate school and began full-time employment. She explained, "This is the first time I've ever made enough money to think about doing something like this. The liposuction will cost $2,000, which is less than it usually costs because I won't have to have general anesthesia, but it's still a lot of money." Bonnie noted that she would never have seriously considered having cosmetic surgery while she was living near her family and friends.

> The other thing is that I wouldn't want any of my friends or family to know about it, only my husband. My family would all be like, "You don't need to have that done. You're crazy. You are thin enough already." That doesn't keep me from thinking these lumps on my thighs are really ugly. They are the only thing I see when I look in the mirror.

Bonnie continued, explaining that her hesitance to discuss her desire to have liposuction with her friends stems from their perception of cosmetic surgery as part of a process of "giving in to pressure, giving in to these ideals about how women should look, when none of us real women are ever going to look like that." Bonnie believed that her friends would react to her interest in plastic surgery by making her "feel so ashamed, like I am not strong enough to accept myself like I am, like I hate my female body."

Bonnie was one of the few women I interviewed who articulated her ambivalence about plastic surgery in what could be construed as political, rather than exclusively personal, terms. Her description of her friends' imagined protests to liposuction was one of many examples of her concern with the political meaning of her actions. Bonnie also explained that her own interpretation of cosmetic surgery was the main source of her dilemma over having the procedure. She said,

I am not worried about problems with the operation itself. I know that Dr. Norris has a great reputation. I've talked to other people at the gym who have used him and they were all really happy. He does so much of this stuff, I'm sure he's really good at it.

Bonnie's concerns focused instead on the social and cultural significance of her action. She said, "If I am proud to be a woman, then I should be proud to look like a woman, with a woman's butt and a woman's thighs." Reacting to her own accusations, she said, "I am proud to be a woman, but I really hate it when I get a glimpse of my backside and I just look *big*. I feel terrible knowing that it is those areas of my body which are understood to be most 'female' that I dislike the most." Expressing her interest in cosmetic surgery as her only viable option for reducing dissatisfaction with her appearance, she added,

> I don't really know how to get around it, though, because I really do not like those parts of my figure. Plastic surgery seems like a pretty good way, and really, a pretty easy way, to deal with that dissatisfaction, to put those negative feelings behind me . . . to move on with the rest of my life. . . . Like, I'd really like to put on a pair of biking shorts and not even have it cross my mind that my butt is going to look big in them. I'd love to get dressed for work in the morning, and have only the work in front of me, rather than, you know, what's literally behind me, be the thing that concerns me the most.

Bonnie is explicitly aware that the body and the self are understood culturally to be equivalent. When she says that she dislikes the "female" parts of her figure, one can easily imagine replacing the term "figure" with the term "self." Indeed, it is Bonnie's ambivalence about her female identity that is most troubling to her; by eradicating the physical signs of femininity—and the imperfection which is necessarily a component of those attributes—she believes she will be able to construct a self that will be less imperfect and more culturally acceptable, and which will, as she puts it, allow her to "move on with the rest of" her life. Bonnie contends that having plastic surgery will allow her to focus more attention on other activities and concerns, including her career, the sports she enjoys, and her new marriage. At the same time, her decision to undergo liposuction comes at a considerable cost for Bonnie, who says explicitly that, if possible, she would prefer to change her perceptions rather than her body. The "pressure" she feels, however, limits Bonnie's ability to actively rework her self-image, leaving her to choose between two options—plastic surgery or a negative self-concept—neither of which is satisfactory. Bonnie's decision to undergo liposuction suggests that, in the end, the costs associated with having plastic surgery were somehow less significant than were those attached to accepting her appearance flaws.

Ann Marie and Bonnie present two quite disparate images of the concerns women face as they consider having cosmetic surgery. While Anne Marie struggled to work out the financial and physical requirements of her face-lift, Bonnie agonized over the political dimension of her decision to have liposuction. So distinct are these preoccupations, in fact, that they can be conceptualized as opposite ends of a continuum, along which the perspectives of the other 18 women I interviewed can be placed. For most of these women, the political implications of cosmetic surgery, though not entirely ignored, were far less significant than they were for Bonnie. Compared to her, the other women I interviewed were more often concerned with the health risks and financial costs involved in cosmetic surgery and, even more significantly, with how they would look after their procedures.

While the character of Anne Marie's and Bonnie's pre-operative anxieties took different forms, both constructed elaborate accounts regarding their entitlement to plastic surgery. Like Anne Marie and the other women whose voices I will recount later in this article, Bonnie justifies her decision to have plastic surgery by explaining that she has done all that is humanly possible to alter a failed body and argues that no act short of plastic surgery will allow her to live peacefully with herself. Significantly, the women I talked to provided accounts in which they attempted to dissociate themselves from responsibility for perceived bodily flaws. Each woman's body was imperfect not because she had erred in her body work but because of aging, genetics, or some other physical condition that the woman could not control. In effect, they argued that their flawed bodies were incorrect indicators of character, and, as such, effectively lie about who the women really are. Accounts like these not only justify cosmetic surgery but attempt to convert it into an expression of a putatively true identity. Plastic surgery becomes for them not an act of deception, but an effort to align body with self.

## 'The Body I Was Meant to Have': Why Women Have Cosmetic Surgery

While some writers have dealt with cosmetic surgery as if it were an attempt to accomplish idealized female beauty in order to gain the approval of men (Wolf 1991), the women I spoke with claimed that the goal of plastic surgery is neither to become beautiful, nor to be beautiful for husbands, boyfriends, or other significant individuals. Indeed, these women adamantly insisted that they altered their bodies for their own satisfaction, in effect utilizing such procedures to create what they conceptualize as a normal appearance—an appearance that reflects a normal self. While I do not accept their accounts without some skepticism, I believe that women who have plastic surgery are not necessarily doing so in order to become beautiful nor to please particular individuals. Instead, when women have plastic surgery, they are responding to highly restrictive notions of normality and the "normal" self, notions which neither apply to the population at large (in fact, quite the reverse) nor leave space for ethnic variation. In effect, plastic surgery, as I have argued earlier, "works" for women who have these procedures, but it works only within the context of a culture of appearance that is highly restrictive and which is less a culture of beauty than it is a system of control based on the physical representations of gender, age, and ethnicity.

Throughout the interviews, my respondents claimed that prior to having surgery, some particular physical feature stood in the way of their looking "normal." This feature distinguished them from others and prohibited them from experiencing, as Marcy, a 25-year-old student, explained, "a happy, regular life." Marcy decided at age 16 to have the bony arch in the middle of her nose removed and its tip shortened. Prior to having the procedure, Marcy had never been involved in a romantic relationship, a fact that she attributed to her "hook" nose and unattractive appearance. Marcy said,

> I have always felt terrible about how pronounced it was. No matter how I wore my hair, it was in the middle of my face and everybody noticed it. It's not like I could just wear my bangs long.

Marcy decided to have rhinoplasty near a date that was particularly symbolic for her. She explained, "I was having my nose done just before Valentine's Day. I thought to myself, maybe if I have my nose done for Valentine's Day, by next Valentine's Day, I'll have a valentine!" Although she did not find a valentine for the following year—she explained that "[dating] didn't happen until a few years later"—Marcy claimed that over time, she was able to experience pleasure that she would have missed without having her nose surgically altered.

Because Marcy uses cosmetic surgery to make herself more appealing to others, her experience seemingly supports the criticisms of authors like Wolf (1991). However, a central feature of Marcy's account is that she does not expect plastic surgery to make her beautiful. Neither does she believe that winning male affection requires her to be beautiful. Quite the contrary, Marcy clearly imagines that a merely normal appearance is sufficient to garner the male attention that she desires.

The women I interviewed frequently described the ways in which their physical features had kept them from living ordinary lives. For example, Barbara, a 29-year-old bookkeeper, told me that her breasts—which were, by her account, too small to fill out attractive clothing—made her appear "dumpy" and ill-proportioned. Her "flaw" had, in turn, contributed to the negative self-image Barbara described having in her teens and early twenties, and this negative self-image served to limit the education and career goals Barbara set for herself, the friendships she attempted to foster, and the romantic and sexual relationships she pursued. Barbara decided to have her breasts augmented (from a 36A to a 36D) to make herself, as she said, "more attractive to myself and others." While her larger breasts have in fact made Barbara feel more attractive, like other patients I interviewed, she nevertheless laments her (and all women's) inability to be self-confident despite self-perceived physical shortcomings. She said,

> For women, the appearance is the important thing. That's too bad that we can't worry about not being judged. [Small breasts] made a big difference in how I felt myself being perceived and how I felt about myself as a person.

Prior to having cosmetic surgery, Barbara was both abnormal (because her small breasts made her appear and feel awkward and self-conscious) and, at the same time, normal for her gender (in that all women are abnormal because they all fail to meet standards for female beauty).

Because physical attractiveness shapes the way women are "judged," appearance must be guarded as women age. Like Ann Marie, several of the patients I interviewed underwent cosmetic procedures aimed at reducing the natural signs of aging. These women claimed that aging had changed an acceptable appearance into an unacceptable one, with the resulting appearance reflecting negatively on identity. For instance, Sue, a 44-year-old optician, decided to have the loose skin around her eyes tightened. She explained why she had the operation:

> My eyes had always been alright, nice eyes. I guess I had always liked my face pretty well, but with age, the skin around them started getting puffy. They just didn't look nice anymore. I looked tired, tired and old. That's why I had them fixed.

While Sue had, according to her own account, once been satisfied with her appearance—even thinking her eyes were "nice"—she grew to dislike her face as the signs of aging became apparent. Basically, Sue had lost an acceptable appearance over time and so used cosmetic surgery to regain the face she liked "pretty well."

The women who had cosmetic surgery told me that they had chosen to have these procedures not to make themselves beautiful or outstanding in any particular way, but instead simply to regain normal physical characteristics that they once had but had lost through the aging process (see Davis 1995 for similar findings). . . . Youth—or at least a youthful appearance—is not the only characteristic women attempt to construct or regain through aesthetic procedures. Indeed, three of the patients I interviewed—all of whom were under the age of 30—had cosmetic surgery in order to reduce the physical markers of ethnicity. These women underwent procedures intended to make their physical features more closely approximate those associated with Anglo-Saxon nationalities. Marcy, a Jewish woman who—as described earlier—had rhinoplasty to diminish the "hook" in her nose, noted that the procedure also removed physical features "more frequently associated with Jewish people." Jodie, a 28-year-old student who also had her nose reshaped, said, "I had this Italian bump on my nose. It required a little shaving. Now, it looks better." By a "better" nose, Jodie implies a more Anglo-Saxon, less Italian, and, therefore, less ethnic nose. And Kim, a 22-year-old Taiwanese-American student, underwent a procedure to make her eyes appear more oval in shape. She said, "We [Taiwanese people] regard girls with wide, bright eyes as beautiful. My eyes used to look a little bit as if I was staring at somebody. The look is not soft; it is a very stiff look." While none of these women are consciously attempting to detach themselves from ethnicity per se, they nevertheless chose to ignore the fact that their efforts to appear more "normal" are, by definition, explicitly intended to diminish the physical markers of that ethnicity. Clearly indifferent to the loss of ethnic identity that their actions imply,

these women simply accept the notion that normalized (i.e., Anglo-Saxon) features are more attractive than ethnic ones.

As I listened to these women's accounts of their cosmetic surgery, I was struck by the fact that all of them claimed—quite adamantly, in fact—to have benefited from their participation in an activity that has garnered widespread and hostile criticism from feminists and nonfeminists alike. These women contended that plastic surgery was, for them, a logical, carefully thought-out response to distressing circumstances that could not otherwise be remedied. Moreover, as a result of their procedures, the women perceive themselves to be more socially acceptable, more normal, and, in several cases, more outgoing. As Bonnie, the woman whose political concerns made her initially reluctant to undergo liposuction, explained, "I got exactly what I wanted from this. My body isn't extraordinarily different, but now I feel like, well, I have a cute bottom. I have a cuter figure. I don't feel like the-one-with-the-big-butt anymore. And for me, that lets me put my body issues away pretty much."

At the same time, implying that some remnants of her original ambivalence about having cosmetic surgery still remained, Bonnie explained that she wishes she could have said, "To hell with it, I am going to love my body the way it is . . . but I had tried to do that for 15 years and it didn't work." She adds, "Now, I know I'll never look like Cindy Crawford, but I can walk around and feel like everything is good enough."

During my interviews with these patients, I was also struck by the fact that plastic surgery provides for the pleasure not only of the observers/lovers/partners of the women who undergo these procedures, but also of the women themselves. For instance, some of these women say that they are able to wear clothes that they did not feel attractive in prior to their operations; others, as I mentioned earlier, claim to have greater self-confidence or to be more extroverted. In one such example, Jennifer, the 29-year-old teacher who had liposuction to remove fatty tissue from the inside of her knees, explained,

When I walk out that door in the morning, my head might be a little bit higher when I'm wearing a certain outfit. Like before I had [liposuction] done, it used to be, I feel good, but I hope no one will notice that my legs aren't too nice.

The clothing these women are now able to wear includes items such as bathing suits, dresses with low-cut necklines, and lingerie—all of which are likely to be feminine and revealing. Wearing these clothes, and perceiving themselves as attractive in them, shapes the women's perceptions of themselves and increases their self-confidence. For example, Tara, a 27-year-old student, told me that before she had breast augmentation surgery, she avoided wearing bathing suits in public and had refused to shop for bras. She said,

> [Breast augmentation] has given me more self-confidence than I ever had. I fit in when I'm with my girlfriends now. Before, I never went to the beach with anybody around. After I had [plastic surgery], I couldn't wait to buy a bra. I could never buy one before because I was so pathetically small.

By her account, prior to having breast augmentation, Tara had been too "pathetically small" to enjoy going to the beach or shopping with friends. Having plastic surgery, however, served to make Tara appear more normal. Being able to "fit in," Tara now participates in activities from which she previously felt excluded.

Barbara, who also had breast augmentation surgery, recounted a similar experience. She said,

> I used to wear super-padded bras when I dressed up but they just never did it for me. I didn't look like the other women. But now, like tonight, I am going to a party and I know I'll be able to fill out the dress.

Barbara added, "[Breast augmentation] has made me feel very confident. I think that's the difference."

Sandra, a 43-year-old office manager who had liposuction to reduce her "thick thighs" and "saddlebag" hips, explained that she underwent the procedure not only to appear youthful or to wear feminine clothing, but also to approximate a cultural ideal involving social class. She said,

> I used to put on nice clothes and still look like a bag lady, you know, unsophisticated. Now I feel like I can wear good clothes and look like they are appropriate for me. Now my *body fits the clothes.*

Here, Sandra likens appearance to a tableau of social class, both in the context of the clothing one chooses and the extent to which one's body appears to be "appropriate" for that clothing (and the social standing that it implies). Simply put, before Sandra's surgery, her "flabby" body suggested a lower social status than did her clothing. Despite her efforts to wear "nice clothes"—i.e., clothes that would not be considered appropriate for a "bag lady"—her body undermined her efforts to use appearance to stake out a particular social location. In effect, Sandra's body not only makes her clothing an ineffective class identifier, but also invalidates Sandra's claims to a particular status. Plastic surgery, however, allows Sandra to more effectively display social class through clothing. Bringing her body into line with her self-appointed social class—particularly as its enactment relies upon clothing—cosmetic surgery serves as a tool for legitimizing Sandra's claims to social status. . . .

## Plastic Surgery and Inauthenticity: The High Price of Body Work

In its own terms, the process of making an abnormal body into a normal one, plastic surgery succeeds. The women who have undergone plastic surgery believe themselves to possess, as they had not before, the bodily expression of a normative self. However, at the same time, plastic surgery fails. If women are attempting to use plastic surgery to recreate themselves—to make claims through the body about who and what they are—they must also deal with charges of shallowness. In high irony, the very same women who are attracted to plastic surgery because of a belief that the body is an indicator of the self must now deal with charges that the surgically altered body is a deception, that it is an inauthentic representation of the self. Some of the costs of cosmetic surgery—including the danger of physical damage and the high financial price—are obvious to those who have undergone these procedures and, perhaps, even to those who have not. Most of the women I talked to had plastic surgery only after serious consideration (often accompanied by research into the medical technology involved in the operations). Likewise, few could easily afford the surgery they underwent; nearly all of them had to sacrifice some other large purchase or to weather some financial hardship in order to have the surgery. Some have accrued considerable debt while others have had to request financial help from relatives. Only a very few of the women I interviewed were able to waylay some of the costs through insurance.

It is, however, the other costs associated with cosmetic surgery that I wish to focus on here. In particular, I want to explore the taint of inauthenticity that women must deal with after surgery. Despite their efforts to tell a story in which they have earned the right to plastic surgery, the women who have undergone that surgery are still alert to charges that they have merely bought a new appearance. At the same time that their bodies approximate normality, the method that they use invites charges that their character is suspect. Not the results of plastic surgery, but the very fact of having had plastic surgery, becomes the primary indicator of identity. Although the women I interviewed do not formulate the complexities and contradictions involved in their activities in the way I have here, the accounts they construct show that they struggle to deal with a self-concept that continues to be deviant despite the women's normal appearances. Indeed, the accounts themselves—which attempt to deny inauthenticity by positioning cosmetic surgery as somehow owed to the women who partake of it—show that plastic surgery fails to align body and self.

While the women's accounts take a variety of forms, they suggest a singular conclusion with regards to the success of plastic surgery for establishing a normative identity. More specifically, women like Anne Marie and

Bonnie invoke their rigorous body work regimens as evidence of moral value and as the basis for their entitlement to cosmetic surgery. At the same time, they remain unsatisfied with the results, physical and moral, of this body work. Unlike the women I studied in an aerobics class—who, by virtue of their hard work, successfully undermined the body's power to reflect character—the women who had plastic surgery seemed unable to escape the social and moral meanings they attributed to their own bodies. Had they accepted the hard work they put into exercise and dieting as an adequate indicator of identity, they would not have needed to turn to plastic surgery to correct what they saw as their bodies' failings. Needing to establish the act of plastic surgery (as distinct from its results) as irrelevant for selfhood and needing to position the surgically altered body as the putatively true indicator of selfhood, women who have had plastic surgery revert to accounts that have already proved unsuccessful. The critical implications for self inherent in cosmetic surgery itself require women to resort to accounts that they know—either consciously or unconsciously—will fail to support the identity claims of youth or ethnicity that they want to make. Indeed, in the very act of making these claims, women who have undergone plastic surgery attest to the failure of that surgery to position the transformed body as a convincing representation of the self.

## Conclusion

My research points to three general conclusions. The first bears on the reasons women have plastic surgery and suggests a modification of the criticisms of such procedures. The second bears on the ways in which women create accounts of plastic surgery, an omission from the criticisms of plastic surgery. The third returns more sympathetically to those criticisms.

First, none of the women I spoke to embarked casually on plastic surgery. The costs of these procedures—measured in dollars and in the risk of physical damage—are well known to those who have undergone cosmetic surgery. Most of these women had plastic surgery only after serious consideration, often accompanied by research into the medical technology involved in the operations. Nearly all either had to sacrifice another large purchase or to weather some sort of financial hardship to pay for the surgery. More importantly, although physicians may serve as gatekeepers, preventing some women from receiving surgery, physicians do not, in any direct sense, recruit patients. Neither did the women I spoke to report that they underwent surgery at the urging of a specific other—husband, parent, lover, or friend. Rather, the decision to seek surgery seems to have been driven by the desires of women themselves, at least in the immediate circumstances. To be sure, the women's decisions to undergo surgery were shaped by broader cultural considerations—by notions of what constitutes beauty, by distinctively ethnic notions of beauty, and, most importantly, by the assumption that a woman's worth is measured by her appearance. Yet to portray the women I talked to as some sort of "cultural dopes," tossed and battered by cultural forces beyond their understanding, as passively submitting to the demands of beauty, is to badly misrepresent them. A more appropriate image, I would suggest, is to present them as savvy cultural negotiators, attempting to "make out" as best they can within a culture that limits their options. Those who undergo plastic surgery may (ultimately) be wrong, but they are not foolish. They know what they are doing. Their goals are realistic and they, in fact, achieve most of what they set out to accomplish with plastic surgery. Although their actions surely do, in the long run, contribute to the reproduction of a beauty culture that carries heavy costs for them and for all women, in the short run they have succeeded in their own more limited purposes.

Second, plastic surgery demands accounts; . . . those who undertook plastic surgery are working hard to justify themselves . . . [and] they do this in two steps. First, they must convince themselves that they deserve the surgery, whether by the hard work they put in at the gym or the effort they invest in saving the money that surgical procedures require. In so doing, they make the surgery,

psychologically and ideologically, their own. Second, they must convince themselves that the revised appearances they *have been given,* however well earned, are somehow connected to the self—i.e., that they are innocent of the charges of inauthenticity. To do this, they invoke essentialist notions of the self and corresponding notions of the body as accidental, somehow inessential, or a degeneration from a younger body that better represented who they truly were. . . .

Finally, I return more sympathetically to the criticisms of plastic surgery. . . . In the other settings I studied, the local production of an alternative culture is very much in evidence. Among the women who chose to have plastic surgery, there are the aesthetic judgments of their plastic surgeon and the ignored expressed opposition of friends and family, but no local culture of their own. Elsewhere women are challenging, however haltingly, however partially, a beauty culture. In contrast, the women who undergo plastic surgery are simply making do, perhaps as best they can, within a culture that they believe rewards them for their looks.

## References

Bordo, S. (1990). "Material girl": The effacements of postmodern culture. *Michigan Quarterly Review, 29,* 653–677.

Dally, A. (1991). *Women Under the Knife: A History of Surgery.* London: Hutchinson Radius.

Davis, K. (1995). *Reshaping the Female Body: The Dilemma of Cosmetic Surgery.* New York: Routledge.

Finkelstein, J. (1991). *The Fashioned Self.* Philadelphia, PA: Temple University Press.

Gimlin, D. (Forthcoming). *Bodywork: The Business of Beauty in Women's Lives.* Berkeley: University of California Press.

Goldwyn, R. M. (Ed.) (1980). *Long-Term Results in Plastic and Reconstructive Surgery.* 2nd edition. Boston: Little, Brown and Company.

Kaw, E. (1994). Opening faces: The politics of cosmetic surgery and Asian American women. In N. Sault (Ed.), *Many Mirrors: Body Image and Social Relations* (pp. 241–265). New Brunswick, NJ: Rutgers University Press.

Meredith, B. (1988). *A Change for the Better.* London: Grafton Books.

Wolf, N. (1991). *The Beauty Myth: How Images of Beauty Are Used Against Women.* New York: William Morrow.

## Review

1. What are the cultural forces behind the use of cosmetic surgery?

2. What kinds of reasons do women give for justifying their cosmetic surgery?

3. How do women feel about themselves after having cosmetic surgery?

## Applications

1. Look at clothing ads in a newspaper or magazine. If you were an alien whose only information about humans was the models in these ads, how would you describe the way humans look? What proportion of people do you think actually look that way?

2. Although this article focuses on women, men undergo a certain amount of cosmetic surgery because they are dissatisfied with their physical appearance. Make an informal survey of friends and acquaintances—try to get an equal number of males and females. Tell them a little about this article and then ask them how they feel about their own bodies. Are they basically satisfied or somewhat dissatisfied with the way they look? If they could change something about their appearance, what would it be? Are there differences between the responses of the males and females? How do your findings square with what Gimlin found in her research?

## Related Web Sites

1. *http://www.cosmeticsurgery.org/.* Home page of the American Academy of Cosmetic Surgery, showing the way that the surgery is presented to prospective patients.

2. *http://www.bodypositive.com/.* A site that offers abundant information and guidance about body image.

# 8

# Culture and Asian Americans' Sexuality

*Sumie Okazaki*

To *paraphrase John Donne, no culture is an island. All modern cultures are the result of both indigenous activity and* **diffusion** *from other cultures. Diffusion occurs as people from diverse cultures have contact with each other through travel, warfare, and the mass media. You will, for example, discover aspects of American culture throughout the world, including such things as blue jeans, Coca-Cola, fast-food restaurants, music, and ideas about democracy and freedom.*

*Similarly, American culture is composed of elements derived from many sources, including the American Indians who were here before the arrival of Europeans. For example, in a famous essay, anthropologist Ralph Linton noted the great number of items we frequently use that originated elsewhere: cotton was domesticated in India; sheep were domesticated in the Near East; silk was discovered in China; pajamas come from India; soap was invented by the ancient Gauls; the process of tanning animal skins arose in ancient Egypt, where glass was also invented; coins are an ancient Lydian invention; steel was first made in southern India; and so on. In other words, our culture, like all others, is a mixture accumulated from cultures throughout the world.*

*Cultures also have* **subcultures,** *groups within a society that share the culture of the larger society while maintaining certain distinctive patterns of their own. American subcultures include the generational, racial and ethnic, regional, and religious. Members of subcultures may find themselves caught between the conflicting norms of their subculture and those of the larger society. In this se-*

*lection, Sumie Okazaki shows how Asian Americans' sexual beliefs and behavior are affected by the intersection of their subculture with the larger American culture.*

While sharing their Asian ancestry and vestiges of Asian cultural heritage to varying degrees, Asian Americans comprise an ethnic minority group that defies simple characterizations. Consisting of approximately 4% of the total U.S. population, Asian Americans trace their roots to one or more of 28 Asian countries of origin or ethnic groups. The largest proportions of Asian Americans in 1990 were Chinese (24%) and Filipino (20%), followed by Japanese, Korean, and Asian Indian at approximately 11% to 12% each and Vietnamese at 9% (U.S. Bureau of the Census, 1993). However, the continuing influx of new immigrants from Southeast Asia and South Asia as well as from China and Korea provide a backdrop for diversity among Americans of Asian ancestry on important dimensions such as national origin, language, nativity, generational status, religion, acculturation to the mainstream American values and customs, and so on. The majority (66%) of Asian Americans in 1990 were born in foreign countries (U.S. Bureau of the Census, 1993).

The present review concerning the impact of Asian and Asian American cultures on sexuality will first examine aspects of various Asian cultural traditions and values that influence sexual attitudes and behavior among Asian Americans, then examine the available scientific literature in several major areas (but excluding materials related to HIV, other STDs, and safe sex practices). . . .

## Cultural Roots

Sexuality is linked to procreation in most Asian cultures. Gupta (1994) argues that sexuality was not a taboo subject in ancient Hindu culture granted that it was not discussed within the context of marriage. Rather, sexuality was openly discussed in religious and fictional texts (e.g., the *Kama Sutra*) and depicted in paintings and sculptures, some with explicit erotic details. Japanese and Chinese erotica also date back to ancient times. On the other hand, sex is a taboo subject in contemporary Chinese culture, where sex education in schools is minimal and parents as well as health professionals are reluctant to discuss sexuality and sexual information (Chan, 1986). Traditional Cambodian society believed that a lack of knowledge regarding sexuality would prevent premarital sexual activity that would tarnish the family honor; consequently, discussions of information regarding sexual intercourse and sexuality were kept to a minimum (Kulig, 1994). Filipino culture, with the strong influence of Catholicism, tends to have a strong moral undercurrent that scorns premarital sex, use of contraceptives, and abortion (Tiongson, 1997).

Regardless of each Asian culture's degree of openness surrounding sexual discourse, expressions of sexuality outside of marriage are considered highly inappropriate in most Asian cultures. Most Asian cultures are highly collectivistic and patriarchical; thus, sexuality that is allowed open expression (particularly among women) would represent a threat to the highly interdependent social order as well as to the integrity of the family. Many Asian cultural traditions place emphasis on propriety and the observance of strict moral and social conduct, thus modesty and restrained sexuality are valued (Abraham, 1999). The sexually conservative beliefs and behavior that many Americans of Asian ancestry may exhibit may, in turn, be misinterpreted by the larger American society as asexual (Tsui, 1985).

## Sexual Knowledge, Attitudes, and Norms

Available data regarding the sexual knowledge, attitudes, and norms among Asian Americans reflect relative conservatism. In a 1993 study in British Columbia comparing 346 Asian Canadian and 356 non-Asian Canadian university students enrolled in introductory psychology courses, Meston, Trapnell, and Gorzalka (1998) found that Asian Canadians held more conservative sexual attitudes and demonstrated

less sexual knowledge than non-Asian Canadians. Among Asian Canadians, the more acculturated they were to the Canadian culture the more permissive their sexual attitudes. In a survey of 574 girls in sixth through eighth grades at public junior high schools in southern California, East (1998) compared the girls' sexual, marital, and birth expectations across four ethnic groups (White, Black, Hispanic, and Southeast Asians). Southeast Asian American (Vietnamese, Cambodian, Laotian; n = 70) girls reported the oldest "best" age for first intercourse (M = 21.7) and first birth (M = 24.4) and the oldest "desired" age for first birth (M = 26.4) of the four ethnic group girls. Southeast Asian American girls indicated the least desire to have children, the least likelihood of having children out of wedlock, and the least intention of having sexual intercourse in the near future. In a survey of 452 unmarried young adults (ages 18 to 25) attending 2-year community colleges, Feldman, Turner, and Araujo (1999) also found that Asian Americans (n = 104) held significantly later normative and personal sexual timetables for initiating all types of sexual behavior relative to other ethnic groups. In another survey with 474 college students in the Southwest (17 of whom were Asian American) regarding sex education, Asian Americans' reported age at which they understood what sexual intercourse was (M = 15.1) and the age at which they plan to begin their future children's sex education (M = 14.1) were older than those of any other ethnic group (Harman & Johnson, 1995).

There are some data suggesting that Asian Americans' sexually conservative attitude may erode with higher degrees of exposure to the American culture. Abramson and Imai-Marquez (1982) administered a measure of sex guilt to three different generations of Japanese American men and women and matched groups of White Americans in the metropolitan Los Angeles area. The researchers found that each subsequent younger generation of Japanese Americans and White Americans reported less guilty thoughts and feelings concerning sexual matters, although Japanese Americans still reported more sex guilt than White Americans within each age cohort group. However, in a different study of 18 Japanese American, 22 Mexican American, 20 African American, and 27 White American parents in Los Angeles regarding their attitudes toward sex education, the attitudes of Japanese American parents were found not to differ from those of other ethnic group parents once father's education and mother's religiosity were controlled for (Abramson, Moriuchi, Waite, & Perry, 1983). Notably, all of the Japanese American parents were born in the U.S.

## Sexual Behavior

Most studies of sexual activity among Asian Americans have been conducted with adolescents and college students. The most comprehensive survey of American adults' sexual behavior, the National Health and Social Life Survey conducted in 1992, did not oversample Asian American individuals (Laumann, Gagnon, Michael, & Michaels, 1994). Consequently, only 2% of the total sample was Asian American, making it difficult to sufficiently characterize the sexual behavior of Asian American (particularly female) adults in the general population.

### Adolescents

In a survey of 2,026 high school students in Los Angeles County, Asian American adolescents (n = 186) were more likely to be virgins (73%) than African American (28%), Latino (43%), and White Americans (50%) (Schuster, Bell, & Kanouse, 1996). Further analyses of the same data revealed that Asian American adolescents were less likely to have initiated vaginal intercourse at an early age and were less likely to report having participated in other heterosexual genital sexual activities during the prior year than their non-Asian counterparts (Schuster, Bell, Nakajima, & Kanouse, 1998). The researchers found that Asian American nonvirgins also reported the lowest number of lifetime partners for vaginal intercourse, even though the reported frequency of sexual activity did not differ from those of other ethnic group adolescents. Asian American adolescents in homes where English is the primary language spoken were more likely

than other Asian Americans to be nonvirgins and to have engaged in heterosexual genital sexual activities. Asian American adolescents were also more likely than non-Asian Americans to think that their parents and friends would disapprove if they had vaginal intercourse and that people their own age should not have vaginal intercourse.

Another study of an ethnically diverse sample of 877 Los Angeles County youths (Upchurch, Levy-Storms, Sucoff, & Aneshensel, 1998) found that Asian American males had the highest median age of first sex (18.1) and that Asian American females (as well as Hispanic females) had rates of first sex about half that of White females. Finally, an analysis of the national Youth Risk Behavior Survey data (total N = 52,985) collected by the Centers for Disease Control and Prevention (Grunbaum, Lowry, Kann, & Pateman, 2000) also found that Asian American high school students were significantly less likely than Black, Hispanic, or White students to have had sexual intercourse or to have had four or more sex partners. Only 28% of Asian American students reported lifetime experience of sexual intercourse compared to 77% of Black, 55% of Hispanic, and 48% of White students. However, among those who were currently sexually active, Asian American students were found to be as likely as other groups to have used alcohol or drugs during last sexual intercourse or to have used a condom at last intercourse. It should be noted that there is variability among Asian ethnic groups with respect to sexual behavior. Horan and DiClemente (1993) reported that among 11th and 12th grade students in San Francisco, only 13% of Chinese American students were sexually active but 32% of Filipino students were sexually active.

### College Students

The patterns found with Asian American adolescents also extend to college students. In a 1982 survey of 114 Chinese American college students in northern California (60% of whom were U.S.-born), Huang and Uba (1992) found that the majority (over 60%) approved of premarital sexual intercourse when partners are in love or engaged to be married; however, only 37% of the men and 46% of the women surveyed had ever engaged in coitus. In this sample, Chinese American women were generally more sexually experienced than men, with more women having engaged in kissing, necking, and petting, although men (M = 18.5) and women (M = 18.8) did not differ in age of first vaginal intercourse experience. There was a positive correlation between the level of acculturation to the U.S. and engagement in premarital sexual intercourse, and those Chinese Americans dating only White Americans consistently had more sexual experience than those dating only Chinese Americans. Huang and Uba concluded that Chinese American college students were not avoiding premarital sex because they do not find it permissible. Rather, the authors speculated that Chinese Americans' sexual behavior and gender differences may reflect internalized racism (e.g., less positive body images), more conservative standards for engaging in premarital sexual relations, and racialized stereotypes of Asian American men as asexual and undesirable sexual partners.

In a 1987–1988 survey of 153 Asian American college students in Southern California (half of who were born in the U.S.), Cochran, Mays, and Leung (1991) found that 44% of the men and 50% of the women had engaged in heterosexual sexual intercourse at least once. The rate of Asian Americans who were sexually active (47%) was significantly lower than their age cohorts in other ethnic groups. Among those who were sexually active, the rates of engagement in oral sex was high (86% for women, 75% for men). In an [analysis] of their 1993 data on 346 Asian and 356 non-Asian Canadian college students, Meston, Trapnell, and Gorzalka (1996) found significant and substantive ethnic differences in all measures of interpersonal sexual behavior (i.e., light and heavy petting, oral sex, intercourse) and intrapersonal sexual behavior (i.e., frequency of fantasies, masturbation incidence and frequency, and ideal frequency of intercourse), and all sociosexual restrictiveness measures (e.g., lifetime number of partners, number of partners in the past year, pre-

dicted number of partners, lifetime number of one-night stands). Overall, 35% of Asian Canadian college students in this survey reported having experienced intercourse. This study did not find any differences among Asian Canadians in their sexual behavior according to their length of residency in Canada.

A survey of 148 White American and 202 Asian American college students in Southern California (McLaughlin, Chen, Greenberger, & Biermeier, 1997) also found that Asian American men (over 55%) and women (60%) were significantly more likely than White American men (25%) and women (<30%) to be virgins. Among those who were sexually experienced, Asian American men (M = 2.3) and women (M = 2.2) reported fewer lifetime sexual partners than White American men (M = 5.5) and women (M = 3.5). Within the Asian American sample, women from least acculturated families were more likely to be virgins (77%) than those from moderately or highly acculturated families (52% and 53%, respectively). This pattern did not hold for Asian American men. Of note, Asian Americans and White Americans endorsed casual sex to a similar degree even though the groups differed significantly in the number of partners. McLaughlin et al. interpreted this attitude-behavior inconsistency among Asian American college students as possibly reflecting the larger and more effective role that their parents play in controlling the adolescents' behavior.

In sum, the available data indicate that Asian Americans tend to be more sexually conservative than non-Asian Americans of the same age group, particularly with regard to the older age of initiation of sexual activity. One exception is a study by Sue (1982), who reported in a survey of 36 Asian American college students enrolled in a human sexuality course that rates of premarital sexual behavior did not differ from those of non-Asian students. However, Sue's anomalous data are likely the result of the selective nature of Asian American students who voluntarily enrolled in a human sexuality course.

## Sexual and Reproductive Help

Almost all studies examining sexual and reproductive health among Asian Americans have been conducted with women. The studies of participation in breast and cervical cancer screening among the Asian American population paint a fragmented picture. Some studies have shown moderate rates of cancer screening among Asian American women. For example, 57% of 189 Chinese American women in Michigan, aged 50 or older, had had mammograms in the past 2 years (Yu, Seetoo, Tsai, & Sun, 1998), and over 70% of the Chinese American women sampled in San Francisco had had a mammogram, Pap test, clinical breast examination (CBE), and breast self examination (BSE) (Lee, 1998).

However, the majority of the studies have found extremely low rates of screening in Asian Americans compared to the non-Asian American population. In a study conducted in the Puget Sound area, Asian American women were found to be less likely than other ethnic group women to enroll in breast cancer screening programs even when out-of-pocket expenses for the screening tests were paid by managed care (Tu, Taplin, Barlow, & Boyko, 1999). In a study of women 18 to 74 years old in the San Francisco Bay Area, Chinese American and Vietnamese American women had the lowest rates of first time utilization and recent utilization of breast and cervical cancer screening among all the ethnic groups (Hiatt et al., 1996). Specifically, 33% of Chinese American women had never obtained a Pap test and 30% had never performed BSE, whereas 58% of Vietnamese American women had never had a Pap test and 66% had never performed BSE. An interview study of 332 Chinese American women (ages 40–69) recruited in the Chinatown area of Chicago (Yu, Kim, Chen, & Brintnall, 2001) also found a low level of knowledge of cancer screening tests and low use rates. Only 52% and 54% of the Chinese American women surveyed had ever heard of the CBE and Pap smear test, respectively, for cancer screening purposes, and much lower percentages had actually undergone screenings (35% for CBE, 12% for mammogram, 26% for BSE, and 36% for Pap test). Levels of education, English fluency, and source of health care (Eastern vs. Western medicine) were significant predictors of reproductive health behavior in this population.

The pattern of low use of screening also extends to younger age groups. Only 14.9% of 174 Chinese American students at a midwestern university practiced BSE (Lu, 1995). In a 1996 reproductive and sexual health survey of 674 Asian American women (age 18–35; the majority foreign-born) in California, 67% of the women reported having had at least one sexual partner in their lifetime, yet half of the women (50%) had not received any reproductive or sexual health services within the past year and 25% had never received such services in their lifetime (National Asian Women's Health Organization, 1997). More than one third of the respondents reported that they had never discussed pregnancy, sexually transmitted diseases, birth control, or sexuality in their households. A survey of high school students in Los Angeles County also found that Asian American adolescents reported lower levels of communication with physicians about sexual activity and risk prevention than other ethnic groups (Schuster, Bell, Petersen, & Kanouse, 1996).

In a rare study that specifically examined the role of Asian cultural variables, Tang, Solomon, Yeh, and Worden (1999) studied BSE and cervical cancer screening behavior in 156 Asian American and 50 White American female college students. In this sample, 48% of Asian American and 68% of White American women reported having had sexual intercourse with a male partner. The ethnic differences extended to screening behavior, as only 27% of Asian American women reported performing BSE at least once in their lifetime in contrast to 47% of White American women. Similarly, only 32% of Asian American but 70% of White American women reported having had at least one Pap test in their lifetime. Asian American women were found to have more cultural barriers to screening (more communication barriers with mother surrounding sexual and gynecological issues, less openness around sexuality and more modesty, less prevention orientation in health care, and less utilization of Western medicine). Even after controlling for differences between the two ethnic groups (e.g., mother's education, year in college, family history of breast or cervical cancer, knowing someone with breast cancer, being sexually active, etc.), Asian Americans were still less likely than White Americans to have BSE and pap test. However, Asian American women who were more acculturated were more likely to participate in these screening behaviors.

Consistent with Tang et al.'s (1999) results, similar cultural reasons for the low utilization of reproductive health services were elucidated through a qualitative analysis of interview data with 9 Asian American health care practitioners and educators who worked with Asian American women and focus group data with 6 second-generation Asian American women (National Asian Women's Health Organization, 1995). This study found that Asian American women's sense of risk regarding reproductive and sexual health appeared to be downplayed, as the women tended to view gynecological services as important and legitimate only when they concerned reproductive functions or when the pain or symptoms of infection became unbearable or interfered with daily functioning. In the interviews, health advocates and practitioners agreed that recent immigrants in particular may perceive gynecological exams such as Pap tests as invasive and inappropriate prior to marriage, and that the perception that gynecological care is only acceptable after marriage likely prevents many Asian American women from accessing appropriate care. Additionally, Mo (1992) argued that the idea of a visit to a medical doctor for a checkup without receiving some form of intervention (namely medication) does not fit immigrant Chinese patients' expectations. Mo explained that a Cantonese term, *ham suup*, which is a colloquial term for sexuality that is most often used in a derogatory manner, is used to describe anyone who is sexually inappropriate. Talking about or touching one's body and being knowledgeable about the body are considered as *ham suup*, thus discouraging traditional and immigrant Chinese women from gaining knowledge regarding sexuality and sexual health. In sum, there appears to be a pervasive tendency for Asian American girls and women to be more reluctant than White American girls and women to seek care for their sexual and reproductive health.

As a possible consequence of their relatively low use of screening, Asian American women tend to be diagnosed with more advanced stages of cervical cancer (Frisch & Goodman, 2000) and breast cancer (Jenkins & Kagawa-Singer, 1994) than White American women, thereby increasing the disease burden at diagnosis (Hedeen, White, & Taylor, 1999). Cervical cancer rates among Vietnamese American women was the highest of all ethnic groups in the U.S., with the incidence of 43 per 100,000, a rate that is almost five times that of White American women (Miller et al., 1996). These statistics indicate that there are high health costs associated with Asian American women's reluctance to become knowledgeable about, and to engage in, sexual and reproductive health practices.

One study regarding the sexual and reproductive health issues of Asian American men does exist. A telephone survey of 802 English speaking Asian American men between the ages of 18 and 65 was conducted in Los Angeles, San Francisco, and New York (National Asian Women's Health Organization, 1999). Over half of the respondents (54%) were single and the majority (75%) was foreign-born. Although 87% of the surveyed Asian American men had at least one sexual partner in the past year, the vast majority of the respondents (89%) had never received sexual or reproductive health care services.

## Sexual Abuse and Aggression

The scope of sexual abuse in the Asian American community is unknown, as most state and national agencies that collect such data fail to segregate the data for Asian American victims. Where data are available, the reported incidence among Asian Americans appears relatively low compared to other ethnic groups, possibly due to their lack of access or reluctance to use mental health services and public agencies (Kenny & McEachern, 2000). However, many service providers assert that the actual incidence is much higher than reported (Okamura, Heras, & Wong-Kerberg, 1995). High rates of history of sexual victimization among Cambodian American refugee women and children, which they suffered during the Khmer Rouge reign of terror or at refugee camps, have been extensively documented (e.g., Mollica, Wyshak, & Lavelle, 1987; Rozee & Van Boemel, 1989; Scully, Kuoch, & Miller, 1995). In a study of abuse history among 102 Vietnamese Amerasian refugee young adults in the Philippine Refugee Processing Center who were awaiting placement in the United States, 12% of men and 9% of women reported having been sexually abused (McKelvey & Webb, 1995).

Those who work with Asian American communities speak of the Asian American victims' extreme reluctance to disclose or report sexual abuse or assault (Okamura et al., 1995; Tsuneyoshi, 1996). For example, most Southeast Asian refugees surveyed by Wong (1987) stated that they would respond to sexual abuse in their own family by keeping it a family secret. Further, sexual abuse within the context of marriage may be fatalistically tolerated among some Asian American communities. As a result, immigrant Asian American women may be at a higher risk of marital sexual abuse than U.S.-born Asian American women because they may have been socialized to believe that they had fewer sexual rights than their husbands (Lum, 1998). An analysis of interviews with 25 South Asian immigrant women who were abused by their spouses found that 60% of the women reported being forced to have sex with their husbands against their will, and sexual abuse took many forms such as marital rape and violence and the husbands' control of women's reproductive choices (e.g., forcing the wife to get an abortion, refusal to allow the use of contraceptives, etc.) (Abraham, 1999). Similarly, an interview study with 150 immigrant Korean American women in Chicago revealed that 60% of the women reported being battered, and 37% of those who were physically abused also re-

ported being forced to have sex by their partners (Song, 1996).

Given the cultural tendency to hide sexual abuse from others, it is difficult to ascertain the accuracy of sexual abuse reports. A review of 158 Asian American cases referred for child maltreatment to a San Diego social service agency serving Asian American immigrants and refugees found that sexual abuse constituted only 5% of the total cases, with most sexual abuse victims being Filipino and female (Ima & Hohm, 1991). Another retrospective chart review study of a child abuse clinic in San Francisco generated 69 substantiated cases of sexual abuse between 1986 and 1988 in which the victims were Asian Americans (Rao, DiClemente, & Ponton, 1992). A comparison of this sample of Asian American child sexual abuse victims with randomly selected samples of other ethnic group counterparts found that Asian American victims tended to be older (M = 11.5 years) and more likely to be living with both parents than other ethnic group victims. Notably, Asian American victims were much less likely to display inappropriate sexual behaviors or express anger and hostility but most likely to express suicidal ideation or attempt suicide. Although Asian American mothers were as likely as White Americans and Hispanic Americans to be the primary caretakers to the child victims, they were much less likely than the other groups to have brought the abuse to the attention of authorities and most likely to disbelieve the report of the abuse. Asian American victims were also the least likely to disclose sexual abuse to their mothers; 61% either never spontaneously disclosed the abuse or disclosed the abuse to someone other than their mothers. Asian American victims were also the most likely group to be abused by a male relative (including the father).

Meston and her colleagues (Meston, Heiman, & Trapnell, 1999; Meston, Heiman, Trapnell, & Carlin, 1999) conducted a survey of 466 Asian Canadian and 566 non-Asian Canadian undergraduates regarding abuse experience before age 18 and their current sexuality. The researchers found that 25% of Asian Canadian women and 11% of Asian

Canadian men had at least one experience with sexual abuse (defined here as being involved in some sexual activity against their wishes). In contrast, 40% of non-Asian Canadian women and 11% of non-Asian Canadian men reported at least one experience with sexual abuse. However, associations between early abuse and adult sexual behavior did not differ significantly between Asian and non-Asian Canadians, and reports of sexual abuse were not significantly correlated with socially desirable responding in either group. In another survey of 243 college women (38 of whom were Asian American), rates of reported childhood sexual abuse and being a victim of rape among Asian American college women (21% and 11%, respectively) were lower than those of their White American and African American counterparts (Urquiza & Goodlin-Jones, 1994). The researchers also found that for White and African Americans, women with a history of childhood sexual abuse were three times as likely to be raped as an adult than women without a history of childhood sexual abuse. However, this pattern did not hold for Asian American women.

Hall and Barongan (1997) noted that there appeared to be a lower prevalence of sexual aggression in Asian American communities. A national survey of sexual aggression found that fewer Asian American men perpetrate rape and fewer Asian American women are victims of rape than other ethnic groups (Koss, Gidycz, & Wisniewski, 1987). In their review of risk and protective factors for sexual aggression among Asian Americans, Hall, Windover, and Maramba (1998) argued that the patriarchical aspects of Asian culture, in which women hold subordinate status to men, may create a risk for, and a tolerance of, sexual aggression by Asian American men. On the other hand, Asian cultural emphases on self-control and interpersonal harmony may serve as protective factors for [sexually] aggressive behavior among Asian Americans. To test culture-specific models of sexual aggression, Hall, Sue, Narang, and Lilly (2000) examined intra- and interpersonal determinants of Asian American and White American men's sexual aggression. In this sample of college students, 33% of Asian American and 38% of White American men reported that they had perpetrated some form of sexual aggression. Whereas a path model for White American men suggested that only an intrapersonal variable (misogynous beliefs) predicted sexual aggression, both interpersonal (concern about social standing) and intrapersonal (misogynous beliefs, alcohol use) variables were predictive of Asian American sexual aggression.

Other studies point to a possible role of Asian cultural factors in the attitudes toward sexual violence. For example, a study of 302 Asian American and White American college students (Mori, Bernat, Glenn, Selle, & Zarate, 1995) found that Asian Americans were more likely to endorse negative attitudes toward rape victims and greater belief in rape myths than their White counterparts. Moreover, less acculturated Asian Americans held more negative attitudes toward rape victims than more acculturated Asian Americans. A telephone survey about domestic violence attitudes with 262 Chinese Americans in Los Angeles County (Yick, 2000) found that although 89% of the respondents agreed that sexual aggression constituted domestic violence, the respondents' gender role beliefs (traditional or egalitarian) emerged as a significant factor that shapes their definitions of abuse. In summary, certain facets of traditional Asian cultures (e.g., traditional gender roles, concerns about loss of face) appear to be implicated in Asian Americans' attitudes toward, reporting of, and perpetration of sexual abuse and aggression.

## Sexual Orientation

Little empirical research exists concerning sexual orientation and sexual identity among Asian Americans apart from the HIV-risk studies, although a body of scholarly work (largely in the humanities) regarding Asian American gay, lesbian, and bisexual identities and sexual orientation exists (e.g., Leong, 1994, 1996). One study of 13 Japanese American gay men revealed that only half of their respondents were open with their families regarding their gay identity

(Wooden, Kawasaki, & Mayeda, 1983). In a survey of 19 women and 16 men (ages 21–36) who identified as both Asian American and lesbian or gay, Chan (1989) found that they tended to be more involved in social and political activities in the lesbian-gay community than in the Asian American community. More than half of the respondents (57%) reported being more comfortable in the lesbian/gay community than in the Asian American community and identified more strongly with the gay or lesbian aspects of their identity, although a minority of the respondents reported synthesized ethnic and sexual identities. Although the majority (77%) had come out to a family member (e.g., sibling), only 26% had disclosed their gay identity to their parents because of fear of rejection.

Finally, in a study investigating whether cultural backgrounds moderate the relationship between sexual orientation and gender-related personality traits, Lippa and Tan (2001) found that participants from more gender-polarized cultural backgrounds (Hispanics and Asian Americans) showed larger homosexual-heterosexual differences in gender-related traits than White Americans for both men and women. That is, Hispanic and Asian American gay men assumed more feminine roles and Hispanic and Asian American lesbians assumed more masculine roles with respect to occupational and hobby preferences as well as self-ascribed masculinity and femininity. Hispanic and Asian American gays and lesbians were also found to fear social disapproval of their homosexuality more than their White counterparts. Taken together, the findings from the few existing studies on sexual orientation among Asian Americans suggest possible influences of cultural and community factors in their sexual identity, disclosure of homosexuality, and gender-related traits.

## Conclusion

Although there are significant gaps in the social science literature concerning Asian Americans' sexuality and sexual behavior, the existing data converge on notable differences between Asian Americans and other ethnic groups on major aspects such as sexual timetables and behaviors and attitudes surrounding sexuality, reproductive health, and sexual abuse.

## References

Abraham, M. (1999). Sexual abuse in South Asian immigrant marriages. *Violence Against Women, 5,* 591–618.

Abramson, P. R., & Imai-Marquez, J. (1982). The Japanese-American: A cross-cultural, cross-sectional study of sex guilt. *Journal of Research in Personality, 16,* 227–237.

Abramson, P. R., Moriuchi, K. D., Waite, M. S., & Perry, L. B. (1983). Parental attitudes about sexual education: Cross-cultural differences and covariate controls. *Archives of Sexual Behavior, 12,* 381–397.

Chan, C. S. (1989). Issues of identity development among Asian-American lesbians and gay men. *Source Journal of Counseling & Development, 68,* 16–20.

Chan, D. W. (1986). Sex misinformation and misconceptions among Chinese medical students in Hong Kong. *Archives of Sexual Behavior, 19,* 73–93.

Cochran, S. D., Mays, V. M., & Leung, L. (1991). Sexual practices of heterosexual Asian-American young adults: Implications for risk of HIV infection. *Archives of Sexual Behavior, 20,* 381–391.

East, P. L. (1998). Racial and ethnic differences in girls' sexual, marital, and birth expectations. *Journal of Marriage & the Family, 60,* 150–162.

Feldman, S. S., Turner, R. A., & Araujo, K. (1999). Interpersonal context as an influence on sexual timetables of youths: Gender and ethnic effects. *Journal of Research on Adolescence, 9,* 25–52.

Frisch, M., & Goodman, M. T. (2000). Human papillomavirus-associated carcinomas in Hawaii and the mainland U.S. *Cancer, 88,* 1464–1469.

Futa, K. T., Hsu, E., & Hansen, D. J. (2001). Child sexual abuse in Asian American families: An examination of cultural factors that influence prevalence, identification, and treatment. *Clinical Psychology: Science & Practice, 8,* 189–209.

Grunbaum, J. A., Lowry, R., Kann, L., & Pateman, B. (2000). Prevalence of health risk behaviors among Asian American/Pacific Islander high school students. *Journal of Adolescent Health, 27,* 322–330.

Gupta, M. (1994). Sexuality in the Indian sub-continent. *Sexual & Marital Therapy, 9,* 57–69.

Hall, G. C. N., & Barongan, C. (1997). Prevention of sexual aggression: Sociocultural risk and protective factors. *American Psychologist, 52,* 5–14.

Hall, G. C. N., Sue, S., Narang, D. S., & Lilly, R. S. (2000). Culture-specific models of men's sexual aggression: Intra- and interpersonal determinants. *Cultural Diversity & Ethnic Minority Psychology, 6,* 252–267.

Hall, G. C. N., Windover, A. K., & Maramba, G. G. (1998). Sexual aggression among Asian Americans: Risk and protective factors. *Cultural Diversity & Ethnic Minority Psychology, 4,* 305–318.

Harman, M. J., & Johnson, J. A. (1995). Cross-cultural sex education: Aspects of age, source, and sex equity. *TCA Journal, 23*(2), 1–11.

Hedeen, A. N., White, E., & Taylor, V. (1999). Ethnicity and birthplace in relation to tumor size and stage in Asian American women with breast cancer. *American Journal of Public Health, 89,* 1248–1252.

Hiatt, R. A., Pasick, R. J., Perez-Stable, E. J., McPhee, S. J., Engelsatd, L., Lee, M., Sabogal, F., D'Onofrio, C. N., & Stewart, S. (1996). Pathways to early cancer detection in the multiethnic population of the San Francisco Bay Area. *Health Education Quarterly, 23* (Suppl.), S10–S27.

Horan, P. F., & DiClemente, R. J. (1993). HIV knowledge, communication, and risk behavior among White, Chinese-, and Filipino-American adolescents in a high-prevalence AIDS epicenter: A comparative analysis. *Ethnicity & Disease, 3,* 97–105.

Huang, K., & Uba, L. (1992). Premarital sexual behavior among Chinese college students in the United States. *Archives of Sexual Behavior, 21,* 227–240.

Ima, K., & Hohm, C. E (1991). Child maltreatment among Asian and Pacific Islander refugees and immigrants: The San Diego case. *Journal of Interpersonal Violence, 6,* 267–285.

Jenkins, C. N. H., & Kagawa-Singer, M. (1994). Cancer. In N W. S. Zane, D. T. Takeuchi, & K. N. J. Young (Eds.), *Confronting critical health issues of Asian and Pacific Islander Americans,* (pp. 105–147). Thousand Oaks, CA: Sage.

Kenny, M. C., & McEachern, A. G. (2000). Racial, ethnic, and cultural factors of childhood sexual abuse: A selected review of the literature. *Clinical Psychology Review, 20,* 905–922.

Koss, M. P., Gidycz, C. A., & Wisniewski, N. (1987). The scope of rape: Incidence and prevalence of sexual aggression and victimization in a national sample of higher education students. *Journal of Consulting & Clinical Psychology, 55,* 162–170.

Kulig, J. C. (1994). Sexuality beliefs among Cambodians: Implications for health care professionals. *Health Care for Women International, 15,* 69–76.

Laumann, E. O., Gagnon, J. H., Michael, R. T., & Michaels, S. (1994). *The social organization of sexuality: Sexual practices in the United States.* Chicago: The University of Chicago Press.

Lee, M. (1998). Breast and cervical cancer early detection in Chinese American women. *Asian American & Pacific Islander Journal of Health, 6,* 351–357.

Leong, R. (Ed.) (1994). Dimensions of desire [Special issue]. *Amerasia Journal, 20* (1).

——. (Ed.) (1996). *Asian American sexualities: Dimensions of the gay and lesbian experience.* New York: Routledge.

Lippa, R. A., & Tan, F. D. (2001). Does culture moderate the relationship between sexual orientation and gender-related personality traits? *Cross-Cultural Research, 35,* 65–87.

Lu, Z. J. (1995). Variables associated with breast self-examination among Chinese women. *Cancer Nursing, 18,* 29–34.

Lum, J. L. (1998). Family violence. In L. C. Lee & N. W. S. Zane (Eds.), *Handbook of Asian American Psychology* (pp. 505–525). Thousand Oaks, CA: Sage.

McKelvey, R. S., & Webb, J. A. (1995). A pilot study of abuse among Vietnamese Amerasians. *Child Abuse & Neglect, 19,* 545–553.

McLaughlin, C. S., Chen, C., Greenberger, E., & Biermeier, C. (1997). Family, peer, and individual correlates of sexual experience among Caucasian and Asian American late adolescents. *Journal of Research on Adolescence, 7,* 33–53.

Meston, C. M., Heiman, J. R., & Trapnell, P. D. (1999). The relation between early abuse and adult sexuality. *The Journal of Sex Research, 36,* 385–395.

Meston, C. M., Heiman, J. R., Trapnell, P. D., & Carlin, A. S. (1999). Ethnicity, desirable responding, and self-reports of abuse: A comparison of European- and Asian-ancestry undergraduates. *Journal of Consulting & Clinical Psychology, 67,* 139–144.

Meston, C. M., Trapnell, P. D., & Gorzalka, B. B. (1996). Ethnic and gender differences in sexuality: Variations in sexual behavior between Asian and non-Asian university students. *Archives of Sexual Behavior, 25,* 33–72.

——. (1998). Ethnic, gender, and length-of-residency influences on sexual knowledge and attitudes. *The Journal of Sex Research, 35,* 176–188.

Miller, B. A., Kolonel, L. N., Bernstein, L., Young, J. L., Swanson, G. M., West, D., Key, C. R., Liffy, J. M., Glover, C. S., Alexander, G. A., et al. (Eds.). (1996). Racial/ethnic patterns of cancer in the United States, 1988–1992, *NIH Publication No. 96 4104.* Bethesda, MD: National Cancer Institute.

Mo, B. (1992). Modesty, sexuality, and breast health in Chinese-American women. *Western Journal of Medicine, 157,* 260–264.

Mollica, R., Wyshak, G., & Lavelle, J. (1987). The psychological impact of war trauma and torture on Southeast Asian refugees. *American Journal of Psychiatry, 144,* 1567–1571.

Mori, L., Bernat, J. A., Glenn, P. A., Selle, L. L., & Zarate, M. G. (1995). Attitudes toward rape: Gender and ethnic differences across Asian and Caucasian college students. *Sex Roles, 32,* 457–467.

National Asian Women's Health Organization. (1995). *Perceptions of risk: An assessment of the factors influencing use of reproductive and sexual health services by Asian American women.* San Francisco: Author.

——. (1997). *Expanding options: A reproductive and sexual health survey of Asian American women.* San Francisco: Author.

——. (1999). *The Asian American men's health survey: Sharing responsibility.* San Francisco: Author.

Okamura, A., Heras, P., & Wong-Kerberg, L. (1995). Asian, Pacific Island, and Filipino Americans and sexual child abuse. In L. A. Fontes (Ed.), *Sexual abuse in nine North American cultures: Treatment and prevention* (pp. 67–93). Thousand Oaks, CA: Sage.

Rao, K., DiClemente, R. J., & Ponton, L. E. (1992). Child sexual abuse of Asians compared with other populations. *Journal of the American Academy of Child & Adolescent Psychiatry, 31,* 880–886.

Rozee, P. D., & Van Boemel, G. (1989). The psychological effects of war trauma and abuse on older Cambodian refugee women. *Women & Therapy, 8*(4), 23–50.

Schuster, M. A., Bell, R. M., & Kanouse, D. E. (1996). The sexual practices of adolescent virgins: Genital sexual activities of high school students who have never had vaginal intercourse. *American Journal of Public Health, 86,* 1570–1576.

Schuster, M. A., Bell, R. M., Nakajima, G. A., & Kanouse, D. E. (1998). The sexual practices of Asian and Pacific Islander high school students. *Journal of Adolescent Health, 23,* 221–231.

Schuster, M. A., Bell, R. M., Petersen, L. P., & Kanouse, D. E. (1996). Communication between adolescents and physicians about sexual behavior and risk prevention. *Archives of Pediatric and Adolescent Medicine, 150,* 906–913.

Scully, M., Kuoch, T., & Miller, R. A. (1995). Cambodians and sexual child abuse. In L. A. Fontes (Ed.), *Sexual abuse in nine North American cultures: Treatment and prevention* (pp. 97–127). Thousand Oaks, CA: Sage.

Song, Y. I. (1996). *Battered women in Korean immigrant families.* New York: Garland.

Sue, D. (1982). Sexual experience and attitudes of Asian American students. *Psychological Report, 51,* 401–402.

Tang, T. S., Solomon, L. J., Yeh, C. J., & Worden, J. K. (1999). The role of cultural variables in breast self-examination and cervical cancer screening behavior in young Asian women living in the United States. *Journal of Behavioral Medicine, 22,* 419–436.

Tiongson, A. T., Jr. (1997). Throwing the baby out with the bathwater: Situating young Filipino mothers and fathers beyond the dominant discourse on adolescent pregnancy. In M. P. P. Root (Ed.), *Filipino Americans: Transformation and identity* (pp. 257–271). Thousand Oaks, CA: Sage.

Tsui, A. M. (1985). Psychotherapeutic considerations in sexual counseling of Asian immigrants. *Psychotherapy, 22,* 357–362.

Tsuneyoshi, S. (1996). Rape trauma syndrome: Case illustration of Elizabeth, an 18-year-old Asian American. In F. H. McClure & E. Teyber (Eds.), *Child and adolescent therapy: A multicultural relational approach* (pp. 287–320). New York: Harcourt Brace College Publishers.

Tu, S., Taplin, S. H., Barlow, W. E., & Boyko, E. J. (1999). Breast cancer screening by Asian-American women in a managed care environment. *American Journal of Preventive Medicine, 17,* 55–61.

Upchurch, D. M., Levy-Storms, L., Sucoff, C. A., & Aneshensel, C. S. (1998). Gender and ethnic differences in the timing of first sexual intercourse. *Family Planning Perspectives, 30,* 121–127.

Urquiza, A. J., & Goodlin-Jones, B. L. (1994). Child sexual abuse and adult revictimization with women of color. *Violence & Victims, 9,* 223–232.

U.S. Bureau of the Census. (1993).*We the Americans: Asians.* Washington, DC: U.S. Government Printing Office.

Wong, D. (1987). Preventing child sexual assault among Southeast Asian refugee families. *Child Today,* 16, 18–22.

Wooden, W. S., Kawasaki, H., & Mayeda, R. (1983). Lifestyles and identity maintenance among gay Japanese-American males. *Alternative Lifestyles,* 5, 236–243.

Yick, A. G. (2000). Domestic violence beliefs and attitudes in the Chinese American community. *Journal of Social Service Research,* 27, 29–51.

Yu, E. S. H., Kim, K. K., Chen, E. H., & Brintnall, R. A. (2001). Breast and cervical cancer screening among Chinese American women. *Cancer Practice,* 9, 81–91.

Yu, M. Y., Seetoo, A. D., Tsai, C. K., & Sun, C. (1998). Sociodemographic predictors of Papanicolaou smear test and mammography use among women of Chinese descent in Southeastern Michigan. *Womens Health Issues,* 8, 372–381.

## Review

1. How would you generally characterize views on sexuality in Asian cultures?

2. In what ways does sexual behavior differ between Asian Americans and other Americans?

3. How does Asian culture affect sexual and reproductive health behavior among Asian Americans?

4. How would you compare the sexual abuse and aggression experienced by Asian Americans with that experienced by other Americans?

## Applications

1. Okazaki provides the median age at which Asian Americans have varied kinds of experiences with their sexuality. How does your own age at having any such experiences compare with the ones she gives? What are your thoughts on the "best" or "most desirable" age for the experiences? If you have or hope to have children, at what ages would you want them to have the experiences?

2. Select one of the topics covered by Okazaki and see what you can find out about it in the popular literature (e.g., use an Internet search engine, or the *Readers' Guide to Periodical Literature* to find articles in popular magazines, and/or check books in your local library). In what ways does the popular treatment differ from, add to, or modify what you learned in this selection? How would you explain any differences you discovered?

## Related Web Sites

1. *http://www.unescap.org/pop/publicat/apss156/chapter5.htm.* A U.N. paper on the sexual and reproductive health needs of Asian adolescents.

2. *http://www.gapsn.org/project2/history/.* Support site for gay Asian young people, including numerous articles and interviews.

# Part Two

## *Becoming a Social Creature*

Socialization occurs throughout life, but some of the most important socialization takes place during childhood. Foremost among the socializing agents is the family. From birth, the family influences a child's development by such things as the way the parents hold the baby, look at it, talk to it, and respond to its needs. As the child grows, the parents teach values and norms. Family socialization is reinforced or modified by experiences at school and with peers, by the mass media, and by interaction with others.

In this part, we look at two of the agents of socialization—family and television. In both, the question addressed is how the particular agent affects the development of gender roles. The third selection explores the results of socialization by looking at how male patrons of strip clubs act out their masculinity. ✦

# 9

# As the Twig Is Bent

## Children Reared in Feminist Households

*Barbara J. Risman*
*Kristen Myers*

*In a perfectly integrated society, everything would work together harmoniously and flawlessly. All the various agents of socialization would be consistent with each other. But no society is perfectly integrated. As a result, the agents of socialization are not always consistent, and sometimes may even contradict each other. An example of contradiction is the admonition by parents and teachers to avoid drugs and the peer pressure to experiment with drugs.*

*Contradictory messages and pressures from socializing agents occur throughout people's lives. For instance, a man who was urged by his parents and encouraged by his new employer to work more than the required minimum found himself facing hostile colleagues when he tried to forego the morning coffee break and remain at his desk.*

*How do people deal with such contradictions? Obviously, there are various options. In this selection, the researchers looked at how children reared in feminist households handle the contradiction between parental efforts to imbue them both with nonsexist attitudes and behavior and with the attitudes and behavior of the less-than-egalitarian world in which they must function. They gathered their material by finding 15 "fair" families (those in which husband and wife agreed that they had an egalitarian relationship) and interviewing the 12 boys and nine girls from those families. They also had some of the children write poetry and free-play.*

*The article illustrates an important sociological principle: How an individual behaves is a function not only of his or her personal attitudes and inclinations but also of the social forces that come to bear upon him or her in particular social contexts. Those who adapt to the social context may pay a price in the sense of compromising their standards or preferences. Those who do not adapt may pay the even heavier price of ostracism. Most people adapt at least enough to be an acceptable part of some group.*

In recent years, sociologists have come to define gender as a social construct to be negotiated rather than as a fixed entity (West and Zimmerman 1987; Connell 1987; Risman and Schwartz 1989; Howard et al. 1996). In this view, gender is neither simply an attribute of individuals nor a constraint of the social structure. Instead, when people interact in their daily lives, they "do gender" which helps to reproduce the larger, gendered social structure. West and Zimmerman (1987) argue that individuals are actors working within structural constraints rather than passive pawns. The conceptualization of gender as behavior that may or may not be enacted allows those concerned with inequality to hope for change: What would happen if we decided not to do gender, or to do it differently? Would we radically alter the social structure as we know it, or are larger social pressures strong enough to override individual insurgency?...

## Learning How to Behave: Acting Versus Reacting

Sociologists have only rarely—and quite recently—studied children's gender. Therefore, much of the literature to be reviewed originates in other disciplines. When children are studied, in both sociology and psychology, the predominant questions center around the ways in which children learn to be boys or girls. We organize this literature analytically, for purposes of discussion, based on the presumptions about children's role in their own socialization. We divide this scholarship into three categories: that which sees children as the primary actors in the gendering process, or cognitive theories; that which sees children's gender as something that is imposed by the larger culture, and that is reinforced through structural constraints, or socialization theories; and that which argues that children are constrained by long-standing gender norms, but which sees children as participating in and negotiating the enactment of gender or social constructionist theories.

We briefly summarize these analytic categories. First, theories where children are the primary actors [including Piaget (1932); Kohlberg (1966); Maccoby (1992); and Martin (1993)] are theories of cognitive development which argue that children play an active role in gender acquisition, rather than passively absorbing appropriate information from their parents and peers. Instead, children seek relevant information, and they organize it into predictable patterns. They begin to do this at a young age in order to make sense out of their worlds. This perspective puts undue emphasis on the child as rational actor freely picking and choosing among the available options, and selecting gender as the most salient organizing force in society (Bem 1993).

The second category—which conceptualizes gender as structurally imposed upon children—includes Parsons and Bales (1955); Inkeles (1968); Bandura (1962, 1971); Cahill (1987); Deaux (1984); Fagot et al. (1992); Hutson (1983); Stern and Karraker (1989); and Eisenberg et al. (1985). This perspective sees the socialization process as a one-way conduit of information from adult to child. Beginning at birth, people in society (parents, teachers, and peers) reward children for learning the behavior of the same sex. Because they receive positive feedback for "correct" behavior, children imitate same-sex behavior, and "encode" it into their behavioral repertoires. Once encoded, the child's gender is set. This socialization perspective offers a static picture of gender with the child as a relatively acquiescent recipient of appropriate models of behavior, which in turn offer little room for improvisation and change. This is typical of role theo-

rists in general (Kreps et al. 1994). It also does not allow for the enactment of multiple masculinities and femininities (Connell 1992), thereby reifying and valorizing a gender dichotomy.

The last category is more consistent with a social constructionist perspective. In recent years, sociologists have taken a more critical look at the gender socialization of children, arguing that socialization is not a one-way conduit of information, with adults providing role models and sanctions, and with the children hitting, missing and eventually getting it "right" [for more, see Corsaro (1985), Alanen (1988), and Giddens (1979)]. Instead, the children participate in the process as social actors. Research in this tradition is quite new. For example, Borman and O'Reilly (1987) find that kindergarten children in same-sex play groups initiate play in similar manners, but that the topics for play vary by gender. That is, boys and girls play different types of games, thereby creating different conversational and negotiation demands. Thorne (1993) examines groups of children in classrooms and school yards, illustrating how "kids" actively create and police gender boundaries, forming various strata among themselves. She asserts that gender relations are not invariant, but instead can change according to the context and the actors involved. Thorne criticizes most socialization and development frameworks for presupposing a certain outcome: that boys will learn appropriate masculinities, girls will learn appropriate femininities; and if they fail to do so, they will either be punished or labeled deviant. She argues that this future-oriented perspective distorts the children's everyday realities, which are crucial to their ongoing gendered negotiations. As she says, "children's interactions are not preparation for life, they are life itself" (p. 3).

Bem (1993) improves upon both cognitive and socialization theories by linking them. Bem argues that children try to make sense of the world by forming categories, or "schema," but these categories are shaped by the ubiquitous presence of existing gender categories in society. She argues that learning gender is subtle, transmitted to children by adults both consciously and unconsciously, so that the dominant way of understanding the social world is seen as the only way to understand it. Existing gender divisions are hegemonic and therefore usually unquestioned by both children and adults. Therefore, calling into question the taken-for-granted gendered organization of society is difficult and unlikely, though not impossible.

It seems quite reasonable that all three processes occur. Children who live in gendered societies do, no doubt, develop gender schema and code themselves as well as the world around them in gendered terms. But this seems much more likely to be the result of their lived experiences in patriarchal societies and not the consequence of some innate drive for cognitive development. While children do indeed develop cognitive gender schema, adults and older children also treat boys and girls quite differently. Gender socialization is apparent in any observation of children's lives. And, while children are being socialized, they react, negotiate, and even reject some of the societal pressures as they interact with each other, and adults. Children are actors in the gendering process, but that does not mean that we must ignore the impact of differential reinforcement of gender-appropriate behavior on them. The cognitive effects of living in a gendered (and sexist) society, the reality of gender socialization, and the active efforts of boys and girls to negotiate their own worlds interact to affect their future options and constraints.

## Unequal Outcomes: Reproducing Gender Inequalities

Even when we recognize that children both act and react throughout the gendering process, we cannot overlook the strong empirical data which suggests that boys and girls are differentially prepared for their adult roles. Boys are still routinely socialized to learn to work in teams and to compete; girls are still routinely socialized to value nurturing (just notice the relative numbers of boys and girls in team sports versus those dedicated readers to the very popular book series, *The Babysitters Club*). Thorne (1993)

has shown very convincingly that there is much more cross-over gender play than dichotomous thinking presumes; and yet other research continues to indicate the consequences of gender socialization on children (Lever 1978; Luttrell 1993; Hawkins 1985; Wilder et al. 1985; Signorelli 1990; Maccoby 1992; Hutson 1993). There is also much evidence that gender socialization differs by social class, ethnicity and religion (Peterson and Rollins 1987; Collins 1990).

Lever's (1978) classic study of boys' and girls' play offers insight into the ways in which boys and girls are differentially prepared for their futures: men are presumed to belong in the public, competitive sphere and women in the private, nurturing sphere. Boys' games were more likely to be outside, involve teams and be age-integrated. Girls were more likely to play make believe games with one or two others, and to break up a game rather than work through conflict. After interviewing two groups of working class women about their gendered experiences in school, Luttrell (1993) suggests that school is politically embattled, and femininity is used to undermine working class girls' academic confidence and success in school. Hawkins (1985) argues that girls often do not receive sufficient support with regard to learning computer skills; they are thereby somewhat handicapped in an increasingly computer-reliant world. Wilder et al. (1985) echo this argument, examining the ideology that technology is a male domain. In surveys of 1,600 children in kindergarten through twelfth grade, they find that girls like computers less than boys and therefore use them less. In a survey of first year college students, they find that women students feel less competent with computer technology, regardless of their skill or experience.

Gender specific experiences aren't limited to play and school. Because human beings are helpless at birth and, in our society, adulthood may not arrive for more [than] two decades, children are dependent upon families for a very long time. Therefore, parents and the immediate family are one source of existing gendered expectations (Maccoby 1992). The research we have discussed above points to the negative impact of gender-typing on their psyches, their acquisition of competitive market skills, necessary nurturing skills, and their interaction with each other. Research indicates that parents participate in gender-typing by often rewarding gender-typical play and punishing gender-atypical play (Hutson 1983). In order to help combat gender inequality, we must carefully attend to both gendering processes and the negotiation of gender among children. While several scholars have documented that some families in our society are moving in the direction of shared parenting, we have as yet little information about how effective such changes in parenting style might be in a society in which gendering processes continue to occur in other social realms (Coltrane 1996; Marsiglio 1995; Schwartz 1994; Segal 1990).

In this paper, we examine children whose parents have attempted to break the chain of gender inequality that begins at birth. We focus particularly on the ways in which children grapple with and enact gender. The children in this study are living in a different context than children in more mainstream families: these are children whose parents . . . have an ideological and practical commitment to organizing their homes and families in an egalitarian manner. Whereas mainstream parents may react with delight when their daughter wants to be Barbie for Halloween and their son wants toy guns for his birthday, the parents in this study are likely to be dismayed. Rather than receiving reinforcement from their parents when they enact hegemonic behavior, these children are likely to encounter disappointment or concern. So, how do these children negotiate gender given their atypical parents? . . .

## The Complicated Worlds of Fair Children

In examining the stories, poems, and conversations of the children, we have drawn two main findings. The inconsistencies between the children's egalitarian beliefs and their experiences with peers are the major and consistent finding in these data. The second finding, also consistent, is that identities seem to be forged more from lived experiences than from ideology. The disjunction between ideology, experience, and identity seems to be a common thread woven through all these children's stories. In discussing the findings and providing the words of the children themselves, we refer to the gender of the child. We recognize that, in focusing repeatedly on gender, we may be reinforcing the notion of gender differences rather than similarities; that is not our intention. It is simply a necessary means of distinguishing subjects and the differential experiences.

We divide our findings into three major categories: ideology, experiences and identities of the children. In analyzing the data, we realized that gender operates on several levels for these children. They all espouse a certain rhetoric of gender which they have learned in part from living in "fair" families. We find that this rhetoric is not always in sync with the children's gendered experiences and behaviors, so we address them separately. And, last, we find that the children have internalized notions of gender which affect their identities as girls and boys.

### Ideology

Approximately 80 percent of the children (16 of 21) entirely adopted their parents' egalitarian or feminist views on gender. Two of the children without such views were four year olds whose answers were better described as inconsistent than traditional. These children knew that occupations were currently sex-segregated but believed they shouldn't be. They didn't see any jobs in families that ought to be either for men or women. One 10 year old boy actually became annoyed as we questioned him about what men and women should do. He retorted in an irritated voice and rolled his eyes: "I told you I think anybody can do these jobs. . . . I think that saying just men or just women could do these jobs isn't being equal." The children over six years of age didn't have any problem differentiating what was true from what should be so.

Most of both boys and girls not only believed that men and women should be free to work in any occupation and share the family labor, they also understood that male privilege existed in contemporary society. This nine year old girl told us that she believed very much in feminism because "I don't think that it is the least bit fair that in most places males have the main power. I think that women play an important part and should be free to do what they want to do." Similarly, a 15 year old told us, in response to a question about what he liked about being a boy, "It's probably easier being a guy at least it is now because of stereotypes and prejudices and everything." Overall, most of these children were sophisticated, true believers in gender equality and the capabilities of men and women to be in the same jobs and family roles. The influence of their parents as ideological conduits and role models was evident in these children's attitudes.

## Experiences

These children may have had "politically correct" attitudes about gender equality for men and women, but when that ideology contradicted their experiences as boys and girls, the experiential data won hands-down. Despite their answers to what should be for grown-ups, these children gave remarkably typical answers about the differences between boys and girls. In order to find out their "gut" beliefs about boys and girls, we probed their experiences with a variety of techniques. We asked them how their lives would be different if a magician turned them into a girl/boy. We provided them short scenarios using stereotypically male and female adjectives (e.g. weak, strong, fearful, adventuresome) and asked them to circle a male or female diagram, and then asked why. We asked what they liked and disliked about being a girl or boy. We asked them to write poems which began with the line "If I were a boy/girl" using the opposite sex category. We showed them different pictures of a boy and a girl (similar in the fact that both sat on the same sofa), and we asked them to tell us a story about each child. We followed up every comment which would help us assess their experiences.

None of the four, five or six year olds had yet begun to believe that boys and girls were different. These egalitarian parents managed to exert some insulation for their preschoolers from typical American norms—perhaps by choice of paid care giving arrangements and selection of friends. This finding differs from theories based on developmental psychological research [e.g. Kohlberg (1966), Kohlberg and Ullian (1974)], which suggests that children necessarily begin sex-stereotyping as early as four years old.

Once children hit seven years of age, however, their non-familial experiences have broadened considerably, as have their ideas about differences between the sexes. We found the descriptions of school age children remarkably consistent—and stereotypical—across sex and age categories. Girls were sweet and neat; boys were athletic and disruptive. . . . These children offered unequivocal support for the belief in major sex differences between boys and girls within minutes of having parroted their parents' [feminist] views about the equality and similarity of men and women.

Three of these children qualified these stereotypical answers. An 8 year old boy made a point of telling us that he knew girls could be into sports or computers, he just didn't personally know any who were. A 7 year old girl was sure that girls were better behaved and boys were mean, but she also sometimes wanted to be a boy because they seemed to have more playful and active games. A 10 year old boy knew that some girls were "like boys," and he even let such a girl try out for his spy club. And one 6 year old boy made the very acute observation that girls played different games on the playground but the same games as boys in the neighborhood [Thorne (1993) finds the same thing]. This little boy had a close neighborhood girl friend, but we observed that when the other boys came around, he left her alone. Crossing gender for play was fine with him, but not at the expense of ridicule from the other boys. Our observation was reinforced by his parents' independently mentioning this pattern.

When family experiences collided head on with experiences with peers, the family influences were dwarfed. For example, one six year old boy told us that if a magician were to turn him into a girl, he'd be different because he'd have long hair. This boy's father had a long straight black ponytail which went to the middle of his back, and his mother's hair hardly reached below her ears. A four year old boy told us that if a magician were to turn him into a girl, he'd have to do housework—despite his father's flexible work schedule, which allowed him to spend more time in domestic pursuits than his wife. Children knew that women and men were equal; it was boys and girls who were totally different. It almost seemed as if these children believed that boys and girls were opposites, but men and women were magically transformed into equal and comparable people.

Seven of these children spoke explicitly about male privilege among peers or at school. A 9 year old girl told us that sometimes she wished to be a boy because when

> teachers need help like to carry a box to their classroom, they always come in and say, like, can I borrow a couple of your boys, and never say, "can I borrow a couple of your students?" And so the girls never get to do any of the stuff and leave the classroom . . . it's always the boys that get to leave. And like, little trips and stuff, when we used to go on field trips, the boys would always have to carry a basket of lunches, and go ahead, and, like, when they had stuff to bring from the car, it'd always be boys that'd get to go to the car and eat and the girls, like, had to stay on the bus and just sit there and wait while some boys got to go there and the girls never got to do it, do that stuff . . . you get left out because you're a girl. . . . But I'm not wimpy.

The 7 year old girl told us that she was "more hyper" than most girls and many of her friends were boys because they were more active and playful. A 10 year old boy mentioned "racism against women" in sports. One 9 year old girl was an avowed feminist who also espoused implicitly essentialist notions about girls' innate cooperativeness versus boys' innate combativeness. She thought girls ought to have more power in the world because they were better people. The following paragraph written by an 8 year old boy was an articulate statement about male privilege, but such an un-

derstanding of such privilege was widely shared by all of the children, though not usually so well articulated.

> If I were a girl I'd have to attract a guy—wear makeup; sometimes, wear the latest style of clothes and try to be likeable. I probably wouldn't play any physical sports like football or soccer. I don't think I would enjoy myself around men in fear of rejection or under the pressure of attracting them.

Therefore, while boys and girls shared the perception that boys were troublemakers, sarcastic, and athletic, they also sensed that boys had advantages. Only a few of the boys were, in fact, conscious that they belonged to a group for which they had internalized negative characteristics. One aware boy answered our question about how he was different from other guys this way[:] "I think I'm taller. I don't like bullying people around that much. When one of my friends starts fighting somebody or arguing with somebody, I don't join in. I steer clear of them. I try to get in as few fights as possible." This boy built his identity in sports (his room was a baseball shrine and his activities were sports, sports, and more sports), but tried to distance himself from the violent aspects of peer group masculinity. Another boy told us that if he were magically transformed into a girl, he would be nicer to his friends. These boys had internalized very negative attitudes toward their own group—and at some level, themselves. In no case did any girl tell us how bad girls as a group were. When girls talked about how they were similar and different from other girls, their answers were idiosyncratic. These children "knew" that boys and girls were very different; they "knew" that boys had advantages; but they also "knew" that girls were nicer people.

### Identity

These boys and girls were consistent when they explained how boys and girls were different. The unanimity dissolved when we began to look at how they forged their own identities. Only six of these children seemed to have fashioned selves which unambiguously fit into their own stereotyped notions of childhood gender. The interview and observational data collected in these families identified six children (the 11 year old Germane girl, the 12 year old Potadman boy, the 8 year old Pretzman boy, the 10 year old Stokes girl, the 6 year old Green girl, and the 9 year old Sykes girl) who described themselves in consistently gendered fashion, and who were so identified in observational data. The first obvious finding was that these children's attitudes and identities were not consistent. The Pretzman boy, Stokes girl, Green girl, and Sykes girl are very self-consciously egalitarian, even feminist. The Germane girl and the Potadman boy, however, were two of the children with more traditional beliefs about gender. The Pretzman and Potadman children were "all-boy;" the Sykes, Stokes, Green and Germane children "all-girl."

What does "all-boy" or "all-girl" mean? In this instance, we refer back to the list created by the children themselves. The children suggested boys were active, into sports, mean, bad, freer than girls, sarcastic, cool, aggressive, athletic, tough, stronger than girls, into fights, troublemakers, competitive, bullies, and into computers. These six children could indeed be described exclusively by characteristics in this list, with no reference to those traits which were used to describe girls. Now, this doesn't mean that every characteristic was applicable, only that no characteristics from the opposite sex list fit at all. For example, there was no indication that the Pretzman boy was mean or a troublemaker, just the opposite. He was an academically gifted child who took school very seriously, and followed directions impeccably, yet all his interests were masculine—sports, [L]eggos, [S]tar-trek, computers. He described himself as "strong" and used that criterion to differentiate boys and girls. He didn't play much with girls, and there was simply no indication of cross-gender behavior or traits either in the interview or as we watched him at home. The Potadman boy was similar. His main interest and identity seemed to be attached to sports. He was interpersonally instrumental, answering us with short, not-too-reflective comments. In traditionally masculine fash-

ion, his friendships were described almost entirely in terms of sharing activities.

The four girls who were "all-girl" could be described by using the characteristics the children provided for us about girls: nice, behave well, quiet, cooperative, good, sweet, not into sports, not sneaky, nice to friends, less free. While none of these girls embodied every one of these traits, it is unlikely that these girls would be described by any of the traits in the "boy" list. One shared characteristic was their distaste for competitive sports. The Germane girl provided an easy comparison to the Potadman boy discussed above. Her very favorite games were make-believe fantasies, and her favorite activity was dance. Her favorite possessions: dolls and stuffed animals. The Stokes 10 year old was similarly gendered. Her very favorite activities were reading, writing poems and art. She was adamant about disliking sports, and she knew why: she didn't like any activity where you had to be pushy or aggressive. The Green daughter had three doll houses, and not a "boy" toy in the house. Because we interviewed the entire family, we knew that this child preferred girl toys in spite of her parents' teaching. Her parents were very conscious of encouraging her to make her own choices and develop her own potential; the mother told us she "was working on" trying to get her daughter to be willing to play some sports, at least at school during recess.

These six children, raised by egalitarian parents and often holding feminist attitudes themselves, nevertheless fashioned selves which are unambiguously gendered. The following poem sums up what these children thought when they imagined being the opposite sex. The essay was written by the Sykes girl in response to our request to write a verse which began with the phrase, "If I were a boy." She wrote,

> If I were a boy, I'd know my parents had made a mistake, and that I should have been a girl. I'd always feel that I didn't belong because the girls were who I wanted to play with; but they wouldn't let me, and I didn't want to be with the boys.

This 9 year old girl provided an interesting and stark example of the disjunction between identity and ideology. She lived in one of our most self-consciously feminist and progressive families. They saw themselves as living outside the mainstream, with no television so their daughter avoided excess materialism. All three Sykes were avowed feminists. And yet, the daughter was one of the most feminine in the sample—her long wavy hair flowed below her waist. She loved and collected china tea cups, hated competitive sports, and loved nature and hiking. She saved a bug from destruction during a home observation, and she carried it tenderly outside. In honor of the interview, she put on her favorite bedclothes, a long nightgown with a pink bow. This child was very smart, and knew it. She intended to succeed professionally, maybe in a scientific career. So perhaps she too, despite her feminine self-presentation and dislike for most things male, was actually more actively crossing over gender boundaries than we could determine in our limited access to her life.

The other 15 children had also fashioned gendered selves. The boys were much more likely to enjoy sports, the girls to enjoy dance. Despite their parents' role-modeling, despite their own ideologies, all of these girls were more feminine than masculine. All of these boys were more masculine [than] feminine. But all of the rest of these children, to varying degrees, crossed over gender lines in interests and interpersonal style. All but one of the girls was either involved in at least one competitive sport or expected to be when she got older. All of the boys stood out some way as exceptions to hegemonic masculinity. An interesting sex difference existed, however. All the girls told us in quite explicit terms just how they were different from other girls, but the boys often denied any differences from other boys, differences that our interview and observational team noted. For example, one girl knew she was different from other girls because she loved team sports and would like to be a boy, except that she knew "they aren't always very nice." A 4 year old liked to climb trees, as well as play fantasy games about babies. She knew she was "nice, like other girls" but wanted to be "cool" like boys. She told us her future goal was to "be a mommy so I can work hard and like my job."

In seeing this child in public settings in the last few years, we know that she has become an enthusiastic baseball player with a square and chunky frame. She looks tough on the field. Another child believed she was more active [than] other girls, but she was also "real sweet," liked horses, and was nice to her friends (all characteristics she sees as different from boys). Yet another child told us she was "not like other girls particularly." She had friends who were boys, although her best friend was another girl. But she liked being a girl because she could do whatever she wanted.

The boys whom we coded as portraying some crossover behaviors and interpersonal style were much less likely to notice it themselves. While some of the data reported here came directly from the interviews, much of it also relied on subtle inconsistencies in their own words, body language, and, to some extent, the "gut" feelings of the interview and observational team as recorded in field notes. Both of the older Potadman boys (15 and 17 years of age) told us some hopes and dreams which seemed to crossover gender stereotypes. The 15 year old babysat and loved domestic work, to vacuum and cook. He would like to stay home with his children if his wife could earn a high enough income. His very tall older brother, whose long pony tail reaching below his waist was his most distinctive visual characteristic, hated to work out, and found it unfair that women can be considered sexy without being muscular but that men can't. He wrote poetry and never has been into sports, although he did like volleyball. He described himself as an intellectual outsider, and seemed comfortable—if somewhat vulnerable—with the status.

Four little boys—all aged 4 or 5—also told us their androgynous preferences. One liked lots of boys' games, particularly baseball. But he also wanted to be like his sister, played housekeeping at day care, and enjoyed playing "dress-up" in his sister's clothes. Another boy's favorite movie characters were Aladdin and the Little Mermaid, and he had shoes adorned with the likenesses of both. A 4 year old boy thought being "silly" was the best part of being a boy.

While he liked guns and had mostly boys as friends, his answers to most questions seemed gender-neutral. Similarly, one 5 year old boy liked boys' toys and baseball, but many of his favorite activities seemed gender-neutral: board games, and playing out of doors with both boys and girls. His body language and self-presentation, his greater enthusiasm for non-gendered subjects, brought to mind the characteristic "gentle." One 6 year old boy preferred stereotypically boy toys, and he took Tae Kwon Do, but like the 15 year old above, he too would like to not work at all, to "spend more time with his children." Even when these boys talked about their stereotypical behaviors, they never seemed rough or tough; they seemed warm and caring.

There were two boys whose words contradicted their behavior (as reported by parents) and our observations. One 10 year old boy seemed to try too hard at his self-presentation. He wanted us to think he was tough, mean, and sneaky—a real boy. But the boy we met was warm, kind, and soft-spoken, even as he told us about his war games. This son of two nonfiction writers wanted a blue-collar job where he could wear "lots of armor" and be tough. But all of these words did not square with what we found—a 10 year old who played gently with his sister. He came back from the bathroom, interrupted our interview and his 4 year old sister's interview, to bring her to look out the bathroom window. He wanted to make sure she didn't miss the full moon. He talked to her quietly, handled her gently. When we noticed some Barbie-dolls in his closet and asked what kind of games he played with them, he answered, "Oh, I mostly kill them. They're my sister's." His mother told us otherwise, that both children played fantasy games with the dolls. He alluded to this himself later on: "I like the Ken doll because he is a basketball star." This boy twitched, visibly, when he spoke about gender preferences. The interview was poignant: he knew that boys were "supposed" to be mean and sneaky, and he wanted very much to fulfill those expectations, or at least to make us believe that he did. But we could not believe it; he gave too many contradictory signals.

We had a similar experience with the 10 year old Woods boy. He was a baseball fanatic and his room was entirely in Carolina Blue, rug and all. He talked about liking to compete. Both of these characteristics are hegemonically masculine, and they were clearly central to his identity. And yet, he described his baby brother in loving terms, and in three straight losses in an UNO card game with his interviewer, he never once showed any competitive spirit nor disappointment in losing. He emanated warmth, as did his father. He also differentiated himself from other boys because he wasn't a bully and didn't like to fight. These children's behavior challenged the boundaries of a rigid gender dichotomy, redefining athletics and competition as less hegemonically masculine.

## Summary

The children in fair families have adopted their parents' egalitarian views. They believe men and women are equal, and that no jobs—inside or outside the family—ought to be sex-linked. But beyond these abstract statements concerning beliefs, these children depend on their own lived experiences for understanding gender in their childhood worlds. And they "know" that boys and girls are different—very different. The children—including the boys themselves—describe boys as a group as not only athletic, but also mean and troublesome. Girls are described as sweet, quiet, and well-behaved. Six of these children met their own criteria for being "all-boy" or "all-girl," while the rest portrayed some examples of cross-gender behavior. The girls knew and reported how they were different from other girls, the boys didn't.

One way to interpret the inconsistencies that we observed between children's ideology and their behavior and identities is that gender socialization has many sources, which are sometimes contradictory. Parents may be the primary socializing agents, but children are influenced by myriad social pressures outside of the family to conform to existing gendered norms. We think this is part of the story. While these parents have struggled to raise their children without oppressive gendered categories, the parents are unable to completely cloister their children. They go to school, synagogue or church, and to their friends' homes—places where gender is done differently.

The closest we came to finding a case where the parents had completely controlled their children's gendered environment was with a family whose two children were under four years old. The children were too young to be interviewed, but one interviewer played with them and observed them for three hours while other team members interviewed their parents. What we saw was remarkable. The parents and their private child care worker had carefully eliminated gender distinctions from their children's lives: they changed pronouns in books to be gender neutral; they never referred to their children as "girls" but as people; and they concentrated instead on teaching love for all people, flora, and fauna. In talking with the older child (who was three years old—her sister was an infant), the interviewer asked her if she was a boy or a girl. The child proudly responded that she was a person. She did not yet differentiate along gendered lines. We wondered what life would be like for this child when her parents could no longer shelter her and her sister from the hegemonically gendered organization of larger society. Nevertheless, she was the only child we observed who lived this seemingly non-gendered life.

Another way to look at these inconsistencies is to see them as a gradual process of gender revolution. These children may be challenging the rigid proscriptions of a gender dichotomy. Sociologists have begun to recognize (see especially Connell 1987 and 1995) that there are multiple masculinities and femininities, but most of society still wholly adopt[s] and enforce[s] a simple dichotomy. These children's actions challenge the existing gender structure of society in that they reject the dichotomy. Being competitive and into sports does not impede a boy's ability to be tender and loving. Girls can wear hair bows and pink dresses and still be feminists. One set of characteristics does not preclude the co-existence of the other. They straddle the boundaries. The strad-

dling makes some children nervous—like the 10 year boy who twitched—because they know they're unusual. But many consider their duality to be normal. These children are not post-gendered in that they obliterate the differences between boys and girls; on the contrary, they embrace and occasionally celebrate them. They are post-gendered because they do not use these differences as dichotomies nor as a basis for ranking each other. What all of these children have in common is a focus on kindness and gentleness. They can be masculine or feminine or both, but they are all humanitarian. . . .

# References

Alanen, L. (1988). Rethinking Childhood. *Acta Sociologica*, 31, 53–67.

Bandura, A. (1962). Social Learning Through Imitation. In M. Jones (Ed.), *Nebraska Symposium on Motivation*, volume 10, (pp. 211–274). Lincoln: University of Nebraska Press.

—— (1971). *Psychological Modeling: Conflicting Theories*. Chicago: Aldine-Atherton.

Bem, S. L. (1993). *The Lenses of Gender*. New Haven: Yale University Press.

Borman, K. M., and P. O'Reilly. (1987). Learning Gender Roles in Three Urban U.S. Kindergarten Classrooms. *Child and Youth Services*, 8, 43–66.

Cahill, S. E. (1987). Language Practices and Self-Definition: The Case of Gender Identity Acquisition. *Sociological Quarterly*, 27, 295–311.

Collins, P. Hill (1990). *Black Feminist Thought*. Boston: Unwin Hyman.

Coltrane, S. (1996). *Family Man: Fatherhood, Housework and Gender Equity*. Oxford: Oxford University Press.

Connell, R. W. (1987). *Gender and Power*. Stanford: Stanford University Press.

—— (1992). A Very Straight Gay: Masculinity, Homosexual Experience, and the Dynamics of Gender. *American Sociological Review*, 57, 735–751.

—— (1995). *Masculinities*. Berkeley: University of California Press.

Corsaro, W. A. (1985). *Friendship and Peer Culture in the Early Years*. Norwood: Ablex Publishing.

Deaux, K. (1984). From Individual Differences to Social Categories: Analysis of a Decade's Research on Gender. *American Psychologist*, 39, 105–116.

Eisenberg, N., S. A. Wolchik, R. Hernandez, and J. F. Pasternack. (1985). Parental Socialization of Young Children's Play: A Short-term Longitudinal Study. *Child Development*, 56, 1506–1513.

Fagot, B. I., M. D. Leinbach, and C. O'Boyle. (1992). Gender Labeling, Gender Stereotyping, and Parenting Behaviors. *Developmental Psychology*, 28, 225–230.

Giddens, A. (1979). *Central Problems in Social Theory*. Berkeley: University of California Press.

—— (1984). *The Constitution of Society*. Berkeley: University of California Press.

Hawkins, J. (1985). Computers and Girls: Rethinking the Issues. *Sex Roles*, 13, 165–180.

Howard, J., B. Risman, M. Romero, and J. Sprague. (1996). *The Gender Lens Book Series*. Thousand Oaks, CA: Forge and Sage Publishers.

Hutson, A. H. (1983). Sex-Typing. In E. M. Hetherington and P. H. Mussen (Eds.) *Handbook of Child Psychology*, volume 4. New York: Wiley.

Inkeles, A. (1968). Society, Social Structure and Child Socialization. In J. Clausen (Ed.) *Socialization and Society*. Boston: Little, Brown.

Kohlberg, L. (1966). A Cognitive-developmental Analysis of Children's Sex-role Concepts and Attitudes. In E. E. Maccoby (Ed.) *The Development of Sex Differences*. Stanford: Stanford University Press.

Kohlberg, L., and D. Z. Ullian. (1974). Stages in the Development of Psychosocial Concepts and Attitudes. In R. C. Friedman, R. N. Richart, and R. L. Vande Wiele (Eds.) *Sex Differences in Behavior*. New York: Wiley.

Kreps, G. A., and S. L. Bosworth; with J. A. Mooney, S. T. Russell, and K. A. Myers. (1994). *Organizing, Role Enactment, and Disaster: A Structural Theory*. Newark: University of Delaware Press.

Lever, J. (1978). Sex Differences in the Complexity of Children's Play and Games. *American Sociological Review*, 43, 471–483.

Luttrell, W. (1993). The Teachers, They All Had Their Pets: Concepts of Gender, Knowledge and Power. *Signs*, 18, 505–546.

Maccoby, E. E. (1992). The Role of Parents in the Socialization of Children: An Historical Overview. *Developmental Psychology*, 28, 1006–1017.

Marsiglio, W. (1995). *Fatherhood: Contemporary Theory, Research, and Social Policy*. Thousand Oaks, CA: Sage.

Martin, C. L. (1993). New Directions for Investigating Children's Gender Knowledge. *Developmental Review*, 13, 184–204.

Parsons, T., and R. Bales. (1955). *Family Socialization and Interaction Process*. Glencoe: Free Press.

Peterson, G. W., and B. C. Rollins. (1987). Parent-child Socialization. In M. Sussman and S. Steinmetz (Eds.) *Handbook of Marriage and the Family*. New York: Plenum.

Piaget, J. (1932). *The Moral Judgement of the Child*. London: Kegan Paul.

Risman, B. (Forthcoming). *Gender Vertigo: American Families in Transition*. New Haven: Yale University Press.

Risman, B., and P. Schwartz. (1989). *Gender in Intimate Relationships: A Microstructural Approach*. Belmont, CA: Wadsworth.

Rosenthal, R., and L. Jacobsen. (1968). *Pygmalion in the Classroom: Teacher Expectations and Pupil's Intellectual Development*. New York: Holt.

Schwartz, P. (1994). *Peer Marriage: How Love Between Equals Really Works*. New York: Free Press.

Segal, L. (1990). *Slow Motion: Changing Masculinities, Changing Men*. New Brunswick: Rutgers University Press.

Signorelli, N. (1990). Children, Television, and Gender Roles. *Journal of Adolescent Health Care*, 11, 50–58.

Stern, M., and K. H. Karraker. (1989). Sex Stereotyping of Infants: A Review of Gender Labeling Studies. *Sex Roles*, 20, 501–522.

Thorne, B. (1993). *Gender Play*. New Brunswick: Rutgers University Press.

West, C., and D. Zimmerman. (1987). Doing Gender. *Gender and Society*, 1, 125–151.

Wilder, G., D. Mackie, and J. Cooper. (1985). Gender and Computers: Two Surveys of Gender-related Attitudes. *Sex Roles*, 13, 215–228.

# Review

1. Explain the three major theories by which social scientists explain how children learn to be boys and girls.

2. Describe the ideology of children reared in feminist homes.

3. How do children reared in feminist homes handle the contradiction between their ideology and their experiences?

4. What happens to the identities of children reared in feminist homes?

## Applications

1. Think about the messages you got while growing up about the meaning of being male and female. Those messages came to you through both what people said and what they did. Compare the messages you got from various sources: parents, friends, teachers, religion, and mass media. Describe any inconsistencies. How do your current beliefs square with these varied messages? Do you, like the children in the above study, find yourself acting in ways that compromise your ideals? Why or why not?

2. One of the issues explored in Risman and Myers' research is the extent to which certain occupations are more appropriate for one sex than the other. Get a list of occupations from the *Statistical Abstract of the United States* or from books about careers. Do you believe that some occupations are more appropriate for one sex than the other? If so, which ones and why? If not, why? Ask the same questions of your friends. Summarize the reasons offered by both those who believe either sex can manage any occupation and those who believe some occupations are more appropriate for one sex over the other.

## Related Web Sites

1. *http://www.sdsmt.edu/online-courses/is/soc100/Socialization.htm*. Numerous materials on socialization from a sociological perspective.

2. *scholar.lib.vt.edu/theses/available/etd-1649101059721601/unrestricted/etd.pdf*. Copy of a dissertation on the influence of feminist mothers on their daughters' career aspirations.

---

# 10

# How Television Shapes Children's Gender Roles

*Susan D. Witt*

"The child is the father of the man," or, perhaps, "mother of the woman." This adage underscores the importance of early socialization, which includes learning **gender roles,** the behavior associated with being either male or female in a particular society.

*Gender roles are not simply the result of biological factors. Sociologists do not deny the importance of biological factors, but they concentrate on the social factors that shape gender behavior. They stress the fact that males and females do not act in particular ways simply because they are biologically different. Rather, every society has norms about what it means to be male or female.*

*The fact that what it means to be male or female in a particular society is not completely rooted in the imperatives of biological makeup is supported by variations in gender roles between societies. Support is also found in gender role norms that have no biological explanation. For example, American women were long barred from many occupations (such as surgeon, police officer, and carpenter) on the grounds that they were emotionally or physically incapable or that the work was simply inappropriate for a woman. Such grounds cannot be defended biologically.*

*How do people learn and accept norms? The agents of socialization include the family, school, religious institutions, and the mass media. In this selection, Susan Witt discusses one of the important tools of gender role socialization among the mass-media television. She points out how television portrayals of males and females perpetuate gender bias. The more that children watch and accept the por-*trayals, the more they are likely to believe that men are decisive leaders and women are dependent followers.*

Children often internalize gender role stereotypes from books, songs, television, and the movies (Thorne 1993). Television, however, is perhaps the most influential form of media (Lauer & Lauer 1994). Research on television viewing and children's socialization indicates that television has a great impact on children's lives.

Studies show preschoolers spend an average of nearly 30 hours a week watching television; some spend more time watching television than doing anything else except sleeping (Anderson, Lorch, Field, Collins, & Nathan 1986; Aulette 1994; Kaplan 1991). Nielsen Media Research has found that by the time children are 16 years old, they have spent more time watching television than going to school (as cited in Basow 1992). As a result, children are exposed to about 20,000 advertisements a year (Stoneman & Brody 1981). By the time a child graduates from high school, he will have witnessed 13,000 violent deaths on television (Gerbner & Gross 1976).

Television influences both children's prosocial and antisocial behaviors (Ahammer & Murray 1979; Bandura 1986; Comstock & Paik 1991; Strasburger 1995), as well as their attitudes about race and gender (Liebert & Sprafkin 1988).

## Development of Children

As children grow and develop, they take in information and acquire knowledge at a rapid pace. As they develop their cognitive abilities, they assimilate new information and accommodate it to what they already know (Piaget 1954). Children's ideas about how the world works come from their experiences and from the attitudes and behaviors they see around them. The young child who believes that only women are nurses and only men are doctors may have developed this understanding because the first doctor he or she saw was a man, who was assisted by a female nurse. This "man as doctor, woman as nurse" idea may have been reinforced further by parents, books, conversations with friends, and television. If the child frequently meets such gender biases and gender stereotypes, this knowledge will be incorporated into future perceptions. Keeping in mind that young children with developing minds watch many hours of television, and recalling how television reinforces gender stereotypes, it is not surprising when children develop stereotyped beliefs.

Of the various factors that help shape gender-typed behaviors, role models and imitation are extremely influential (Bandura 1977; Basow 1992; Beal 1994; Hargreaves & Colley 1986). Research suggests that children who view violent programming on television will behave more aggressively with peers (Bandura 1977; Strasburger 1995). It is also true that children who view prosocial behaviors on television are more likely to exhibit those types of behaviors themselves. Young children will imitate and repeat behaviors they see on television. Consequently, children may exhibit these gender-biased behaviors and develop the gender-biased attitudes that they see modeled on television.

Developing autonomy, initiative, and a sense of industriousness [is] critical to young children's positive development (Erikson 1964). Children who witness female characters on television programs who are passive, indecisive, and subordinate to men, and who see this reinforced by their environment, will likely believe that this is the appropriate way for females to behave. Female children are less likely to develop autonomy, initiative, and industriousness if they rarely see those traits modeled. Similarly, because male characters on television programs are more likely to be shown in leadership roles and exhibiting assertive, decisive behavior, children learn this is the appropriate way for males to behave (Cantor 1977; Carter 1991; Seidman 1999).

## Gender Bias in Television

The National Institute of Mental Health has determined:

- Men are usually more dominant in male-female interactions.
- Men on television are often portrayed as rational, ambitious, smart, competitive, powerful, stable, violent, and tolerant, while women are sensitive, romantic, attractive, happy, warm, sociable, peaceful, fair, submissive, and timid.
- Television programming emphasizes male characters' strength, performance, and skill; for women, it focuses on attractiveness and desirability.
- Marriage and family are not important to television's men. One study found that for nearly half the men, it wasn't possible to tell if they were married, a fact that was true for only 11 percent of the women (National Institute of Mental Health, as cited in Lauer & Lauer 1994, p. 73).

About two-thirds of characters in television programs are male, a figure that has remained constant since the 1950s (Condry 1989; Huston et al. 1992; Seidman 1999). In interactions between men and women, women frequently are defined by their relationships with men (Beal 1994).

Furthermore, television often does not reflect the reality of the work force. For example, 75 percent of the women on TV are depicted as being in the labor force, compared with the truer figure of about 56 percent (Basow 1992; Lauer & Lauer 1994). Most women on television are shown working in a profession. Most women in real life, however, are in low-paying, low-status jobs (Basow 1992). Less than 10 percent of women in the United States make more than $50,000 a year (Beal 1994).

Most females on prime time television are young, attractive, thin, and have an ornamental quality (Davis 1990). Most of these characters are either under 35 or over 50—middle-age women are rare (Beal 1994). Females consistently are placed in situations where looks count more than brains, and helpless and incompetent behaviors are expected of them (Boyer 1986). Men are twice as likely as women to be shown as competent and able to solve problems (Boyer 1986). Gender stereotypes abound on television, with women being depicted as sex objects more frequently than men, and men portrayed as inept when handling children's needs (Horovitz, as cited in Basow 1992; Seidman 1999).

On music television, a popular program choice among young viewers, females often are shown in degrading positions. Music videos frequently show women as sex objects, and as trying to gain the attention of a male who ignores them (Sherman & Dominick 1986). Rap music videos, for example, frequently portray women as objects of lust (Basow 1992; Seidman 1999). Women are four times more likely than men to be provocatively dressed in these videos (Atkin, Moorman, & Lin 1991), while men are almost always fully clothed (Tavris & Wade 1984).

While early television commercials were criticized for being overwhelmingly biased in favor of males, a study of commercials broadcast between 1971 and 1985 indicated a better balance of male and female characters (Bretl & Cantor 1988). Even so, women are most often shown in the role of wife and mother, or demonstrating products for the home (Osborn, as cited in Basow 1992). Another aspect of television advertising that is overwhelmingly a masculine province is voiceovers and narration, in which 83–90 percent of the voices are male (Basow 1992).

## What Children Are Watching

While some children's programming has come under attack for being violent, irrelevant, or sexist (Carter 1991; Streicher 1974), other programs for children, such as "Sesame Street," are regularly lauded for attempting to meet children's developmental needs. Sexism, however, can be found even among the Muppets, most of whom all have male names or male voices (Cobb, Stevens-Long, & Goldstein 1982). Even Miss Piggy, a female character, is voiced by a male.

A study of Saturday morning cartoons revealed that females were pictured less often than males, were less active than males, played fewer roles than males, played fewer lead roles than males, and worked primarily in the home (Streicher 1974). Although these findings were obtained more than 25 years ago, no significant improvement is evident. Recent studies of children's Saturday morning programs feature males in dominant roles, while showing females in peripheral roles (Carter 1991; Thompson & Zerbinos 1995). Children's programs on the Public Broadcasting System consistently show fewer females than males. Furthermore, television programs evidence a greater range of occupations for males than females (Cantor 1977; Thompson & Zerbinos 1995). This discrepancy in occupations between males and females also appears in music videos, where more than nine out of 10 occupational roles that were classified as stereotypically male (e.g., physician, mechanic, firefighter) were played by male actors (Seidman 1999). It has been suggested the preferences of boys are given precedence over those of girls because boys represent 53 percent of the Saturday viewing audience (Watson, as cited in Basow 1992).

Gender stereotypes are common on daytime soap operas as well; women often are shown as hopeless individuals, unable to solve problems without assistance (Basow 1992). Children frequently watch these programs after school, reinforcing notions of women as subordinate, passive, and indecisive.

In commercials for children's programs, boys are shown more frequently and in more active roles; girls' behavior is much more likely to be passive (O'Connor 1989). Advertisers indicate that using male models generates more product sales to children of both sexes than using female models (Schneider 1987). It also has been suggested that girls watch male-dominated programs and commercials simply because that is what is available. Given the option, however, girls will become loyal to programming that is more gender-neutral (Schneider 1987).

Children without television have been shown to be less stereotyped in their gender role attitudes (Kimball 1986). Furthermore, children who view programs with non-traditional gender roles tend to have non-traditional gender role perceptions (Rosenwasser, Lingenfelter, & Harrington 1989). Because children model the behavior they see on television, they are likely to perpetuate gender stereotypes they view (Basow 1992; Strasburger 1995).

## Summary

Research indicates that television has a socializing influence on children regarding their attitudes toward gender roles. Gender role stereotypes seen on television are, in turn, reinforced by parents, friends, and school, contributing to the child's sense of what it means to be male or female in society. Television sends forceful and compelling messages about societally approved gender roles, which are often stereotyped, biased, and outdated. As children continue to develop and grow, they are exposed to more and more examples of such gender biases and stereotypes.

Traditional gender roles, wherein men are encouraged to be decisive and to show leadership qualities while women are encouraged to be deferential and dependent, do not benefit anyone, particularly women. Traditional gender roles discourage the full range of expression and accomplishment. Children should be allowed to develop a sense of self in a gender-fair environment that encourages everyone to fully feel a part of society.

## References

Ahammer, I. M., & Murray, J. P. (1979). Kindness in the kindergarten: The relative influence of role playing and prosocial television in facilitating altruism. *International Journal of Behavioral Development*, 2, 133–157.

Anderson, D. R., Lorch, E. P., Field, D. E., Collins, P., & Nathan, J. G. (1986). Television viewing at home: Age trends in visual attention and time with TV. *Child Development*, 57, 1024–1033.

Atkin, D. J., Moorman, J., & Lin, C. A. (1991). Ready for prime time: Network series devoted to working women in the 1980s. *Sex Roles*, 25, 677–685.

Aulette, J. R. (1994). *Changing Families*. Belmont, CA: Wadsworth Publishing Company.

Bandura, A. (1977). *Social Learning Theory*. Englewood Cliffs, NJ: Prentice-Hall.

Bandura, A. (1986). *Social Foundations of Thought and Action: A Social Cognitive Theory*. Englewood Cliffs, NJ: Prentice-Hall.

Basow, S. A. (1992). *Gender Stereotypes and Roles* (3rd ed.). Pacific Grove, CA: Brooks/Cole Publishing.

Beal, C. (1994). *Boys and Girls: The Development of Gender Roles*. New York: McGraw-Hill.

Boyer, P. J. (1986). TV turns to the hard boiled male. *New York Times*, February 16, pp. H1, H29.

Bretl, D. J., & Cantor, J. (1988). The portrayal of men and women in U.S. television commercials: A recent content analysis and trends over 15 years. *Sex Roles*, 18, 595–609.

Cantor, M. (1977). Women and public broadcasting. *Journal of Communication*, 27, 14–19.

Carter, B. (1991). Children's TV, where boys are king. *New York Times*, May 1, pp. A1, C18.

Cobb, N. J., Stevens-Long, J., & Goldstein, S. (1982). The influence of televised models on toy preference in children. *Sex Roles*, 8, 1075–1080.

Comstock, G., & Paik, H. (1991). *Television and the American Child*. San Diego, CA: Academic Press.

Condry, J. (1989). *The Psychology of Television*. Hillsdale, NJ: Erlbaum.

Davis, D. M. (1990). Portrayals of women in prime time network television: Some demographic characteristics. *Sex Roles*, 23, 325–332.

Erikson, E. (1964). *Childhood and Society* (2nd ed.). New York: Norton.

Gerbner, G., & Gross, L. (1976). The scary world of TV's heavy viewer. *Psychology Today*, April, 41–45.

Hargreaves, D., & Colley, A. (1986). *The Psychology of Sex Roles*. London: Harper & Row, Publishers.

Huston, A. C., Donnerstein, E., Fairchild, H., Feshbach, N. D., Katz, P., Murray, J. P., Rubenstein, E. A., Wilcox, B. L., & Zuckerman, D. (1992). *Big World, Small Screen: The Role of Television in American Society*. Lincoln, NE: University of Nebraska Press.

Kaplan, P. (1991). *A Child's Odyssey*. St. Paul, MN: West Publishing.

Kimball, M. M. (1986). Television and sex role attitudes. In T. M. Williams (Ed.), *The Impact of Television: A Natural Experiment in Three Communities* (pp. 265–301). Orlando, FL: Academic Press.

Lauer, R. H., & Lauer, J. C. (1994). *Marriage and Family: The Quest for Intimacy*. Madison, WI: Brown & Benchmark.

Liebert, R. M., & Sprafkin, J. (1988). *The Early Window: Effects of Television on Children and Youth* (3rd ed.). New York: Pergamon Press.

Lott, B. (1989). Sexist discrimination as distancing behavior: II. Prime time television. *Psychology of Women Quarterly*, 13, 341–355.

O'Connor, J. J. (1989). What are commercials selling to children? *New York Times*, June 6, p. A28.

Piaget, J. (1954). *The Construction of Reality in the Child*. New York: Basic Books.

Rosenwasser, S. M., Lingenfelter, M., & Harrington, A. F. (1989). Nontraditional gender role portrayals on television and children's gender role perceptions. *Journal of Applied Developmental Psychology*, 10, 97–105.

Schneider, C. (1987). *Children's Television: The Art, the Business, and How It Works*. Lincolnwood, NJ: NTC Business Books.

Seidman, S. A. (1999). Revisiting sex role stereotyping in MTV videos. *International Journal of Instructional Media*, 26, 11–22.

Sherman, B. L., & Dominick, J. R. (1986). Violence and sex in music videos, TV, and rock-n-roll. *Journal of Communication*, 36, 79–93.

Stoneman, Z., & Brody, G. H. (1981). Peers as mediators of television food advertisements aimed at children. *Developmental Psychology*, 17, 853–858.

Strasburger, V. C. (1995). *Adolescents and the Media*. Newbury Park, CA: Sage.

Streicher, H. (1974). The girls in the cartoons. *Journal of Communication*, 24, 125–129.

Tavris, C., & Wade, C. (1984). *The Longest War: Sex Differences in Perspective* (2nd ed.). San Diego, CA: Harcourt, Brace, Jovanovich.

Thompson, T. L., & Zerbinos, E. (1995). Gender roles in animated cartoons: Has the picture changed in 20 years? *Sex Roles: A Journal of Research*, 32(9–10), 651–673.

Thorne, B. (1993). *Gender Play: Girls and Boys in School*. New Brunswick, NJ: Rutgers University Press.

## Review

1. How does television influence children's development, including their attitudes and beliefs?

2. How are males and females portrayed on television?

3. What images of males and females emerge from children's cartoons?

4. How would you summarize the net impact of television on children's images of males and females?

## Applications

1. Recall the television programs you watched most when you were a child. What do you remember about the ways males and females were portrayed? Did those programs reflect some of the same biases described by Witt? How do your beliefs about appropriate gender roles square with the programs you watched? What other factors have influenced your beliefs?

2. Watch a number of prime-time television programs. Use the various forms of bias Witt identifies as a checklist for each of the programs and for the commercials as well. How would you rate the programs? Are some more biased than others? How do the commercials compare with the programs? If the programs you watched are typical of all programming, what conclusions would you draw about the extent of gender bias today?

## Related Web Sites

1. *http://www.aber.ac.uk/media/Students/hzi9402.html*. Critical review of the evidence about television's influence on the development of gender roles.

2. *http://www.eldis.org/static/DOC9726.htm*. A short article on socialization to gender roles among Egyptian adolescents.

# 11

# 'Just Trying to Relax'

## Masculinity, Masculinizing Practices, and Strip Club Regulars

*Katherine Frank*

*Although we know that gender roles provide people with guidelines for behavior and can state in general terms what the gender roles are in a particular society, there will be variations in the ways that individuals conform to the roles. Thus, men will strive to behave in ways that are consistent with their understanding of masculinity, but this doesn't mean they must all like the same kinds of activities or relate in exactly the same way to others.*

*For example, in American society, being masculine means that a man must be strong, independent, and aggressive. One man may choose to express those qualities by being a fervent supporter of his local football team and coaching boys' football teams, while another may prefer to express the same qualities through success in business.*

*In this selection, Katherine Frank investigates why some men are regular customers at heterosexual strip clubs. She discusses the ways in which the regulars see it both as a "masculinizing" activity and as an escape from situations where what it means to be a man is confused because of changing gender roles. Her analysis also illustrates some of the differences between male and female gender roles.*

Strip clubs are a visible, profitable, and growing form of entertainment in the contemporary United States and are primarily, though not exclusively, marketed to and visited by heterosexual men. Not all American men, of course, enjoy visiting strip clubs. The focus here is on those regular male customers who visit strip clubs often enough to consider this a significant personal practice, returning again and again to venues where contact and sexual release are prohibited and for whom voyeurism and conversation are the eroticized practices. What exactly is the appeal of modern strip clubs in this particular voyeuristic form for certain groups of late 20th-century heterosexually identified American men?

One assumption in the literature has been that men are motivated to use the sex industry out of a desire to maintain sexual mastery and power over women (Edwards, 1993). Granted, strip clubs as they now exist are indeed intertwined with male privilege. Although euphemistically called "adult entertainment," most commodified sexual productions, from strip clubs to pornography to erotic massages, are still aimed at male consumers. Most strip clubs are owned and operated by men, and many also have rules prohibiting women from entering unless escorted by a male, precluding some women from becoming customers even if they so desire. Men may do business in strip clubs on corporate expense, something for which there is no comparable practice for women. Further, despite the fact that men experience some stigma as a result of being customers, this stigma is relatively small when compared with that experienced by the women who work in the clubs. Customers also often have particular advantages over dancers in terms of educational and social capital. And finally, there are also often large discrepancies between the earning power of male customers and female dancers (even though dancers may do quite well compared with women working in other service industry jobs).

Yet the idea that strip clubs, or the sex industry more generally, inherently exist to reproduce male privilege has been challenged by texts that highlight the agency of sex workers and the "sex negative" cultural context in which such transactions take place (Bell, 1994; Chapkis, 1997; McElroy, 1995;

Nagle, 1997). Further, many men declare that sex workers have the upper hand in commodified sexual transactions, and very few men understand their visits to strip clubs or their use of other venues in terms of an exercise of personal power or a desire for dominance. Although it is a mistake to assert that transactions in strip clubs are unrelated to social structures of inequality, it is clearly necessary to explore the experiences and subjectivity of men in relation to power and commodified sexualized services in more detail (Cornwall & Lindisfarne, 1994; Segal, 1990).

My primary argument is that the customers' understandings of their visits to strip clubs are deeply intertwined with cultural discourses about masculinity, sexuality, leisure, and consumption, and that these visits become meaningful in relation to their everyday lives and relationships and their own personal and emotional experiences of gender and sexuality. Rather than fulfilling a universal masculine need for domination or a biological male need for sexual release, strip clubs provide a kind of intermediate space (not work and not home, although related to both) in which men can experience their bodies and identities in particular pleasurable ways. . . .

## Methods

My ethnographic material is drawn from over 7 years of research on the adult entertainment industry in the contemporary United States. The data for this paper were gathered through participant observation, a traditional anthropological fieldwork technique, and through a series of multiple, in-depth interviews with 30 male customers of strip clubs in a large Southern city, which I refer to as "Laurelton." As a participant observer, I worked at five Laurelton strip clubs intermittently over a period of 14 months as a nude entertainer. Because contemporary strip clubs are highly stratified in terms of "classiness," field sites were selected that represented different positions on this social hierarchy: from the highest ranked clubs in the city to more stereotypical "dive" bars. Each venue offered stage performances by

the dancers, along with the opportunity to purchase "private" table dances. Table dances were offered to the customers at their seats, on a raised platform or table or while standing on the ground between the men's knees. These private dances involved a more individualized interaction between the dancers and their customers, but although dancers could disrobe completely and place their hands on the customers' shoulders, other forms of bodily contact were prohibited. Dancers were also required to keep at least 1 foot of space between themselves and the customers during dances. Customers were not allowed to touch either the dancers or their own genitals. As the dancers circulated among the customers to sell table dances, the individualized interactions that took place became an important part of the experience. Dancers also sat with customers between their sets and their table dances, and thus conversation became a (public) service in and of itself. . . .

In addition to conducting participant observation, I collected qualitative interview data. Except for two men who were employees of the strip clubs, all of the men [whom] I interviewed were customers of the strip clubs in which I worked. While working in Laurelton, I spoke with hundreds of male customers about my research and almost always approached those customers as potential interviewees. That is, I was immediately forthcoming about my research purposes whenever possible and provided the customers with my real name (in addition to my stage name) and information about how to contact me for an interview. Many men declined to do formal interviews but commented on my research, telling me their reasons for visiting the clubs and discussing their opinions about adult entertainment, commodification, masculinity, and sexuality. The taped interview sessions with the interviewees were conducted at their workplaces or at restaurants or coffee shops. Interviews usually lasted from 2 to 4 hours, with follow-up interviews several weeks later. Some follow-up interviews were conducted over e-mail or by telephone if the respondents were not native to the city. The interviews were structured with open-ended questions and often became conversational as I responded to the men's questions about dancing as well. The interviewees have been given pseudonyms, and their quotes have been edited for repetitive verbal tics and for length. Short pauses in their answers have not been indicated here.

The interviewees ranged in age from 28 to 57. All identified as heterosexual and as somewhere in the middle socioeconomic class and had at least some college education. Twenty-seven were White Americans, two were African Americans, and one was a White British citizen who frequently traveled to the United States on business. . . .

## Why Men Become and Remain Customers

So why are some men loyal customers of strip clubs while others find them boring or are contemptuous of their very existence? Significantly, not one man that I interviewed said that he went to the clubs specifically for sexual release, even in the form of masturbation at a later time. This may be because the Laurelton sex industry was large and varied, and men who wanted sexual contact or release had many other venues to choose from in the area. Most men [whom] I spoke with, especially the regulars, realized that sexual activity was available in other venues of the industry and were explicit about their knowledge of this fact. As Joe said, "It's not a place to go find somebody if you're trying to get sex! You might as well go someplace where you can get sex. There's plenty of them around." Similarly, Steven said, "The bottom line is if you want to get laid, I know where and how and when to get laid." Those few men who did enter the Laurelton clubs expecting sexual release usually were from out of the country or were unfamiliar with the various sectors of the sex industry. Regular customers laughed at young, inexperienced, or foreign men who thought that sex was part of the deal being struck between dancers and customers. . . .

Instead, by far the most prevalent (and usually the first given) spoken motivation of the interviewees for visiting strip clubs was a desire to "relax." Nearly every man that I spoke with gave this response in some form or another: "I go there to relax and have a good time, get my mind off of work. It does all those things" (Tim); "It's a business. Where people can just come in and let their hair down, so to speak, and relax" (Herb); "It's definitely more of a relaxing thing than anything" (William). I heard this off-hand response so many times that I began to focus on why the men thought that going to a strip club was relaxing. The reasons fell into several categories: a strip club provided (a) an escape from both work and home, (b) a relative degree of "safety" as well as "excitement," (c) an opportunity for both personal and sexual acceptance from women, and (d) the pleasure of a sexualized encounter without the pressure of physical performance. Although these categories overlap and are not exhaustive, they also highlight particular themes that ran through the interviews. In the following sections, these themes are explored as they relate to several prominent discourses of masculinity, as well as to understandings of leisure practice more generally.

### Searching for Escape From Work and Home

Initially, men tended to explain that strip clubs were relaxing because they were entertainment complexes and leisure spaces: sites that by definition connote relaxation and escape as opposed to responsibility. Several men pointed to entertainment as their main motive for visiting the clubs. Mick said, for example,

> they're like going to a game arcade . . . you know, it's public . . . go out and have fun in a big bar kind of thing, as opposed to the lingerie [parlors] and the prostitution. That's pure sex whereas the other's like a little bit of sex tease with . . . real entertainment. So there's a difference there. My sex life's always been good so it's the entertainment that's more exciting to me.

Yet why visit a strip club rather than some other entertainment venue? As strip clubs have come under fire in conservative communities across the country, the claim that strip clubs are a form of entertainment is often one that is used to maintain that leisure is being sold rather than sexual contact. In fact, what is often being sold is a gendered combination of leisure, entertainment, and service. After all, visiting a strip club is significantly different from attending a play or going to the cinema. In the clubs, the male customers will be attended to by women who are young, accepting, usually attractive, and friendly and whose services (in the form of conversation or dancing) can be purchased for an agreed-upon price. It is also a kind of entertainment that men overwhelmingly pursue alone or with other men, not in mixed sex groups. Further, despite the fact that some dancers' appearances, physiques, or on-stage sexual displays (public nudity, direct gazes, simulations of sexual thrusting, etc.) may challenge mainstream middle-class definitions of femininity, one will rarely encounter a performer in a conventional strip club that caters to heterosexual male customers who does not have female genitals. This may seem obvious; it is, however, important to customers seeking a place where, as Jay Bildstein (1996), creator of the famous Scores strip club in New York City, put it, "a man could be a man" (p. 22).

Going to strip clubs obviously presents the opportunity to look at women, and it is this focus on looking in a public atmosphere that differentiates the strip club from many other forms of adult entertainment. Some men initially explained their visits to strip clubs by claiming a desire to see women's bodies:

> I'm drawn by the attraction of sexuality. You know, sex sells. Sex and beautiful women are very appealing. And they're very appealing to able-bodied men. And what can I say? You know. . . . It's just a fact. (Jim)

"Who wouldn't like to drink beer and watch naked women running around?" Alex asked. Some of these men believed that the desire to look at women's bodies is an expression of natural male biology. Whether or not they understood their desire to look at women in this format as a result of biological influences, however, there were always elements other than the visual that were important to customers.

After all, the desire to visit strip clubs is more than just a desire to see women's bodies, even for the most scopophilic of customers. There are many ways to potentially view naked women: peeping, viewing pornography, reading medical texts, or developing intimate relationships with them, for example. These visits, then, must also be seen as a desire to have a particular kind of experience rooted in the complex web of relationships among home, work, and "away." Touristic practices, according to Urry (1990), "involve the notion of 'departure,' of a limited breaking with established routines and practices of everyday life and allowing one's senses to engage with a set of stimuli that contrasts with the everyday and the mundane" (p. 2). The sights gazed upon are chosen because they offer "distinctive contrasts" with work and home and because "there is an anticipation, especially through daydreaming and fantasy, of intense pleasures, either on a different scale or involving different senses from those customarily encountered" (Urry, 1990, p. 3).

My interviewees corroborated that these sites/sights are "out of the ordinary," at least initially. Even when a customer pays a woman to sit with him and asks her to remain fully clothed, for example, he is doing so in an atmosphere in which he simultaneously has the privilege of asking her to remove her dress, and the significance of this possibility cannot be underestimated. For regulars, of course, the experience of just looking at undressed women eventually becomes almost ordinary ("almost" ordinary because even for the regulars the fact that women were displaying their bodies meant that this was a very different environment from work and home). Matthew and Steven, for example, spoke about how this display became "boring" and "routine" after time and how they began to desire other types of interactions, such as intriguing conversations and even ongoing friendships with the dancers. Several other regulars also discussed this process. In all of these cases, what kept the regulars returning to the various clubs was the opportunity to interact with women whom they would not generally meet in their everyday lives and to cultivate the relationships that they developed with particular dancers and club employees.

There are other ways that strip clubs offer a distinctive space, whether they are seen as transgressive because of the exhibition of nude bodies or experienced as but one more destination on a man's daily geographic trajectories, "a good place to stop for a beer." The behavioral structures of everyday life are inverted for many customers inside the clubs. Women do the approaching rather than men and thus face the possibility of rejection; women ask to be looked at naked; and usually private performances of sexual desire or sexual display are suddenly made public. Further, although intimate relationships between individuals may be covertly facilitated with money in everyday realms, inside the clubs this facilitation is blatant, immediate, and far less apologetic. Thus, although the significance of the dancers' nudity was often minimized by the men and was described by the regulars as something that eventually became "routine," it was still an essential part of the encounters in the clubs, serving as a visual reminder of these social inversions.

Strip clubs also provide an environment where men, singularly or in groups, can engage in traditionally "masculine" activities and forms of consumption often frowned upon in other spheres, such as drinking, smoking cigars, and even being "rowdy," vulgar, or aggressive. Phillip said that in the strip clubs he "sometimes acted like an asshole because I could," a form of release for him. Herb was married to a "very conservative" woman who did not smoke or drink, pleasures that he could thus not indulge in at home. At the club, however, "You got your cold beer, you got your shooters, you got your good-looking girls, you got your music, you got your smokes. You can smoke a cigar if you want. And when you're ready to go, you leave it all behind and that stays there and you go home." Herb usually came to the club on his way home from work, sometimes with friends from the office and other times alone. Either way, his time in the club was described as "personal" time that was pleasurable because it allowed him to engage in activities that were inappropriate in the other spheres of his life.

Another reason that the distinctiveness from work and home was experienced as relaxing was related to the kinds of relationships that could be developed with women in the clubs. For these customers, everyday relationships with women were often seen as a source of pressure and expectations. Indeed, many men that I spoke with described relations between women and men in general as being "strained," "confused," or "tense." Beck, for example, thought that there was a "chasm" between contemporary men and women in terms of understanding and expectations, and Kenneth referred to the "war between the sexes." Over half of the men that I interviewed specifically said that they found the clubs relaxing because they provided an escape from the rules of conduct and the social games involved in entering into interactions with other women in an unregulated setting. If "dating is the institutionalization of romantic encounters without the goal of commitment" (Illouz, 1997, p. 289), relationships formed in strip clubs take this institutionalization a step further; there is no longer need for pretenses, specific social niceties, elaborate plans, or mutual exchanges of personal information. Romantic props can be used to set a scene or to individualize an interaction but are not necessary to move the encounter to a sexualized level (involving nudity, erotic conversation, the sharing of fantasies, etc.). At the same time, the encounters were to some extent "predictable." Phillip called his interactions with dancers "relationships of convenience," explaining that he worked so much he could never find the time to meet women outside of the clubs and move through the expected steps of courtship. In the clubs, he knew exactly how to proceed to obtain the kind of encounter that he desired.

Even a simple conversation with a woman in a singles bar or at another location had its own set of rules and expectations that were sometimes experienced by these men as stressful. . . . Interactions with women in the workplace were also often thought to be constraining. One interviewee pointed out that in the workplace he felt nervous about giving compliments to women for fear that they would accuse him of sexual harassment. Phillip said that club visits "let frustration out": "With all of this sexual harassment stuff going around these days, men need somewhere to go where they can say and act like they want." Roger said that in the clubs, "everybody knows what the rules are." This implies that there are other spaces where the rules are not so transparent, where men do not understand exactly what is going to get them into trouble. Some men, like Gary, explicitly stated a desire to interact with women who were not "feminist," and who still wanted to interact with men in "more traditional" ways. This sentiment was frequently corroborated by other customers that I interacted with in the clubs who said that men had to continually "be on guard" against offending women. Here I do not wish to defend male inability to respect women's demands for comfortable working environments. Indeed, several of the above comments could be analyzed as part of a backlash against feminism. Rather, I am highlighting the fact that these men experienced their visits to the clubs (and also, in part, justified them) within a framework of confusion and frustration rather than simply one of privilege or domination. The rapid increase in the number of strip clubs across the United States in the mid-1980s, after all, was concurrent with a massive increase of women into the workforce and an upsurge of attention paid to issues of sexual harassment, date rape, and the condemnation of the sex industry. Although this is not a case of simple cause and effect, such developments and the discourses surrounding them shape some of the ways that the men's visits to the clubs were spoken about and understood.

Many of the men that I spoke with discussed their confusion as to what was expected of them as men in relationships with women. Tim said that he thought that men were under a good deal of "strain" because their wives were also working nowadays, bringing in their own income and insisting that they be allowed to take an active part in planning the couple's future. "She's not taking a back seat to decisions about careers and moves, and I think that a lot of men have

a hard time dealing with that," he said. Other men complained that they were expected to be strong and assertive, both at home and in their workplaces, but their female partners were at the same time interested in greater communication and emotional expression. Joe summarized this succinctly:

> My wife expects me to be strong emotionally, physically, and I expect spiritually too. . . . But emotionally, she wants me to be strong but she doesn't want me to be overbearing. She wants me to cry and be sensitive, to be the leader and the rock. . . . I'm confused as hell. I wouldn't say that openly in public but I'm definitely confused about what it is to be a man.

Zachary, Eric, Kenneth, and Jason made nearly identical comments. Strip clubs offered a temporary respite from both changing definitions of masculinity and requests from women for either instrumental support or reciprocal emotional communication.

The home, then, was seen as a different sphere with its own set of obligations, commitments, and conflicts. Certainly, the men received a great deal of enjoyment from their families, and almost all were adamant that they did not want to change the structure of their private lives. The home, however, among these interviewees and for many other men that I interacted with, was not necessarily a "haven" from the workplace (Lasch, 1977) where the men could simply relax and be themselves. This is not to say that somehow a more authentic self was being expressed in the strip club than in the workplace or at home. Rather, a man might have multiple selves, or self-representations, that are experienced in different contexts. Certain self-representations, for example, are expressed in work and marriage, and for many men it is these self-representations that are first invoked to identify themselves. These selves, however, were also often premised on responsibilities and commitments. Because the interactions in a strip club (through the gendered performances of both parties) spoke to a male self-representation that was not involved with family or work responsibilities and commitments, the club became an ideal space for some men to access a fantasy of freedom, independence, and idealized masculinity. In addition, confusion about gender roles ("what it is to be a man") may be disturbing to some men because such confusion, change, or deviation may still be taken as evidence of a nonheterosexual orientation (despite the existence of masculinities such as those discussed by Halberstam, 1998, or Levine, 1998). Changing expectations about male economic providership and emotional communication in committed relationships may have contributed to some men's experiences of stress and confusion about their gender identities and roles (Levant & Brooks, 1997). Arguably, these changes and sentiments may be most intense in the middle classes; however, nearly all of the men I interviewed identified as middle class. In a context of contradictory or changing expectations, a man might find it relaxing to be in an environment such as a strip club, where he does not necessarily have any role to perform except for that of a desiring male (though other roles are available). These issues are discussed in more depth in the next section.

The transactions that occur in strip clubs should not merely be seen as providing an escape from responsibilities and commitments. As I have argued elsewhere (Frank, 1998) and as discussed in the next sections, some men were also actively seeking an escape to a kind of interaction with women that was not available to them in their everyday lives. It would also be a mistake to assert that such interactions are only compensatory, whether for the men's alienation as producers or because of an inability to develop intimate relationships with other women. Visits to strip clubs can usefully be seen as masculinizing practices as well as touristic practices. Connell (2000) defined masculinizing practices as practices that are governed by a gender regime, are embedded in social relations, and work to produce masculinities in particular settings and by certain institutions (p. 155). Masculinizing practices may be readily apparent, as in the case of fraternity initiations or boot camp drills that emphasize toughness and physical hierarchy, or much more subtle, involving comportment, dress, sexuality, sport, work, and other ev-

eryday or ritualistic practices. "Masculinities," Connell argued, "do not exist prior to social interaction, but come into existence as people act" (p. 218). People's acts, as they become meaningful, link them to larger-scale structures of the gendered order—structures of power relations, production relations (or divisions of labor), relations of cathexis (or emotional relations), and symbolism (p. 59). To say that a practice is "masculinizing" does not mean that it always or unproblematically constructs a particular stable kind of male subjectivity. Yet, although "men's bodies do not fix patterns of masculinity" (p. 218), their experiences, pleasures, and vulnerabilities are still significant in the constructions and expressions of masculinities. Masculinity, like social class, can thus be seen as a process rather than an achievement or a state of being. Consumption, especially the gendered combination of leisure, entertainment, and service available in strip clubs, can be seen as an important part of that process.

## Safety and Excitement

Strip clubs are appealing, in part, because they are both safe and exciting, and when the tension between these boundaries disappears for a customer, he may cease to be a regular. A touristic practice might be understood as part of a larger process that makes "the habitual desirable as well as making escape from the habits of labor seem possible through everyday practices of consumptive pleasure" (Allison, 1996, p. xv). Strip clubs exist because they are profitable, not as a challenge to the existing social order. Despite recognizing this fact, however, customers often talked about their visits in terms of freedoms—from work, from the demands of women, from the restrictions of marriage, from social mores. Yet at the same time as it promises escape or freedom, the image constructed out of tourist gazes also "serves to validate and legitimize routine experience, domestic and working life, and the social structure within which they are located" (Manderson, 1995, p. 307). The temporary nature of the customers' excursions was highly significant to them, for example, and the desire to return to work and home were unquestioned elements of the men's visits, reflected in the balance between risk and safety that was often being sought. Though some customers expressed the desire for an affair with a dancer or for more "excitement" in their sexual relationships outside of the clubs, few of them seemed prepared to give up their positions in these other realms to pursue such desires. Most of the married customers claimed that they were not interested in leaving their wives, and even the men who described their jobs as "boring," "unfulfilling," or even "intolerable" seemed to have no intention of changing these circumstances. Further, though customers sometimes tried to find out information about a dancer's life or ask a dancer out on a date, for example, the possibility of an outside relationship was often more desirable than a real encounter (Frank, 1998).

One customer, for example, spent an entire afternoon telling me his fantasies about visiting a legal brothel in Nevada. He had never used any aspect of the sex industry except for looking at a few pornographic magazines and visiting strip clubs. "I just want to do it once," he said, "and then I want to go home to Mama" (his wife of 30 years). However, he explained, she would never condone it, and it was not worth the risk. His hours in the strip club provided him with a transgressive and exciting experience—indeed, provided him an opportunity to share this even more transgressive fantasy and develop it further through our interaction—yet still allowed him to return home. Because most of the men kept their activities in the clubs a secret from their coworkers, wives, or partners, they were careful to remove traces of these visits before returning to the office or home: checking for lipstick on their cheeks (remnants of a thank you peck on the cheek) or perfume on their clothes, for example. Such illicit remains were clearly inappropriate in these other spheres, even more literally marking the separateness of the clubs as well as the desire to maintain that separateness.

Many of the interviewees discussed their experiences in the language of "variety," "travel," "fun," "escape," and "adventure." One man consistently described himself as a "pioneer," pointing out that he always visited new clubs in Laurelton on their opening night and sought out strip clubs whenever he passed through a new city. Many of the men enjoyed sharing tales of their travels to strip clubs in other cities and states: "I could tell stories about the places I've been to for hours," one man told me. Other men described themselves as "hunters," "adventurers," or "explorers." Nick said that strip clubs provided "adventure" and "excitement" to balance out the more mundane "compartments" of his life such as work and home and that such sexualized ventures "make life worth living". . . .

Though compared to lower tier clubs, upscale clubs were not as often described as sinister spaces, the customers still fantasized about the dangerous, glamorous, or exciting individuals or the vice that might be encountered in them, despite their lack of proof that such things occurred: rich New York gangsters laundering money or dealing cocaine, beautiful women who could lure a man into a private room and out of his monthly income, or famous athletes buying oral sex from ex-Playboy bunnies.

Despite descriptions of strip clubs as places with "no rules" and as "outside the law," and although customers experience and express feelings of freedom, adventure, or excitement during their excursions to strip clubs, they are actually passing over ground that has been tightly regulated to produce this particular kind of experience. The city has delineated where such clubs can be located and (for the most part) what types of interactions can be had inside. Bouncers physically monitor and control the men's behavior inside the clubs. Other kinds of behaviors—such as proper etiquette in regard to watching table dances, tipping procedures, and customer-to-customer interactions—are policed by both the dancers and the other customers. The men also police their own behavior; few bachelors really need their hands to be tied behind a chair during a table dance, and even men who claim to be wild with desire or testosterone are usually found sitting docilely in their chairs. Some of the men's talk about safety, then, can be seen as a derivative both of restrictive interventions on the part of the law, the club, and the employees and of their own expectations and boundaries. Men's talk about danger and adventure, on the other hand, is connected to historical discourses about masculinity, travel, and encounters with various categories of Others that must be further explored.

Public spaces have long been occupied by men in the cultural imagination, and although this is changing, the gendered split between public and private realms is important in thinking about how discourses of travel have been masculinized over time. Indeed, the sociological figures of the tourist, the stranger, the adventurer, and the flaneur are also implicitly masculine metaphors for particular kinds of subjectivities (Jokinen & Veijola, 1997). The 19th-century flaneur, or stroller, is the "forerunner of the twentieth century tourist," the strolling pedestrian who "poetically confronts the 'dark corners' of a town or city, occupied by the dispossessed and the marginal, and experiences supposedly real authentic life" (Jokinen & Veijola, 1997, p. 26). These spaces in the fast-growing cities were assumed to be dangerous as well as authentic because of their connection with promiscuity, contagion, and contamination, and those who sought them out were said to be "slumming." Underprivileged and disreputable areas "came to be redefined as tourist sights" (Rojek & Urry, 1997, p. 7). The connection of slumming to privilege means that the figure of the flaneur is also often racialized and classed as well as gendered.

For many customers, especially (but not exclusively) those who preferred the lower tier clubs, the fact that visits to strip clubs often implied a journey into "bad" areas of town was seen as risky and dangerous but also exciting, a form of erotic slumming. Alex said that strip clubs were appealing because they "had that sinister type feel," "you know, the whole place is just kind of like dark and there's an underground there." He said that he thought I was "very brave" for conducting interviews with the customers and admitted that he had fantasized that by meeting me, the "worst case scenario" could be that "she drugs me and steals all my money." Saul preferred visiting "dive" bars that were located in "seedy areas of town." At the same time, however, he also worried about crime and "getting rolled in the parking lot." For Saul this danger (often fantasized, given the high security of most Laurelton clubs) was an important part of his excursions. Even though we met for our initial interview in a coffee shop, for example, he also said that he had been warned about showing up for our meeting. "Who knows?" he said. "I've heard of men being robbed and killed this way." ("At Starbucks?" I was tempted to ask.) He continued, "You never know by looking at somebody . . . I mean, I would never know if you were like, a crack dealer, you know? Or like living day to day? Or somebody that's going to school for your future." Yet despite his spoken fears, he showed up on time and participated enthusiastically in the interviews. Further, I continued to see him around town at the various clubs in which I worked. Significantly, then, whereas strip clubs were relatively safe, they were also dangerous enough to be alluring, a bit "less civilized" than the places these middle-class men would ordinarily enter. Race was also important in structuring such fantasies. White customers expressed concerns about visiting the primarily Black clubs in Laurelton, for example, because of the "aggressive" nature of Black dancers, the "rough crowds," and the more "graphic displays" that were supposedly found there (though few of the men who expressed such hesitations had actually visited the clubs in question). . . .

Excursions into the sex industry are not only related to the allure of supposedly bad or dangerous areas of town or of the individuals who populate those "dark corners," but also to the adventure of sexual discovery. Sexual experiences (not necessarily heterosexual, of course) coupled with travel away from the safety of home have often been portrayed as a form of masculinized adventure; one only needs to think of Henry Miller, the adventures of Don Juan, or stories about Charles Bukowski or Jack Kerouac. Many of the men with whom I spoke agreed with this idea, even though they were not pursuing sexual contact or release. Steven said that "what a guy gets in a men's club, he doesn't get at home any more". . . .

At the same time as they offered adventure in the form of sexual discovery, however, many men also explicitly claimed that strip clubs provided safety in relation to marriages or long-term partnerships. For many of my interviewees, "looking" was the final limit with which they felt comfortable. As legal venues in which no overt sexual acts were supposed to take place, the clubs were seen by many of these men as supportive of heterosexual monogamy (though pushing at its borders). Although visiting a prostitute, a massage parlor, or a "jack shack" is relaxing for some men, it caused conflicts for these particular men. For example, although some of the interviewees admitted to periodically reading *Playboy* or renting pornographic videos, such practices were not as significant or enjoyable to them as their experiences in strip clubs. None of the interviewees or other customers admitted to regularly using escort services, prostitutes, or massage parlors. Several interviewees discussed occasional experiences with prostitutes, describing them as riddled with much more ambiguity, distaste, or guilt than their visits to strip clubs, and none considered this a practice they were likely to take up again.

The strip club, then, was relaxing because it provided a safe space in which to be both married or committed and sexually aroused (or at least, interacting with women in a sexualized setting). A variety of ideas about the requirement of sexual exclusivity in marriage and intimate relationships exist among individuals in the United States. However, regardless of any individual's personal views or practices, the predominant representation of commitment is that of lifetime (or increasingly, serial) monogamy, and one must usually position oneself in relation to this representation. Men draw their lines in different places as to how far they can explore their desire for others without being unfaithful to their wives or partners. As Beck said, "there's a certain point you just don't want to go past if you want to maintain a marriage." Jim said that he often felt guilty because of the influence of his wife's Roman Catholic beliefs on his own conscience. At the same time, however, the fact that he had to "sneak" around to visit the clubs gave him a thrill. "Stolen watermelons taste better than the ones you buy," he said. He did not believe that his "thoughts and fantasies about breaking a covenant" were the same thing as doing so, however, and Jim considered himself "faithful" in his 23 year marriage. . . .

Of course, as strip clubs vary around the country, customers cannot always be certain of the kinds of interactions in which they will be involved. My experience in the industry has led me to believe that although men do become accustomed to the services that are offered in their own locales (men who frequented lap-dancing clubs in Tampa or San Francisco, for example, often expressed disappointment in the limited interactions available in the Laurelton clubs), there are also many men who set limits on the kinds of commodified sexual contacts that they find acceptable. Though the customers' spoken reasons for discomfort with other kinds of sexualized service varied—from commitments to worries about sexually transmitted diseases, ambivalence about commercialized sexual activities, and legal concerns—the point is that this kind of no-contact strip club offered the customers a "safe" space in which this discomfort was eased.

## Personal and Sexual Acceptance

All of the men I interviewed noted that the conversations they had in strip clubs were a significant and pleasurable part of the experience. This claim could be dismissed as the men's attempt to justify a sometimes inflammatory practice or defray masturbatory guilt (as when men say they read *Playboy* "for the articles"). However, I believe that the conversations were indeed significant to a large number of customers beyond being a way to legitimate their visits; after all, I was a participant in thousands of these transactions. The men's enjoyment may or may not have been influenced by the content of the conversations; for some men, just talking to a beautiful woman about anything was considered to be a luxury. As Beck said, the moment that he had some free time, "the first place I'd be interested in going to would be someplace where I could talk to a beautiful woman." Jim said that he went to the clubs to have "an idealized social interaction with gorgeous women." Dancers offered an opportunity to talk to women with whom these men would not generally be able to interact, for any number of reasons: a lack of attractiveness, age differences, class differences (in either direction), proximity, and the women's willingness to interact outside of the clubs, for example.

Sometimes, the conversation was valued because it was a kind of interaction that the men felt they had difficulty finding elsewhere, especially in male-dominated workplaces. As Joe said,

> sometimes I go there just to talk because I feel like I can talk to somebody there without any rules. There's no boundaries. I don't necessarily have to talk about sex, but I can go there and just talk about anything and sometimes that's kind of nice. You know? It's almost like therapy. You're not there to judge me.

Roger said that his male friends were good to talk to about "sports, women, or work" but that he felt more engaged with women in conversation about other things. Brett said that though "men can open up to women," men "don't know what their emotions are" and have difficulty communicating with each other because their egos are "too big" and "too fragile." Stoic masculinity may be idealized in the workplace, and eventually may come to pervade other areas of men's lives, preventing emotional sharing in male friendships. Oliker (1989) suggested a possible nonsexual motive for male infidelity: Because men seldom develop intimate friendships with other men, sexual affairs with women may be the only route to intimacy that they think they have (p. 57). Indeed, strip clubs can be seen as offering similar kinds of releases and connections, without the entanglements, obligations, or repercussions of an affair.

Though the men may have valued the conversation, this is not to say that this conversation was always or necessarily based on mutual disclosure or engagement. As long as they paid for the dancer's time, customers could still maintain a sense of control over the situation by dictating how long the conversation would last, what would be discussed, and whether or not the dancer took off her clothes during the interaction. There was an unspoken understanding that if a dancer was not pleasing, she would not be paid. Granted, any dancer could walk away from a customer or group if she did not want to engage in a given interaction or found it offensive, yet there was usually someone else willing to take her place, if only for the money.

Some men noted that the interactions they purchased in strip clubs were an ego boost because they provided safe opportunities for close interactions with women without the risk of rejection. Sexuality and sexual conquest, after all, can be experienced by men as humiliating and stressful as well as thrilling. Men with physical disabilities are frequent visitors of such clubs and appreciate the female companionship that is available to them there (e.g., Reed, 1997; Shuttleworth, 2000). Even men who are not impotent, disabled, or unattractive, however, may feel insecure in interactions with women. The desire for an ego boost was almost never the first motivation that men mentioned, but eventually arose in many interviews and conversations:

> I guess it is kind of an ego thing too . . . if I haven't been feeling that great about myself and I go in there it doesn't matter if it's real or not but after a while, it gets in your head, in your memory. (Jason)

> There's no way you're going to go in [the strip club] and get the cold shoulder, that's for sure. It's just absolutely an ego trip because you go in there, and if you're a warthog, bald, and got a pot belly, some good looking girl's gonna come up and go, "Hey, do you want me to dance for you?" Seducing women is something all men wish they were better at, you know? And this seems like you're doing it, and it's easy! (Roger)

David described his visits to a strip club during a failing marriage as "good for my ego to build me up, to make me feel like I was a man again." Many sex workers joked about really being "therapists" and understood their jobs to be about boosting a man's ego by convincing him that he is desirable, masculine, and successful. Thus customers were at times seeking an otherness within themselves, a sense of escape from those aspects of the self that felt oppressive in other spheres, such as old age, ugliness, insecurity, a lack of social skills, or intimate failures.

Bordo (1999) discussed male anxiety about female attractiveness and argued that "just as the beautiful bodies [in cultural representations] subject us women to (generally) unrealizable models of the kind of female we must become in order to be worthy of attention and love, they also subject men and boys to (generally) unrealizable models of the kind of female they must win—with equally destructive consequences" (p. 285). Though most heterosexual boys settle for "inferior fixes," women who may be attractive but do not quite succeed in approximating the ideal, many men still "remain haunted by the beauties." Images of female perfection thus "not only shape perception, they also shape sexual desire," she argued, and "straight male sexuality is honed on the images, even fixated on them" (p. 287). Bordo argued that the male perception of female beauty as powerful—able to "invade male consciousness and arouse desire and then to reject that desire, leaving the man humiliated, shamed, frustrated" (p. 290)—may lead some men to seek both solace and excitement in pornography. In strip clubs, the "beauties" are there as a live fantasy, young, available, interested, and accepting.

These customers were keenly aware of the fact that, in addition to male bonding, competition between men also often centered on the struggle to gain attention from women and many welcomed the opportunity to avoid this competition. In strip clubs, Gary said, "the pressure's off. I have to be accepted." Similarly, David said,

> I don't get excited about going to your local bars and you know, just trying to pick up chicks and be the cool suave dude at the bar. I don't like using the lines, and I think the competitive nature of that is just sort of silly to me. The girls at the strip joints might be there not only to talk to; they're there because they're working. They have a reason to be there. There's fi-

nancial considerations pushing that, and they'll talk to you whether you're Black, you're big, you're fat, you're small, you're 46, or you're 24.

Customers also sometimes wanted to be accepted as objects of desire. I was constantly asked questions about how it felt to be a dancer by the customers, both on the job and during the interviews, for instance, and they were fascinated with the details of performing. Often the men said things like "It must be nice to have everybody want you"; "How does it feel to be perfect?"; "Is it fun to be the one up on the pedestal?"; or "I'd trade places with you if I could." The cross-identificatory wishes being expressed in such statements are rooted in complex fantasies of power, exposure, degradation, and idealization (see Frank, 2002).

Some men were searching for acceptance of their sexual desires. In addition to the customers who enjoyed the everyday conversation about work, current events, their families, or any number of other topics, I also interacted with a number of men who seemed thrilled by the thought of talking about sex with a woman. Because such conversations are often inappropriate between strangers in the everyday world (and even sometimes between lovers), the fact that we could engage in such talk with impunity was relaxing and enjoyable to some customers. Customers also told dancers things that they claimed they had never told their wives or lovers, usually specific fantasies or experiences that they thought the other women in their lives would not understand. At times, the desires the customers expressed were simply to look at female anatomy without shame or apology, and many told stories about not being allowed to look at their wives' or partners' bodies. Paul, Gary, and Saul all mentioned that they had been made to feel like "perverts" numerous times because of their "voyeuristic" desires to look at women, both at home and on the streets.

Other men wanted to express their desires verbally but not necessarily to act on them. One regular customer was an older married man who considered himself and his wife to be "very Catholic." He enjoyed telling me his sexual fantasies, which he thought that he could not share with his wife. His fantasies were fairly standard pornographic fare that I personally did not find upsetting or surprising. Still, he experienced these fantasies as deviant and was relieved to find a nonjudgmental ear. Other times, customers had fantasies they wanted to share that had caused extreme reactions from the other women in their lives. Another customer, for example, begged me to anally penetrate him with my high-heeled shoes. When I refused, he became distraught and told me his wife had left him because she thought that he was a "pervert" because this was what he wanted. Another married man came to the same club several nights in a row, each night offering more money in an attempt to find someone who would have sex with him after work while wearing a strap-on dildo. He told me that he was certain his wife would leave him if he asked her to do so, yet he still found this fantasy compelling. Although the dancers may not have accepted his actual offer, and to my knowledge none did, the expression of his fantasy did not lead to rejection within the confines of the club, and he was provided with information about anal sex in addition to a forum for aural fantasizing.

Many of the customers were also concerned with seeking women's approval and even enjoyment of the sexual practices that they found appealing. Certainly, in some cases the idea that dancers would be more accepting of their sexual fantasies was based on the men's ideas about the ethical inadequacies of women who would dance nude. Joe, for example, said that dancers were less likely to pass judgment than other women because of their stigmatized position: "They're not gonna tell you what's right or wrong because here they are, dancers!" Gary made several references to dancers as "sluts," the kind of girls that he could "get" when other women rejected him. Other times, however, men who were involved in alternative lifestyles or who had risqué fantasies seemed to genuinely appreciate women who could talk openly about sex and sexual desire. Swingers sometimes visited the clubs, with or without their partners, as did other individuals whose ideas about monogamy and relationships differed from the norm, and they seemed to enjoy discussing their experiences and desires with the dancers as well.

## Performing Desire and the Fantasy of the 'Perfect Penis'

It is essential to recognize that the dancers are not the only performers in these venues; the customers, sometimes consciously and sometimes not, are also part of the scene, intricately involved in performances of identity, sexuality, and desire that generate meaning and pleasure out of their interactions. Though the regulars, in my experience, rarely took advantage of the on-stage performance opportunities that were available for men in the clubs, the fact that they engaged in sexualized encounters with the dancers in a public place, and in the presence of a live audience, was significant to the meanings of the experiences. In such encounters heterosexuality could be comfortably secured, at least temporarily or in fantasy, through a public performance of desire for a woman. Men could observe themselves desiring, both literally, in the mirrored walls of the clubs, and figuratively, in the sense of self-reflection and fantasy. Further, the experience or performance of sexual desire could in turn serve as an affirmation of gender identity both to oneself and to others (although sexual desire can feel different from or independent of gender, it can also serve to reinforce ideas of oneself as masculine or feminine).

This is not to say that all of the participants in the exchanges that occur in heterosexual strip clubs are "straight," for they definitely are not. Many bisexual and lesbian women work as dancers or visit clubs as customers, and many heterosexual women enjoy looking at other women's bodies and visit the clubs as customers if they are allowed. Not all of the male customers are straight either, and some men enjoy watching other men in the clubs. At times, customers visited the clubs seeking gratification of certain fetishes such as the desire to interact with a dominant woman or to experience public humiliation or pain. On the other hand, although strip shows may construct heterosexual desire as problematic in some ways through their geographies and choreographies—as dirty, illegitimate, or artificial, for example (see Liepe-Levinson, 2002)—and although the desires of the customers were not always straightforward or stereotypical, the transactions did not overtly question the connection of heterosexuality to normative patterns of masculinity.

The customers' interactions with the dancers provided not just proof of heterosexual identity, but also a fantasy of sexual potency. A strip club offers a certain protection from vulnerability that other arenas, including the bedroom at home, may not. Significantly, the men remain clothed during the interactions and are never physically exposed or expected to perform (and, indeed, are prohibited from doing so). Ejaculation, after all, is not really necessary in order to enhance a man's feelings of masculinity, especially in a commodified encounter. As Allison (1993) wrote of male patrons of hostess clubs in Japan, when a man desires to feel good about himself as a man, "it is less sex as an act of penetration and release than a talk about sex" (p. 12) that is effective in these settings: specifically, talk about sex with a woman who indulges him and does not counter his assertions. In a strip club, a customer can fantasize about a sexual encounter with a woman, yet is not responsible for physically performing or providing pleasure to her. He is also prohibited from revealing his naked body to the dancers, which can provide another form of refuge from judgment. Some of the talk about the relaxing aspects of strip clubs must be understood in this context, as interconnected with the vulnerabilities of the body as well as with the pleasures.

The clubs provided some customers with a space in which a disjunction between desire and bodily performance could be negotiated. Some interviewees and other customers described difficulties with sexual performance in their relationships, for example. During our second interview, Ross explained that his marriage had become "asexual" in recent years because of his inability to get erections due to a disastrous surgical error. Yet he had slept with a number of women before marriage and said, "My work and my sexual identity are the lynchpins of who I am." He linked this to the fact that no matter what he did as a youth, his physically and emotionally abusive father repeatedly called him a "faggot" and told him that he would amount to nothing. In strip clubs, Ross could interact with the dancers, express his desire for them verbally, and be seen doing so by others. In this way, visits to the clubs allowed him to access the body that he remembered from his youth, a fantasy body that could respond and perform when bidden to, that did not need to be explained in a sexual encounter, along with a chance to express his "real" identity (or, to put it differently, a self-representation that was already experienced as real or original).

Of course, I do not want to reify stereotypes about the sexual inadequacies of men who might use the sex industry. There are, after all, many men who visit strip clubs whose bodies are agreeable to them and for whom sexual functioning is not an issue. Rather, my argument is that part of what strip clubs provide for their customers is the fantasy of the "perfect penis" (Tiefer, 1995) without the need to prove it either visually or through sexual performance. The fantasy of the perfect penis is, of course, linked to hegemonic ideologies of an aggressive or uncontrollable male sexuality, with the penis as a "power tool" (Bordo, 1999). Yet, it has some of its roots in feelings of vulnerability as well. After all, as Tiefer (1995) argued, "sexual competence is part—some would say the central part—of contemporary masculinity" (p. 142), despite the variety of ways masculinity is understood and expressed by individual men. Although increasingly there are ways to be masculine without relying on physical validation, she argued, the increasing importance of sexuality in contemporary relationships has meant that "there seems to be no apparent reduction in the male sexual focus on physical performance" (p. 152).

Youthfulness was an issue that emerged frequently in conversations and interactions that I had in the clubs, as the majority of the regular customers were men middle-aged or older. The clubs, in some ways, provide an interesting and complicated return to a site of adolescent fantasy. . . . Youthfulness was something that the men desired for themselves and not simply in the bodies that they chose to view in the clubs, though the youthfulness of the dancers helped facilitate this fantasy. "These places keep me young," a customer told me during a table dance, "because you're so young." For some customers, effortless sexual response was something that was associated with youth. Some of the older men, for example, expressed difficulties becoming aroused by their wives or long-term partners, yet claimed that they wanted to be able to be excited by them. As Joe said,

> when a man is 20 years old . . . he's a walking erection. Any port in a storm. I think as you get older, though, you need to be excited a little bit more. It takes a little bit more stimulation. And the variety is what actually does that. At least, from my perspective. The same thing over and over, you kind of get desensitized to it. . . . I love my wife's body. I get turned on by my wife. . . . But I find that the older I get, I can be turned on but still not have an erection. . . . I can certainly try and give her pleasure. That turns me on but I don't necessarily have to have an orgasm from it. . . . I think I've finally got my wife to understand that . . . but yet there's this stigma that women think that if a man doesn't have an orgasm he didn't have a good time.

Other customers also discussed the stigma associated with an inability to maintain an erection.

Customers discussed the difficulties that their wives and partners had with "losing beauty and youth" and with "not wanting to be reminded that it was still out there" by their husbands' visits to strip clubs. They also cautiously discussed the importance of their wives' losses of youth and beauty to themselves, sometimes explicitly comparing the bodies of the dancers to those of their wives. This reference to women's bodies was not simply an exercise in male privilege or misogyny, however. Although these men's visits could possibly have contributed to their wives' or partners' insecurities about aging or sexual attractiveness (and several interviewees explicitly stated that they be-

lieved there were connections), and although the ability to purchase the attentions of others to make oneself feel younger and more desirable is a privileged position (and one their wives might not be able to occupy, for a variety of reasons), the visits were also intertwined with the men's own insecurities about losing a youthful body, an attractive body, a body that would and could perform sexually when the opportunity or need arose, especially in the context of an ongoing intimate relationship. The relationship between the dancers' bodies, the men's partners' bodies, and their own bodies and sexual performances was thus complex and multifaceted.

Not every regular claimed that interactions in the clubs improved his sexual relationship at home or were related to his ideas about sexual performance, however. Some men claimed to compartmentalize their fantasy encounters in the clubs and their outside intimacies. As Steven said, "It's not like I'm making love to my wife and fantasizing about a dancer or something." Herb, Kenneth, Brett, Roger, and Tim spoke similarly, as did many other customers with whom I spoke informally in the clubs. In addition to arguing that their encounters in the clubs did not affect their sexual relationships, other men also argued that their commodified interactions did not affect their bodies. In fact, the number of times that I heard men say, "This doesn't affect me physically," exceeded the number of times that the interviewees explicitly claimed a physical response or even a desire for a response. "I don't get hard-ons while I'm watching dancers or anything," Carl said when I asked him about how he responded to table dances, for example. Men's anxieties about out-of-control bodily responses or a lack of responses influenced their interpretations of their sexualized encounters in strip clubs and elsewhere.

## Anxieties About Being a Strip Club Customer

Although the men expressed numerous motivations for their visits to strip clubs, they also experienced a degree of ambivalence about these motivations and about

their practices, some of which have been alluded to above. Many men were ambivalent
toward sexual arousal in the clubs; whereas
performances of desire were encouraged in
some situations, especially by male friends,
actual evidence of desire (an erection, a dependence on a particular dancer, or an inability to control one's spending) was often
seen as humiliating. There are many reasons
for this: the cultural shame that often arises
for individuals around issues of sex, especially around materials and experiences associated with masturbation (even if masturbation does not actually take place); the
social stigma that surrounds the sex industry
and its users; moral discomfort, depending
on one's religious background and one's
other relationships with women; and political discomfort, given the prominence of certain strands of feminism and ideas about
"political correctness" in popular discourse,
as well as one's own beliefs about how relationships should be conducted. Some men
find their desire for commercialized sexual
experiences or materials to be an unpleasant
compulsion (Brooks, 1995; Stock, 1997).
Conflicting conceptions of masculinity also
interact with ideas of clienthood to create
anxiety for some male customers. There are
times, for example, when availing oneself of
commodified sexual services is seen as a deficit in one's masculinity. That is, having to
"pay for it" is demeaning if other men can
(presumably) get the same female attention
for free. There is still a forceful stereotype
that "sex workers provide sexual relief to society's 'wretched': the old, the unattractive,
the unpartnered" instead of to men in a variety of positions and with varying privileges
(Queen, 1997, p. 130). Some of the interviewees went out of their way to point out to
me that their sex life was enjoyable, possibly anticipating and trying to deflect this
stigma.

Certainly, there are some men who, on
some occasions, talk openly and with pride
about their visits to strip clubs, perhaps even
in a way calculated to make others around
them (especially women) uncomfortable.
Some visits, such as bachelor parties, are
seen as socially legitimate and even as normal male behavior. On the other hand, men
who visit too often or who talk about using
any sector of the sex industry too openly risk
censure, rejection, and ostracism from
friends, families, employers, and lovers, especially if they visit alone. Most of the men
discussed the need for their visits to be "private entertainment," and Alex termed his desire not to be seen at the clubs when he visited alone a "healthy paranoia." Further,
although talk about women's bodies is often
a means of bonding with other men and may
reflect misogynistic attitudes, such behavior
may be laden with conflicting personal emotional meaning. Many men claimed to feel
guilty, for example, because they knew their
wives or girlfriends would disapprove of
their visits to strip clubs, even at the same
time as they enjoyed the male camaraderie
and the sexualized nature of the encounters.
Others felt guilty spending "family money"
on private entertainment and tried to find
ways to justify their visits to themselves.

Finally, visits to strip clubs were usually
premised on the ability to spend significant
amounts of money on tips, private dances,
conversations with dancers, drinks, and
cover charges. Although some men might
visit a club and spend only a few dollars on
tips, men who desired longer or more personal interactions were expected to pay
(sometimes highly) for a dancer's time. Visits
to strip clubs, then, could serve both to enhance a man's feelings of financial power
and status—and thus, for some men, feelings
of masculinity—and to function as reminders of his need for continued or future monetary success. Increasing commodification
and concerns about authenticity are progressively more in conflict in consumer cultures more generally as well, intensifying the
potential for uneasiness with such transactions. Becoming and remaining a customer,
then, is a complicated process that is rife
with ambivalence. There are indeed privileges associated with being able to avail oneself of the services offered in strip clubs, but
recognizing the subjective feelings of vulnerability that infuse such practices with meaning is essential in trying to assess their place
in social life more generally.

# Conclusion

Men have many different motivations for visiting strip clubs that, although related to male social power, complicate this connection as well. Men's consumption practices in these kinds of strip clubs are premised on a range of possible desires: a desire to publicly display a particular masculine self free of obligations and commitments, a touristic desire for adventure through mingling with Others who are seen as "wild" or visiting spaces believed to be "dangerous," a desire to feel desirable (at least in fantasy), or a desire to have a sexualized interaction with a woman that does not involve the vulnerability of actual sexual activity. As part of each customer's repertoire of masculinizing practices, visits to strip clubs offered the men opportunities to think of their bodies not as "prison houses" (Ross, 1989) or working machines, but as sources of desire, pleasure, and freedom. The visits also offered the men an opportunity to experience their selves in pleasurable ways: as young, virile, attractive, independent, sometimes as powerful, and other times as vulnerable. . . .

## References

Allison, A. (1993). Dominating men: Male dominance on company expense in a Japanese hostess club. *Genders*, 16, 1–16.

———. (1996). *Permitted and prohibited desires: Mothers, comics, and censorship in Japan.* Boulder, CO: Westview Press.

Bell, S. (1994). *Reading, writing, and rewriting the prostitute body.* Bloomington: Indiana University Press.

Bildstein, J. (1996). *The king of clubs.* New York: Barricade Books.

Bordo, S. (1999). *The male body: A new look at men in public and in private.* New York: Farrar, Straus, and Giroux.

Brooks, G. R. (1995). *The centerfold syndrome: How men can overcome objectification and achieve intimacy with women.* San Francisco: Jossey-Bass.

Chapkis, W. (1997). *Live sex acts: Women performing erotic labour.* London: Cassell.

Connell, R. W. (2000). *The men and the boys.* Berkeley: University of California Press.

Cornwall, A., & Lindisfarne, N. (Eds.). (1994). *Dislocating masculinity: Comparative ethnographies.* London: Routledge.

Edwards, S. S. M. (1993). Selling the body, keeping the soul: Sexuality, power, the theories and realities of prostitution. In S. Scott & D. Morgan (Eds.), *Body matters: Essays on the sociology of the body* (pp. 89–104). Washington, DC: Falmer Press.

Frank, K. (1998). The production of identity and the negotiation of intimacy in a "gentleman's club." *Sexualities*, 1, 175–202.

———. (2002). *G-Strings and sympathy: Strip club regulars and male desire.* Durham, NC: Duke University Press.

Halberstam, J. (1998). *Female masculinity.* Durham, NC: Duke University Press.

Illouz, E. (1997). *Consuming the romantic utopia: Love and the contradictions of capitalism.* Berkeley: University of California Press.

Jokinen, E., & Veijola, S. (1997). The disoriented tourist: The figuration of the tourist in contemporary cultural critique. In C. Rojek & J. Urry (Eds.), *Touring cultures: Transformations of travel and theory* (pp. 23–51). London: Routledge.

Lasch, C. (1977). *Haven in a heartless world: The family besieged.* New York: Basic Books.

Levant, R. F., & Brooks, G. R. (Eds.). (1997). *Men and sex: New psychological perspectives.* New York: Wiley.

Levine, M. P. (1998). *Gay macho: The life and death of the homosexual clone.* New York: New York University Press.

Liepe-Levinson, K. (2002). *Strip show: Performances of gender and desire.* New York: Routledge.

Manderson, L. (1995). The pursuit of pleasure and the sale of sex. In P. R. Abramson & S. D. Pinkerton (Eds.), *Sexual nature, sexual culture* (pp. 305–329). Chicago: University of Chicago Press.

McElroy, W. (1995). *XXX: A woman's right to pornography.* New York: St. Martin's Press.

Myerhoff, B. (1978). *Number our days.* New York: Simon and Schuster.

Nagle, J. (1997). *Whores and other feminists.* New York: Routledge.

Oliker, S. J. (1989). *Best friends and marriage: Exchange among women.* Berkeley: University of California Press.

Queen, C. (1997). *Real live nude girl.* Pittsburgh, PA: Cleis Press.

Reed, S. (1997). All stripped off. In J. Nagle (Ed.), *Whores and other feminists* (pp. 179–188). New York: Routledge.

Rojek, C., & Urry, J. (Eds.). (1997). *Touring cultures: Transformations of travel and theory.* London: Routledge.

Ross, A. (1989). *No respect: Intellectuals and popular culture.* New York: Routledge.

Segal, L. (1990). *Slow motion: Changing masculinities, changing men.* New Brunswick, NJ: Rutgers University Press.

Shuttleworth, R. P. (2000). The pursuit of sexual intimacy for men with cerebral palsy. Unpublished doctoral dissertation, University of California, San Francisco and University of California, Berkeley.

Stock, W. (1997). Sex as commodity: Men and the sex industry. In R. F. Levant & G. R. Brooks (Eds.), *Men and sex: New psychological perspectives* (pp. 100–132). New York: Wiley.

Tiefer, L. (1995). *Sex is not a natural act & other essays.* Boulder, CO: Westview Press.

Urry, J. (1990). *The tourist gaze: Leisure and travel in contemporary societies.* London: Sage.

## Review

1. Describe some of the explanations given for men going to strip clubs.

2. What are the reasons given by the customers for going to strip clubs?

3. In what ways does patronizing a strip club help a man to feel more masculine?

4. Frank argues that strip clubs are both safe and exciting for men. Explain.

## Application

According to Frank's respondents, men go to strip clubs because, among other things, they find that the clubs are relaxing and entertaining, allow them to engage in "masculine" activities, and enable them to be in a setting that is both safe and exciting. Interview 10 men about their own preferred forms of leisure activity. Ask each: "what kinds of things do you do or would you like to do that you would consider relaxing? Entertaining? A masculine activity? Something that is both safe and exciting?" Record their answers. Then ask: "How about a strip club? Would that fit into any of these for you? Why or why not?"

How would you summarize your results? Assuming the men you interviewed are typical of American men, and assuming they gave you honest answers rather than ones they thought would be socially acceptable, what conclusions would you draw from the combination of your results and Frank's?

## Related Web Sites

1. *http://www.otal.umd.edu/~jpaolett/grad/amst628j.htm.* Papers and links dealing with the topic of masculinity in American culture.

2. *www.un-instraw.org/docs/mensroles/vss_1_4.pdf.* A paper on the sociology of men and new international research on masculinity.

Reprinted from: Katherine Frank, "'Just Trying to Relax'; Masculinity, Masculinizing Practices, and Strip Club Regulars." *Journal of Sex Research* 40 (2003): 61–75. Copyright © 2003 by Society for the Scientific Study of Sexuality. Reproduced with permission of Society for the Scientific Study of Sexuality in the format Textbook via Copyright Clearance Center. ✦

# Part Three

## *Social Interaction*

Interaction with others has two crucial functions in human life. First, it maintains people's values and beliefs. No human can retain his or her sanity and hold to purely idiosyncratic ways. We believe what we do, value what we do, and act as we do because we share those things with a certain number of others. Interaction, in other words, maintains the culture. In turn, the culture bears upon the kind of interaction that occurs.

Second, interaction shapes people's development. You are the kind of person you are because of your interaction experiences. You learn through interaction, for example, what it means to engage in social roles. Interaction helps you to understand a particular role both by explicit teaching ("good girls don't act that way") and by example (observing others who hold that role).

Your roles, then, reflect your culture and they guide the way you behave. In this part, we see first how gender roles and culture interact to affect touching behavior in interaction (selection 12). We also see how race affects roles (selection 13), for "couple" is not the same as "interracial couple" when it comes to engaging in leisure activities. ◆

# 12

# Gender and Culture Differences in Touching

*Rosemarie Dibiase*
*Jaime Gunnoe*

*There is a tendency for each of us to believe that the way we do things is the "normal" or "right" way. But what is considered normal or right or appropriate varies both between cultures and between people within a particular culture. For example, you may regard kissing as a natural expression of romantic love. But there are some cultures where kissing on the lips is considered disgusting. And the extent to which, and the kind of, kissing that people in your own culture find enjoyable varies.*

*Similarly, what is considered normal or right or appropriate varies somewhat between men and women. For example, in conversations women tend to like details, while men tend to prefer a more "bottom line" approach. Women are more likely to complain about a man's reticence in conversations, while men are more likely to complain about a woman's extended discussion of something the men find uninteresting.*

*In this selection, Dibiase and Gunnoe examine the ways in which culture and gender roles influence another aspect of interaction— touching behavior. In a conversation between a man and a woman, which one is more likely to touch the other? Or is there any difference? What does it mean to touch someone while talking with that person? Or does it have any particular meaning? Do people in some countries engage in more touching than those in other countries? Or is touching similar among people everywhere? Touching behavior raises some fascinating questions about the nature of human interaction and the social factors that affect that interaction.*

Touch is a universal aspect of human interaction. All people touch and are touched by others, but there are vast differences in the amount of touching that people do. For example, touching appears to vary by gender, culture, and even age. Although these particular differences in touching behavior are not well understood, historically investigators have thought of touch as expressing control and dominance (Henley, 1973; Summerhayes & Suchner, 1978). This conception of touch was primarily based on early research by Henley (1973, 1977, 2001) that has shown that men touched women more than women touched men. Since Henley's original work, her ideas have been a driving force in research on interpersonal touch. However, a number of more recent reviews have revealed a complex relation between gender and touching behavior that seems to detract from rather than directly support Henley's work (Hall & Friedman, 1999; Hall & Veccia, 1990; Jones, 1986; Major, 1981; Major, Schmidlin, & Williams, 1990; Stier & Hall, 1984; Willis & Dodds, 1998).

Furthermore, in addition to gender differences, there also seem to be large cultural differences in touching behavior. That is, the amount of touching that people accept and expect is determined by each particular society and varies from culture to culture (Frank, 1957). In the present study, we propose that using gender and culture together to reexamine existing theory will further investigators' understanding of touching behavior.

## Gender, Status, and Touching Behavior

Early research on individual differences in touching behavior in the United States showed that men touched women more than women touched men. Thus, Henley (1973) conjectured that high-status individuals

113

have a touching privilege that they exercise to maintain their high-status advantage. Therefore, because people considered men to be of higher status than women, men expressed their high-status advantage through such touching of women. For example, male bosses were more likely to touch the female secretaries than vice versa, underscoring the status difference in the relationship.

Early researchers postulated that this power differential could be used to explain gender differences in touching (Henley, 1973, 1977). Later researchers, looking at hand-holding patterns in men and women and at peoples' perceptions of dominance who were touching others compared to people who were being touched, seemed to find data that supported this notion (Chapell, Basso, et al., 1998; Chapell, Beltran, et al., 1999; Henley, 2001; Summerhayes & Suchner, 1978).

Further evidence for the idea that power and status moderate touch came from research on social class, professional status, and cultural differences in touching. Henley (1977) found that high-status individuals in Western countries were more likely to touch others than to be touched by others, whereas low-status individuals were more likely to be touched by their superiors than to touch them. However, this pattern occurred only when the power roles were disparate. Thayer (1988) found that when roles were similar in power, slightly lower status people tried to establish connections with their more powerful and higher status colleagues through physical contact. In addition, although people of high status and those of low status touch each other with approximately equal frequency, they use different types of touches. That is, people of lower status initiate more formal touches like handshakes while people of higher status initiate more intimate touches such as placing one's hand on the other's shoulder (Hall, 1996).

Recently Hall and Veccia (1990) and Major et al. (1990) and less recently Stier and Hall (1984) have scrutinized Henley's work by examining different types of touching and the meaning of these touches. These studies have demonstrated that among other things, type of touch, age, and relationship also are

significant factors in gender differences in touching. In contrast with Henley's data, Hall and Veccia (1990) found that overall, men and women touched each other with equal frequency. However, there was a tendency for men to use their hands to touch women more than women used their hands to touch men and for women to use other parts of their bodies to touch men more than men used other parts of their bodies to touch women. Thus, contrary to Henley's findings, while men tend to use more hand touch than do women, men do not use more of other types of touches than do women. One explanation for this apparent equity in touching among men and women in the United States may be that in that country, only hand touching expresses dominance. Alternatively, gender roles may be becoming less well defined, and men may not be as clearly dominant as they were 25 years ago.

The differential pattern of touching in men and women was more striking when investigators considered age (Hall & Veccia, 1990; Willis & Dodds, 1998). Hall and Veccia (1990) reported that in people under 30 years of age, men touched women significantly more than women touched men. Hall and Veccia speculated that this pattern might occur because young adults' relationships are typically less well established than those of older adults, compelling young men to behave possessively and women to behave submissively. It may be that traditional gender roles and perceptions of power are more germane to young adults trying to attract one another. This is in line with the findings of Willis and his colleagues (Willis & Briggs, 1992; Willis & Dodds, 1998) that men in dating relationships touch women more than vice versa but that this pattern does not persist in married people. Willis and his colleagues have suggested that the differential pattern of touching behavior between men and women at different ages and stages of relationships is a function of gender differences in evolutionary reproductive strategies. That is, men, who seek to reproduce quickly, initiate touch to obtain sex, whereas women, who wish to preserve male parental involvement, use it to maintain relationships with the men.

# Culture and Touching Behavior

There also seem to be large cultural differences in touching behavior that are determined by the particular society (Frank, 1957). The most well known research is in the area of proxemics. A typical finding in this area is that people in colder climates use relatively large physical distances when they communicate, whereas people in warmer climates prefer closer distances (Lustig & Koester, 1996; Sussman & Rosenfeld, 1982). For example, the range of distances that Germans, Scandinavians, and English find to be intimate for conversations overlaps with the range of distances regarded as normal for conversation in France and the Mediterranean countries of Italy, Greece, and Spain. In the same way, Hall (1966) found that Latin Americans are comfortable at a closer range (have smaller personal space zones) than Northern Americans.

Furthermore, researchers have suggested that some cultures, such as the Middle Eastern, Latin American, and southern European ones, could be considered high-contact cultures (Hall, 1966; Lustig & Koester, 1996). People in these countries seem to interact at closer distances and touch each other much more in social conversations than people from noncontact cultures. Interpersonal touching is infrequent in noncontact cultures, such as those of northern Europe, the United States, and Asia (Mazur, 1977; Thayer, 1988). Also, Southern Europeans are reported to be more affectionate than Northern Europeans (LaFrance & Mayo, 1978). This characteristic too is likely to influence their touching behavior. Typically, these differences in touching translate to greeting behaviors such that in high-contact cultures, hugging or kissing is commonly used in greetings, whereas in noncontact cultures, people often greet with a handshake but no hugging or kissing.

The few studies that have examined touching behavior by culture support the idea that there are cultural differences in touching in the expected directions. For example, Jourard (1966) reported that people in Paris and Puerto Rico touched more than people in London, England, and the United States. In addition, Remland, Jones, and Brinkman (1995) found that Greek and Italian dyads used touch during their interactions more than English, French, and Dutch dyads. Lastly, Regan, Jerry, Darell, Narvaez, and Johnson (1999) found that college age Latino couples touched more in public than their Asian counterparts.

What defines specific touching norms may be clarified by examining culture and gender together. There appear to be large differences in status among men and women depending on the country being examined. In many European countries, men are still in clearly dominant positions, and women are expected to adhere to the traditional gender role stereotypes (e.g., those of keeping house; raising children; and being loving, nurturing, and warm companions). If touch were a noninverse function of dominance, men in these cultures would be likely to touch more than women. However, the overall amount of touching would depend on the normative amount of touching in the particular culture that was being examined.

# Italy

One country with historically well-delineated gender roles is Italy. Italian society is built on deep division of gender roles. In the past, women in Italy were seen as inferior to men and responsible for running the household and caring for others. Their most accepted roles have been (a) self-sacrificing wife and mother, (b) nun, and (c) spinster schoolteacher (Merenda & Mattioni, 1995). Women were not granted the vote until 1946, and it was not until 1975 that a law, in this case the Family Rights Reform Law, established a standard of complete legal equality between husband and wife. However, over the past 25 years, there has been tremendous progress in the area of gender equality. For example, in 1991 a special equal opportunity law abolished all forms of gender inequality regarding schooling, job training, and access to jobs. It even attempted to level out inequality in the area of domestic duties. Along with other legal, social, and religious policies, this law has led to a much more liberated attitude in Italian women, especially those living in urban areas. On the other hand, in Italian men the law has led to confusion and loss of self-esteem (Merenda & Mattioni). Despite these dramatic changes, women are still primarily responsible for running the home and caring for the children. But overall, gender roles in Italy today appear to be in transition and clearly moving toward equality.

Investigators might consider the Italian culture, which is southern European, to be a high-contact culture (Lustig & Koester, 1996), seeing Italians as more likely to be comfortable with touching than people in low-contact cultures, including Americans. Also, Italians ate known for their expressive communication, and touching appears to be an important aspect of their social behavior. Thus, greeting behavior includes not only kisses but kisses on both cheeks.

## The United States

In the United States, there is a history of both equality for and subordination of women (Denmark, Nielson, & Scholl, 1995). At particular times in their history, such as the colonial times of the late 1700s, American women have been valued and afforded many of the same opportunities as men. In other periods, like the industrial period of the mid 1800s, women's status was lowered as they filled lower factory positions with lower pay and lower mobility than did men. It was not until the 1920s that women were allowed to vote. In spite of the vote, the status differential continued up until the late 1960s when the modern women's liberation movement was founded. At that time, women's status was reexamined, and women were allowed expanded employment opportunities. However, an Equal Rights Amendment to the U.S. Constitution has never been passed, and the majority of women in the United States, even those employed outside of the home, continue to be primarily responsible for domestic tasks. Thus, while there has been a definite trend toward gender equality, vestiges of traditional gender roles remain (Denmark, Nielson, & Scholl).

American culture has been depicted as a noncontact culture (Lustig & Koester, 1996).

Americans' interpersonal space is more akin to that of Northern Europeans than to that of Southern Europeans, and greeting behavior includes only a handshake.

## The Czech Republic

Highly traditional gender roles exist in the Czech Republic. A communist country until 1989, Czechoslovakia was split up into the Czech Republic and Slovakia in 1993. In the Czech Republic, men and women appear to have even more polarized roles in society than do Italians or Americans because this country is highly stratified along gender lines (Wolchik, 1991). Although during the Communist period, women in the Czech Republic had access to education and participated in the labor force, there then were and still are substantial inequalities. Typically, women bear the sole responsibility for the home and children regardless of whether they participate in the labor force. Evidence even suggests that since the fall of Communism, there has been a backlash against equality and a rejection of the goal of gender equality in favor of more traditional gender roles (Wolchik). In general, since there has been no recent effort to change women's status, men in the Czech Republic appear to be more dominant than are men in Italy and the United States.

Like Italians, Czechs are emotionally expressive people. Women in particular are reported to be highly affectionate (Kuras, 1996). Unfortunately, there is a paucity of information in the literature on their actual touching behavior, and even though their greeting behavior involves hugging and kissing, the central European location of the Czech Republic would not typically be considered a high-contact area.

## The Present Study

The purpose of the present study was to examine concurrently gender and cultural influences in touching. While previous studies have examined touching behaviors in relation to gender and culture separately, none have examined these variables together. Doing so will allow us to examine the dominance issue from a cultural context. In general, if Henley's theory of dominance is to be supported, we should see men in traditional, male-dominated cultures doing more of certain types of touching than women do. However, that touching will be relative to the particular culture being examined such that men and women in high-contact cultures will do more overall touching than people in low-contact cultures do.

Previous studies have suggested that age, setting, and relationship all influence the amount of touching that men and women do (e.g., Major, Schmidlin, & Williams, 1990; Willis & Dodds, 1998). To level these variables, our observations were conducted in recreational settings frequented by young unmarried people. We observed these young adults in Italy, the Czech Republic, and the United States. These countries have different cultural standards regarding touching in general. For example, Italians are typically portrayed as a high-contact culture, whereas the United States is typically considered a low-contact culture. Little research on touching behavior has included the Czechs, but their greeting behavior suggests that they are a high-contact culture. Thus, our first hypothesis, related exclusively to culture, proposes that Italians will do the most touching and that Americans will do the least touching. Czechs will likely be more like Italians than Americans. This trend should hold for all types of touching.

These countries also have different expectations about gender roles and appear to have different commitments to legislating equality for men and women. Specifically, the Czechs appear to have highly traditional gender role expectations relative to both Italy and the United States. To explore how these culturally derived differences in gender role may be related to touching behavior, two types of touch, hand touch and nonhand touch, were examined separately. Previous studies (e.g., Hall & Veccia, 1990) established that there is typically asymmetry in hand touching such that in general men do more hand touching than women.

Our second hypothesis, which is related to hand touching and gender, proposes that our findings will be in line with those of Hall and Veccia and Major, Schmidlin, and Williams (1990) so that men will touch more with their hands than women. If hand touch is a function of dominance, as Henley's (1977, 2001) work suggests, these findings should be magnified when examining gender and culture together. Here, we expect hand touch to be a function of both dominance and culture such that men in high-contact, highly traditional male-dominant cultures will touch women more with their hands than men in low-contact, nontraditional cultures.

Specifically, our third hypothesis, which is concerned with both gender and culture, is that in the Czech Republic, where there continues to be substantial gender stratification and perceived male dominance, men will hand-touch women more than women will hand-touch men. In the United States and Italy, where changing gender roles and societal striving for equality seem to be occurring, there should be fewer gender-related differences with respect to hand-touch. However, as predicted in our first hypothesis, while gender differences in hand touching between Italian men and women are not expected to be as great as those of Czechs, Italian men (high-contact culture) should do more hand touching than American men (low-contact culture).

Fewer gender differences in nonhand touching have been found, and in fact women tend to nonhand touch men more than vice versa (Hall & Veccia, 1990). This suggests that nonhand touch may not be related to the expression of dominance. If this is the case, we would expect women in all cultures to engage in more nonhand touching than men. Thus, our fourth hypothesis, which is related to gender and nonhand touching, is that, overall, women will do more nonhand touching than men and that as predicted in our first hypothesis, women in Italy and the Czech Republic (high-contact cultures) will do more nonhand touching than will Americans (low-contact culture).

## Method

### Participants

Participants were 120 people whom we visually judged to be in their early-to-mid 20s of age. There were 40 Italians (20 men and 20 women), 40 Czechs (20 men and 20 women), and 40 Americans (20 men and 20 women). All were observed early in the evening in dance clubs in their respective countries in the cities of Rome, Prague, or Boston. All of these clubs were in neighborhoods that were frequented primarily by locals as opposed to tourists, and the clubs primarily attracted white patrons of mid-to-high socioeconomic status. We made observations as unobtrusively as possible so that the participants would not know that they were being observed.

## Procedure

The procedure and measures were modified versions of those that Hall (1996) used. We made observations over a 6-month period, visiting each location two or three times. In each city, raters entered dance clubs early in the evening and sat in a central location. To assure that the participants were of the expected nationality, raters got close enough to hear that they were speaking the native language before doing the observations. All male-female dyads within the rater's field of vision were observed. After a rater evaluated all the couples in one location, the rater moved to a new location within the dance club. Raters brought with them magazines containing precoded sheets on which to record their observations. These sheets contained space for gender of participant, number of hand touches, number of nonhand touches, and rater comments.

***Interrater reliability.*** Two female raters collected the data. Prior to data collection, a senior investigator trained raters on coding of touch and judgment of age (within 5 years). Raters then went into a dance club and rated 10 randomly selected men and women on frequency of touching behavior and age. Interrater reliability for frequency of touching was established using a standard procedure: the number of agreements divided by the sum of the number of agreements and the number of disagreements, all times 100. Given the straightforward nature of the observations, the mean percentage of agreement was better than 95%.

To examine reliability for age agreement, we used a Pearson correlation. As with the touching, there was a high level of agreement, $r = .90$. Reliability was reestablished after every 15 participants were rated.

***Sampling.*** Raters flipped a coin to select the gender of the first participant to be observed. After this selection, subsequent selections alternated by gender. The rater observed and recorded touching behavior for 5 min. Two types of touching, hand touch and nonhand touch, were used as our dependant variables. Examples of hand touches included touches from hand to body, touches from hand to hand, touches from hand to face, touches from hand to leg, and touches from hand to shoulder. Examples of nonhand touches included touches from body to body, hugging, and kissing. Raters recorded only touches initiated after the rating began (in-progress touches were not recorded), because in-progress touches have been controversial in previous research (Willis & Dodds, 1998). For each participant, the total number of new hand touches and the total number of new nonhand touches for a 5-min period were recorded and used in the analyses. If any partcipants left the area before the 5 min were up, they were eliminated from the sample.

## Discussion

We designed the present study to examine gender and cultural influences on touching behavior. Earlier research and theory had suggested that people in high-contact cultures would do more of all kinds of touching than those in low-contact cultures. Thus, we first predicted that people in Italy and the Czech Republic would do more overall touching than those in the United States would. As expected, for both hand touch and nonhand touch, Americans initiate touch less frequently than both Italians and Czechs. This difference is most pronounced for nonhand touch, with Italians touching the most and Czechs touching second-to-most.

These findings support the work of Jourard (1966) and Remland, Jones, and Brinkman (1995), indicating the possibility that there are cultural differences in touching behavior and that these behaviors are likely to be the product of socialization. This is the first study in English to empirically demonstrate that Czechs' touching behavior is more like that of people in high-contact cultures than it is like that of people in low-contact cultures.

We also were interested in the question of whether there were gender differences in touching that paralleled cultural norms of gender roles. Earlier research had demonstrated that such differences are likely to be more apparent when hand touch as opposed to nonhand touch is observed (e.g., Hall & Veccia, 1990). Thus, in an extension of Henley's (1973) work on dominance and touch, our second hypothesis predicted that men would do more hand touching than women. We extended this idea further with our third hypothesis, which predicted that in cultures with the most traditional gender roles, in this case the Czech Republic, men would be more likely to initiate touch with their hands than men in currently less traditional cultures, such as Italy and the United States. As expected, there was a tendency across cultures for men to touch women with their hands more frequently than women touched men with their hands. However, only in the Czech Republic did men touch women with their hands significantly more than women touched men with their hands. While this finding does not demonstrate with certainty that hand touching is more indicative of dominance than are other types of touches, as noted earlier the Czech Republic appears to have more traditional gender role delineation than the United States and Italy. In addition, if an absence of legislative efforts toward equality can be taken as evidence, working toward gender equality does not appear to be a current priority for the Czech Republic. The fact that only Czechs demonstrate this distinctive difference in touching supports (a) the idea that hand touch is associated with dominance or at least power and (b) Henley's theory suggesting that men in dominant positions touch women more than women touch men. In keeping with Thayer (1988), it follows that in societies where gender roles are less well

defined, this touching differential is similarly less well defined.

These findings are only applicable to young men and women and may not hold for people of other ages. Earlier studies have shown that touching patterns among men and women of different ages vary greatly (Hall & Veccia, 1990; Major, Schmidlin, & Williams, 1990; Willis & Dodds, 1998). The present authors' work is generally consistent with others' findings that men in their twenties touch women in general more than women in their twenties touch men. However, in keeping with Hall's work (Hall & Veccia), this finding is only relevant for hand touching.

For the nonhand touch data, the present authors expected to see women doing more touching than men did, and in all 3 groups there was a tendency for women to do more nonhand touching than men did, which was quite the opposite of what we found for hand touching. However, there were not significant differences between men and women living in the United States, and there were only trends toward differences in Italy. There were significant differences between Czech men and women such that women touched men more than men touched women. Thus, as with the hand touch data, there was a striking asymmetry in touching behavior in the most traditional society examined but not in those societies where gender roles are less traditionally defined or in transition. The meaning is unclear and forces this question: Do hand touches reflect dominance or something like it, whereas other touches express something else? The present research suggests that this may be the case and further suggests that there may be gender-related motivations for nonhand touch as well as for hand touch. Certainly, along with the research of Hall and her colleagues, it demonstrates that not all types of touches are the same. In fact, over the past few decades of research on this topic, it has become quite clear that touch is a complex behavior with many different origins, meanings, and functions. Treating all touch as one unit is no longer an effective research strategy.

Because we examined different cultural groups, our study is unique. One seemingly unambiguous finding is that male and female touching patterns are not universal and as such are unlikely to be the result of biological predispositions only. In fact, quite different patterns of gender-related touch are evident in the three cultures that we examined. Thus, although Willis and his colleagues have suggested that the gender-related asymmetry in touching behavior reflects differential evolutionary reproductive strategies, that hypothesis is not entirely supported by the present data. Although it is conceivable that touch, like other human behaviors, has some survival function (from an evolutionary perspective), there are other factors in play here as well. In fact, the present results suggest that touching behavior has at least some culturally infused learning components.

One aspect of the present study that investigators should carefully consider is that the present investigators conducted our research in only one type of setting and that this setting was unarguably a social setting where there may have been intimate relationships among participants. Previous studies have demonstrated that setting is a potent mediator of touching behavior. It is not certain whether our findings would hold in other settings with formal relationships. Some research in nonprofessional settings has demonstrated that touch is often used for purposes other than dominance and that there is less gender asymmetry in casual settings than in public, nonintimate settings (Major, Schmidlin, & Williams, 1990). In fact, a number of studies have suggested that touch in casual settings may be used to show affection, nurturing, warmth, sexual interest, and intimacy rather than dominance (Burgoon, 1991; Jourard & Rubin, 1968; Major, 1981; Major, Schmidlin, & Williams, 1990; Mehrabian, 1972; Nguyen, Heslin, & Nguyen, 1976; Willis & Briggs, 1992; Willis & Dodds, 1998). Thus, we concur with Major, Schmidlin, and Williams (1990) in asserting that the relationship between the toucher and the recipient is extremely important yet has been much neglected in the research in this area. Future investigators should examine this issue more carefully in studies akin to that of Willis and Dodds in which they asked participants about their relationships after touching behaviors had been observed. Looking at what types of touching people do in different types of relationships and how this changes over time could further extend this research.

In fact, going beyond anonymous observations and gathering more personal data will further elucidate our understanding of many aspects of the relation between touching behavior and power. For example, one could make a direct examination of some of the intermediary variables, like men and women's perceptions of their own dominance and power and their impressions of the power of their gender in the greater society, as they are related to how men and women touch. Similarly, investigators should examine gender role also in the context of touching behavior. If touch is an expression of dominance, it could be hypothesized that those men with a more masculine gender role would touch women more frequently, especially with their hands, than those with a more neutral gender role. Future studies should extend the current work by measuring both gender and gender role, as well as observing touching patterns.

Lastly, while the present investigators have undertaken a study of three culturally diverse groups, there are clearly more groups to be examined. In the present study, all of the groups that we examined were of the European tradition in which there are many underlying similarities. It also would be of great interest to examine more diverse cultures such as those of the Middle East, Asia, and the developing world. The more culturally diverse the groups that we examine are, the more likely we are to uncover patterns of associations that will augment and extend understanding of touching behavior.

## References

Burgoon, J. K. (1991, Winter). Relational message interpretations of touch, conversation distance, and posture. *Journal of Nonverbal Behavior*, 15 (4), 233–259.

Chapell, M. S., Basso, E., DeCola, A., Hossack, J., Keebler, J. J., Marm, J., et al. (1998). Men and women holding hands: Whose hand is uppermost? *Perceptual and Motor Skills, 87,* 127–130.

Chapell, M. S., Beltran, W., Santanello, M., Takahashi, M., Bantom, S. R., Donovan, J. S., et al. (1999). Men and women holding hands: II. Whose hand is uppermost? *Perceptual and Motor Skills, 89,* 537–549.

Denmark, F. L., Nielson, K. A., & Scholl, K. (1995). United States of America. In L. L. Adler (Ed.), *International handbook on gender roles* (pp. 159–173). Westport, CT: Greenwood Press.

Frank, L. K. (1957). Tactile communication. *Genetic Psychology Monographs, 56,* 209–255.

Hall, E. T. (1966). *The hidden dimension* (2nd ed.). Gardner City, NY: Anchor Books/Doubleday.

Hall, J. A. (1996). Touch, status, and gender at professional meetings. *Journal of Nonverbal Behavior, 20* (1), 23–44.

Hall, J. A., & Friedman, G. B. (1999). Status, gender and nonverbal behavior: A study of structured interactions between employees of a company. *Personality and Social Psychology Bulletin, 25* (9), 1082–1091.

Hall, J. A., & Veccia, E. M. (1990). More "touching" observations: New insights on men, women, and interpersonal touch. *Journal of Personality and Social Psychology, 59* (6), 1155–1162.

Henley, N. M. (1973). Status and sex: Some touching observations. *Bulletin of the Psychonomic Society, 2,* 91–93.

——. (1977). *Body politics: Power, sex, and nonverbal communication.* Englewood Cliffs, NJ: Prentice-Hall.

——. (2001). Body politics. In A. Branaman (Ed.), *Self and society: Blackwell readers in sociology* (pp. 288–297). Malden, MA: Blackwell Publishers.

Jones, S. E. (1986). Sex differences in touch communication. *Western Journal of Speech Communication, 50,* 227–241.

Jourard, S. M. (1966). An exploratory study on body-accessibility. *British Journal of Social and Clinical Psychology, 5,* 221–231.

Jourard, S. M., & Rubin, J. E. (1968). Self disclosure and touching: A study of two modes of interpersonal encounter and their inter-relation. *Journal of Humanistic Psychology, 8* (1), 39–48.

Kuras, B. (1996). *Czechs and balances: A nation's survival kit.* Praha, Czech Republic: Baronet.

LaFrance, M., & Mayo, C. (1978). Cultural aspects of nonverbal communication: A review essay. *International Journal of Intercultural Relations, 2,* 71–89.

Lustig, M. W., & Koester, J. (1996). *Intercultural competence: Interpersonal communication across cultures* (2nd ed.). New York: HarperCollins.

Major, B. (1981). Gender patterns in touching behavior. In C. Mayo & N. M. Henley (Eds.), *Gender and nonverbal behavior* (pp. 15–37). New York, NY: Springer-Verlag.

Major, B., Schmidlin, A. M., & Williams, L. (1990). Gender patterns in social touch: The impact of setting and age. *Journal of Personality and Social Psychology, 58* (4), 634–643.

Mazur, A. (1977). Interpersonal spacing on public benches in contact vs. noncontact cultures. *The Journal of Social Psychology, 101,* 53–58.

Mehrabian, A. (1972). *Nonverbal communication.* Chicago: Aldine-Atherton.

Merenda, R., & Mattioni, M. (1995). Italy. In L. L. Adler (Ed.), *International handbook on gender roles* (pp. 159–173). Westport, CT: Greenwood Press.

Nguyen, T., Heslin, R., & Nguyen, M. L. (1976). The meanings of touch: Sex and marital status differences. *Representative Research in Social Psychology, 7,* 13–18.

Regan, P. C., Darell, J., Narvaez, M., & Johnson, D. (1999). Public displays of affection among Asian and Latino heterosexual couples. *Psychological Report, 84,* 1201–1202.

Remland, M. S., Jones, T. S., & Brinkman, H. (1995). Interpersonal distance, body orientation, and touch: Effects of culture, gender, and age. *The Journal of Social Psychology, 135,* 281–297.

Stier, D. S., & Hall, J. A. (1984). Gender differences in touching: An empirical and theoretical review. *Journal of Personality and Social Psychology, 47* (2), 440–459.

Summerhayes, D. L., & Suchner, R. W. (1978). Power implications of touch in male-female relationships. *Sex Roles, 4,* 103–110.

Sussman, N. M., & Rosenfeld, H. M. (1982). Influence of culture, language, and sex on conversation distance. *Journal of Personality and Social Psychology, 42,* 66–74.

Thayer, S. (1988, March). Close encounters. *Psychology Today, 22,* 31–36.

Willis, F. N., Jr., & Briggs, L. F. (1992). Relationship and touch in public settings. *Journal of Nonverbal Behavior, 16,* 55–63.

Willis, F. N., Jr., & Dodds, R. A. (1998). Age, relationship and touch initiation. *The Journal of Social Psychology, 138,* 115–124.

Wolchik, S. L. (1991). *Czechoslovakia in transition: Politics, economics, and society.* London, England: Printers Publishers Limited.

## Review

1. How does touching behavior differ among humans?

2. Explain the following terms: traditional gender roles, a contact culture, and a noncontact culture. Give examples.

3. How does touching behavior vary between the United States, Italy, and the Czech Republic?

4. How would you respond to the claim that because touching behavior is universal, it reflects some kind of biological predisposition?

## Application

Sit in a public place where there are a number of couples (either opposite sex or same sex) talking. Watch a number of couples—one at a time—for five to ten minutes each. Count the number of times touching occurs. Also note the kind of touching and, for opposite-sex couples, whether the touch is by the male or the female. How do your results square with the findings of this selection? If a number of students in the class do this, compare your results. Are there differences in the amount and/or kind of touching between male-female, male-male, and female-female couples? Someone can also be assigned to observe groups of three or more, and see if the additional numbers seem to affect the kind or amount of touching behavior.

## Related Web Sites

1. *http://digilander.libero.it/linguaggiodel corpo/biblio/*. The site of the Nonverbal Library; click the button for "Touch, Skin" for articles and other resources on touching behavior.

2. *http://wrc.lingnet.org/mec.htm*. An article on the way touch enters into various Arab customs and gestures.

Reprinted from: Rosemarie Dibiase and Jaime Gunnoe, "Gender and Culture Differences in Touching Behavior." In *The Journal of Social Psychology* 144 (2004): 49–62. Reprinted with permission of the Helen Dwight Reid Educational Foundation. Published by Heldref Publishers. Copyright © 2004. ✦

# 13
# The Social Life of Interracial Couples

*Dan K. Hibbler*
*Kimberly J. Shinew*

*As noted in the introduction to Part Three, interaction shapes your development. The kind of interaction you have, in fact, is crucial to your well-being. Consider, for example, what happens to the child who grows up unloved or abused by parents, or the young person who is labeled a "nerd," or the woman who is sexually harassed by male co-workers. Such negative interaction experiences depress the quality of life.*

*An important question, therefore, is why people have various kinds of interaction. Do others interact with you simply on the basis of your personality? Or do various social factors affect the nature of your interaction? As the last selection showed, social factors such as gender and culture are important factors in understanding the nature of interaction. In this selection, the researchers look at how* **race** *comes to bear on the way that people interact. In particular, they raise the question of how being an interracial couple has a dramatic impact on leisure activities.*

According to recent empirical studies, various types of interracial relationships have become more common over the course of this century (Kalmijn, 1993). Spickard (1989) explained that romantic relationships between African Americans and European Americans have a long, though not necessarily celebrated, history in America dating back to the nation's colonial past. However, Spickard pointed out that the concept of intermarriage is, by and large, a more recent phenomenon and has recently gained increased attention in the media and in the popular literature. Interracial marriages are more acceptable and common than in the past (Kalmijn, 1993). Today, there are nearly 3 million married interracial couples in the U.S., representing approximately 5% of all marriages (Suro, 1999). Furthermore, Sandor (1994) estimated that there were 2.5 million interracial couples dating. Demographers argue that interracial relationships will continue to grow, producing children and families with their own unique set of social issues (Xie & Goyette, 1997), including issues related to leisure behavior.

A substantial historical literature base suggests that interracial marriage may have a number of negative effects on the couples and their children (Bowles, 1993; Gordon, 1964; Henriques, 1974; McDermott & Fukunagua, 1977; Washington, 1970; Xie & Goyette, 1997). Among the suggested negative effects are anxiety, insecurity, guilt, anger, depression, and identity conflicts (Stephan & Stephan, 1991). On the rare occasions that biracial people and/or interracial couples are asked about their social reality, they often report that the psychological and sociological problems that they face are manifestations of racism and overall societal pressure (Porterfield, 1982; Reddy, 1994; Rosenblatt, Karis, & Powell, 1995; Stephan & Stephan, 1991). This suggests that, perhaps the broader concern is not the issues affecting those involved in interracial relationships, but rather the societal issue of race and the "possessive investment in whiteness" (Lipsitz, 1998, p. vii). Lipsitz explained that "Whiteness" has cash value, which provides advantages to Whites in such areas as employment, housing, education, and health care. He argued that European Americans are encouraged to invest in "Whiteness," to remain true to an identity that provides them with resources, power, and opportunity. This would include making a concerted effort to preserve the purity of the so-called "superior White race" and not allow inferior people of color to pollute that purity. . . .

A related concern is interracial families' perceptions of discrimination (in public places (Feagin, 1991) or more specifically in leisure settings (Floyd, 1998; Philipp, 1999; West, 1989)) and how this impacts their leisure behavior and choices. Feagin (1991) found that African Americans "remain vulnerable targets in public places." Feagin stated, "When blatant acts of avoidance, verbal harassment, and physical attack combine with subtle and covert slights, and these accumulate over months, years, and lifetimes, the impact on a black person is far more than the sum of the individual instances" (p. 115). West (1989) stated that leisure settings are not immune to interracial conflict, and Floyd (1998) suggested that more work needs to be done to investigate the types of range of discrimination and how they impact leisure choices and constraints.

To build on this research, this study examined interracial couples and the role of leisure in addressing the problems they face as a racialized couple. Social network theory was selected as the framework for the study. Floyd and Shinew (1999) stated that understanding social groups and social interaction provides critical insight into leisure choices and meanings.

### Theory

Social network theory was utilized as the theoretical framework to guide the systematic inquiry into the phenomenon of interracial families and leisure. "Network analysis is a style of social science research that focuses on people's social networks as a means toward understanding their behavior" (Fischer, 1977, p. 63). The primary focus of network analysis is on the interpersonal relationships of an individual and his or her various associations. Individuals are linked to their society primarily through relations with other individuals, such as relatives, friends, co-workers, and acquaintances. Each individual is the center of a web of social bonds that radiates outward to people that are known both intimately and casually, and to the wider society (Fischer, 1977). These relationships are considered to be our personal social networks. Researchers (Fischer, 1977; Wellman & Wortley, 1989; Wireman, 1984) have found that Americans utilize social networks to gain support, establish group norms and values, and maintain a modified version of community in spite of the changes taking place in America's social and economic culture. According to Wellman and Wortley (1989), this support is provided in four major dimensions: emotional aid, information, companionship, and financial aid. These four dimensions are frequently utilized to study the depth of an individual's support system and are the foundation of network analysis. Further, Stokowski (1994) explained that one's leisure patterns are significantly influenced by one's social network. Therefore, this theory has been used to help explain leisure behavior in previous research studies. . . .

## Methods

### Sample Selection

The six interracial couples or 12 married "conversational partners" (Rubin & Rubin, 1995, p. 10) who participated in this study were drawn from the Champaign-Urbana (CU), Illinois, community. Conversational partners are individuals who are treated as partners in the research process rather than objects of research. The study was limited to only married African American and European American couples.

Champaign is a city of 65,000 residents with its neighboring city to the East, Urbana, having a population of 35,000 residents. The two cities are also the home of the University of Illinois with an enrollment of approximately 35,000 students. CU is typical of a middle class American university community and has a mean family income level of $36,950 (Destination Champaign, 1993). Currently, the African American population is approximately 14.2% with an Asian population at approximately 4.1%, and a Hispanic and Native American population at less than 1%, respectively (Destination Champaign, 1993). The remaining 80.7% of the population is European American.

To gain a comprehensive understanding of interracial couples and their leisure experiences, attempts were made to diversify the sample in terms of length of time together. The sample included married interracial couples who had been together less than 5 years, more than 10 years, and a couple who has been together more than 15 years. All the conversational partners had a minimum of one child in the home. Same race couples were not interviewed. The data were collected during the spring, summer and fall of 1999 utilizing a purposeful sampling technique. Specifically, a snowballing technique was used to locate the couples, beginning with a couple that was referred by a key informant. . . .

## Data Collection

Long interviewing was selected as the data gathering method for this study. In using long interviews, conversational partners were allowed to expand on general orienting questions. Field notes were taken before and after each interview session, and took the form of a field journal to record thoughts, impressions, initial ideas, working hypotheses, and issues to pursue. Observational data related to the home environment, how the family dressed, mannerisms, and any other data of interest, such as leisure paraphernalia, were also recorded. . . .

Each member of the couple participated in a minimum of one individual interview and one interview as a couple. Some conversational partners participated in additional interviews as part of the member checking process. Each session lasted on average 90 minutes. This was necessary to reach a data saturation point. Also, the interviews were approximately ten days apart. The ten days between sessions allowed time to transcribe tapes, "process," and "internalize" interviews in order to make the most effective use of subsequent interviews.

An interview protocol was used to give the interview sessions a semistructure[d] format. The interview protocol consisted of 19 guiding questions within specific topical areas. The topical areas were interracial relationships, race, socioeconomic class, gender, family, leisure, social networks, and societal issues concerning interracial relationships. All interviews were recorded with an audio recorder and were transcribed verbatim following the interviews. The interviews took place in a combination of mutually agreeable locations—in couples' homes, restaurants, the researcher's office at the University of Illinois, and a public park. The optimal location was in the couples' homes. This provided an opportunity to gather field notes related to the physical setting in which the couples negotiated their daily lives. This information illuminated other issues surrounding the couples' reality and provided dialogue for subsequent interviews. All the conversational partners were assigned a pseudonym to conceal their identity and to ensure confidentiality (results below use these pseudonyms). . . .

## Results

After careful analysis of the study data, one major theme emerged. The interracial couples in this study had limited social networks due to perceived negative societal reactions. The limitations on the couples' social networks were found in the areas of family, work, and leisure. Therefore, the results have been organized by reporting the couples' social network isolation into these three categories.

### Social Networks and Isolation

The couples in this study spoke of being socially isolated due to racism and indicated that this isolation was manifested in family, work, and leisure. Over the years, the conversational partners in this study married, had their first child (and in some cases several children), yet were still navigating through a complex understanding of the nuances related to the uniqueness of being in an interracial relationship. Settling into their newly formed, racialized social network was particularly salient for these couples. As a unit, they were no longer exclusively European American or African American.

A theme that ran through the data was that interracial families have limited social networks due to societal pressures. Friends and family members tended to withdraw from these couples due to issues of race and racism. Therefore, the social network support was limited and affected the physical, emotional, and financial well being of the interracial families. This also significantly impacted the couples' leisure behavior. According to Burch (1969), the nature of intimate social circles of individuals may be the crucial determinate of leisure behavior. The absence of such network support can greatly influence a family's ability to maintain a healthy lifestyle, including leisure, within the societal structure. In reporting the contextual realities of their leisure experience, the couples in this study confirmed the social isolation of interracial families.

## Social Network Isolation: Family

> Nikki: I'm Italian and the majority are very prejudice. My dad said, "That's just how it's going to be Nikki." "You should have married your own race." I said, "If you can't love me for me, then I guess you don't need to be a part of my life. Cause I ain't gonna change for nobody . . ." So, I don't talk to my dad anymore.

As a result of her interracial relationship, Nikki has not spoken to her father in several years. Prior to dating interracially, Nikki had frequent and substantial contact with her father. In fact, she readily admits that he was a major source of various forms of support for her prior to his knowledge of her dating pattern, which she kept secret for three years. However, as Nikki settled into adulthood and fell in love with an African American man, she took full responsibility for her life. She did not allow her friends or family members to dictate how she lived her life, even if that resulted in them no longer being involved with her. Nonetheless, as documented by Fisher (1990), the absence of the support of one's father may play a role in one's ability to maintain a healthy lifestyle and could conceivably affect one's overall long-term quality of life.

The literature related to interracial relationships has historically reported that family members often withdraw from those who choose to marry outside of their race (Rosenblatt et al., 1995). Spickard (1989) argued that this is especially true of the European American partner's family. The African American partner's family has been far more accepting toward interracial marriage than the often violent reactions of the European American partner's family. This tended to be the case with the couples in this study. Nonetheless, European Americans and African Americans agree that the support of family

and friends can be a crucial element in the success and overall health of individuals and families. However, the withdrawal of family members and/or friends appeared to be a frequent pattern among all the couples in this study. Further, in some instances, because of negative reactions from friends and family, it was the couples themselves who made the decision to detach themselves from people, places and situations that made them uncomfortable:

> Phil: I don't _ _ _ _ around with these small towns . . . sometimes her family would end up in small towns and they'll wanna go somewhere. Cori knows me . . . I ain't going. Ya don't _ _ _ _ around in these small towns.

> Tressa: Half of his dad's side of the family didn't like me, so we stay away.

Interracial couples frequently found themselves in situations where they had to deal with racism, discrimination, and prejudice within their own families. Therefore, over time they developed strong coping skills to buffer them from familial and societal influences. It also appeared to bond them as a couple because many of them did not receive the type of support that same-race couples often receive from immediate and extended family members. Paul explains difficulties with family:

> Paul: Things were really bad for a long time. But I think that it strengthens you because you're able to really see yourself and get the support from your spouse. And I think that it helps to clarify your relationship in a way because it helps you get at the root of why you're together as a couple in the first place. But I think it's . . . it's . . . who knows. I mean, I think some people get married for the wrong reasons. And we got married because we loved each other . . . I mean I didn't marry my wife because she was . . . because her grandmother was from Syria or because her father was from Italy. I married her because I loved her. We had some fun doing things together. We had the same vision of where we were going to go in our life. And that's what we did . . . So anyway, it was horrifying for me. The family thing. Because it pointed things out to me

in a way . . . and it made us rely on ourselves . . . much more than maybe we would have if my family had been very supportive. Because other than my father, you know we knew we weren't getting a whole lot of support from very many other people.

Same-race couples may find themselves in situations where they are estranged from their families, but interracial couples frequently experience these estranged relationships specifically due to their partner's racial background. Given the nature of societal reactions to interracial couples, withdrawal of family members becomes increasingly salient to the couple. Although, as Paul stated, a potentially positive outcome of being socially isolated from family members is a strengthened bond between the couple, it should be noted that the lack of familial support can have a long-term, negative impact on couples' lives.

### Social Network Isolation: Work

Wellman and Wortley (1989) indicated that contact with co-workers within the work environment can extend one's social network. Therefore, the potential to extend one's leisure-related personal community through one's work activity is often an extension of social network development. However, the couples in this study reported that they had difficulty establishing relationships with co-workers that extended into their personal leisure time and spaces.

One may never again see the person at the park who stares or, for that matter, the racist uncle who could never accept the relationship from the beginning, if it is a job that the individual enjoys and the income is essential to the financial well being of the family, the people at work may be a part of one's daily life for years. Thus, racism in the workplace can be especially burdensome because work can be a constant and important part of one's life (Rosenblatt et al., 1995). Cori explained a work related situation she encountered as she began her career as an engineer:

Cori: In corporate America . . . I was working in Dubuque, Iowa, which I found out later was a pretty racist place and he [Phil] didn't know that. There had

been Ku Klux Klan people come there a couple of years before I moved there . . . a pretty hot place. Um . . . and he came to visit me and I . . . um . . . asked the management if I could take him on . . . I told him my boyfriend's coming in town and I want to take him on a plant tour. And um . . . he said, "That's great! Wonderful!" So they scheduled the little trucks and the guide and then . . . Phil came and we got on it and they started . . . and uh . . . I think that we got called in. I don't think we . . . I'm almost positive we didn't make it through the whole um . . . tour. And I got called into one of the top executive's office. And I think he said something . . . I don't remember exactly . . . something to the effect that I had made . . . I had um . . . exhibited poor judgment and I was causing disruption in the uh . . . factory. And that he thought that my boyfriend should leave. And I got pretty shy about those sorts of things afterwards. And more so it was . . . it wasn't because of my reputation anyway, but it was because I really made Phil uncomfortable. The fact that he had come out of his way to come there, and then I had to send him home. Just the worst, worst thing! And I never wanted to put him in that sort of position again . . . personal things and race-based things . . . seem to complicate things . . . if I introduce him into my work environment.

Cori explained how from that point on she was ostracized at work, felt uncomfortable, and isolated from her co-workers. Soon after, Cori resigned from that position, but more importantly, she did not introduce her husband and children into her work situation again, which further isolated her family and reduced the possible social support co-workers could have provided. In fact, Cori and Phil ultimately decided to go into business for themselves in an effort to escape the racist treatment experienced in corporate America. The experience was similar for Tressa in her work environment:

Tressa: A guy I worked with knew I was dating a Black man. I can't remember what it was but, whatever it was he was like, "well if you want it, have your boyfriend just steal it." Ted's brother worked there at the time and I guess he set him straight, and I never had any problems with him since . . . in fact, he will hardly say two words to me.

As noted from the self-reports of Cori and Tressa, interracial couples can experience very hurtful situations within the workforce due to being in an interracial relationship. These two women were middle-class, college-educated people who had heavily invested in their careers. It was evident that their work was important to them and represented a major part of their self-identity. Therefore, to be ostracized at work simply because of who they marry was extremely burdensome. The couples in this study were cautious about letting co-workers know that they were involved in an interracial relationship for fear of some form of retaliation.

Therefore, these interracial couples did not have the opportunity to extend their social networks through their work activity. These conversational partners indicated that most of their work acquaintances are just that, acquaintances. They reported that they did not have significant, meaningful relationships with those whom they worked and typically did not extend their relationships with co-workers beyond the realm of the work environment into their personal leisure spaces. In fact, only one of twelve conversational partners indicated that they spent time with a co-worker outside of the work environment. This may have been due to the fact that he was the only White male in the study, affording him an increased level of privilege and access.

## Social Network Isolation: Leisure

Leisure spaces, places, and activities are important locales for the development of social networks. However, these interracial couples found it difficult to establish network ties through their leisure participation. Dominant views of social network formation did not hold for these couples. All the couples involved in this study reported multiple instances of negative leisure experiences due to racism and discrimination, suggesting the Champaign-Urbana community, and perhaps the United States as a whole, are not culturally sensitive to interracial couples and biracial children. These negative experiences constantly affected how they perceived and selected activities. Moreover, this status negatively affected the ultimate outcome of their leisure experiences.

Many U.S. cities are segregated by race, which poses particular problems for interracial couples because they often find themselves attempting to participate in leisure activities in racially homogeneous environments. Whether they participate in leisure within a predominately African American or European American environment, there are issues of comfort for one or both partners and also for their biracial children. The issue of "comfort" based on race and leisure participation must be considered when discussing leisure participation for interracial couples. Philipp (1995) indicated that African Americans felt less comfortable in many leisure spaces than did European Americans. Further, Philipp (1999) found that African Americans felt less welcome in leisure activities than many European Americans thought.

Therefore, it is important to note that some leisure theorists have suggested that leisure may have a negative side as well (Curtis, 1979; Jacobson & Samdahl, 1998; Robertson, 1994; Rojek, 1999). This might include leisure as a context for deviant leisure, sexism or for criminal activities. In this case, it is a setting for racism and discrimination. For example, Ted and Tressa experienced stares, intrusiveness, and hostility when attempting to enjoy leisure experiences. Ted described an evening in a public park when trying to enjoy an outdoor concert:

> Ted: . . . there were stares and that's what's _ _ _ _ _ up . . . which is funny, the stares were from upper class people. Ya know, that I've encountered . . . people who dress nice. Ya know, Tressa came over and sat by me and I gave her a kiss and I saw this guy just . . . him and his wife . . . ya know . . . almost like their mouth dropped . . . people staring and just looking in shock . . . there are always stares.

Ted also explained that he has always enjoyed traveling. According to Edginton, Jordon, DeGraaf, and Edginton (1998), visiting family and friends is one of the primary reasons that people travel, to extend and deepen social network ties. However, since being in an interracial relationship, not only Ted, but also several of the couples had difficulty pursing their passion to travel and to subsequently deepen their social network associations because of the constraints placed upon them by society. Oftentimes the couples could not be assured of safety, and thus elected to withdraw and remain at home or develop an alternative leisure plan. For example, all the couples were averse to traveling in the Southern states:

> Ted: Going through Georgia, I felt unsafe. Going through Virginia I really felt unsafe. I had a person who was dating a White girl, who actually lived there, tell me how bad it was. This was in my mind . . . after that guy in Georgia told me how bad it was. I never encountered it myself, but then I was even more cautious. . . .

> Jan: Um . . . when we were, you know, planning our wedding and all that kind of stuff, and what we were going to do on our honeymoon, I said, "Well," um . . . we kind of got out the MAP and said, "you know, Which direction should we go?" And Bob says to me, "Well, we can't go South." And I said, "Why not?" "What do you mean we can't go South?" He said, "Because it's not going to go over well down there."

It is interesting to note, as is evidenced in the quote above, that whether or not the couple had actually experienced trouble traveling in the South, they all perceived it to be unsafe for them as a couple or as a family.

A recurring theme among these couples was being very "careful" where they go for leisure experiences. It became obvious from the interviews that there was an awareness involved in selecting and participating in leisure activities for interracial couples. There are times when people are able to minimize the likelihood of encountering problems, or diminishing their impact, by being very aware of their surroundings and the places they frequent (McNamara, Tempenis, & Walton, 1999). The couples in this study accomplished this by doing research prior to becoming involved in a leisure experience. For example, they would call ahead, visit a

leisure site prior to exposing family members, or ask friends about the possibility of encountering problems. Nonetheless, even when caution was taken in the leisure selection process, the feelings of real or perceived constraint were rarely forgone due to the constant need to be on guard and feeling the need to protect oneself and family. While probing for deeper explanations, Phil gave the following response when asked why he was constantly on guard:

> Phil: Um . . . for me it is because I am always in protector mode, always . . . always. Ya know and I tell Cori, ya know, you might be relaxed, but I'm not cause I'm always making decisions, looking around, making certain that nobody's runnin up on us . . . I'm very cautious that way . . . in today's climate I'm concerned with racist mentality you know . . . I'm concerned that mutha _ _ _ _ _ are not running up on us . . . my kids and wife are the most precious things in my life. We're pretty nervous folk.

The recurring theme of not feeling "normal" and often being met with hostility was very problematic for the couples. Darla and Pat gave further explanations of experiences and feelings related to interracial couples' leisure experiences:

> Darla: When we go out and stuff we get stares ya know people looking to see if we're together or ya know, my children are all African-American so people are like . . . ya know what's going on with that?

During a vacation to Wrightsville Beach, Pat and her family were refused service at a restaurant and generally received "poor" and "rude" treatment while attempting to experience leisure.

> Pat: We would never go back to Wrightsville Beach. It's on the outer banks of North Carolina. We hope they're about to be devastated by Hurricane ah . . . Daniel. Because my attitude is why should I give my money to someone who . . . can't appreciate the fact that I'm the same as everyone else and why should I give my money to someone who's a jerk.

Along with attempts to research safe places for leisure participation, another pattern for coping with the racism and discrimination was for the couples to withdraw from public spaces as much as possible. Reported directly and implied, many couples just preferred to stay at home and not be seen in public because the aggravation and fear that accompanied their visibility was simply not worth the trouble. Obviously, this limited the couples' social networks, since isolation reduced opportunities to maintain friendships and extended contacts. This placed a greater reliance on family members for support, but as discussed earlier, extended family members were often unsupportive because of their opposition to interracial relationships. Tressa amplifies her feelings of withdrawal:

> Tressa: I don't want to go out and do anything in public any more. Like . . . I used to want to go out if we'd be done with school and stuff . . . when like I didn't have to work or whatever. But now it's like I don't want to because I'd rather just be safe at home and just sit . . . so we can relax, so yeah. So, . . . cause it's so much more relaxing just to sit here and you know, not do anything and not deal with stuff.

The interracial couples preferred to participate in those leisure activities that did not require a great deal of contact with those outside of their relationship, including other extended family members. For example, renting movies for home viewing was reported as a favorite leisure activity by at least one partner of all the couples studied. As previously stated, it was not necessarily the actual activity that was the distinction of interracial families' leisure, but rather the process they went through to in order to engage in leisure. Interracial couples' constant concern for safety and comfort limited their ability to establish and maintain meaningful social network ties within a leisure context.

## Discussion and Implications

This research suggests that the construction of attitudes and opinions concerning leisure among interracial couples and their families are distinct from those of same-race couples and families. The essential difference in participation patterns seem[s] to relate to the social and cultural practices that influenced and defined the range and reach of leisure activities chosen from, as well as ultimately selected. For example, a major finding of this study was the process that interracial couples went through in order to participate in leisure activities. The couples did extensive research regarding a leisure opportunity prior to participation to ensure comfort and even psychological and physical safety. Often times the couples would send the White or Black partner into a leisure setting as a tester to "get a feel" for the environment prior to exposing the entire family to a situation. The couples would frequently call a leisure service provider to inquire about multiculturalism and issues of safety to interracial families. Also, they indicated that they would "read up" or ask friends about leisure experiences before investing time and emotional energy. For all the couples in this study, it became part of their standard operating procedure to thoroughly investigate leisure offerings prior to participation, in an attempt to not subject themselves or their children to overt racism.

It was found that interracial couples in this study experienced significant levels of social isolation due to issues related to racism. The results clearly indicated that racism was an important leisure constraint for interracial couples. The couples were very vocal in reporting how racism, discrimination and prejudices affected their leisure participation. Whether perceived or real, interracial couples felt uncomfortable in various leisure settings due to their racialized status. Philipp (1995) found that African Americans and European Americans had different levels of comfort on a wide variety of leisure activities. Philipp argued that African Americans tended to feel more uncomfortable in a greater number of activities than did European Americans, due to issues of race and discrimination. This study supports his findings in that all the couples reported that they have experienced "racist treatment" while attempting to participate in family leisure. Further, in the initial stages of the couples' relationships, the European

American partner was often personally unaware of the depth of racial discriminatory treatment, but later in the relationship that partner also began to feel that the discrimination was transferred onto them and their children, causing tension in their racial ideology. The European American partner was faced with losing much of his or her White privilege due to being involved with an African American partner. The White partner would appear to lose much of their social status by being in a relationship with a nonwhite person. The salient issue was that due to issues of race, interracial couples' social networks were limited and this negatively impacted their leisure involvement.

The information collected from these conversational partners did not support all aspects of social network theory, but did demonstrate the significant practice of social network theory in the daily lives of interracial couples. For example, this study supported Stokowski and Lee's (1991) findings that social network relationships facilitate and also constrain social behaviors within a leisure context. In listening to the couples' stories, it became clear that social relationships were extremely meaningful in the day-to-day social realities of these families. Further, by examining the families' social networks, certain aspects of their leisure behavior were better understood. For example, due to social network isolation, interracial families tended to gravitate toward home-based leisure activities to avoid the negative influences of societal pressure. Stokowski and Lee (1991) identified several social network interactions within a leisure setting, including social isolates. Social isolates are those who reported no or weak ties with others within a given community. Further, Stokowski and Lee's study indicated that the recreation patterns of socially isolated people reflected the constraints of their life-style or limited social connections. There is congruence between their findings and the findings of this study related to interracial families' leisure participation. However, for interracial couples in this study, the core of their isolation was perceived to be externally imposed by the negative influences of society, whereas other social isolates may have chosen to withdraw from network participation. . . .

## References

Bowles, D. D. (1993). Bi-racial identity: Children born to African-American and white couples. *Clinical Social Work Journal*, 21 (4), 417–428.

Burch, W. R. (1969). The social circles of leisure: Competing explanations. *Journal of Leisure Research*, 1 (2), 125–147.

Curtis, J. E. (1979). *Recreation: Theory and practice*. St. Louis: Mosby.

Destination Champaign: 21st Century. (1993). Comprehensive plan update (City inventory). August 1993.

Edginton, C., Jordan, D., DeGraaf D., & Edginton, S. (1998). *Leisure and life satisfaction: Foundational perspectives*. Boston: McGraw-Hill.

Feagin, J. R. (1991). The continuing significance of race: Antiblack discrimination in public places. *American Sociological Review*, 56 (1), 101–116.

Fischer, C. (1977). *Network and places: Social relations in the urban setting*. New York: The Free Press.

Fisher, W. A. (1990). A theory-based framework for intervention and evaluation in STD/HIV prevention. *The Canadian Journal of Human Sexuality* [On-line]. Available: *http://hweweb.hwe.ca/hpb/lede/publicat/cjhs/cjhs3.html*.

Floyd, M. F. (1998). Getting beyond marginality and ethnicity: The challenge for race and ethnic studies in leisure research. *Journal of Leisure Research*, 30, 3–22.

Floyd, M. F., & Shinew, K. J. (1999). Convergence and divergence in leisure style among Whites and African Americans: Toward an interracial contact hypothesis. *Journal of Leisure Research*, 31, 359–384.

Gordon, A. I. (1964). *Intermarriage: Interfaith, interracial interethnic*. Boston: Beacon Press.

Henriques, F. (1974). *Children of Caliban: Miscegenation*. London: Seeker & Warburg.

Jacobson, S., & Samdahl, D. M. (1998). Leisure in the lives of old lesbians: Experiences with and responses to discrimination. *Journal of Leisure Research*, 30 (2), 233–255.

Kalmijn, M. (1993). Trends in black/white intermarriage. *Social Forces*, 72 (1), 1196.

Lipsitz, G. (1998). *The possessive investment in whiteness: How white people profit from identity politics*. Philadelphia: Temple University Press.

McDermott, J. F., & Fukunagua, C. (1977). Intercultural family interaction patterns. In WenShing Teng, J. F. McDermott, & T. W. Maretzki (Eds.), *Adjustment to intercultural marriage*. Honolulu: University Press of Hawaii.

McNarmara, K. P., Tempenis, M., & Walton, B. (1999). *Crossing the line: Interracial couples in the South*. Westport, CT: Praeger.

Philipp, S. F. (1995). Race and leisure constraints. *Leisure Sciences*, 17, 109–120.

———. (1999). Are we welcome? African-American racial acceptance in leisure activities and the importance given to children's leisure. *Journal of Leisure Research*, 31 (4), 385–403.

Porterfield, E. (1982). Black-American intermarriage in the United States. *Marriage & Family Review*, 5 (1), 17–34.

Reddy, M. T. (1994). *Crossing the color line: Race, parenting, and culture*. New Brunswick, NJ: Rutgers University Press.

Robertson, B. J. (1994). An investigation of leisure in the lives of adolescents who engage in delinquent behavior for fun, thrills, and excitement. *Dissertation Abstracts International Section A: Humanities & Social Sciences*, 54 (12-A), 4587.

Rojek, C. (1999). Deviant leisure: The dark side of free-time activity. In E. L. Jackson and T. L. Burton (Eds.), *Leisure studies: Prospects for the twenty-first century* (81–95). State College, PA: Venture Publishing, Inc.

Rosenblatt, P. C., Karis, T. A., & Powell, R. D. (1995). *Multiracial couples: Black and white voices*. Thousand Oaks, CA: Sage.

Rubin, H. J., & Rubin, I. S. (1995). *Qualitative interviewing: The art of hearing data*. Thousand Oaks, CA: Sage.

Sandor, G. (1994). The other Americans. *American Demographics*, 16 (6), 21–29.

Spickard, P. R. (1989). *Mixed blood: Intermarriage and ethnic identity in twentieth-century America*. Madison: The University of Wisconsin Press.

Stephan, W. G., & Stephan, C. W. (1991). Intermarriage: Effects on personality, adjustment, and intergroup relations in two samples of students. *Journal of Marriage and the Family*, 53, 241–250.

Stokowski, P. A. (1994). *Leisure in society: A network structural perspective*. New York: Mansell.

Stokowski, P. A., & Lee, K. G. (1991). The influence of social network ties on recreation and leisure: An exploratory study. *Journal of Leisure Research*, 23 (2), 95–113.

Suro, R. (1999). Mixed doubles. *American Demographics*, 11, 57–62.

Washington, J. R. (1970). *Marriage in black and white*. Boston: Beacon Press.

———. (1990). Different strokes from different folks: Community ties and social support. *American Journal of Sociology*, 96 (3), 558–588.

Wellman, B., & Wortley, S. (1989). Brothers' keepers: Situating kinship relations in broader networks of social support. *Sociological Perspectives*, 32 (3), 273–306.

West, P. C. (1989). Urban region parks and black minorities: Subculture, marginality, and interracial relations in park use in the Detroit metropolitan area. *Leisure Sciences*, 11, 11–28.

Wireman, P. (1984). *Urban neighborhoods, networks, and families: New forms for old values*. Lexington: Lexington Books.

Xie, Y., & Goyette, K. (1997). The racial identification of biracial children with one Asian parent: Evidence from the 1990 census. *Social Forces*, 76 (2), 547–570.

## Review

1. What are some of the social consequences of being in an interracial marriage?

2. Describe the family life experienced by interracial couples.

3. How does being in an interracial marriage affect one's relationships with co-workers?

4. Discuss the way in which interracial couples deal with leisure activities.

## Applications

1. Use one or more of the newspaper indices available in the library to find articles over the past two years about interracial marriages. Compare the information you find in the articles with that in this selection. What conclusions would you draw about interracial marriage?

2. Find an interracial couple—dating, cohabiting, or married. Briefly share with them the information from this selection. Ask them to comment in terms of their own experiences. Do they give you a similar or different picture than does

this selection of the social life of interracial couples?

## Related Web Sites

1. *http://www.multiracial.com/links/links-interracial.html.* A site that offers support and guidance to interracial couples.

2. *http://www.delawareonline.com/newsjournal/life/2003/03/07interracial* *coup.html.* A newspaper article on the growing acceptance of interracial couples.

---

# Unit III

## *Inequality*

Inequality is a central concept in sociological analysis. Inequality exists in all societies, because every society has a **stratification** system—an arrangement of the society into groups that are unequal with regard to things valued in that society. In the United States and other modern societies, the groups are called **social classes** and the "things valued" include wealth and possessions, power, and prestige. In general, those at the top of the stratification system have the highest incomes, the best occupations (which bring them prestige as well as income), and the most power.

Although all societies are unequal, equality is one of humanity's most profound ideals. Whether embodied in the Founding Fathers' notion that "all men are created equal," Marx's vision of a communist society of equal rewards, or the feminist goal of an Equal Rights Amendment, the desire for equality has stirred the passions of the masses throughout history.

Nevertheless, a society with complete equality has never existed. And, while the ideal itself is still important to many people, others deny its value or at least its practicality. For instance, the prominent sociological theory of structural functionalism asserts that unequal rewards must necessarily be at-tached to various positions in a society in order to motivate people to hold those positions. In this view, the complete equality of rewards would be a "sociological monstrosity." How could people be motivated to take up important but arduous jobs without concomitant higher rewards? Such a society, according to these theorists, could not work.

Another way to look at the issue is more pragmatic. We accept the fact that inequality always has and always will exist. The issue then is, how much inequality is acceptable? It is unlikely that consensus can be obtained on this issue. Therefore, society will experience ongoing conflict as various groups strive to obtain what they view as their fair share of valued things.

The selections in this unit (selections 14–23) illustrate this last point. They each involve some kind of conflict between groups over the fairness of the distribution of valued things. Many people not only have less but also feel deprived by those above them. For them inequality means not just that they have fewer valued things than others, but that they have less than their rightful share. The deprived groups include the lower social classes, people in lower-level occupations, the homeless, racial/ethnic groups, women, and those in poorer nations. ✦

# Part One

## *The Nature of Inequality*

While structural functionalism can be used to justify a certain amount of inequality, conflict theory generally is used to attack inequalities. There are, in other words, different perspectives on the causes and consequences of inequality in a society.

One point, however, is indisputable: Everyone in the world lives in a system of inequality. There are no societies where perfect equality exists. The kind of inequality any particular individual faces, however, may vary from one society to another. The selections in this part probe the causes and nature of inequality. Selection 14 offers Marx's classic statement about social classes. Selection 15 argues that poverty is rooted in the social structure, not in individual failings. Selection 16 examines the plight of those at the bottom of America's stratification system. ✦

# 14
# The Communist Manifesto

*Karl Marx*
*Friedrich Engels*

*The work of Marx must be regarded as the starting point for the sociological analysis of* **stratification** *in societies. His fundamental insight here is that societies are divided into potentially conflicting groups on the basis of the ownership or control of productive property (i.e., land, natural resources, commercial and industrial enterprises, etc.). In Marx's view, the primary division in industrial society was between the* **capitalists** *or bourgeoisie and the workers or proletariat. While he recognized the existence of other classes in industrial society, they were of secondary importance. After all, it was the class conflict between the bourgeoisie and the proletariat which was to propel society on to its next historical stage, socialism.*

*While Marx was incorrect in a number of his predictions about the future of capitalism, many of his ideas have stood the test of time and continue to illuminate current events. For instance, Marx observed that the ruling class in a society is dominant by virtue of its superior material or economic position; but this dominance is also reflected in the legal and political system and in the whole range of beliefs and ideology. Ideas, then, simply mirror material reality. Therefore, revolutionary ideas are impotent without a basis in material reality, such as a proletarian class experiencing privation and misery.*

*Marx overestimated the extent to which capitalism would inflict miserable working and living conditions on the proletariat. He never anticipated the welfare state or government intervention on behalf of workers. Yet his insight into the inherent conflict of interest between the owners and the workers is still*

*valid. As the history of the labor movement dramatizes, any gains made by those in the lower levels of the stratification system come through struggle, threat, and coercive action rather than through the generosity and sense of fair play of those in positions of power.*

## I. Bourgeois and Proletarians

The history of all hitherto existing society is the history of class struggles.

Freeman and slave, patrician and plebeian, lord and serf, guild-master and journeyman, in a word, oppressor and oppressed, stood in constant opposition to one another, carried on an uninterrupted, now hidden, now open fight, a fight that each time ended either in a revolutionary reconstitution of society at large, or in the common ruin of the contending classes.

In the earlier epochs of history, we find almost everywhere a complicated arrangement of society into various orders, a manifold gradation of social rank. In ancient Rome we have patricians, knights, plebeians, slaves; in the Middle Ages, feudal lords, vassals, guild-masters, journeymen, apprentices, serfs; in almost all of these classes, again, subordinate gradations.

The modern bourgeois society that has sprouted from the ruins of feudal society has not done away with class antagonisms. It has but established new classes, new conditions of oppression, new forms of struggle in place of the old ones.

Our epoch, the epoch of the bourgeoisie, possesses, however, this distinctive feature; it has simplified the class antagonisms. Society as a whole is more and more splitting up into two great hostile camps, into two great classes directly facing each other: Bourgeoisie and Proletariat.

From the serfs of the Middle Ages sprang the chartered burghers of the earliest towns. From these burgesses the first elements of the bourgeoisie were developed.

The discovery of America, the rounding of the Cape, opened up fresh ground for the rising bourgeoisie. The East-Indian and Chinese markets, the colonization of America, trade with the colonies, the increase in the means of exchange and in commodities generally, gave to commerce, to navigation, to industry, an impulse never before known, and thereby, to the revolutionary element in the tottering feudal society, a rapid development.

The feudal system of industry, in which industrial production was monopolized by closed guilds, now no longer sufficed for the growing wants of the new markets. The manufacturing system took its place. The guild-masters were pushed on one side by the manufacturing middle-class; division of labor between the different corporate guilds vanished in the face of division of labor in each single workshop. Meantime the markets kept ever growing, the demand, ever rising. Even manufacture no longer sufficed. Thereupon steam and machinery revolutionized industrial production. The place of manufacture was now taken by the giant, modern industry, the place of the industrial middle-class, by industrial millionaires, the leaders of whole industrial armies, the modern bourgeoisie.

Modern industry has established the world market, for which the discovery of America paved the way. This market has given an immense development to commerce, to navigation, to communication by land. This development has, in its turn, reacted on the extension of industry; and in proportion as industry, commerce, navigation, railways extended, in the same proportion the bourgeoisie developed, increased its capital, and pushed into the background every class handed down from the Middle Ages. We see, therefore, how the modern bourgeoisie is itself the product of a long course of development, of a series of revolutions in the modes of production and of exchange. . . .

The bourgeoisie has played a most revolutionary role in history. The bourgeoisie, wherever it has got the upper hand, has put an end to all feudal, patriarchal, idyllic relations. It has pitilessly torn asunder the motley feudal ties that bound man to his natural superiors, and has left remaining no other bond between man and man than naked self-interest, than callous cash payment. It has drowned the most heavenly ecstacies of religious fervor, of chivalrous enthusiasm, of philistine sentimentalism, in the icy water of egotistical calculation. It has resolved personal worth into exchange value, and in place of the numberless indefeasible chartered freedoms, has set up that single, unconscionable freedom, Free Trade. In one word, for exploitation, veiled by religious and political illusions, it has substituted naked, shameless, direct, brutal exploitation.

The bourgeoisie has stripped of its halo every occupation hitherto honored and looked up to with reverent awe. It has converted the physician, the lawyer, the priest, the poet, the man of science, into its paid wage-laborers.

The bourgeoisie has torn away from the family its sentimental veil, and has reduced the family relation to a mere money relation.

The bourgeoisie has disclosed how it came to pass that the brutal display of vigor in the Middle Ages, which Reactionists so much admire, found its fitting complement in the most slothful indolence. It has been the first to show what man's activity can bring about. It has accomplished wonders far surpassing Egyptian pyramids, Roman aqueducts, and Gothic cathedrals; it has conducted expeditions that put in the shade all former migrations of nations and crusades.

The bourgeoisie cannot exist without constantly revolutionizing the instruments of production, and thereby the relations of production, and with them the whole relations of society. Conservation of the old modes of production in unaltered form was, on the contrary, the first condition of existence for all earlier industrial classes. Constant revolutionizing of production, uninterrupted disturbance of all social conditions, everlasting certainty and agitation distinguish the bourgeois epoch from all earlier ones. All fixed, fast-frozen relations, with their train of ancient and venerable prejudices and opinions, are swept away, all new-formed ones become antiquated before they can ossify. All that is solid melts into air, all that is holy is profaned, and man is at last compelled to face with sober senses his real conditions of life, and his relations with his kind. The need of a constantly expanding market chases the bourgeoisie over the whole surface of the globe. It must nestle everywhere, settle everywhere, establish connections everywhere.

The bourgeoisie has through its exploitation of the world-market given a cosmopolitan character to production and consumption in every country. To the great chagrin of Reactionists, it has drawn from under the feet of industry the national ground on which it stood. All old-established national industries have been destroyed or are daily being destroyed. They are dislodged by new industries, whose introduction becomes a life and death question for all civilized nations, by industries that no longer work up indigenous raw material, but raw material drawn from the remotest zones; industries whose products are consumed, not only at home, but in every quarter of the globe. In place of the old wants, satisfied by the production of the country, we find new wants, requiring for their satisfaction the products of distant lands and climes. In place of the old local and national seclusion and self-sufficiency, we have intercourse in every direction, universal interdependence of nations. And as in material, so also in intellectual production. The intellectual creations of individual nations become common property. National one-sidedness and narrow-mindedness become more and more impossible, and from the numerous national and local literatures there arises a world literature.

The bourgeoisie, by the rapid improvement of all instruments of production, by the immensely facilitated means of communication, draws all, even the most barbarian, nations into civilization. The cheap prices of its commodities are the heavy artillery with which it batters down all Chinese walls, with which it forces the barbarians' intensely obstinate hatred of foreigners to capitulate. It compels all nations, on pain of extinction, to adopt the bourgeois mode of production; it compels them to introduce what it calls civilization into their midst, i.e., to become bourgeois themselves. In a word, it creates a world after its own image.

The bourgeoisie has subjected the country to the rule of the towns. It has created enormous cities, has greatly increased the urban population as compared with the rural, and has thus rescued a considerable part of the population from the idiocy of rural life. Just as it has made the country dependent on the towns, so it has made barbarian and semi-barbarian countries dependent on the civilized ones, nations of peasants on nations of bourgeois, the East on the West.

The bourgeoisie keeps more and more doing away with the scattered state of the population, of the means of production, and of property. It has agglomerated population, centralized means of production, and has concentrated property in a few hands. The necessary consequence of this was political centralization. Independent, or but loosely connected provinces, with separate interests, laws, systems of taxation, and governments, became lumped together in one nation, with one government, one code of laws, one national class-interest, one frontier, and one customs tariff.

The bourgeoisie, during its rule of scarce one hundred years, has created more massive and more colossal productive forces than have all preceding generations together. Subjection of Nature's forces to man, machinery, application of chemistry to industry and agriculture, steam-navigation, railways, electric telegraphs, clearing of whole continents for cultivation, canalization of rivers, whole populations conjured out of the ground. What earlier century had even a presentiment that such productive forces slumbered in the lap of social labor?. . .

Modern bourgeois society with its relations of production, of exchange and of property, a society that has conjured up such gigantic means of production and of exchange, is like the sorcerer, who is no longer able to control the powers of the nether world whom he has called up by his spells. For many a decade past the history of industry and commerce is but the history of the revolt of modern productive forces against modern conditions of production, against the property relations that are the conditions for the existence of the bourgeoisie and of its rule. It is enough to mention the commercial crises that by their periodical return put on its trial, each time more threateningly, the existence of the entire bourgeois society. In these crises a great part not only of the existing products but also of the previously created forces are periodically destroyed. In these crises, there breaks out an epidemic that, in all earlier epochs, would have seemed an absurdity, the epidemic of overproduction. Society suddenly finds itself put back into a state of momentary barbarism, it appears as if a famine, a universal war of devastation had cut off the supply of every means of subsistence, industry and commerce seem to be destroyed; and why? Because there is too much civilization, too much means of subsistence, too much industry, too much commerce. . . .

And how does the bourgeoisie get over these crises? On the one hand by enforced destruction of a mass of productive forces; on the other, by the conquest of new markets, and by the more thorough exploitation of the old ones. That is to say, by paving the way for more extensive and more destructive crises, and by diminishing the means whereby crises are prevented.

The weapons with which the bourgeoisie felled feudalism to the ground are now turned against the bourgeoisie itself.

But not only has the bourgeoisie forged the weapons that bring death to itself, it has also called into existence the men who are to wield those weapons, the modern workingclass, the proletarians.

In proportion as the bourgeoisie, i.e., capital, is developed, in the same proportion is the proletariat, the modern working-class, developed a class of laborers, who live only so long as they find work, and who find work only so long as their labor increases capital. These laborers, who must sell themselves piecemeal, are a commodity, like every other article of commerce, and are consequently exposed to all the vicissitudes of the market.

Owing to the extensive use of machinery and to division of labor, the work of the proletarians has lost all individual character, and, consequently, all charm for the workman. He becomes an appendage of the machine, and it is only the most simple, most monotonous, and most easily acquired knack that is required of him. . . .

Modern industry has converted the little workshop of the patriarchal master into the great factory of the industrial capitalist. Masses of laborers, crowded into the factory, are organized like soldiers. As privates of the industrial army they are placed under the command of a perfect hierarchy of officers and sergeants. Not only are they the slaves of the bourgeois class, and of the bourgeois State, they are daily and hourly enslaved by the machine, by the overlooker, and, above all, by the individual bourgeois manufacturer himself. The more openly this despotism proclaims gain to be its end and aim, the more petty, the more hateful and the more embittering it is. . . .

The lower strata of the middle class, the small tradespeople, shopkeepers, and retired tradesmen generally, the handicraftsman and peasants, all these sink gradually into the proletariat, partly because their diminutive capital does not suffice for the scale on which Modern Industry is carried on, and is swamped in the competition with the large capitalists, partly because their specialized skill is rendered worthless by new methods of production. Thus the proletariat is recruited from all classes of the population.

The proletariat goes through various stages of development.With its birth begins its struggle with the bourgeoisie. At first the contest is carried on by individual laborers, then by the workpeople of a factory, then by the operatives of one trade, in one locality, against the individual bourgeois who directly exploits them. They direct their attacks not against the bourgeois conditions of production, but against the instruments of production themselves; they destroy imported wares that compete with their labor, they smash to pieces machinery, they set factories ablaze, they seek to restore by force the vanished status of the workman of the Middle Ages.

At this stage the laborers still form an incoherent mass scattered over the whole country, and broken up by their mutual competition. If anywhere they unite to form more compact bodies, this is not yet the consequence of their own active union, but of the union of the bourgeoisie, which class, in order to attain its own political ends, is compelled to set the whole proletariat in motion, and is moreover yet, for a time, able to do so. At this stage, therefore, the proletarians do not fight their enemies, but the enemies of their enemies, the remnants of absolute monarchy, the landowners, the non-industrial bourgeois, the petty bourgeoisie. Thus the whole historical movement is concentrated in the hands of the bourgeoisie; every victory so obtained is a victory for the bourgeoisie.

But with the development of industry the proletariat not only increases in number, it becomes concentrated in greater masses, its strength grows, and it feels that strength more. The various interests and conditions of life within the ranks of the proletariat are more and more equalized, in proportion as machinery obliterates all distinctions of labor and nearly everywhere reduces wages to the same low level. The growing competition among the bourgeoisie, and the resulting commercial crises, make the wages of the workers ever more fluctuating. The unceasing improvement of machinery, ever more rapidly developing, makes their livelihood more and more precarious; the collisions between individual workmen and individual bourgeoisie take more and more the character of collisions between two classes. Thereupon the workers begin to form combinations (Trades' Unions) against the bourgeois, they club together in order to keep up the rate of wages; they found permanent associations in order to make provision beforehand for these occasional revolts. Here and there the contest breaks out into riots.

Now and then the workers are victorious, but only for a time. The real fruit of their battles lies not in the immediate result, but in the ever expanding union of the workers. This union is helped on by the improved means of communication that are created by modern industry, and that place the workers of different localities in contact with one another. It was just this contact that was needed to centralize the numerous local struggles, all of the same character, into one national struggle between classes. But every class struggle is a political struggle. And that union, to attain which the burghers of the Middle Ages, with their miserable highways, required centuries, the modern proletarians, thanks to railways, achieve in a few years.

This organization of the proletarians into a class, and consequently into a political party, is continually being upset again by the competition between the workers themselves. But it ever rises up again, stronger, firmer, mightier. . . .

Further, as we have already seen, entire sections of the ruling classes are, by the advance of industry, precipitated into the proletariat, or are at least threatened in their conditions of existence. These also supply the proletariat with fresh elements of enlightenment and progress.

Finally, in times when the class-struggle nears the decisive hour, the process of dissolution going on within the ruling class, in fact, within the whole range of old society, assumes such a violent, glaring character, that a small section of the ruling class cuts itself adrift, and joins the revolutionary class, the class that holds the future in its hands. Just as, therefore, at an earlier period, a section of the nobility went over to the bourgeoisie, so now a portion of the bourgeoisie goes over to the proletariat, and in particular, a portion of the bourgeois ideologists, who have raised themselves to the level of comprehending theoretically the historical movements as a whole.

Of all the classes that stand face to face with the bourgeoisie today, the proletariat alone is a really revolutionary class. The other classes decay and finally disappear in the face of modern industry; the proletariat is its special and essential product.

The lower middle class, the small manufacturer, the shopkeeper, the artisan, the peasant, all these fight against the bourgeoisie, to save from extinction their existence as fractions of the middle class. They are, therefore, not revolutionary, but conservative. Even more, they are reactionary, for they try to roll back the wheel of history. If by chance they are revolutionary, they are so, only in view of their impending transfer into the proletariat, they thus defend not their present, but their future interests, they desert their own standpoint to place themselves at that of the proletariat. . . .

All previous historical movements were movements of minorities, or in the interest of minorities. The proletarian movement is the self-conscious, independent movement of the immense majority, in the interest of the immense majority. The proletariat, the lowest stratum of our present society, cannot stir, cannot raise itself up, without the whole super-incumbent strata of official society being sprung into the air.

Though not in substance, yet in form, the struggle of the proletariat with the bourgeoisie is at first a national struggle. The proletariat of each country must first of all settle matters with its bourgeoisie.

In depicting the most general phases of the development of the proletariat, we traced the more or less veiled civil war, raging within existing society, up to the point where that war breaks out into open revolution, and where the violent overthrow of the bourgeoisie lays the foundation for the sway of the proletariat.

Hitherto, every form of society has been based, as we have already seen, on the antagonism of oppressing and oppressed classes. But in order to oppress a class, certain conditions must be assured to it under which it can, at least, continue its slavish existence. The serf, in the period of serfdom, raised himself to membership in the commune, just as the petty bourgeois, under the yoke of feudal absolutism, managed to develop into a bourgeois. The modern laborer, on the contrary, instead of rising with the progress of industry, sinks deeper and deeper below the conditions of existence of his own class. He becomes a pauper, and pauperism develops more rapidly than population and wealth. And here it becomes evident that the bourgeoisie is unfit any longer to be the ruling class in society, and to impose its conditions of existence upon society, as an overriding law. It is unfit to rule, because it is incompetent to assure an existence to its slave within his slavery, because it cannot help letting him sink into such a state that it has to feed him. Society can no longer live under this bourgeoisie, in other words, its existence is no longer compatible with society.

The essential condition for the existence, and for the sway, of the bourgeois class is the formation and augmentation of capital; the condition for capital is wage-labor. Wage-labor rests exclusively on competition between the laborers. The advance of industry, whose involuntary promoter is the bourgeoisie, replaces the isolation of the laborers, due to competition, by their involuntary combination, due to association. The development of Modern Industry therefore cuts from under its feet the very foundation on which the bourgeoisie produces and appropriates products. What the bourgeoisie therefore produces, above all, are its own grave-diggers. Its fall and the victory of the proletariat are equal. . . .

The Communist revolution is the most radical rupture with traditional property relations; no wonder its development involves the most radical rupture with the traditional ideas of all of the bourgeoisie. But let us have done with the bourgeois objections to Communism.

We have seen above, that the first step in the revolution by the working class, is to raise the proletariat to the position of ruling class, to win the battle of democracy.

The proletariat will use its political supremacy to wrest, by degrees, all capital from the bourgeoisie, to centralize all instruments of production in the hands of the State, i.e., of the proletariat organized as the ruling class, and to increase the total of productive forces as rapidly as possible.

Of course, in the beginning, this cannot be effected except by means of despotic inroads on the rights of property, and on the conditions of bourgeois production; by means of measures, therefore, which appear economically insufficient and untenable, but which, in the course of the movement, outstrip themselves, necessitate further inroads upon the old social order, and are unavoidable as a means of entirely revolutionizing the mode of production.

These measures will of course be different in different countries.

Nevertheless in the most advanced countries the following will be found pretty generally applicable:

1. Abolition of property in land and application of all rents of land to public purposes.

2. A heavy progressive or graduated income tax.

3. Abolition of all right of inheritance.

4. Confiscation of property of emigrants and rebels.

5. Centralization of credit in the hands of the State, by means of a national bank with State capital and an exclusive monopoly.

6. Centralization of the means of communication and transport in the hands of the State.

7. Extension of factories and instruments of production owned by the State; the bringing into cultivation of waste lands, and the improvement of soil generally in accordance with a common plan.

8. Equal liability of all to labor. Establishment of industrial armies, especially for agriculture.

9. Combination of agriculture with manufacturing industries; gradual abolition of the distinction between town and country, by a more equable distribution of population over the country.

10. Free education for all children in public schools. Abolition of children's factory labor in its present form. Combination of education with industrial production, etc.

When, in the course of development, class distinctions have disappeared, and all production has been concentrated in the hands of a vast association of the whole nation, the public power will lose its political character. Political power, properly so called, is merely the organized power of one class for oppressing another. If the proletariat during its contest with the bourgeoisie is compelled, by the force of circumstances, to organize itself as a class, if, by means of a revolution, it makes itself the ruling class, and, as such, sweeps away by force the old conditions of produc-

tion, then it will, along with these conditions, have swept away the conditions for the existence of class antagonisms, and of classes generally, and will thereby have abolished its own supremacy as a class.

In place of the old bourgeois society, with its classes and class antagonisms, we shall have an association, in which the free development of each is the condition for the free development of all.

## Review

1. What has been the role of the bourgeoisie in history?

2. How does the bourgeoisie handle crises?

3. Describe the development and life of the proletariat.

4. How will communism change the nature of social life?

## Application

Interview one person in the working class (a member of a labor union) and another person who is an owner or executive. Develop and use a questionnaire that addresses the following:

a. perception of the existence and types of classes in the United States

b. perception of how class conflict is manifested

c. advantages and disadvantages of being in the different classes

d. opinion about Marx's ideas

e. opinion about the amount of inequality in the United States. Is it too much? Why or why not? If so, how could it be reduced?

Summarize your findings, contrasting the responses given by the two respondents.

## Related Web Sites

1. *http://www.marxists.org/*. Archives of Marxist writers, with access to over 300 authors.

2. *http://www.marxist.com/150years/trotskyintro.html.* Leon Trotsky's commentary on the Communist Manifesto 90 years after its publication.

# 15
# American Poverty as a Structural Failing

*Mark R. Rank*
*Hong-Sik Yoon*
*Thomas A. Hirschl*

*In the first selection of this reader, C. Wright Mills used the problem of unemployment to illustrate the difference between an individualistic and a sociological understanding. In essence, an individualistic approach asks what is wrong with the person who has a problem, while the sociological approach asks what is happening in the social structure that creates problems for people. Marx and Engels, in the last selection, also took a sociological approach. They argued that the problems of a capitalistic society are built into its very structure. Inequality, then, is not the result of those at the top of the social order being more motivated or capable than all others. Rather, inequality reflects the nature of the social structure itself.*

*In this selection, Rank, Yoon, and Hirschl further elaborate the sociological approach by showing how poverty is an inevitable outcome of the American political economy as it is now structured. Indeed, that structure guarantees that there will always be a certain number of people living in poverty. If, therefore, Americans continue to place the blame for such problems as poverty on individual deficiencies or failings, efforts to resolve the problems necessarily will fail.*

Few questions have generated as much discussion across time as that of the causes of human impoverishment. The sources and origins of poverty have been debated for centuries. As the historian R. M. Hartwell notes, "The causes of poverty, its relief and cure, have been a matter of serious concern to theologians, statesmen, civil servants, intellectuals, tax-payers and humanitarians since the Middle Ages" (1986: 16). The question of causality has found itself at the heart of most debates surrounding poverty and the poor.

In recent times these debates have often been divided into two ideological camps. On one hand, poverty has been viewed as the result of individual failings. From this perspective, specific attributes of the impoverished individual have brought about their poverty. These include a wide set of characteristics, ranging from the lack of an industrious work ethic or virtuous morality, to low levels of education or competitive labor market skills. On the other hand, poverty has periodically been interpreted as the result of failings at the structural level, such as the inability of the economy to produce enough decent paying jobs.

Within the United States, the dominant perspective has been that of poverty as an individual failing. From Ben Franklin's Poor Richard's Almanac to the recent welfare reform changes, poverty has been conceptualized primarily as a consequence of individual failings and deficiencies. Indeed, social surveys asking about the causes of poverty have consistently found that Americans tend to rank individual reasons (such as laziness, lack of effort, and low ability) as the most important factors related to poverty, while structural reasons such as unemployment or discrimination are viewed as significantly less important (Feagin, 1975; Gilens, 1999; Kluegel and Smith, 1986).

This emphasis on individual attributes as the primary cause of poverty has also been reinforced by social scientists engaged in poverty research (O'Connor, 2001). As the social survey has become the dominant methodological approach during the past 50 years, and with multivariate modeling becoming the principal statistical technique, the research emphasis has increasingly fallen on understanding poverty and welfare dependency in terms of individual attributes. The unit of analysis in these studies is by definition the individual rather than the wider social or economic structures, resulting in statistical models of individual characteristics predicting individual behavior. Consequently, the long standing tension between structural versus individual approaches to explaining poverty has largely been tilted within the empirical poverty research community towards that of the individual. . . .

The argument in this article is that such an emphasis is misplaced and misdirected. By focusing on individual attributes as the cause of poverty, social scientists have largely missed the underlying dynamic of American impoverishment. Poverty researchers have in effect focused on who loses out at the economic game, rather than addressing the fact that the game produces losers in the first place. An analysis into this underlying dynamic is critical to advancing our state of knowledge regarding American poverty.

Of course, not all social scientists have abandoned the importance of structural considerations with respect to poverty. The work of William Ryan (1971), Michael Katz (1989), Herbert Gans (1995), Douglass Massey (1996) and Joe Feagin (2000) come[s] to mind. However, it should not be a surprise that most of these scholars have taken a theoretical or historical approach, rather than a statistical one. There is a need to articulate the quantitative evidence supporting the argument that U.S. poverty is ultimately the result of structural failings at the economic, political, and social levels.

## Current Understanding of American Poverty

The current research emphasis upon understanding American poverty has largely focused on the individual and demographic characteristics of the poor. These characteristics have, in turn, been used to explain why particular individuals and households experience poverty. This approach has revealed the extent to which the risk of poverty varies across particular individual and household attributes.

Repeated cross-sectional national surveys such as the Current Population Survey have indicated that the likelihood of poverty varies sharply with respect to age, race, gender, family structure, and residence. For example, the U.S. Census Bureau (2003a) reports that while the overall U.S. poverty rate in 2002 was 12.1 percent, it was 16.7 percent for children and for those residing in central cities, 24.1 percent for African Americans, and 28.8 percent for persons in female headed households. Other demographic characteristics closely associated with the risk of poverty include giving birth outside of marriage, families with larger numbers of children, and having children at an early age (Maynard, 1997).

In addition, cross-sectional research has shown a close association between human capital characteristics and an individual's risk of poverty—those who are lacking in human capital are much more likely to experience poverty than individuals with greater levels of human capital. Specifically, lower levels of education, less marketable work skills and experience, and having a physical disability that interferes with an individual's ability to participate in the labor market are all highly correlated with an elevated risk of poverty (Blank, 1997; Schiller, 2004). On the other hand, research comparing the attitudes and motivation of the poor versus the non-poor, have found relatively few differences between these two groups (Goodwin, 1972; 1983; Lichter and Crowley, 2002; Rank, 1994; Seccombe, 1999) and little in the way of their being a causal factor leading to poverty (Duncan, 1984; Edwards et al., 2001).

Longitudinal studies examining the dynamics of poverty have addressed the length of time and particular factors related to a spell of poverty. This body of work indicates that most spells of poverty are of modest length. The typical pattern is that households are impoverished for one, two, or three years, and then manage to get above the poverty line (Bane and Ellwood, 1986; Blank, 1997; Duncan, 1984; Walker, 1994). They may stay there for a period of time, only to experience an additional fall into poverty at some later point. For example, Stevens

(1994, 1999) calculated that of all persons who had managed to get themselves above the poverty line, over half would return to poverty within five years. Since their economic distance above the poverty threshold is often modest, a detrimental economic or social event can push a household back below the poverty line.

Longitudinal research has also focused on the nature of such events and individual changes that result in a spell of poverty (Devine and Wright, 1993; Duncan, 1984; Walker, 1994). The most important of these have been the loss of employment and earnings, along with changes in family structure. For example, using the Panel Study of Income Dynamics (PSID) data, Duncan et al. (1995) found that two thirds of all entries into poverty were associated with either a reduction in work (48 percent) or the loss of work (18 percent). Divorce and separation were associated with triggering approximately 10 percent of all spells of poverty. Blank (1997) found that employment and family structure changes were also influential in ending spells of poverty. Two thirds of those below the poverty line escaped impoverishment as a result of increases in the individual earnings of family members or increases from other sources of income, while the remaining third had their spells of poverty end as a result of changes in family structure (such as marriage or a child leaving the household). In addition, research has shown that illness and incapacitation are also important factors contributing to falls into poverty (Schiller, 2004).

A substantial body of work has also examined the dynamics of welfare use and dependency. This research has shown that individuals utilizing public assistance programs and who experience longer spells of welfare are often at a distinct disadvantage vis-à-vis the labor market (Bane and Ellwood, 1994; Boisjoly et al., 1998; Harris, 1996; Moffitt, 1992; Pavetti, 1992; Rank, 1988; Sandefur and Cook, 1998). Consequently, those with work disabilities, low education, greater numbers of children, and/or living in inner-city areas are more likely to extensively utilize the welfare system. The results from these studies largely mirror the findings that

have been gathered regarding the length and duration of poverty spells.

The above body of work has provided an important understanding into who are the economic losers in American society. Yet at the same time it has failed to address the question of why there are economic losers in the first place? The premise of this article is that in order [to] answer this question, it is essential to analyze specific failings at the structural level.

## The Structural Nature of Poverty

Three lines of evidence are detailed in order to illustrate the structural nature of poverty—(1) the inability of the U.S. labor market to provide enough decent paying jobs for all families to avoid poverty or near poverty; (2) the ineffectiveness of American social policy to reduce levels of poverty through governmental social safety net programs; and (3) the fact that the majority of the population will experience poverty during their adult lifetimes, indicative of the systemic nature of U.S. poverty. Each of these lines of evidence [is] intended to empirically illustrate that American poverty is by and large the result of structural failures and processes.

## The Inability of the Labor Market to Support All Families

Several of the pioneering large scale studies of poverty conducted at the end of the 19th and beginning of the 20th centur[ies] focused heavily on the importance of labor market failings to explain poverty. The work of Charles Booth (1892–1897), Seebohm Rowntree (1901), Hull House (1895), Robert Hunter (1904), and W. E. B. DuBois (1899) all emphasized the importance of inadequate wages, lack of jobs, and unstable working conditions as a primary cause of poverty. For example, Rowntree (1901) estimated that approximately 57 percent of individuals in poverty were there as a direct result of labor market failures (low wages, unemployment, irregularity of work).

Yet by the 1960's the emphasis had shifted from a critique of the economic structure as a primary cause of poverty, to an analysis of individual deficiencies (e.g., the lack of human capital) as the underlying reason for poverty. As Timothy Bartik (2001) notes, U.S. antipoverty policy has focused heavily on labor supply policies (e.g. increasing individual's human capital or incentives to work through welfare reform) rather than labor demand policies (increasing the number and quality of jobs). As mentioned earlier, social scientific research has reinforced this policy approach by focusing on individual deficiencies to explain individual poverty.

Yet it can be demonstrated that irrespective of the specific characteristics that Americans possess, there simply are not enough decent paying jobs to support all of those (and their families) who are looking for work. During the past 25 years the American economy has increasingly produced larger numbers of low paying jobs, jobs that are part-time, and jobs that are lacking in benefits (Seccombe, 2000). For example, the Census Bureau estimated that the median hourly earning of workers who were paid hourly wages in 2000 was $9.91, while at the same time approximately three million Americans were working part-time as a result of the lack of sufficient full-time work being available (U.S. Census Bureau, 2001). In addition, 43.6 million Americans were lacking in health insurance, largely because their employer did not provide such benefits (U.S. Census Bureau, 2003b).

Studies analyzing the percentage of the U.S. workforce falling into the low wage sector have shown that a much higher percentage of American workers fall into this category when compared with their counterparts in other developed countries. For example, Smeeding, Rainwater, and Burtless (2000) found that 25 percent of all U.S. full-time workers could be classified as working in low wage work (defined as earning less than 65 percent of the national median earnings on full-time jobs). This was by far the highest percentage of the countries analyzed, with the overall average falling at 12.9 percent.

One of the reasons for this has been the fact that the minimum wage has remained at low levels and has not been indexed to infla-

tion. Changes in the minimum wage must come through Congressional legislation. This often leads to years going by before Congress acts to adjust the minimum wage upward, causing it to lag further behind the cost of living.

Beyond the low wages, part-time work, and lack of benefits, there is also a mismatch between the actual number of available jobs and the number of those who need them. Economists frequently discuss what is known as a natural unemployment rate—that in order for a free market economy to effectively function, a certain percentage of laborers need to be out of work. For example, full employment would impede the ability of employers to attract and hire workers, particularly within the low wage sector. Consequently, a certain degree of unemployment appears systematic within a capitalist economy, irrespective of the individual characteristics possessed by those participating in that economy.

During the past 40 years, U.S. monthly unemployment rates have averaged between 4 and 10 percent (U.S. Census Bureau, 2001). These percentages represent individuals who are out of work but are actively looking for employment. In 2001 this translated into nearly 7 million people unemployed at any particular point in time throughout the year, while over 15 million people experienced unemployment at some point during the year (Schiller, 2004). Certainly some of these individuals have voluntarily left their jobs in order to locate another job (known as frictional unemployment), while in other cases the unemployed may include individuals whose famil[ies] are not dependent upon their job for its economic survival, such as teenagers looking for summer work. Nevertheless, a good proportion of unemployment is the result of involuntary reasons, such as layoffs and downsizing, directly affecting millions of heads of households.

Bartik (2001, 2002) used several different approaches and assumptions to estimate the number of jobs that would be needed to significantly address the issue of poverty in the United States. Data were analyzed from the 1998 Current Population Survey. His conclusion? Even in the booming economy of the late 1990's, between five and nine million more jobs were needed in order to meet the needs of the poor and disadvantaged.

The structural failing of the labor market to support the pool of labor that currently exists can be further illustrated through an analysis of the Survey of Income and Program Participation (SIPP). The SIPP is a large ongoing longitudinal study that interviews households every four months over the course of three or four years, gathering detailed monthly information regarding individual[s'] employment and income across these periods of time. It allows one to map the patterns of labor force participation for a large nationally representative sample (for an in-depth discussion of the history, methodology, and specific details of the SIPP data set, see Westat, 2001).

An analysis of the SIPP illustrates the mismatch between the number of jobs in the labor market that will enable a family to subsist above the threshold of poverty, versus the number of heads of families in need of such jobs. Table 15.1 is based upon the jobs and work behavior of family heads across all 12 months of 1999. From this we can esti-

mate the annual number of hours worked, the annual amount of pay received, and whether such earnings were sufficient to raise a family above the poverty line. The analysis is confined to heads of families who are between the ages of 18 and 64.

In Table 15.1, we examine whether the jobs that family heads were working at during the year were able to get their current families out of poverty. Three poverty thresholds are examined—below 1.00 (the official poverty line); below 1.25 of the poverty line (the official poverty line raised by 25 percent); and below 1.50 of the poverty line (the official poverty line raised by 50 percent). To illustrate, the poverty line for a family of 4 in 1999 was $17,029. Consequently the 1.25 poverty threshold for this family would be $21,286, while the 1.50 poverty threshold would be $25,544. These thresholds provide us with several alternative levels of poverty and near poverty.

Our focus is on the availability of jobs in the labor market to lift various families out of poverty. We examine this question for three different populations of family heads who are in the labor market. The first panel

### Table 15.1
*Inability of the Labor Market to Support Various Family Structures Above Different Poverty Thresholds*

| Current Family Status Poverty Threshold | All Families | Married Couple Families | One Parent Families | Single Families |
|---|---|---|---|---|
| **Heads of Families Working Full-Time** | | | | |
| Below 1.00 | 9.4 | 9.9 | 16.9 | 3.2 |
| Below 1.25 | 15.3 | 16.0 | 26.4 | 6.6 |
| Below 1.50 | 22.0 | 23.0 | 36.6 | 10.2 |
| N (1000s) | 9,891 | 6,053 | 1,557 | 2,281 |
| **Heads of Families Working Half-Time or More** | | | | |
| Below 1.00 | 14.9 | 13.5 | 27.7 | 9.5 |
| Below 1.25 | 21.4 | 19.8 | 37.0 | 14.3 |
| Below 1.50 | 28.0 | 26.7 | 46.5 | 18.3 |
| N (1000s) | 11,312 | 6,623 | 1,969 | 2,720 |
| **Heads of Families in the Labor Market** | | | | |
| Below 1.00 | 20.3 | 17.1 | 36.8 | 15.8 |
| Below 1.25 | 26.5 | 23.3 | 44.9 | 20.4 |
| Below 1.50 | 32.7 | 30.0 | 53.4 | 24.2 |
| N (1000s) | 12,190 | 6,972 | 2,259 | 2,959 |

Source: Survey of Income and Program Participation, authors' computations.

focuses only on those heads of families who are working full-time throughout the year (defined as averaging 35 or more hours per week across the 52 weeks of the year). The second panel includes those working full-time as well as those who are working at least half-time throughout the year (defined as working an average of 20 or more hours per week across 52 weeks). The third panel includes all heads of families in the labor market (defined as any head of family who has either worked at some point during the year or who has been actively looking for work).

For those employed full-time during 1999, 9.4 percent are working in jobs where their annual earnings will not get their families above the poverty line, 15.3 percent are at jobs in which their earnings will not get their families above 1.25 of the poverty line, and 22.0 percent are employed at jobs that will not get their families above 1.50 of the poverty line. We can clearly see that the jobs one parent family heads are working at are much less able to sustain these households above the level of poverty than that for all families. On the other hand, single men and women are more likely to be able to lift themselves out of poverty through their work. Married couples fall in between these two family types (it should be kept in mind that for these couples, we are only focusing on the ability of the family head's job to lift the household above the threshold of poverty, rather than the earnings of both partners).

The middle panel illustrates that if we include family heads who are working either full-time or at least half-time throughout the year, nearly 15 percent were working at jobs in which their income would not raise their families above the poverty line, 21.4 percent were at jobs that would not get their families over 1.25 of the poverty line, while 28 percent fell below 1.50 of the poverty line. Finally, the bottom panel includes all family heads that were in the labor market at some point during the year. Here we can see that the percentages for the three poverty thresholds are 20.3, 26.5, and 32.7.

Consequently, depending on the level of poverty and the size of the pool of labor, the failure of the labor market to raise families out of poverty ranges from 9.4 percent (uti-

lizing the official poverty line for those working full-time) to 32.7 percent (applying 1.50 of the poverty line for all who are in the labor market). To use an analogy that will be developed later, the supply of jobs versus the demand for labor might be thought of as an ongoing game of musical chairs. That is, there is a finite number of jobs available in the labor market that pay enough to support a family above the threshold of poverty (which might be thought of as the chairs in this analogy). On the other hand, the amount of labor, as represented by the number of family heads in the labor market (and hence the players in the game), is greater than the number of adequately paying jobs. As indicated in Table 15.1, this imbalance ranges from 9.4 percent to 32.7 percent. Consequently, the structure of the labor market basically ensures that some families will lose out at this musical chairs game of finding a decent paying job able to lift a family above the threshold of poverty.

Table 15.2 illustrates this in a slightly different fashion. Here we estimate the earnings capacity of jobs held by family heads to support various hypothetical family sizes above our three different thresholds of poverty. What is clear from this table is that for the pool of family heads who are working full-time, the jobs that they are employed at are quite able to support a one or two person family above the official poverty line. For example, only 2.4 percent are in full-time jobs in which their earnings would not raise a one person family above the official poverty line, while 4.7 percent of family heads are working at jobs that would not raise a family of two above the poverty line.

However, as we look at the ability of such jobs to get larger sized families above the thresholds of poverty, we can see their increasing failure to do so. Consequently, 15 percent of these jobs will not raise a family of four above 1.00 of the poverty line. At the 1.25 level the figure is 25.1 percent, and at the 1.50 level it is 36 percent. Thus, the current supply of full-time jobs in the labor market would appear able to lift most one or two person families out of poverty, but it becomes much less effective in raising moderate sized families out of poverty. As we in-

**Table 15.2**
*Inability of the Labor Market to Support Various Family Sizes
Above Different Poverty Thresholds*

| | Hypothetical Family Size | | | | | |
|---|---|---|---|---|---|---|
| Poverty Threshold | 1 Person Family | 2 Person Family | 3 Person Family | 4 Person Family | 5 Person Family | 6 Person Family |
| **Heads of Families Working Full-Time** | | | | | | |
| Below 1.00 | 2.4 | 4.7 | 7.6 | 15.0 | 22.3 | 29.0 |
| Below 1.25 | 4.3 | 8.9 | 14.0 | 25.1 | 35.0 | 42.4 |
| Below 1.50 | 7.2 | 14.5 | 21.8 | 36.0 | 46.3 | 54.6 |
| **Heads of Families Working Half-Time or More** | | | | | | |
| Below 1.00 | 6.3 | 10.2 | 13.8 | 21.6 | 28.9 | 35.3 |
| Below 1.25 | 9.6 | 15.2 | 20.6 | 31.6 | 41.0 | 47.9 |
| Below 1.50 | 13.2 | 21.1 | 28.3 | 42.0 | 51.6 | 59.3 |
| **Heads of Families in the Labor Market** | | | | | | |
| Below 1.00 | 12.0 | 15.8 | 19.3 | 26.9 | 33.7 | 39.7 |
| Below 1.25 | 15.3 | 20.8 | 25.9 | 36.3 | 45.0 | 51.5 |
| Below 1.50 | 18.8 | 26.4 | 33.2 | 46.0 | 54.9 | 62.1 |

Source: Survey of Income and Program Participation, authors' computations.

clude family heads who are working at least half-time (the middle panel of Table 15.2) or who are in the labor market (the bottom panel of Table 15.2) the percentages rise significantly.

Finally, we can illustrate this in yet another manner. Using the SIPP data again for 1999, we estimated the annual average hourly wages for heads of families. This analysis indicates that 12.1 percent of family heads were working at jobs which paid an average of less than 6 dollars an hour, 21.2 percent worked at jobs paying less than 8 dollars an hour, 31.7 percent worked at jobs paying less than 10 dollars an hour, and 42.7 percent were earning less than 12 dollars an hour. In order to raise a family of three above the official poverty line in 1999 one would have to be working full-time (defined as averaging 35 hours per week across the 52 weeks of the year) at $7.30 an hour, and for a family of four the figure would be $9.36 an hour. The fact that nearly one third of family heads are working at jobs paying less than $10.00 an hour, is indicative of the significant risk of poverty that they face.

To summarize, the data presented in this section indicates that a major factor leading to poverty in the United States is a failing of the economic structure to provide viable opportunities for all who are participating in that system. In particular, the labor market simply does not provide enough decent paying jobs for all who need them. As a result, millions of families find themselves struggling below or precariously close to the poverty line.

## The Ineffectiveness of the Social Safety Net to Prevent Poverty

A second major structural failure is found at the political level. Contrary to the popular rhetoric of vast amounts of tax dollars being spent on public assistance, the American welfare state, and particularly its social safety net, can be more accurately described in minimalist terms (Esping-Andersen, 1990). Compared to other Western industrialized countries, the United States devotes far fewer resources to programs aimed at assisting the economically vulnerable (Organization for Economic Cooperation and Development, 1999). As Charles Noble writes, "The U.S. welfare state is striking precisely because it is so limited in scope and ambition" (1997: 3).

On the other hand, most European countries provide a wide range of social and insurance programs that largely prevent families from falling into poverty. These include substantial family or children's allowances, designed to transfer cash assistance to families with children. Unemployment assistance is far more generous in these countries than in the United States, often providing support for more than a year following the loss of a job. Furthermore, universal health coverage is routinely provided, along with considerable support for child care.

The result of these social policy differences is that they substantially reduce the extent of poverty in Europe and Canada, while U.S. social policy has had only a small impact upon poverty reduction. As Rebecca Blank notes, "the national choice in the United States to provide relatively less generous transfers to low-income families has meant higher relative poverty rates in the country. While low-income families in the United States work more than in many other countries, they are not able to make up for lower governmental income support relative to their European counterparts" (Blank, 1997: 141–142).

This effect can be clearly seen in Table 15.3. The data in this table are based upon an analysis of the Luxembourg Income Study (LIS) conducted by Veli-Matti Ritakallio (2001). Initiated in the 1980s, the LIS contains income and demographic information on households in over 25 different nations from 1967 to the present. Variables have been standardized across 70 data sets, allowing researchers to conduct cross-national analyses regarding poverty and the effectiveness of governmental programs in alleviating such poverty (for further detail regarding the LIS, see Luxembourg Income Study, 2000). Poverty in this analysis is defined as being in a household in which its disposable income is less than one half of the median annual income.

Table 15.3 compares eight European countries and Canada with the United States in terms of their pre-transfer and post-transfer rates of poverty. The pre-transfer rates (column one) indicate what the level of poverty would be in each country in the absence of any governmental income transfers such as welfare payments, unemployment compensation, or social security payments. The post-transfer rates (column two) represent the level of poverty after governmental transfers are included (which is how poverty is officially measured in the United States and many other countries). In-kind benefits such as medical insurance are not included in the analysis. Comparing these two levels of poverty (column three) reveals how effective (or ineffective) governmental policy is in reducing the overall extent of poverty in a country.

Looking first at the rates of pre-transfer poverty, we can see that the United States is on the lower end of the scale. Norway's pre-

---

***Table 15.3***
*Comparative Analysis of Governmental Effectiveness in*
*Reducing Poverty Across Selected Countries*

| Country | Pre-transfer Poverty Rates | Post-transfer Poverty Rates | Reduction Factor |
|---|---|---|---|
| Canada (1994) | 29 | 10 | 66 |
| Finland (1995) | 33 | 4 | 88 |
| France (1994) | 39 | 8 | 79 |
| Germany (1994) | 29 | 7 | 76 |
| Netherlands (1994) | 30 | 7 | 77 |
| Norway (1995) | 27 | 4 | 85 |
| Sweden (1995) | 36 | 3 | 92 |
| United Kingdom (1995) | 38 | 13 | 66 |
| United States (1994) | 29 | 18 | 38 |

Source: Luxembourg Income Study, adapted from Veli-Matti Ritakallio (2001) computations.

transfer poverty rate is 27 percent, followed by the United States, Canada, and Germany at 29 percent. The Netherlands pre-transfer rate is 30 percent, Finland stands at 33 percent, Sweden is at 36 percent, the United Kingdom rate is 38 percent, and finally, France possesses the highest level of pre-transfer poverty at 39 percent.

When we examine the post-transfer rates of poverty found in column two, a dramatic reversal takes place in terms of where the United States stands vis-à-vis the comparison countries. The average post-transfer poverty rate for the eight comparison countries in Table 15.3 is 7 percent, whereas the United States' post-transfer poverty rate stands at 18 percent. As a result of their more active social policies, Canada and the European countries are able to significantly cut their overall rates of poverty. For example, Sweden is able to reduce the number of people that would be poor (in the absence of any governmental help) by 92 percent as a result of social policies. The overall average reduction factor for the eight countries is 79 percent. In contrast, the United States poverty reduction factor is only 38 percent (with much of this being the result of Social Security).

Table 15.3 clearly illustrates a second major structural failing leading to the high rates of U.S. poverty. It is a failure at the political and policy level. Specifically, social and economic programs directed to the economically vulnerable populations in the United States are minimal in their ability to raise families out of poverty. While America has always been a "reluctant welfare state," the past 25 years have witnessed several critical retrenchments and reductions in the social safety net. These reductions have included scaling back both the amount of benefits being transferred, as well as a tightening of program eligibility (Noble, 1997; Patterson, 2000). In addition, the United States has failed to offer the type of universal coverage for child care, medical insurance, or child allowances that most other developed countries routinely provide. As a result, the overall U.S. poverty rates remain at extremely high levels.

Once again, this failure has virtually nothing to do with the individual. Rather it is emblematic of a failure at the structural level. By focusing on individual characteristics, we lose sight of the fact that governments can and do exert a sizeable impact on reducing the extent of poverty within their jurisdictions. In the analysis presented here, Canada and Europe are able to lift a significant percentage of their economically vulnerable above the threshold of poverty through governmental transfer and assistance policies. In contrast, the United States provides substantially less support through its social safety net, resulting in poverty rates that are currently the highest in the industrialized world.

The one case where the U.S. has effectively reduced the rate of poverty for a particular group has been that of the elderly. Their substantial reduction in the risk of poverty over the past 40 years has been directly attributed to the increasing generosity of the Social Security program, as well as the introduction of Medicare in 1965 and the Supplemental Security Income Program in 1974. During the 1960's and 1970's, Social Security benefits were substantially increased and indexed to the rate of inflation, helping many of the elderly escape from poverty. It is estimated today that without the Social Security program, the poverty rate for the elderly would be close to 50 percent (rather than its current 10 percent). Put another way, Social Security is responsible for getting 80 percent of the elderly above the poverty line who would otherwise be poor in its absence.

## The Widespread Life Course Risk of Poverty

A third approach revealing the structural nature of American poverty can be found in a life course analysis of poverty. As discussed earlier, previous work on poverty has examined the cross-sectional and spell dynamic risk. Yet there is another way in which the incidence of poverty can be examined. Such an approach places the risk of poverty within the context of the American life course. By doing so, the systematic nature of American poverty can be revealed.

The work of Rank and Hirschl (1999a, 1999b, 1999c, 2001a, 2001b) has developed this approach. Building upon the longitudinal design of the Panel Study of Income Dynamics, Rank and Hirschl have utilized a technique for constructing a series of life tables estimating the probability that Americans will experience poverty at some point during their adulthood (see Rank and Hirschl, 2001c, for a more detailed description of their methodology and approach, and Hill, 1992, for a further discussion of the PSID).

Table 15.4 is based upon three separate life tables estimating the age specific and cumulative probabilities of experiencing poverty between the ages of 20 and 75 for the following poverty thresholds—1.00 (the official poverty line); 1.25 (the poverty line raised by 25 percent), and 1.50 (the poverty line raised by 50 percent). Table 15.4 reports the cumulative percentages of the American population that will encounter poverty at various points of adulthood.

At age 20 (the starting point of the analysis), we can see that 10.6 percent of Americans fell below the poverty line (which is similar to the cross-sectional rate of poverty

for 20 year olds), with 15 percent falling below the 1.25 threshold and 19.1 percent falling below the 1.50 threshold. By the age of 35, the percent of Americans experiencing poverty has increased sharply—31.4 percent of Americans have experienced at least one year below the poverty line; 39 percent have experienced at least one year below 1.25 of the poverty line; and 46.9 percent have experienced a year below 1.50 of the poverty line. At age 55 the percentages stand at 45.0, 52.8, and 61.0, and by the age of 75, they have risen to 58.5 percent, 68 percent and 76 percent.

What these numbers indicate is that a clear majority of Americans will at some point experience poverty during their lifetimes. Rather than an isolated event that occurs only among what has been labeled the "underclass," the reality is that the majority of Americans will encounter poverty firsthand during their adulthoods.

Such patterns illuminate the systematic essence of American poverty, which in turn points to the structural nature of poverty. Occasionally we can physically see widespread examples of this. For instance, the economic collapse during the Great Depression of the 1930's. Given the enormity of this collapse, it became clear to many Americans that most of their neighbors were not directly responsible for the dire economic situation they found themselves in. This awareness helped provide much of the impetus and justification behind the New Deal (Patterson, 2000).

Similarly, the existence of the "other" America as noted by Michael Harrington (1962) during the early 1960's, pointed again to the widespread nature of U.S. poverty. The other America was represented by the extremely high rates of poverty found in economically depressed areas such as rural Appalachia and the urban inner city. The War on Poverty during the 1960's was an attempt to address these large scale structural pockets of poverty amidst plenty.

The analysis in this section indicates that poverty may be as widespread and systematic today as in these more visible examples. Yet we have been unable to see this as a result of not looking in the right direction. By focusing on the life span risks, the prevalent

**Table 15.4**
**The Cumulative Percent of Americans Experiencing Poverty Across Adulthood**

| | Level of Poverty | | |
|---|---|---|---|
| Age | Below 1.00 Poverty Line | Below 1.25 Poverty Line | Below 1.50 Poverty Line |
| 20 | 10.6 | 15.0 | 19.1 |
| 25 | 21.6 | 27.8 | 34.3 |
| 30 | 27.1 | 34.1 | 41.3 |
| 35 | 31.4 | 39.0 | 46.9 |
| 40 | 35.6 | 43.6 | 51.7 |
| 45 | 38.8 | 46.7 | 55.0 |
| 50 | 41.8 | 49.6 | 57.9 |
| 55 | 45.0 | 52.8 | 61.0 |
| 60 | 48.2 | 56.1 | 64.2 |
| 65 | 51.4 | 59.7 | 67.5 |
| 70 | 55.0 | 63.6 | 71.8 |
| 75 | 58.5 | 68.0 | 76.0 |

Source: Panel Study of Income Dynamics, authors' computations.

nature of American poverty is revealed. At some point during adulthood, the bulk of Americans will face impoverishment. The approach of emphasizing individual failings or attributes as the primary cause of poverty loses much of its explanatory power in the face of such patterns. Rather, given the widespread occurrence of economic vulnerability, a life span analysis points to a third line of evidence indicating that poverty is more appropriately viewed as a structural failing of American society. . . .

## Discussion

Given the above arguments and evidence indicating that American poverty is primarily the result of structural failings, how might we reconcile this perspective with the earlier discussed research findings indicating that human capital and individual attributes largely explain who is at risk of experiencing poverty? An approach that bridges the empirical importance of individual attributes with the significance of structural forces has been the concept of structural vulnerability (Rank, 1994, 2000, 2001, 2004). This framework recognizes that human capital and other labor market attributes are associated with who loses out at the economic game (and hence will be more likely to experience poverty), but that structural factors predominately ensure that there will be losers in the first place.

An analogy can be used to illustrate the basic concept. Imagine a game of musical chairs in which there are ten players but only eight chairs. On one hand, individual success or failure in the game depends on the skill and luck of each player. Those who are less agile or less well placed when the music stops are more likely to lose. These are appropriately cited as the reasons a particular individual has lost the game. On the other hand, given that there are only eight chairs available, two players are bound to lose regardless of their characteristics. Even if all the players were suddenly to double their speed and agility, there would still be two losers. From this broader context, the characteristics of the individual players are no longer important in terms of understanding

that the structure of the game ensures that someone must inevitably lose.

We would argue that this analogy applies with respect to poverty. For every ten American households, there are good jobs and opportunities at any point in time to adequately support roughly eight of those ten. The remaining two households will be locked out of such opportunities, often resulting in poverty or near poverty. Individuals experiencing such economic deprivation are likely to have characteristics putting them at a disadvantage in terms of competing in the economy (lower education, fewer skills, single-parent families, illness or incapacitation, minorities residing in inner cities, etc.). These characteristics help to explain why particular individuals and households are at a greater risk of poverty.

However, given the earlier discussed structural failures, a certain percentage of the American population will experience economic vulnerability regardless of what their characteristics are. As in the musical chairs analogy, increasing everyone's human capital will do little to alter the fact that there are only so many decent paying jobs available. In such a case, employers will simply raise the bar in terms of the employee qualifications they are seeking, but nevertheless there will remain a percentage of the population at risk of economic deprivation. Consequently, although a lack of human capital and its accompanying vulnerability leads to an understanding of who the losers of the economic game are likely to be, the structural components of our economic, social, and political systems explain why there are losers in the first place. . . .

The recognition of this dynamic represents a fundamental shift in thinking from the old paradigm. It helps to explain why the social policies of the past two decades have largely been ineffective in reducing the rates of poverty. We have focused our attention and resources on either altering the incentives and disincentives for those playing the game, or in a very limited way, upgrading their skills and ability to compete in the game, while at the same time leaving the structure of the game untouched.

When the overall poverty rates in the United States do in fact go up or down, they do so primarily as a result of impacts on the structural level that increase or decrease the number of available chairs. In particular, the performance of the economy has been historically important. Why? Because when the economy is expanding, more opportunities (or chairs) are available for the competing pool of labor and their families. The reverse occurs when the economy slows down and contracts. Consequently, during the 1930's or early 1980's when the economy was doing badly, poverty rates went up, while during periods of economic prosperity such as the 1960's or the middle to later 1990's, the overall rates of poverty declined.

Similarly, changes in various social supports and the social safety net available to families will make a difference in terms of how well such households are able to avoid poverty or near poverty. When such supports were increased through the War on Poverty initiatives in the 1960's, poverty rates declined. Likewise, when Social Security benefits were expanded during the 1960's and 1970's, the elderly's poverty rates declined precipitously. Conversely, when social supports have been weakened and eroded, as in the case of children's programs over the past 25 years, their rates of poverty have gone up.

The recognition of poverty as a result of the way the game is structured also makes it quite clear why the United States has such high rates of poverty when compared to other Western countries. These rates have nothing to do with Americans being less motivated or less skilled than those in other countries, but with the fact that our economy has been producing a plethora of low wage jobs in the face of global competition and that our social policies have done relatively little to support families compared to our European neighbors. From this perspective, one of the keys to addressing poverty is to increase the labor market opportunities and social supports available to American households.

The structural vulnerability perspective thus recognizes the importance of human capital in being able to predict who is more likely to experience economic deprivation, while at the same time emphasizing the importance of structural constraints in guaranteeing that some Americans will be left out of the economic mainstream. In short, the structure of the American economy, accompanied by a weak social safety net and public policies directed to the economically vulnerable, ensure that a certain percentage of the American population will experience impoverishment at any point in time, and that a much larger percentage of the population will experience poverty over the course of a lifetime. The fact that three quarters of Americans will experience poverty or near poverty (at the 1.50 level) during their adulthoods is emblematic of these structural level failings. . . .

## References

Bane, M. J., & Ellwood, D. T. (1986). Slipping into and out of poverty: The dynamics of spells. *Journal of Human Resources*, 21, 1–23.

———. (1994). *Welfare realities: From rhetoric to reform*. Cambridge, MA: Harvard University Press.

Bartik, T. H. (2001). *Jobs for the poor: Can labor demand policies help?* New York: Russell Sage Foundation.

———. (2002). Poverty, jobs, and subsidized employment. *Challenge*, 45, 100–111.

Blank, R. M. (1997). *It takes a nation: A new agenda for fighting poverty*. Princeton, NJ: Princeton University Press.

Boisjoly, J., Harris, K. M., & Duncan, G. J. (1998). Trends, events, and duration of initial welfare spells. *Social Service Review*, 72, 466–492.

Booth, C. (1892–97). *Life and labour of the people of London, first series: Poverty*. London: Macmillan.

Devine, J. A., & Wright, J. D. (1993). *The greatest of evils: Urban poverty and the American underclass*. New York: Aldine De Gruyter.

DuBois, W. E. B. (1899). *The Philadelphia Negro*. Philadelphia: University of Pennsylvania Press.

Duncan, G. J. (1984). *Years of poverty, years of plenty: The changing economic fortunes of American workers and families*. Ann Arbor, MI: Institute for Social Research.

Duncan, G. J., Gustafsson, B., Hauser, R., Schmaus, G., Jenkins, S., Messinger, H., Muffels, R., Nolan, B., Ray, J., & Voges, W. (1995). Poverty and social-assistance dynamics in the United States, Canada, and Europe.

In K. McFate, R. Lawson, & W. J. Wilson (Eds.), *Poverty, inequality and the future of social policy: Western states in the new world order* (pp. 67–108). New York: Russell Sage Foundation.

Edwards, M. E., Plotnick, R., & Klawitter, M. (2001). Do attitudes and personality characteristics affect socioeconomic outcomes? The case of welfare use by young women. *Social Science Quarterly, 82*, 827–843.

Esping-Andersen, G. (1990). *The three worlds of welfare capitalism.* Princeton, NJ: Princeton University Press.

Feagin, J. R. (1975). *Subordinating the poor: Welfare and American beliefs.* Englewood Cliffs, NJ: Prentice-Hall.

——. (2000). *Racist America: Roots, current realities, and future reparations.* New York: Routledge.

Gans, H. J. (1995). *The war against the poor: The underclass and antipoverty policy.* New York: Basic Books.

Gilens, M. (1999). *Why Americans hate welfare: Race, media, and the politics of antipoverty policy.* Chicago: University of Chicago Press.

Goodwin, L. (1972). *Do the poor want to work? A social-psychological study of work orientations.* Washington, DC: Brookings Institution.

——. (1983). *Causes and cures of welfare: New evidence on the social psychology.* Lexington, MA: Lexington Books.

Harrington, M. (1962). *The other America: Poverty in the United States.* New York: Macmillan.

Harris, K. M. (1996). Life after welfare: Women, work, and repeat dependency. *American Sociological Review, 61*, 407–426.

Hartwell, R. M. (1986). The long debate on poverty. Paper presented at the Political Economy Seminar Series, Washington University, St. Louis, Missouri.

Hill, M. S. (1992). *The Panel Study of Income Dynamics: A user's guide.* Newbury Park, CA: Sage Publications.

Hull House (1895). Hull House maps and papers. New York: Thomas Y. Crowell.

Hunter, R. (1904). *Poverty.* New York: Macmillan.

Katz, M. B. (1989). *The undeserving poor: From the war on poverty to the war on welfare.* New York: Pantheon Books.

Kluegel, J. R., & Smith, E. R. (1986). *Beliefs about inequality: Americans' views of what is and what ought to be.* New York: Aldine de Gruyter.

Lichter, D. T., & Crowley, M. L. (2002). Poverty in America: Beyond welfare reform. *Population Bulletin, 57*, 1–36.

Luxembourg Income Study (2000). LIS quick reference guide. Syracuse, NY: Maxwell School of Citizenship and Public Affairs, Syracuse University.

Massey, D. S. (1996). The age of extremes: Concentrated affluence and poverty in the twenty-first century. *Demography, 33*, 395–412.

Maynard, R. A. (1997). *Kids having kids: Economic costs and social consequences of teen pregnancy.* Washington, DC: The Urban Institute Press.

Moffitt, R. (1992). Incentive effects of the U.S. welfare system: A review. *Journal of Economic Literature, 30*, 1–61.

Noble, C. (1997). *Welfare as we knew it: A political history of the American welfare state.* New York: Oxford University Press.

O'Connor, A. (2001). *Poverty knowledge: Social science, social policy, and the poor in twentieth-century U.S. history.* Princeton: Princeton University Press.

Organization for Economic Cooperation and Development (1999). Social expenditure database 1980–1996. Paris: Organization for Economic Cooperation and Development.

Patterson, J. T. (2000). *America's struggle against poverty in the twentieth century.* Cambridge, MA: Harvard University Press.

Pavetti, L. A. (1992). The dynamics of welfare and work: Exploring the process by which young women work their way off welfare. Paper presented at the APPAM Annual Research Conference, October, Denver, Colorado.

Rank, M. R. (1988). Racial differences in length of welfare use. *Social Forces, 66*, 1080–1101.

——. (1994). *Living on the edge: The realities of welfare in America.* New York: Columbia University Press.

——. (2000). Poverty and economic hardship in families. In D. H. Demo, K. R. Allen, & M. A. Fine (Eds.), *Handbook of family diversity* (pp. 293–315). New York: Oxford University Press.

——. (2001). The effect of poverty on America's families: Assessing our research knowledge. *Journal of Family Issues, 22*, 882–903.

——. (2004). *One nation, underprivileged: Why American poverty affects us all.* New York: Oxford University Press.

Rank, M. R., & Hirschl, T. A. (1999a). The likelihood of poverty across the American adult life span. *Social Work, 44*, 201–216.

——. (1999b). Estimating the proportion of Americans ever experiencing poverty during their elderly years. *Journal of Gerontology: Social Sciences, 54B*, S184–S193.

——. (1999c). The economic risk of childhood in America: Estimating the probability of poverty across the formative years. *Journal of Marriage and the Family,* 61, 1058–1067.

———. (2001a). The occurrence of poverty across the life cycle: Evidence from the PSID. *Journal of Policy Analysis and Management,* 20, 737–755.

———. (2001b). Rags or riches? Estimating the probabilities of poverty and affluence across the adult American life span. *Social Science Quarterly,* 82, 651–669.

———. (2001c). The measurement of long term risks across the life course. *Social Science Quarterly,* 82, 680–686.

Ritakallio, V. M. (2001). Trends of poverty and income inequality in cross-national comparison. Luxembourg Income Study Working Paper No. 272, Maxwell School of Citizenship and Public Affairs, Syracuse University, Syracuse, New York.

Rowntree, B. S. (1901). *Poverty: A study of town life.* London: Macmillan.

Ryan, W. (1971). *Blaming the victim.* New York: Pantheon Books.

Sandefur, G. D., & Cook, S. T. (1998). Permanent exits from public assistance: The impact of duration, family, and work. *Social Forces,* 77, 763–786.

Schiller, B. R. (2004). *The economics of poverty and discrimination.* Upper Saddle River, NJ: Prentice Hall.

Seccombe, K. (1999). *So you think I drive a Cadillac? Welfare recipients' perspectives on the system.* Needham Heights, MA: Allyn and Bacon.

———. (2000). Families in poverty in the 1990s: Trends, causes, consequences, and lessons learned. *Journal of Marriage and the Family,* 62, 1094–1113.

Smeeding, T. M., Rainwater, L., & Burtless, G. (2000). United States poverty in a cross-national context. Luxembourg Income Study Working Paper No. 244, Maxwell School of Citizenship and Public Affairs, Syracuse University, Syracuse, New York.

Stevens, A. H. (1994). The dynamics of poverty spells: Updating Bane and Ellwood. *American Economic Review,* 84, 34–37.

———. (1999). Climbing out of poverty, falling back in: Measuring the persistence of poverty over multiple spells. *The Journal of Human Resources,* 34, 557–588.

U.S. Bureau of the Census (2001). Statistical Abstract of the United States: 2001 (121st edition.) Washington, DC: U.S. Government Printing Office.

———. (2003a). Poverty in the United States: 2002. Current Population Reports, Series P60-222.

Washington, DC: U.S. Government Printing Office.

———. (2003b). Health Insurance Coverage: 2002. Current Population Reports, Series P60-223. Washington, DC: U.S. Government Printing Office.

Walker, R. (1994). *Poverty dynamics: Issues and examples.* Aldershot, England: Avebury.

Westat (2001). *Survey of Income and Program Participation Users' Guide, Third Edition.* Rockville, MD: Westat.

## Review

1. Explain and illustrate the individual explanation of poverty in American society.

2. Discuss the emphasis of the current research into American poverty.

3. What do Rank, Yoon, and Hirschl mean by the "inability of the labor market to support all families?" What data support their argument?

4. Discuss the ineffectiveness of social policy to reduce poverty through safety net programs.

5. Describe the main conclusions of Rank, Yoon, and Hirschl about the proportion of Americans who will experience poverty during their lifetimes.

## Application

Spend one or two weeks trying to live like someone who is poor. Specifically, spend only as much money for food as a poor person would—the government estimates this as one-third of your income. In 2001, an individual under 65 living alone was poor if he or she had an annual income of $9214 or less (check the Statistical Abstract of the United States for the latest figures). That comes to $59.06 a week, or $8.44 a day. How well did you eat on this amount? How would the food you could afford affect your long-term health if you were poor indefinitely? Did the experience give you a better sense of the struggles of the poor?

## Related Web Sites

1. *http://www.census.gov/hhes/www/poverty.html.* The latest data on poverty from the U.S. Census Bureau.

2. *http://www.ssc.wisc.edu/irp/*. Home page of the Institute for Research on Poverty, providing access to numerous publications.

# 16
# America's Shame
## Women and Children in Shelter

*Barbara A. Arrighi*

*The homeless are at the bottom of the stratification system in the United States. While the United States has always had a population of transients, the character of this segment of the poor has changed in several ways in recent decades. The homeless have become more numerous since about 1980. They have become more visible, no longer confined to the "skid row" areas of the larger cities. The composition of the homeless has also changed. More women and children are now living on the streets. A third or more of the homeless population are families with children.*

*In this selection, Barbara Arrighi discusses the ways in which homelessness affects the development of children. Homeless children are deprived of the major benefits of social institutions such as a stable and secure family life and a good education. The children are living examples of the deprivations and emotional trauma endured by those at the bottom of the stratification system.*

What are children who live in poverty, in substandard housing, and in unsafe neighborhoods to believe of a society that claims to revere the family and to hold family values superior to all other values? How does temporary housing affect children? Children who live in a transitional state know no structure, no order, no predictability; they know only chaos. For a child who looks to the adults in her life for security, the sight of her mother or father losing control over life's basic needs can damage her development of trust and sense of security. Many factors can influence the impact of such a transitional state, including the length of time in which the family is without a home, the availability of a support system for the family, and the child's age, sex, and temperament. Even so, the child is influenced by the emotional and physical environment of the available temporary housing.

Loss of home is not the only event that affects a child's sense of security. The process of poverty begins with one or a combination of crises, including separation, divorce, or death of a parent or caretaker, the head of household's loss of employment, declining household income, loss of extended-kin support system, and/or increased family conflict. Any of these factors can affect a child profoundly, and in combination they can have long-term consequences for a child's emotional and physical development. Children require a nurturing, supportive, caring, safe, predictable home life in order to thrive and acquire a sense of self-worth, and a lack of a permanent home disrupts that process.

The institutional environment of a shelter can heighten the crisis of an already tenuous familial relationship and compound the trauma experienced by a child without a home. A parent who is feeling powerless and helpless because of the family's situation is emotionally unable to reassure a frightened child, whose feelings mirror those of the parent. Children typically subjected to conflicting behavior expectations from mothers and staff become overwhelmed and confused. Their anxiety is heightened, not alleviated, by shelter life.

When a child remains largely uncomforted and insecure, she is more likely to exhibit any of an array of maladaptive behaviors, including depression, aggressiveness, restlessness, regressive behavior, hyperactivity, and anxiety. The child's sense of self is traumatized. There is some evidence that the emotional assault that is entwined with being without a permanent space negatively affects a child's expectations about his or her future.

Frequent changes in home environment, structure, and neighborhood can affect a child's sense that she belongs to some place and that some place belongs to her—the child's personal space or turf. Although the environment lacks permanence, one factor that generally remains constant for children living in poverty is the ghettoization of their lives. Typically, any area that they call home has been abandoned by the more affluent and is isolated from the economically vibrant portions of the city.

## Poor Children and Schools

For children without a home, school could be a "haven in a heartless world." The few hours a day these children spend at school might well be the only time when they enjoy a sense of order or predictability. Even so, feelings of insecurity and inferiority surrounding these children's home lives can harm them in various areas, including formation of friendships, schoolwork, and attendance. Children who have stayed in a shelter spoke of the ridicule they encountered because of their situation. They coped in various ways. Sometimes they feigned illness to avoid going to school and facing the other children. Another tactic was to get off the school bus before their stop at the shelter so the other children would not see them enter their "home." Children described the pain of being stigmatized by classmates, who frequently taunted them because of their temporary residence.

Unfortunately, some teachers' treatment of the children can be as callous as the taunting by their schoolmates. Often teachers view the issues that children without homes, who live in poverty, bring to the classroom as interfering with teaching. Because any negative reaction on the part of classmates and/or teacher heightens the child's sense of alienation, the child might feel the need to become secretive, protective, and deceptive about her or his personal life. The more often the child employs these defense mechanisms, the more isolated she will be.

Thus life can be a catch-22 for a child without a home. The more she attempts to keep her family situation secret, the more distrusted, suspect, and marginalized she becomes. The most effective way to keep the family secret is to play truant; one study found that 43 percent of school-age children who lacked a permanent home did not attend school. For many children, then, especially adolescents, dropping out is the solution.

### Education: Not an Equalizer

Frequently the desperate day-to-day life of poor children and their parents clashes with the educational system. Pierre Bordieu's perspective on education explains the disadvantaged position of poor children in the classroom. Children living in poverty experience the world at a primitive level. Their parents exhaust their psychic energy in search of life's basic needs—food, shelter, and clothing. These children and their families live a concrete existence and speak concrete language about problems relating to their survival. However, the culture of education, disseminated through abstract concepts, presupposes that children have transcended the concrete, essentials of life. Teachers assume that children are prepared for conceptualizing, but children living in poverty generally are not. They have not had the luxury of experiencing abstract ways of thinking. The progressive nature of schoolwork is a constant struggle for them. Bordieu's thinking underscores the point that children living in poverty are excluded from the language and culture of education, and further, that the educational system, portrayed as neutral, is laden with the ideas of the elite. Bordieu's perspective would explain the dropout rate of children in poverty and/or without homes as well as the high proportion of working class and poor children in vocational classes. The language of vocational coursework is familiar. Only 29 percent of children who are poor are placed in the college preparatory track, compared with 65 percent of students from high-income families.

Without a conceptual understanding of their world, the probability intensifies that poor children will be left out of the school curriculum and instruction. Equally important, because of their situation, they risk being excluded from most circles of friends. Thus over time they resort to the most effective exclusion, self-exclusion, which severely decreases their chances for upward mobility. Current research on intergenerational mobility provides evidence supporting the assertion that children whose parents belong to today's underclass have a higher than average probability of taking their parents' place as adults.

The McKinney Act of 1987 mandated that children without homes are entitled to receive an education like all other children. In response to the mandate, the state of Kentucky formed Family Resource Centers in schools in which the majority of students are at or below poverty level. The resource centers facilitate children's attendance in school by assisting them with material needs such as clothing, food, and school supplies, and nonmaterial needs such as counseling and tutoring. In addition, Family Resource Center staff members emphasize to parents the importance of parental involvement with a child's education and encourage parents to volunteer in some way at school. Personnel at the resource center attempt to work with school faculty members to encourage parental involvement. In an interview with a former staff member at a northern Kentucky resource center, however, I learned that school faculty members often do not encourage involvement on the part of these parents. Mothers with whom I spoke told of feeling welcome at the resource center, but not in other areas of the school, especially as classroom mothers. Each mother who had attempted to become an assistant in the classroom told of the teacher's lack of encouragement for the parent's participation. One mother told of an experience where she repeatedly volunteered to assist the teacher while the teacher never asked the mother to assist. Further, the mother maintained that the teacher seemed irritated every time the mother volunteered for classroom activities.

Again, from Bordieu's perspective, teachers typically bring middle-class value systems to education. If they are ill equipped to cope with children living in poverty, their judgment of the children's parents is likely to be even less tolerant, less empathic, less accepting. Indeed, it would be anathema for classrooms laden with middle-class ideology and for the teachers in those classrooms to view a mother who receives AFDC as a potential role model for the students.

If children of parents who are poor and without housing are to reach even half (national test scores indicate many are not achieving even half) of their potential in school, educators must go beyond legal mandates. Flexible school systems and empathic teachers are needed for coping with children's socioeconomic and sociocultural diversity.

### Unwelcoming School Structures

Unfortunately, the forbidding atmosphere of school buildings in poor neighborhoods can and does reinforce negative messages that poor children receive from the educational system. Antiquated structures, peeling paint, crumbling plaster, and restrooms in constant disrepair tell children they are unimportant. Children learn a lesson that is as lasting as any classroom instruction, if not more so: not to expect much from any situation they enter. For these children, the atmosphere at school is consistent with the atmosphere at home. They grow up believing that this is all there is, this is all they can expect in life, and this is all they deserve.

As middle-class families continue to flee inner-city school systems, the quality of education in those systems has little chance of improving. Because the proportion of households with children in public schools continues to decrease (currently it is about 24 percent), school levies cannot easily muster support. Increasingly, school systems heavily populated by poor Anglos and members of minorities have fewer resources for basic instructional materials. Poor children are the initial losers, but eventually the whole society loses. Taking care of all children early in their lives is a cost-effective investment; certainly it is less costly to society than rehabilitating or incarcerating adults.

## The Role of the Community Environment

Research has established a relationship between dilapidated, economically deprived communities and maladaptive childhood development. Yet there is evidence that even a homogeneous, poor neighborhood can provide children with a buffer against some of the stressors of poverty. Because children living in a totally poor environment are not likely to be in contact with children who enjoy greater material comfort, their self-esteem is less likely to become bruised. They are less likely to be judged by appearances.

Athletic competition frequently brings together children who are disparate in income and race or ethnicity. Differences between lower-income neighborhood schools and middle-income suburban schools are discerned easily in the neighborhood setting, the age and condition of the structure, the quality of the gymnasium, and the team uniforms. Thus even seemingly innocuous athletic meetings have the potential to affect the self-concept of students from schools in poor communities.

On the other hand, children who interact exclusively with persons in their poverty-ridden communities run the risk of adopting characteristics of their neighborhood role models. Two of the children interviewed for this study, sisters aged 9 and 11, spoke matter-of-factly about living in an apartment building in which drug dealers also lived. They recalled the fear they felt when they saw a SWAT (Special Weapons and Tactics) team surround their building in order to apprehend the traffickers. They also reported that the police did not bother to verify whether other tenants were present in the building. Normal police procedure should include ensuring the safety of those in the vicinity of a potentially dangerous arrest. One study suggests that 38 percent of youngsters aged 10 to 17 fear that they could be hurt by someone using drugs. Children should not have to fear being injured by police who are in pursuit of those suspected of committing a crime. Are safety procedures routinely ignored in lower-income neighborhoods? Besides the obvious physical risk to children living among drug dealers, there is the danger that deviance will become normalized in their minds. Children living in such conditions become acutely sensitive to deviance and develop a high tolerance. The sisters giggled, for example, when they described the drug dealers as kind, generous men who gave neighborhood children candy, money, and motorcycle rides. Perhaps it is to their

advantage that they did not fully grasp the immediate danger or the long-term consequences of their circumstances. Yet occasional face-to-face encounters with others outside their community, whose lifestyle is very different, might not be the solution. It might simply emphasize the inequities.

## Bringing Order to Unordered Lives

Because the lives of children in poverty and those without housing are out of control, they often fight for control in any arena they enter, such as the classroom, the school playground, the football field, or the gymnasium. In a society that reveres the home, children without a home soon learn from their environment—their classmates, television, films, and the print media—that their situation is considered abnormal and undesirable. And as these children progress through adolescence—these children who have never been allowed to be children, and who live in a society where middle- and upper-class children are idolized and overindulged by their parents—some rebel against their parents, some vandalize their own community, and some choose the safest victims for destruction: themselves. Those who survive childhood will take their place at the lower levels of the class structure, believing that they will achieve parity with those in other social classes if they only work harder and longer. The great majority will never do so.

According to Charles Cooley's "looking glass" theory, which maintains that we see ourselves reflected in the eyes of others, children who lack permanent housing are likely to see themselves as undesirable. Depending on the child's age, temperament, and familial relationships, he or she will develop protective coping mechanisms such as extreme introversion (as in withdrawal) or extreme extroversion (as in acting out in various ways such as aggressive behavior).

Staff members at Hope House have experienced a variety of coping strategies on the part of children. They stated that age is a factor in determining behavior. Older children who could comprehend the total picture were embarrassed about the situation and the lack of privacy; they tended to withdraw. Younger children, who could not verbalize their insecurity, tended to cling to their mothers. Still others, who sensed their mothers' loss of power over them in the shelter, became disruptive.

# Children and Shelter Life

Despite the best efforts on the part of an excellent shelter like Hope House, staff members acknowledge that the artificial home environment cannot replace the stabilizing, secure effect of permanent housing for children and their parents. If the familiar constantly gives way to the unfamiliar, a child often ceases to form attachments to people and places. This behavior pattern affects performance of adult roles and places the next generation at risk. The two sisters introduced earlier discussed the difficulty of adapting to shelter life, in which they had lived for 3½ months. Within the shelter, the most troublesome features were sharing their room with another family and the resulting lack of privacy. Another issue (less serious but nonetheless irritating) was the abundance of rules in the shelter: rules that contradicted their way of life outside the shelter, rules for minor things such as snacks in the evening or doing homework at a specified time, rules for everything.

One mother told of her preadolescent son's crying spells. He, his mother, and a younger sibling had to share a room with a family with adolescent girls. Although he had little contact with the girls, sharing a room with strangers was experienced as a tremendous loss of control in his life. He had a sense of dread and mortification about the possibilities the situation presented. Changing his clothes became a battle for the mother because he was afraid the girls would walk in on him. He was fearful, too, of having his few possessions taken. One can only imagine the lifelong consequences for this traumatized child.

Outside the shelter, a major concern for children was hiding their shelter life. The sisters described the measures they took to keep their "home" a secret from their classmates. They made certain that none of their schoolmates ever saw them enter or leave the shelter. Ridicule from classmates who knew

they were staying in a shelter was one of their most painful experiences. Former shelter guests confirmed the girls' perceptions and observed that their adolescent children were mortified about their temporary residence. Even at that, not all their experiences with the shelter were negative. The girls spoke positively about some of their shelter experiences. Looking surprised by their own admission, they happily reported that their mother could not whip them when they disobeyed, as was her custom. The girls also pointed out that as shelter guests, they were offered recreational opportunities that would not have been available. Some of the amenities included tickets to concerts and ball games donated by local corporations. A favorite activity was going to the local Boys and Girls Club for swimming and other activities.

An agency in the role of the good provider presents a double-edged sword for families in shelter. Parents, by definition, are supposed to be the providers of the good things in life, including recreational events for children. Parents living in poverty cannot indulge their children in costly leisure activities. Therefore, when an agency replace[d] the parents as provider, mothers expressed mixed emotions. They were happy to see their children enjoying the event, but they also felt saddened about their inability to be the one making their child's life more enjoyable. It threatened their status as a parent. Perhaps one of the hardest things for us to understand about those living in poverty is their seeming lack of gratitude for works of charity and philanthropy. It is difficult to comprehend that dependency breeds hostility, not gratitude. Most people, given the choice, would choose independence over being on the receiving end of charity.

## Familial Relationships in Shelters

When asked about the familial relationships that shelter guests reveal to case managers, Ms. Mayerson and the staff responded without hesitation and almost in unison. Recounting frequent observations of blurred boundaries between mothers and children, they said, "Parents do not parent, and children are not children." Childhood appears to be lost for the youngsters they see. The eldest child or the older children frequently serve as caretakers for the parent as well as the younger children. Although daughters are more likely to be caregivers for all others, staff members reported that typically the sons act like adult male partners for their mothers. Mothers rely on their sons as a wife would rely on a husband. Staff members also pointed out that it was not uncommon for mothers to sleep with their preteen sons . . . (males over age 12 may not stay at Hope House).

Although the mother-child relationships observed by workers seemed to be outside normative expectations from a sociological perspective, a mother's reliance on her children can be understood in several ways. First, from a material standpoint, mothers existing at a survival level have a vague notion of the current cultural prescriptions for performing the mother role, but they have little hope of enacting it. These women have no home, no money, no food, few belongings, and no support system that offers them sustained protection.

Second, the women and their children exhibit vestiges of paradigmatic kin relationships of other eras. For example, families living in poverty resemble members of hunting-and-gathering societies but lack the security and community of a kinship group. The children, like the young of hunting-and-gathering societies, who assisted with sustenance as soon as they could take their place in the group, forage with and sometimes substitute for their parents. Contemporary children whose parents cannot provide for them adequately are producers as well as consumers, like the children of the hunters and gatherers.

Further, families in poverty reflect medieval times, when boundaries between childhood and adulthood hardly existed. During that period, children were treated like small adults (but without the privileges), and took on the roles of caretaker and provider at very young ages. Young boys assumed men's responsibilities; if the father died or departed, the son acted as head of the family. Because housing was scarce and living space inadequate for the poor in the burgeoning cities of that time (just as they are now), family members frequently slept together.

Families living in poverty today cannot be expected to exhibit twentieth-century middle-class Western norms. Earlier models of family and kinship groups might provide more useful explanations of their existence than the current cultural paradigms of motherhood and parenthood. The latter appear almost irrelevant to the material conditions in which these families find themselves.

We must not assume that such behavior is limited to poor persons and those without homes. We do not know the extent to which the familial relationships revealed to workers in shelters are unique to the guest population and to what extent they reflect the larger society. Certainly the research does not support the conclusion that "deviant" familial behavior is the exclusive domain of the poor. The evidence indicates that maladaptive treatment of children, including incest, cuts across all income levels but too often escapes attention unless the family is forced into public scrutiny for some reason. Families are subjected to public examination, for example, when they apply for assistance with income, housing, and/or food. Although behavior bordering on the incestuous is not to be condoned, we cannot assume that incest is class bound or that it is the cause or the consequence of the circumstances surrounding families without homes.

Deviance of any kind is more likely to be uncovered among persons seeking income assistance than among other families, because higher-income families generally can avoid confrontations with an intrusive legal system. The once-private lives of families who seek federal, state, or local assistance are subjected to scrutiny by numerous strangers. Often such families are asked repeatedly to explain their income and budgetary actions, their lifestyle, and their parenting techniques.

Hope House staff members have been trained to understand and accept the uniqueness of each family's situation. While staying alert to behavior that could harm the children, they work with families without passing judgment. They know the realities of shelter guests' lives and remain alert to their self-conscious struggle to achieve the status of the "normative American family."

## Societal Response to Those Without Homes

Our society's response to the growing numbers of people without homes has been ill conceived. It is almost too little, too late. Policies supporting temporary shelter as a solution are based on the assumption that individuals' and families' housing problems are temporary and that people need only a brief stay in a shelter to regain economic solvency. Yet systemic factors beyond individuals' control, such as a shortage of full-time jobs, increased part-time and temporary service work, declining wages, a decrease in affordable housing, and cuts in federal and state assistance for families, have contributed to a crisis-based way of life for increasing numbers of people. Because of unfavorable economic conditions, temporary shelters have become more than a one-time respite; they are a recurring reality for more and more lower-income individuals and families. The dismantling of federal welfare programs that is about to begin means that the chronic crisis of living conditions of poor families will reach epidemic proportions. Temporary housing has not been enough. What will happen when federal funding is completely gone?

## Review

1. Why is education "not an equalizer" for homeless children?

2. How do homelessness and poverty affect the self-concept of children?

3. Describe the effects on children of living in a shelter.

4. What has been the societal response to homelessness?

## Applications

1. Contact city, county, and state offices and obtain information about the latest official statistics on the number of homeless in your community. Get as much demographic information—sex, race, age, number of dependents, etc.— as you can. Contact a local homeless shelter and ask for a demographic breakdown of the people they serve. Are they similar to the official figures? If not, what could account for the discrepancies?

2. Use the library to consult the archives of your local newspaper. Search for stories on homelessness. How often was the issue addressed? When did the majority of the stories appear? What did the stories indicate about the demographics of the homeless, the causes of homelessness, and efforts to deal with it? Summarize your findings in a brief data table and essay.

## Related Web Sites

1. *http://www.nlchp.org/.* Home page of the National Law Center on Homelessness and Poverty, offering many reports and information.

2. *http://www.nationalhomeless.org/families.html.* A fact sheet from the National Coalition for the Homeless about families with children who are homeless.

# Part Two

## *Racial/Ethinic Inequality*

The United States has an increasingly diverse population.

The proportion of the population that is white and non-Hispanic continues to decline (from 79.9 percent in 1980 to 71.3 percent in 2000). As the number of racial/ethnic Americans increases, their demands for an equitable share in American life grow stronger. Historically, the minorities have not had equal access to the American dream. They have endured considerable **prejudice** (a negative attitude toward those in a different racial/ethnic group that justifies discriminatory behavior) and **discrimination** (arbitrary, unfavorable treatment of people in a different racial/ethnic group). Discrimination of racial/ethnic minorities has been maintained through the policies and practices of institutions, a process that sociologists call **institutional racism.**

In this part, selections 17 and 18 examine the struggles of racial/ethnic minorities, including an example of institutional racism. Selection 19 shows how prejudice enters into the way we interpret aspects of our culture like motion pictures. ✦

# 17

# Women of Color in Academe

## Living With Multiple Marginality

*Caroline Sotello Viernes Turner*

*In the first part of the 20th century, sociologists developed the notion of marginality to explain the plight of second-generation immigrants. In essence, the children of immigrants tried to be a part of mainstream American society as they grew up, but their obvious immigrant roots hindered their efforts. They were not fully accepted by the larger society, but neither were they fully part of the immigrant culture in which they grew up. Thus, the term "marginal" signified people who were living in two different social worlds but who were not fully part of either of them.*

*Racial/ethnic groups continue to be marginalized in varying degrees. And unlike the European immigrants, who became indistinguishable from other Americans over the course of time, most racial/ethnic groups are identifiable by skin color or other physical characteristics. In this selection, Turner discusses the problems women of color face even in the academic setting where one might expect greater acceptance. In fact, women of color experience double jeopardy—from both their color and their gender. In the next part, we'll deal with gender inequality. Here, you'll see that many women of color are not sure whether it's their color or their gender or both that underlies the inequality, while others are convinced that color is even more important than gender as a source of their struggles.*

## Introduction

I recall a personal example of how multiple social identities may shape one's opportunities in higher education. As a woman of color from a "no collar" class (I come from a farm labor background), when first exploring graduate school options I was discouraged from applying to a master's level program in business by an admissions officer. The admissions officer stated that I would not fit. I was a woman, a minority, a single parent, I had a background in the public sector, and I had some but not enough math background. This would make it nearly impossible for me to succeed as others in the program fit another and opposite profile. Although all of this may be true, it did not occur to the admissions officer that this might not be an appropriate state of affairs for student enrollment in the program. It was merely accepted as the way things are and should remain. I remember being struck by the many ways I could be defined as not "fitting" and, therefore, not encouraged and, more than likely, not admitted. I was so easily "defined out" rather than "defined in."

I am now a faculty member at a major research university. My current work focuses on the experiences of faculty of color in higher education. While pursuing this work, I have had many opportunities to interview, converse with, and read about the lives of other faculty women of color. Many continue to speak, although in different ways, about the experience of multiple marginality and being defined out. The following quotations from the literature give insight into the lives of faculty women of color, including my own.

## Lived Contradiction

"I am struck by my lived contradiction: To be a professor is to be an Anglo; to be a Latina is not to be an Anglo. So how can I be both a Latina and a professor? To be a Latina professor, I conclude, means to be unlike and like me. *Que locura!* What madness! . . . As Latina professors, we are newcomers to a world defined and controlled by discourses that do not address our realities, that do not affirm our intellectual contributions, that do not seriously examine our worlds. Can I be both Latina and professor without compromise?" (Ana M. Martinez Aleman in Padilla & Chavez, 1995, pp. 74–75).

## Ambiguous Empowerment

"Readers who have listened to any group of professional women talk about their work experiences will likely find these stories familiar. Like other successful women who work in male and white-dominated professions, women superintendents have much to say about the way they managed to get into such positions despite the anomaly of their gender or race, how they developed confidence in their competence and authority, and what they have accomplished by exercising their professional power. They also talk about various forms of gender and race inequality that structure the profession and how they respond to discriminatory treatment . . . I study these familiar stories in order to understand how professional women make sense of their ambiguous empowerment—in the context of contemporary American culture." (Chase, 1995, p. x).

The narrative data presented here portray the lives of faculty women of color as filled with lived contradictions and ambiguous empowerment. Chase's (1995) "ambiguous empowerment" based on the lives of women school superintendents also applies to the experiences of faculty women of color. Although faculty women of color have obtained academic positions, even when tenured they often confront situations that limit their authority and, as they address these situations, drain their energy. For example, in an interview[1] a woman of color who is a full professor and chair of her department observes:

"I'm the department chair . . . and I meet with a lot of people who don't know me— you know, prospective students and their parents. And I know that their first reaction to me is that I'm an Asian American woman, not that I'm a scientist or that I'm competent."

Statements by faculty women of color typically relay such observations. Unfortunately, the lives of faculty women of color are often invisible, hidden within studies that look at the experiences of women faculty and within studies that examine the lives of faculty of color. Women of color fit both categories, experience multiple marginality, and their stories are often masked within these contexts.[2] This article seeks to redress such shortcomings by presenting experiences expressed by faculty women of color in interviews conducted by the author and in statements published in the higher education literature. At times I include personal observations.

## How Do Proportions Count?

To begin, it is informative to discuss the importance and implications of representation or lack of representation within organizations. Kanter's theory of proportions (1977) first made me aware of the potential effects of marginality on social interactions and mobility in a corporate setting. Briefly, Kanter describes the effect of being a "token." She states that the numerical distribution of men and women in the upper reaches of the corporation provide different interaction contexts for those in the majority versus those in the minority (p. 206). For example, women in the minority (in very small proportion) inhabit a context characterized by the following:

- Being more visible and on display
- Feeling more pressure to conform, to make fewer mistakes
- Becoming socially invisible, not to stand out
- Finding it harder to gain credibility
- Being more isolated and peripheral
- Being more likely to be excluded from informal peer networks, having limited sources of power through alliances
- Having fewer opportunities to be sponsored
- Facing misperceptions of their identity and role in the organization
- Being stereotyped

• Facing more personal stress

Those in the majority (in very high proportion) face the opposite social context. They are seen as one of the group, preferred for sponsorship by others inhabiting higher level positions (pp. 248–249).

Although Kanter's work articulates the social situation for "tokens" quite well, she primarily speaks to the situation of White women in an organizational setting. Kanter's argument suggests that those who differ from the norm within the corporate hierarchy encounter a cycle of cumulative disadvantage, whereas those who fit the norm experience a cycle of cumulative advantage. Her theories imply that the more ways in which one differs from the "norm," the more social interactions will be affected within multiple contexts. Situations in which a woman of color might experience marginality are multiplied depending on her marginal status within various contexts. Often it is difficult to tell whether race or gender stereotyping is operating. When asked if she experienced any barriers, one woman of color in academe, quoted in Hune (1998), responded: "The answer is yes. I think for me personally, it's hard to know if it's because I am a woman or because I am Asian, or both" (p. 11). In a conversation with me, another faculty member stated: "Dealing with the senior, [mostly white] males in my department has been a huge challenge. . . . I don't know if they tend to discount my contributions because I'm new, female, Latina, young, or what. Perhaps a combination of all of the above." Rains (1999) calls attention to the complexities that daily pervade the experiences of many women of color in the academy (p. 152).

Cho (1996) sheds light on the complexities of defining parity. Her work describes bias suffered by Asian Pacific Americans in the academic workplace even though the perception is that they are well represented and, therefore, successful. She contends the following: (1) numbers showing over-parity in some fields or disciplines mask related under-parity in other fields; (2) over-parity status at the entry level does not mean over-parity status higher up on the promotion lad-

der; and (3) inferences drawn from an aggregated over-parity status serve to make invisible the varied needs of a heterogeneous population (p. 34). Cho's work made me realize that drawing a statistical picture of numerical "inclusion" without reflecting on the context of that inclusion and "quality of life" factors paints an incomplete portrait.

## Representation and the Creation of Campus Climate

Studies by Harvey (1991) and Spann (1990) further illuminate the importance and complexity of representation in the development of the campus climates within which faculty women of color work. According to Harvey, "campus climate" is a "term used to describe the culture, habits, decisions, practices, and policies that make up campus life. The degree to which the climate is hospitable determines the 'comfort factor' for African Americans and other nonwhite persons on campus" (p. 128). In defining the chilly climate within an academic setting, Spann gives voice to discussions by her study respondents (referred to as panelists):

> Panelists defined climate as the quality of respect and support accorded to women and minorities on individual campuses and in individual departments. They believed that climates were created by institutions and could be measured in specific ways, . . . by the number of women and minority faculty members at junior and senior levels, . . . by the social distance between majority and minority group faculty and administrators, . . . by the equitability of work assignments. (p. 1)

Spann's study implies that nontraditional faculty representation within different locations (i.e., junior and senior faculty status as well as administrative positions) in the organization determines, in large part, what her respondents describe as campus climate. Providing support for the impact of social distance argument, Etzkowitz, Kemelgor, and Uzzi (2000) stress that the existence of a "critical mass" (i.e., at least 15% of women in an organization) to address tokenism will not fully address the situation of the minority in an organization. They state that "the precise number is less important than the nature of the response the new minority receives from the majority" (p.107).

## Representation and Distribution: Demographic Data

The Chronicle of Higher Education Almanac (2001) reports that the total of full-time faculty members, including instructor and lecturer, is 568,719, of which 204,794 (36%) are women. Of the total women, 29,546 (14%) are women of color. Table 17.1 shows the underrepresentation of women of color in the professorate by rank and racial/ethnic breakdown.

Similar patterns are reported for the Instructor and Lecturer categories, with women of color represented in small numbers in each academic rank. Contrary to the "model minority" myth, women in the Asian category are not the most represented of the faculty women of color. Hune and Chan (1997) note that Asian Pacific American (APA) men represent three-quarters of all APA faculty, and that APAs have the largest gender gap of any racial/ethnic group (p. 57). In the main, faculty women of color primarily occupy the junior, untenured ranks whereas men of color occupy the more senior, tenured ranks. For more information on within group patterns, see Carter and Wilson (1997). The American Council on Education (ACE) data also report lower tenure rates for women of color in tenure-track positions (Wilds, 2000, p. 101).[3]

## Interviews With Faculty Women of Color

In this section I draw from and elaborate on interviews with 64 faculty members of color to analyze the consequences of underrepresentation for women faculty of color.[4] Four Asian Pacific American females, fifteen African American females, four Native American females, and eight Latinas were interviewed. Most of these women occupy tenured positions; some are high-level academic administrators.[5] They spoke about the interlocking effects of race and gender bias in the academic workplace.

## Manifestation of Interlocking Race and Gender Bias

In general, faculty of color describe racial and ethnic bias in ways that overlap with the concerns raised by women.[6] Yet the interlocking effects of gender and race compound the pressures of the workplace environment for faculty women of color. They perceive that being both minority and female hampers their success as faculty members.[7] This respondent talks about being defined out of consideration for an administrative position because she is an Asian female.

"A [university administrative] position opened up and there were a lot of names mentioned—it was clear that an active [internal] person would be named. I would hear on the grapevine 'so-and-so's' name. . . . I felt that if I were a white male,

---

**Table 17.1**
*Full-Time Women in the Professorate by Rank, Race/Ethnicity 1997*

| Women Faculty by Race/Ethnicity | Rank | | |
| --- | --- | --- | --- |
| | Full Professor | Associate Professor | Assistant Professor |
| Total Women | 32,353 | 43,522 | 57,354 |
| American Indian | 92 | 145 | 285 |
| Asian | 1,243 | 1,633 | 3,113 |
| Black | 1,924 | 2,674 | 4,288 |
| Hispanic | 767 | 1,088 | 1,753 |
| White | 28,107 | 37,586 | 46,385 |

Source: The Chronicle of Higher Education Almanac, 2001.

my name would have been out there. I
mean I am sure of that. But it never was
and, you know, . . . there is no question in
my mind that race and gender influenced
that."[8]

## Challenges From Academic Old Boy Networks

Although noted in the literature, I uncovered only indirect mention of challenges from academic old boy networks in the interviews. One American Indian woman alludes to this situation in her comment: "This is hard to believe—for a long time I was the only woman of color on this faculty—for years. . . . This campus is very, very white. Almost all of the Indian faculty have been men." Montero-Sieburth (1996) similarly states that Latina professors must overcome more obstacles to gain support for academic advancement, because they are farther removed from the academic old-boy network than Latino or White female counterparts. Although instances of mentorship across and within racial/ethnic and gender groups exist, scarce resources such as tenured faculty positions and chairs of Chicano studies programs can pit Latinas against Latinos. In a similar vein, Hooks (1991) states that scholars writing about Black intellectual life focus solely on the lives and works of Black men, ignoring and devaluing the scholarship of Black women intellectuals.

Themes that emerge from the study interviews include: (1) feeling isolated and underrespected; (2) salience of race over gender; (3) being underemployed and overused by departments and/or institutions; (4) being torn between family, community, and career; and (5) being challenged by students. I describe these themes below.

## Feeling Isolated and Underrespected

One professor expresses the isolation and the added pressure to perform as a woman of color:

"I have to think about the fact that black females or any female in the field of [name] that has been predominantly a white male profession, has a problem.

Many [white] females in the college complain about the fact that up until recently . . . we had never had a full professor in [department name]. It's changing, but it's not changing fast. And then you add to that being the black female who has to be superwoman."

Focusing more on slots filled rather than on expertise or potential programmatic contributions are reported by this newly hired faculty member:

"This one dean . . . was writing down all the federal slots that I would fit in as far as hiring. . . . And he says, "Okay, you're a woman, you're over fifty-five, you're an American Indian," and then he looks at me and grins. He said, "Do you have a handicap?" . . . These schools have to fulfill these guidelines and in getting me they can check a lot of boxes."

## Salience of Race Over Gender

Despite shared gender discrimination, women faculty of color cannot always expect support from their white female colleagues. A sense that white women have fared and are faring better than are women or men of color exists. This perception speaks to the salience of race over gender. An American Indian woman notes: "Even the white females they've hired still have a problem with minority students and minority perspectives. This is particularly true in [discipline]. It is really dominated by Western European notions."

Montero-Sieburth (1996) points out that "being female does not necessarily guarantee the sympathy of mainstream women toward them nor does it offer entry into mainstream academic domains" (p. 84). She quotes one Latina professor commenting on an experience with White female researchers: "I was always singled out when we needed to present research about underserved communities or make statements about the Latino population; otherwise, my research was ignored" (p. 84).

Gains made by white women resulting from affirmative action are not reflected for women of color. A report by the Women's Environment and Development Organization entitled Women's Equality: An Unfinished Agenda (2000) supports this perception:

> "Although all women benefit from affirmative action, white women have been the major beneficiaries in the areas of education, contracting and employment. Indeed, white women have progressed to such a significant degree in the area of education that the challenge of affirmative action is no longer in college admissions but in graduate schools and in such areas as engineering and science for which the numbers of women are woefully small. . . . However, affirmative action is still a vital necessity in higher education for women of color, particularly African American and Latino women, whose numbers still lag in undergraduate admissions and in all levels of graduate and professional schools." (*www.wedo.org/book.txt*)

However, as stated previously, statistical representation is not entirely revealing of the quality of inclusion or equitable distribution in higher education even for white women in the academy. Within the higher education literature (i.e., Glazer-Raymo, 1999), exclusion and the "glass ceiling" phenomenon are well documented as affecting all women. Nonetheless, such statistics fuel the perception that white women, not women of color, have been the primary benefactors of affirmative action.

## Being Underemployed and Overused by Departments and/or Institutions

Unlike White male faculty members, women of color say they are expected to handle minority and gender affairs, representing two constituencies. An American Indian female faculty member states: "Issues of pedagogy and cultural diversity and gender are not the province of just women or just faculty of color. I think that happens too often and that puts the faculty of color person or woman on the spot, to kind of convince or persuade—be this change agent. . . . The faculty members feel the added pressure, but are caught in a 'Catch-22' because minority issues are also important to them."

Mitchell (1994) notes that the small numbers of faculty women of color compels them to serve simultaneously as a role model for their profession, race, and gender: "The accountability and time demands that the female ethnic professor encounters are especially pressing, given the fact that minority women occupy even fewer positions than minority men"[9] (p. 387). In retrospect, this African American woman, who did not attain tenure in her first university states: "I am a female and African American. . . . I was doing a lot of things in terms of serving on this board, serving on that board, being faculty adviser for one of the professional fraternities." A Latina notes: "When you are one of three or four Latinos and being a woman, almost every committee wants you to be on it. It gives you opportunities, at the same time, I think, you are expected to do a lot of things not expected of other faculty."

These quotes bring attention to the apparent contradiction and "double whammy" faced by women of color. On the one hand, there is too little opportunity and support for the work that is valued (research) (Fairweather, 1996); on the other hand, there is too much demand for work that is not rewarded (committee work, student club advisor, etc.). In most instances, service does not lead to tenure or to prestigious positions related to committee service, such as administration. Junior faculty members are particularly at risk. Institutional reward systems can deny tenure and security of employment to those who spend more time on service than on research and scholarship, even when the service is assigned to meet institutional needs.

## Being Torn Between Family, Community, and Career

Many faculty women of color speak about being "psychologically divided between home and career" or between community and career. They seemingly have two choices: sacrifice family and community commitments for several years to focus almost exclusively on their careers, or honor nonwork commitments, an essential part of their identity, at the risk of not earning tenure. Although policies to accommodate faculty needs for maternity and family leave and childcare are becoming common, little attention has been paid in the academy to minority faculty's desire to contribute actively to their racial or ethnic community (for further discussion see Townsend & Turner, 2000). For example, for many Native Americans, including faculty members (Stein, 1996), "the social value and preeminent goal in life . . . is the survival of the Indian people" (Cross, 1996, p. 335). Similarly, some Chicano faculty "maintain a strong affiliation with their community and feel a strong sense of responsibility to improve the status of other Chicanos in the larger community" (de la Luz Reyes & Halcon, 1988/1996, p. 345; see also Rendon, 1992/1996). For most African American faculty, ties with the Black community are extremely important partly because of "the African heritage of communalism" (Gregory, 1995, p. 7).

## Being Challenged by Students

Faculty women of color perceive that they are more likely to have their authority challenged by students than are White male professors.[10] As examples, consider the following:

"If a white male professor says something that's wrong in class, my observation is that even if the students perceive that it's wrong, they may say something outside of class, but they hesitate to challenge a 50+ white male professor. They feel quite comfortable challenging an African American woman in class."

"Regarding interaction with students, there's a different expectation for us when we walk in as a minority, they automatically assume that we know less than our colleagues in the same department. . . . It doesn't matter whether it's undergraduate level or graduate level. . . . They challenge females more. . . . So, I wear dark, tailored suits and I am very well prepared. They don't hire us unless we're prepared anyway, but students think we are here because of our color."

Many women faculty of color are called on to advise students of color and others studying in similar fields. Because of their scarcity, faculty women of color can face great out-of-class instructional loads. One junior faculty member of color describes her experience as teacher/mentor:

"As teacher/mentor, the main issue has been balancing. When I first arrived, I was overwhelmed by the amounts of students who came to me to ask for guidance (not always in so many words)—mostly women of color, feeling like most other faculty did not acknowledge their existence. It is difficult to balance this with the research and publication pressures, and course preparation."

Another female faculty member states:

"It is hard to say no, especially on minority issues, when there are so few people. . . . I realize how few people are available [to address these issues]. . . . I sit on 53 doctoral committees. Doctoral students take a lot of time for the dissertation process. I turned down being chair of one doctoral student's committee and she nearly cried. She was a good student studying multicultural issues, but I can't chair these committees. I'll wind up spending all my time correcting dissertations and not doing my own writing."

Andrews (1993) describes this situation as an "emotional drain":

"The Black woman professor is often called upon to serve as mentor, mother, and counselor in addition to educator in these settings. The consequences of these multifaceted role expectations by students are compounded by the existence of similar demands placed upon Black women by colleagues and administrators. . . . If we consider the fact that Black women often also have these same expectations to meet at home, it is abundantly clear that in many cases something has to give." (p. 190).

Cruz (1995) summarizes her reaction to such experiences: "It was not simply that my colleagues and students made me feel different; it was that my difference was equated with inferiority" (in Padilla & Chavez, 1995, p. 93). . . .

## Conclusion

Over the last decade, I have interviewed many women of color who are undergraduate students, graduate students, and who are faculty members. Many of these individuals feel that to succeed in academe requires them to leave themselves, who they are, at the door of graduate education and the tenure process. This loss would be a tragedy for both current and future faculty women of color. Acknowledging who we are and how that affects our approaches to research as well as what we find of scholarly interest may result in a more viable work environment for women faculty of color now and in the future:

"Each person brings a unique cultural background to their experience. Who you are shapes the types of questions you ask, the kinds of issues which interest you, and the ways in which you go about seeking solutions. . . . Although doctoral student and faculty socialization processes are very strong, we must not lose ourselves in the process of fitting in. . . . [Also, as demonstrated here,] the backgrounds [faculty women of color] bring to academia need not take a back seat. . . . They can be placed in the foreground of our work." (Turner, 2000, p. 133).

By bringing ourselves through the door and supporting others in doing so as well, we can define ourselves in and claim unambiguous empowerment, creating discourses that address our realities, affirm our intellectual contributions, and seriously examine our worlds.

## Notes

1. Throughout this text I use quotations to exemplify issues discussed. Quotations from interviews are observations made by faculty women of color who participated in a study conducted by the author and Samuel L. Myers, Jr. (2000).

2. Even though common themes are noted in this essay, it is also important to acknowledge that all women of color are not the same and that institutions should not expect them to behave as such. Furthermore, women of color have a range of interests and ways in which they choose to contribute to the academy.

3. Numbers of full-time faculty in higher education are also noted in the latest American Council on Education (ACE) Status Report (Wilds, 2000, p. 98). These numbers show that women of color comprise 14% of the professorate, the same percent as reported in The Chronicle of Higher Education Almanac for Fall, 1997. Of the total full-time faculty (538,023) in 1995, 187,267 (35%) were women; 26,247 of the women were women of color (14%). These data show that across ranks and tenure status the proportion of full-time women faculty of color is low.

4. See Turner and Myers (2000) for a detailed description of the study design.

5. Respondents were located in the biological and physical sciences as well as in the social sciences, humanities, and education. Interviews solicited views on reasons for pursuing an academic career, the pathways that led them to the current position, professional development experiences, experiences as faculty members, general experiences in the academic workplace, future plans and expectations with regard to leaving academia, and recommendations for improving the recruitment and retention of faculty of color.

6. Respondents of color in the Turner and Myers study (2000) reveal that they face covert and overt forms of racial and ethnic bias. Manifestations of bias described by faculty respondents include: (1) Denial of tenure or promotion due to race/ethnicity; (2) being expected to work harder than whites; (3) having their color/ethnicity given more attention than their credentials; (4) being treated like a token; (5) lack of support or validation of research on minority issues; (6) being expected to handle minority affairs; (7) too few minorities on campus.

7. Similar results are reflected in Through My Lens, a video production by Women of Color in the Academy Project at the University of Michigan (Aparicio, 1999). One featured participant speaks of the intersection of race and gender in the academy: "I think that the university is committed but oftentimes has a hard time understanding the position of women of color, certainly understanding how color, how culture and race, make an impact on one's career is a challenge. And then, understanding how being a woman impacts one's career is a challenge as well."

8. In the literature, Ideta and Cooper (1999) note that "Asian women leaders seem to live in the confines of paradoxes. As Asian females they struggle in organizations which define leaders as primarily male and White. . . . Behaviors which are typical of leaders (displays of power, authority, and fortitude) are considered atypical for women and doubly atypical for Asian women . . . expected to be compliant and subservient in their behavior" (p. 141).

9. Padilla (1994) refers to being expected to handle minority affairs as "cultural taxation," "the obligation to show good citizenship toward the institution by serving its needs for ethnic representation on committees, or to demonstrate knowledge and commitment to a cultural group, which may even bring accolades to the institution but which is not usually rewarded by the institution on whose behalf the service was performed" (p. 26). He goes on to state that as long as people of color are scarce, such expectations will continue to be the norm.

10. One White male professor quoted in "Silences as weapons: Challenges of a Black professor teaching white students" (Ladson-Billings, 1996, p. 79) states that students will perceive him as objective, scholarly, and disinterested when teaching issues related to class, race, and gender. On the other hand, minority females teaching in these areas are often seen as self-interested, bitter, and espousing political agendas. His observations mirror comments made by women of color about their classroom experiences (see Committee on Women in Psychology and American Psychological Association Committee, *Surviving and Thriving in Academia: A Guide for Women and Ethnic Minorities*, 1998).

## References

Aleman, A. M. (1995). Actuando. In R. Padilla & R. Chavez (Eds.), *The leaning ivory tower: Latino professors in American universities* (pp. 67–76). Albany: State University of New York Press.

Andrews, A. R. (1993). Balancing personal and professional. In J. James & R. Farmer (Eds.), *Spirit, space, and survival: African American women in (White) academe*. New York: Routledge.

Aparicio, F. R. (1999). Through my lens: A video project about women of color faculty at the University of Michigan. *Feminist Studies, 25,* 119–130.

Carter, D. J., & Wilson, R. (1997). *Minorities in higher education: Fifteenth annual status report*. Washington, DC: American Council on Education.

Chase, S. E. (1995). *Ambiguous empowerment: The work narratives of women school superintendents*. Amherst: The University of Massachusetts Press.

Cho, S. (1996). Confronting the myths: Asian Pacific American faculty in higher education. Ninth Annual APAHE Conference Proceedings (pp. 31–56). San Francisco: APAHE.

The Chronicle of Higher Education Almanac. (2001). Volume 48, Number 1. Washington, DC.

Committee on Women in Psychology and APA Commission on Ethnic Minority Recruitment, Retention, and Training in Psychology. (1998). *Surviving and thriving in academia: A guide for women and ethnic minorities*. Washington, DC: American Psychological Association.

Cross, W. T. (1996). Pathway to the professorate: The American Indian faculty pipeline. In C. Turner, M. Garcia, A. Nora, & L. I. Rendon (Eds.), *Racial and ethnic diversity in higher education* (pp. 327–336). Needham Heights, MA: Simon & Schuster Custom Publishing.

Cruz, D. M. (1995). Struggling with the labels that mark my identity. In R. Padilla & R. Chavez (Eds.), *The leaning ivory tower: Latino professors in American universities* (pp. 91–100). Albany: State University of New York Press.

De la Luz Reyes, M., & Halcon, J. J. (1988/1996). Racism in academia: The old wolf revisited. In C. Turner, M. Garcia, A. Nora, & L. I. Rendon (Eds.), *Racial and ethnic diversity in higher education* (pp. 337–348). Needham Heights, MA: Simon & Schuster Custom Publishing.

Etzkowitz, H., Kemelgor, C., & Uzzi, B. (2000). *Athena unbound: The advancement of women in science and technology*. New York: Cambridge University Press.

Fairweather, J. (1996). *Faculty work and the public trust*. Boston: Allyn & Bacon.

Glazer-Raymo, J. (1999). *Shattering the myths: Women in academe*. Baltimore, MD: The Johns Hopkins University Press.

Gregory, S. (1995). *Black women in the academy: The secrets to success and achievement*. New York: University Press of America.

Harvey, W. B. (1991). Faculty responsibility and tolerance. *Thought and Action, 7,* 115–136.

Hooks, B. (1991). *Breaking bread: Insurgent Black intellectual life.* Boston, MA: South End Press.

Hune, S. (1998). *Asian Pacific American women in higher education: Claiming visibility and voice.* Washington, DC: Association of American Colleges and Universities.

Hune, S., & Chan, K. S. (1997). Special focus: Asian Pacific American demographic and educational trends. In D. Carter & R. Wilson (Eds.), *Minorities in higher education: Fifteenth annual status report* (pp. 39–67). Washington, DC: American Council on Education.

Ideta, L. M., & Cooper, J. E. (1999). Asian women leaders of higher education: Stories of strength and self-discovery. In L. Christian-Smith & K. Kellor (Eds.), *Everyday knowledge and uncommon truths: Women of the academy* (pp. 129–146). Boulder, CO: Westview Press.

Kanter, R. M. (1977). *Men and women of the corporation.* New York: Basic Books.

Ladson-Billings, G. (1996). Silences as weapons: Challenges of a Black professor teaching white students. *Theory into Practice, 35* (2), 79–85.

Mitchell, J. (1994). Visible, vulnerable, and viable: Emerging perspectives of a minority professor. In K. Feldman & M. Paulsen (Eds.), *Teaching and learning in the college classroom* (pp. 383–390). Needham Heights, MA: Simon & Schuster Custom Publishing.

Montero-Sieburth, M. (1996). Beyond affirmative action: An inquiry into the experiences of Latinas in academia. *New England Journal of Public Policy, 2,* 65–98.

Padilla, A. M. (1994). Ethnic minority scholars, research, and mentoring: Current and future issues. *Educational Researcher, 23* (4), 24–27.

Padilla, R. V., & Chavez, R. C. (1995). *The leaning ivory tower: Latino professors in American universities.* Albany: State University of New York Press.

Rains, F. V. (1999). Dancing on the sharp edge of the sword: Women faculty of color in white academe. In L. Christian-Smith & K. Kellor (Eds.), *Everyday knowledge and uncommon truths: Women of the academy* (pp. 147–174). Boulder, CO: Westview Press.

Rendon, L. I. (1992/1996). From the barrio to the academy: Revelations of a Mexican American "scholarship girl." In C. Turner, M. Garcia, A. Nora, & L. I. Rendon (Eds.), *Racial and ethnic diversity in higher education* (pp. 281–287). Needham Heights, MA: Simon & Schuster Custom Publishing.

Spann, J. (1990). *Retaining and promoting minority faculty members: Problems and possibilities.* Madison: The University of Wisconsin System.

Stein, W. (1996). The survival of American Indian faculty. In C. Turner, M. Garcia, A. Nora, & L. I. Rendon (Eds.), *Racial and ethnic diversity in higher education* (pp. 390–397). Needham Heights, MA: Simon & Schuster Custom Publishing.

Townsend, B., & Turner, C. (2000, March 27). Reshaping the academy to accommodate conflicts of commitment: Then what? Paper presented at the Shaping a National Agenda for Women in Higher Education conference. Minneapolis, MN.

Turner, C. S. V. (2000). Defining success: Promotion and tenure—Planning for each career stage and beyond. In M. Garcia (Ed.), *Succeeding in an academic career: A guide for faculty of color* (pp. 111–140). Westport, CT: Greenwood Press.

Turner, C. S. V., & Myers, S. L., Jr. (2000). *Faculty of color in academe: Bittersweet success.* Needham Heights, MA: Allyn and Bacon.

Wilds, D. J. (2000). *Minorities in higher education: Seventeenth annual status report.* Washington, DC: American Council on Education, Office of Minorities in Higher Education.

Women's Environment and Development Organization. (2000). Women 's equality 1995–2000: An unfinished agenda. Retrieved December 2000 from *www.wedo.org/book.txt.* New York: Women's Environment and Development Organization.

## Review

1. What does Turner mean by "ambiguous empowerment"?

2. What are some of the consequences for minorities of being a low proportion of the workers in a job setting?

3. Identify and briefly illustrate some of the negative experiences of women of color in academe.

4. What does it mean to be "underemployed and overused" in a university?

## Application

Interview two professors in your school who represent a racial/ethnic minority. If possible, choose one male and one female. Ask them to describe any problems minority teachers have that white teachers do not have. Briefly summarize for them the main points made in Turner's article. Ask them to respond in terms of their own experience (personal or what they know of other minorities). If you interview a male and female, how did their experiences compare? Do you believe that racial/ethnic background is more important than gender, or the reverse? Why? If the professors you interview are typical, what conclusions would you draw?

## Related Web Sites

1. *http://www.eeoc.gov/stats/reports/womenofcolor/women6.html*. Data from the EEOC on the total employment of minority women as officials and managers from 1990 to 2001.

2. *http://www.apa.org/pi/wpo/academe/resources.html*. A list of books and articles that explore the issues faced by women of color in academe.

---

# 18

# Policies of Prejudice

## Gregory Squires

*While one might expect that prejudice and discrimination go hand in hand, this is not always the case. An important study done in the United States during the 1930s illustrates this point. Richard LaPiere, a social psychologist, accompanied a Chinese couple on a journey across the country and found that fewer than 1 percent of the food and lodging establishments along the way refused the couple service. However, when LaPiere later wrote the same businesses asking whether they would serve Chinese customers, over 90 percent said they would not. Obviously, action was not consistent with **attitude** in this instance.*

*In the United States today, we are likely to find the opposite situation. That is, public expressions of prejudice are less likely to occur, but discrimination in some forms persists. It is important to distinguish between de jure and de facto forms of discrimination. De jure discrimination is formally written into law; de facto is more subtle and informal, based on customs and existing social arrangements. De jure discrimination against minorities has been eliminated in the United States. De facto discrimination has been more difficult to eliminate in this country, because in some instances it derives from the normal workings of institutions (i.e., institutional racism).*

*While specific governmental remedies have been utilized to overcome de facto discrimination in education (e.g., voluntary or mandatory busing) and in employment (e.g., affirmative action), residential segregation has been more difficult to address. In this selection, Squires shows how so-called redlining practices perpetuate discrimination against minorities in the housing market and in their efforts to develop businesses.*

Racial discrimination in the home mortgage market has finally been acknowledged by lenders and regulators in recent years after decades of organizing efforts by community groups around the country. But equally harmful redlining practices by property insurers have received far less attention. Yet property insurance is essential for home ownership, business development, or any urban revitalization effort. The vital role of property insurance for the development of the nation's cities was captured in the following statement of a federal advisory report almost thirty years ago:

> Insurance is essential to revitalize our cities. It is a cornerstone of credit. Without insurance, banks and other financial institutions will not and cannot make loans. New housing cannot be constructed, and existing housing cannot be repaired. New businesses cannot be opened, and existing businesses cannot expand or even survive.

Without insurance, buildings are left to deteriorate; services, goods, and jobs diminish. Efforts to rebuild our nation's inner cities cannot move forward. Communities without insurance are communities without hope.[1]

Despite widespread evidence of discrimination by the property insurance industry, public officials have not pursued remedies to insurance redlining as aggressively as federal financial regulatory agencies have begun to address redlining by mortgage lenders. Where many lenders now acknowledge, perhaps grudgingly, their responsibilities under federal law, the insurance industry's basic response continues to be resistance. However, things may be changing.

## The Evidence

The insurance industry, like the housing industry generally, has long utilized race as a factor in appraising and underwriting property. In the past, the Federal Housing Administration (FHA) has warned of "inharmonious racial groups" in its underwriting manuals. Lenders have considered "pride of ownership" in mortgage applications, and homeowners have incorporated racially restrictive covenants in home sales contracts. But insurers were no less concerned with race, sometimes indirectly through vague references to such terms as "character," but often explicitly as well.

In a 1958 report called "Report on Negro Areas of Chicago," the National Inspection Company, which provided technical underwriting consulting services to insurers, noted the "encroachment of Negroes" and observed that "The Puerto Ricans, Mexicans, Japanese and 'Hillbillies' have worked into some colored areas, particularly on the fringe of the cheaper or poorer districts and, in some cases, are in the same category with the lower-class Negroes." The report went on to describe a racially mixed neighborhood in Chicago and concluded, "Any liability in the areas described should be carefully scrutinized and in case of Negro dwellings, usually only the better maintained, owner-occupied risks are considered acceptable for profitable underwriting."

In 1977, the Chief Actuary of the New York Department of Insurance stated, "Take Harlem, for example. They don't need any insurance because they don't have anything of value to insure."

That same year, the Michigan Insurance Commissioner stated that "many of the underwriting rules are not rules at all, but are a conglomeration of myths, notions, perceptions, and beliefs. They are often subjective, not based upon scientific, empirical fact." And in 1994 the Texas Insurance Commissioner told the Senate Banking Committee, "We still find insurance companies making underwriting decisions based on all kinds of factors that have nothing to do with a statistically measured or measurable probability of risk."

The overt use of race in underwriting and pricing of insurance has been reduced in recent years, but it has not disappeared. The sales manager of American Family Insurance, a large insurer, told one agent, "I think you write too many blacks," and instructed several other agents in writing to "quit writing all those blacks. . . ." Until a few years ago, American Family produced a document called "Red Flags for Underwriting," which included "population or racial changes" as

one of the flags. And in a 1993 underwriting manual, Nationwide stated that an "applicant must be a person of integrity and financial stability who takes pride in his property"—a phrase that can be understood to mean white people.

More systematic evidence also indicates the continuing role of race in property insurance markets. In 1993, the Missouri Department of Insurance found that residents of low-income minority neighborhoods in St. Louis paid 50 percent more than did residents of low-income white areas for comparable policies, even though losses over the previous five years had been higher in the white communities. Back in 1995, an economist with the department also found that the number of agents in a community was directly related to the racial composition of the area even after controlling for loss history. Ironically, loss costs turned out not to be a significant factor in accounting for the distribution of agents in St. Louis.

The National Association of Insurance Commissioners (NAIC) recently obtained loss data from a sample of insurers in forty-seven communities across thirteen states. Again, even after controlling for losses, the number of policies and the price of those policies in a community remained significantly associated with racial composition of the neighborhood. In their 1995 report, the researchers concluded that the results "lend greater support to concerns that the causes are not confined to higher losses in urban areas."

The National Fair Housing Alliance recently completed a series of paired tests of insurance companies in nine cities. The housing group matched "mystery shoppers" in terms of the structure and value of their homes, their incomes and occupations, and other socioeconomic factors. The only difference was the racial composition of their neighborhoods. In 1995 they reported that discrimination occurred in over half the tests. They found, for example, that when testers from white areas called to inquire about the availability of insurance, agents generally attempted to sell them a policy. But when callers from minority areas inquired about the same insurance needs, the same insurers often denied coverage, offered inferior policies and/or higher rates, referred the caller to a FAIR Plan (publicly administered insurance services that generally provide inferior yet more expensive policies than those available in the regular or "voluntary" insurance market), did not return phone calls, failed to meet scheduled appointments, or otherwise discouraged the callers from pursuing a policy with them.

The industry contends it is risk, not race, that governs its underwriting activities. As the National Association of Independent Insurers—a trade association representing 570 companies who write about one-third of all homeowners insurance—stated in 1978:

> The insurance industry refrains from moral pronouncements about its customers. We measure risk as accurately as we can, applying experience and objective criteria refined for more than two centuries. We leave it to others to speak of discrimination and other such moral terms.

This sentiment has been echoed repeatedly over the years. Insurers often state that underwriting is as much an art as it is a science and, therefore, subjectivity is inevitable. Yet the mounting evidence that has accumulated in recent years demonstrates that race, as well as risk, enters into underwriting, marketing, and sales practices. Even the arguably more objective dimensions of underwriting can have a discriminatory impact on minority applicants and communities and may violate the Federal Fair Housing Act even if there is no evidence of any intent to discriminate. For example, many insurers maintain maximum housing age and minimum housing value requirements to qualify for particular insurance products. Common thresholds exclude homes that are over fifty years of age or valued at less than $50,000. Nationwide, almost half of all black households but less than one-quarter of white households reside in homes valued under $50,000. Similarly about 40 percent of black households but less than 30 percent of white households live in homes that are more than fifty years old.

The Office of the Public Insurance Counsel in Texas reviewed underwriting guidelines used by major insurers and found that 90 percent of the market in that state was served by companies with age and value restrictions. No doubt Texas is not unique. Such practices have a clear adverse racial impact. Unless there is a business necessity for such practices and no less discriminatory alternative is available that would serve the same business purpose, these practices would violate the Fair Housing Act.

## The Law

Insurers contend that even if discrimination occurs, a little-known 1945 statute, the McCarran-Ferguson Act, exempts the industry from the Federal Fair Housing Act. McCarran-Ferguson grants the industry limited immunity from federal antitrust laws and provides for state regulation of the industry. The law states, in part, that "No act of Congress shall be construed to invalidate, impair, or supersede any law enacted by any state for the purpose of regulating the business of insurance." Therefore, insurers contend it is state, not federal, law that would apply to them.

But contrary to the industry's assertions, a proper reading of the law clearly shows that the Federal Fair Housing Act does apply to insurance companies. Under the Fair Housing Act it is unlawful to "otherwise make unavailable or deny a dwelling to any person because of race" or other prohibited classifications (42 U.S.C. Section 3604a) or to "discriminate against any person . . . in the provision of services or facilities in connection therewith" (42 U.S.C. Section 3604b). Because insurance is required to qualify for a mortgage loan, and because home ownership depends on access to mortgage financing, enjoyment of the full rights provided by the Fair Housing Act requires nondiscrimination in the provision of property insurance. HUD made this explicit when it enacted regulations implementing the Fair Housing Amendments Act of 1988 defining as prohibited conduct "Refusing to provide . . . property or hazard insurance for dwellings or providing such services or insurance differently because of race, color, religion, sex, handicap, familial status, or national origin" (24 C.F.R. Section 100.70d [4]).

The courts have consistently interpreted the Fair Housing Act as applying to insurance. In several district court cases, application of the Fair Housing Act has been reaffirmed.[2]

In 1984 the Fourth Circuit ruled to the contrary (Mackey v. Nationwide, 724 F. 2d 419 [Fourth Circuit 1984]). Subsequent to this decision, however, HUD issued its rule explicitly applying the Fair Housing Act to insurance. Pointing to this rule, in 1992 the Seventh Circuit concluded in the American Family case that "events have bypassed Mackey" and found the act did apply. In the Nationwide case the Sixth Circuit observed, "we conclude that HUD's interpretation of the act is consistent with goals of the act and a reasonable interpretation of the statute. . . . We hold that the McCarran-Ferguson Act does not preclude HUD's interpretation of the act." Nationwide filed a petition requesting that the U.S. Supreme Court review this decision, but in February the Court declined, as it did in the 1993 American Family case. Thus, for the second time the Court reaffirmed a circuit court opinion that property insurance is covered by the Fair Housing Act.

State laws do address discrimination, but they do not provide the same protection as the Federal Fair Housing Act. Most states do not provide the same coverage, procedural rights, or range of remedies, such as civil penalties and punitive damages. So, it is not coincidental that virtually all the significant legal challenges to insurance discrimination have been brought under the Fair Housing Act by private attorneys or the federal government rather than under state law by state insurance commissioners. Not only do state laws fail to provide the protections offered by the Fair Housing Act, but state regulators have, in general, failed to enforce state values aggressively and have been unenthusiastic about utilizing the tools available to them.

## Responses to Redlining

Some aggressive steps have been taken in recent years to combat insurance redlining. Much more could be done, but the current political climate does not lend itself to optimism on this front, at least for the immediate future.

The most significant development was the 1995 settlement reached by the NAACP and the Justice Department in their lawsuit against American Family. As indicated above, American Family had provided agents with explicit instructions to avoid writing insurance for black applicants. The company also took race into consideration in deciding whether or not to inspect homes and provided different types of policies and levels of service to predominantly black and white neighborhoods.

In a $16 million settlement, the insurer agreed to finance various programs to encourage homeownership in Milwaukee's central city, eliminate the use of housing age and value in its underwriting, appoint four new agents in the central city, expand advertising in electronic and print media directed to the African American community, contract with an independent organization to conduct paired-testing of American Family agents, increase its share of the homeowners insurance market in the central city by at least 1,200 policies within five years, as well as to take other steps to expand its services in Milwaukee's black community. This settlement reverberated throughout the industry. The National Association of Insurance Commissioners labeled it the "mother of all affirmative action plans" and chastised the Justice Department for using "litigation scare tactics" that constituted "Big Brother central planning at its worst."

As a result of its testing program, the National Fair Housing Alliance filed discrimination complaints with HUD against three of the nation's largest insurers: State Farm, Allstate, and Nationwide. And HUD has sponsored similar testing programs in several additional cities that will likely result in more complaints or lawsuits over the next few years.

Several voluntary industry initiatives and partnership activities involving insurers, community-based organizations, and state insurance commissioners have been launched in recent years to increase the insurability of urban properties and educate the industry on business opportunities that currently exist in underserved areas. Among the companies involved in such efforts are Travelers, Hartford, State Farm, Allstate, and Nationwide. Participating community organizations include Habitat for Humanity, Neighborhood Housing Services, and the Association of Community Organizations for Reform Now (ACORN).

For example, Travelers and ACORN recently launched a program in several cities where the company will provide discounts on policies that are tied to anti-crime, fire prevention, and other safety programs that ACORN organizes within its communities. In Atlanta, several insurers are working with the Urban League, the Insurance Commissioner, and industry trade associations to identify and appoint more minority agents in order to increase insurance availability in underserved (often minority) neighborhoods. Several companies and trade associations have initiated mentoring programs enabling more minority agents to obtain contracts with major insurers, again for the primary purpose of expanding business in previously underinsured communities.

More aggressive actions could be taken, but only if a more effective political constituency for such actions can be mobilized. One obvious next step would be an insurance disclosure requirement similar to the Home Mortgage Disclosure Act that currently requires lenders to report lending activity publicly by census tract, the disposition of all loan applications (i.e., whether they were approved or denied), and the race, gender, and income of each applicant. Zip code disclosure bills for insurers were rejected in 1994 and there is little prospect for such legislation in the near future.

Along these same lines, a Community Reinvestment Act (CRA) for insurers similar to the current CRA law requiring federally chartered lenders to be responsive to the credit needs of their entire service, has often been proposed, but not seriously considered at the national level. CRA-type provisions were issued in California in 1994 at the urging of then-Democratic state insurance commissioner, John Garamendi. His Republican successor has proposed new rules that would enable insurers to circumvent these requirements.

HUD could, once again, announce its intent to issue detailed regulations that clarify how the Fair Housing Act applies to insurance. The agency was directed to do so in a 1994 Presidential Executive Order. But the Department recently announced that it would not issue such regulations in the near future.

Linkage requirements could also be established whereby municipalities, unions, churches, and other nonprofit organizations would purchase insurance products only from those companies that demonstrate a commitment to urban communities and to racial minorities wherever they live. But the ethos of the era of privatization and the limited public information documenting where insurers do business make this unlikely in the near future as well.

In sum, the 1994 elections dramatically changed the politics of the insurance redlining debate. Unless there is a reversal of those returns, the likelihood of concerted action to limit the prerogatives of the property insurance industry in the near future is minimal. A major barrier to such action is the political and financial clout of the insurance industry. Property insurance companies control more than $704.6 billion in assets. The 3,300 companies that write property insurance, along with affiliated agencies and technical service organizations, employ more than one million people. Several insurance trade associations lobby actively in state capitals across the country and in Washington, D.C. The American Insurance Association, one of several industry groups with headquarters in the nation's capital, employs a staff of 150 people on an annual budget of $20 million. No doubt the industry's visible presence in Washington is a significant factor in the preservation of state regulation.

Property insurance, and the dynamics of insurance redlining and discrimination, constitute critical components of the uneven development of metropolitan areas. Million-man marches, the debate over the genetic base of racial inequality, and the alleged end of racism and the rationality of discrimination may be more newsworthy. But the fact remains that "communities without insurance are communities without hope."

Any set of long-term recommendations for the development of a healthy city, and stable race relations within those environs, must include detailed attention to some of the more mundane building blocks. Insurance, a risky business as much for consumers as for providers, is an essential part of the formulation.

## Endnotes

1. President's National Advisory Panel on Insurance in Riot-Affected Areas, Meeting the Insurance Crisis of Our Cities, 1968.

2. Dunn v. Midwestern, 472 F. Supp. 1106 (S.D. Ohio 1979), McDiarmid v. Economy Fire and Casualty Co., 604 F. Supp. 105 (S.D. Ohio 1984), and Strange v. Nationwide, No. 93-6585 (E.D. Pa. 9-22-94) and two circuit court cases (NAACP v. American Family, 978 F. Circuit 1992) certiorari denied, 113 S. Ct. 2335 (1993), and Nationwide v. Cisneros, No. 94-3296 (Sixth Circuit May 1, 1995).

## Review

1. What is meant by the practice of redlining?

2. How much redlining is there, and why does it occur?

3. What kind of legal protection is there against redlining?

4. What action has been taken in recent years to combat redlining?

## Application

1. Prepare a map of residential patterns of race or ethnicity in your city. Gather the necessary information by interviewing real estate agents or people in the neighborhood, or by examining U.S. census data.

2. Obtain information from an insurance company or from the state insurance commission on rates of home and auto insurance for the various areas of the city.

3. Compare the two sets of information. Do people in areas with high concentrations of racial/ethnic minorities pay higher rates? If so, ask an insurance agent to explain the rates.

## Web Sites

1. *http://www.census.gov/hhes/www/housing/resseg/ch5.html.* A Census Bureau report on the residential segregation of African Americans.

2. *http://www.civilrightsproject.harvard.edu/research/reseg03/resegregation03.php.* A report from the Civil Rights Project of Harvard University on racial segregation in schools.

# 19

# Cowboys and Indians

## Perceptions of Western Films Among American Indians and Anglos

*JoEllen Shively*

*The French philosopher Pascal once observed that what is true on one side of the Pyrenees, a mountain range separating France and Spain, may not be true on the other side. This basic insight—that one's perception is influenced by one's culture and social identity—has been broadened by sociologists to say that all our social identities shape our view of reality. If, for example, a U.S. political leader is supported by a majority of voters, sociologists will examine how the leader's appeal differs according to the gender, social class, and race/ethnicity of voters. Or they will research a new fashion according to its effect on such variables as sex and social class.*

*In this selection, Shively investigates how different groups respond to the same movie—in this case the "classic" Western* The Searchers. *Shively shows how Indian and Anglo males (Anglos are defined as non-Indian, non-Hispanic white Americans) identified with the movie's characters, what qualities they perceived in a certain heroic character, what values they interpreted from the story, and why they did or did not like the story. In doing so, Shively goes beyond the common assumptions about how perceptions differ on the basis of race and ethnicity.*

*For this study, Shively developed an innovative method for exploring this topic and produced intriguing results. Rather than merely examine the content of the movie in a critical light, she selected specific groups with varying expected attitudes, screened the movie for* them, and then elicited their responses in focused discussion groups. Consequently, her findings offer a striking contrast to the expected predictions of armchair speculation.*

In the major sociological study of Western films, Wright (1977) used his own viewing of the most popular Western movies from 1931 to 1972 to argue that Westerns resemble primitive myths. Wright's main thesis is that the narrative themes of the Western resolve crucial contradictions in modern capitalism and provide viewers with strategies to deal with their economic worlds. The popularity of Westerns, Wright argued, lies in the genre's reflection of the changing economic system, which allows the viewers to use the Western as a guide for living.

While growing up on an Indian reservation in the Midwestern United States, I observed that fellow Indians loved Western movies and paperbacks. Subsequently, I observed this phenomenon on Indian reservations in Oregon and North Dakota, as well as among Indians who lived off the reservations. As scholars have noted (McNickle 1973; Cornell 1987; Snipp 1991), American Indians have always lived in a culturally, economically, and politically marginal subculture and are ambivalent about American values of achievement and acquisition of material wealth. Thus, it seemed unlikely that Indians who like Westerns would need them as conceptual guides for economic action as Wright alleged. The popularity of Westerns among Indians must be explained in other ways.

In an argument similar to Wright's, Swidler (1986) suggested that cultural works are tools used by people to contend with immediate problems. Swidler discussed "culture" in a broad sense as comprising "symbolic vehicles of meaning including beliefs, ritual practices, art forms, ceremonies as well as language, gossip, stories and rituals of daily life" (p. 272). Swidler was concerned with how culture shapes action and with how people "use" culture. Assuming that Western movies are a story or an art form,

**185**

how do American Indians use this cultural product?

I address several issues that previous studies have made assumptions about but have not addressed clearly. One issue is the general question of how different groups appropriate and find meaning in cultural products. In particular, does Wright's theory about the cultural use of Westerns hold true for American Indians watching a "cowboys vs. Indians" film? Is the mythic structure of a drama—the "good guy/bad guy" opposition in the Western—more salient than the ethnic aspect of the cultural product, or do Indians in the audience identify with Indians on the screen, regardless of who the good guys and bad guys are? Do Indians prefer Westerns that portray sympathetic and positive images of Indians, e.g., *Broken Arrow* and other movies described by Aleiss (1987) and Parish and Pitts (1976)? Do Indians like only Westerns that show a tribal group other than their own as the villains? Fundamentally, how do Indians link their own ethnic identity to the Western, or limit this identity so they can enter the narrative frame of the Western?

## Research Design

Matched samples of 20 Indian males and 20 Anglo[1] males living in a town on an Indian reservation on the Western Plains of the United States watched a Western film, *The Searchers*. Ethnically pure groups were assembled by one Anglo informant and one Indian informant who invited five ethnically similar friends to their homes to watch the film. Written questionnaires were administered immediately after the film, followed by focus-group interviews. An Anglo female conducted the focus-group interviews with Anglos; I conducted the focus-group interviews with Indians. (I am Chippewa.) (Transcripts of the focus interviews are available from the author on request.)

Respondents were asked why they liked or did not like *The Searchers* in particular and Western movies in general. Basic demographic questions included racial identification, including "blood quantum" for Indians.

The research site is the second largest town on the reservation and has a popula-

tion of about 1,200. Equal numbers of Indians and Anglos live in the town.[2] According to the Tribal Headquarters Enrollment Officer (Bighorn, 12 May 1988), of the 600 Indians approximately 40 percent are Sioux, 10 percent are Assiniboine, 10 percent are Indians of mixed Indian origins, and approximately 40 percent of the self-identified Indians are "mixed-blood," i.e., Indian and white ancestry. Because I wanted to avoid the possible ambiguity of asking how mixed-bloods understand Westerns, all Indians in my sample claim to be "full-blood" Sioux, and all Anglos claim to be white.[3] Because the Western genre is primarily about males, only males were included in the sample.[4]

The respondents did not constitute a representative sample, but were assembled in an effort to create roughly matched groups. I attempted to match Indians and Anglos on age, income, years of education, occupation, and employment status, but succeeded in matching mainly on age, education, and occupation, and was less successful on income and employment status.[5] In the analysis, neither employment status nor income appear to affect the dependent variables. Matching Indians and Anglos on education required me to exclude college-educated respondents.[6] All subjects were between the ages of 36 and 64—the average age of Indian respondents was 51, and the average age of Anglo respondents was 52. Most of the respondents were married.[7]

I chose *The Searchers* (1956) as the Western film to show because its major conflict is between cowboys and Indians. According to Wright (1977), *The Searchers* was one of the period's top-grossing films, a sign of mythical resonance. The film stars John Wayne—a critical advantage for a Western according to Indian and Anglo informants. Briefly, *The Searchers* is about Indian-hating Ethan Edwards's (John Wayne) and Martin Polly's (Jeff Hunter) five-year search to find Debbie Edwards, Ethan's niece (Natalie Wood), who has been kidnapped by Comanche Chief Scar (Henry Brandon). In the end, Scar is killed, and Debbie, who was married to Scar, is taken back to the white civilized world.

# Findings

I began my research with the assumption that people understand movies based on their own cultural backgrounds. Therefore, the experience of watching Western movies should be different for Indians and Anglos, especially when watching scenes in which Indians are portrayed in distorted, negative ways. My most striking finding, however, is an overall similarity in the ways Indians and Anglos experienced *The Searchers*.

All respondents—Indians and Anglos—indicated that they liked Western movies in general. Furthermore, in the focus interviews, they said they wished more Westerns were being produced in Hollywood. I asked the respondents to rank the three types of films they most liked to watch from a list of 10 (musical, gangster, horror, and so on). All 40 subjects—both Anglo and Indian—ranked Westerns first or second; the Western was far and away the most popular genre. Seventy-five percent ranked Westerns first. Combat movies were a distant second, and science fiction movies were third.

On both the written questionnaires and in the focus interviews, all respondents indicated that they liked *The Searchers* and considered it a typical Western. One Indian and two Anglos reported that they had seen the film before.

In response to the question, "With whom did you identify most in the film?" 60 percent of the Indians and 50 percent of the Anglos identified with John Wayne, while 40 percent of the Indians and 45 percent of the Anglos identified with Jeff Hunter.[8] None of the Indians (or Anglos) identified with the Indian chief, Scar. Indians did not link their own ethnic identity to Scar and his band of Indians, but instead distanced themselves from the Indians in the film. The Indians, like the Anglos, identified with the characters that the narrative structure tells them to identify with—the good guys. In the focus-group interviews, both Indians and Anglos reiterated their fondness for John Wayne. For both audiences, the Indians in the film were either neutral or negative. What stood out was not that there were Indians on the screen, but that the Indians were the "bad guys." For example, in the focus groups respondents were asked, "Do you ever root for the Indians?" Both Indians and Anglos consistently responded, "Sometimes, when they're the good guys." Their responses suggest that there is no strong ethnic bias governing whom the respondents root for and identify with. Instead, antagonism is directed against the bad guys. The structure of oppositions that defines the heroes in a film seems to guide viewers' identification with the characters in the film and overrides any ethnic empathy.

The Indians' identification with the good guys in the film is similar to Jahoda's (1961, p. 104) observations of African audiences reacting to films set in Africa that portray Africans as "rude, barbaric savages." Jahoda found that the majority of Africans did not identify with the Africans on the screen—only a minority of highly educated Africans identified with the Africans.

Although Indians and Anglos relied on cues in *The Searchers* about whom to identify with, in other ways the fictional frame of the film did not completely capture these viewers. When discussing *The Searchers*, Indians and Anglos rarely used the main characters' story names. Instead they used the actors' names—John Wayne and Jeff Hunter—which suggests a strong "star effect." Although John Wayne plays different characters in different films, these audiences associated his "cowboy" personality with the off-screen John Wayne, not with specific movie characters. On one level, they saw the actor as embodying all his movie roles. For example, when asked, "Why do you think Ethan Edwards hated the Indians in this movie?" the Indians and Anglos responded in similar ways:

## Indians

Well, John Wayne might have hated Indians in this movie, but in other movies he doesn't hate them.
(Mechanic, age 51)

Well, they've killed his brother and his brother's wife. He doesn't hate Indians in all his movies.
(Cook, age 56)

### Anglos

John Wayne doesn't like the Indians here because they've killed his brother's family. But in other movies, he's on their side. He sticks up for them.
(Foreman, age 56)

Sometimes he fights for the Indians like in *Fort Apache*.
(Bartender, age 48)

Both Indians and Anglos reported that they liked all of John Wayne's movies, whether he played a boxing champion, a pilot, or a cowboy. In all of his films, they see the strong personality characteristics of "the Duke," or "Dude," as some of the respondents referred to him. For both Indians and Anglos on this reservation, being called "cowboy" or one of John Wayne's nicknames, often "Dude" or "Duke," is a token of respect. Indians often see themselves as "cowboys," greeting each other with, "How ya doing, cowboy?" or "Long time no see, cowboy," and refer to their girlfriends or wives as "cowgirls." Fixico (1986) described a similar emulation of the cowboy among reservation Indians in Arizona and South Dakota.

The respondents talked about John Wayne as if he were one of them and they knew him personally—like a good friend. Believing in John Wayne the man is part of the charisma attached to the cowboy role. It is a self-reinforcing cycle: Because John Wayne always plays good guys—characters with whom viewers empathize—it is easy to identify with John Wayne and all he represents. Levy (1990) noted that, "because acting involves actual role playing and because of the 'realistic' nature of motion pictures, audiences sometimes fail to separate between players' roles onscreen and their real lives offscreen. The difference between life on and offscreen seems to blur" (p. 281). For respondents, John Wayne *is* the Cowboy, both in his movies and in real life. This focus on "John Wayne in real life" is similar to Liebes and Katz's (1990) finding that, when retelling episodes of the TV series "Dallas," Americans and Kibbutzniks talk about the "real life" (behind-the-scene) personalities of the actors.

## The Real and the Fictional: Patterns of Differences

Although Anglos and Indians responded in similar ways to the structure of oppositions in the narrative, the two groups interpreted and valued characteristics of the cultural product differently once they "entered" the narrative. The narrative was (re)interpreted to fit their own interests. Although both Indians and Anglos saw some aspects of *The Searchers* as real and others as fictional, the two groups differed on what they saw as authentic and what they saw as fictional.

Table 19.1 shows how the two groups responded when asked to rank their three most

*Table 19.1*
*Ranks of Reasons for Liking The Searchers, by Ethnicity*

| Reason | American Indians | | | | Anglos | | | |
|---|---|---|---|---|---|---|---|---|
| | Ranked 1st | Ranked 2nd | Ranked 3rd | Weighted Sum of Ranks[a] | Ranked 1st | Ranked 2nd | Ranked 3rd | Weighted Sum of Ranks[a] |
| Action/Fights | 2 | 4 | 5 | 19 | 2 | 6 | 4 | 22 |
| John Wayne | 5 | 3 | 2 | 23 | 2 | 3 | 0 | 12 |
| It had Cowboys and Indians | 6 | 5 | 3 | 31 | 3 | 2 | 5 | 18 |
| Humor | 1 | 5 | 6 | 19 | 0 | 1 | 1 | 3 |
| Romance | 0 | 0 | 1 | 1 | 0 | 0 | 1 | 1 |
| Authentic Portrayal of Old West | 0 | 0 | 0 | 0 | 10 | 3 | 3 | 39 |
| Other | 0 | 0 | 1 | 1 | 0 | 0 | 0 | 0 |

[a]Ranks are weighted: 1st x 3; 2nd x 2; 3rd x 1.

important reasons for liking the film. The Kendall rank-order correlation coefficient of $\tau = .29$ indicates that Indians' and Anglos' reasons often differed. The two groups agreed on the importance of "action and fights," "it had cowboys and Indians," and "the scenery and landscape" as reasons for liking the film. They also agreed that "romance" was not an important reason for liking the film. But the differences between Indians and Anglos in Table 19.1 are striking: None of the Indians ranked "authentic portrayal of the Old West" as an important reason for liking the movie, while 50 percent of the Anglos ranked it as the most important reason.

The results in Table 19.1 suggest that the distinctive appeal of the Western for Indians has two elements: (1) the cowboy's way of life—the idealized Western lifestyle seems to make this cultural product resonate for Indians; and (2) the setting of the film, the beauty of the landscape (Monument Valley) moves Indian viewers. When asked in the focus groups, "Why did you like this film, and what makes Westerns better (or worse) than other kinds of movies?" Indians reported: "Westerns relate to the way I wish I could live;" "The cowboy is free;" "He's not tied down to an eight-to-five job, day after day;" "He's his own man;" and "He has friends who are like him." What makes Westerns meaningful to Indians is the fantasy of being free and independent like the cowboy and the familiarity of the landscape or setting.

The setting also resonated for Anglos, but Anglos perceived these films as authentic portrayals of their past. In the focus groups, Anglos, but not Indians, talked about Westerns as accurate chronicles of their history. When asked, "Why did you like this film, and what makes Westerns better (or worse) than other kinds of movies?" Anglos said, "My grandparents were immigrants and Westerns show us the hard life they had;" "Westerns are about my heritage and how we settled the frontier and is about all the problems they had;" "Westerns give us an idea about how things were in the old days;" and "Westerns are true to life." What is meaningful to Anglos is not the fantasy of an idealized lifestyle, but that Western films

link Anglos to their own history. For them, Western films are like primitive myths: They affirm and justify that their ancestors' actions when "settling this country" were right and good and necessary.[9]

Indians seemed ambivalent about how the Old West was portrayed in *The Searchers*. In the focus groups, I asked Indians if the film was an authentic portrayal of the Old West and they responded:

> As far as the cowboy's life goes, it's real, but you don't get to know the Indians, so it's hard to say it's totally authentic.
> (Bartender, age 42)

> I think it's real in some ways, like when you see the cowboy and how he was.
> (Mechanic, age 51)

> The cowboys are real to me. That's the way they were. But I don't know about the Indians 'cause you never see much of them.
> (Farm worker, age 50)

> Yeah, the movie is more about the good guys than the bad guys. I mean, the bad guys are there, but you don't get to know them very well. Mostly the movie is about the cowboys, the good guys, anyway.
> (Carpenter, age 48)

For Indians, the film was more about cowboys than about Indians. This does not hinder their enjoyment of the film or make it less meaningful, because they did not view the Indians on the screen as real Indians.

Both Indians and Anglos were asked, "Are Indians and cowboys in this film like Indians and cowboys in the past?" and "Are they like Indians and cowboys today?" Anglos replied:

> I think the cowboys and the settlers are pretty much like those in the old days. It's hard to say if the Indians are like Indians in the past.
> (Mechanic, age 39)

> They're not like Indians today.
> (Foreman, age 56)

> Indians don't go around kidnapping white women and children these days.
> (Bartender, age 48)

> Probably they're similar to how some of the Indians were in the past, I mean Indi-

ans really did scalp white men.
(Postal worker, age 49)

Yeah, and they kidnapped white children and white women.

My grandparents used to tell stories about how their parents told them to be careful when they played outside. They had to stay close to their homes, 'cause the Indians used to kidnap children.
(Bus driver, age 49)

Anglos thought the cowboys in the Western were similar to cowboys of the past, and they suggested that Indians in the film were similar to Indians in the past. However, they did not think Indians today are like Indians in the film.

When asked the same questions about whether Indians and cowboys in the film are like Indians and cowboys today and in the past, Indians replied somewhat differently:

The cowboys are like cowboys in the past. Maybe some Indians in the past were like the Indians in the films.
(Bartender, age 58)

They're not like Indians today. I mean, the only time Indians dress up is for pow-wows.
(Cook, age 60)

In this movie and other movies with Indians, you don't get to know them. I mean, they're not really people, like the cowboys are. It's hard to say they're like Indians in the past. For sure they're not like Indians today.
(Bartender, age 42)

The Indians aren't at all like any of the Indians I know.
(Unemployed factory worker, age 44)

Indians today are the cowboys.
(Bartender, age 42)

The phrase "Indians today are the cowboys" means that contemporary Indians are more like cowboys than Anglos are, in the sense that it is Indians who preserve some commitment to an autonomous way of life that is not fully tied to modern industrial society. Indians want to be, and value being, independent and free—separate from society—more than Anglos do.

Because *The Searchers* portrays Indians not as human beings, but as "wild, blood-thirsty animals," Indians might be expected to report that the Indians on the screen are not like Indians they know today or like Indians in the past. How could they identify with the Indians on the screen when Indians are portrayed in such a caricatured fashion? The only connections that Indians made between the Indians on the screen and Indians of the past and present were with the costumes worn by the Indians on the screen.

On some deeper level, however, Indian respondents may have identified with the Indians on the screen. For example, when asked in the focus groups, "What's a bad Western like?" Indians reported that they like all Westerns except for films like *Soldier Blue*. All of the Indian respondents were familiar with this film. *Soldier Blue* is a 1970 film based on the Sand Creek massacre of 1864, when Colonel Chivington of the U.S. Cavalry ambushed and slaughtered a village of peaceful Arapaho and Cheyenne children, women, and men in Colorado. In all of the Indian focus groups, this title was mentioned as one Western they did not like. This suggests that when films are too realistic and evoke unpleasant emotions, they are no longer enjoyable. This finding resembles Radway's (1984, p. 184) findings about "failed" romance novels. A "failed" romance is one that evokes overly intense feelings of anger, fear, and violence. Such novels are discarded by readers because they are not enjoyable. *Soldier Blue*, however, is sympathetic to the Indians, and the narrative leads the viewer to empathize with the Indians. Unlike the Indians, Anglos reported that they like all Westerns and could not think of an example of a bad Western.

Another striking difference revealed in Table 19.1 is that Indians cited "humor" as an important reason for liking the film, while Anglos did not. In the focus groups, Indians talked about several comic scenes in the film. When asked if humor was important in Western films, they all said, "Yeah." They reported that they liked humor and wit in Western movies and valued this trait in their friends. Humor is a source of joy for them—a gift.

Anglos, in contrast, never mentioned John Wayne's humor. Why did Indians and not Anglos respond to the humor? If Anglos perceived the film as an authentic story of their past, they may have concentrated on the serious problems in the film, i.e., getting the white girl back. Perhaps Anglos were so preoccupied with the film as an affirmation of their past that they were unable to focus on the intended humor, or at least other characteristics of the film were more important. On the other hand, Indians, who did not see the film as an authentic story of their own past, may have focused more on the intended humor in the film.

## Ideal Heroes

Indians and Anglos also valued individual traits of the cowboy differently. Table 19.2 shows how the two groups responded when asked to rank the three most important qualities that make a good hero in a good Western. A Kendall rank-order correlation coefficient of $\tau = .167$ shows little agreement between Indian and Anglo rankings. Indians ranked "toughness" and "bravery" as the two most important qualities of a good hero in a good Western, whereas Anglos ranked "integrity/honesty" and "intelligence" as most important. Perhaps audiences look for exceptional characteristics in a good hero—qualities they would like to see in themselves. To live free and close to the land like Indians wish to live, exceptional bravery and toughness are necessary. Because Anglos do not want to live like cowboys, bravery and toughness are not as important. Responses of Indians in Table 19.2 are similar to responses in Table 19.1 and to the oral responses. For example, when the Indians described John Wayne as a reason why they liked *The Searchers*, they concentrated on John Wayne's toughness.

While the two groups differed on the qualities that make a good hero, Indians and Anglos tended to agree on the characteristics of a good Western. When asked what characteristics they liked in a good Western, a Kendall's rank-order correlation coefficient between Indian and Anglo responses was high, $\tau = .78$, i.e., there were no pronounced differences between Indians and Anglos. For both groups, the three most important characteristics of a good Western were: "a happy ending;" "action/fights;" and "authentic portrayal of Old West." Like the ranking of "a happy ending" as the most important ingredient in a good romance novel (Radway 1984, p. 59), Indian and Anglo viewers ranked "a happy ending" as the most desirable characteristic of a good Western.

For Indians, the importance of a "happy ending" in a good Western film also reflects on their evaluation of *Soldier Blue* as a bad Western—*Soldier Blue* does not fulfill the

---

### Table 19.2
#### Ranks of Qualities That Make a Good Western, by Ethnicity

| Quality | American Indians | | | | Anglos | | | |
|---|---|---|---|---|---|---|---|---|
| | Ranked 1st | Ranked 2nd | Ranked 3rd | Weighted Sum of Ranks[a] | Ranked 1st | Ranked 2nd | Ranked 3rd | Weighted Sum of Ranks[a] |
| Bravery | 8 | 4 | 4 | 40 | 3 | 4 | 1 | 18 |
| Integrity/Honesty | 2 | 2 | 0 | 10 | 8 | 9 | 5 | 47 |
| Independence | 0 | 0 | 2 | 2 | 0 | 0 | 1 | 1 |
| Toughness | 8 | 8 | 4 | 44 | 0 | 0 | 0 | 0 |
| Sense of Humor | 0 | 2 | 8 | 12 | 0 | 1 | 1 | 3 |
| Strength | 2 | 0 | 0 | 6 | 0 | 0 | 0 | 0 |
| Loyalty | 0 | 0 | 0 | 0 | 1 | 0 | 7 | 10 |
| Intelligence | 0 | 2 | 2 | 6 | 8 | 6 | 5 | 41 |
| Other | 0 | 0 | 0 | 0 | 0 | 0 | 0 | 0 |

[a]Ranks are weighted: 1st x 3; 2nd x 2; 3rd x 1.

"happy ending" criterion of a good Western. Although Indians like action or fights, they are discerning about what kinds of action or fights they enjoy.

For both Anglos and Indians, the three least liked characteristics of a good Western were: "hero rides off into the sunset alone;" "Indians as bad guys;" and "romance between hero and woman."[10]

## The Politics of Perception

Some Indians do identify with the Indians in the Western[s] and are not affected by the film's signals about whom to identify with. Before taking my research procedures into the field, I pretested them with 15 American Indian college students at a West Coast university (10 males, 5 females). Because Indians in the reservation sample differed in important characteristics from the Indians in the pretests (9 of the Indian students were "mixed-bloods"), systematic comparisons were not possible.

However, Indian students responded differently from Indians in the reservation sample. Ethnicity was a salient issue for the majority of the students. The narrative of *The Searchers* did not "work" for the students and they were unable to fully enter the drama. For example, unlike the reservation Indians, a majority of the Indian students identified with and rooted for Scar and his Indians or Debbie, the kidnapped girl. They thought Debbie should have been allowed to stay with Scar and that the search should not have taken place at all.

Like the reservation Indians, the college-educated Indians did not view *The Searchers* as an authentic portrayal of the "Old West" and were quick to point out stereotypical portrayals of Indians in the film. They reacted against the negative message in the film that "the only good Indian is a dead one." They also pointed out many inaccuracies in the film, such as the use of Navajos and the Navajo language for Comanche, "Comanche" Indians wearing Sioux war bonnets, and Indians sometimes wearing war bonnets while fishing. Neither the Indians nor the Anglos in the reservation sample mentioned any of these inaccuracies.

All students but one reported that they liked Westerns in general, but preferred Westerns whose plots are about "cowboys vs. cowboys" or "Indians vs. Indians," or a "cowboys vs. Indians" plot in which the Indian point of view is shown. Several male students indicated that they and their friends often rent Western videos and named the video stores nearest the university that had the best selection of Westerns.

None of the students particularly liked John Wayne. Like the reservation sample, the students talked about John Wayne in "real life" and referred to what they considered racist statements he made off-screen in various interviews.

I asked each student, "Do Indians back home on the reservation like Westerns?" and "Do they root for the cowboys?" All of them said, "Oh yeah, sure." One Sioux student said his father had most of John Wayne's films on video, and a Chippewa said that his uncle was named after John Wayne. One Navajo said of his reservation town, "Ever since they closed down the movie theater several years ago, every Friday night they show a movie in the cafeteria room at the high school, and most of the time it's a Western. Everybody goes."

The heightened ethnic awareness of the college students interferes with, or overrides, their responses to the Western so that they do not get caught up in the structure of oppositions in the narrative. Because they identify with their ethnic group, they see *The Searchers* through a different lens. Education increases their awareness of anti-Indian bias in the film, producing a "revised eye" that frames these films in ethnic terms. In this context, ethnicity is a construct of a particular culture or subculture.

## Conclusion

Although it would seem problematic for Indians to know which characters to identify with in *The Searchers*, it was not a problem for them at all—they identified with the cowboy and his lifestyle. Indians did not focus on the Indians, who are often portrayed on-screen as a faceless, screaming horde. Instead, they saw the cowboys as they want to see themselves—as the good guys.

What appears to make Westerns meaningful to Indians is the fantasy of being free and independent like the cowboy. In addition, the familiarity of the setting is important. Anglos, on the other hand, respond to the Western as a story about their past and their ancestors. The Western narrative becomes an affirmation of their own social experience—the way they are and what their ancestors strove for and imposed on the West are "good." Thus, for Anglos, the Western resembles a primitive myth. But it is not a myth in this sense for Indians—Indians do not view the Western as authentic.

Both Indians and Anglos found a fantasy in the cowboy story in which the important parts of their ways of life triumph and are morally good, validating their own cultural group in the context of a dramatically satisfying story. Perhaps this motive for ethnic group validation is more general and not peculiar to cowboy movies.

The Indian college students, who by attending college have opted for some of the values of white society, find other meanings in *The Searchers*. Because they are immersed in the intellectual world of the university, the symbolic importance of the film for them lies in its false representation of their ancestry and history.

## Endnotes

1. "Anglo" refers to non-Indian white Americans and does not include those of Spanish or Mexican descent.

2. Of the approximately 50,000 residents living on the seven federally recognized reservations in this state in 1980, 48.5 percent are Indian and 51.5 percent are Anglo (Confederation of American Indians 1986, pp. 125–34). Under the 1887 General Allotment Act, more than 100 Indian Reservations on the Plains, along the Pacific Coast and in the Great Lakes states, were divided up and allotted to individual Indians. The remaining land was declared "surplus" and opened up to white homesteaders. Under the terms of this Act, Indians were eventually dispossessed of almost 90 million acres (Talbot 1981, pp. 111–12). Today, whites continue to own land and live on these reservations where their land is "checker-boarded" between Indian-owned land. On some of these reservations, non-Indians own as much or more land than the tribe or Indians do, and the proportion white is equal to or higher than the proportion Indian. The research site is on one of these reservations.

3. I have observed that "mixed-blood" Indians acknowledge and respect both their Indian and white ancestries. To avoid speculation about whether the findings might be associated with the self-identified Indians' "Indianness" or "whiteness," I included only full-bloods.

4. My data show that the Western genre is popular among women, but because the major focus of this study is on racial differences and because I had a limited budget, I controlled for gender by looking [at] males only.

5. The median annual household income for the Indians was $9,000; the median annual household income for the Anglos was $13,000. Seven of the 20 Indian men were unemployed at the time of the research compared to 3 of the Anglo men. Of currently employed Indians, 4 were working part-time; 3 of currently employed Anglos were working part-time. There are no significant differences between the Indians in my study and the 1980 Census data on income and unemployment (U.S. Bureau of the Census 1986, Tables 9, 10, 25; U.S. Bureau of the Census 1988, Table 234). Occupations of the Indians included bartender, farm worker, mechanic, factory worker, carpenter, and food-service worker. Occupations of the Anglos included janitor, school bus driver, bartender, store clerk, factory worker, carpenter, mechanic, foreman, and postal worker.

6. Indians and Anglos differed in the proportion who completed high school, but this difference had no effect on the analysis. Among Indian respondents, 25 percent had completed high school and 60 percent had some high school. For Anglo respondents, 80 percent had completed high school and 20 percent had some high school.

7. To obtain matched 20-person samples, 11 groups comprising 30 Indians and 25 Anglos watched the film. Of these, 2 Indians and 3 Anglos had "some college education" and 8 Indians and 2 Anglos were mixed-blood. These respondents' questionnaires were not used and the respondents were not involved in the focus interviews.

8. One Anglo identified with Laurie, Jeff Hunter's girlfriend. It was difficult to tell why.

9. Describing the role of the myth among Trobriand Islanders, Malinowski (1948) wrote: "The *myth* comes into play when rite, ceremony, or a social or moral rule demands justification, warrant of antiquity, reality, and sanctity" (pp. 84–85).

10. I collected some data in the field on female reservation Indians and female Anglos. These data reveal gender differences as well as differences by ethnicity. For example, women identified with the women in the film, while the men did not. Women ranked "romance" as one of the most important reasons for liking the film, whereas the men ranked it as the least important reason. Women ranked "action/fights" as one of the least important reasons for liking the film, while the men ranked it as one of the most important reasons. Like Anglo men, Anglo women saw the film as an authentic portrayal of the past, while the Indian women, like the Indian men, did not. Indian women, like Indian men, also distanced themselves from the Indians on the screen.

## References

Aleiss, Angela. 1987. "Hollywood Addresses Postwar Assimilation: Indian/White Attitudes in *Broken Arrow*."*American Indian Culture and Research Journal* 11:67–79.

Bighorn, Spike N. 1988. Personal communication with author. 12 May.

Confederation of American Indians. 1986. *Indian Reservations: A State and Federal Handbook*. Jefferson, NC: McFarland.

Cornell, Stephen. 1987. "American Indians, American Dreams, and the Meaning of Success." *American Indian Culture and Research Journal* 11:59–70.

Fixico, Donald L. 1986. "From Indians to Cowboys: The Country Western Trend." Pp. 8–14 in *American Indian Identity: Today's Changing Perspectives*, edited by C. E. Trafzer. Sacramento, CA: Sierra Oaks Publishing Company.

Jahoda, Gustav. 1961. *White Man: A Study of the Attitudes of Africans to Europeans in Ghana before Independence*. London: Oxford University Press.

Levy, Emanuel. 1990. *And the Winner Is . . . : The History and Politics of the Oscar Awards*. New York: Continuum.

Liebes, Tamar and Elihu Katz. 1990. *The Export of Meaning: Cross Cultural Readings of DALLAS*. New York: Oxford University Press.

McNickle, DArcy. 1973. *Native American Tribalism: Indian Survivals and Renewals*. New York: Oxford University Press.

Malinowski, Bronislaw. 1948. *Magic, Science, and Religion and Other Essays*. Glencoe, IL: The Free Press.

Parish, James R. and Michael R. Pitts. 1976. *The Great Western Pictures*. Metuchen, NJ: The Scarecrow Press, Inc.

Radway, Janice A. 1984. *Reading the Romance: Women, Patriarchy, and Popular Literature*. Chapel Hill, NC: University of North Carolina Press.

Snipp, C. Matthew. 1991. *American Indians: The First of This Land*. New York: Russell Sage Foundation.

Swidler, Ann. 1986. "Culture in Action: Symbols and Strategies." *American Sociological Review* 51:272–279.

Talbot, Steve. 1981. *Roots of Oppression: The American Indian Question*. New York: International Publishers.

U.S. Bureau of the Census. 1986. *1980 Census of Population. American Indians, Eskimos, and Aleuts on Identified Reservations and in the Historical Areas of Oklahoma*. Vols. 1–2. Subject Report prepared by the U.S. Department of Commerce. Washington, DC: U.S. Government Printing Office.

——. 1988. *1980 County and City Data Book*. Prepared by the U.S. Department of Commerce. Washington, DC: U.S. Government Printing Office.

Wright, Will. 1977. *Sixguns and Society: A Structural Analysis of the Western*. Berkeley, CA: University of California Press.

## Review

1. What did Shively expect to find using the film *The Searchers*? Why did she choose this particular film?

2. In what ways were the two audiences similar and different in their views about the film's content?

3. Shively found that Native American college students viewed the film differently from the Native Americans on the reservation. How does she interpret these differences?

4. Contrast the differences between the reservation Native Americans' understanding and the Anglos' understanding of the film's image of the West.

## Application

Visit a video store and find a film with a racial or ethnic theme involving both "good" and "bad" guys. View the film with friends from that racial or ethnic group, and then note who they identify with and why. Compare your findings with Shively's in a short essay.

## Related Web Sites

1. *http://www.hanksville.org/sand/stereotypes/*. This site offers a number of papers about stereotypes and other challenges faced by American Indians.

2. *http://www.usc.edu/isd/archives/ethnicstudies/media_stereotypes.html*. A list of resources on racial stereotypes and images in American media.

# Part Three

## *Gender Inequality*

Prejudice and discrimination against women is called **sexism.** Some Americans believe that women no longer suffer from sexism, that women today face no barriers to their aspirations. Sociological studies, however, identify significant gender inequality. Women more than men are the victims of **sexual harassment,** unwanted sexual advances by someone in a position of superior power. Inequality also continues in the area of work (income and opportunities for advancement), politics (office holding), religion (clerical positions), and family (amount of time spent on household tasks).

Selection 20 looks at inequality in the area of work, namely the high-status profession of medicine. Selection 21 examines violence in families–another aspect of inequality. For while considerable violence occurs by both men and women in families, women are far more likely than men to be the victims of severe violence. Selection 22 looks at sexism as experienced in everyday life by both women and men. ◆

196

# 20

# How Unhappy Are Women Doctors?

*Robert Lowes*

For *women who want to work or pursue a ca-*
*reer outside of the home, there is good news*
*and bad news. The good news is that the pro-*
*portion of the labor force that is female has*
*grown dramatically in recent decades, and*
*women are found in increasing numbers even*
*in occupations once reserved for men. The bad*
*news is that women who opt for an occupation*
*traditionally considered more appropriate for*
*men continue to encounter problems of resis-*
*tance, harassment, and discrimination.*

*Discrimination occurs both in hiring and*
*in promotions. In many occupational catego-*
*ries, women are found disproportionately in*
*the lower-echelon positions. For example, far*
*more women than men are teachers, but far*
*more men than women hold the top adminis-*
*trative jobs in education. In the area of medi-*
*cine, women constitute an increasing propor-*
*tion of admissions to medical schools. But*
*women are often encouraged to pursue the*
*more traditional "female" specialties of pediat-*
*rics, psychiatry, and preventive medicine.*

*In this selection, Lowes looks at the world*
*of women doctors. He, too, finds good news*
*and bad news. It is considerably less difficult*
*for a woman to be a physician today than it*
*was in the past. Still, women who want to*
*practice medicine face obstacles, pressures,*
*and problems—in both their professional life*
*and their family life—that men typically do*
*not face. There has been much progress, but*
*medicine is still far from being an area of gen-*
*der equality.*

## A Look at the Complex World of Female Physicians

St. Louis ob/gyn Kathy Maupin is a classic multitasker. Once the alarm clock goes off, Maupin's making breakfast for her daughter, Rachel, and husband, John, loading the clothes washer, e-mailing other doctors, and reviewing medical charts. After a day at the office, she comes home to juggle again—dinner, another pile of laundry, more charts.

"I have three businesses," says Maupin. "I practice medicine, I run my office, and I run my household."

Physicians of either sex hustle nonstop in this era of bottom-line medicine, but women such as Maupin encounter other sources of stress. Shouldering a disproportionate share of domestic duties is just one of them. Female doctors also contend with family-un-friendly schedules, gender bias, and sexual harassment.

You'd think that all these challenges would add up to deep demoralization, but by and large, women physicians are a robust, healthy group that's sold on medicine, according to Atlanta preventive medicine specialist Erica Frank, who surveyed 4,500 women about their well-being. In a study published in the *Archives of Internal Medicine* last year, she reported that 84 percent were generally satisfied with their careers. Maupin is part of that group. "I love being a physician," she says. "I would never be anything else."

Interestingly enough, the popular press presented Frank's research as bad news by emphasizing another finding: 31 percent of women physicians, when asked whether they would choose to become a doctor again, said maybe not, probably not, or definitely not. But Frank doesn't find these figures alarming, particularly since half of this group consisted of maybes. And at least one other study indicates this degree of career remorse holds true for all doctors.

Actually, the good news of Frank's research goes deeper than the 84 percent satisfaction rate. The most contented female doctors, it turns out, are the ones who have children. "It's a really toxic myth that if you're a doctor, having children tears you apart," says Frank. "The doctors we studied prove otherwise." And despite all the strikes against women physicians, their rate of depression is about the same as it is for all U.S. women, she adds.

Frank's findings come at a time when women physicians can celebrate much progress—if not complete success—in transforming a male-dominated profession into a more inclusive and hospitable one. In the space of 30 years, the percentage of physicians who are women has grown from a tokenish 8 percent to 23 percent. Almost half of first-year medical school students in 1999 were women. It will take decades, but someday one of every two physicians will be female. And with these rising numbers, old inequities are crumbling.

Medical historian Ellen S. More, author of *Restoring the Balance*, a history of American women doctors from 1850 through 1995, believes that the morale of women physicians has vastly improved since 1970. "It's gotten to the point where younger women have forgotten the degree of discrimination that used to exist. But we still can't afford to lower our guard," says More, who teaches at the University of Texas Medical Branch at Galveston.

To a lesser degree, the career satisfaction of women physicians ebbs and flows on industry and societal trends that doctors in general can't control. The shift to managed care has been a downer, for example. Research suggests that the pressure to squeeze more patients into a day is discouraging female doctors to a greater degree than their male counterparts because women practitioners favor longer patient encounters.

To More and others, though, the knottiest issue is how to accommodate the needs of women physicians who are bearing and rearing children. Yet there's good news on that front, too. Men are beginning to realize that harmonizing home and career isn't just a "chick issue." They're grasping what Frank's study suggests: Doctors who live with balance are happier.

## Women Are Closing the Gaps in Income and Leadership

Women physicians don't enjoy playing catch-up with male counterparts when it comes to easily observed measures of equality. Take money. "When women doctors talk to me about gender issues," says AMA past president Nancy Dickey, an FP [family practitioner] at College Station, TX, "one of the first things they mention is unequal pay."

However, women physicians are catching up. In 1991, they earned on average 65 percent of what male physicians earned, according to *Medical Economics' Continuing Survey*. By 1998, they were up to the 72 percent mark.

The gap between male and female earnings isn't entirely the product of discrimination. Women tend to gravitate to lower-paying primary care specialties and work seven fewer hours per week than men, according to the AMA. And because they're younger than the men on the whole, they haven't built their practices up as much.

Yet bald-faced economic injustice continues. One female primary care physician on the East Coast recalls when she and another woman shared a full-time job and a $95,000 salary. Then their employer hired a less experienced man in their specialty on a full-time basis for $120,000. "I told them that was sexist," says the doctor, whose protest led to a small raise, but not enough to bring her pay to half of the [man's].

Women are particularly vulnerable to lowball salaries because 56 percent of them are employees, as opposed to practice partners or shareholders. In contrast, only 35 percent of male doctors are employees.

Leadership is another area of tension. Again, women have made gains, rising to some of the top spots in medicine. Nancy Dickey became the first female president of the AMA in 1998. And just last October, *The Journal of the American Medical Association* hired its first female editor, pediatrician Catherine D. DeAngelis.

Dickey and DeAngelis are more than window-dressing. Leadership by women physicians also is broader. In 1980, when women accounted for 12 percent of all doctors, they made up only 5 percent of the membership in the Tampa, FL-based American College of Physician Executives. Today, however, this group is 17 percent female—far closer to the actual proportion of women in medicine.

Not all the statistics are as sunny. While women constituted about 43 percent of medical school enrollment in 1999, only 27 percent of med school faculty and a mere 11 percent of full professors were female. After-hours faculty meetings and lack of on-site day care penalize women with children, according to those who've researched the problem. Plus, instructors who work part time often aren't eligible for tenure.

"Promotion is tied not to skill, but to schedule, and that's not right," says DeWitt, NY, internist Janice Scully, who was an assistant professor at a New York medical school for eight years.

The same obstacles face part-timers in private practice. Traditionally, they haven't been considered partner or stockholder material, much less potential leaders. To doctors from the 80-hour-a-week generation, the words "part time" translated into "not truly committed to medicine." However, for the sake of accommodating women physicians with children, practices are changing the rules. The Camino Medical Group in Sunnyvale, CA, for example, allows doctors working a three-quarters schedule to become shareholders. They even can slow down to a half-time pace, but only for three years; otherwise, they become employees. Several of those part-time shareholders head up satellite offices while others chair group-wide departments, says internist and board chairman Elizabeth Vilardo.

However, there's no denying that for part-timers, leadership is a stretch. "Leadership takes time—attending meetings, networking, educating yourself about the business of medicine," says Edina, MN, ob/gyn Janette H. Strathy, a member of the Park Nicollet Clinic. "That's going to deter some part-timers."

Strathy, who has a 15-year-old son, predicts that the part-time quandary will disappear for women doctors in her generation when they finish raising their children. "We'll have more time to devote to our

groups and organized medicine," she says. "They won't know what to do with us!"

## More Freedom to Be Feminine

"You don't change society quickly," observes internist Janice Scully. There's no better proof of that for women physicians than the persistence of harassment, which Erica Frank calls a strong predictor of career dissatisfaction. In Frank's Women Physicians' Health Study, 48 percent of those surveyed reported being hassled in a nonsexual manner simply because they were women, although it was more likely to have happened in medical school and residency than in private practice. Scully recalls such an incident: "When I was a new intern, up all night and exhausted, a male attending told me half-seriously during hospital rounds that he wouldn't talk to me because I was a girl. I went to a stairwell and cried."

Thirty-seven percent of those surveyed reported having been sexually harassed. If you're a man who's too embarrassed to ask a female colleague what it's like, you can read stories posted on the Association of Women Surgeons' Web site (womensurgeons.org). In one recent posting, a West fashion model turned cardiothoracic surgeon described her problems with male doctors: "They stare at my chest and don't take me for my surgical skills. Does anybody have any experience being extremely attractive and a medical professional, too?" Another ex-model ruefully replied: "I tried cutting my hair, dressing in scrubs, no makeup—nothing works. I do, however, wear T-shirts under the scrubs so the V-neck is less enticing."

Discussing what wardrobe will reduce male leers points to a subtler, but no less disconcerting problem: the pressure to deemphasize your femininity to fit in with the boys. That pressure still exists, but to a lesser degree than 30 years ago, say women doctors.

"In the past, the need to conform was critical," says Yarmouth, ME, general surgeon Dixie Mills, president of the AWS. "If you stood out as a woman, you got rejected and didn't make it. But now that there are more women in medicine, we can stand out."

Ferndale, WA, family physician Bertha "Berdi" Safford has experienced that freedom, too. "At first, I didn't let my female self come through," says Safford, who earned her MD in 1976. "I was less personal with people, and tended to give more orders. Today, I'm more myself with my patients—I talk with them about my children. And I'm collaborative as opposed to directive. Its easier now because there are so many more women to reinforce each other."

## Maternity Leave: Male Doctors Show Their True Colors

If you take away the pay inequities, the glass ceiling, and the unwanted sexual advances, women physicians still have another challenge—societal attitudes toward mothers in the workplace. "There's one thing that young women doctors often don't understand," says Janice Scully. "Once they have children, the differences between men and women really show up. Before that, they get along fine."

In a classic case of an irresistible force meeting an immovable object, women who want to alter their schedules to fulfill parental roles run headlong into unsympathetic male colleagues. When this happens, mothers feel as if they've lost control of their work environment, says Erica Frank.

The great divide usually begins with maternity leave. According to practice management consultant Gray Tuttle Jr. in Lansing, MI, as recently as the 1970s women found that some practices wouldn't even let them use sick time to cover maternity leave. And there was always the pressure to get back to work fast. "I took five weeks off," says ob/gyn Kathy Maupin, whose daughter is 14, "and after three weeks, my two male partners were telling me over the phone, 'We're tired of doing your work.' They were deplorable."

Granted, there's been progress. The 1993 Family and Medical Leave Act (FMLA) guarantees that in companies of 50 or more employees, a new mother can stay home up to 12 weeks and still keep her job. Uncle Sam doesn't guarantee she'll be paid during that time, but some practices voluntarily compensate their women physicians during maternity leave. Park Nicollet Clinic, for example, lets new mothers take off 12 weeks, eight of them with pay under a short-term disability insurance policy—even for normal childbirth and recovery.

But other groups opt for less expensive disability policies that don't pay anything until 90 days or more of disability. In that scenario, new mothers normally must use up any accrued sick leave and vacation time if they want to maintain cash flow. They have the right to apply such paid leave to their 12 guaranteed weeks under FMLA, but the loss of vacation time is a sore point, says practice management consultant Mike Parshall with The Health Care Group in Plymouth Meeting, PA. "Women don't see maternity leave as a vacation," he explains, "so they don't want to forfeit vacation time."

Consultant Sandra McGraw, also at The Health Care Group, says groups should be more generous about granting paid maternity leave for the sake of retaining women physicians. "Look at the big picture," says McGraw. "We're talking about six to eight weeks, and it may happen only two or three times in the woman's career. Men as well as women need time off on special occasions. They get divorced. A kid gets sick. Stuff will happen."

Requests for part-time schedules after maternity leave also spark discord. More groups are conceding part-time hours, but some still demand that the part-timer take full-time call duty. Others give the part-timers a break and prorate call. The same arguments for liberalizing maternity leave also apply to part-time schedules and variations such as job-sharing. "If you don't treat your part-timers well, you'll lose them," says Ellen More.

## Sharing the 50-Pound Knapsack Called Child Rearing

The gains that women have made in medicine are all the more remarkable given the extra burdens that society places on them as wives and mothers; in most cases, they're the default homemakers.

"If medicine is a footrace, then women are running it with a 50-pound knapsack on their back," says Janice Scully. "That knapsack is the work of raising children."

Do men know how heavy that knapsack feels? Memphis pediatrician Nancy Mitchell remembers the efforts she made to breastfeed her third child as a part-timer at a large group practice. "On my lunch hours at the office, I would close the door and pump my breasts, eat lunch, and dictate charts at the same time," says Mitchell. "I was doing it all."

However, multitasking has a dark side. "You're always feeling like you're not getting everything done," says Mitchell. For multitaskers, the result is often guilt. Are they shortchanging their families at the expense of their patients—and vice versa? "When I go home at night, I'm thinking about food, homework, and baths, but I'm also worrying about patients," says Mitchell. "I work in a few telephone calls on some of them, and my kids are saying, 'Read me a book, read me a book.'"

"Would I choose medicine again? On some days, medicine is the most satisfying thing I can do, but on other days, I think, 'This would be great if I were a man.' I used to tell younger women doctors that they could do it all, but now I have some doubts. You can have it all, but at a price." She's hanging in, though.

Mitchell's frustration notwithstanding, Erica Frank's study suggests that immersion in family life actually gives women physicians a brighter outlook on their careers. Frank found that those with no children were less happy. Multiple roles, according to Frank, seem to have benefits that mitigate the wear and tear. The more children female doctors had, in fact, the more content they were. "Children bring us joy," says Frank, the mother of a 3-year-old. And perspective, adds Elizabeth Vilardo. "I have a couple of children," she says. "They help you focus on things besides sick patients."

Author Ellen More echoes these thoughts. "Frank's study indicates that women who experience overall satisfaction with life are better able to cope with the frustrations of work," she says.

If the blend of family and career called the "mommy track" is rewarding, why not a "daddy track" for men? Well, it's under construction. Men are expecting more from themselves as husbands and fathers, which should come as a relief to hard-pressed working mothers. A 1997 study by the Families and Work Institute showed that working fathers spent 4.4 hours per workday caring for their children and doing chores, up from not quite 3 hours in 1977. Working women, in contrast, put in 6.1 hours, a half-hour less than they did 20 years earlier. True, women still shoulder about 60 percent of the load, but ob/gyn Kathy Maupin observes that most women would just as soon have it that way. "We feel the need to have the bigger role," says Maupin. "Maybe we're wired differently."

The awakening of men to hearth and home carries over into medicine. Research shows that young male doctors are twice as likely as older counterparts to make career adjustments—reduce their hours, for example—for the sake of family. Elizabeth Vilardo sees evidence of that in her circle. "The newer male doctors make it a priority to spend more time with their kids and lead a balanced life," says Vilardo, whose husband is a stay-at-home engineer. "The world is changing."

Ellen More sounds a similarly hopeful note at the end of her book: Male physicians are taking up the concerns of their female counterparts as their own. "Can women physicians restore the balance in their profession, in their own lives, and perhaps even in the lives of their patients?" asks More. "It seems clear that the answer is Yes, but they cannot, should not—and may no longer have to—do it alone."

## Here's How Women Physicians Can Achieve Balance: Clone John Hruby

FP Bertha "Berdi" Safford in Ferndale, WA, is living proof that if a woman physician wants to balance career and home, she should marry someone who thinks like she does.

Safford and her husband, FP John Hruby, have gotten balance down to a science. Since 1979, the two doctors have shared a practice and split domestic duties on a 50-50 basis.

"I'm blessed with a husband who does the same thing I do," says Safford. "As a result, I don't think I've given up as much for medicine as other women have."

Here's how they slice the pie of life. Safford works in the office on Tuesdays and Fridays; Hruby, on Mondays and Wednesdays. They take Thursdays off together and, when they can, head off to the mountains for skiing and hiking. On the days when one spouse is practicing medicine, the other takes charge of domestic duties from dawn to bedtime (those duties are lighter lately since one of the couple's two children has left the nest).

Safford and Hruby count as one full-timer in their four-doctor practice, so they pull the equivalent of a full-time call schedule. They divide the duty so that the doctor-for-the-day is responsible for any call on his or her evening. "By doing this, we draw boundaries around our jobs," says Hruby. "If I stay home all day, I wash the dishes that night instead of seeing a patient in the ER." On Thursdays and weekends, deciding who takes call comes down to "heavy negotiating," he adds.

Part-time medical schedules have allowed Safford and Hruby to devote more time not only to parenthood, but to labors of love in the outside world. Safford is active in the American Academy of Family Physicians, having served as president of her state chapter. She also squeezes in another part-time job on Wednesdays as medical director of a family physician network. Hruby has [sat] on the local school board for 12 years.

Safford and Hruby married before they entered the University of Washington School of Medicine together. They graduated in 1976. "We knew we wanted children, and we agreed that full-time practice wasn't compatible with raising a family," says Safford. "When we started job-sharing after residency training, nobody else was doing this. It puzzled other doctors. They'd ask John, 'Did you go fishing on your day off?' They couldn't imagine that he was changing diapers instead."

"Today, the reaction is different," adds Hruby. "As doctors have gotten overwhelmed by managed care, they've been envious of us. Some have followed in our foot-steps. There are six or seven other physician couples in our area who are job-sharing."

Hruby would like to win over more converts, though. "Society has to allow parents to be parents," he says. "We need more flexibility. Kids come first. Our jobs come second."

## What a Mom-Friendly Medical Practice Looks Like

When Memphis pediatrician Aimee Christian wanted to attend her 7-year-old daughter's school play at 9am on a recent Tuesday, nobody at her five-doctor practice objected to rescheduling her patients so she could do so. That's because the other doctors in Memphis Pediatrics are mothers, too. And like Christian, they work less than full-time schedules for the sake of parenting.

Christian, one of three founders, says the group didn't set out to be an all-female—much less all-mom—practice when it formed in 1998. "We were friends in residency, and we wanted to be in a small group," says Christian, a mother of four. Nevertheless, the group oozes the kind of flexibility that working mothers yearn for when they need to take a child to the dentist, watch a softball game, or drive a carpool. "When one of us is rounding at the hospital, somebody else will occasionally have her kids over and watch them," says Christian.

Pediatrician Nancy Mitchell, a mother of three who joined Memphis Pediatrics in 1998, says she used to hear condescending comments from male colleagues in her old practice when she asked for time off to attend to her children. "They acted as if I had something to apologize for," says Mitchell. Not so at Memphis Pediatrics. "There's a more relaxed atmosphere," she says. "Everybody covers for everybody else. We all know, for example, that our kids will get sick and need us. It's not a big deal."

Memphis Pediatrics makes it easier on doctors when illness strikes by maintaining a veritable sick bay in the back of the office, away from patients. It's outfitted with a TV, a VCR, sleeping bags, and toys. Doctors can drop off their sick children here and not miss work, although the room is mostly meant for older children who don't require constant supervision. Other local doctors jokingly refer to Memphis Pediatrics as the "mom group," but the moms are having the last laugh as they watch their practice prosper.

"It took us only a year to pay off the bank loan that got us started," says Christian. "We've been very successful."

## What Advice Would You Give Brand-New Women Physicians?

Hold on to your goals, hold on to your passion. You can balance family and career. I used to take my son on hospital rounds when there was nobody to watch him. He would wait at the nurse's station or outside the patient's door. Sometimes a patient would ask to see him and he'd step inside and smile. If you expand your vision, you can make it work.

—General surgeon Dixie Mills, Yarmouth, ME

Maintain at least one hobby or sport in your life that has nothing to do with being a wife, mother, or doctor. I have two—downhill skiing and flying a Cessna TR-1 82.

Exercise. Young mothers often put that last on their list of things to do; they think that chasing their kids equals a workout. But at least take 30 minutes a day for a brisk walk. You'll have more energy to deal with stress.

Pay people to do domestic work that you don't want to do—house cleaning, for example. And pay your child care people well. The best thing I ever did was to employ a live-in nanny for seven years. It gave me peace of mind and made me more productive at work.

—Ob/gyn Janette Strathy, Edina, MN

Become a good negotiator. You can command top dollar from employers by selling the advantages of having a woman physician. Your name on the door will bring in new patients.

Before you sign a contract, hash out the terms of maternity leave. You'll be in a better negotiating position than if you bring this up when you're three months pregnant. And if you decide on three months of maternity leave, stick to your handshake and come back to work after three months. Don't change your mind and take off for another three months. You have an obligation not only to your employer and patients, but to the women physicians who follow you. If you don't stand by your agreement, your employers will be skeptical about hiring the next female applicant.

—FP Nancy Dickey, College Station, TX

### Review

1. According to Lowes, women doctors are closing the gaps in income and leadership. What evidence does he present?

2. Discuss the situation of women doctors with regard to looking feminine and taking maternity leave.

3. What are the problems women doctors face when they have children?

### Applications

1. Do as the author suggests and go to the Association of Women Surgeons' Web site (womensurgeons.org) to find stories of sexual harassment. What kind of measures would you institute to prevent such incidents?

2. The problems women doctors face are similar to those of women in other professions. Make a list of both the gains and the problems that Lowes notes. Then talk with a woman in another profession about the extent to which she has experienced, or knows of someone

who has experienced, similar gains and problems.

## Related Web Sites

1. *http://www.aamc.org/members/wim/resources.htm.* This site gives access to newsletters and reports that deal with the statistics and the issues facing women in medicine.

2. *http://www.findarticles.com/cf_1/m4339/3_20/57816042/p3/article.jhtml?term=.* A journal article dealing with the struggles and challenges of professional women.

# 21

# How Women Experience Battering

## The Process of Victimization

*Kathleen J. Ferraro*
*John M. Johnson*

*One of the most tragic expressions of women's inequality in American society is their violent victimization by spouses and lovers. A surprising aspect of this abuse is the extraordinary length of time some women stay in these relationships. In certain cases women have tolerated so long their mates' beating that some observers have concluded they were willing victims. Such a view is naive. As Ferraro and Johnson make clear, this victimization is closely connected to our culture's conception of women and their position in society. Many women feel they have no choice but to stay in an abusive relationship; they are socialized to accept their subordinate role as natural and are often financially and emotionally dependent on a man. Moreover, some women accept physical violence as a burden to be borne to save their husband, children, or home. Unfortunately, about half of the women in this study returned to their abusive relationships. The same dependencies and patriarchal perceptions that initially prevented their leaving probably contributed to their return.*

$W$hy do battered women stay in abusive relationships?

The socialization of women emphasizes the primary value of being a good wife and mother, at the expense of personal achievement in other spheres of life. The patriarchal ordering of society assigns a secondary status to women, and provides men with ultimate authority, both within and outside the family unit. Economic conditions contribute to the dependency of women on men. In sum, the position of women in U.S. society makes it extremely difficult for them to reject the authority of men and develop independent lives free of marital violence (Dobash and Dobash, 1979; Pagelow, 1981).

Material and cultural conditions are the background in which personal interpretations of events are developed. Women who depend on their husbands for practical support also depend on them as sources of self-esteem, emotional support, and continuity. This paper looks at how women make sense of their victimization within the context of these dependencies.

We first describe six techniques of rationalization used by women who are in relationships where battering has occurred. We then turn to catalysts which may serve as forces to reevaluate rationalizations and to initiate serious attempts at escape. Finally, we outline the consequences of leaving or attempting to leave a violent relationship.

## The Data

From July, 1978, to September, 1979, we were participant observers at a shelter for battered women located in the southwestern United States. The shelter was located in a suburban city of a major urban center. The shelter served five cities as well as the downtown population, resulting in a service population of 170,000.

During the time of the research, 120 women passed through the shelters; they brought with them 165 children. The women ranged in age from 17 to 68, generally had family incomes below $15,000, and did not work outside the home.

We established personal relationships with each of these women, and kept records of their experiences and verbal accounts. We also tape-recorded informal conversations, staff meetings, and crisis phone conversations with battered women. This daily interaction with shelter residents and staff permitted first-hand observation of feelings and thoughts about the battering experience. Finally, we taped interviews with 10 residents and five battered women who had left their abusers without entering the shelter. All quotes in this paper are taken from our notes and tapes.

The term battered woman is used in this paper to describe women who are battered repeatedly by men with whom they live as lovers. Marriage is not a prerequisite for being a battered woman. Many of the women who entered the shelter we studied were living with, but were not legally married to, the men who abused them.

## Rationalizing Violence

Rather than seeking help or escaping, as people typically do when attacked by strangers, battered women often rationalize violence from their husbands, at least initially. Although remaining with a violent man does not indicate that a woman views violence as an acceptable aspect of the relationship, the length of time that a woman stays in the marriage after abuse begins is a rough index of her efforts to accommodate the situation. In a U.S. study of 350 battered women, Pagelow (1981) found the median length of stay after violence began was four years; some left in less than one year, others stayed as long as 42 years.

Battered women have good reasons to rationalize violence. There are few institutional, legal, or cultural supports for women fleeing violent marriages. Eighty percent of Pagelow's (1981) sample indicated previous, failed attempts to leave their husbands. Despite the development of the international shelter movement, changes in police practices, and legislation to protect battered women since 1975, it remains extraordinarily difficult for a battered woman to escape a violent husband determined to maintain his control. At least one woman, Mary Parziale, has been murdered by an abusive husband while residing in a shelter (Beverly, 1978); others have been murdered after leaving shelters to establish new, independent homes (Garcia, 1978). When practical and social constraints are combined with love for and commitment to an abuser, it is obvious that

there is a strong incentive—often a practical necessity—to rationalize violence.

Previous research on the rationalizations of deviant offenders has revealed a typology of "techniques of neutralization," which allow offenders to view their actions as normal, acceptable, or at least justifiable (Sykes and Matza, 1957). A similar typology can be constructed for victims. Extending the concepts developed by Sykes and Matza, we assigned the responses of battered women we interviewed to one of six categories of rationalization: (1) the appeal to the salvation ethic; (2) the denial of the victimizer; (3) the denial of injury; (4) the denial of victimization; (5) the denial of options; and (6) the appeal to higher loyalties. The women usually employed at least one of these techniques to make sense of their situations; often they employed two or more, simultaneously or over time.

1) *The appeal to the salvation ethic:* This rationalization is grounded in a woman's desire to be of service to others. Abusing husbands are viewed as deeply troubled, perhaps "sick" individuals, dependent on their wives' nurturance for survival. Battered women place their own safety and happiness below their commitment to "saving my man" from whatever malady they perceive as the source of their husbands' problems (Ferraro, 1979). The appeal to the salvation ethic is a common response to an alcoholic or drug-dependent abuser. The battered partners of substance-abusers frequently describe the charming, charismatic personality of their sober mates, viewing this appealing personality as the "real man" being destroyed by disease. They then assume responsibility for helping their partners to overcome their problems, viewing the batterings they receive as an index of their partners' pathology. Abuse must be endured while helping the man return to his "normal" self. One woman said:

> I thought I was going to be Florence Nightingale. He had so much potential; I could see how good he really was, and I was going to "save" him. I thought I was the only thing keeping him going, and that if I left he'd lose his job and wind up in jail. I'd make excuses to everybody for him. I'd call work and lie when he was

drunk, saying he was sick. I never criticized him, because he needed my approval.

2) *The denial of the victimizer:* This technique is similar to the salvation ethic, except that victims do not assume responsibility for solving their abusers' problems. Women perceive battering as an event beyond the control of both spouses, and blame it on some external force. The violence is judged situational and temporary, because it is linked to unusual circumstances or a sickness which can be cured. Pressures at work, the loss of a job, or legal problems are all situations which battered women assume as the causes of their partners' violence. Mental illness, alcoholism, and drug addiction are also viewed as external, uncontrollable afflictions by many battered women who accept the medical perspective on such problems. By focusing on factors beyond the control of their abuser, women deny their husbands' intent to do them harm, and thus rationalize violent episodes.

> He's sick. He didn't used to be this way, but he can't handle alcohol. It's really like a disease, being an alcoholic. . . . I think too that this is what he saw at home, his father is a very violent man, and alcoholic too, so it's really not his fault, because this is all he has ever known.

3) *The denial of injury:* For some women, the experience of being battered by a spouse is so discordant with their expectations that they simply refuse to acknowledge it. When hospitalization is not required, routines quickly return to normal. Meals are served, jobs and schools are attended, and daily chores completed. Even with lingering pain, bruises, and cuts, the normality of everyday life overrides the strange, confusing memory of the attack. When husbands refuse to discuss or acknowledge the event, in some cases even accusing their wives of insanity, women sometimes come to believe the violence never occurred. The denial of injury does not mean that women feel no pain. They know they are hurt, but define the hurt as tolerable or normal. Just as individuals tolerate a wide range of physical discomfort before seeking medical help, battered women tolerate a wide range of physical abuse before defining it as an injurious assault. One woman explained her disbelief at her first battering:

> I laid in bed and cried all night. I could not believe it had happened, and I didn't want to believe it. We had only been married a year, and I was pregnant and excited about starting a family. Then all of a sudden, this! The next morning he told me he was sorry and it wouldn't happen again, and I gladly kissed and made up. I wanted to forget the whole thing, and wouldn't let myself worry about what it meant for us.

4) *The denial of victimization:* Victims often blame themselves for the violence, thereby neutralizing the responsibility of the spouse. Pagelow (1981) found that 99.4 percent of battered women felt they did not deserve to be beaten, and 51 percent said they had done nothing to provoke an attack. The battered women in our sample did not believe violence against them was justified, but some felt it could have been avoided if they had been more passive and conciliatory. Both Pagelow's and our samples are biased in this area, because they were made up almost entirely of women who had already left their abusers, and thus would have been likely to feel major responsibility for the abuse they received. Retrospective accounts of victimization in our sample, however, did reveal evidence that some women believed their right to leave violent men was restricted by their participation in the conflicts. One subject said:

> Well, I couldn't really do anything about it, because I did ask for it. I knew how to get at him, and I'd keep after it and keep after it until he got fed up and knocked me right out. I can't say I like it, but I shouldn't have nagged him like I did.

As Pagelow (1981) noted, there is a difference between provocation and justification. A battered woman's belief that her actions angered her spouse to the point of violence is not synonymous with the belief that violence was therefore *justified.* But belief in provocation may diminish a woman's capacity for retaliation or self-defense, because it blurs her concept of responsibility. A woman's acceptance of responsibility for the violent incident is encouraged by an abuser who continually denigrates her and makes unrealistic demands. Depending on the social supports available, and the personality of the battered woman, the man's accusations of inadequacy may assume the status of truth. Such beliefs of inferiority inhibit the development of a notion of victimization.

5) *The denial of options:* This technique is composed of two elements: practical options and emotional options. Practical options, including alternative housing, source of income, and protection from an abuser, are clearly limited by the patriarchal structure of Western society. However, there are differences in the ways battered women respond to these obstacles, ranging from determined struggle to acquiescence. For a variety of reasons, some battered women do not take full advantage of the practical opportunities which are available to escape, and some return to abusers voluntarily even after establishing an independent lifestyle. Others ignore the most severe constraints in their efforts to escape their relationships. For example, one resident of the shelter we observed walked 30 miles in her bedroom slippers to get to the shelter, and required medical attention for blisters and cuts to her feet. On the other hand, a woman who had a full-time job, had rented an apartment, and had been given by the shelter all the clothes, furniture, and basics necessary to set up housekeeping, returned to her husband two weeks after leaving the shelter. Other women refused to go to job interviews, keep appointments with social workers, or move out of the state for their own protection (Ferraro, 1981b). Such actions are frightening for women who have led relatively isolated or protected lives, but failure to take action leaves few alternatives to violent marriage. The belief of battered women that they will not be able to make it on their own—a belief often fueled by years of abuse and oppression—is a major impediment to acknowledg[ing] that one is a victim and taking action.

The denial of *emotional* options imposes still further restrictions. Battered women may feel that no one else can provide intimacy and companionship. While physical beating is painful and dangerous, the pros-

pect of a lonely, celibate existence is often too frightening to risk. It is not uncommon for battered women to express the belief that their abuser is the only man they could love, thus severely limiting their opportunities to discover new, more supportive relationships. One woman said:

> He's all I've got. My dad's gone, and my mother disowned me when I married him. And he's really special. He understands me, and I understand him. Nobody could take his place.

6) *The appeal to higher loyalties:* This appeal involves enduring battering for the sake of some higher commitment, either religious or traditional. The Christian belief that women should serve their husbands as men serve God is invoked as a rationalization to endure a husband's violence for later rewards in the afterlife. Clergy may support this view by advising women to pray and try harder to please their husbands (Davidson, 1978; McGlinchey, 1981). Other women have a strong commitment to the nuclear family, and find divorce repugnant. They may believe that for their children's sake, any marriage is better than no marriage. One woman divorced her husband of 35 years after her last child left home. More commonly women who have survived violent relationships for that long do not have the desire or strength to divorce and begin a new life. When the appeal to higher loyalties is employed as a strategy to cope with battering, commitment to and involvement with an ideal overshadows the mundane reality of violence.

## Catalysts for Change

Rationalization is a way of coping with a situation in which, for either practical or emotional reasons, or both, a battered woman is stuck. For some women, the situation and the beliefs that rationalize it may continue for a lifetime. For others, changes may occur within the relationship, within individuals, or in available resources which serve as catalysts for redefining the violence. When battered women reject prior rationalizations and begin to view themselves as true victims of abuse, the victimization process begins.

There are a variety of catalysts for redefining abuse; we discuss six: (1) a change in the level of violence; (2) a change in resources; (3) a change in the relationship; (4) despair; (5) a change in the visibility of violence; and (6) external definitions of the relationship.

1) *A change in the level of violence:* Although Gelles (1976) reports that the severity of abuse is an important factor in women's decisions to leave violent situations, Pagelow (1981) found no significant correlation between the number of years spent cohabiting with an abuser and the severity of abuse. On the contrary: the longer women lived with an abuser, the more severe the violence they endured, since violence increased in severity over time. What does seem to serve as a catalyst is a sudden change in the relative level of violence. Women who suddenly realize that battering may be fatal may reject rationalizations in order to save their lives. One woman who had been severely beaten by an alcoholic husband for many years explained her decision to leave on the basis of a direct threat to her life:

> It was like a pendulum. He'd swing to the extremes both ways. He'd get drunk and beat me up, then he'd get sober and treat me like a queen. One day he put a gun to my head and pulled the trigger. It wasn't loaded. But that's when I decided I'd had it. I sued for separation of property. I knew what was coming again, so I got out. I didn't want to. I still loved the guy, but I knew I had to for my own sanity.

There are, of course, many cases of homicide in which women did not escape soon enough. In 1979, 7.6 percent of all murders in the United States where the relationship between the victim and the offender was known were murders of wives by husbands (Flanagan et al., 1982). Increases in severity do not guarantee a reinterpretation of the situation, but may play a part in the process.

2) *A change in resources:* Although some women rationalize cohabiting with an abuser by claiming they have no option, others begin reinterpreting violence when the resources necessary for escape become available. The emergence of safe homes or shelters since 1970 has produced a new resource for battered women. While not completely adequate or satisfactory, the mere existence of a place to go alters the situation in which battering is experienced (Johnson, 1981). Public support of shelters is a statement to battered women that abuse need not be tolerated. Conversely, political trends which limit resources available to women, such as cutbacks in government funding to social programs, increase fears that life outside a violent marriage is economically impossible. One 55-year-old woman discussed this catalyst:

> I stayed with him because I didn't want my kids to have the same life I did. My parents were divorced, and I was always so ashamed of that. . . . Yes, they're all on their own now, so there's no reason left to stay.

3) *A change in the relationship:* Walker (1979), in discussing the stages of a battering relationship, notes that violent incidents are usually followed by periods of remorse and solitude. Such phases deepen the emotional bonds, and make rejection of an abuser more difficult. But as battering progresses, periods of remorse may shorten, or disappear, eliminating the basis for maintaining a positive outlook on the marriage. After a number of episodes of violence, a man may realize that this victim will not retaliate or escape, and thus feel no need to express remorse. Extended periods devoid of kindness or love may alter a woman's feelings toward her partner so much so that she eventually begins to define herself as a victim of abuse. One woman said:

> At first, you know, we used to have so much fun together. He has kind've, you know, a magnetic personality; he can be really charming. But it isn't fun anymore. Since the baby came, it's changed completely. He just wants me to stay at home, while he goes out with his friends. He doesn't even talk to me, most of the time. . . . No, I don't really love him anymore, not like I did.

4) *Despair:* Changes in the relationship may result in a loss of hope that "things will get better." When hope is destroyed and replaced by despair, rationalizations of violence may give way to the recognition of victimization. Feelings of hopelessness or despair are the basis for some efforts to assist battered

women, such as Al-Anon. The director of an Al-Anon organized shelter explained the concept of "hitting bottom":

> Before the Al-Anon program can really be of benefit, a woman has to hit bottom. When you hit bottom, you realize that all of your own efforts to control the situation have failed; you feel helpless and lost and worthless and completely disenchanted with the world. Women can't really be helped unless they're ready for it and want it. Some women come here when things get bad, but they aren't really ready to be committed to Al-Anon. Things haven't gotten bad enough for them, and they go right back. We see this all the time.

5) *A change in the visibility of violence:* Creating a web of rationalizations to overlook violence is accomplished more easily if no intruders are present to question their validity. Since most violence between couples occurs in private, there are seldom conflicting interpretations of the event from outsiders. Only 7 percent of the respondents in Gelles' (1976) study who discussed spatial location of violence indicated events which took place outside the home, but all reported incidents within the home. Others report similar findings (Pittman and Handy, 1964; Pokorny, 1965; Wolfgang, 1958). If violence does occur in the presence of others, it may trigger a reinterpretation process. Battering in private is degrading, but battering in public is humiliating, for it is a statement of subordination and powerlessness. Having others witness abuse may create intolerable feelings of shame which undermine prior rationalizations.

> He never hit me in public before—it was always at home. But the Saturday I got back [returned to husband from shelter], we went Christmas shopping and he slapped me in the store because of some stupid joke I made. People saw it, I know, I felt so stupid, like, they must all think what a jerk I am, what a sick couple, and I thought, "God, I must be crazy to let him do this."

6) *External definitions of the relationship:* A change in visibility is usually accomplished by the interjection of external definitions of abuse. External definitions vary depending on their source and the situation; they either reinforce or undermine rationalizations. Battered women who request help frequently find others—and especially officials—don't believe their story or are unsympathetic (Pagelow, 1981; Pizzey, 1974). Experimental research by Shotland and Straw (1976) supports these reports. Observers usually fail to respond when a woman is attacked by a man, and justify nonintervention on the grounds that they assumed the victim and offender were married. One young woman discussed how lack of support from her family left her without hope:

> It wouldn't be so bad if my own family gave a damn about me. . . . Yeah, they know I'm here, and they don't care. They didn't care about me when I was a kid, so why should they care now? I got raped and beat as a kid, and now I get beat as an adult. Life is a big joke.

Clearly, such responses from family members contribute to the belief among battered women that there are no alternatives and that they must tolerate the abuse. However, when outsiders respond with unqualified support of the victim and condemnation of violent men, their definitions can be a potent catalyst toward victimization. Friends and relatives who show genuine concern for a woman's well-being may initiate an awareness of danger which contradicts previous rationalizations.

> My mother-in-law knew what was going on, but she wouldn't admit it. . . . I said, "Mom, what do you think these bruises are?" and she said "Well, some people just bruise easy. I do it all the time, bumping into things.". . . And he just denied it, pretended like nothing happened, and if I'd said I wanted to talk about it, he'd say, "life goes on, you can't just dwell on things. . . ." But this time, my neighbor knew what happened, she saw it, and when he denied it, she said, "I can't believe it! You know that's not true!". . . And I was so happy that finally, somebody else saw what was goin' on, and I just told him then that this time I wasn't gonna come home!

Shelters for battered women serve not only as material resources, but as sources of external definitions which contribute to the victimization process. They offer refuge from a violent situation in which a woman may contemplate her circumstances and what she wants to do about them. Within a shelter, women meet counselors and other battered women who are familiar with rationalizations of violence and the reluctance to give up commitment to a spouse. In counseling sessions, and informal conversations with other residents, women hear horror stories from others who have already defined themselves as victims. They are supported for expressing anger and reflecting responsibility for their abuse (Ferraro, 1981a). The goal of many shelters is to overcome feelings of guilt and inadequacy so that women can make choices in their best interests. In this atmosphere, violent incidents are reexamined and redefined as assaults in which the woman was victimized.

How others respond to a battered woman's situation is critical. The closer the relationship of others, the more significant their response is to a woman's perception of the situation. Thus, children can either help or hinder the victim. Pizzey (1974) found adolescent boys at a shelter in Chiswick, England, often assumed the role of the abusing father and themselves abused their mothers, both verbally and physically. On the other hand, children at the shelter we observed often became extremely protective and nurturing toward their mothers. This phenomenon has been thoroughly described elsewhere (Ferraro, 1981a). Children who have been abused by [fathers] who also beat their mothers experience high levels of anxiety, and rarely want to be reunited with their fathers. A 13-year-old abused daughter of a shelter resident wrote the following message to her stepfather:

> I am going to be honest and not lie. No, I don't want you to come back. It's not that I am jealous because mom loves you. It is [I] am afraid I won't live to see 18. I did care about you a long time ago, but now I can't care, for the simple reason you['re] always calling us names, even my friends. And another reason is, I am tired of seeing mom hurt. She has been hurt enough in her life, and I don't want her to be hurt any more.

No systematic research has been conducted on the influence children exert on their bat-

tered mothers, but it seems obvious that the willingness of children to leave a violent father would be an important factor in a woman's own decision to leave.

The relevance of these catalysts to a woman's interpretation of violence var[ies] with her own situation and personality. The process of rejecting rationalizations and becoming a victim is ambiguous, confusing, and emotional. We now turn to the feelings involved in victimization.

## The Aftermath

The consequences of leaving a violent husband vary widely and depend on such situational variables as the atmosphere of a shelter, the availability of new partners, success at employment, and the response of the spouse. Interestingly, most battered women, like most divorcees, are optimistic about future relationships (Scanzoni, 1972). When the opportunity presented itself, battered women at the shelter we observed were happy to date and establish new relationships. The idea that battered women seek out violent men has been refuted by both Pagelow (1981) and Walker (1979). However, entering a new relationship shortly after escaping a violent one does interfere with a woman's opportunity to develop autonomy and overcome problems created by years of abuse. Involvement in a new relationship is, however, appealing, because it cushions the impact of divorce and the prospect of making it alone.

Some battered women, however, develop a feeling of repugnance to romantic involvements. They may feel that "men are no good," or simply enjoy their freedom too much to consider entering a relationship. Most women in shelters reject feminism as a total philosophy, but adopt many of its tenets. Living in a shelter operated by and for women changes ideas about the role of women and their ability to run their own lives. It also provides an opportunity to develop female friendships, and to overcome the view of other women as "competitors." The rights of women to defend themselves and to make their own decisions are not easily given up once they are found. So, while women who have extricated themselves from violent relationships may not call themselves feminists, or become politically active, they do gain a commitment to certain feminist goals (Ridington, 1978).

Some formerly battered women do join in political activity to help other victims. Many of the grass-roots shelters now in existence in the United States and Europe were created by formerly battered women (Warrior, 1978), and some shelters make a special effort to recruit such women for their staffs. Entry into the battered women's movement provides an opportunity to develop a new support group, as well as build feelings of self-worth by contributing service to others.

Of course, some women return to violent relationships. There is a tendency for observers to view such decisions as failures, but they are often part of the process of gaining independence. Women may leave and return to violent relationships a number of times before making a final break. As Pagelow (1981, 219) explains it:

> Women who return home are not "failures" in any sense of the word. If there was only a short history of abuse and their spouses recognize they have a problem and begin to correct it, there is a possibility of no further violence. But these women had the courage to leave the first time; they were exposed to alternatives and new ideas; they found out that other people outside their homes can and do care for their welfare; they learned that they are not ugly "freaks" with a rare, individual problem. They may return to the men that abused them, but they do not return the same women they were when they left.

Most shelters are too overworked and understaffed to conduct systematic follow-ups for more than a month or two after women leave. Because our research was participatory, we were able to develop personal knowledge about each resident of the shelter, allowing for a more complete understanding of their post-shelter experiences. If success is defined in terms of life satisfaction (positive relationships with others, self confidence, and optimism about the future), only 30 of the 120 women we met during the study period could be said to have successfully dealt with their battering. An additional 30 women did not re-

turn to their marriages, to anyone's knowledge, but continued to face severe problems, either financially, interpersonally, or emotionally. The other 60 shelter residents (50 percent of the sample) returned to their marriages. Further, systematic research on the experiences of battered women who permanently leave violent marriages is needed to expand our knowledge of the battering phenomenon.

## Conclusion

The process of victimization is not synonymous with experiencing violent attacks from a spouse. Rationalizing the violence inhibits a sense of outrage and efforts to escape abuse. Only after rationalizations are rejected, through the impact of one or more catalysts, does the victimization process begin. When previously rationalized violence is reinterpreted as dangerous, unjustified assault, battered women actively seek alternatives. The success of their efforts to seek help depends on available resources, external supports, reactions of husbands and children, and their own adaptation to the situation. Victimization includes not only cognitive interpretations, but feelings and physiological responses. Creating a satisfying, peaceful environment after being battered involves emotional confusion and ambiguity, as well as enormous practical and economic obstacles. It may take years of struggle and aborted attempts before a battered woman is able to establish a safe and stable lifestyle; for some, this goal is never achieved.

## References

Beverly, "Shelter Resident Murdered by Husband," *Aegis*, September/October, 1978, p. 13.

Davidson, Terry, *Conjugal Crime* (New York: Hawthorn, 1978).

Dobash, R. Emerson, and Russell P. Dobash, *Violence Against Wives* (New York: Free Press, 1979).

Ferraro, Kathleen J., "Hard Love: Letting Go of an Abusive Husband," *Frontiers*, 4, 1979, 2:16–18.

——, "Battered Women and the Shelter Movement," unpublished doctoral dissertation, Arizona State University, 1981a.

——, "Processing Battered Women," *Journal of Family Issues*, 2, 1981b, 4:415–438.

Flanagan, Timothy J., David J. Van Alstyne, and Michael R. Gottfredson (eds.), *Sourcebook of*

*Criminal Justice Statistics 1981*, U.S. Department of Justice, Bureau of Justice Statistics (Washington, D.C.: U.S. Government Printing Office, 1982).

Garcia, Dick, "Slain Women 'Lived in Fear,'" *The Times* (Erie, PA), June 14, 1978, B1.

Gelles, Richard J., "Abused Wives: Why Do They Stay?" *Journal of Marriage and the Family*, 38, 1976, 4:659–668.

Johnson, John M., "Program Enterprise and Official Cooptation of the Battered Women's Shelter Movement," *American Behavioral Scientist*, 24, 1981, 6:827–842.

McGlinchey, Anne, "Woman Battering and the Church's Response," in *Sheltering Battered Women*, ed. Albert R. Roberts (New York: Springer, 1981), pp. 133–140.

Pagelow, Mildred Daley, *Woman-Battering* (Beverly Hills: Sage, 1981).

Pittman, D.J., and W. Handy, "Patterns in Criminal Aggravated Assault," *Journal of Criminal Law, Criminology, and Police Science*, 55, 1964, 4:462–470.

Pizzey, Erin, *Scream Quietly or the Neighbors Will Hear* (Baltimore: Penguin, 1974).

Pokorny, Alex D., "Human Violence: A Comparison of Homicide, Aggravated Assault, Suicide, and Attempted Suicide," *Journal of Criminal Law, Criminology, and Police Science*, 56, December, 1965, pp. 488–497.

Ridington, Jillian, "The Transition Process: A Feminist Environment as Reconstitutive Milieu," *Victimology*, 2, 1978, 3–4:563–576.

Scanzoni, John, *Sexual Bargaining* (Englewood Cliffs, NJ: Prentice-Hall, 1972).

Shotland, R. Lance, and Margret K. Straw, "Bystander Response to an Assault: When a Man Attacks a Woman," *Journal of Personality and Social Psychology*, 34, 1976, 5:990–999.

Sykes, Gresham M., and David Matza, "Techniques of Neutralization: A Theory of Delinquency," *American Sociological Review*, 22, 1957, 6:667–670.

Walker, Lenore E., *The Battered Woman* (New York: Harper and Row, 1979).

Warrior, Betsy, *Working on Wife Abuse* (Cambridge, MA: Betsy Warrior, 1978).

Wolfgang, Marvin E., *Patterns in Criminal Homicide* (New York: John Wiley, 1958).

## Review

1. How do Ferraro and Johnson define the term "battered women"?

2. Briefly describe each of the six categories of rationalization used by battered women.

3. What are the six catalysts for redefining abuse? Describe each.

4. What consequences do Ferraro and Johnson find for battered women leaving their violent husbands?

## Application

Develop a questionnaire for interviewing a staff member of a shelter for battered women. Address the following points in your interview:

a. shelter's definition of battered women

b. objectives and activities of the shelter

c. statistics about residents, e.g., age, ethnicity, marital status, length of time with their men, average duration of abuse prior to leaving, prior attempts at leaving, number of children, etc.

d. use of rationalization or other techniques of neutralization by residents

e. six catalysts present in redefinition of abuse by victims or others

f. consequences for women of leaving their men and percentage of those who return to their men

If possible, interview one or more of the residents or sit in on a group counseling session.

## Related Web Sites

1. *http://www.omsys.com/fivers/waits_houston.htm*. Lessons about battered women and their children gained from one woman's story.

2. *http://www.ojp.usdoj.gov/vawo/*. Information and publications from the Justice Department's Office on Violence Against Women.

# 22
# Everyday Sexism

*Janet K. Swim*
*Lauri L. Hyers*
*Laurie L. Cohen*
*Melissa J. Ferguson*

*Being victimized by discrimination in the workplace or by violence in intimate relationships—the topics discussed in the two previous selections—are forms of inequality of which nearly all Americans disapprove. But what about other kinds of behavior? What about such things as sexual innuendo: "hitting" on a woman, or using derogatory names like "bitch" and "chick"? What about groups of men who sit around joking about women's bodies? Are these also examples of sexism or are they only a form of fun and teasing?*

*In this selection, the researchers look at "everyday" sexism, the incidents that some men would define as trivial or "just having fun," but that women may perceive as assaults on them individually and on women generally. As the authors point out, such incidents may be so common that many women may not even notice them until they are pointed out to them. The authors also examine sexist acts against men. While women are much more likely than men to be victims of sexism, the fact that men are also victimized by sexist behavior should underscore the point that sexism leaves only victims, not victors, in its wake.*

Everyday incidents make up the basic substance of people's lives, and for members of traditionally oppressed or stigmatized groups, everyday experiences with prejudice likely represent a substantial subset of these experiences. Everyday experiences with prejudice can emerge in one's home from one's family or on the street from strangers.

These types of experiences have been referred to as everyday prejudice or interpersonal discrimination and represent the expression of prejudice and the display of discriminatory behavior embedded in people's daily lives (Essed, 1991; Lott, 1995; Swim, Cohen, & Hyers, 1998). These incidents have the potential, like any type of daily hassle, to have a significant impact on people's psychological well-being. Understanding these incidents can help provide concrete information about the way that stigmatized individuals' lives differ from those of non-stigmatized individuals and increase awareness of the issues that must be addressed in order to obtain social justice. In the research presented here, we focus on everyday sexism by examining the incidence and nature of women's and men's experiences with everyday sexism on a college campus and the impact of these incidents on their psychological well-being.

Much of the existing research on people's experiences with sexism is in the form of retrospective accounts in which participants were asked to characterize what they typically experience, sometimes for more than a year's worth of experiences. For instance, investigations of women's experiences with sexual harassment (Fitzgerald et al., 1988) and rape (Koss & Oros, 1982) use retrospective reporting methods. These studies have been effective in assessing people's recall of relatively blatant incidents of sexism. However, they often neglect more mundane or "everyday" types of experiences and thus may provide an incomplete picture of the extent and variety of daily experiences with sexism. Even when everyday sexism has been examined, retrospective survey methods have been used (e.g., Klonoff & Landrine, 1995; Fitzgerald & Ormerod, 1993).

Retrospective surveys and interviews may not accurately reflect the extent and nature of experiences people have with prejudice for several reasons. First, uncertainty about labeling subtle and ambiguous incidents as prejudicial may decrease the likelihood that such incidents are encoded and recalled as prejudicial. Second, isolated incidents may be minimized over time or seen as insignificant and therefore forgotten, even though

214

continual experiences with minor or isolated incidents may ultimately have a cumulative detrimental effect. Third, the similarity and commonness of incidents that constitute everyday prejudice may make it difficult to assess the frequency with which they occur through expansive retrospection. For instance, a woman may perceive that people are more likely to attend to male partners in conversations than to female partners but, if she experiences this often, she may not keep track of individual incidents and may even come to perceive it as typical or usual, rather than discrimination. Finally, retrospective reports are subject to distortion (Reis & Wheeler, 1991) as moods dissipate and contexts change, leaving only salient incidents to take on a more central role in recall. In contrast, daily diary studies minimize many of these problems, providing a more accurate and complete report of incidents and responses to them without the distorting processing that may result in errors (e.g., Crosby, Clayton, Alskins, & Hemker, 1986).

### Purpose of Present Research

The purpose of the present research is to examine the incidence and nature of everyday sexism and the ways it affects the daily lives of those who are its targets. Over a 2-week period, participants in our first two studies were asked to describe any gender-related experiences throughout the day and to indicate the degree to which the incidents were indicative of prejudice. Participants in the third study reported their experiences on a checklist, which included examples of sexist hassles (taken from Studies 1 and 2). In addition, the first study examined the immediate effects of the sexist incidents on women's psychological well-being, and the third study examined the effects of sexist and nonsexist incidents on women's and men's psychological well-being.

*Individual differences in experiences with everyday sexism.* We predicted that the nature of reported incidents directed at women and men would differ such that women would experience more sexual objectification than men (e.g., Plous & Neptune, 1997). Our data also enabled us to compare gender differences in reported experi-

ences with both sexist and nonsexist daily hassles. Previous research has indicated that women report more daily hassles than men (Kohn, Lafreniere, & Gurevich, 1990; Osman, Barrios, Langnecker, & Osman, 1994). One possible reason for this gender difference in general hassles is that women may experience more sexist hassles. More experiences with sexist hassles can be a result of the greater stigmatization of women than men. Lastly, we predicted that those who have feminist-related beliefs (e.g., disagreements with sexist beliefs and involvement in women's issues) would be more sensitive to sexism and thus report more sexist incidents.

*Psychological well-being.* We also examined the psychological effects of these incidents on individuals' mood and state self-esteem. We predicted that experiences with everyday sexism would lead to distressed mood and lowered state self-esteem. This prediction is congruent with research on the negative effects of other daily hassles on mood (Bolger, DeLongis, Kessler, & Schilling, 1989) and with retrospective and experimental research on the negative psychological effects of sexism (Haslett & Lipman, 1997; . . . Landrine, Klonoff, Gibbs, Manning, & Lund, 1995; Ruggiero & Taylor, 1997. Moreover, everyday sexism can be threatening because it can activate feelings of stereotype threat . . . and elevate concerns about future provocation (Fitzgerald & Ormerod, 1993). In our third study, we tested the effects of sexist and nonsexist hassles on women's and men's experiences, which allowed us to test the unique and possibly differential contribution of these experiences to well-being.

## Study 1

### Method

*Participants.* Participants were 40 female students enrolled in an undergraduate Psychology of Gender course whose age ranged from 19 to 26, with a median age of 22. Participants received extra credit for their participation in the study.

*Procedure.* Participants completed prediary measures in class prior to the explanation of the diary portion of the study. The prediary measures assessed endorsement of traditional gender stereotypes and roles (the Old Fashioned Sexism Scale; Swim, Aikin, Hall, & Hunter, 1995), Modern Sexist beliefs (Swim et al., 1995), Benevolent and Hostile Sexist beliefs (Glick & Fiske, 1996), and self-reported personal activism against sexism (e.g., "I express my anger and frustration due to sexism"; O'Neil, Egan, Owen, & Murry, 1993). Prediary measures also included assessments of women's typical emotions when interacting with men, to be used as a baseline for comparisons with emotions reported in the diaries (see below).

In introducing the diary portion of the study, participants were told that the study was designed to gain the target's perspective on prejudice and that they would be participant-observers. The concept of a participant-observer study was explained as one in which they could serve in a dual role as participant in an interaction and an observer of that interaction, like a researcher. They were told that their role would be to record incidents they witnessed in which they, someone else, or women in general were treated differently because of their gender. They were told to note incidents that were directed toward them, someone else, or women in general. In order to obtain a manageable number of incidents to record, participants were told to exclude observations from the media, such as television programming or advertisements.

If they observed a gender-related incident, they were to complete the forms as soon as possible after the incident had occurred. If more than one incident occurred on one day they were to complete a form for each incident. If they did not observe any gender-related incidents on any particular day, they were to note this on one of the forms at the end of each day. Participants turned in their data three times over a 2-week time period rather than only at the end of the study, to encourage them to complete the measures on a daily basis.

Postdiary measures were completed after all other materials were turned in. Participants indicated whether they reported all relevant incidents in their diaries and provided their assessment of whether participating in the study increased, decreased, or did not affect their tendency to notice gender-related incidents. . . .

## Results and Discussion

*Frequency.* Women reported a mean of 2.05 and a median of 1.50 incidents that they considered to be probably or definitely prejudiced, which means that they reported experiencing about one incident per week. The number of incidents ranged from 0 to 9, with 35% (n = 14) of the women reporting no incidents. Counter to our expectations, none of the scales measuring sexist beliefs or activism correlated with the number of incidents that women reported.

*Characteristics of incidents.* To obtain a description of the full range of sexist incidents, coders classified all incidents that participants had rated as being uncertain, probably, or definitely prejudiced. Although some incidents could potentially be classified in more than one category, we asked coders to select one category that appeared to fit the description best.

*Traditional gender role prejudice and stereotyping.* The first category of incidents involved comments or behaviors that reflected or enforced traditional gender role prejudice and stereotyping (e.g., endorsement of traditional gender roles or general dislike of women or subtypes of women). This included (a) comments indicating that certain roles were more appropriate for either men or women (e.g., one participant reported someone saying to her, "You're a woman, so fold my laundry," another reported that a man had said, "It's not my job to wash dishes," and a third reported that during a class exercise one of her female friends role-played a professor, and the actual male professor insisted on calling her friend "sir." When asked if she had to be a sir the professor said, "In my mind she does."); (b) comments indicating that men have greater ability in gender-stereotypic domains (e.g., a professor in one participant's class stressed that all the great scientists in the world were men, and another participant reported that her husband was discussing a bill with a receptionist and he told his wife that she should not "worry her pretty little head about these complex insurance issues"); (c) comments indicating that women possess stereotypic traits (e.g., women are more passive); (d) comments where it is assumed that women have different interests and preferences or enjoy different activities (e.g., one woman noted that a male responded to her confusion about an exam question by saying that "girls aren't into that stuff, I guess"; others noted assumptions about women not being interested or capable in sports); (e) expressions of a double standard for men and women (e.g., one participant reported a discussion in which a man said it was all right for men to see female strippers but not for women to see male strippers); and (f) general dislike of women.

***Demeaning and derogatory comments and behaviors.*** The second type of incident was using demeaning labels (such as "bitch" or "chick"), making sexist jokes, exclusion in conversations, exclusion through the use of sexist language, violence toward women, and negative attitudes toward equality. For example, one woman noted, "I was hanging out with some friends when one guy in the apartment said, 'Yo bitch, get me some beer!'" Another woman noted that a man she just met came up to her, put his arm around her, and called her "his woman." Another woman noted that a man had said, "Stupid women's lib shit—their plugs are crocked." Although many of these comments and behaviors reflect traditional gender roles and can be sexually objectifying, the element that ties these incidents together is that they are more obviously negative and directly degrading to women.

***Sexual objectification.*** The final type of incident included comments and behaviors of a sexual nature. One woman reported that she was on a trip that included two male friends who were discussing women and they decided that females were okay only if they were "easy." Another woman reported that she was walking home from a party and was approached by three men. One complimented her on her Harley Davidson belt, and the other one stared at her chest and said, "Forget the belt, look at her rack." Another woman noted that she was standing at a party and a guy whom she did not know walked past her and squeezed her waist. In general, the sexual comments included offensive comments about one's body parts or clothing (e.g., "that's a nice boulder holder"), references to sexual acts, threats of sexual contact, and street remarks such as making catcalls. Behaviors in this category included unwanted flirting, staring, and touching, such as being intimately touched by men they did not know.

***Likelihood of experiencing different types of incidents.*** To correct for over-representation of data from participants who reported a greater number of incidents, we randomly selected one incident that participants rated probably or definitely prejudiced from each participant's set of diaries. Excluding the uncertain incidents allowed us to assess the relative frequency of different types of incidents that participants were fairly certain were prejudicial. The pattern of findings reveals that, first, the incidents tended to fall fairly evenly across the categories noted above. Second, based upon participants' own ratings of incidents, just under half of incidents that women reported were those directed at women in general, whereas the remainder were directed at themselves, another specific woman, or some combination of these three targets.

***Psychological well-being.*** We were interested in the emotional impact that the incidents had on participants. For the same reasons noted above, we again analyzed only the randomly selected incidents that participants rated as probably or definitely prejudiced. Coding of the open-ended responses revealed that the most commonly experienced emotional response to prejudice was being angry or upset. Women indicated that they were angry in 75% of the incidents. In addition, paired comparisons revealed significant differences between the emotions participants reported typically experiencing with men (from the premeasures) and the emotions they reported experiencing during and after the incidents. Specifically, the results indicate that encountering sexism decreased women's comfort relative to their typical emotions they felt and that their comfort levels returned to the level that they typically felt after the incident was over. Similarly, women reported an increase in their surprise levels during the incident and that their surprise levels returned to their baseline after the incident was over. A different pattern emerged for feelings of threat, with women reporting no change from baseline in threat during the incident and a decrease in feelings of threat compared to baseline after the incident was over.

***Postdiary measures.*** The postdiary measures indicated that about a third of the participants (36%) did not report all the incidents that they observed, thus the average number of incidents reported is likely an underestimate to some degree. Participants also indicated that participation in the study affected their responses, with 80% reporting that being in the study increased the likelihood that they noticed gender-related incidents.

## Study 2

The results for Study 1 indicated that encountering everyday sexism was not an uncommon experience for most participants. However, the women in the first sample were from a Psychology of Gender class and may have been more likely to endorse feminist belief systems than the typical student, which could increase the likelihood that they would observe and report sexist incidents. . . . In Study 2, we recruited a less feminist-oriented sample from two introductory psychology classes and an advanced marketing course. Furthermore, in order to compare sexism directed at women and men, we also recruited men and asked both men and women to report on incidents of sexism directed at women and men.

### Method

***Participants.*** Participants in the second sample were 20 women and 17 men from two introductory psychology courses and an advanced marketing course, who received extra credit for their participation in the study. Demographic information assessed during the prediary measures indicated participants' age ranged from 18 to 44, with a median age of 22. Compared to women in

Study 1, women in Study 2 had higher Modern Sexism scores, but did not differ in personal activism.

***Procedure and materials.*** Participants completed prediary measures data in a separate mass screening that occurred in their class. The prediary measures assessed traditional gender stereotypes (the Attitudes Toward Women Scale; Spence, Helmreich & Strapp, 1973), Modern Sexist beliefs (Swim et al., 1995), and personal activism against sexism (O'Neil et al., 1993).

The instructions for keeping the diaries were the same as those in the first study, except that participants were explicitly told in this study that incidents could represent sexism directed at either women or men. . . . One difference between the diaries in Studies 1 and 2 is that in Study 2, participants rated separately the extent to which each of the incidents they reported was prejudiced against women and against men using the following scale ratings: definitely not prejudiced, probably not prejudiced, uncertain, probably prejudiced, definitely prejudiced, a discussion of prejudice but did not reveal prejudice itself, or not applicable. Hence, they could indicate, for example, that an incident was definitely prejudiced against women and probably prejudiced against men or they could indicate that the incident was prejudiced against women but not applicable to men.

Postdiary measures assessed whether participants reported all incidents in their diaries that they had observed, and whether participating in the study increased, decreased, or did not affect their tendency to report observing sexist incidents.

### Results and Discussion

#### Frequency

***Incidents directed at women.*** Women reported a mean of 3.45 and a median of 3.5 incidents directed at women, which is about one to two per week. The number ranged from 0 to 9, with 9% (n = 1) reporting no incidents. Men reported significantly fewer events directed at women than women reported. More specifically, men observed a mean of 2.06 and a median of 2.00 incidents, which is about one incident per week. The number ranged from 1 to 5, with none reporting no incidents.

It is interesting to note that women in Study 2 actually reported more incidents than women in Study 1, and all men in Study 2 reported at least one incident, even though participants in Study 2 were less feminist and thus likely to be less generally sensitive to gender prejudice (Pinel, 1999). It is possible that women from the Psychology of Gender class experienced fewer incidents because feminist women may self-select into situations in which they are less likely to encounter gender prejudice. Additionally, the acquaintances of more feminist women may refrain from expressing sexist prejudice in their presence.

***Incidents directed at men.*** There were no significant differences between the number of events men and women reported as being directed at men, such that they both tended to perceive that men experienced one event about every other week. Men reported a mean of 1.35 and a median of 1.00 incidents directed at men, with a range of 0 to 5. Similarly, women reported a mean of 1.05 and a median of 1.0 incidents directed at men, with a range of 0 to 4. 35% of men and 40% of women reported no incidents. . . .

***Characteristics of incidents.*** In order to assess the characteristics of the incidents and to compare the results with those in Study 1, we examined, for each female participant in the sample, a randomly selected incident that was rated as probably or definitely prejudiced directed at women, and for each male participant, an incident that was rated as probably or definitely prejudiced directed at men. A comparison of the incidents reported by women and men indicates that men's experiences are most likely to consist of traditional gender role prejudice, whereas, as in Study 1, women's responses are more evenly distributed across the three categories of prejudice. Men's experiences included people calling men "jerks," "pigs," or "worthless," characterizing men as attending too much to women's appearances, or noting that certain groups of men are unsafe for women because of sex crimes. The likelihood that the target of the incident was

the self versus another specific person was about the same in Study 1, among women in Study 2, and among men in Study 2. However, women in Study 2 were less likely than women in Study 1 and men in Study 2 to note that the incidents they observed were directed at their own gender group in general. Women in Study 2 were more likely than women in Study 1 and men in Study 2 to say that the events they observed were directed at some combination of the self, another person, or their gender group in general.

***Postdiary measures.*** As in Study 1, some participants reported that they did not record all incidents. Fewer women (14%) did this in Study 2, however, than in Study 1. This could also explain the greater number of incidents women recorded in Study 2 than Study 1. Similar to the women in Study 1, about 37% of the men reported not recording all incidents. Participants again indicated that participation in the study affected their responses. Seventy-three percent of women and 81% of men reported that being in the study increased the likelihood that they noticed gender-related incidents.

# Study 3

In Study 3, we further explored the frequency of everyday sexist incidents that women and men experience. Participants in this study used a checklist method to record their experiences with a range of incidents, including both sexist and nonsexist incidents. The sexist incidents in the checklist were based upon the incidents reported in Study 1. We also expanded our set of prediary measures to test whether other individual differences might predict reported experiences with sexism. . . .

## Method

***Participants.*** Participants were students enrolled in a Psychology of Gender class and their male friends. . . .

***Procedure.*** Students in the Psychology of Gender class were given oral and written instructions in class. Students in the class then gave the materials to their male friends, who were told to follow the procedures outlined in class. Participants completed prediary measures prior to the explanation of the diary portion of the study. . . .

Participants were again instructed as to their participant-observer role in the research. However, instead of using an incident-sampling procedure as was done in the first two studies, participants in the third study completed two types of diary forms at the end of each day. The diary form to be completed first each day was a report of their psychological well-being. The next form to be completed each day was a checklist of possible hassles they might have experienced over the course of the day. Participants were asked to turn in their forms three times over the 2-week course of the study to encourage timely completion of the forms. Postdiary measures, completed at the end of the 2-week period, assessed the extent to which the participants perceived that the study increased, decreased, or did not affect their reporting of incidents.

**Diaries.** At the end of every day, participants reported how they currently felt on 18 different mood states on a scale of 0 (not at all) to 4 (extremely). Half of the moods were positive and half were negative. The positive moods were used as filler items. The negative mood items derived from Lorr and McNair's (1971) Profile of Mood States, measuring anger (annoyed, peeved, resentful), anxiety (on edge, uneasy, nervous), and depression (sad, hopeless, discouraged). Participants also noted their state self-esteem based on Heatherton and Polivy's (1991) measures of appearance, social, and performance state self-esteem.

After completing the psychological well-being measures, participants noted whether they had experienced any of 14 possible incidents presented in a checklist. Brief descriptions of sexist and nonsexist incidents were alternated in the checklist. Six of the items on the checklist were sexist incidents drawn from the descriptions of experiences in the first two studies (treated stereotypically, comments reflecting dislike or stereotypes of people of one's own gender, unwanted sexual attention, demeaning or degrading labels, threat or experience of sexual or physical violence, words that exclude people of your gender, and negative attitudes about

gender equality). A seventh sexist incident in the checklist involved sexism in the media, but it was not included in the analyses presented below. Seven of the incidents in the checklist represented typical daily hassles that college students report having (academic challenges, time pressure, feeling alienated, assorted annoyances, general social mistreatment, and friendship or romantic relationship problems; Kohn et al., 1990; Osman et al., 1994). An "other" category allowed participants to check off and describe an incident not captured in the other 14 categories. . . .

## Results and Discussion

*Frequency.* . . . Both women and men in Study 3 reported many more sexist incidents than those in Studies 1 and 2 reported. On average women reported observing 6.11 incidents that they rated as probably or definitely sexist, which is about one per day. It is possible that demand characteristics increased the reporting of sexist incidents or that providing participants with a list of possible incidents made them more likely to notice or think about certain incidents as being sexist. It is also possible that participants included reports of more trivial incidents when using the checklist method than when using the open-ended reporting method because it took less effort to check them off than to describe them using the structured diaries of Studies 1 and 2. For instance, some participants in the first two studies had mentioned in the postdiary measures that they did not report some incidents because they did not think they were very important. Thus, a more conservative estimate of everyday sexism from the checklists would be to examine only those sexist incidents that participants indicated had the most impact. Women reported that 1.38 of these incidents with the greatest impact were sexist, which is comparable to the frequencies reported in Studies 1 and 2.

Consistent with findings from Study 2, men reported fewer incidents directed at men than women had reported directed at women. Men reported observing on average 2.86 sexist incidents directed toward men per week. Considering only the sexist incidents with the greatest impact, men reported observing less than one incident per week (M = .61), which is also comparable to the frequencies reported in Study 2.

We tested whether the inclusion of sexist hassles might be able to account for the general tendency for women to report more daily hassles than men (Kohn et al., 1990; Osman et al., 1994). Consistent with past research, women reported a higher total number of hassles than men. There was no difference, however, in women's and men's tendency to report incidents that they labeled as nonsexist, and no difference in their tendency to report incidents that they labeled as being uncertain as to whether or not they were sexist. The gender difference emerged only in their reports of experiences they had labeled as sexist. Similarly, gender differences emerged for the number of sexist hassles but not for other types of hassles when examining only those incidents reported as having the greatest impact on them each day.

As in Studies 1 and 2, Modern Sexism, traditional gender role beliefs, and feminist activism did not predict the number of sexist incidents reported (with one exception: The more men endorsed Modern Sexist beliefs, the fewer sexist hassles they reported). There was also no tendency for neuroticism to predict number of incidents reported. However, the feminist-related measures included in Study 3 that had not been included in Studies 1 and 2 did predict the total number of sexist incidents reported. More specifically, the more women and men endorsed more gender-feminist beliefs and the more women felt threatened by the possibility of being stereotyped, the more incidents they reported. . . .

***Psychological well-being.*** . . . [T]he more participants reported experiencing either nonsexist or sexist incidents, the more likely they were to report that they were angry, anxious, and depressed. With regard to state self-esteem, sexist and nonsexist incidents had different effects. The more people reported experiencing sexist incidents, the lower their social state self-esteem. Sexist incidents did not influence their appearance or performance state self-esteem. In contrast, the more people reported experiencing nonsexist incidents, the lower their appearance and performance state self-esteem. Nonsexist incidents did not influence their social state self-esteem. The findings confirm the results from retrospective studies illustrating the relationship between women's experiences with everyday sexist incidents and psychological well-being (Landrine et al., 1995) and from laboratory studies illustrating that attributions to discrimination can lower one's social state self-esteem (Ruggiero & Taylor, 1997). . . .

## General Discussion

Across all three studies, it is clear that experiences with sexist hassles are a common occurrence, especially for women, who experience incidents with a personal impact an average of once or twice a week. The qualitative information about women's and men's experiences obtained in the studies gives insight into modern forms of sexism. Traditional gender role beliefs and prejudices, demeaning comments and behaviors, and sexual objectification characterized these incidents. Although women are more likely to experience all of these types of prejudice than men, the greatest difference occurs in their experience with sexual objectification, with men rarely, if ever, reporting these experiences. This may be one reason women objectify their own bodies, internalizing an observer's perspective on their own appearance, which has the potential of threatening women's psychological well-being, including increasing their levels of depression (Frederickson & Roberts, 1997).

It has been argued that modern forms of sexism include both overt displays of inequality and subtle and covert forms of sexism as well (Benokraitis & Feagin, 1995). The presence of traditional forms of sexism in our results is consistent with the argument that overt forms of prejudice still exist. If one focused only on these traditional forms of sexism, however, one would miss other forms of sexism. Subtle sexism consists of displays of inequality that might typically go unnoticed or might not be specifically remembered because they are considered normal parts of our lives. The tendency for many participants to indicate that the study made them more aware of sexist incidents suggests that incidents are occurring but can go unnoticed. The tendency of relatively strong feminist beliefs and perceptions of stereotype threat to predict reporting of sexist incidents, more than endorsement of sexist beliefs, suggests that a more defensive and perhaps self-protective reaction to sexism increases one's sensitivity to sexism. The lack of effect of the other forms of sexist beliefs may be a result of the instructions making the less feminist participants more similar to the feminist participants in sensitivity. Yet even controlling for the effect of relatively strong feminist beliefs and feelings of stereotype threat, sexist incidents affected psychological well-being.

Everyday sexist incidents have important psychological ramifications, especially for women. Women's greater experience with sexist hassles compared to men accounts for the total difference in experiences with daily hassles. Everyday sexist incidents are a significant source of anger, with about 75% of the sexist incidents reported in Study 1 resulting in anger, and the more experiences women (and men) had with sexist incidents, the more angry they felt in Study 3. These incidents are likely to affect other aspects of women's psychological well-being. Study 1 indicates that encounters with sexism affected women's comfort, and there was a trend in Study 3 for women and not men to experience more anxiety the more incidents they reported in a day. Further, even though reporting more sexist incidents was associated with more anger, more depression, and lower social state self-esteem for both women and men, the tendency for women to report more sexist incidents than men suggests a greater impact on women than men because women will experience these effects more frequently than men. . . .

## References

Benokraitis, N. V., & Feagin, J. R. (1995). *Modern Sexism* (2nd ed.). Englewood Cliffs, NJ: Prentice Hall.

Bolger, N., DeLongis, A., Kessler, R. C., & Schilling, E. A. (1989). Effects of daily stress on negative mood. *Journal of Personality and Social Psychology, 57,* 808–818.

Crosby, F., Clayton, S., Alskins, O., & Hemker, K. (1986). Cognitive biases in the perception of discrimination: The importance of format. *Sex Roles, 14,* 637–646.

Essed, P. (1991). Understanding everyday racism: An interdisciplinary theory. *Sage series on race and ethnic relations, Vol. 2.* Newbury Park, CA: Sage.

Fitzgerald, L. F., & Ormerod, A. J. (1993). Breaking silence: The sexual harassment of women in academia and the workplace. In F. Denmark and M. Paludi (Eds.), *The psychology of women: Handbook of issues and theories* (pp. 553–581). Westport CT: Greenwood.

Fitzgerald, L. F., Shullman, S. L., Bailey, N., Richards, M., Swecker, J., Gold, Y., Ormerod, M., & Weitzman, L. (1988). The incidence and dimensions of sexual harassment in academia and the workplace. *Journal of Vocational Behavior, 32,* 152–175.

Fredrickson, B. L., & Roberts, T. (1997). Objectification theory: Toward understanding women's lived experiences and mental health risks. *Psychology of Women Quarterly, 21,* 173–206.

Glick, P., & Fiske, S. T. (1996). The Ambivalent Sexism Inventory: Differentiating hostile and benevolent sexism. *Journal of Personality and Social Psychology, 70,* 491–512.

Haslett, B. B., & Lipman, S. (1997). Micro inequalities: Up close and personal. In N. V. Benokraitis (Ed.), *Subtle sexism* (pp. 34–53). Thousand Oaks, CA: Sage.

Heatherton, T. F., & Polivy, J. (1991). Development and validation of a scale for measuring state self-esteem. *Journal of Personality and Social Psychology, 60,* 895–910.

Klonoff, E. A., & Landrine, H. (1995). The schedule of sexist incidents: A measure of lifetime and recent sexist discrimination in women's lives. *Psychology of Women Quarterly, 19,* 439–473.

Kohn, P. M., Lafreniere, K., & Gurevich, M. (1990). The Inventory of College Students' Recent Life Experiences: A decontaminated hassles scale for a special population. *Journal of Behavioral Medicine, 13,* 619–630.

Koss, M. P., & Oros, C. J. (1982). Sexual experiences survey: A research instrument investigating sexual aggression and victimization. *Journal of Consulting and Clinical Psychology, 50,* 455–457.

Landrine, H., Klonoff, E. A., Gibbs, J., Manning, V., & Lund, M. (1995). Physical and psychiatric correlates of gender discrimination: An application of the schedule of sexist incidents. *Psychology of Women Quarterly, 19,* 473–492.

Lorr, M., & McNair, D. M. (1971). *The Profile of Mood States manual.* San Diego, CA: Educational and Industrial Testing Service.

Lott, B. (1995). Distancing from women: Interpersonal sexist discrimination. In B. Lott & D. Maluso (Eds.), *The social psychology of interpersonal discrimination* (pp. 12–49). New York: Guilford.

O'Neil, J. M., Egan, J., Owen, S., & Murry, V. M. (1993). The gender role journey measure: Scale development and psychometric evaluation. *Sex Roles, 38,* 167–185.

Osman, A., Barrios, F. X., Langnecker, J., & Osman, J. (1994). Validation of the Inventory of College Students' Recent Life Experiences in an American college sample. *Journal of Clinical Psychology, 50,* 856–863.

Pinel, E. C. (1999). Stigma consciousness: The psychological legacy of social stereotypes. *Journal of Personality and Social Psychology, 76,* 114–128.

Plous, S., & Neptune, D. (1997). Racial and gender biases in magazine advertising: A content-analytic study. *Psychology of Women Quarterly, 21,* 627–644.

Reis, H. T., & Wheeler, L. (1991). Studying social interaction with the Rochester Interaction Record. *Advances in Experimental Social Psychology, 24,* 269–318.

Ruggiero, K. M., & Taylor, D. M. (1997). Why minority group members perceive or do not perceive the discrimination that confronts them: The role of self-esteem and perceived control. *Journal of Personality and Social Psychology, 72,* 373–389.

Spence, J. T., Helmreich, R., & Strapp, Joy. (1973). A short version of The Attitudes Toward Women Scale (AWS). *Bulletin of the Psychonomic Society,* Vol. 2 (4), Oct. 1973, 219–220.

Swim, J. K., Aikin, K. J., Hall, W. S., & Hunter, B. A. (1995). Sexism and racism: Old-fashioned and modern prejudices. *Journal of Personality and Social Psychology, 68,* 199–214.

Swim, J. K., Cohen, L. L., & Hyers, L. L. (1998). Experiencing everyday prejudice and discrimination. In J. K. Swim & C. Stangor (Eds.), *Prejudice: The target's perspective* (pp. 37–60). New York: Academic.

## Review

1. What are the advantages of the diary method of studying sexism over methods used in other research?

2. Name and briefly define the various categories of incidents that Swim and her associates defined as everyday sexism.

3. How do men's and women's experiences of sexism compare in terms of frequency and types of incidents?

## Application

Conduct your own research similar to the way the students did in this selection. Keep a diary for two weeks. Note any sexist incidents directed against either yourself or someone else. Watch for incidents against both males and females. Compare your results with those of Swim and her associates. Did doing this research make you more sensitive to sexism? Based on your observations, what course of action would you recommend to those who want to reduce the amount of sexism in our society?

## Related Web Sites

1. *http://www.understandingprejudice.org/links/sexism.htm*. This site offers a multitude of links to sites dealing with sexism, sexual harassment, and women's rights.

2. *http://www.geocities.com/youth4sa/advertising.html*. An article on sexism in advertising.

Source: Janet K. Swim, Lauri L. Hyers, Laurie L. Cohen, and Melissa J. Ferguson, "Everyday Sexism: Evidence for Its Incidence, Nature, and Psychological Impact From Three Daily Diary Studies," In *Journal of Social Issues* 57 (2001): 31–53. Copyright © 2001 by Blackwell Publishing Ltd. Reprinted with permission. ✦

# Part Four

## *International Inequality*

Inequality exists not only between groups within a society, but between societies as well. There is, in other words, a global stratification system. The **gross national product** per capita in rich nations is 400 or more times higher than that of the poorest nations. This difference translates into such things as lower life expectancy, higher rates of disease and infant mortality, lower educational levels, and higher rates of poverty in the poor nations. As selection 23 shows, the rich nations must bear some responsibility for the plight of the poor nations, for the rich nations are able to use those in the poor nations for their own benefit. ◆

# 23
# Sweatshop Barbie
## Exploitation of Third World Labor

*Anton Foek*

*The industrialized nations owe much of their current prosperity to the use of extremely cheap labor in Third World countries. One perspective on this economic relationship, called* **modernization theory,** *holds that the money and models provided by more advanced nations promote the development of industrial economies and democratic governments in the Third World.* **World system theory,** *in contrast, views the relationship as exploitative of Third World countries and detrimental to their economic development. Researchers have found some support for both positions, suggesting that different outcomes may occur for different nations (for reasons that are not yet clear).*

*Whatever the eventual outcome for a Third World nation, the situation of the workers is often deplorable. In this selection, Anton Foek depicts one such situation—women and children in Thailand who make Barbie dolls. Why do they stay in jobs that are killing them? Simple survival is one motivation. Another is the role obligations they have as family members who are expected to help poorer relatives.*

My daughter Zsa Zsa, seven years old, stands in front of the toy store and can't make up her mind which Barbie doll she wants. Barbie is her idol and role model. I urge her to pick out another present for her birthday but, if I insist, I'll spoil her day altogether. So Barbie it is: four or five to keep the peace and save her birthday.

There is no way for me to explain to her that there is something fundamentally wrong with Barbie. For as financially successful as the doll has been, the story of Barbie is appalling.

Barbie dolls are manufactured in factories in China, Thailand, and Indonesia, where working conditions are radically different from what Americans are used to. Factory workers in these Far Eastern countries are underpaid, overworked, and getting sick—even dying. Just arrived in Bangkok, I see banners that say, "We are not salve labour!" (They were intended to say "slave labour," but the message gets through anyway.) The banners are carried by women and children who work in the Dynamics factory just outside of Bangkok. Only a few men have shown up to support them. I ask these protestors what they want and they answer: to be treated like human beings. They regard themselves as modern-day slaves of a system that exploits them.

One woman, Karim, tells me that more than half of these women are sick. They make Mattel's Barbie dolls in an environment that would probably have been banned as dangerous anywhere in the First World. Many of the workers have respiratory infections, their lungs filled with dust from fabrics in the factory. And not only dust: others work with lead and other chemicals and suffer from chronic lead poisoning. They can wear masks, of course, but first they have to buy them. And as they make a mere four to five dollars a day—from which they must also buy their uniforms and scissors—most simply can't afford the protection.

Thanks to John Osolnick, an American working in Bangkok, I obtained access to the Dynamics factory (naturally, no tape or video recorders were allowed inside). I saw hundreds of women and children stuffing, cutting, dressing, and assembling Barbie dolls—as well as the Lion Kings my daughter worships and other Disney properties that dazzle me.

Many of these factory workers suffer from pains in their hands, necks, and shoulders. Others experience nausea and dizziness and suffer from hair and memory loss. They sleep badly. The most common complaints, however, are a shortage of breath and infections in and around the throat. More than 75 percent

225

of the people working here have breathing problems. The air in the factory is so dusty that even the managers don't come in for fear of being contaminated. And of the hundreds of workers I saw, all of them, without exception, have black circles under their eyes.

One woman told me, "It sometimes gets so hot and moist in here that some of us faint." A small number of workers have tried to organize, she said, but there is an overall fear that they will be fired and that "no one will take care of us if we do not work." There is also the fear of physical harm. "Women in Thailand are vulnerable," another worker tells me. "We have to think of our parents in Chiang Mai and our small brothers and sisters who go to school. Who is going to pay for them if we don't?" It is a catch-22 situation: if they don't work, their relatives get nothing, if they do work, they get sick from all the chemicals and dust.

"I am an old woman even before my twentieth birthday," a third woman said to me. "Maybe I should move to Taiwan or Korea." But even if she wanted to, she wouldn't be allowed to emigrate, because she is too young. This job is a nightmare for her and the 4,500 other people who work at the Dynamics factory, and it is almost standard that Asian women and children are exploited this way. It doesn't really matter what industry you work in, as a woman or child you are always on the bottom of the heap—long hours, low wages, and poor health care. I can't help thinking that health organizations in the West should be able to do something more for them.

Pramitwa doesn't exactly know what to say to me when we meet in a Bangkok hospital. At first, she doesn't really understand why I am there. Dr. Orapun has asked her to come down from the outskirts of this hellish city of six million to the inner city, which is filled with exhaust fumes, noise, and poisoned air.

Dr. Orapun knows that Pramitwa has trouble breathing, but the physician thinks it is important that her story be told to the outside world. Otherwise, Pramitwa does not have a voice. Dr. Orapun is a 42-year-old woman who has an energy and power that is the envy of anyone who meets her. Her office is small but very well known among the underprivileged here. She has been investigating the widespread illnesses and even deaths of workers at several different factories and assembly plants in and around Bangkok. She knows her work will stir controversy; Thai society is closed and prefers to settle disputes its own way.

Pramitwa is a shy, 22-year-old woman. She is accompanied by two friends, who are also suffering from diseases related to their work at the Dynamics plant. Eye contact with these women is difficult to make, and they all suffer from hair loss and have trouble breathing. When I ask one of them, Sunanta, how she is, she diverts her eyes to the ground and asks me in a whisper if I want to buy a souvenir.

Sunanta is a little older than the rest. I can hear her breathing is heavy and irregular. Dr. Orapun says that Sunanta is in terrible shape. Indeed, most of the women and children working in these toy factories are in terrible shape: besides the asthma, hair and memory loss, and constant pain in their hands, necks, and shoulders, they have episodes of vomiting and the women have irregular periods. Moreover, and without exception, they sleep badly, resulting in fatigue.

Sunanta is a bit more outspoken than the rest and bluntly states that the factory is exploiting them. Most of the Dynamics plant's 4,500 workers come from northeastern Thailand, where the poverty is abject and appalling. It is a frequent practice for parents there to sell their daughters—often not more than 11 or 12 years old—into sex slavery or as cheap labor to Thai gangsters or mafiosi from neighboring countries. The parents generate some income from that—a one-time flat fee of a couple of hundred dollars.

Those who aren't sold outright into slavery at an early age often are sent to the bigger cities like Bangkok, where they generate an even more stable income working in factories. They send the money back home to their parents and very often help pay for their little brothers and sisters to go to school.

Sunanta describes how she has to get up every morning at five o'clock to cook a meal and get ready for work. She also takes care of her neighbor's two children and gets them ready for kindergarten. Then, after a shower from a bucket outside the hut, Sunanta gets dressed and waits for the motorcycle that will pick up both her and the woman she shares the hut with and take them to the factory. She does this six days a week.

Dr. Orapun translates her words to me: "I have been working there for over six years now. After one year, I already started to have these problems." Sunanta's eyes still don't make contact with mine, and her voice is so low that the doctor has to ask her to repeat what she's saying.

I understand that working conditions, not just at the Dynamics plant but in all factories throughout Thailand and Southeast Asia, are appalling: long hours, hard work, low pay, no vacations, no sick days, no rights. No union and thus no voice.

"When we get sick, they throw us out," Sunanta tells me. "It isn't even the factory itself. The factory knows the standards set by the U.S. mother companies. But as the workers are hired by someone else for a period of 120 days, it is easy to fire us after 118 days of work. Very often we are hired again the very same day we are fired for another period of 120 days."

She says that complaining is of no use and that she wants to start a movement. She would like to get in contact with women from overseas, from countries where rights are guaranteed and a part of daily life. Eventually, the souvenir she wanted to sell me becomes a present simply for listening to her.

Sunanta gets up to go to the bathroom and, when she comes back, I notice that she has put some lipstick on. Her eyes are hollow, but they are making contact now with mine. I discover a proud woman who has redefined her identity.

Dr. Orapun started investigating sweatshops in 1991 as the director of Thailand's National Institute of Occupational and Environmental Medicine. At that time, she was looking into the deaths of several factory workers at Seagate Technology, the subsidiary of a computer company located in Silicon Valley. Seagate was, at that time, one of the world's largest independent computer hard-disk producers. It had opened two assembly plants in Thailand and was said to be one of the country's largest employers, with some 21,000 workers.

Seagate was profitable for a long time because it had based its operations in a low-wage country. Seagate's chief executive officer, Alan Shugart, even stated in a 1991 interview with *Electronic Business* magazine that his company was not very employee-oriented. And when Seagate's profits finally started to fall in the fluid and ever-changing computer market, the last thing the company wanted was to allow its employees to form a union to demand higher wages and better working conditions.

It was in this atmosphere that Dr. Orapun started her investigation. One day, while she was walking the factory assembly line, she was summoned to the company boardroom. There she was confronted by Stapron Kavitanon, the first secretary of the then-prime minister of Thailand and the director-general of the Thai Board of Investment. That meeting confirmed one of Dr. Orapun's misgivings about the goals of Thailand's foreign investors. "I am still furious," she tells me now, "because it was then I began to understand how these companies work. If they think Thailand is becoming too expensive or the workers too difficult, they simply move to cheaper labor countries like Indonesia or China."

Dr. Orapun recalls what Stapron said to her: "What you are doing is hurting your country. You cannot continue to investigate Seagate or any other foreign investor. You are a threat to the workers of this country."

Dr. Orapun refused to be intimidated and continued her investigations. Within a few weeks, she was removed as head of the National Institute of Occupational and Environmental Medicine. But that didn't stop her. She began analyzing blood samples from more than 2,000 workers at several factories (including the Dynamics plant where the Barbie dolls are made) in order to discover what was causing the worker illnesses and deaths.

At this point in the interview, Sunanta again makes eye contact with me and says that, at the Dynamics plant, at least four of her friends have died. I look at her and her almost bald head and listen to her heavy breathing, and I cannot help thinking that she may be dead soon, too.

"I think of quitting work, because it is very difficult for me," she says, gasping for air. "I have to rest. I am very tired." Her eyes turn away again, tiny tears in the corners and her cheeks gaunt.

Days before this interview, Sunanta was at the rally I witnessed upon my arrival in Bangkok. She believes that if she doesn't help the other workers, her life will have had no meaning. Before she dies she wants to do something to help her friends and colleagues keep alive the dream of a better life.

Dr. Orapun takes Sunanta's hands and holds them. She says that the blood samples she analyzed from the Seagate workers had levels of lead greater than 20 micrograms per 100 milliliters. "The fatalities at Seagate may have been caused by chronic poisoning," she tells me. "The main source of lead in electronics factories is the solder that is used to attach components to the circuit boards."

Seagate maintains that the high levels of lead in their workers are more likely the result of their living in a dangerously polluted part of the city. But Dr. Orapun says that this isn't true, because another study indicates that only 4 percent of the traffic police in Bangkok—many of whom are continually exposed to the air pollution caused by the city's traffic—had more lead in their blood than the workers at Seagate. Only 4 percent. So what's going on here?

In other factories, like the Dynamics plant where Sunanta and Pramitwa work, illness is more likely caused by the inhalation of dust and solvents. Sunanta says that, for her, becoming ill without health insurance would be possibly the most humiliating thing of all, because she would have to go back home. She does not want to face her relatives again and spend her remaining days dependent upon their benevolence. She is afraid that, if she loses her job—even a job that has caused her to get sick in the first place—she may end up losing her integrity, her self-esteem, and even her identity. And so she doesn't want to complain much about being paid six or seven dollars for a 12-hour workday. Indeed, by Bangkok standards, she is considered lucky to have found such a good job.

Sunanta herself has never played with a Barbie doll. The Dynamics workers are not allowed to buy them—not at the regular price and certainly not at a discount. She is astonished when I tell her that there are two Barbie dolls sold somewhere in the world every second, and that Mattel made more than $3.2 billion in 1994. Nor does she know that more than a billion pairs of shoes have been made for Barbie, many of them here in Bangkok, or that Barbie has 35 dogs, 10 horses, scores of cats, a panda, a chimpanzee, lion cubs, a giraffe, and a zebra. Sunanta cannot grasp the luxury of Barbie's world, but she certainly is not jealous. She just wishes that she could breathe more easily and that she wouldn't be so tired and that her hair would grow back again. She tells me how pretty she used to be when she was still living at home and even during the years when she had first come to Bangkok. But after working at the Dynamics plant for only a year, she started to develop problems: first, with her period, then headaches, memory loss, and now hair loss. Her health problems have left her depressed and embarrassed, shy and ashamed.

The local press eventually picked up on Dr. Orapun's research but concluded that she never proved her case. John Osolnick, an American researcher working in Bangkok, says that this is par for the course. He is furious over the way factory workers are being treated in Thailand: "They try to raise their voices, and they're fired without any benefit whatsoever. The companies know that, if they support the workers' demands, the American mother companies can easily move to even lower-wage countries. So the pressure from lobbyists is enormous." In Osolnick's office, the very air seems to be filled with his disappointment, anger, and frustration. He is particularly incensed by the way Dr. Orapun was treated. Six weeks after she filed her report, her medical institute was closed. "One day," he recalls, "a bunch of people arrived at her office only to remove the name board."

Dr. Orapun confirms the story and adds that she was informed by the director of the hospital that she no longer had a job there and should start looking elsewhere. Not surprisingly, both the Seagate and Dynamics plants have been officially cleared of any wrongdoing in the Kingdom of Thailand. Osolnick also informs me that another Dynamics employee, Metha, is hospitalized just outside of Bangkok and suggests that I speak with her myself.

The hospital is neat and clean. As it is a national holiday, the Dynamics plant is closed, so two friends are visiting Metha to cheer her up and tell her the latest gossip. Metha is a militant woman in her early twenties, who also came to Bangkok to improve the quality of her life. But she is afraid to talk to me. "Barbie is powerful," she says. "Three friends have already died. If they kill me, who will ever know I lived?"

Metha tried to start a union at the Dynamics plant. She claims that the company not only fired her but threatened to shut her up forever. Then she developed respiratory problems and was transferred to this hospital. It remains unclear who is going to pay the bill: Metha has no money and no insurance, and the company refuses to recognize her illness as work-related. Her illness has left her worn out, weak, and thin.

Metha says that she began to feel sick early in 1995, after having worked at the Dynamics plant since 1992 sorting parts for Barbie dolls. She reports, "When my head and body started to ache, I'd go to the factory doctor, but he wouldn't take me seriously. He said it would go away with time. But then my periods stopped, too, and I really started to worry. I told the manager at the factory, but he laughed at me. The doctor then withdrew the diagnosis of my sickness after he was called by the factory. That set me thinking about the rights and responsibilities we have."

Like the other Dynamics workers I have met, Metha avoids eye contact and speaks in a monotone. The only time she ever shows emotion is when she begins to cry and wonders aloud when it is all going to end.

I cannot help thinking of Cindy Jackson, an American photographer in London who has had 19 cosmetic-surgery operations to make herself look like Barbie—at a cost of some $165,000. I wonder what Jackson would say if she could see these sick and dying women and know how brutally they have been exploited in order to make dolls for First World children. Pramitwa, Sunanta, and Metha have never heard of Cindy Jackson, but my guess is they are glad not to be in her shoes. For them, it would be unbearable to live a life looking like Barbie.

## Review

1. In what sense are the workers in the Barbie factory "modern-day slaves of a system that exploits them"?

2. Why do the workers accept the jobs, and why do they remain in them?

3. What happens when someone tries to improve the conditions of the workers?

## Application

Make a personal or telephone interview of several buyers or suppliers for department stores, clothing retailers, or toy stores. Find out the following:

a. The proportion of products that are made in Third World countries

b. How the wholesale prices of these products compare with those of products made in the United States

c. Whether the proportion of products made in Third World countries has increased or decreased over the past decade

d. Whether the respondent knows the wages and working conditions of the Third World workers who make the products

Discuss your findings in light of the information found in this article.

## Related Web Sites

1. *http://barbie.everythinggirl.com/.* The Barbie home page is instructive in light of the materials offered in this selection.

2. *http://www.nmass.org/nmass/index.html.* This site offers information about sweatshops in the U.S., along with ideas about how to eliminate them.

---

# Unit IV

## *Social Institutions*

Social institutions are the pillars of society. An **institution** is a collective solution to a problem of social life. Thus, the institutions of any society provide a framework for carrying out that society's essential functions, and they enhance social stability. The institutions found in all societies include family, government, the economy, education, religion, and health care. Note that sociologists define "institution" differently from its common usage. A mental hospital is not an institution in sociological terms; it is an organization, which is one kind of group. The family, in the sense of all families rather than a particular family, is an institution.

Examining a society in terms of its institutions can be revealing, especially when comparing one society with another. For instance, contrast our practice of marrying for romantic love with the dowry and bride-price systems of certain societies. Or compare the working conditions of those in Third World countries with those in modern nations such as the United States and Canada (selection 23).

The connections between institutions within a single society are also worthy of exploration. For example, what are the effects of rising unemployment on family problems such as divorce and child abuse? Similarly, one might look at how power is apportioned among a society's institutions and the implications of that distribution. Religious institutions were dominant in medieval Europe, for instance, but political institutions are much more powerful today. Finally, technological developments both tie institutions together and affect all institutions individually.

Selections 24 through 38 in this unit touch on each of the social institutions mentioned above. As you read the selections, think about how each institution has affected your life. It should be clear that social institutions are the matrix in which each of us are embedded as we live out our lives. ✦

# Part One

## *The Family*

Some kind of family is found in every human society, suggesting that the family has crucial functions for both individuals and society as a whole. Those functions include socialization, regulation of sexual relationships (in most societies people are expected to confine sex to marriage), reproduction, and the economic cooperation necessary to sustain life and well-being.

Family life has varied over time in the United States. In colonial America, a man was expected to be financially secure before marriage. Once married, children tended to come rapidly, creating large families. The family was stable; divorce was stigmatized. Because colonial America was primarily an agrarian society, the family also tended to be a self-contained economic unit, producing a great deal of what it consumed.

In contrast, today the family is small, divorce is frequent, and the family is no longer a self-contained economic unit. Selections 24 and 25 address some of the challenges faced by the modern family. Selection 26 points out that we may be in a time of transition into new understandings about family life. ✦

# 24
# Home Work Time

*Marilyn Snell*

A *century ago, women and men were widely regarded as having separate spheres of life. Women were viewed as "naturally" suited to child rearing and housework. Men, on the other hand, were regarded as competitive and logical—well equipped for the world of work and public affairs. While some people still hold these beliefs, the massive influx of women into the labor force makes it difficult to maintain the illusion that they are unsuited to work outside the home. And what about men? Are they suited to, and willing to engage in, household work? When wives share in producing family income, do husbands balance this out by helping with the "second shift" of household work and child care?*

*In the 1980s, Arlie Hochschild and Anne Machung addressed the issue and concluded that husbands did little to help with household chores; wives simply added a "second shift" to their workday. In the 1990s, Hochschild used participant observation to continue her study of families in which both husband and wife work outside the home. The following interview summarizes and expands somewhat on the major findings reported in her book,* The Time Bind.

*In the interview, Hochschild notes a number of social factors that draw people's commitment away from family time and toward work time. One such factor is the possibility of* **social mobility,** *the movement within or between social classes. Upward mobility is a strong value in American society. It is a value that is not always consistent with the most satisfying family life.*

I n her latest book, *The Time Bind: When Work Becomes Home and Home Becomes Work* (New York: Metropolitan Books,

1997), UC Berkeley sociologist Arlie Hochschild takes a detective's eye to the problem of what's keeping parents at work so long. What she discovered were men and women apparently happily married to their jobs and not the least inclined to take advantage of family-friendly company policies—programs that would have allowed employees to spend more time at home.

Hochschild, who made waves with *The Second Shift*—her groundbreaking 1989 book on gender roles in two-career marriages—this time spent three summers observing employees of a Fortune 500 company she calls "Amerco" to protect the privacy of those she studied. She chose the Northeastern manufacturer precisely for its reputation as a good place for parents to work: A 1991 survey by the Families and Work Institute named it one of the 10 most family-friendly companies in the US.

After visiting company-sponsored child-care centers, tagging along on errands with stressed-out, upper-management moms, and interviewing employees in all sectors of the company—from "Bill," a high-ranking corporate executive, to "Becky," a factory-line worker—Hochschild discovered myriad ways in which the home is being invaded by the pressures of work, while the workplace is becoming a haven from a hectic, unrewarding home life. Her findings offer eloquent, sad, and sometimes chilling evidence of the "time bind" many employees find themselves in and, more broadly, suggest a disturbing cultural transformation in the way Americans feel about home, family, work, and even time itself.

Q: You argue that people are having trouble arranging their work hours to spend more time with their families. But you also contend that men and women alike are choosing to spend less time at home. What's going on? Where's the bind?

A: The bind is between work and home for both women and men. In *The Second Shift*, I put forward the argument that women have changed more rapidly than men. Women are spending more and more time at work, but men are not spending much more time taking care of needs at home (the second shift). We're still stuck in this stalled revolution,

**233**

and we've come to think of that stall as "normal." In *The Time Bind*, I've explored ways in which the first shift (paid work) is staging a quiet takeover of life at home.

When I began my research, I thought we were working more for external reasons—for example, we needed the money. When I took a hard look, that explanation didn't fit the facts: At the company I studied, the richer the employees the less interested they were in time at home. The poorer they were, the more interested.

Another explanation I tried out was that with all the downsizing going on, people are working very hard so that they don't get on the layoff list. But when I asked people, "Are you working your 60-hour week because you're afraid of being laid off?" they said, "No. I'm doing it because I love my work." Disbelieving these responses at first, I looked at two different departments of this company, one which was adding people and another which was subtracting people. In comparing the two, I found that there weren't any differences in the number of people applying for family-friendly work schedules.

I'm not saying that fear of being laid off or the financial need to work long hours aren't real issues for people. It's just that they didn't account for the absence of a cultural resistance to long hours at work. I was looking for that kind of cultural resistance. What I found was a company that offered policies that we say we want—paternity and maternity leave, part-time, job sharing, flex-time—but very few employees who were interested in them.

Q: Were these policies really available? I got the sense that while the policies were on company books, they often didn't exist in practice.

A: Indeed, there were some managers who really wanted to sabotage the policies. It was just an extra headache for them. But there were also managers who took pride in offering flexible work arrangements. When I compared people working for rigid managers to those who were working for flexible managers, I found little difference in the number of people who came forward to ask for shorter hours.

Then I thought that perhaps people just didn't know about these policies. Wrong. In fact some workers said, "I'm really proud to be working for an enlightened company." Or, "I really don't know the policy specifics, but I know how I can find out should I need them in an emergency." But they weren't defining the scarcity of time at home as an emergency.

All of these explanations—that people wouldn't want more time at home because they couldn't afford it, or they wouldn't want more time because they were working scared, or they wouldn't want more time because they didn't dare ask a bad boss, or they wouldn't want more time because they didn't know about the policies—hold a little water and, in some cases, were definitive explanations. But they didn't account for the absence of a cultural resistance to long hours at work.

Q: Have we become a workaholic, anti-family culture?

A: This country has become more workaholic, but I don't think Americans are anti-family. It's not a family values issue. We live in two separate cultural worlds, one encompassing the workplace and one encompassing home and family. Over time, the world of the workplace has been transformed by a new kind of cultural engineering—especially in Fortune 500 companies—where the worker is invited to be empowered, to work closely with a team, to be a part of a quality circle, etc. In this new work culture, there is a great premium on reward. Moreover, if you get into a problem, there is somebody there to help you. For all its aggravations, many people like being at work.

I don't think that this new culture is necessarily bad. Rather, I think we need the same kinds of support at home that we are now getting at work. Today we have more recognition ceremonies at work, and fewer recognition ceremonies, so to speak, at home. We're asked to value the individual at work, and nobody's quite holding that ideology at home. It's tempting, therefore, to emotionally relocate to the workplace.

Of course, there are many kinds of workplaces and many kinds of homes. There is also a complicated set of corporate work-family strategies. Some corporations are going in the high-investment direction I saw at Amerco: "We're going to put a lot of effort into making a good workplace, and we're going to get a lot of work out of these folks." Others are following the strategy of divestment: "We're going to lay workers off; we're going to speed up; we're going to go back to Frederick Taylor's efficiency model." [In the early 1900s, Taylor engineered highly rigorous and mechanistic standards for factory work.]

Q: But isn't the company you studied in fact doing this? It has laid people off, it has encouraged a speedup in the sense that people are working a lot longer at their jobs for the same amount of pay. It's Taylorism with a smiley face.

A: You're right. But now workers buy into it. They internalize the speedup; they think their hurry is due to their work ethic. At Amerco, people began to think it was exciting to be in a workaholic environment. They would say, "We're our own worst enemy"; "It's hard to scrape myself up and get home, there's just so much to do"; and "No one does it to us, we're like that to ourselves."

They simply felt very rewarded by work. Moreover, their best friends were at work. Essentially, the neighborhood has gone to work. Corporate engineers have looked at how women are with each other, borrowing the best tips from female neighborhood culture and then transporting them back into the bosom of capitalism. They've feminized capitalism. You have to marvel at such corporate engineering, and then you have to watch it like a hawk because it's stealing family time away from families.

Q: Are you suggesting the workplace has been feminized but that the effect of this feminization has been far different than what the original women's movement might have hoped for?

A: Yes. Absolutely. A lot of feminists in the 1970s were calling for an equality in the workplace based on a female sensibility, as well as for an equality in which men participated more actively at home. But the corporate world was holding out the carrot of another equality in which women became equal on traditionally male terms. And there have been more rewards for women to throw themselves into work, frankly, than there

have been rewards for men to go in the other direction.

I'm a feminist. And I'm certainly not saying it was a mistake for women to enter the labor force. I believe work outside the home is good for women and it's good for families. All the data we have show that working women are more likely to feel good about themselves and positive about their lives, and to feel that their contributions at home are honored and valued—more so than women who permanently stay home.

However, women have entered the work world on male terms, and because of power arrangements they haven't felt able to push back. The strategy we need to pursue is one of recovering our time to push back on our hours of work. We need to form a new alliance between feminist groups, labor unions, child advocates, progressive corporations, and the federal government insofar as it's willing to pursue a family-friendly agenda.

Q: But if people really like to work and they don't want to go home, why should we care about starting a "time movement" that would give us more time away from work to spend with our families?

A: I hope to open up a conversation about the costs of settling for the wrong terms at work. And I think there are enough people who don't feel good about the conditions under which they're working to begin this conversation. People are ambivalent. They feel confused. I hope to appeal to this ambivalence.

Q: Men who would like to take more responsibility for child rearing seem to be in an untenable position, almost worse than that of women, because in today's corporate culture wanting to spend more time with one's family—to be a family man—is taken as a sign of lack of ambition.

A: Yes. I think that when you allow a market culture to prevail, those new men, those heroes of an alternative culture, suffer. For example, I interviewed a young engineer, the first man to apply for formal paternity leave at Amerco—two weeks, unpaid. His own father had left home early in his childhood, and he felt strongly about becoming a real daddy to his child, from the very start. His wife appreciated his doing this. The women in his office appreciated it. But his male co-workers divided into two groups. Acquaintances pretended they didn't know why he'd been absent, though they did know. Friends kidded him, "So, did you catch up on the soaps?" They could understand his wanting to take a holiday, but they couldn't understand paternity leave. They thought family-friendly policies were for women, not men. Of course, if he'd been living in Sweden he wouldn't have gotten the soaps jokes, since he'd be among the 80 percent of all employed fathers who take two weeks paternity leave there.

Q: What's happening to the kids in this time-deprived family dynamic?

A: The children I saw were doing fine in school and weren't beating up kids on the playground. But children feel starved for time, and adults feel guilty for starving children of time. That's a huge problem, not because your kid won't grow up to be bright and successful, but what if they grow up to be bright and successful and replay the same time-starved life that was taught to them? I talked to one child, who said to her grandmother on the telephone: "Grandma, I don't have time to talk to you." Well, this kid was doing beautifully in school, but is that what really matters? If that's what matters most, aren't we missing an important emotional piece of the picture?

We want to live fully human lives. Not only is that the feminist project, it's the progressive project. What I'm talking about is very radical. The time movement is an extension of the labor movement, only it's fundamentally different because it puts family and private life center stage in a way that the labor movement has not done. Even portions of the feminist movement have not yet dared to do it.

A new time movement needs to be critical of market culture; it also needs to critique the ways in which capitalism has incorporated the useful aspects of neighborhood female culture and given itself a humanitarian face.

The subtraction of effort from community life has been seen as the absence of civic virtue. I see it as the result of increasing the number of hours at work. The marketplace has been absorbing more people's time, and that time is coming not just from families but from communities.

The focus of our public discourse has been on how American companies are competing with Japanese, German, and other foreign companies. What this allows us to ignore is how each of those American companies is really in competition with the families of the workers. That's the real competition. And in that competition the American companies are winning hands down.

Q: Why haven't we been able to hold the line, like other nations, against the invasion of work, into the home?

A: I think we have a rawer version of capitalism and a more fragile community and family base than other nations. We are a more individualistic culture. From the Boston Tea Party on, we've had too little faith in government. We also have a higher rate of mobility from one community to another. These American characteristics didn't wreak havoc until other factors came into play—the decline of labor movements and the globalization of capital. We could get along with rugged individualism, social mobility, and the absence of dedication to community before. But when you add on these two extra factors, the balance is tipped in favor of the marketplace. And the marketplace has won—for the moment.

## Review

1. What is the "time bind" for men and women working outside the home?

2. Describe the new work culture discussed by Hochschild.

3. In what sense has the workplace been feminized?

4. What are the consequences of the new work culture for children?

## Application

Make a list of all the things that consume time for families—work, school, meals, individual recreation, couple (husband and wife) activities, family leisure activities, household chores, and so forth. Provide a separate list for each member of a family in which husband and wife both work outside the home and the children are in school. Ask them to write down an estimate of the amount of time they spend during an average week on each of the activities.

Compare the lists. Discuss possible reasons for any discrepancies. If other families are similar to the one you interviewed, what are the implications for family life today?

## Related Web Sites

1. *http://www.census.gov/*. The home page of the Census Bureau, which keeps data on the number and proportion of mothers who work outside the home.

2. *http://www.e-thepeople.org/article/ 26728/*. Conversations about whether two-income families are good or bad.

Reprinted from: Marilyn Snell, "Home Work Time." In *Mother Jones*, May/June, 1997, pp. 26–30. Reprinted with permission from *Mother Jones* magazine, Copyright © 1997, Foundation for National Progress. ✦

# 25
# The Transformation of Family Life

*Lillian B. Rubin*

Life is quite different for people in the various social classes. Obviously, those with less education, income, and power have fewer resources and fewer options than do those with more of these things. Sociologists have noted, in fact, a great many differences—ranging from health to lifestyles to values and attitudes—between people of different social classes. In studying the family, therefore, it is important to know the social class of the families involved. While Hochschild's research focuses on dual-career couples in the middle and upper-middle class, the author of this selection, Lillian Rubin, has spent much of her career studying working-class families.

*Like their middle-class counterparts, working-class wives and mothers are likely to work outside the home. How do working-class couples handle the tensions? In this selection, based on her in-depth interviews with working-class men and women, Rubin describes some of their struggles with money, child care, sex, and men's attitudes toward housework. She also points out some racial/ethnic differences among the families she studied.*

*Note that the men and women in her study often have differing perceptions of what's going on in the home. Rubin doesn't use the term* **definition of the situation,** *but it is an important concept that applies well to her research. It means that if people define a situation as real, it is real in its consequences. Thus, if a husband defines himself as overworked, he will act like someone overworked whether or not his wife or an outside observer agrees with his definition. And if a wife defines herself as not getting a fair amount of help* from her husband, she will act accordingly regardless of his perceptions or those of an outside observer. People act on the basis of how they define the situation. To understand their behavior, therefore, you need to understand their definitions, their perceptions.

"I know my wife works all day, just like I do," says Gary Braunswig, a twenty-nine-year-old white drill press operator, "but it's not the same. She doesn't have to do it. I mean, she has to because we need the money, but it's different. It's not really her job to have to be working; it's mine." He stops, irritated with himself because he can't find exactly the words he wants, and asks, "Know what I mean? I'm not saying it right; I mean, it's the man who's supposed to support his family, so I've got to be responsible for that, not her. And that makes one damn big difference.

"I mean, women complain all the time about how hard they work with the house and the kids and all. I'm not saying it's not hard, but that's her responsibility, just like the finances are mine."

"But she's now sharing that burden with you, isn't she?" I remark.

"Yeah, and I do my share around the house, only she doesn't see it that way. Maybe if you add it all up, I don't do as much as she does, but then she doesn't bring in as much money as I do. And she doesn't always have to be looking for overtime to make an extra buck. I got no complaints about that, so how come she's always complaining about me? I mean, she helps me out financially, and I help her out with the kids and stuff. What's wrong with that? It seems pretty equal to me."

Cast that way, his formulation seems reasonable: They're each responsible for one part of family life; they each help out with the other. But the abstract formula doesn't square with the lived reality. For him, helping her adds relatively little to the burden of household tasks he must do each day. A recent study by University of Wisconsin researchers, for example, found that in families where both wife and husband work full-

238

time, the women average over twenty-six hours a week in household labor, while the men do about ten. That's because there's nothing in the family system to force him to accountability or responsibility on a daily basis. He may "help her out with the kids and stuff" one day and be too busy or preoccupied the next. But for Gary's wife, Irene, helping him means an extra eight hours every working day. Consequently, she wants something more consistent from him than a helping hand with a particular task when he has the time, desire, or feels guilty enough. "Sure, he helps me out," she says, her words tinged with resentment. "He'll give the kids a bath or help with the dishes. But only when I ask him. He doesn't have to ask me to go to work every day, does he? Why should I have to ask him?" "Why should I have to ask him?"—words that suggest a radically different consciousness from the working-class women I met twenty years ago. Then, they counted their blessings. "He's a steady worker; he doesn't drink; he doesn't hit me," they told me by way of explaining why they had "no right to complain." True, these words were reminders to themselves that life could be worse, that they shouldn't take these things for granted—reminders that didn't wholly work to obscure their discontent with other aspects of the marriage. But they were nevertheless meaningful statements of value that put a brake on the kinds of demands they felt they could make of their men, whether about the unequal division of household tasks or about the emotional content of their lives together.

Now, the same women who reminded themselves to be thankful two decades ago speak openly about their dissatisfaction with the role divisions in the family. Some husbands, especially the younger ones, greet their wives' demands sympathetically. "I try to do as much as I can for Sue, and when I can't, I feel bad about it," says twenty-nine-year-old Don Dominguez, a Latino father of three children, who is a construction worker.

Others are more ambivalent. "I don't know, as long as she's got a job, too, I guess it's right that I should help out in the house. But that doesn't mean I've got to like it," says twenty-eight-year-old Joe Kempinski, a white warehouse worker with two children.

Some men are hostile, insisting that their wives' complaints are unreasonable, unjust, and oppressive. "I'm damn tired of women griping all the time; it's nothing but nags and complaints," Ralph Danesen, a thirty-six-year-old white factory worker and the father of three children, says indignantly. "It's enough! You'd think they're the only ones who've got it hard. What about me? I'm not living in a bed of roses either." "Christ, what does a guy have to do to keep a wife quiet these days? What does she want? It's not like I don't do anything to help her out, but it's never enough."

In the past there was a clear understanding about the obligations and entitlements each partner took on when they married. He was obliged to work outside the home; she would take care of life inside. He was entitled to her ministrations, she to his financial support. But this neat division of labor with its clear-cut separation of rights and obligations no longer works. Now, women feel obliged to hold up their share of the family economy—a partnership men welcome. In return, women believe they're entitled to their husband[s'] full participation in domestic labor. And here is the rub. For while men enjoy the fruits of their wives' paid work outside the home, they have been slow to accept the reciprocal responsibilities—that is, to become real partners in the work inside the home.

The women, exhausted from doing two days' work in one, angry at the need to assume obligations without corresponding entitlements, push their men in ways unknown before. The men, battered by economic uncertainty and by the escalating demands of their wives, feel embattled and victimized on two fronts—one outside the home, the other inside. Consequently, when their wives seem not to see the family work they do, when they don't acknowledge and credit it, when they fail to appreciate them, the men feel violated and betrayed. "You come home and you want to be appreciated a little. But it doesn't work that way, leastwise not here anymore," complains Gary Braunswig, his angry words at odds with sadness in his eyes. "There's no peace, I guess that's the real problem; there's no peace anywhere anymore."

The women often understand what motivates their husbands' sense of victimization and even speak sympathetically about it at times. But to understand and sympathize is not to condone, especially when they feel equally assaulted on both the home and the economic fronts. "I know I complain a lot, but I really don't ask for that much. I just want him to help out a little more," explains Ralph Danesen's wife, Helen, a thirty-five-year-old office worker. "It isn't like I'm asking him to cook the meals or anything like that. I know he can't do that, and I don't expect him to. But every time I try to talk to him, you know, to ask him if I couldn't get a little more help around here, there's a fight."

One of the ways the men excuse their behavior toward family work is by insisting that their responsibility as breadwinner burdens them in ways that are alien to their wives. "The plant's laying off people left and right; it could be me tomorrow. Then what'll we do? Isn't it enough I got to worry about that? I'm the one who's got all the worries; she doesn't. How come that doesn't count?" demands Bob Duckworth, a twenty-nine-year-old factory worker.

But, in fact, the women don't take second place to their men in worrying about what will happen to the family if the husband loses his job. True, the burden of finding another one that will pay the bills isn't theirs—not a trivial difference. But the other side of this truth is that women are stuck with the reality that the financial welfare of the family is out of their control, that they're helpless to do anything to prevent its economic collapse or to rectify it should it happen. "He thinks I've got it easy because it's not my job to support the family," says Bob's wife, Ruthanne. "But sometimes I think it's worse for me. I worry all the time that he's going to get laid off, just like he does. But I can't do anything about it. And if I try to talk to him about it, you know, like maybe make a plan in case it happens, he won't even listen. How does he think *that* makes me feel? It's my life, too, and I can't even talk to him about it."

Not surprisingly, there are generational differences in what fuels the conflict around the division of labor in these families. For the older couples—those who grew up in a different time, whose marriages started with another set of ground rules—the struggle is not simply around how much men do or about whether they take responsibility for the daily tasks of living without being pushed, prodded, and reminded. That's the overt manifestation of the discord, the trigger that starts the fight. But the noise of the explosion when it comes serves to conceal the more fundamental issue underlying the dissension: legitimacy. What does she have a right to expect? "What do I know about doing stuff around the house?" asks Frank Moreno, a forty-eight-year-old foreman in a warehouse. "I wasn't brought up like that. My pop, he never did one damn thing, and my mother never complained. It was her job; she did it and kept quiet. Besides, I work my ass off every day. Isn't that enough?"

For the younger couples, those under forty, the problem is somewhat different. The men may complain about the expectation that they'll participate more fully in the care and feeding of the family, but talk to them about it quietly and they'll usually admit that it's not really unfair, given that their wives also work outside the home. In these homes, the issue between husband and wife isn't only who does what. That's there, and it's a source of more or less conflict, depending upon what the men actually do and how forceful their wives are in their demands. But in most of these families there's at least a verbal consensus that men *ought* to participate in the tasks of daily life. Which raises the next and perhaps more difficult issue in contest between them: Who feels responsible for getting the tasks done? Who regards them as a duty, and for whom are they an option? On this, tradition rules.

Even in families where husbands now share many of the tasks, their wives still bear full responsibility for the organization of family life. A man may help cook the meal these days, but a woman is most likely to be the one who has planned it. He may take the children to child care, but she virtually always has had to arrange it. It's she also who is accountable for the emotional life of the family, for monitoring the emotional temperature of its members and making the necessary corrections. It's this need to be responsible for it all that often feels as burdensome as the tasks themselves. "It's not just doing all the stuff that needs doing," explains Maria Jankowicz, a white twenty-eight-year-old assembler in an electronics factory. "It's worrying all the time about everything and always having to arrange everything, you know what I mean. It's like I run the whole show. If I don't stay on top of it all, things fall apart because nobody else is going to do it. The kids can't and Nick, well, forget it," she concludes angrily.

If, regardless of age, life stage, or verbal consensus, women usually still carry the greatest share of the household burdens, why is it important to notice that younger men grant legitimacy to their wives' demands and older men generally do not? Because men who believe their wives have a right to expect their participation tend to suffer guilt and discomfort when they don't live up to those expectations. And no one lives comfortably with guilt. "I know I don't always help enough, and I feel bad about it, you know, guilty sometimes," explains Bob Beardsley, a thirty-year-old white machine operator, his eyes registering the discomfort he feels as he speaks.

"Does it change anything when you feel guilty?" I ask.

A small smile flits across his face, and he says, "Sometimes. I try to do a little more, but then I get busy with something and forget that she needs me to help out. My wife says I don't pay attention, that's why I forget. But I don't know. Seems like I've just got my mind on other things."

It's possible, of course, that the men who speak of guilt and rights are only trying to impress me by mouthing the politically correct words. But even if true, they display a sensitivity to the issue that's missing from the men who don't speak those words. For words are more than just words. They embody ideas; they are the symbols that give meaning to our thoughts; they shape our consciousness. New ideas come to us on the wings of words. It's words that bring those ideas to life, that allow us to see possibilities unrecognized before we gave them words. Indeed, without words, there is no conscious thought, no possibility for the kind of self-reflection that lights the path of change.

True, there's often a long way between word and deed. But the man who feels guilty when he disappoints his wife's expectations has a different consciousness than the one who doesn't—a difference that usually makes for at least some small change in his behavior. Although the emergence of this changing male consciousness is visible in all the racial groups in this study, there also are differences among them that are worthy of comment.

Virtually all the men do some work inside the family—tending the children, washing dishes, running the vacuum, going to the market. And they generally also remain responsible for those tasks that have always been traditionally male—mowing the lawn, shoveling the snow, fixing the car, cleaning the garage, doing repairs around the house. Among the white families in this study, 16 percent of the men share the family work relatively equally, almost always those who live in families where they and their wives work different shifts or where the men are unemployed. "What choice do I have?" asks Don Bartlett, a thirty-year-old white handyman who works days while his wife is on the swing shift. "I'm the only one here, so I do what's got to be done."

Asian and Latino men of all ages, however, tend to operate more often on the old male model, even when they work different shifts or are unemployed, a finding that puzzled me at first. Why, I wondered, did I find only two Asian men and one Latino who are real partners in the work of the family? Aren't these men subject to the same social and personal pressures others experience?

The answer is both yes and no. The pressures are there but, depending upon where they live, there's more or less support for resisting them. The Latino and Asian men who live in ethnic neighborhoods—settings where they are embedded in an intergenerational community and where the language and culture of the home country is kept alive by a steady stream of new immigrants—find strong support for clinging to the old ways. Therefore, change comes much more slowly in those families. The men who live outside the ethnic quarter are freer from the mandates and constraints of these often tight-knit communities [and] therefore are more responsive to the winds of change in the larger society.

These distinctions notwithstanding, it's clear that Asian and Latino men generally participate least in the work of the household and are the least likely to believe they have much responsibility there beyond bringing home a paycheck. "Taking care of the house and kids is my wife's job, that's all," says Joe Gomez flatly.

"A Chinese man mopping a floor? I've never seen it yet," says Amy Lee angrily. Her husband, Dennis, trying to make a joke of the conflict with his wife, says with a smile, "In Chinese families men don't do floors and windows. I help with the dishes sometimes if she needs me to or," he laughs, "if she screams loud enough. The rest, well, it's pretty much her job."

The commonly held stereotype about black men abandoning women and children, however, doesn't square with the families in this study. In fact, black men are the most likely to be real participants in the daily life of the family and are more intimately involved in raising their children than any of the others. True, the men's family work load doesn't always match their wives', and the women are articulate in their complaints about this. Nevertheless, compared to their white, Asian, or Latino counterparts, the black families look like models of egalitarianism.

Nearly three-quarters of the men in the African-American families in this study do a substantial amount of the cooking, cleaning, and child care, sometimes even more than their wives. All explain it by saying one version or another of: "I just figure it's my job, too." Which simply says what is, without explaining how it came to be that way.

To understand that, we have to look at family histories that tell the story of generations of African-American women who could find work and men who could not, and to the family culture that grew from this difficult and painful reality. "My mother worked six days a week cleaning other people's houses, and my father was an ordinary laborer, when he could find work, which wasn't very often," explains thirty-two-year-old Troy Payne, a black waiter and father of two children. "So he was home a lot more than she was, and he'd do what he had to do around the house. The kids all had to do their share, too. It seemed only fair, I guess."

Difficult as the conflict around the division of labor is, it's only one of the many issues that have become flash points in family life since mother went to work. Most important, perhaps, is the question: Who will care for the children? For the lack of decent, affordable facilities for the care of the children creates unbearable problems and tensions for these working-class families.

It's hardly news that child care is an enormous headache and expense for all two-job families. In many professional middle-class families, where the child-care bill can be $1,500–2,000 a month, it competes with the mortgage payment as the biggest single monthly expenditure. Problematic as this may be, however, these families are the lucky ones when compared to working-class families, many of whom don't earn much more than the cost of child care in these upper middle-class families. Even the families in this study at the highest end of the earnings scale, those who earn $42,000 a year, can't dream of such costly arrangements.

For most working-class families, therefore, child care often is patched together in ways that leave parents anxious and children in jeopardy. "Care for the little ones, that's a real big problem," says Beverly Waldov, a thirty-year-old white mother of three children, the youngest two, products of a second marriage, under three years old. "My oldest girl is nine, so she's not such a problem. I hate the idea of her being a latchkey kid, but what can I do? We don't even have the money to put the little ones in one of those good day-care places, so I don't have any choice with her. She's just got to be able to take care of herself after school," she says, her words a contest between anxiety and hope.

"We have a kind of complicated arrangement for the little kids. Two days a week, my mom takes care of them. We pay her, but at least I don't have to worry when they're with her; I know it's fine. But she works the rest of the time, so the other days we take them to this woman's house. It's the best we can afford, but it's not great because she keeps too many kids, and I know they don't get good attention. Especially the little one; she's just a baby, you know." She pauses and looks away, anguished. "She's so clingy when I bring her home; she can't let go of me, like nobody's paid her any mind all day. But it's not like I have a choice. We barely make it now; if I stop working, we'd be in real trouble."

Even such makeshift solutions don't work for many families. Some speak of being unable to afford day care at all. "We couldn't pay our bills if we had to pay for somebody to take care of the kids."

Some say they're unwilling to leave the children in the care of strangers. "I just don't believe someone else should be raising our kids, that's all."

Some have tried a variety of child-care arrangements, only to have them fail in a moment of need. "We tried a whole bunch of things, and maybe they work for a little while," says Faye Ensey, a black twenty-eight-year-old office worker. "But what happens when your kid gets sick? Or when the baby sitter's kids get sick? I lost two jobs in a row because my kids kept getting sick and I couldn't go to work. Or else I couldn't take my little one to the baby sitter because her kids were sick. They finally fired me for absenteeism. I didn't really blame them, but it felt terrible anyway. It's such a hassle, I sometimes think I'd be glad to just stay home. But we can't afford for me not to work, so we had to figure out something else."

For such families, that "something else" is the decision to take jobs on different shifts—a decision made by one-fifth of the families in this study. With one working days and the other on swing or graveyard, one parent is home with the children at all times. "We were getting along okay before Daryl junior was born, because Shona, my daughter, was getting on. You know, she didn't need somebody with her all the time, so we could both work days," explains Daryl Adams, a black thirty-year-old postal clerk with a ten-year-old daughter and a nine-month-old son. "I used to work the early shift—seven to three—so I'd get home a little bit after she got here. It worked out okay. But then this here big surprise came along." He stops, smiles down fondly at his young son and runs his hand over his nearly bald head.

"Now between the two of us working, we don't make enough money to pay for child care and have anything left over, so this is the only way we can manage. Besides, both of us, Alesha and me, we think it's better for one of us to be here, not just for the baby, for my daughter, too. She's growing up and, you know, I think maybe they need even more watching than when they were younger. She's coming to the time when she could get into all kinds of trouble if we're not here to put the brakes on."

But the cost such arrangements exact on a marriage can be very high. When I asked these husbands and wives when they have time to talk, more often than not I got a look of annoyance at a question that, on its face, seemed stupid to them. "Talk? How can we talk when we hardly see each other?" "Talk? What's that?" "Talk? Ha, that's a joke."

Mostly, conversation is limited to the logistics that take place at shift-changing time when children and chores are handed off from one to the other. With children dancing around underfoot, the incoming parent gets a quick summary of the day's or night's events, a list of reminders about things to be done, perhaps about what's cooking in the pot on the stove. "Sometimes when I'm coming home and it's been a hard day, I think: Wouldn't it be wonderful if I could just sit down with Leon for half an hour and we could have a quiet beer together?" thirty-one-year-old Emma Guerrero, a Latina baker, says wistfully.

But it's not to be. If the arriving spouse gets home early enough, there may be an hour when both are there together. But with the pressures of the workday fresh for one and awaiting the other, and with children clamoring for parental attention, this isn't a promising moment for any serious conversation. "I usually get home about forty-five minutes or so before my wife has to leave for work," says Ralph Jo, a thirty-six-year-old Asian repairman whose children, ages three and five, are the product of a second marriage. "So we try to take a few minutes just to make contact. But it's hard with the kids and all. Most days the whole time gets spent with taking care of business—you know, who did what, what the kids need, what's for supper, what bill collector was hassling her while I was gone—all the damn garbage of living. It makes me nuts."

Most of the time even this brief hour isn't available. Then the ritual changing of the guard takes only a few minutes—a quick peck on the cheek in greeting, a few words, and it's over. "It's like we pass each other. He comes in; I go out; that's it."

Some of the luckier couples work different shifts on the same days, so they're home together on weekends. But even in these families there's so little time for normal family life that there's hardly any room for anyone or anything outside. "There's so much to do when I get home that there's no time for anything but the chores and the kids," says Daryl's wife, Alesha Adams. "I never get to see anybody or do anything else anymore and, even so, I'm always feeling upset and guilty because there's not enough time for them. Daryl leaves a few minutes after I get home, and the rest of the night is like a blur—Shona's homework, getting the kids fed and down for the night, cleaning up, getting everything ready for tomorrow. I don't know; there's always something I'm running around doing. I sometimes feel like—What do you call them?—one of those whirling dervishes, rushing around all the time and never getting everything done.

"Then on the weekends, you sort of want to make things nice for the kids—and for us, too. It's the only time we're here together, like a real family, so we always eat with the kids. And we try to take them someplace nice one of the days, like to the park or something. But sometimes we're too tired, or there's too many other catch-up things you have to do. I don't even get to see my sister anymore. She's been working weekends for the last year or so, and I'm too busy week nights, so there's no time.

"I don't mean to complain; we're lucky in a lot of ways. We've got two great kids, and we're a pretty good team, Daryl and me. But I worry sometimes. When you live on this kind of schedule, communication's not so good."

For those whose days off don't match, the problems of sustaining both the couple relationship and family life are magnified enormously. "The last two years have been hell for us," says thirty-five-year-old Tina Mulvaney, a white mother of two teenagers. "My son got into bad company and had some trouble, so Mike and I decided one of us had to be home. But we can't make it without my check, so I can't quit.

"Mike drives a cab and I work in a hospital, so we figured one of us could transfer to nights. We talked it over and decided it would be best if I was here during the day and he was here at night. He controls the kids, especially my son, better than I do. When he lays down the law, they listen." She interrupts her narrative to reflect on the difficulty of raising children. "You know, when they were little, I used to think about how much easier it would be when they got older. But now I see it's not true; that's when you really have to begin to worry about them. This is when they need someone to be here all the time to make sure they stay out of trouble."

She stops again, this time fighting tears, then takes up where she left off. "So now Mike works days and I work graveyard. I hate it, but it's the only answer; at least this way somebody's here all the time. I get home about 8:30 in the morning. The kids and Mike are gone. It's the best time of the day because it's the only time I have a little quiet here. I clean up the house a little, do the shopping and the laundry and whatever, then I go to sleep for a couple of hours until the kids come home from school.

"Mike gets home at five; we eat; then he takes over for the night, and I go back to sleep for another couple of hours. I try to get up by 9 so we can all have a little time together, but I'm so tired that I don't make it a lot of times. And by 10, he's sleeping because he has to be up by 6 in the morning. So if I don't get up, we hardly see each other at all. Mike's here on weekends, but I'm not. Right now I have Tuesday and Wednesday off. I keep hoping for a Monday–Friday shift, but it's what everybody wants, and I don't have the seniority yet. It's hard, very hard; there's no time to live or anything," she concludes with a listless sigh.

Even in families where wife and husband work the same shift, there's less time for leisure pursuits and social activities than ever before, not just because both parents work full-time but also because people work longer hours now than they did twenty years ago. Two decades ago, weekends saw occasional family outings, Friday-evening bowling, a Saturday trip to the shopping mall, a Sunday with extended family, once in a while an evening out without the children. In summer, when the children weren't in school, a week night might find the family paying a short visit to a friend, a relative, or a neighbor. Now almost everyone I speak with complains that it's hard to find time for even these occasional outings. Instead, most off-work hours are spent trying to catch up with the dozens of family and household tasks that were left undone during the regular work week. When they aren't doing chores, parents guiltily try to do in two days a week what usually takes seven—that is, to establish a sense of family life for themselves and their children.

"Leisure," snorts Peter Pittman, a twenty-eight-year-old African-American father of two, married six years. "With both of us working like we do, there's no time for anything. We got two little kids; I commute better than an hour each way to my job. Then we live here for half rent because I take care of the place for the landlord. So if somebody's got a complaint, I've got to take care of it, you know, fix it myself or get the landlord to get somebody out to do it if I can't. Most things I can do myself, but it takes time. I sometimes wonder what this life's all about, because this sure ain't what I call living. We don't go anyplace; we don't do anything; Christ, we hardly have time to go to the toilet. There's always some damn thing, that's waiting that you've got to do."

Clearly, such complaints aren't unique to the working class. The pressures of time, the impoverishment of social life, the anxieties about child care, the fear that children will live in a world of increasing scarcity, the threat of divorce—all these are part of family life today, regardless of class. Nevertheless, there are important differences between those in the higher reaches of the class structure and the families of the working class. The simple fact that middle-class families have more discretionary income is enough to make a big difference in the quality of their social life. For they generally have enough money to pay for a baby-sitter once in a while so that parents can have some time to themselves; enough, too, for a family vacation, for tickets to a concert, a play, or a movie. At $7.50 a ticket in a New York or San Francisco movie house, a working-class couple will settle for a $3.00 rental that the whole family can watch together.

Finding time and energy for sex is also a problem, one that's obviously an issue for two-job families of any class. But it's harder to resolve in working-class families because they have so few resources with which to buy some time and privacy for themselves. Ask about their sex lives and you'll be met with an angry, "What's that?" or a wistful, "I wish." When it happens, it is, as one woman put it, "on the run"—a situation that's particularly unsatisfactory for most women. For them, the pleasure of sex is related to the whole of the interaction—to a sense of intimacy and connection, to at least a few relaxed, loving moments. When they can't have these, they're likely to avoid sex altogether—a situation the men find equally unsatisfactory.

"Sex?" asks Lisa Scranton, a white twenty-nine-year-old mother of three who feigns a puzzled frown, as if she doesn't quite know the meaning of the word. "Oh yeah, that; I remember now," she says, her lips smiling, her eyes sad. "At the beginning, when we first got together, it was, WOW, real hot, great. But after a while it cools down, doesn't it? Right now, it's down the toilet. I wonder, does it happen to everybody like that?" she asks dejectedly.

"I guess the worst is when you work different shifts like we do and you get to see each other maybe six minutes a day. There's no time for sex. Sometimes we try to steal a few minutes for ourselves but, I don't know, I can't get into it that way. He can. You know how men are; they can do it any time. Give them two minutes, and they can get off. But it takes me time; I mean, I like to feel close, and you can't do that in three minutes. And there's the kids; they're right here all the time. I don't want to do it if it means being interrupted. Then he gets mad, so sometimes I do. But it's a problem, a real problem."

The men aren't content with these quick sexual exchanges either. But for them it's generally better than no sex at all, while for the women it's often the other way around. "You want to talk about sex, huh?" asks Lisa's husband, Chuck, his voice crackling with anger. "Yeah, I don't mind; it's fine, only I got nothing to talk about. Far as I'm concerned, that's one of the things I found out about marriage. You get married, you give up sex. We hardly ever do it anymore, and when we do, it's like she's doing me a favor.

"Christ, I know the way we've got to do things now isn't great," he protests, running a hand through his hair agitatedly. "We don't see each other but a few minutes a day, but I don't see why we can't take five and have a little fun in the sack. Sure, I like it better when we've got more time, too. But for her, if it can't be perfect, she gets all wound and uptight and it's like . . ." He stops, groping for words, then explodes, "It's like screwing a cold fish."

She isn't just a "cold fish," however. The problems they face are deeper than that. For once such conflicts arise, spontaneity takes flight and sex becomes a problem that needs attention rather than a time out for pleasure and renewal. Between times, therefore, he's busy calculating how much time has passed: "It's been over two weeks"; nursing his wounds: "I don't want to have to beg her"; feeling deprived and angry: "I don't know why I got married." When they finally do come together, he's disappointed. How could it be otherwise, given the mix of feelings he brings to the bed with him—the frustration and anger, the humiliation of feeling he has to beg her, the wounded sense of manhood.

Meanwhile, she, too, is preoccupied with sex, not with thoughts of pleasure but with figuring out how much time she has before, as she puts it, "he walks around with his mouth stuck out. I know I'm in real big trouble if we don't do it once a week. So I make sure we do, even if I don't want to." She doesn't say those words to him, of course. But he knows. And it's precisely this, the knowledge that she's servicing him rather than desiring him that's so hard for him to take.

The sexual arena is one of the most common places to find a "his and her" marriage—one marriage, two different sex lives. Each partner has a different story to tell; each is convinced that his or her version is the real one. A husband says mournfully, "I'm lucky if we get to make love once a week." His wife reports with irritation, "It's two, sometimes three times a week." It's impossible to know whose account is closest to the reality. And it's irrelevant. If that's what they were after, they could keep tabs and get it straight. But facts and feelings are often at war in family life. And nowhere does right or wrong, true or false count for less than in their sexual interactions. It isn't that people arbitrarily distort the truth. They simply report their experience, and it's feeling, not fact, that dominates that experience; feeling, not fact, that is their truth.

But it's also true that, especially for women, the difference in frequency of sexual desire can be a response—sometimes conscious, sometimes not—to other conflicts in the marriage. It isn't that men never withhold sex as a weapon in the family wars, only that they're much more likely than women to be able to split sex from emotion, to feel their anger and still experience sexual desire. For a man, too, a sexual connection with his wife can relieve the pressures and tensions of the day, can make him feel whole again, even if they've barely spoken a word to each other.

For a woman it's different. What happens—or, more likely, what doesn't happen—in the kitchen, the living room, and the laundry room profoundly affects what's possible in the bedroom. When she feels distant, unconnected, angry; when her pressured life leaves her feeling fragmented; when she hasn't had a real conversation with her husband for a couple of days, sex is very far from either her mind or her loins. "I run around busy all the time, and he just sits there, so by the time we go to bed, I'm too tired," explains

Linda Bloodworth, a white thirty-one-year-old telephone operator.

"Do you think your lack of sexual response has something to do with your anger at your husband's refusal to participate more fully in the household?" I ask.

Her eyes smoldering, her voice tight, she snaps, "No, I'm just tired, that's all." Then noticing something in my response, she adds, "I know what you're thinking; I saw that look. But really, I don't think it's because I'm angry; I really am tired. I have to admit, though, that I tell him if he helped more, maybe I wouldn't be so tired all the time. And," she adds defiantly, "maybe I wouldn't be."

Some couples, of course, manage their sexual relationship with greater ease. Often that's because they have less conflict in other areas of living. But whether they accommodate well or poorly, for all two-job families, sex requires a level of attention and concern that leaves most people wanting much of the time. "It's a problem, and I tell you, it has to be well planned," explains thirty-four-year-old Dan Stolman, a black construction worker. "But we manage okay; we make dates or try to slip it in when the baby's asleep and my daughter's out with a friend or something. I don't mean things are great in that department. I'm not always satisfied and neither is Lorraine. But what can you do? We try to do the best we can. Sex isn't all there is to a marriage, you know. We get along really well, so that makes up for a lot.

"What I really miss is that we don't ever make love anymore. I mean, we have sex like I said, but we don't have the kind of time you need to make love. We talk about getting away for an overnight by ourselves once in a while. Lorraine's mother would come watch the kids if we asked her; the problem is we don't have any extra cash to spare right now."

Time and money—precious commodities in short supply. These are the twin plagues of family life, the missing ingredients that combine to create families that are both frantic and fragile. Yet there's no mystery about what would alleviate the crisis that now threatens to engulf them: A job that pays a living wage, quality child-care facilities at rates people can pay, health care for all, parental leave, flexible work schedules, decent and affordable housing, a shorter work week so that parents and children have time to spend together, tax breaks for those in need rather than for those in greed, to mention just a few. These are the policies we need to put in place if we're to have any hope of making our families stable and healthy.

What we have, instead, are families in which mother goes to work to relieve financial distress, only to find that time takes its place next to money as a source of strain, tension, and conflict. Time for the children, time for the couple's relationship, time for self, time for social life—none of it easily available for anyone in two-job families, not even for the children, who are hurried along at every step of the way. And money! Never enough, not for the clothes children need, not for the doctor's bill, not for a vacation, not even for the kind of child care that would allow parents to go to work in peace. But large as these problems loom in the lives of working-class families, difficult as they are to manage, they pale beside those they face when unemployment strikes, especially if it's father who loses his job.

## Review

1. How would you characterize the attitudes of working-class husbands toward housework?

2. What differences did Rubin find between white men and those from other racial/ethnic groups?

3. Describe the problems of child-care arrangements for working-class families.

4. What is the nature of the sex life of the working-class couples Rubin studied?

## Application

Interview a working-class couple (interview the husband and wife separately) or two students from working-class homes. Conduct an in-depth interview about the following topics: division of labor in the home (who does what); perception of time and financial pressures and the reasons for them; perceptions of what an ideal marriage and an ideal family life would look like.

How do your results compare with Rubin's descriptions? How do they compare with your own experiences? What are your own ideals for marriage and family life?

## Related Web Sites

1. *http://nieer.org/news/index.php?NewsID= 79.* An article from the Boston Globe on the dilemmas working-class families face as they deal with the need for child care.

2. *http://www.monthlyreview.org/ 500editr.htm.* An article on how the burden of debt affects working-class families.

# 26

# The Death of 'Till Death Us Do Part'

## Pair-bonding Transformed

*William M. Pinsof*

*Much has been said and written recently about "family values." Some of those who affirm what they call family values think that American society is in jeopardy because of the decline of the "traditional" family (a family with a father, a stay-at-home mother, and children). They also are alarmed by the divorce rate, the number of couples cohabiting rather than marrying, the number of unmarried women having babies, and the number of single-parent homes. What does all of this mean?*

*Experts disagree about how to interpret the trends. Some assert that we should be concerned, that family life is threatened and, thus, our whole way of life is threatened as well. The ideal, they argue, is for a home to have both a mother and a father; otherwise any children will suffer a variety of negative consequences. Others argue that the trends simply reflect changes rather than societal decline or degeneration. In this selection, William Pinsof analyzes some of the changes that have occurred and takes the position that marriage is only one form of pair-bonding. There is no question about the trends he notes; his interpretation of those trends and what to do about them is another matter. He sees the challenge as one of adapting to the transformation rather than recapturing what has been lost. As such, his position will elicit both attack and defense, depending on people's values about marriage and family.*

To have and to hold from this day forward, for better or worse, for richer or poorer, in sickness and in health, to love and to cherish, till death us do part.

Solemnization of Matrimony, *The Book of Common Prayer* (p. 301)

During the 20th century, human life was transformed in a number of substantial ways. These transformations pertained primarily to human life in the West, but also to certain industrially developed parts of Asia, South America, and Africa. In regard to the family, perhaps the most fundamental transformation concerned marriage. Prior to the 20th century, the most common endpoint of marriage was death. During the 20th century, the most common endpoint of marriage became divorce. In 1900, two-thirds of all marriages ended as a result of partner death within 40 years; by 1976 that figure had gone down to just over one-third (Uhlenberg, 1980). Nineteen seventy-four marked the point at which more marriages ended as a result of divorce rather than death (Hagestad, 1988). In 1867, less than 10% of all marriages in the U.S. ended in divorce; by 1985 that figure had grown to over 50% (Cherlin, 1992). By the end of the 20th century in the West, divorce replaced death as the "normal" endpoint of most marriages.

This transformation in the way the majority of marriages end has had numerous consequences for families and society. Two consequences, or at least correlates of this transition, were that during the last half of the 20th century marriage became an object of therapeutic intervention (Gurman & Fraenkel, 2002) and scientific inquiry (Gottman & Notarius, 2002). Additionally, in the last 30 years, divorce became a major topic of social and political discourse. In almost all of these contexts, and with few exceptions (Ahrons, 1994; Goldsmith, 1982), divorce has been defined as an undesirable end to marriage. Many studies have documented the deleterious short- and long-term effects of divorce on children and adults (Bray & Hetherington, 1993), and divorce has been viewed as a "social disorder" whose frequency approaches "epidemic" proportions and urgently needs to be reduced.

At the beginning of the 21st century, when divorce has become the statistically, if not culturally "normal" endpoint of marriage, the time has come to examine the shift from death-to-divorce from a more historical, evolutionary, and ethological perspective. It is time to move beyond thinking about the divorce rate as an indicator of a social disorder that must be reduced, to thinking about it more neutrally and inquisitively. The trend, initiated with Goldsmith's (1982) pioneering efforts to define the postdivorce family as a "normal unit," needs to be intensified and expanded.

New questions need to be asked, such as, what does this death-to-divorce shift mean? What may it reveal about human beings' capacities and inclinations for permanent pairbonding? What does it imply for expectations about the permanence of marriage and the theories that are needed to encompass these expectations? What are the implications of this shift in regard to the kind of social and legal structures and procedures that could and should be created to support couples living the new "marital reality?". . . Lastly, and most fundamentally, does this shift require a new paradigm for marriage in the 21st century and beyond? This article represents an initial attempt to address these questions.

## Monogamous Marriage Within Western Civilization

This article conceptualizes, contextualizes, and defines marriage in specific ways. Marriage is conceptualized from an interspecies perspective as a form of pairbonding. Pair-bonding is a concept from ethology (Eibl-Eibesfeldt, 1989) that refers to a species' establishment and maintenance of mutually exclusive and enduring dyadic relationships. Pair-bonding typically implies the existence of a sexual relationship between the partners, which defines the couple as potentially procreative. Pair-bonding has been typically thought of as a heterosexual phenomenon, although heterosexuality is not a necessary or inherent part of the concept as used in this article. Some species apparently pair-bond for life, whereas others pair-bond more flexibly (Barash & Lipton, 2001).

From an intraspecies or human perspective, this article locates marriage within a specific systemic context—"Western civilization." It includes Europe, North America, Australia, and New Zealand and is essentially European-American civilization. The concept of marriage targeted in this article does not include marriage as generally defined and practiced within the non-Western civilizations—the Islamic, Hindu, Sinic (Chinese), African, Japanese, and Latin American. This is not to deny that there may be certain Westernized groups within these civilizations to which this definition of marriage applies.

In addition to contextualizing permanent pair-bonding within Western civilization, this article addresses marriage as a relationship that is predicated on a mutual and voluntary commitment to a lifelong, monogamous partnership. "Monogamy" refers to sexual exclusivity (Laumann, Gagnon, Michael, & Michaels, 1994) and means that the partners in a marriage pledge sexual fidelity as part of their commitment. Additionally, they commit to stay married for life—"till-death-us do part." That many partners fail to honor these pledges and commitments does not deny their role in defining the type of relationship to which the partners originally committed themselves.

In conclusion, the type of marriage addressed in this article can be thought of as romantic or love-based marriage: from this perspective, marriage is primarily love-driven. Secondarily it may be economically, politically, or socially-driven. This type of marriage primarily expresses the desires, goals, and interests of the partners, as opposed to their families or others. In this kind of Western marriage, the partners marry primarily because they want to, and they do it primarily for love and for life.

## Transition From Death-to-Divorce

To contextualize the death-to-divorce transition adequately, it is necessary to understand what marriage was like historically, when the endpoint of death predominated.

## Pre-modern Marital Experience

Beatrice Gottlieb (1993), the historian, has written extensively about the family in the Western world from 1400 to 1800—from the end of the Black Death Plague to the dawn of industrialization. . . .

Marriages were viewed as permanent, but relatively unstable and short-lived. "In the past when a couple got married they could not help but have ambivalent expectations about the durability of their relationship. They were tightly locked into it and could not easily get out of it by legal means, but they knew very well that the time was probably not far off when death was going to part them" (p. 105).

Along the same lines, writing about pre-industrial, Catholic Poland, Kuklo (1990) reports 15 years as the average duration of marriage in most towns. Once again, most of these marriages ended as a result of death. Furthermore, in normal years in pre-industrial Warsaw, two-thirds of all marriages were first marriages. However, in years of natural calamities, spousal mortality decreased this proportion to 50%.

## The Modern Marital Experience

Some form of divorce or formal marital dissolution has always been part of the human species. The divorce rate has varied depending on the era and restrictions placed on divorce; but even under the most divorce-restricting regimes (e.g., the Catholic Church in Europe before the Reformation) people found ingenious and even bizarre ways to annul marriages and essentially divorce (Gies & Gies, 1987). Prior to the dawn of industrialization, in the middle of the 19th century, the probability that a marriage would end in divorce (or annulment) hovered below 10% (Cherlin, 1992). In the U.S., the proportion of marriages begun in each year that will end in divorce has steadily increased from less than 10% for 1867 to over 55% for 1985 (Cherlin, 1992). The statistics for Western Europe have shown a similar trend. However, by the mid-1980s that 115 year trend stopped. The divorce rate in the U.S. and Europe leveled off and even decreased slightly through the rest of the 20th century. . . .

Integrating the data that have emerged in the last quarter of the 20th century about the divorce rate and the longevity of marriages, it is reasonable to conclude that one-quarter of all marriages will dissolve by their seventh year, and approximately half of all marriages will end before their 20th year as a result of divorce or separation. The remaining 50% of marriages will end primarily as a result of death over the next 40 to 50 years.

# Factors Behind the Death-to-Divorce Transition

The shift from death-to-divorce as the most common endpoint of marriage in the 20th century was associated with and perhaps driven by three major factors: the increased lifespan in Western civilization; the shift in the biopsychosocial roles of women; and legal and social value changes. The extent to which these factors can be viewed as causally related to the death-to-divorce transition varies across the factors and different studies.

## Increased Lifespan

A fundamental and unprecedented transformation in the lives of people in the West in the 20th century was the increase in the human lifespan. From 1900 to 2000, the average human lifespan for white Americans increased over 25 years (for men from 48 to 74; for women from 51 to 80); for non-white Americans, who started with a shorter average lifespan in 1900, it increased over 30 years (Caplow, Hicks, & Wittenberg, 2001). Western Europeans experienced a similar lifespan increase (Hall, 1993). "The mortality decline in this century is greater than the total mortality decline that occurred during the 250 years preceding 1900" (Uhlenberg, 1980).

If the most common endpoint of marriage is death, an increased lifespan should result in longer marriages. The assumption is that as people live longer, they will stay married longer. However, this has not been the case. As people in the West came to live longer, it appears that the average duration of their marriages did not substantially increase. Instead, people dramatically increased their use of divorce. . . .

## Biopsychosocial Roles of Women

Michael (1988), an economist and disciple of Gary Becker (1981), the first economist to focus primarily on family systems, used statistics systematically to examine the contributions of various factors to the doubling of the divorce rate in the U.S. between 1960 and 1980. Michael ruled out U.S.-specific phenomena because of the comparable (if slightly smaller) rise in the divorce rate in Western Europe. Furthermore, his analyses led him to dismiss arguments attributing the rise to the increased aging of the U.S. population, the increasing rate of second and third marriages, and geographical location within the U.S.

Employing a complex regression analysis, Michael found evidence to support the impact of the reduced fertility rate in the U.S. (which decreased from 3.42 in 1961 to 1.63, below replacement, in 1974) and Western Europe on the divorce rate. In his and Becker's analyses, having one child reduced the likelihood of divorce approximately 30% between the fifth and fifteenth year of marriage; having two children reduced the rate another 30%. The reduced fertility rate directly links to Michael's finding that the diffusion of modern contraceptive technology accounts for approximately 50% of the variance in the rise in the divorce rate into the late 1970s. Additionally, Michael unequivocally concludes that "the rise in women's income is a dominant force affecting the divorce rate" (1988, p. 392). The power of the findings on women's income in almost all analyses of the rise of divorce from the early 1960s to 1978 is particularly intriguing because it emerges in the face of the rise in men's income during this period, a variable that has been consistently associated with a diminished likelihood of divorce.

The two variables that account most consistently for the rise of the divorce rate in Michael's analysis are women's income and the diffusion of contraceptive technology. The impact of the latter variable was further substantiated, in Michael's opinion, by the much slower rise in the divorce rate in Japan during the same period, and Japan's reluctance to adopt the contraceptive pill through the early 1970s. What is most striking about these two variables is that they greatly increased women's choice. The income variable provided women with economic opportunity and choice. It reduced women's economic dependence on men and provided them with opportunities to support themselves that had not existed prior to the last half of the 20th century. The contraceptive variable provided women with choice about when and if to become pregnant. It opened biological options that did not exist heretofore. The radically reduced fertility rate in the entire Western world reflects the impact of this contraceptive breakthrough and the elective options it offered women (and men).

## Social Value and Legal Changes

Undoubtedly, one of the most debated factors in the effort to explain and account for the increase in divorce in the 20th century is the transformation of divorce laws, specifically the implementation of no-fault divorce laws. Michael dismissed the often-cited explanation tying the rate rise from 1960 to 1980 to the easing of divorce laws within the U.S. "Many states exhibited rising divorce rates several years before a change in the law occurred" (Michael, 1988, p. 369). Going beyond Michael's analysis, Marvell (1989) studied the impact of different types of divorce laws on divorce rates in 38 states to challenge the results of at least ten studies which "explored the impact of no-fault divorce laws on divorce rates, with most concluding that there is none" (p. 546). He found that different types of laws had different effects, some of which were significant. However, he concluded that his "findings only mildly contradict the earlier studies finding no such impact" (p. 564).

The extent to which changes in divorce laws drove or were driven by the rising divorce rate up to 1980 is probably impossible to determine. However, it is clear that the change in divorce laws in the last half of the 20th century reflected a change in social values—a change that simultaneously attempted to: (1) make divorces easier to obtain; (2) reduce the social and legal stigma associated with divorce; and (3) reduce the psychosocial trauma (blame and character assassination) associated with divorce.

It is impossible to understand the transition to divorce in the last half of the 20th century without considering the value shift associated with the rise of feminism. As cited above, the role of women changed dramatically in the course of the 20th century, economically and reproductively. However, these changes were closely associated with dramatic and profound shifts in the roles women took on in the family, in marriage, and in society in general. These shifts also began a transformation in men's roles within the family and marriage, as well as a general reduction in patriarchy within the broader society. They also led to a sustained series of critiques of marriage as an institution. Rampage (2002) explores the impact of this feminist and ultimately gender-role revolution in the 20th century on marriage and divorce.

## African American Experience

In general, African Americans experienced the same trends as white and Hispanic Americans, but only more so. The divorce rate per 1000 women in the African American community increased from 78 in 1960 to 358 in 1990, whereas the rate for whites changed from 38 to 153 (Tucker & Mitchell-Kernan, 1995). However, the greatest change in the African American community during this period was in the marriage rate. As of 1992, "fewer than three of four black women overall can expect to marry compared to nine of ten white women" (1995, p. 12).

The increasing divorce rate and the huge reduction in the marriage rate in the African American community can be partially attributed to the factors that have influenced these rates in the white community (lifespan; women's economic and reproductive choice; and social/legal values), but there are significant additional factors. The two primary additional factors that have emerged in the analysis of these trends in the African American community are changes in the demographic sex ratio and male employment.

In regard to sex ratios, over the last half of the 20th century the male/female sex ratio has changed dramatically, such that there are substantially more women than men in the appropriate age cohorts. This gender disparity has been attributed to relatively high (compared to white) adolescent homicide/suicide rates (gang violence and drug overdoses), and the high rate of adolescent and young adult incarceration. Secondly, the disappearance of blue-collar jobs in the industrial Northeast and Midwest had a devastating impact on male employment and income in African American communities (Wilson, 1996). Simply stated, in the last 20 years of the 20th century, in the African American community, there have not been enough men for the available women, and many of the men who have been available as potential marriage partners, have been unattractive as providers because of unemployment or relative (to female) underemployment (Patterson, 1998). Pinderhughes (2002) explores the African American marital experience in the 20th century in greater detail.

## Leveling of Divorce Rate After 1980

Along with the skyrocketing divorce rate between 1960 and 1980, many social demographers have noted another dramatic trend: the divorce rate dropped slightly after its 1981-high and stayed around 22 divorces per 1000 married women (50% lifetime probability of divorce) through the rest of the 20th century (Caplow et al., 2001). The same leveling of the divorce rate also occurred in Western Europe after the early 1980s (Hall, 1993).

Goldstein (1999) statistically examined various predictors to test their capacity to explain this leveling off in the United States. First of all, his analysis suggests that the leveling trend is sufficiently robust that it can be viewed as a "real" phenomenon as opposed to a temporary depression in the century-long increase. Secondly his compositional analysis failed to explain the leveling as a result of any of the following variables: age structure of the population, age at marriage, marriage order (first, second, etc.), educational attainment, number of children, and the timing of childbearing. Lastly, his analysis suggests that "any increased selectivity of marriage linked to co-habitation appears to be only a small part of the story behind the leveling of marital instability" (p. 414). He concludes that the current divorce rate will continue at its present level and that "new theories are needed to explain the determinants of divorce rates at the population level" (p. 409).

A possible explanation may reside in the hypothesis that the overall level of marital stability has not changed, but rather the means by which that level is maintained have changed. If this is true, that the level of marital stability has remained the same, it may well be that, from a population perspective, the increasing divorce rate over the last century maintained the 20-year average or median duration of marriage in the face of the largest human lifespan increase in recorded history. The divorce rate increased until the median duration of marriage returned to the 20-year level and then it stopped.

It is puzzling that the divorce rate stopped growing after 1980, despite the continuing increase in women's income and employment, the primary statistical predictors (and correlates) of the rise in divorce rates between 1960 and 1980. From 1980 to 1997 the percentage of married women in the work force in the U.S. increased from 50% to 65% and women's earnings as a percentage of men's earnings increased from 60% to 74% (Caplow et al., 2001). In other words, the primary "drivers" of the rise in divorce rates continued increasing after the rise in the divorce rate stopped, a finding that is statistically counterintuitive. Based on these data, it is not unreasonable to hypothesize that as long as the increased lifespan, the increase in women's income and employment, the availability of effective and cheap contraceptive technology, and divorce-friendly laws and values remain facts of life, the 50% divorce rate is here to stay. It fits the evolved human level of monogamous marital stability.

## Human Pair-Bonding

The data on the death-to-divorce transition raise important questions about the ex-

tent to which human beings, at least human beings in the West, have evolved to be permanent, monogamous pair-bonders. In the context of a 50-year lifespan, no economic independence or reproductive choice for women, and divorce-hostile social and legal values, marrying till death us do part was realistic. However, these changes in the 20th century have created a new context in which the majority of couples will not sustain marriage until death. Why? What, if anything, have the increased lifespan and the other biopsychosocial changes associated with death-to-divorce transition revealed about the human capacity and inclination to pair-bond permanently and monogamously?

### Capacity to Pair-bond as a Set of Individual Factors

A major issue that emerges from this question is whether it would be useful to view the capacity for permanent, monogamous pair-bonding as a complex set of factors located within an individual? This individual capacity may be normally distributed, with certain individuals having a lot of it, others (the majority) having a moderate amount, and others having very little. This capacity might include the following set of factors: the ability to select an appropriate partner; the ability to commit to an intimate relationship; the ability to attach to another human being; the ability to maintain a certain level of personal integrity, morality, and responsibility; the ability to regulate emotion (particularly anger) and impulses (particularly sexuality); the ability to get along with another person over an extended period of time; and the ability to love another person.

Undoubtedly, like all individual abilities, the capacity to pair-bond permanently and monogamously would be influenced by genetic and environmental factors. Viewed as an individual capacity, a substantial amount of the variance in this set of factors could be accounted for by personality variables. . . .

### Capacity to Pair-Bond as a Set of Couple Factors

It is not sufficient to think about the capacity for pair-bonding as solely a set of individual factors. It denies the systemic nature of marriage. From a systemic perspective, it is less the characteristics of the individuals in the marriage that predict whether or not they will get divorced, but rather the characteristics of the couple, including the characteristics of the individuals in relationship to each other. A step in this direction is the homophily hypothesis, which states that individuals who are more alike demographically (age, religion, socioeconomic status, etc.) and attitudinally (beliefs and values) have a higher probability of staying married than individuals who differ on these dimensions (Laumann et al., 1994). The homophilic couple characteristic is demographic similarity, whereas the narrative couple characteristic is compatibility.

However, systems theorists would argue that the homophilic and narrative approaches are still additive—for them, the whole never becomes greater than the sum of the parts. To do that, theorists need to move to a level of description of the couple that is not based on individual attributes. In four studies over 25 years, Gottman (1993; Gottman & Notarius, 2002) found that married couples with a set of specific interactional characteristics have almost a 100% probability of getting divorced within four years. The characteristics of these couples, which emerge in a relatively brief face-to-face interaction in Gottman's laboratory, are criticism, defensiveness, contempt, and stonewalling—a quartet of factors called the "Four Horsemen of the Apocalypse."

The identification of this highly at-risk group of couples constitutes a major step forward in the study of divorce. However, family psychology is still far away from being able to predict over longer (than four years) periods of time which couples will and which couples will not divorce. What is clear at this point, however, is that the capacity to pair-bond is a product of capacities of the individuals in a relationship as well as capacities of the couple. There is emerging evidence that suggests that whether or not a couple will divorce is not just a function of their individual upbringing or their history and current functioning as a couple, but also of their genetic heritages (McGue & Lykken,

1992; Reiss, Neiderhiser, Hetherington, & Plomin, 2000). Thus, the capacity to pair-bond monogamously for life is a complex set of biopsychosocial factors that science has just begun to differentiate and study (Gottman & Notarius, 2002).

## Inclination to Stay Married/Capacity to Divorce

In the preceding examination of the psychosocial factors that influence whether or not a couple will stay married, staying married is viewed as a capacity. The capacity perspective on marriage typically assumes that the capacity to stay married is a good thing and that having more of it is better than having less of it. This perspective takes a deficit view of divorce. However, it is possible to take a different perspective that considers the capacity to divorce as a characteristic of an individual and/or a couple. This perspective does not just view divorce as a failure of the capacity to stay married, but as a potential positive event or outcome. Any marital therapist who has treated a wide variety of couples over a number of years, knows that in certain circumstances, getting a divorce is a courageous and positive act. In such circumstances, staying married may reflect an inability to pursue what may be in the best interests of oneself, one's partner, and even one's children.

In this regard, Becker's (1981) and Michael's (1988) economically based theory views individuals as decision-makers who are constantly evaluating the benefits and costs of marriage. The decision to divorce, from their perspective, derives from one or both individuals in a couple concluding that the benefits of divorce outweigh the benefits of staying married. In essence, they define people as rational decision makers, and the decision to divorce as a rational act that is perceived by the individual making that decision as a beneficial step in his or her life.

No discussion of marital stability would be complete however without considering the inclination of a person to get divorced. The inclination to divorce is another complex phenomenon that contains a variety of individually anchored factors that collectively determine the extent to which an individual is disposed or inclined to consider divorce as a realistic and positive option. Although linked to factors like reproductive choice and socioeconomic opportunity, the inclination to divorce is distinct. It targets what might be thought [of] as a person's unencumbered attitude toward divorce. Some of the factors that comprise this phenomenon are an individual's: degree of religious conviction; beliefs about the sacrosanctity of marriage and relational commitment; sense of entitlement to relational happiness; family history of divorce; social context; and perception of the damage that a divorce will inflict on loved ones.

## Adult Development and Marital Stability

Another factor behind the death-to-divorce transition is the human capacity for growth over the life course. It is not coincidental that developmental psychology expanded beyond childhood and adolescence in the second half of the 20th century as the human lifespan lengthened and a healthy and vigorous life became a reality for many people into their 80s. The capacity for adult development in the context of an expanded lifespan means that people are changing and evolving values, goals, and beliefs as they age. People are not the same people at 40 that they were at 20, nor will they be the same at 60 and 80. Since most people now marry between 25 and 35, in all probability, they will have changed (grown) substantially by the time they reach 40.

The findings that half of all divorces occur by the seventh year of marriage and that the vast majority of divorces will have occurred by the 20th year of marriage do not support the idea that as people age and differentiate the likelihood increases that they will become incompatible and divorce. An alternative life-course explanation is that people's sense of their relational future at 35 and 40 is very different now than the sense of the future 35- and 40-year-olds had before the 20th century. The prospect of another forty to fifty years with decent health and possibilities for individual growth in an unhappy relationship is very different than the prospect of another 10 to 15 years under the same conditions.

## Evolution of the Capacity to Pair-bond Flexibly

The capacity to divorce and remarry may also derive in part from human beings' evolutionary heritage. The human capacity for serial monogamy and pair-bonding is an essential characteristic of the human species. With death as the primary terminator of marriage, human beings were left with basically two options after the loss of a spouse—remain single the rest of one's life or remarry. The capacity to bond, lose a spouse, and bond again is critical to the survival of the human species, particularly after events like the Black Plague, famines, and wars. Natural selection favored the survival of people with the capacity for flexible and serial pair-bonding. The result of this selection process over millennia is that human beings have the capacity to lose a spouse through divorce or death and to find another partner to marry. If human beings did not have this capacity, it would make marriage more secure, but it might jeopardize the survival of the species.

# The Impact of the Death-to-Divorce Transition

A secondary hypothesis of this article is that the death-to-divorce transition in the last half of the 20th century, and in particular the doubling of the divorce rate between 1960 and 1980 had a profound, if not traumatic impact on the children of parents who divorced during the rate rise (up to 1980). Furthermore, that impact resulted in a variety of new pair-bonding patterns that clearly emerged in the last 25 years of the 20th century and that will probably endure as long as men and women enjoy an increased lifespan, have economic and contraceptive choice, and live in a society that defines divorce as an acceptable option.

Approximately half of the children born after 1960 in the Western world experienced parental divorce. This experience occurred within societies in North America and Europe that were not equipped legally, socially, and emotionally to deal with this experience. In fact, divorce did not become an object of serious scientific study until the last quarter of the 20th century (Goldsmith, 1982;

Gottman & Notarius, 2002). These children felt shame, isolation (despite their numbers), and a lack of social and emotional support. They were told that their families were "broken," and many of these children felt emotionally responsible for the breakdown. There were no models for bi-nuclear families (Ahrons, 1994). Only after this period did research begin to reveal the critical role of a good co-parental relationship between divorced ex-spouses and the importance of sustained and significant involvement by the nonresidential parent. In other words, these children experienced divorce at a time when there were no psychosocial road maps, social facilitators, or societal supports. Traumatology since the Vietnam War has revealed that negative posttraumatic sequelae are greater when the traumatized individual feels socially isolated, lacks social support, and feels ashamed and/or embarrassed about the trauma. These children of the escalating divorce rate were a psychologically traumatized generation, traumatized by their parents' divorces and their own sense of social isolation and shame.

This traumatic experience created great suspicion about marriage. If half of that generation's parents made life-long commitments to each other which they eventually abrogated, what did that say about marriage? Was it really forever, if the majority of people who pledged forever did not stick to the agreement? This suspicion has led that generation, and to a significant extent following generations, to question the meaning of marriage and the pathways that historically led to it. In doing so, they began experimenting with a variety of pair-bonding alternatives and alternative perspectives on pair-bonding that were in full bloom by the dawn of the 21st century.

However, it would be a mistake to reduce the new perspectives on pair-bonding that emerged from the generation that came of age after 1970 to the traumatic effects of their parents' divorces and society's failure to support and integrate them and their experience. The changes in values, beliefs, and behavior in regard to marriage, divorce, and pair-bonding alternatives that occurred in the last 40 years of the 20th century also de-

rived from broader and nontraumatic factors like the rise of feminist values (Rampage, 2002), beliefs about individuals' right to personal happiness and fulfillment, and heightened expectations for intimate relationships.

## Redefining Marriage, Cohabitation, and Co-parenting

As the divorce rate soared after 1960, three other major trends started to emerge that were part of the 20th century's transformation in pair-bonding in the Western world: the rate of marriage decreased, while the rates of cohabitation without marriage and nonmarital births increased. In the U.S., the marriage rate (per 1000 unmarried women per year) decreased from approximately 80 in 1970 to a low of 50 in 1996. "The marriage rate generally rose and fell with the business cycle. The 1990s, with conspicuously low marriage rates in years of unprecedented prosperity, were exceptional" (Caplow et al., 2001, p. 68). A slightly greater drop occurred in the marriage rate in Western Europe. The percentage of cohabiting, unmarried couples in the U.S. increased from less than 1% in 1960 to over 7% of all couples by 1998. The rates for Western Europe were higher, e.g., 19% in the U.K. (Hall, 1993). In the U.S., the percentage of nonmarital births for white women increased from around 2% in 1960 to 26% by 1997, and from 24% to 69% for black women over the same period (Caplow et al., 2001). Across Europe, the nonmarital birthrate in 1960 was 5% or less, depending on the country. In 1988, over 25% of the births in the U.K. and France were nonmarital, whereas in Denmark and Sweden the rates were 48% and 52% respectively (Hall, 1993). This nonmarital birthrate increase is particularly impressive because it occurred at the same time that women in the West had more contraceptive choice than ever before in the history of the human species.

These three trends represent what might be thought of as a collective deconstruction of marriage by the generations that came of age in the last quarter of the 20th century. Historically, cohabitation, marriage, and childbearing were all part of one inseparable package. Marriage and cohabitation were usually co-occurring, and both were typically followed by the birth of children. These three trends reflect an unprecedented separation of cohabitation, marriage, and childbearing.

Data from the National Survey of Family Growth in 1995 found that over half of the women between the ages of 30 to 34 were either cohabiting at the time of the survey or had cohabited before they got married (Caplow et al., 2001). These data suggest that for most of the women in this age cohort, cohabitation and marriage were distinct events. However, distinct does not mean unrelated. For many, if not most cohabiting couples, cohabitation represented a major step toward marriage, as opposed to an end in itself.

The fact that in 1997, over one-quarter of the Caucasian babies and over two-thirds of the African American babies in the U.S., and almost half of the babies in Scandinavia were born to unmarried women suggests that for many women (and couples), the decision to have a baby had become distinct from the decision to marry. Once again, being distinct does not mean unrelated. Caplow et al. noted that the white "parents of a considerable number of these infants eventually married" (2001, p. 86).

These trends reflect the emergence of a new, nondeviant pair-bonding sequence in the last twenty years of the 20th century. This sequence typically began with cohabitation. For the majority of couples this was followed by marriage, but for a very substantial minority in the white community and for many in the African American community, cohabitation was followed by the birth of children. Subsequently, many of these couples married. What emerged was a pattern in which the three events began to represent three somewhat independent choices. Initially, a couple committed to live together—to share property, expenses, and space. Then many couples decided to have children—to commit to being co-parents. A substantial number of these couples then decided to marry—to commit to being life partners. For many couples that followed this pattern, cohabita-

tion represented an opportunity to check each other out, to get to know the other person and the relationship better before making the decision to have children and/or marry.

Many African American families did not follow this alternative pattern. For many families, cohabitation did not precede or follow nonmarital childbirth. Due to the paucity of good statistical data and the flexibility and unofficial nature of many cohabitating arrangements, it is hard to estimate the exact numbers of families in which the unmarried parents did not live together before or after the birth of their child. Official statistics report that in 1998, 57% of black families with children under 18 were headed by a single female parent (Caplow et al., 2001). This distinct trend of nonmarital and noncohabiting childbirth and childrearing within the African American community still supports the hypothesis that African Americans, along with white North Americans and Europeans, in the last half of the 20th century, engaged in a process of disaggregating cohabitation, childbirth, and marriage.

It will be very interesting in the coming years to see whether the marriages that occur after cohabitation and childbearing are more enduring than those that are not preceded by cohabitation and/or childbearing. There is currently a widespread debate as to the meaning of recent findings that couples that cohabit before marriage appear to have a higher incidence of divorce than couples that do not cohabit before marriage (Axinn & Thornton, 1992; Bumpass & Sweet, 1989). It will also be interesting to see the extent to which the trends of the last twenty years of the 20th century continue into the 21st. Were the decrease in the rate of marriage and the increase in the rates of nonmarital cohabitation and childbearing primarily characteristics of a psychologically traumatized generation that came of age between 1960 and 1980, or in the case of the African American community, characteristics of an economically and socially traumatized generation, or will these trends characterize subsequent generations that experienced divorce in a more normalized and supportive context?

# Implications of the Death-to-Divorce Transition

The emergence of the death-to-divorce transition and many people's subsequent redefinition of pair-bonding in the latter half of the 20th century, present numerous challenges to social policy and law makers, social scientists, and mental health practitioners. Despite the fact that the death-to-divorce transition was apparent for at least the last twenty-five years of the 20th century, the currently predominant social policies, laws, research practices, and clinical intervention models pertaining to marriage are predicated upon the life-long, till-death-us-do-part traditional model of marriage. As a result, they are and will continue to be unsynchronized with the new emerging normal realities of pair-bonding in the West. They have been tweaked somewhat in order to accommodate the increase in divorce and the realities of single-parent and bi-nuclear families, but by and large they are still based on a normative and traditional life-long marriage model.

## Toward a New Pair-bonding Paradigm for Western Civilization

For social policies, laws, research practices, and clinical interventions to incorporate the new marital realities of the 21st century in Western civilization, they need to be based on a new pair-bonding paradigm that integrates the implications of the death-to-divorce transition. It is probably presumptuous to attempt to articulate a new pair-bonding paradigm at this early stage, before it is possible to determine the enduring nature of the pair-bond changes that occurred in the 20th century. Instead, the following represent an initial set of precepts that could constitute part of the foundation of a new pair-bonding paradigm.

1. Marital theory needs to become pair-bonding theory: The theory of intimate relations that has guided most policies, research, and intervention in the 20th century has been a dichotomous model that looks at people as married or unmarried: the only serious pair-bonding state is marriage. Many couples in the last half of the 20th century defined four serious pair-bonding states—cohabitation without children, cohabitation with children, marriage, and a relatively new phenomenon that might be called elder pair-bonding. Replacing dichotomous marital theory with a pluralistic theory of human pair-bonding lays a theoretical foundation for identifying, acknowledging, and addressing the multiplicity of serious pair-bonding structures that have evolved over the last 30 years.

2. The existence and viability of a multiplicity of pair-bonding arrangements need to be acknowledged and addressed: This precept derives from and extends the first. At a minimum, the four arrangements listed above need to be recognized as legitimate pair-bond structures that fulfill important functions for their participants.

3. Entering into any particular pair-bond structure entails a distinct and legitimate decision-making process: This precept disaggregates the one-decision model of traditional marriage in which the commitment to cohabit, have children, and marry, are all part of the same package.

4. Young adults, contemplating pair-bonding, need to be able to consider a variety of pair-bond options that fit their cultural beliefs, personal preferences, and relational goals: As young adults consider pair-bonding, they need to be freely able to choose the pair-bond that best fits who they are and where they want to go. They also need to be able to understand that there is a multiplicity of structures that can be entered into sequentially, as their needs and objectives change.

5. Marriage should continue to be defined as the lifelong, monogamous pair-bond: Marriage should continue to function as an objective for those who desire such a bond, representing the most committed and enduring pair-bond.

6. Marriage, as a life-long, monogamous committed relationship, should be available to all mentally competent adults who desire to enter into such a legal and formal relationship. This precept pertains particularly to gays and lesbians, but also potentially to other groups whose right to marry has been or could be restricted.

7. Co-parenting without marriage needs to be recognized as a legitimate and life-long, nonmonogamous pair-bond: Once couples who are not married have children, they are co-parents for the rest of their lives. Their commitment as co-parents needs to be recognized and legitimated.

8. Co-habitation without children or marriage needs to be viewed not only as a legitimate end-state in itself, but also as a legitimate form of pre-marriage: Premarital cohabitation is clearly being used by many couples in the West to determine compatibility and the potential for co-parenting and marriage. In 1981–82, in a national survey of 18–34 year olds in Australia, 55% of females and 62% of males agreed that "it is good to have a trial marriage," by which they meant cohabitation (Carmichael, 1985, pp. 98–100). These findings clearly reflect the way in which many Western young adults use and view premarital cohabitation. As of 1988, approximately 60% of all first cohabitations in the U.S. ended in marriage (Bumpass & Sweet, 1989).

9. Divorce and relational dissolution need to be viewed and treated as normal social events in the life course of modern families: Public societal discourses on divorce, and relational dissolution in general, need to acknowledge the normality of these events in the life course of families.

10. The decision to divorce needs to be viewed with greater complexity, thoughtfulness, and neutrality: Rather than viewing divorce as a failure, it needs to be treated as a complex relational process that can have good and poor outcomes. It is not inherently good or bad (Hetherington & Kelly, 2002). In fact, under certain circumstances, it can be a positive and even courageous act.

These ten precepts represent an initial foray into the task of articulating a new pair-bonding paradigm. That paradigm remains to be fully articulated. Nevertheless, these ten precepts offer a pre-paradigmatic foundation that can inform subsequent examinations of the implications of the death-to-divorce transition for social policy, law, social science research, and intervention. . . .

## References

Ahrons, C. (1994). *The good divorce: Keeping your family together when your marriage comes apart.* New York: Harper Collins.

Axinn, W. G., & Thornton, A. (1992). The relationship between cohabitation and divorce: Selectivity or causal influence. *Demography* 29, 357–374.

Barash, D. P., & Lipton, J. E. (2001). *The myth of monogamy: Fidelity and infidelity in animals and people.* New York: W. H. Freeman.

Becker, G. S. (1981). *A treatise on the family.* Cambridge: Harvard University Press.

Bray, J., & Hetherington, E. M. (1993). Families in transition: Introduction and overview. *Journal of Family Psychology* 7: 3–9.

Bumpass, L. L., & Sweet, J. A. (1989). National estimates of cohabitation. *Demography* 26 (4): 615–625.

Caplow, T., Hicks, L., & Wattenberg, B. J. (2001). *The first measured century: An illustrated guide to trends in America, 1900–2000.* Washington, DC: American Enterprise Institute (AEI) Press.

Carmichael, G. A. (1985). The changing structure of Australian families. *The Australian Quarterly,* Autumn/Winter: 95–104.

Cherlin, A. J. (1992). *Marriage, divorce, and remarriage.* Cambridge: Harvard University Press.

Eibl-Eibesfeldt, I. (1989). *Human ethology.* New York: Aldine de Gruyter.

Gies, F., & Gies, J. (1987). *Marriage and the family in the middle ages.* New York: Harper & Row.

Goldsmith, J. (1982). The postdivorce family system (pp. 297–330). In F. Walsh (ed.), *Normal family processes.* New York: Guilford Press.

Goldstein, J. R. (1999). The leveling of divorce in the United States. *Demography* 36 (3): 409–414.

Gottlieb, B. (1993). *The family in the Western world: From the Black Death to the industrial revolution.* New York: Oxford University Press.

Gottman, J. M. (1993). A theory of marital dissolution and stability. *Journal of Family Psychology* 7: 57–75.

Gottman, J. M., & Notarius, C. I. (2002). Marital research in the 20th century and a research agenda for the 21st century. *Family Process* 41: 159–197.

Gurman, A. S., & Fraenkel, P. (2002). The history of couple therapy: A millennial review. *Family Process* 41: 199–260.

Hagestad, G. O. (1988). Demographic change and the life course: Some emerging trends in the family realm. *Family Relations* 37: 405–410.

Hall, R. (1993). Europe's changing population. *Geography* 78: 3–15.

Hetherington, E. M., & Kelly, J. (2002). *For better or for worse: Divorce reconsidered.* New York: W. W. Norton.

Kuklo, C. (1990). Marriage in pre-industrial Warsaw in the light of demographic studies. *Journal of Family History* 15 (3): 239–259.

Laumann, E. O., Gagnon, J. H., Michael, R. T., & Michaels, S. (1994). *The social organization of sexuality: Sexual practices in the United States.* Chicago: University of Chicago Press.

Marvell, T. B. (1989). Divorce rates and the fault requirement. *Law and Society Review* 23 (4): 543–567.

McGue, M., & Lykken, D. T. (1992). Genetic influence on risk of divorce. *Psychological Science* 3 (6): 368–373.

Michael, R. T. (1988). Why did the U.S. divorce rate double within a decade? *Research in Population Economics* 6: 367–399.

Patterson, O. (1998). *Rituals of blood: Consequences of slavery in two American centuries.* New York: Basic Civitas Books.

Pinderhughes, E. B. (2002). African American marriage in the 20th century. *Family Process* 41: 1269–1282.

Rampage, C. (2002). Marriage in the 20th century: A feminist perspective. *Family Process* 41: 261–268.

Reiss, D., Neiderhiser, J. M., Hetherington, E. M., & Plomin, R. (2000). *The relationship code: Deciphering genetic and social influences on adolescent development.* Cambridge: Harvard University Press.

Tucker, M., & Mitchell-Kernan, C. (1995). Trends in African American family formation: A theoretical and statistical overview (pp. 3–27). In M. Tucker & C. Mitchell-Kernan (eds.), *The decline in marriage among African Americans.* New York: Russell Sage Foundation.

Uhlenberg, P. (1980). Death and the family. *Journal of Family History* 5: 313–320.

Wilson, W. J. (1996). *When work disappears.* New York: Random House (Vintage).

## Review

1. Give a brief historical overview of marriage and of how marriages ended from the pre-modern to the modern era in Western civilization.

2. Discuss the three major factors in the death-to-divorce transition.

3. Describe some of the differences between the African American and white American experience of marriage and divorce.

4. How can you explain the development of humans as permanent, monogamous pair-bonders?

5. Discuss the implications of the death-to-divorce transition in pair-bonding.

## Application

The author notes that many couples now follow the pattern of cohabitation, marriage, and childbearing. A large number, however, cohabit, have children, then marry. And some have children without ever getting married. What is your own preferred pattern? Why? Which pattern do you think is best for a healthy society? Why? Ask the same questions of six couples—three who are just dating or newly cohabiting or married and three who have been married for 10 or more years. Based on your results, what would you predict about pair-bonding for the future?

## Related Web Sites

1. *http://human-nature.com/ep/articles/ ep01138154.html.* An article on pair-bonding from the perspective of evolutionary psychology.

2. *http://www.usatoday.com/news/opin-ion/columnists/lovemarriage/love4.htm.*
An article by a social scientist on the problems faced by those who cohabit.

# Part Two

## Government and Politics

**G**overnment is the social institution responsible for protecting the citizenry from foreign enemies and for maintaining law and order within the society. **Politics** are the ways that people attempt to influence or control the government. Through government, **power** (control over the behavior of others) is exercised by those in authority. Through politics, various individuals and groups seek to use the power of government for their own interests.

The first selection in this part deals with the issue of whether it makes any difference which party is in power (some Americans believe it doesn't). The second deals with the current concern with civil liberties in the face of terrorist activities. How much power should the government be able to exercise? ✦

# 27

# In Economic Policy, How Much Does It Matter Which Party Governs?

*Robert Blendon*
*John Benson*
*Mollyann Brodie*
*Drew Altman*
*Kathleen Weldon*

*Political parties date back to the early years of the nation. The current party system, composed primarily of the Democratic and Republican parties, developed in the years preceding the Civil War. For the past 70 years or more the presidential candidates from those two parties have received 85 percent or more of the votes cast. Various other parties (e.g., the Socialist, Progressive, States' Rights, Libertarian, and Reform parties) have tried to gain office, but few of their candidates have been elected at any level of government.*

*The two parties are divided to some extent along socioeconomic lines. A higher proportion of those in the lower strata vote Democratic, while a higher proportion of upper-strata Americans are Republicans. This should mean that the two parties would have very different agendas. Contrary to the notion of some Americans that all politicians are basically alike and that it matters little to the average person which party is in power, Blendon and his associates show in this selection that there can be important economic consequences when one party or the other governs*

*the nation because registered Democrats and registered Republicans have contrary views on many issues. This selection also illustrates the complexity of the issue because it shows the divisions of opinion within the parties as well as those between the parties.*

The United States has now witnessed three consecutive presidential elections and three straight congressional elections in which neither party has won 50 percent of the vote (Barone 2001). The presidency and the U.S. Senate have each changed partisan hands twice during the past decade. Republicans gained control of the U.S. House of Representatives in 1994, but they currently enjoy only a nine-seat advantage.

These election results accurately represent the close partisan balance prevailing in the country as a whole. Perhaps less obvious is that philosophical divisions within both Congress and the American public have been growing for several decades (Jacobson 2001). One element often missed by the press and economic commentators is just how large the differences in economic-policy attitudes are between the two parties' core constituencies. These differences will probably be suspended for some time during the military conflict that is likely to follow the attacks on the United States that took place September 11, 2001. But after the conflict is resolved, the differences between the parties will reemerge.

But if at some time during the next decade either of the major parties gains both the presidency and large majorities in Congress, economic policy is likely to be profoundly affected.[1] Political dominance by one or the other party would affect policy with regard to federal government spending, regulation of business, economic equity, tax cuts and the flatness of the tax system, and energy and environmental policy. These differences would be even more important if an economic downturn or serious energy crisis occurred on one or the other party's watch.

In two major areas of economic policy—free trade and immigration—both parties are internally divided. During a recession, tensions within each party are likely to increase, and this situation could once again lead to the rise of a third party based on these two issues.

Public opinion surveys can provide an important insight into the core beliefs of the two parties' politicians and activists. Members of Congress and presidential candidates pay attention to members of their party and are affected by their party's own culture. By looking at the views of Republicans and Democrats in the general public, we can have a glimpse of the underlying values and beliefs that prevail within each party. This insight, in turn, allows us to draw some conclusions about how dominance by one party or the other could affect the nation's economic policy.

## Federal Government Spending

If Democrats gained political dominance, the federal government would play a more activist role—principally meaning increased government spending in areas such as education, health care, and job training—than if Republicans were ascendant. This conclu-

sion reflects a philosophical difference between the two parties' constituencies. Democrats are far more likely than Republicans (76 percent to 47 percent) to believe that the federal government should do everything possible to improve the standard of living of all Americans (WP/Kaiser/Harvard 2000b). (See Table 27.1.)

More than three-fourths (79 percent) of Republicans prefer a smaller government with fewer services, while Democrats are nearly equally divided, with a plurality favoring a larger government with many services (WP/Kaiser/Harvard 2000c). Regarded from a different angle, three-fourths (76 percent) of Democrats say that providing needed services is more important to them than holding down the size of government (18 percent). Republican opinion is nearly split, with 50 percent preferring to hold down the size of government (ABC/WP 2001a).

Democratic voters generally favor having the government do more to help middle-class Americans. This assistance would involve increased spending to make social security and Medicare financially secure, helping to pay for the cost of a college education,

### Table 27.1
### Federal Government Spending

| | Percent of Registered Voters | |
| --- | --- | --- |
| | **Republicans** | **Democrats** |
| The government in Washington should do everything possible to improve the standard of living of all Americans | 47 | 76 |
| More important to you: | | |
| Holding down size of government | 50 | 18 |
| Providing needed services | 43 | 76 |
| Helping the middle class is very important in deciding 2000 presidential vote | 48 | 72 |
| Paying doctor and hospital bills: | | |
| Responsibility of government in Washington | 33 | 65 |
| People should take care of these themselves | 31 | 8 |
| Agree with both/neither | 36 | 27 |
| What the federal government should do about increasing the number of Americans' health insurance: | | |
| Major effort that would require a tax increase | 23 | 51 |
| Limited effort that would not require a tax increase | 32 | 30 |
| Not something the federal government should be doing | 40 | 11 |

and providing subsidies for day care to help working families. Republicans—who distrust government, like tax cuts, and emphasize the role of the market economy and individual responsibility—are less likely to want a direct government role. When asked prior to the 2000 election, Democrats (72 percent) were far more likely than Republicans (48 percent) to say that helping the middle class was very important in deciding their presidential vote (WP/Kaiser/Harvard 2000c).

Differences between the parties can be seen in the health care area. Nearly two-thirds (65 percent) of Democrats believe it is the responsibility of the federal government to help people pay doctor and hospital bills. Republican opinion is almost evenly divided, with 33 percent saying it is the responsibility of the federal government and 31 percent believing that people should take care of these bills themselves (Davis et al. 2000).

Half (51 percent) of Democrats believe the federal government should make a major effort to raise the number of Americans with health insurance, even if it requires a tax increase. Only one-fourth (23 percent) of Republicans favor such a major effort. Most Republicans either think the federal government should not be involved in such an enterprise (40 percent) or favor a limited effort that requires no tax increase (32 percent) (WP/Kaiser/Harvard 2000a). Three-fourths

(77 percent) of Democrats, compared with half (51 percent) of Republicans, consider expanding health-care coverage to all Americans to be a moral issue (WP/Kaiser/Harvard 2000b).

## Government Regulation

If Democrats gained the upper hand, we could expect more government regulation of the pharmaceutical, health insurance, energy, and banking industries. Republican political dominance would likely result in a push to deregulate certain industries.

More than three-fourths (82 percent) of Republicans believe that government has gone too far in regulating business, while Democrats are nearly evenly split in their views, with 49 percent agreeing and 46 percent disagreeing (WP/Kaiser/Harvard 2000c) (see Table 27.2). A majority (56 percent) of Republicans believe that government regulation does more harm than good, while a majority (58 percent) of Democrats believe that such regulation protects the public (Pew/PSRA 1999). Similarly, Democrats are significantly more likely than Republicans (59 percent to 43 percent) to agree that government regulation of big business is necessary to protect the public (WP/Kaiser/Harvard 1998).

In part, Democrats' more populist views reflect their attitude about corporate profits.

**Table 27.2**
*Government Regulation*

| | Percent of Registered Voters | |
|---|---|---|
| | **Republicans** | **Democrats** |
| Government has gone too far in regulating business | | |
| Agree | 82 | 49 |
| Disagree | 15 | 46 |
| Government regulation does more harm than good | 56 | 34 |
| Government regulation protects the public | 38 | 58 |
| Government regulation of big business and corporations is necessary to protect the public | 43 | 59 |
| Corporations make reasonable profit | 54 | 35 |
| Corporations make too much profit | 40 | 59 |
| Immigration should be decreased | 51 | 38 |

A majority of Democrats (59 percent) believe that corporations make too much profit, while a majority (54 percent) of Republicans believe corporations make reasonable profits (Pew/PSRA 1999).

The issue of immigration is likely to be a continuing thicket for both parties, since Latinos are a rapidly growing group that could be critical in one party's gaining a clear majority. At the same time, a substantial share of voters in both parties are concerned about increased immigration. While both parties are divided, there is a larger constituency among Republicans (51 percent) than among Democrats (38 percent) for decreasing immigration (Gallup 2001a).

## Economic Equity

The great debate about leveling income differences in the United States is over, at least for the foreseeable future. But concerns among Democrats about various issues of equity are likely to arise. Although Democrats are about twice as likely as Republicans (39 percent to 20 percent) to agree that it is the responsibility of government to reduce income differences between those of high and low incomes, a majority of both parties disagree with that contention (WP/Kaiser/Harvard 1998). (See Table 27.3.) Democrats may not generally be concerned with income differences between upper-income people and the rest of society, but they are more con-

### Table 27.3
#### Economic Equity

| | Percent of Registered Voters | |
| | Republicans | Democrats |
|---|---|---|
| Responsibility of government to reduce income differences between those of high and low incomes: | 20 | 39 |
| Income differences between rich and poor: | | |
| Government in Washington ought to reduce differences | 28 | 53 |
| Government should not concern itself | 57 | 24 |
| Are the following items moral issues (% answering yes)? | | |
| The differences in income between people with high incomes and people with low incomes | 23 | 53 |
| Taxes and the tax system | 41 | 44 |
| Money and wealth in this country: | | |
| Distribution is fair | 53 | 20 |
| Should be more evenly distributed | 43 | 75 |
| Government should do more to help the needy | 44 | 67 |
| Government can't afford more help for the needy | 48 | 27 |
| Favor increasing minimum wage | 74 | 93 |
| It is the responsibility of the federal government to make sure minorities have jobs equal in quality to whites | 32 | 59 |
| Favor employers and colleges making an extra effort to find and recruit qualified minorities | 48 | 64 |
| Affirmative action: | | |
| Race/ethnicity should be a factor when deciding who is hired, promoted, or admitted to college | 2 | 8 |
| Should be based strictly on merit | 97 | 87 |
| Because of past discrimination, blacks should be given preferences in hiring and promotion | 11 | 27 |
| It is the responsibility of the federal government to make sure blacks have schools equal in quality to whites | 59 | 79 |

cerned than Republicans are with any tax changes that help the very wealthy. This sensitivity is shown by what happens when the word "rich" is used in the question. About half (53 percent) of Democrats believe the federal government should reduce income differences between the rich and the poor, while about one-fourth believe government should not concern itself. For Republicans, the figures are reversed (Davis et al. 2000).

About half (53 percent) of Democrats, compared with only 23 percent of Republicans, consider the differences in income between high- and low-income people to be a moral issue. Although Republicans and Democrats differ in their attitudes about economic equity, a majority of neither party's constituency considers taxes and the tax system to be a moral issue (WP/Kaiser/Harvard 2000b).

Democrats (75 percent) are far more likely than Republicans (43 percent) to believe that money and wealth in this country should be more evenly distributed (WP/Kaiser/Harvard 2000c). Similarly, two-thirds of Democrats (67 percent) believe government should do more to help the needy. Republican opinion is nearly evenly divided, with a plurality (48 percent) believing that government cannot afford more help for the needy (Pew/PSRA 1999).

While the Democrats are unlikely to make major efforts to redistribute income, their views are likely to make them more supportive of labor union goals and highly resistant to efforts to flatten out the progressive income tax and eliminate the inheritance tax. On the other hand, the Republicans would move in the opposite direction in each of these areas.

The minimum wage represents one major exception to party differences. Large majorities of both Democrats (93 percent) and Republicans (74 percent) favor raising the minimum wage (Pew/PSRA 2001b).

## Economic Equity Related to Race

The two parties disagree on whether the federal government needs to play an aggressive role in trying to bring minorities into the economic mainstream and establish fairer treatment in jobs and health care. A majority (59 percent) of Democrats believe it is the responsibility of the federal government to make sure that minorities have jobs equal in quality to those held by whites. Only one-third (32 percent) of Republicans see this intervention as a role for the federal government. Nearly two-thirds (64 percent) of Democrats, compared with about half (48 percent) of Republicans, want employers and colleges to make an extra effort to find and recruit qualified minorities (WP/Kaiser/Harvard 2001).

However, policies that promote the stricter forms of affirmative action are likely to decline, no matter which party is in power. Less than 10 percent of either party thinks race or ethnicity should be a factor when deciding who is hired, promoted, or admitted to college. Overwhelming majorities of both parties believe that hiring, promotion, and admissions should be based strictly on merit and qualifications other than race or ethnicity (WP/Kaiser/Harvard 2001). Similarly, only 27 percent of Democrats and 11 percent of Republicans believe that because of past discrimination, African-Americans should be given preference in hiring and promotion (Davis et al. 2000).

Equality of educational opportunity is one area where the parties' constituencies agree. Majorities of both Democrats amid Republicans believe it is the responsibility of the federal government to make sure minorities have schools equal in quality to whites' (WP/Kaiser/Harvard 2001).

## Economic Priorities and Tax Cuts

Republicans and Democrats have fundamentally different views about economic priorities, how to use the federal budget surplus, and tax policy.

Republicans are more likely than Democratic voters to say that cutting income taxes is the top priority for using the budget surplus. Democrats, on the other hand, tend to prefer strengthening social security and Medicare or increasing spending on domestic programs (ABC/WP 2001a).

Republicans are more likely to favor an across-the-board tax cut for all taxpayers,

**Table 27.4**
*Economic Priorities and Tax Cuts*

| | Percent of Registered Voters | |
| --- | --- | --- |
| | Republicans | Democrats |
| Priorities for budget surplus: | | |
| Strengthen social security and Medicare | 16 | 33 |
| Increase spending on domestic programs, such as education or health care | 24 | 41 |
| Reduce national debt | 18 | 18 |
| Cut federal income taxes | 40 | 8 |
| Preferred type of tax cut: | | |
| Across-the-board for all taxpayers | 74 | 30 |
| Smaller, targeted mainly to lower and middle income | 25 | 67 |
| Large tax cut will help the economy | 47 | 19 |
| Tax cuts are: | | |
| Good for the economy | 68 | 53 |
| Bad for the economy | 9 | 19 |

while Democrats generally prefer a smaller tax cut targeted at middle- and lower-income Americans. Republicans are also more likely than Democrats (47 percent to 19 percent) to think a large tax cut helps the economy (WP/Kaiser/Harvard 2000c). Even aside from the recent tax-cut debate, Republicans are more likely than Democrats (68 percent to 53 percent) to think that tax cuts in general are good for the economy (WP/Kaiser/Harvard 1996). (See Table 27.4.)

## Private Investment of Social Security Funds

Democrats, worried that efforts to privatize social security will lead to substantial inequities, are much less interested in introducing private investment into the system than Republicans are. Republicans are more likely to see these changes as opportunities for individual financial growth amid greater consumer responsibility.

More than two-thirds of Republicans, compared with less than half of Democrats, support a plan in which people could choose to invest some of their social security payroll contributions in the stock market (ABC/WP 2001a). This partisan difference may be due in part to the investments people currently have. About two-thirds (68 percent) of Republicans, compared with 45 percent of Democrats, say they own stocks, bonds, or mutual funds, either directly or through a 401(k) plan (WP/Kaiser/Harvard 2001). (See Table 27.5.)

## The 'New Economy' and Trade Agreements

Reflecting a division within the country as a whole, both parties' constituencies are di-

**Table 27.5**
*Social Security*

| | Percent of Registered Voters | |
| --- | --- | --- |
| | Republicans | Democrats |
| Support plan in which people could choose to invest some of their social security contributions in stock market | 69 | 42 |
| Respondent owns stocks, bonds, or mutual funds— either directly or through 401(k) plan | 68 | 45 |

vided in their attitudes about the "new economy" and trade agreements. About four in ten Republicans (41 percent) and Democrats (39 percent) think that most jobs being created in this country in recent years pay well, while about half of each (46 percent of Republicans, 50 percent of Democrats) think the new jobs are mostly low-paying. (See Table 27.6.) Similarly, almost four in ten Republicans (38 percent) and Democrats (36 percent) think that globalization of the world economy is mostly beneficial. Surprisingly, Republicans are more likely (29 percent to 17 percent) to say it is detrimental. About half of both Republicans (50 percent) and Democrats (49 percent) believe that trade agreements between the United States and other countries have cost U.S. jobs rather than created them (22 percent, 20 percent) (WP/Kaiser/Harvard 2000c).

Democrats are more likely than Republicans (43 percent to 31 percent) to believe that the "new economy" actually just helps people who are already rich. A majority of each party's constituency disagrees, but once again, a sizable portion of each party's constituency is less sanguine about the "new economy" (WP/Kaiser/Harvard 2000c).

When it comes to trade with China, opinion within each party is divided. A substantial number of both Democrats (43 percent) and Republicans (49 percent) oppose having free trade with China on the same terms the United States gives its main trading partners (ABC/WP 2001a).

Because both parties contain a number of voters who are skeptical about some of the effects of globalization and free trade, an administration of either party is likely to meet some resistance within Congress and encounter bipartisan efforts to protect particular U.S. industries from foreign competition. A recent example was the bipartisan protectionist effort on behalf of the U.S. steel industry.

## Energy and the Environment

The recent conflict between a Democratic governor of California and a Republican president foreshadows future debates between the parties over energy policy. Republicans put a higher premium on developing long-term energy supplies, while Democrats are more likely to favor conservation and dealing with current energy shortages and prices. Two-thirds (67 percent) of Republi-

***Table 27.6***
*"The New Economy" and Trade Agreements*

| | Percent of Registered Voters | |
| --- | --- | --- |
| | **Republicans** | **Democrats** |
| Most jobs being created in the country today: | | |
| Pay well | 41 | 39 |
| Are low-paying | 46 | 50 |
| Globalization of world economy: | | |
| Is mostly good | 38 | 36 |
| Does not make much difference | 20 | 31 |
| Is mostly bad | 29 | 17 |
| Trade agreements between United States and other countries have: | | |
| Created U.S. jobs | 22 | 20 |
| Cost U.S. jobs | 50 | 49 |
| New economy really just helps people who are already rich | 31 | 43 |
| United States should have free trade with China on the same terms it gives its main trading partners: | | |
| Agree | 44 | 51 |
| Disagree | 49 | 43 |

cans, compared with about half (49 percent) of Democrats, believe that the higher energy priority for the president and Congress is to find long-term energy supplies rather than to control rising gasoline prices and deal with present shortages (Pew/PSRA 2001a). A majority (62 percent) of Democrats favor federal limits on the price of electricity to prevent perceived "price gouging" by suppliers, while 51 percent of Republicans oppose price controls (ABC/WP 2001b). (See Table 27.7.)

Nearly two-thirds (64 percent) of Republicans believe that developing new sources of energy is a higher priority for the country than protecting the environment (28 percent). More Democrats give priority to protecting the environment (50 percent to 40 percent). Moreover, a majority (61 percent) of Republicans believe that expanding exploration and constructing new power plants is the more important priority for U.S. energy policy, while a majority (62 percent) of Democrats see energy conservation and regulation as the more important priority (Pew/PSRA 2001a).

Three-fourths (76 percent) of Republicans, compared with just over half (54 percent) of Democrats, favor investing in more gas pipelines as a way to deal with the energy situation. A majority of Republicans (58 percent) favor building more nuclear power plants, while a majority of Democrats are opposed (ABC/WP 2001b). While a majority of Republicans favor oil exploration or drilling in the Arctic National Wildlife Refuge, Democrats are overwhelmingly opposed (Gallup 2001b, ABC/WP 2001a). This split is reflected in the divergent views expressed by Senate Democratic and House Republican leaders.

Democrats (54 percent) are also more likely than Republicans (39 percent) to say that the greenhouse effect is very dangerous to the environment (Davis et al. 2000).

## What Difference Do All These Results Make?

Economic policy is likely to be strongly affected if one party gains political dominance. Republican ascendancy would likely

### Table 27.7
### Energy and the Environment

| | Percent of Registered Voters | |
| --- | --- | --- |
| | Republicans | Democrats |
| Higher energy priority for president and Congress: | | |
|   Control rising gasoline prices and deal with current shortages | 24 | 37 |
|   Find long-term supplies | 67 | 49 |
| Federal limits on price of electricity to prevent "price gouging" by suppliers: | | |
|   Favor | 46 | 62 |
|   Oppose | 51 | 34 |
| Higher priority for country: | | |
|   Protect environment | 28 | 50 |
|   Develop new sources of energy | 64 | 40 |
| More important priority for U.S. energy policy: | | |
|   Expand exploration/construct new power plants | 61 | 32 |
|   More energy conservation/energy regulations | 33 | 62 |
| As a way to deal with the energy situation, favor: | | |
|   Investing in more gas pipelines | 76 | 54 |
|   Building more nuclear power plants | 58 | 39 |
|   Allowing oil drilling in Arctic National Wildlife Refuge | 62 | 28 |
| Greenhouse effect is very dangerous | 39 | 54 |

result in less federal government spending for services than if Democrats were in power; less regulation of business in general and deregulation of certain industries; larger tax cuts; a flatter tax system and the end of the inheritance tax; more aggressive attempts to create private investment accounts in social security; and more emphasis on expanding domestic energy supplies.

If Democrats gain a dominant position politically, we are likely to see more government spending for services to help middle- and lower-income people; greater government regulation of certain aspects of the economy; less tax-cut activity; less expansion of private investment accounts in social security; and more emphasis on energy conservation.

In the areas where the two parties agree, future election outcomes are unlikely to affect economic policy. For instance, neither party's constituents favor major income redistribution. On the other hand, support is strong in both parties for increasing the minimum wage. Both Republicans and Democrats believe that the federal government is responsible for ensuring that minorities have educational opportunity equal to that of whites. But large majorities of both parties oppose strict forms of affirmative action.

## Wild Cards: An Economic Downturn or an Energy Crisis

Differences between the two parties would matter most if the United States were to experience serious economic problems or a severe energy crisis while one or the other party holds political dominance. If an economic downturn occurred on the Democrats' watch, the federal government would likely intervene by grabbing whatever budget surplus remains and spending it to cushion the downturn's effects. The Democrats would probably also cancel some of the planned tax cuts. If the recession continued for a long time, the Democrats would be willing to return to deficit spending in order to ease the impact of the recession.

In response to a serious economic downturn, Republicans would try to ride out the business cycle, relying on monetary policy. If the recession continued, Republicans are also likely to have a deficit, but by different means than the Democrats. Republicans would probably propose additional tax cuts as a way of stimulating the economy, while avoiding increases in spending.

An economic downturn could also create considerable instability in that a third party candidate could, like Ross Perot and Pat Buchanan, appeal to the substantial minorities in both major parties who do not like free trade agreements or our current immigration policy. Such a third party candidate would likely call for limiting free trade agreements, particularly those with China, while at the same time arguing for tough new restrictions on immigration. In addition, incumbent members of Congress could face serious primary challenges from opponents campaigning on these issues.

An energy crisis would also elicit substantially different responses, depending on which party was in power. Republicans would likely avoid major federal government regulation of the marketplace. At the same time, they would encourage increasing energy supplies even if it meant difficult environmental tradeoffs. Democrats, on the other hand, would emphasize energy conservation and be less likely to make environmental tradeoffs. They would also increase regulation of the pricing policies of the energy industry and increase subsidies for low-income people affected by sharply rising fuel costs.

To many in the media, congressional debates about economic policy sound like partisan bickering and individual contests of will. However, these debates reflect real philosophical differences about economic policy issues. Thus, if the party composition of Congress and the presidency changes strongly in favor of one party or the other, a substantial shift in economic policy would occur. But if the balance continues to be nearly even as it is today, economic policies are likely to remain muddled and to represent compromises on issues where the parties substantially disagree.

## Note

1. Even if one party gains such clear dominance, structures within the country's pluralistic political system will resist sweeping change. Constraints include independent regulatory agencies, trade agreements and treaties, and prerogatives that can be exercised by individual members of the U.S. Senate. Also, on specific issues, members of Congress sometimes do not vote with their own party.

## For Further Reading

ABC News/Washington Post Poll (ABC/WP). 2001a. Storrs, CT: Roper Center for Public Opinion Research, April 19–22.

———. 2001b. Storrs, CT: Roper Center for Public Opinion Research, May 31–June 3.

Barone, Michael. 2001. "The 49 Percent Nation." *National Journal* 33, no. 23: 1710–16.

Davis, James A., Tom W. Smith, and Peter V. Marsden. 2000. General Social Surveys, 1972–2000 (machine-readable data file). Chicago: National Opinion Research Center.

Gallup Poll. 2001a. Storrs, CT: Roper Center for Public Opinion Research, March 26–28.

———. 2001b. Storrs, CT: Roper Center for Public Opinion Research, May 7–9.

Jacobson, Gary C. 2001. "A House and Senate Divided: The Clinton Legacy and the Congressional Elections of 2000." *Political Science Quarterly* 116, no. 1: 5–27.

Pew Research Center/Princeton Survey Research Associates (Pew/PSRA). 1999. Storrs, CT: Roper Center for Public Opinion Research, July 14–September 9.

———. 2001a. Storrs, CT: Roper Center for Public Opinion Research, May 15–20.

———. 2001b. Storrs, CT: Roper Center for Public Opinion Research, June 13–17.

Washington Post/Henry J. Kaiser Family Foundation/Harvard University (WP/Kaiser/Harvard). 1996. Economy Survey. Storrs, CT: Roper Center for Public Opinion Research, July 22–August 2.

———. 1998. Values Survey. Storrs, CT: Roper Center for Public Opinion Research, July 29–August 18.

———. 2000a. Issue Survey 2: Health Care and Medicare. Storrs, CT: Roper Center for Public Opinion Research, July 5–18, 2000.

———. 2000b. Issue Survey 3: Moral Values. Storrs, CT: Roper Center for Public Opinion Research, September 7–17, 2000.

———. 2000c. Issue Survey 4: The Economy and Taxes. Storrs, CT: Roper Center for Public Opinion Research, October 12–19, 2000.

———. 2001. Racial Attitudes Survey. Storrs, CT: Roper Center for Public Opinion Research, March 8–April 22.

## Review

1. Briefly summarize the differences between Republicans and Democrats on the issue of Federal government spending and government regulation.

2. What is meant by economic equity, and how would you characterize the attitudes of Republicans and Democrats on the issue?

3. How do Republicans and Democrats differ on the issue of economic priorities and tax cuts?

4. Discuss the positions of those in the two parties on private investment in Social Security and on the "new economy" and trade agreements.

5. How would you characterize the position of Republicans and Democrats on issues related to energy and the environment?

6. Why would differences between the two parties matter most in an economic downturn or an energy crisis?

## Application

Make a list of all the issues discussed in this selection, and where the majority of those in each party stand on each. Note your own position. Are you consistently on the same side as one or the other party? If so, or if not, why? What factors do you believe have influenced your political attitudes? If you favor the Democratic position on some issues and the Republican on others, how would you decide which party to support? How would you compare your political position with those of other members of your family? If there are differences, how would you explain them? Have a close friend answer all of these same questions. What would you conclude about the political leanings of Americans?

## Related Web Sites

1. *http://www.democrats.org/* and *http://www.rnc.org/* are the sites, respectively, for the Democratic National Committee and Republican National Committee. They offer perspectives on current events from the two parties' points of view.

2. *http://www.politics.com/* This site is a non-partisan portal for political resources, news, and information on party politics, campaigns, and government.

Reprinted from: Robert Blendon, John Benson, Mollyann Brodie, Drew Altman, and Kathleen Weldon, "In Economic Policy, How Much Does It Matter Which Party Governs?" In *Challenge* 44 (2001): 59–77. Copyright © 2001 by M.E. Sharpe, Inc. Reprinted with permission. ✦

# 28

# National Security Versus Civil Liberties

*Nancy V. Baker*

**Terrorism** *has become a major focus of concern in America since the September 11, 2001, hijacking of four passenger jets resulted in the destruction of the Twin Towers of the World Trade Center in New York and considerable damage to the Pentagon in Washington, D.C. This was not the first terrorist act in the United States. Between 1980 and 2000, the F.B.I. identified 335 incidents or suspected incidents of terrorism. Of those, 247 were attributed to domestic terrorists (e.g., the bombing of the federal building in Oklahoma City) and 88 to international terrorists. The more than 3,000 people killed in the 2001 attacks, however, galvanized the nation into both concern and action.*

*Some of the actions initiated by the federal government in response to terrorist attacks raise serious questions about civil liberties. In the immediate aftermath of the 2001 attacks, more than 1,200 people suspected of violating immigration laws or of being material witnesses to terrorist activity were detained for considerable periods of time without being charged. Attorney General John Ashcroft changed federal rules to give the government more power to monitor conversations and activities. A Department of Homeland Security was created to combat terrorism and was given broad powers that could infringe on civil liberties.*

*Nancy Baker details some of the ways in which civil liberties are threatened by the war against terrorism. Her work raises the question of whether the American people are willing to forego civil liberties and give the government much broader power to intrude into*

*their lives in order to gain a measure of security.*

Soon after the George W. Bush administration began crafting its response to the terrorist attacks of September 11, 2001, voices could be heard questioning the impact of its antiterrorism measures on civil liberty. The Patriot Act would give the FBI "a blank warrant," warned the *Village Voice* (Hentoff 2001). When names of the detained were not released, one editorial asked "Why Not Disclose?" (Editorial 2001). The debate has not died down. In fact, according to the *Washington Post*, it has crystallized around opposing views of the nature of threat and the best way to confront it (Lane 2002a). Almost two years after the attacks, *The New York Times* discussed calculating the benefits and costs of the limits on liberty (Andrews 2003), and *The Economist* (2003) posed "A question of freedom." In the intervening months, publications ranging from *The Christian Science Monitor* (Kiefer 2002) to the Sunday newspaper insert *Parade Magazine* (Klein 2002) have covered the debate summarized as national security versus civil liberties.

The debate has special saliency during wartime, because the suggestion that there is another side than the government's implies dissension and even subversion. This was the point raised by Attorney General John Ashcroft in Senate hearings in December 2001: "To those who scare peace-loving people with phantoms of lost liberty, my message is this: Your tactics only aid terrorists—for they erode our national unity and diminish our resolve . . . " (U.S. Senate 2001, 316). This grim warning is particularly disturbing in the context of a war against terrorism, because the war has no clear end or scope; it is not waged against a nation-state or even an ideology, but against age-old methods of violence and terror; it is bound neither by time, geography, nor specific adversaries. President Bush has noted the difference as well, commenting that, "We're at war in a different kind of war" (CNN 2003). . . .

Another product of wartime is that civil liberties are generally categorized as luxury items, like silk stockings during World War II, that divert valuable resources from the war effort. Historically, once war is over, those luxuries are again embraced. The White House, Congress, and the courts then reassert civil liberty values, perhaps even chiding themselves for their earlier restrictions. But a war on terrorism, bringing a securitization of domestic life, creates a different metaphor. Liberties are not luxuries to be sacrificed in the short term until we can afford them again. Liberties are gaping holes in the security fabric; they must be sealed off permanently if the nation is to be safe. The demands of a war on terrorism also undercut the likelihood that liberties can be reasserted, because a war without a clear end will never produce the peace of mind necessary to reflect on what we have lost.

***"Firmly rooted in the Constitution."*** The administration characterizes its antiterrorism measures as fully consistent with civil liberties and denies that any of its actions constitute restrictions. A commitment to civil liberties extends up to the president, according to Ashcroft: "President Bush insists that our responses to evil respect the Constitution and value the freedoms of justice the Constitution guaranteed" (CNN 2003). The attorney general has been the most outspoken member of the administration on this theme. He told Senators this past spring, "The Department of Justice has acted thoughtfully, carefully, and within the Constitution of the United States, that framework for freedom" (U.S. Senate 2003). Throughout the past two years, he has made similar assurances in press releases and public statements when discussing antiterrorism measures. For example, he described the plan to end informational firewalls between federal prosecutors and intelligence officers as "rooted in our Constitutional liberties" (U.S. Senate 2002), and the post-9/11 interrogation of thousands of foreign nationals as exhibiting "full respect for the rights and dignity of the individuals being interviewed" (Attorney General Transcript 2002a). He called the revised guidelines permitting FBI agents to monitor public gatherings as a demonstration to the American public that the agency would protect them from terror-

ism "with a scrupulous respect for civil rights and personal freedoms" (Attorney General Remarks 2002a). He reassured a conference of federal appellate judges that "our post-September 11 policies have been carefully crafted to prevent terrorist attacks while protecting the privacy and civil liberties of Americans" (Attorney General Remarks 2002b). In a similar vein, he told a conference of U.S. attorneys that "our actions are firmly rooted in the Constitution . . . and consistent with the laws passed by Congress" (Attorney General Remarks 2002c), using the same phrase a week later when addressing the International Association of Chiefs of Police (Attorney General Remarks 2002d). He said he tells his staff every day, "'Think outside the box,' but . . . 'Think inside the Constitution'" (Anderson 2003a).

The attorney general's continued references to civil liberties and the Constitution have not settled the debate. His steady insistence that liberties are not affected has not satisfied the critics, largely because it appears to be contradicted by the actual impact of some of the new policies and procedures. Furthermore, Ashcroft himself has framed civil liberties as a point of vulnerability from a national security perspective. Terrorists, he has argued, "exploit our openness—not randomly or haphazardly—but by deliberate, premeditated design." Our freedoms, he has said, are being turned against us, as "means of freedom's destruction" (Attorney General Remarks 2002d). He told senators in December 2001, "We are at war with an enemy who abuses individual rights as it abuses jet airliners: as weapons with which to kill Americans" (U.S. Senate 2001). In other words, a system of civil liberties makes the country more vulnerable to future attack; it is part of the terrorist arsenal.

## Restrictions on Civil Liberties

John Ashcroft sees two broad areas of civil liberties as particular weaknesses waiting to be exploited by terrorists—free press and due process rights. He described a seized al Qaeda training manual where "terrorists are told how to use America's freedom as a weapon against us. They are instructed to use the benefits of a free press—newspapers, magazines and broadcasts—to stalk and kill their victims. They are instructed to exploit our judicial process for the success of their operations" (U.S. Senate 2001). The logic is clear: to foil the terrorist plot, the administration must enact antiterrorism measures that ensure greater governmental control of information, fewer procedural protections for people linked to terrorism (as either suspects or material witnesses), and enhanced government surveillance. Not surprisingly, these are the civil liberty encroachments most lamented by policy critics.

Civil liberty concerns raised in federal courts have varied from free speech to discrimination to criminal procedural rights, as a report from the American Civil Liberties Union illustrates. Documenting its litigation activities from September 11, 2001 to March 14, 2003, as either a party or a friend of court, the ACLU chronicled thirty cases involving allegations of religious profiling, closed immigration hearings, government refusal to release names of detainees, misuse of material witness warrants, and unsuccessful efforts to obtain government documents through the Freedom of Information Act. The organization has been involved in some of the higher profile challenges to the administration's antiterrorism efforts, including enemy combatant cases, the gag order on the attorney of convicted shoe bomber Richard Reid, and the use of Foreign Intelligence Surveillance search warrants for criminal investigations (ACLU Report 2003)....

## Limiting the Flow of Information

Control of information has been a core component of the Bush administration's antiterrorism agenda. However, even before September 11, 2001, the administration had sought to limit press and public access to some information, including refusing to release the Reagan administration papers in January 2001, as stipulated in the Presidential Records Act. The White House from the start has been concerned with the erosion of confidentiality and executive privilege in previous administrations.

National security and the war against terrorism have heightened the administration's determination to control the flow of information to an unprecedented degree. Government agencies stripped their web sites of reports, data, and maps. FBI agents visited government repositories and libraries to ensure that other sensitive material was destroyed (Cha 2002). All federal departments and agencies were instructed to safeguard "information that could be misused to harm the security of our Nation and the safety of our people," including protecting from disclosure unclassified but sensitive information (White House Chief of Staff 2002). The attorney general has reportedly resisted providing Congress with information on the implementation of the Patriot Act and other antiterrorism measures (Bettelheim 2002; Koszczuk 2002).

A month following the 9/11 attacks, Ashcroft issued a new policy governing Freedom of Information requests, shifting the presumption away from disclosure by promising department and agency heads that the Justice Department would defend their decisions not to disclose unless that decision lacked "a sound legal basis" (U.S. Department of Justice 2001a). Using this new interpretation of the statute, the Justice Department then refused to release aggregated government data to the Transactional Records Access Clearinghouse (TRAC) at Syracuse University, where it had been available since 1989 to researchers, members of the press, Congress, and others interested in gauging how well the government was doing its job. The department cited a concern that the data could "interfere with anti-terrorism investigations and endanger lives," although others suggested the action could be tied to the release of a TRAC study showing that the FBI exaggerated the number of terrorism cases it referred (Grimaldi 2002). These and other actions have led some critics, such as Larry Klayman of the conservative Judicial Watch, to categorize the administration as "the most secretive of our lifetime, even more secretive than the Nixon administration" (quoted in Elsner 2002). In terms of free press and free expression since 9/11, detentions and immigration hearings have triggered the most questions concerning secrecy.

## Nondisclosure of Names of the Detained

Several free press cases involve due process and privacy questions as well. Such was the case when the federal government refused to disclose the names, locations, and charges against the approximately 1,200 people detained in the aftermath of the attacks. The exact number of people held and other details about their cases are unknown, because the government stopped issuing that information in November 2001 (Goldstein and Eggen 2001). Both the media and defense attorneys protested what they saw as violations of the First and Sixth Amendments to the Constitution. At their annual meeting, the American Bar Association condemned the secret detentions and denial of counsel (*Washington Post* 2002). Reportedly, secrecy went even further in some cases, where defense attorneys were not permitted to remove documents from court and were placed under federal gag orders to bar public discussion about their clients (Goldstein 2001; Fainaru and Williams 2002).

Making an early challenge to this secrecy, nineteen organizations filed a Freedom of Information Act request with the Justice Department to compel disclosure of the names and locations of the detainees, the identities of their counsel, and any relevant legal orders (*Center for National Security Studies, et al., v. Department of Justice* 2001). Refusing the request, Ashcroft relied on his new policy governing the Freedom of Information Act. A lawsuit was filed. The federal district judge, Gladys Kessler, ordered the government to release the names of the detainees and their attorneys, but not the other requested information. Then she issued a stay when the government announced it would seek an expedited appeal to the DC Circuit Court. Oral arguments were held in November 2002 and the decision is pending (*Center for National Security Studies, et al., v. Department of Justice* 2002).

Another challenge to the secrecy rule was raised by a New Jersey state judge who, in March 2002, ordered Justice to release the names of those held in New Jersey county jails on an INS contract. The state judge, finding that secret detentions violate state laws, gave the department a deadline by which to comply, adding that "the federal government was still required to obey the law" (Edwards 2002a). Two weeks later, the judge shortened the length of time that the Justice Department had to comply (Edwards 2002b). At that point, the department issued an interim INS rule that barred state or other non-federal prison facilities from releasing any information relating to INS detainees held under a federal contract. Justice argued that "The courts . . . are ill-equipped to become sufficiently steeped in foreign intelligence matters to serve effectively in the review of secrecy classifications in that area." Furthermore, "application of state law in this area has the potential to threaten the Attorney General's [national security] mission" (INS 2002a). When the rule became part of the Federal Register a few days later (INS 2002b), the state court of appeals reversed the state judge, and the New Jersey Supreme Court denied review (*ACLU of N.J. v. County of Hudson*).

The attorney general has provided a number of explanations for the decision to close hearings and keep confidential the names of people detained by the government. When asked initially, Ashcroft referred to legal constraints that tied his hands, but when asked by a reporter what law would be broken if the names were released, Ashcroft replied that no law compelled him to release the names and so he was upholding the law (Transcript 2001). He gave a slightly different explanation to the Senate Judiciary Committee, telling them, "All persons being detained have the right to contact their lawyers and their families. Out of respect for their privacy, and concern for saving lives, we will not publicize the names of those detained" (U.S. Senate 2001).

## Closure of Immigration Hearings

Citing national security concerns, the Justice Department also has closed hundreds of immigration hearings of foreign nationals detained after 9/11. The "Creppy Directive," issued by Chief Immigration Judge Michael Creppy ten days after the attacks, institutionalized new security precautions for immigration cases deemed to be of "special interest." The new provisions were initiated by the attorney general and disseminated through Creppy to other immigration judges. Immigration judges are Justice Department employees and not part of the regular judiciary (Fainaru 2002). The Creppy Directive requires that hearings be closed to the public, judges not discuss these cases with anyone outside the Immigration Court, and judges involved in special interest cases have secret clearance because "some of these cases may ultimately involve classified evidence" (U.S. Department of Justice Memo 2001b). In July 2002, the Justice Department issued an interim operating policy and procedures memorandum authorizing immigration judges to issue protective orders and seal case records to shield information that is not classified "but whose disclosure could nonetheless jeopardize investigations" (U.S. Department of Justice OPPM 2002a). These measures have triggered a number of legal challenges.

Rabih Haddad, a Lebanese national living in Ann Arbor, Michigan, was facing deportation proceedings for overstaying his visa when, without prior notice to him or his attorney, his hearing was ordered closed to his family, the press, and the public, including Michigan Congressman John Conyers. He was detained and denied bail. Haddad, Conyers, and *The Detroit Free Press* and *Detroit News* sought an injunction to stop the government from closing his future hearings. Haddad claimed the blanket closure not only violated statutory and administrative law, but also the Due Process Clause of the Fifth Amendment. The newspapers argued that the Creppy Directive, both on its face and as applied in Haddad's case, violated their right of access under the First Amendment. Government attorneys—as-

serting that hearings are not criminal trials covered by the Sixth Amendment—argued "no constitutional rights are abridged by exclusion of the press and public from the hearings." They added that, because immigration matters rest with the president and Congress, the U.S. District Court lacked jurisdiction; therefore, the court should dismiss the case or at least "apply a deferential level of scrutiny" (*Haddad v. Ashcroft* 2002, 3).

Judge Nancy Edmunds of the district court ruled that blanket closures of deportation hearings are unconstitutional, and she granted the injunction (*Detroit Free Press, et al., v. Ashcroft* 2002a). The government appealed the ruling to the Sixth Circuit, which affirmed the district court. Circuit Judge Damon Keith penned a now famous phrase, "Democracies die behind closed doors," writing later in the opinion that, "Open proceedings, with a vigorous and scrutinizing press, serve to ensure the durability of our democracy" (*Detroit Free Press, et al., v. Ashcroft* 2002b). Keith acknowledged that the "political branches" have plenary authority over substantive immigration laws and decisions, but that non-substantive laws and policies—ones that involve procedural questions—are subject to judicial review when they abridge constitutional rights. He noted, "The Government certainly has a compelling interest in preventing terrorism," but the Creppy Directive and interim Protective Orders and Sealing of Records were both over-broad by closing all special interest cases without a case-by-case assessment, and under-inclusive by permitting some disclosure of sensitive information. He concluded, "By the simple assertion of 'national security,' the Government seeks a process where it may, without review, designate certain classes of cases as 'special interest cases' and, behind closed doors, adjudicate the merits of these cases to deprive non-citizens of their fundamental liberty interests. This, we simply may not countenance" (*Detroit Free Press, et al., v. Ashcroft* 2002b). Later, in Haddad's case, Judge Edmunds granted another preliminary injunction and denied the government's motion to dismiss. Taking cognizance of the securitized environment, she noted that, in the "climate of fear" since 9/11, Haddad's designation as a special interest case was likely to have "tainted the immigration judge's decision" to continue to detain him. Because he had a right to due process and a fair hearing, the government had to either release him from detention within ten days or hold an open detention hearing with a new judge (*Haddad v. Ashcroft* 2002). . . .

## The Secrecy Rationale

The government insists that "the Constitution does not require immigration proceedings to be opened in a way that provides valuable information to terrorist organizations or others who wish to harm Americans" (U.S. Department of Justice Press Release 2002b). Elsewhere, it has argued that opening these hearings threatens American lives because terrorists would then be able to glean information about ongoing terrorist investigations (Schulhofer 2003). Ashcroft believes that such information has to be kept confidential lest it make the nation vulnerable to attack. "When the United States is at war," he said, "I will not share valuable intelligence with our enemies" (Transcript 2001). In other words, law enforcement information—available in the past to the public—constitutes valuable intelligence during a war against terrorism.

These comments point to the Justice Department's legal reasoning in support of government secrecy, the so-called mosaic theory. This theory, developed by the CIA, draws an analogy between building a mosaic and gathering bits of seemingly unimportant information (Goldstein 2001). Even facially inconsequential pieces could be critical to constructing the whole picture. For example, in Haddad's case, the government warned that an open hearing could result in the disclosure of "bits and pieces of information that seem innocuous in isolation, but when pieced together with other bits and pieces, aid [terrorists] in creating a bigger picture of the Government's anti-terrorism investigation" (*Detroit Free Press, et al., v. Ashcroft* 2002b). Such information, Justice warned, "allows terrorist organizations to alter their patterns of activity to [evade] detection"

(U.S. Department of Justice 2002c). In fighting the New Jersey state judge's order to release the names of detainees, the Justice Department defended the secrecy as necessary to ensure that seemingly innocuous but vital information not be communicated to terrorists on the outside (INS 2002a).

Supporting this view, William Barr, former attorney general in the first Bush administration, told the Senate Judiciary Committee, "Information about who is presently detained by the government, when and where they were arrested, their citizenship, and like information could be of great value to criminal associates who remain free" (quoted in Knickerbocker 2001). The mosaic theory has also been applied to justify deprivations of due process. The government has cited the theory to defend its incarceration of hundreds of people for relatively minor immigration violations. In some immigration cases, for example, a seven-page FBI affidavit outlining the mosaic theory has been used to argue that individuals accused of even minor violations should be denied bail, because the government might later find that they fit into the larger terrorist picture (Goldstein 2001). Even individuals innocent of any crime still might need to be detained as material witnesses because they could have some small piece of knowledge that could aid investigators in understanding the terrorist threat.

## Limiting Rights to Due Process

Antiterrorism measures have raised multiple questions relating to due process, specifically the presumption of innocence, the writ of habeas corpus, and the rights to counsel, a speedy and public jury trial, confront witnesses, and search and arrest warrants based on probable cause. Many of these procedural rights are implicated in the president's military order that "terrorists and those who support them" can be "detained and, when tried . . . tried for violations of the laws of war and other applicable laws by military tribunals" (Bush 2001).

Some administration officials agree with civil libertarians that the government's aggressive legal response in pursuing suspected terrorists alters traditional law enforcement and court practice. According to one official, the process followed for suspected terrorists "is different than the criminal procedure system we all know and love. It's a separate track for people we catch in the war" against terrorism (quoted in Lane 2002b, 30). Unlike ordinary crime, the government asserts, terrorism must be stopped in advance as well as prosecuted, and this compelling proactive mission necessitates different procedures.

But the national security mandate has not produced consistent procedures "or even understandable principles" in government prosecutions for terrorism, as Fisher noted after reviewing the cases of John Walker Lindh, Richard Reid, Zacarias Moussaoui, Yaser Esam Hamdi, and Jose Padilla (Fisher 2003). Padilla and Hamdi, U.S. citizens who have been designated enemy combatants by the president, appear to face indefinite detention in military custody without charges. Lindh, a U.S. citizen, and Reid, a British citizen, were tried in federal civilian courts, as is Moussaoui, a French citizen, although the administration hinted that it might transfer his case to a military tribunal because the district court granted a request by his attorneys to interview an al Qaeda leader in U.S. custody (Shenon 2003).

In effect, instead of following even a broad reading of due process, whatever that process is, executive decision making in this area has been characterized by an element of arbitrariness. Solicitor General Theodore Olson, who heads the government's litigation work in the Justice Department, suggests that following established guidelines is incompatible with new security demands. He described the method of designating a person an enemy combatant this way: "There will be judgments and instincts and evaluations and implementations that have to be made by the executive that are probably going to be different from day to day, depending on the circumstances" (Lane 2002b, 30). Such subjective and changeable criteria undercut the very notion of due process....

## Presumption of Innocence

A key feature of the American legal system is the presumption that a person is innocent until proven guilty by the state; in criminal cases, the state must prove its case beyond a reasonable doubt. However, since the attacks of 9/11, this presumption has been suspended as it applies to people—particularly younger men—who are Muslim and/or Middle Eastern.

The first due process issue to emerge in the immediate wake of the terror attacks concerned the detention of approximately 1,200 foreign nationals as part of the Justice Department's "preventive campaign of arrest and detention" of people presumed to be national security threats or material witnesses of such threats. The foreign nationals were held on suspicion of minor crimes, but, according to Ashcroft's chief policy adviser, Assistant Attorney General Viet Dinh, such detentions were "within our prosecutorial discretion. If we suspect you of terrorist activity, we will use our prosecutorial discretion to keep you off the streets" (Oliphant 2001, 1). Ashcroft has argued that this approach is an effective strategy to stop future terrorist attacks, the department's new overarching mission. Consistent with this new mission, the detentions have been aimed less at investigating past attacks than at disrupting potential future attacks (Goldstein 2001; Attorney General Transcript 2002a). The USA Patriot Act, passed a month after 9/11, grants the attorney general broad authority to detain until deportation any foreign national whom he certifies to be a terrorist or "engaged in any other activity that endangers the national security of the United States." Within seven days of their detention, people must be placed in deportation proceedings or charged with a criminal offense, unless—in the attorney general's opinion—"removal is unlikely in the reasonably foreseeable future" and if release "will threaten the national security of the United States or the safety of the community or any person" (Patriot Act, Sec. 412).

Eight weeks following the terrorist attacks, the *Washington Post* identified 235 of the 1,147 people detained at that time, and found that three fifths were being held on immigration charges and 75 had been released. A small number were detained on material witness warrants and about ten were believed to have some link to al Qaeda or the hijackers. Despite the government's formal position condemning profiling of Muslim or Arab Americans (see, for example, Patriot Act, Sec. 102), most of those detained were from Saudi Arabia, Egypt, and Pakistan, almost all men in their twenties and thirties. A few were U.S. citizens (Goldstein 2001). Those held specifically as material witnesses also were primarily from the Middle East, according to a December 2002 report (Fainaru and Williams 2002).

In addition to the detentions, the FBI sought in the months following the terrorist attacks to interview 5,000 foreign nationals in the U.S., most from Muslim and Arab states. Denying that the interviews were coercive or that they constituted profiling, Ashcroft said people were selected for interviews "because they fit criteria designed to identify persons who might have knowledge of foreign-based terrorists" (Attorney General Transcript 2002a). Late in 2002, the government implemented another program targeting primarily Muslims and Arabs when it required tens of thousands to report to Immigration and Naturalization offices to be questioned, fingerprinted, and photographed. The first set of immigrants to report in California faced mass arrests, with estimates ranging from 250 by the INS to 1,000 by immigration lawyers (Loney 2003). When war with Iraq erupted in March 2003, the government issued an order to jail people from 33 mostly Muslim countries who seek asylum in the United States on the grounds of political persecution. The countries were selected because they have a terrorism presence. This new policy, according to Homeland Security Secretary Tom Ridge, provides time for U.S. officials to determine whether asylum seekers are genuinely in danger in their home states, or if they are seeking entry to the U.S. for other—perhaps criminal—reasons (Anderson 2003b; Mintz 2003).

These and other measures appear to target people on the basis of their ethnic or religious backgrounds instead of any particular-

ized suspicion. As a result, says a spokesman for the Council on American-Islamic Relations, "All Muslims are now suspects" (Lichtblau and Liptak 2003). The burden of proof is on them to establish their innocence.

## Material Witness Warrants

FBI agents used the Material Witness Statute of 1984 as the legal basis to arrest and jail persons suspected of knowing something in the investigation of terrorism. The statute was intended to apply to the reluctant witness whose testimony is material in a criminal trial; those held are entitled to counsel and a bond hearing. As of December 2002, the Washington Post was able to identify 44 people held as material witnesses, 20 of whom had never been called to testify before a grand jury. Detentions ranged from a few days to more than 400 days. Many people were held under maximum security conditions, such as solitary confinement and 24 hour lighting. Many had difficulty contacting family members or attorneys in their first weeks of incarceration. Most of the cases were under judicial sealing orders, which left some defense attorneys uncertain about what information they could disclose about their clients (Fainaru and Williams 2002). . . .

## Writ of Habeas Corpus

One of the most dramatic breaks from precedent is the president's designation of two U.S. citizens as enemy combatants, thereby removing them from the regular criminal justice process and even stripping them of the right to petition for a writ of habeas corpus. The administration has placed the men, Yaser Esam Hamdi and Jose Padilla, in indefinite military detention without charge and without counsel. Hamdi was captured on the battlefield in Afghanistan; Padilla was arrested in Chicago in connection with a plan to make and detonate a "dirty bomb." The Hamdi and Padilla cases illustrate how the securitized environment as framed by the administration is fundamentally altering the relationship between the citizen and the state. At issue is the writ of habeas corpus. Enshrined in the body of the Constitution itself, it is, in the words of habeas corpus scholar Eric Freedman, "perhaps the most cherished remedy in Anglo-American jurisprudence" (2000). A petition for a writ compels the government to produce a person it holds before a court, so that the court may determine whether the detention is lawful. In the enemy combatant cases, particularly those involving U.S. citizens, both the executive branch and some federal judges are treating the right as optional and even irrelevant in the face of the terrorist threat.

Some lawyers outside of government, such as Alan Dershowitz of Harvard Law School, defend the detentions as necessary in a time of national emergency. "No civilized nation confronting serious danger has ever relied exclusively on criminal convictions for past offenses," Dershowitz writes, noting that every country has applied administrative or preventive detention to those "who are thought to be dangerous but who might not be convictable under conventional criminal law" (quoted in Taylor 2002). Dershowitz's position accords with the administration's contention that Hamdi and Padilla constitute security threats that are so severe that regular constitutional processes must be bypassed. For example, after inaccurately describing a dirty bomb as capable of causing "mass death and injury," Ashcroft announced that "the safety of all Americans and the national security interests of the United States require that Abdullah Al Muhajir—Padilla's Muslim name—be detained by the Defense Department as an enemy combatant" (Attorney General Transcript 2002b). President Bush determined that Padilla constituted "a continuing, present and grave danger to the national security of the United States" and that his detention "was necessary to prevent him from aiding al Qaeda in its efforts to attack the United States or its armed forces, other government personnel or citizens" (Mobbs Declaration on Padilla 2002, 5).

Yet the mere assertion that a person poses a threat, absent a meaningful judicial opportunity to challenge the basis of that asser-

tion, guts the habeas corpus protection in the Constitution. The Mobbs Declaration poses this problem. The government insists that it provides a sufficient factual basis for both Hamdi's and Padilla's designations as enemy combatants, although some federal judges have disagreed, finding instead that the record as established by Michael Mobbs is subject to challenge. Mobbs is the special advisor to the Undersecretary of Defense Policy, who handles national security and defense policy. Charged with heading the Detainee Policy Group, Mobbs drafted a declaration for the court for each man, laying out the evidence that led the president to make his determination. The courts were told not to second-guess that assessment. The declaration for Padilla, however, raises some questions of fact that Padilla, with counsel, might be able to challenge. For example, Mobbs notes in a footnote some problems with the two primary confidential sources on Padilla. One of the sources had recanted some of his testimony, their statements on Padilla were only partially corroborated independently, and one source was on drugs for a medical condition during the interview (Mobbs Declaration on Padilla 2002).

The federal district judges in both cases came to similar conclusions, that both men should have access to counsel, even if in a limited capacity to assist with a challenge to the factual record on which the designation was based. Judge Robert Doumar permitted Hamdi a private meeting with his federal public defenders, a decision that was immediately appealed by the Justice Department to the Fourth Circuit Court of Appeals (Amon 2002). In the government brief, the Justice Department asserted that civilian courts "may not second-guess the military's enemy combatant determination," because it constitutes a core executive power. The brief argued, "A court's inquiry should come to an end once the military has shown in the return that it has determined that the detainee is an enemy combatant" (Brief 2002). While not conceding that federal courts have no role to play, Chief Judge Harvie Wilkinson for the Fourth Circuit gave government attorneys the decision they wanted, ruling that further judicial inquiry into Hamdi's status would undermine "the efficiency and morale of American forces" (*Hamdi v. Rumsfeld*). Wilkinson cited the Mobbs Declaration as providing a legally valid basis on its face for Hamdi's detention. Freedman compares the Fourth Circuit's decision with the case of the five knights held in the Tower of London in 1627. When they applied for a writ of habeas corpus to the keeper of the tower and then the court, they were told that they were held by his "Majesty's special command," and the court was not competent to look into the king's reasoning (Freedman 2003). . . .

## Curtailing Privacy Expectations

Many of the privacy concerns triggered by the war against terrorism can be traced directly to the Patriot Act. Title II of the statute, entitled Enhanced Surveillance Procedures, expands the government's power to intercept wire, oral, and electronic communications; to engage in open register and trap and trace searches; to get access to certain business, library, and medical records; to utilize a single search warrant for nation-wide searches; to expand the scope of subpoenas for electronic communications; to block notification of the search to the person whose records have been searched; to limit the liability of persons who disclose required records to the government and thereby violate privacy laws; and to permit information sharing between law enforcement and intelligence-gathering agencies (Patriot Act 2001). Even in the rush of passage, legislators were concerned enough by privacy encroachments that they instituted a sunset clause of December 31, 2005 for many of these provisions (Patriot Act, Sec. 224).

Title II expands the application of the Foreign Intelligence Surveillance Act (FISA), which permits surveillance under a much lower standard (preponderance of evidence versus probable cause) and establishes a separate and secret court process to consider search warrant applications, the FISA court. When passed in 1978, the Foreign Intelligence Surveillance Act permitted an otherwise unconstitutional wiretap or search if the purpose was to monitor a suspected spy or agent of a foreign power. Evidence gathered would be for intelligence uses and not introduced in a criminal trial.

One of the fiercest battles in the Senate during the Patriot Act's passage reportedly dealt with the phrasing of an amendment expanding FISA's purpose. Ashcroft advocated broadening the language so that foreign intelligence was simply "a purpose" and not "the purpose" of a FISA warrant, thus making the FISA process generally available to law enforcement not engaged in foreign intelligence work. Concerned with the implications, some senators preferred that foreign intelligence remain the "primary purpose" of a FISA search. In the end, compromise language produced "a significant purpose" (Patriot Act, Sec. 218). According to Assistant Attorney General Michael Chertoff, this language still gives the administration the leeway it wanted to conduct electronic and physical searches under FISA (McGee 2001b). . . .

## Conclusion

The terrorist strikes of two years ago, coupled with the ongoing threat of future attacks, have posed an enormous challenge to each level and branch of government, especially the national executive. President Bush and his administration could have pursued a number of possible courses of action. When Bush framed the crisis as a war against terrorism, the homefront became a battlefront, and the markers of an open society—a free press, individual protections in criminal proceedings, and privacy from government snooping—were conceptually transformed by the administration into opportunities for the enemy. That vision of 9/11 necessarily has led to greater restrictions on the flow of information about government, fewer due process protections, and less privacy from government surveillance, as documented in this study. The administration seems to see civil liberties as security problems that require strong executive action. Limits on civil liberties are not simply byproducts of security measures, as they often have been in previous national crises. Instead, limits on liberties are the point of many of the security measures.

Whereas a desire for security has motivated these antiterrorism policies, some of these measures may undermine the government's ability to address the terrorist threat in the long run. For example, the Justice Department's new mission of stopping a terrorist attack requires replacing the traditionally patient investigative approach of the FBI with a preemptive strategy to arrest suspected terrorists quickly, before informants can be developed, leads can be exhausted, or full criminal cases can been built (Locy and Johnson 2003). The policy of preemptive arrest and detentions has been criticized by several former high-ranking members of the FBI, including former FBI Director William H. Webster, who said that the approach may disrupt terrorist activities but will not eradicate the threat. Using a different approach, that is, long-term criminal investigations coupled with intelligence gathering, the FBI was able to prevent 131 terrorist attacks from 1981 to 2000, according to Webster and others. And the measures did not "jump all over people's private lives," he added (quoted in McGee 2001a, 8).

Regrettably, the national security versus civil liberties debate is difficult to engage at the national level, because many who serve in the Bush administration deny that rights are violated in any way. This denial is not a misrepresentation from their point of view; rather, it can be understood as part of the larger security picture: an open debate on rights would be a sign of disunity that the national security interest as defined by this administration cannot allow.

## References

*ACLU of New Jersey v. County of Hudson.* 2002. Supreme Court of New Jersey. 174 N.J. 190; 803 A.2d 1162; 2002 N.J. LEXIS 1159.

ACLU Report. 2003. The ACLU in the courts since 9/11. Updated March 14. Available from *http://www.aclu.org/SafeaodFree*.

Amon, Elizabeth. 2002. The fight over access to terror suspects; judges aren't giving the U.S. all it asks. *National Law Journal*, June 10, p. A-1.

Anderson, Curt. 2003a. Ashcroft cites progress in war on terror. Associated Press online, February 13. Available from *http://news.findlaw.com*.

———. 2003b. FBI arrest power for immigration violations. Associated Press online, March 19. Available from *http://news.findlaw.com*.

Andrews, Edmund L. 2003. Measuring lost freedom vs. security in dollars. *New York Times*, March 11.

Attorney General Remarks. 2002a. Attorney general guidelines. May 30. Available from *http://www.usdoj.gov/ag/speeches2002.html*.

———. 2002b. Eighth Circuit Judges Conference, Duluth, MN. August 7. Available from *http://www.usdoj.gov/ag/speeches2002.html*.

———. 2002c. U.S. Attorneys Conference, New York City. October 1. Available from *http://www.usdoj.gov/ag/speeches2002.html*.

———. 2002d. International Association of Chiefs of Police Conference, Minneapolis, MN. October 7. Available from *http://www.usdoj.gov/ag/speeches2002.html*.

Attorney General Transcript. 2002a. Eastern District of Virginia/Interview projects results announcement. March 20. Available from *http://www.usdoj.gov/ag/speeches2002.html*.

———. 2002b. Regarding the transfer of Abdullah Al Muhajir (born Jose Padilla) to the Department of Defense as an enemy combatant. June 10. Available from *http://www.usdoj.gov/ag/speeches2002.html*.

Bettelheim, Adriel. 2002. Changing tone of homeland security debate. *Congressional Quarterly*, August 1, p. 2222.

Brief for Respondents-Appellants. 2002. *Yaser Esam Hamdi, et al., v. Donald Rumsfeld, et al. U.S. Court of Appeals for the Fourth Circuit*. No. 02-6895.

Bush, George W. 2001. Military Order. Detention, treatment and trial of certain non-citizens in the war against terrorism. Office of the Press Secretary, November 13.

*Center for National Security Studies, American Civil Liberties Union, Electronic Privacy Information Center, et al., v. Department of Justice.* 2001. Complaint for injunctive relief, filed in the U.S. District Court for the District of Columbia. December 5.

———. 2002. 215 F. Supp. 2d 94; 2002 U.S. Dist. LEXIS 14168; 30 Media L. Rep. 2569. Decided August 2.

Cha, Ariana Eunjung. 2002. Risks prompt U.S. to limit access to data. *Washington Post*, February 24, p. A01.

CNN–Cable News Network. 2003. Bush speaks at Justice Department. Paula Zahn, CNN anchor, February 14. Transcript #021404CN.V54.

*Detroit Free Press, et al., v. John Ashcroft.* 2002a. 195 F. Supp. 2d 937 (E.D. Mich.).

——. 2002b. U.S. Court of Appeals for the Sixth Circuit. 2002 FED App. 0291P (6th Cir.). Decided August 26.

*The Economist.* 2003. A question of freedom. U.S. edition, March 8.

Editorial. 2001. Why not disclose? *Washington Post*, October 31. Available from *http:// www.washingtonpost.com*.

Edwards, Jim. 2002a. Judge orders end to secret detention of federal inmates in county jails ruling stayed while U.S. Department of Justice appeals. *New Jersey Law Journal*, April 1.

——. 2002b. Inadmissible: Fine tuning. *New Jersey Law Journal*, April 15.

Elsner, Alan. 2002. Bush expands government secrecy, arouses critics. Reuters, September 3. Available from *http://news.findlaw.com*.

Fainaru, Steve. 2002. Immigration hearings case goes to high court. *Washington Post*, June 22, p. A-11.

Fainaru, Steve, and Margot Williams. 2002. Is the law being bent? The material witness statute keeps detainees in jail, but many have never testified. *Washington Post*, national weekly edition, December 2–8, p. 29.

Fisher, Louis. 2003. Who's minding the courts on rights? *Los Angeles Times*, February 23.

Freedman, Eric M. 2000. Milestones in habeas corpus: Part I: Just because John Marshall said it, doesn't make it so: Ex parte Bollman and the illusory prohibition on the federal writ of habeas corpus for state prisoners in the Judiciary Act of 1789. *Alabama Law Review*, 51 Ala. L. Rev. 531, winter.

——. 2003. Hamdi and the case of the five knights. *Legal Times*, February 3.

Goldstein, Amy. 2001. A deliberate strategy of disruption: Massive, secret detention effort aimed mainly at preventing more terror. *Washington Post*, November 4, p. A01.

Goldstein, Amy, and Dan Eggen. 2001. U.S. to stop issuing detention tallies. *Washington Post*, November 9, p. A16.

Grimaldi, James V. 2002. At Justice, freedom not to release information. *Washington Post*, December 2, p. E01.

*Haddad v. Ashcroft.* 2002. 221 F. Supp. 2d 799; 2002 U.S. Dist. LEXIS 17990. September 17.

*Hamdi v. Rumsfeld.* 2003. 316 F. 3d 450; 2003 U.S. App. LEXIS 198. January 8.

Hentoff, Natt. 2001. John Ashcroft v. the Constitution: Giving the FBI a "blank warrant." *The Village Voice*, November 26.

Immigration and Naturalization Service. 2002a. Release of information regarding Immigration and Naturalization Service detainees in non-federal facilities: Interim rule. 8 CFR Parts 236 and 241. Effective date April 17.

——. 2002b. Release of information regarding Immigration and Naturalization Service detainees in non-federal facilities. *Federal Register*, Vol. 67, No. 77. April 22.

Kiefer, Francine. 2002. Backlash grows against White House secrecy. *Christian Science Monitor*, March 25, p. 3.

Klein, Edward. 2002. We're not destroying rights, we're protecting rights. *Parade Magazine*, May 19.

Knickerbocker, Brad. 2001. Security concerns drive rise in secrecy. *Christian Science Monitor*, December 3.

Koszczuk, Jackie. 2002. Ashcroft drawing criticism from both sides of the aisle. *Congressional Quarterly*, September 7.

Lane, Charles. 2002a. Fighting terror vs. defending liberties: A new debate has crystallized since Sept. 11. *Washington Post*, national weekly edition, September 9–15, p. 30.

——. 2002b. A second tier of justice: A parallel legal system—without constitutional protections—is in the works for terror suspects. *Washington Post*, national weekly edition, December 9–15, p. 30.

Lichtblau, Eric, with Adam Liptak. 2003. On terror and spying, Ashcroft expands reach. *New York Times*, March 15, p. A-1.

Locy, Toni, and Kevin Johnson. 2003. How the US watches suspects of terrorism. *USA Today*, February 12.

Loney, Jim. 2003. Controversial anti-terror program in new state. *Reuters*, January 10.

McGee, Jim. 2001a. The dragnet's downside. *Washington Post*, national weekly edition, December 3, p. 8.

——. 2001b. An intelligence giant in the making. *Washington Post*, November 4. Available from *http://www.washingtonpost.com*.

Mintz, John. 2003. Rights groups protest jailing of asylum seekers. *Washington Post*, March 18. Available from *http://www.washingtonpost. com*.

Mobbs Declaration on Padilla. 2002. Declaration of Michael H. Mobbs, Special Advisor to the Undersecretary of Defense for Policy. August 27.

Oliphant, Jim. 2001. Justice during wartime: Order on military trials final piece of Sept. 11 response. *Legal Times*, November 19, p. 1.

Schulhofer, Stephen. 2003. At war with liberty: Post 9–11, due process and security have taken a beating. *The American Prospect* 14: A5–A8.

Shenon, Philip. 2003. Justice Department will appeal ruling in trial linked to 9/11. *New York Times*, February 8.

Taylor, Stuart Jr. 2002. Let's not allow a fiat to undermine the Bill of Rights. *The Atlantic* online, July 23.

Transcript: Ashcroft on terror probe suspects. 2001. On Politics, *Washington Post*, November 27. Available from *http://www.washingtonpost.com*.

USA Patriot Act. 2001. HR 3162—PL 107-56. Signed October 26.

U.S. Department of Justice. 2001a. John Ashcroft memorandum to heads of all federal departments and agencies. Subject: The Freedom of Information Act. October 12.

——. 2001b. Michael Creppy memorandum to all immigration judges and court administrators. Subject: Cases requiring special procedures. September 21.

——. 2002a. OPPM. Office of the Chief Immigration Judge. Interim operating policies and procedures memorandum. Protective orders and the sealing of records in immigration proceedings. July 16.

——. 2002b. Press Release. Statement of Associate Attorney General Jay Stephens. Regarding the Sixth Circuit Decision in the Haddad case. April 19.

——. 2002c. Statement of Barbara Comstock, Director of Public Affairs. Regarding the Sixth Circuit Opinion in Detroit Free Press v. Ashcroft. August 27.

U.S. Senate. 2001. Testimony of Attorney General John Ashcroft. Department of Justice oversight: Preserving our freedoms while defending against terrorism. Hearings before the Senate Committee on the Judiciary. 107th Cong., 1st sess.

——. 2002. Testimony of Attorney General John Ashcroft. Committee on the Judiciary concerning oversight of the Department of Justice. July 25.

——. 2003. Hearings on the war against terrorism. Testimony of U.S. Attorney General John Ashcroft; Homeland Security Secretary Tom Ridge; Federal Bureau of Investigation Director Robert Mueller. Judiciary Committee. Federal News Service, March 4.

*Washington Post*. 2002. ABA opposes secret custody in 9/11 probe. August 14, p. A10.

White House Chief of Staff. 2002. Memorandum for the heads of executive departments and agencies. Subject: Action to safeguard information regarding weapons of mass destruction and other sensitive documents related to homeland security. March 19.

## Review

1. Briefly discuss the two broad areas of civil liberties that Attorney General Ashcroft called particular weaknesses waiting to be exploited by terrorists.

2. How are nondisclosure of names of people detained and closed immigration hearings threats to civil liberties?

3. Explain the "mosaic theory" as a rationale for secrecy.

4. Discuss the rights to due process that antiterrorism measures limit.

5. How have the presumption of innocence and habeas corpus been violated in the war against terrorism?

## Application

What are your feelings about the tradeoff between security and civil liberties? Do the actions taken by the government as described in this article make you feel more secure? Do you believe the government's actions are justified under the circumstances or that they pose as much a threat as does terrorism? Write a brief paper stating and defending your position and read it to the class. Have someone with an opposing point of view also read his or her paper. Have the class debate the issue.

## Related Web Sites

1. *http://washingtontimes.com/national/20030615-123422-5163r.htm*. A newspaper article that summarizes some of the powers granted the government under the Patriot Act.

2. *http://www.aclu.org/*. Site of the American Civil Liberties Union, with numerous articles and papers on various aspects of civil liberties.

# Part Three

## *The Economy*

The **economy** is the institution that regulates the production and distribution of goods and services. Some of those goods and services are necessary for the maintenance of life and some are believed to enhance the quality of life. Today, the two basic forms of economy among the nations of the world are capitalism and socialism, including a few nations that combine the two in some way.

**Capitalism** is an economic system with private ownership of the means of production and competitive, for-profit distribution of goods and services. **Socialism** is an economic system with state ownership of the means of production and cooperative distribution of goods and services.

The first two selections in this part examine capitalism from two very different perspectives. The third selection addresses an increasingly troublesome aspect of our economy today—underemployment. ✦

# 29
# Alienation in Work

*Karl Marx*

In Marx's view, a central problem of labor in a capitalist society is **alienation,** estrangement from the social environment that includes feelings of isolation, powerlessness, and meaninglessness. He believed that it is human nature for humans to fulfill their creative potential through labor. In this respect he differed from other early social scientists such as Adam Smith, the eighteenth-century political economist who held that human beings were lazy by nature and would not be productive without the incentives of profit and property. Marx maintained that people's distaste for work is the result of a capitalistic system that serves to alienate workers from the processes and products of their labor, from other workers, and, ultimately, from themselves.

This selection discusses the nature, causes, and effects of work-related alienation and the dehumanizing power of money in capitalist society. Although Marx first put forth these ideas more than a century and a half ago, they are still relevant and thought-provoking today.

We shall begin from a *contemporary* economic fact. The worker becomes poorer the more wealth he produces and the more production increases in power and extent. The worker becomes an ever cheaper commodity the more goods he creates. The *devaluation* of the human world increases in direct relation with the *increase in value* of the world of things. Labour does not only create goods; it also produces itself and the worker as a *commodity,* and indeed in the same proportion as it produces goods.

This fact simply implies that the object produced by labour, its product, now stands opposed to it as an *alien being,* as a *power independent* of the producer. The product of labour is labour which has been embodied in an object and turned into a physical thing; this product is an *objectification* of labour. The performance of work is at the same time its objectification.

These consequences follow the fact that the worker is related to the *product of his labour* as to an alien object. For it is clear on this presupposition that the more the worker expends himself in work the more powerful becomes the world of objects which he creates in place of himself, the poorer he becomes in his inner life, and the less he belongs to himself. It is just the same as in religion. The more of himself man attributes to God the less he has left in himself. The worker puts his life into the object, and his life then belongs no longer to himself but to the object. The greater his activity, therefore, the less he possesses. What is embodied in the product of his labour is no longer his own. The greater this product is, therefore, the more he is diminished. The *alienation* of the worker in his product means not only that his labour becomes an object, assumes an *external* existence, but that it exists independently, *outside himself,* and alien to him, and that it stands opposed to him as an autonomous power. The life which he has given to the object sets itself against him as an alien and hostile force.

Labour certainly produces marvels for the rich but it produces privation for the worker. It produces palaces, but hovels for the worker. It produces beauty, but deformity for the worker. It replaces labour by machinery, but it casts some of the workers back into a barbarous kind of work and turns the others into machines. It produces intelligence, but also stupidity and cretinism for the workers.

So far we have considered the alienation of the worker only from one aspect; namely, *his relationship with the products of his labour.* However, alienation appears not merely in the result but also in the *process of production,* within productive activity itself. How could the worker stand in an alien relationship to the product of his activity if he did not alienate himself in the act of production itself? The product is indeed only the *résumé* of activity, of production. Consequently, if the product of labour is alienation, production itself must be active alienation—the alienation of activity and the activity of alienation. The alienation of the object of labour merely summarizes the alienation in the work activity itself.

What constitutes the alienation of labour? First, that the work is *external* to the worker, that it is not part of his nature; and that, consequently, he does not fulfill himself in his work but denies himself, has a feeling of misery rather than well-being, does not develop freely his mental and physical energies but is physically exhausted and mentally debased. The worker, therefore, feels himself at home only during his leisure time, whereas at work he feels homeless. His work is not voluntary but imposed, *forced labour.* It is not the satisfaction of a need, but only a *means* for satisfying other needs. Its alien character is clearly shown by the fact that as soon as there is no physical or other compulsion it is avoided like the plague. External labour, labour in which man alienates himself, is a labour of self-sacrifice, of mortification. Finally, the external character of work for the worker is shown by the fact that it is not his own work but work for someone else, that in work he does not belong to himself but to another person.

We arrive at the result that man (the worker) feels himself to be freely active only in his animal functions—eating, drinking and procreating, or at most also in his dwelling and in personal adornment—while in his human functions he is reduced to an animal.

For labour, *life activity, productive life,* now appear to man only as *means* for the satisfaction of a need, the need to maintain his physical existence. Productive life is, however, species-life. It is life creating life. In the type of life activity resides the whole character of a species, its species-character; and free, conscious activity is the species-character of human beings. Life itself appears only as a *means of life.*

The animal is one with its life activity. It does not distinguish the activity from itself. It is *its activity.* But man makes his life activity itself an object of his will and consciousness. He has a conscious life activity. It is not a determination with which he is completely identified. Conscious life activity distinguishes man from the life activity of animals. Only for this reason is his activity free activity. Alienated labour reverses the relationship, in that man because he is a self-conscious *being* makes his life activity, his being, only a means for his *existence.*

The practical construction of an *objective world*, the *manipulation* of inorganic nature, is the confirmation of man as a conscious species-being, i.e., a being who treats the species as his own being or himself as a species-being. Of course, animals also produce. They construct nests, dwellings, as in the case of bees, beavers, ants, etc. But they only produce what is strictly necessary for themselves or their young. They produce only in a single direction, while man produces universally. They produce only under the compulsion of direct physical needs, while man produces when he is free from physical need and only truly produces in freedom from such need. Animals produce only themselves, while man reproduces the whole of nature. The products of animal production belong directly to their physical bodies, while man is free in face of his product. Animals construct only in accordance with the standards and needs of the species to which they belong, while man knows how to produce in accordance with the standards of every species and knows how to apply the appropriate standard to the object. Thus man constructs also in accordance with the laws of beauty.

A direct consequence of the alienation of man from the product of his labour, from his life activity and from his species-life, is that man is *alienated* from *other* men. When man confronts himself he also confronts *other* men. What is true of man's relationship to his work, to the product of his work and to himself, is also true of his relationship to other men, to their labour and to the objects of their nature.

Thus in the relationship of alienated labour every man regards other men according to the standards and relationships in which he finds himself placed as a worker.

If the product of labour is alien to me and confronts me as an alien power, to whom does it belong?

The *alien* being to whom labour and the product of labour belong, to whose service labour is devoted, and to whose enjoyment the product of labour goes, can only be *man* himself. If the product of labour does not belong to the worker, but confronts him as an alien power, this can only be because it belongs to a *man other than the worker*. If his activity is a torment to him it must be a source of *enjoyment* and pleasure to another. Not the gods, nor nature, but only man himself can be this alien power over men.

Thus, through alienated labour the worker creates the relation of another man, who does not work and is outside the work process, to this labour. The relation of the worker to work also produces the relation of the capitalist (or whatever one likes to call the lord of labour) to work.

## Money

Money, since it has the *property* of purchasing everything, of appropriating objects to itself, is, therefore, the *object par excellence*. The universal character of this *property* corresponds to the omnipotence of money, which is regarded as an omnipotent being . . . money is the *pander* between need and object, between human life and the means of subsistence. But *that which* mediates *my* life mediates also the existence of other men for me. It is for me the *other* person.

That which exists for me through the medium of *money*, that which I can pay for (i.e., which money can buy), that *I am*, the possessor of the money. My own power is as great as the power of money. The properties of money are my own (the possessor's) properties and faculties. What *I am* and *can do* is, therefore, not at all determined by my individuality. I *am* ugly, but I can buy the most beautiful woman for myself. Consequently, I am not *ugly*, for the effect of ugliness, its power to repel, is annulled by money. I am a detestable, dishonourable, unscrupulous and stupid man, but money is honoured and so also is its possessor. Money is the highest good, and so its possessor is good. Besides, money saves me the trouble of being dishonest; therefore, I am presumed honest. I who can have, through the power of money, *everything* for which the human heart longs, do I not possess all human abilities? Does not my money, therefore, transform all my incapacities into their opposites?

If *money* is the bond which binds me to *human* life, and society to me, and which links me with nature and man, is it not the bond of all *bonds*? It is the real means of both *separation* and *union*. The difference between effective demand, supported by money, and ineffective demand, based upon my need, my passion, my desire, etc. is the difference between *being* and *thought*, between the merely inner representation and the representation which exists outside myself as a *real object*.

If I have no money for travel I have no *need*—no real and self-realizing need—for travel. If I have a *vocation* for study but no money for it, then I have *no* vocation, i.e., no *effective*, genuine vocation. Conversely, if I really have *no* vocation for study, but have money and the urge for it, then I have an *effective* vocation. *Money* is the external, universal means and power (not derived from man as man nor from human society as society) to change *representation* into *reality* and *reality* into *mere representation*.

Let us assume *man* to be *man*, and his relation to the world to be a human one. Then love can only be exchanged for love, trust for trust, etc. If you wish to enjoy art you must be an artistically cultivated person; if you wish to influence other people you must be a person who really has a stimulating and encouraging effect upon others. Every one of your relations to man and to nature must be a *specific expression*, corresponding to the object of your will, of your *real individual* life.

## Review

1. What is the product of labor, according to Marx?

2. What does he mean by the alienation of the worker from the worker's products?

3. When do human beings feel themselves to be freely active, according to Marx?

4. What is the direct consequence of the alienation of humans from the product of their labor?

5. What property and power does money have, according to Marx?

## Application

Interview two or three people who have worked at a variety of jobs. Ask what the best and worst of these jobs were and what aspects of the work made them good or bad. Relate their descriptions to these notions from Marx:

a. low pay (exploitation)

b. monotony versus variety of tasks

c. excessive supervision versus autonomy

d. personal profit versus service to others

e. narrowly defined tasks versus creativity

What other aspects of work were seen as particularly satisfying or burdensome? Summarize your findings and use them in evaluating Marx's discussion of work.

## Related Web Sites

1. *http://www.marxists.org/.* Archives of Marxist writers, with access to over 300 authors.

2. *http://www.socialistworker.org/2003-2/ 467/467_09_Alienation.shtml.* An article on alienation from a socialist journal.

---

# 30

# The Protestant Ethic and the Spirit of Capitalism

*Max Weber*

Weber's thesis about the historical relationship between the rise of capitalism and the Protestant Reformation is one of the most widely discussed works in social science. Weber believed that modern capitalism is distinguished by its rationality, which involves the pursuit of profit through ethically controlled competition.

In the Middle Ages, however, there was no specific moral code that applied to economic activity. Thus, tradesmen, merchants, and financiers were free to use force or fraud for profit. But in the sixteenth century, new economic attitudes began to emerge from various Protestant denominations, most notably the **Calvinists**—Puritans and others who followed the beliefs of the Protestant reformer John Calvin (1509–1564). Presbyterians and Reformed groups are present-day descendants of the early Calvinists.

Puritans believed that, because an individual's calling in life was a duty to God, economic activity must be pursued in strict accordance with ethical rules. They also believed that worldly success was a sign of God's salvation. In recognition of this distinctive Puritan contribution, Weber, in his writings, refers to all ascetic Protestant religions as Puritan.

It should be noted that Weber regarded the relationship between Protestantism and capitalism with irony. In his view, the early Protestants were driven by concern for their fate in the next world to transform this world into its modern form. But the materialism engendered by this transformation proved so alluring it killed off the very spirituality that fostered it.

## An Overview of Weber's Thesis

The basic dogma of strict Calvinism, the doctrine of predestination, makes it impossible for the church to administer sacraments whose reception can have any significance for eternal salvation. Moreover, the actual behavior of the believer is irrelevant to his fate, which has been determined from eternity through God's inscrutable and immutable will.

The inscrutability of predestination to either salvation or damnation was naturally intolerable to the believer; he searched for the *certitudo saluris*, for an indication that he belonged to the elect. He could find this certainty, on the one hand, in the conviction that he was acting according to the letter of the law and according to reason, repressing all animal drives; on the other, he could find it in visible proofs that God blessed his work. "Good works" of the Catholic variety were meaningless in the face of God's unchangeable decree; however, for the believer and his community, his own ethical conduct and fate in the secular social order became supremely important as an indication of his state of grace. A person was judged elect or condemned as an entity; no confession and absolution could relieve him and change his position before God and, in contrast to Catholicism, no individual "good deed" could compensate for his sins. Therefore, the individual could only be sure of his state of grace if he felt reason to believe that, by adhering to a principle of methodical conduct, he pursued the sole correct path in all his action—that he worked for God's glory. Methodical conduct, the rational form of asceticism, is thus carried from the monastery into the world. The ascetic means are in principle identical: Rejected are all vain glorification of the self and of all other things of the flesh, feudal pride, the spontaneous enjoyment of art and life, "levity," all waste of money and time, eroticism, or any other activity that detracts from the rational work in one's private vocation and within the God-willed social order. The curtailment of all feudal ostentation and of all irrational consumption facilitates capital accumulation and the ever-renewed utilization of property for productive purposes.

Life is focused not on persons but on impersonal rational goals. Charity becomes an impersonal operation of poor relief for the greater glory of God. And since the success of work is the surest symptom that it pleases God, capitalist profit is one of the most important criteria for establishing that God's blessing rests on the enterprise.

It is clear that this style of life is very closely related to the self-justification that is customary for bourgeois acquisition: profit and property appear not as ends in themselves but as indications of personal ability. Here has been attained the union of religious postulate and bourgeois style of life that promotes capitalism. Of course, this was not the purpose of the Puritan ethic, especially not the encouragement of money making; on the contrary, as in all Christian denominations, wealth was regarded as dangerous and full of temptation. However, just as the monasteries time and again brought this temptation on themselves by virtue of the ascetic rational work and conduct of their members, so did now the pious bourgeois who lived and worked ascetically.

## The Contrast of Catholicism With Protestant Asceticism

The normal mediaeval Catholic layman lived ethically, so to speak, from hand to mouth. In the first place he conscientiously fulfilled his traditional duties. But beyond that minimum his good works did not necessarily form a connected, or at least not a rationalized, system of life, but rather remained a succession of individual acts. He could use them as occasion demanded, to atone for particular sins, to better his chances for salvation, or, toward the end of his life, as a sort of insurance premium. Of course the Catholic ethic was an ethic of intentions. But the concrete *intentio* of the single act determined its value. And the single

good or bad action was credited to the doer determining his temporal and eternal fate. Quite realistically the Church recognized that man was not an absolutely clearly defined unity to be judged one way or the other, but that his moral life was normally subject to conflicting motives and his action contradictory. Of course, it required as an ideal a change of life in principle. But it weakened just this requirement (for the average) by one of its most important means of power and education, the sacrament of absolution, the function of which was connected with the deepest roots of the peculiarly Catholic religion.

To the Catholic, the absolution of his Church was a compensation for his own imperfection. The priest was a magician who performed the miracle of transubstantiation, and who held the key to eternal life in his hand. One could turn to him in grief and penitence. He dispensed atonement, hope of grace, certainty of forgiveness, and thereby granted release from that tremendous tension to which the Calvinist was doomed by an inexorable fate, admitting of no mitigation. For him such friendly and human comforts did not exist. He could not hope to atone for hours of weakness or of thoughtlessness by increased good will at other times, as the Catholic or even the Lutheran could. The God of Calvinism demanded of his believers not single good works, but a life of good works combined into a unified system. There was no place for the very human Catholic cycle of sin, repentance, atonement, release, followed by renewed sin.

The moral conduct of the average man was thus deprived of its planless and unsystematic character and subjected to a consistent method for conduct as a whole. It is no accident that the name of Methodists stuck to the participants in the last great revival of Puritan ideas in the eighteenth century.

Only by a fundamental change in the whole meaning of life at every moment and in every action could the effects of grace . . . be proved.

# The Effects of Protestant Asceticism on Everyday Life

If a demonstration of religious fidelity is still to be made within the institutional structure of the world, then the world, for the very reason that it inevitably remains a natural vessel of sin, becomes a challenge for the demonstration of the ascetic temper and for the strongest possible attacks against the world's sins. The world abides in the lowly state appropriate to its status as a created thing. Therefore, any sensuous surrender to the world's goods may imperil concentration upon and possession of the ultimate good of salvation, and may be a symptom of unholiness of spirit and impossibility of rebirth. Nevertheless, the world as a creation of God, whose power comes to expression in it despite its creatureliness, provides the only medium through which one's unique religious charisma may prove itself by means of rational ethical conduct, so that one may become and remain certain of one's own state of grace.

Hence, as the field provided for this active certification, the order of the world in which the ascetic is situated becomes for him a vocation which he must fulfill rationally. As a consequence, and although the enjoyment of wealth is forbidden to the ascetic, it becomes his vocation to engage in economic activity which is faithful to rationalized ethical requirements and which conforms to strict legality. If success supervenes upon such acquisitive activity, it is regarded as the manifestation of God's blessing upon the labor of the pious man and of God's pleasure with his economic pattern of life.

Certain other manifestations of inner-worldly asceticism must be noted. Any excess of emotional feeling for one's fellow man is prohibited as being a deification of the creaturely, which denies the unique value of the divine gift of grace. Yet it is man's vocation to participate rationally and soberly in the various rational, purposive institutions of the world and in their objective goals as set by God's creation. Similarly, any eroticism that tends to deify the human creature is proscribed. On the other hand, it is a divinely imposed vocation of man "to soberly produce children" (as the Puritans expressed it) within marriage. Then, too, there is a prohibition against the exercise of force by an individual against other human beings for reasons of passion or revenge, and above all for purely personal motives. However, it is divinely enjoined that the rationally ordered state shall suppress and punish sins and rebelliousness. Finally, all personal secular enjoyment of power is forbidden as a deification of the creaturely, though it is held that a rational legal order within society is pleasing to God.

The person who lives as a worldly ascetic is a rationalist, not only in the sense that he rationally systematizes his own personal patterning of life, but also in his rejection of everything that is ethically irrational, esthetic, or dependent upon his own emotional reactions to the world and its institutions. The distinctive goal always remains the alert, methodical control of one's own pattern of life and behavior.

\*\*\*

Waste of time is the first and in principle the deadliest of sins. The span of human life is infinitely short and precious to make sure of one's own election. Loss of time through sociability, idle talk, luxury, even more sleep than is necessary for health, six to at most eight hours, is worthy of absolute moral condemnation. It does not yet hold that time is money, but the proposition is true in a certain spiritual sense. It is infinitely valuable because every hour lost is lost to labour for the glory of God. Thus inactive contemplation is also valueless, or even directly reprehensible if it is at the expense of one's daily work. For it is less pleasing to God than the active performance of His will in a calling.

\*\*\*

The sexual asceticism of Puritanism differs only in degree, not in fundamental principle, from that of monasticism; and on account of the Puritan conception of marriage, its practical influence is more far-reaching than that of the latter. For sexual intercourse is permitted, even within marriage, only as the means willed by God for the increase of His glory according to the commandment, "Be fruitful and multiply." Along with a moderate vegetable diet and cold baths, the same prescription is given for all sexual temptations as is used against religious doubts and a sense of moral unworthiness: "Work hard in your calling." But the most important thing was that even beyond that labour came to be considered in itself the end of life, ordained as such by God. St. Paul's "He who will not work shall not eat" holds unconditionally for everyone. Unwillingness to work is symptomatic of the lack of grace.

***

The Puritan aversion to sport was by no means simply one of principle. Sport was accepted if it served a rational purpose, that of recreation necessary for physical efficiency. But as a means for the spontaneous expression of undisciplined impulses, it was under suspicion; and in so far as it became purely a means of enjoyment, or awakened pride, raw instincts or the irrational gambling instinct, it was of course strictly condemned. Impulsive enjoyment of life, which leads away both from work in a calling and from religion, was as such the enemy of rational asceticism.

***

The theatre was obnoxious to the Puritans, and with the strict exclusion of the erotic and of nudity from the realm of toleration, a radical view of either literature or art could not exist. The conceptions of idle talk, of superfluities, and of vain ostentation, all designations of an irrational attitude without objective purpose, thus not ascetic, and especially not serving the glory of God, but of man, were always at hand to serve in deciding in favour of sober utility as against any artistic tendencies. This was especially true in the case of decoration of the person, for instance clothing. That powerful tendency toward uniformity of life, which today so immensely aids the capitalistic interest in the standardization of production, had its ideal foundations in the repudiation of all idolatry of the flesh.

***

One of the most notable economic effects of Calvinism was its destruction of the traditional forms of charity. First it eliminated miscellaneous almsgiving . . . and especially any benevolent attitude toward the beggar. For Calvinism held that the unsearchable God possessed good reasons for having distributed the gifts of fortune unequally. It never ceased to stress the notion that a man proved himself exclusively in his vocational work. Consequently, begging was explicitly stigmatized as a violation of the injunction to love one's neighbor, in this case the person from whom the beggar solicits.

What is more, all Puritan preachers proceeded from the assumption that the idleness of a person capable of work was inevitably his own fault. But it was felt necessary to organize charity systematically for those incapable of work, such as orphans and cripples, for the greater glory of God. This notion often resulted in such striking phenomena as dressing institutionalized orphans in uniforms reminiscent of fool's attire and parading them through the streets of Amsterdam to divine services with the greatest possible fanfare. Care for the poor was oriented to the goal of discouraging the slothful. In any case, charity itself became a rationalized "enterprise," and its religious significance was therefore eliminated or even transformed into the opposite significance. This was the situation in consistent ascetic and rationalized religions.

***

The pious Puritan could demonstrate his religious merit through his economic activity because he did nothing ethically reprehensible, he did not resort to any lax interpretations of religious codes or to systems of double moralities, and he did not act in a manner that could be indifferent or even reprehensible in the general realm of ethical validity. On the contrary, the Puritan could demonstrate his religious merit precisely in his economic activity. He acted in business with the best possible conscience, since through his rationalistic and legal behavior in his business activity he was factually objectifying the rational methodology of his total life pattern. He legitimated his ethical pattern in his own eyes, and indeed within the circle of his own community, by the extent to which the absolute—not relativized—unassailability of his economic conduct remained beyond question. No really pious Puritan—and this is the crucial point—could have regarded as pleasing to God any profit derived from usury, exploitation of another's mistake, haggling and sharp dealing, or participation in political or colonial exploitation. Quakers and Baptists believed their religious merit to be certified before all mankind by such practices as their fixed prices and their absolutely reliable business relationships with everyone, unconditionally legal and devoid of cupidity. Precisely such practices promoted the irreligious to trade with them rather than with their own kind, and to entrust their money to the trust companies or limited liability enterprises of the religious sectarians rather than those of their own people—all of which made the religious sectarians wealthy, even as their business practices certified them before their God.

## The Ironic Consequences of Protestant Asceticism

One of the fundamental elements of the spirit of modern capitalism, and not only of that but of all modern culture, rational conduct on the basis of the idea of the calling was born—that is what this discussion has sought to demonstrate—from the spirit of Christian asceticism.

The Puritan wanted to work in a calling; we are forced to do so. For when asceticism was carried out of monastic cells into everyday life, and began to dominate worldly morality, it did its part in building the tremendous cosmos of the modern economic order. This order is now bound to the technical and economic conditions of machine production which today determine the lives of all the individuals who are born into this mechanism, not only those directly [concerned] with economic acquisition, with irresistible force. Perhaps it will so determine them until the last ton of fossilized coal is burnt.

Since asceticism undertook to remodel the world and to work out its ideals in the world, material goods have gained an increasing and finally an inexorable power over the lives of men as at no previous period in history. The idea of duty in one's calling prowls about in our lives like the ghost of dead religious beliefs. Where the fulfillment of the calling cannot directly be related to the highest spiritual and cultural values, or when, on the other hand, it need not be felt simply as economic compulsion, the individual generally abandons the attempt to justify it at all. In the field of its highest development, in the United States, the pursuit of wealth, stripped of its religious and ethical meaning, tends to become associated with purely mundane passions, which often actually give it the character of sport.

No one knows who will live in this cage in the future, or whether at the end of this tremendous development entirely new prophets will arise, or there will be a great rebirth of old ideas and ideals, or, if neither, mechanized petrification, embellished with a sort of convulsive self-importance. For of the last stage of this cultural development, it might well be truly said: "Specialists without spirit, sensualists without heart; this nullity imagines that it has attained a level of civilization never before achieved."

## Review

1. In what ways are ascetic means and ascetic principles identical, according to Weber?

2. How does Weber define and describe the Puritan Ethic?

3. What function do the sacraments have for Catholics?

4. According to Weber, how has the rise of Protestantism determined the role of material goods in people's lives?

## Application

Interview a Catholic and a member of a very traditional Protestant denomination. Address the following, relating to each person's attitudes on each:

a. fate and salvation and the existence of an afterlife

b. money, wealth, profit, and property ownership

c. work—a necessary evil, pleasure, or means to salvation

d. atonement for sins

e. asceticism—a rational, disciplined life versus enjoyment of people and worldly pleasures

f. time

g. sex

h. sports participation

i. beggars, the poor, and charity

## Related Web Sites

1. *http://www.faculty.rsu.edu/~felwell/Theorists/Weber/Whome.htm.* This site features the life and work of Max Weber, including articles on his teachings.

2. *http://www.j-bradford-delong.net/pdf_files/Protestant_Ethic.pdf.* A contemporary examination of the Protestant Ethic.

---

# 31

# Underemployment in America

*Leif Jensen*

*Tim Slack*

*Politicians debate the health of the economy by noting the unemployment rate and the number of jobs created or lost. These are certainly two important indicators of economic well-being. But as the authors of this selection point out, the unemployment rate cannot tell the whole story. There are workers who are employed, but only part-time when they want full-time work. There are others who work full-time, but their wages are so low that they must live in poverty. These are two examples of the important concept of **underemployment.***

*When underemployment is taken into account, the economic challenges of the nation loom much larger. Underemployment results in frustration, financial worry, and stress for people—people who don't show up in data on unemployment and number of jobs in the nation. Underemployment usually means that the worker has not found work that is meaningful and yields more than a paycheck. Many underemployed Americans are working in the growing number of temporary jobs. Such jobs not only deprive the worker of security but also subject the worker to the degradation of being a "second-class citizen" at the workplace.*

*As Jensen and Slack point out, it is very difficult to measure underemployment, but it is also very important to take it into account in any analysis of the economy. It both underscores the deficiencies of the economy and points out the way in which minorities once again bear a disproportionate share of the burden.*

The economic turmoil of the Great Depression changed the way Americans thought about poverty at the time (Levitan, Mangum, & Mangum, 1998). To that point the prevailing view held that poverty was caused by individual deficiencies among the poor. Able-bodied people who were poor because they were not working were regarded as lazy and undeserving of societal aid. With the Depression came widespread joblessness, and a recognition that to some extent the causes of poverty were rooted in the structure of the economy and society, rather than the blameworthy individual characteristics of the poor themselves. It is no coincidence that in the 1930s industrializing nations of the West began to collect unemployment statistics as a way to gauge the performance of the labor market and the social circumstances of its workers (Clogg, 1979). The unemployment rate has been a mainstay of social indicators ever since. Clogg (1979, p. 2) writes, "[i]t is difficult indeed to conceive of another socioeconomic statistic that has been more influential in public policy debate, more critical in the shaping of modern political cleavage, or more central to social scientific theory about the socioeconomic order."

The calculation of the unemployment rate is relatively simple. The numerator of the rate is the number of people in a population who are unemployed, that is, who are not currently working and are actively looking for a job, plus the number who are on layoff. The base (denominator) of the rate is the number of people in a population who are economically active. Often referred to simply as the "labor force," this economically active population consists of those people who are unemployed (as defined above) plus those who are currently working. Thus, the unemployment rate is simply the number unemployed divided by the number in the labor force (employed plus unemployed). Assuming it is calculated monthly or annually, the unemployment rate can be used to track the state of the labor market over time. Within a given point in time, it can also be used to describe inequalities between groups (Whites vs. Blacks, men vs. women, Floridians vs. Texans) in their prevalence of joblessness.

Despite its centrality, labor market scientists have long pointed out the inadequacies of the unemployment rate in capturing the full array of types of employment hardship (Hauser, 1974). As an alternative, some have proposed and advocated the broader concept of underemployment which goes beyond mere unemployment to include additional forms of inadequate employment (Clogg, 1979; Hauser, 1974; Sullivan & Hauser, 1978). These include those who are working part-time, but would like full-time work; those who are working full-time, but for poverty-level wages; those who are not working and would like to be, but have given up looking for a job (since they are not looking, they are not counted as unemployed); and those whose occupational status falls far below what one would expect given their level of education.

While on the rise at this writing, unemployment rates neared historic lows during the very strong economy of the mid- to late-1990s. Ironically, despite this prosperity, concerns over employment adequacy and underemployment in the United States continue to be voiced. The reasons for this are twofold (Jensen & Slack, 2000). First, it has been suggested that the globalization of the world economy and the corresponding industrial restructuring of the U.S. economy (away from manufacturing and toward services), have given rise to a bifurcation of the U.S. labor force into good jobs and bad jobs (Nelson & Smith, 1999). Good jobs are stable, full-time, and well-paying, offer advancement opportunities, and tend to be held by those who are highly skilled and/or well educated. Bad jobs tend to be unstable, poorly paying, and often part-time, and they are lacking in benefits and prospects for advancement. The worry is that despite a hot economy, the relative rise in the prevalence of bad jobs has consigned a sizable portion of the labor force to a high risk of underemployment. Second, in recent years the United States has reoriented its social welfare system to encourage employment and work preparedness. Specifically, the Personal Responsibility and Work Opportunity Recon-

ciliation Act of 1996 (or "welfare reform") placed strict time limits on Public Assistance receipt and, for most, made work or work-skills training a prerequisite for assistance. As welfare rolls have plummeted, and employment among erstwhile welfare recipients had increased (Lichter & Jensen, 2001), employment adequacy has become even more important for determining economic well-being among those at the bottom. The worry is that the influx of low-skilled workers has lowered wages and labor demand, and increased the risk of underemployment for those who are most vulnerable. That governments are foisting more responsibility for economic well-being on the labor market and workers themselves at the very time that questions are being raised about the implications of macroeconomic change for the quality of jobs available for low-skilled groups only heightens concern over the specter of underemployment (Jensen & Slack, 2000). . . .

## Trends and Correlates

In this section we offer an up to date portrait of underemployment in the United States today. Figure 31.1 shows the prevalence of underemployment by type and year for the period 1990–2000. The point estimates are derived from original analysis of the March Current Population Surveys for those years. . . .

Overall, underemployment began the decade at roughly 17% and rose to over 20% amidst a sluggish economy early in the decade. Underemployment declined steadily to around 14% by the year 2000, clearly reflecting the very strong economy during those years. In all years except one (1992) the modal type of underemployment was that by low income. The working poor comprised about 40 to almost 50% of all underemployed workers throughout the 1990s, or around 7% of the entire labor force. Unemployment is the second most common form of underemployment (except in 1992 when it was the most common form), and appears especially susceptible to macroeconomic swings, varying from a high of 7.5% of the labor force in 1992, to 4.1% by decade's end.

Underemployment by low-hours is the third most prevalent form, and decline[d] steadily from a maximum of 5.2% of the labor force in 1992, to 4.1% in 2000. Finally, discouraged workers hovered around 1% of the labor force throughout the period, and in

***Table 31.1***
*Percentage Distribution of Underemployment by Selected Characteristics*

|  | Total | Nonmetropolitan | Metropolitan | | |
|---|---|---|---|---|---|
|  |  |  | Total | Central city | Suburb |
| **Total** | 13.5% | 16.2% | 13.0% | 15.5% | 11.3% |
| **Age** | | | | | |
| 18-24 | 29.1 | 29.7 | 29.0 | 33.0 | 26.4 |
| 25-34 | 12.4 | 16.3 | 11.7 | 12.9 | 10.2 |
| 35-44 | 10.9 | 13.9 | 10.2 | 12.7 | 8.8 |
| 45-54 | 9.5 | 11.9 | 8.9 | 11.2 | 7.9 |
| 55-64 | 11.0 | 14.2 | 10.2 | 11.6 | 9.5 |
| **Gender** | | | | | |
| Men | 12.0 | 14.0 | 11.6 | 14.2 | 10.0 |
| Women | 15.3 | 18.8 | 14.5 | 17.0 | 12.7 |
| **Race/ethnicity** | | | | | |
| Non-Hispanic White | 11.3 | 15.0 | 10.3 | 10.6 | 9.8 |
| Non-Hispanic Black | 19.9 | 24.9 | 19.3 | 22.1 | 15.2 |
| Hispanic | 21.3 | 21.8 | 21.3 | 22.8 | 18.9 |
| Native American | 23.3 | 27.1 | 21.3 | 25.5 | 15.1 |
| Asian | 12.7 | 15.9 | 12.6 | 13.8 | 10.5 |
| **Marital status** | | | | | |
| Married | 9.3 | 12.0 | 8.6 | 10.3 | 7.6 |
| Never married | 22.1 | 27.3 | 21.2 | 22.1 | 19.8 |
| Divorced/separated | 14.1 | 18.3 | 13.3 | 15.5 | 11.8 |
| Widowed | 18.5 | 24.2 | 17.3 | 19.5 | 15.1 |
| **Education** | | | | | |
| Less than high school | 29.0 | 28.4 | 29.3 | 32.5 | 26.0 |
| High school or GED | 16.0 | 17.9 | 15.5 | 19.2 | 13.6 |
| Some college | 13.3 | 15.4 | 12.8 | 15.1 | 11.7 |
| College degree or more | 6.6 | 8.9 | 6.2 | 6.8 | 5.7 |
| **Industry** | | | | | |
| Extractive | 22.7 | 21.6 | 23.5 | 27.2 | 22.9 |
| Manufacturing | 11.3 | 13.5 | 10.6 | 12.0 | 9.5 |
| Transportation/utilities | 8.8 | 11.1 | 8.4 | 10.1 | 7.3 |
| Wholesale and retail trade | 19.2 | 22.4 | 18.6 | 22.2 | 16.1 |
| Finance, insurance, real estate | 6.8 | 7.8 | 6.6 | 9.5 | 5.0 |
| Services | 12.0 | 14.7 | 11.5 | 13.6 | 10.0 |
| **Region** | | | | | |
| Northeast | 13.1 | 16.6 | 12.7 | 17.5 | 10.6 |
| Midwest | 12.2 | 14.0 | 11.7 | 15.7 | 9.5 |
| South | 13.9 | 17.2 | 13.0 | 14.6 | 11.4 |
| West | 14.7 | 18.2 | 14.3 | 15.1 | 13.3 |

Source: Original calculations from the March 2000 Current Population Survey.

2000 represented less than 5% of all underemployed workers.

Table 31.1 describes the nature and severity of inequality in underemployment prevalence across key sociodemographic groups using data from the March 2000 CPS. The table is broken down by residence in nonmetropolitan (nonmetro) versus metropolitan (metro) areas (and within the latter, by central city versus suburbs), in order to underscore the important residential variation in this regard. Essentially, a metro area is defined as a county with a city of 50,000 or more population (or total urbanized area of 100,000 or more), plus surrounding counties with significant economic ties to the central county as evidenced by commuting patterns. All other counties are defined as nonmetro. About three quarters of all counties are nonmetro, but nonmetro residents account for less than one quarter of the U.S. population.

Table 31.1 shows that the overall prevalence of underemployment in 2000 (13.5%) masks substantial residential variation in this regard. Residents of nonmetro areas are the most disadvantaged (16.2%), but underemployment also is high in the most urban category—the central cities of metro areas (15.5%). Only 11.3% of suburban residents are underemployed. The risk of underemployment also is strongly related to age, with those in the youngest age category (18–24) having by far the highest risk. Underemployment prevalence decreases steadily with age, but increases again among those who are nearing retirement age (55–64). In the U.S. job market, men continue to carry an advantage over women (e.g., with respect to wages), and the same is true in regard to underemployment. About 15.3% of all women, and 18.8% of nonmetro women workers are underemployed. There also are stark differences by race and ethnicity which echo well chronicled disadvantages of minorities in U.S. society. Indeed, the prevalence of underemployment among non-Hispanic Whites (11.3%) is much lower than it is for Blacks (19.9%), Hispanics (21.3%), and American Indians (23.3%). Aside from Whites, Asians are the only other group to have an underemployment rate less than the national average.

In general, rural (nonmetro) minorities have among the highest rates of underemployment. Essentially one quarter of nonmetro Blacks, and over one quarter of nonmetro Native Americans are underemployed. Interestingly, relatively little residential variation is seen among Hispanics—they have high rates across the board. Marital status also makes a big difference, with distinct disadvantages seen among those who have never been married (22.1%) and widows (18.5%)—a pattern which is clearly reflective of the nonlinear age gradient in underemployment noted above. Human capital theory holds that workers are remunerated in direct proportion to the bundle of skills they bring to the labor force. It is little surprise then that of all these variables the one with the strongest association with underemployment is education. Nearly three in 10 workers who never completed high school are underemployed, versus 16.0% among high school graduates, and only 6.6% among college graduates. There are clear differences also with respect to industry of employment, with those in extractive industries (farming, forestry, fishing, mining) having particularly high rates of underemployment. Finally, regional differences in underemployment are not substantial—though residents of the South and West appear at a slight disadvantage.

## Conclusion

Americans make ends meet principally through income earned in the formal labor market. As that market has bifurcated to some degree into good and bad jobs, and as the new welfare system has placed unprecedented emphasis on employment as a route out of poverty, concerns have been raised about employment hardship among the most vulnerable Americans. Concerns about employment adequacy are not at all new; they can be traced back at least to the Great Depression. An important way in which employment hardship has been conceptualized and defined is as underemployment. The overarching purpose of this paper has been [to provide] a history and critique of underemployment, by reviewing the prevailing literature on this topic, and offering a brief statistical portrait of underemployment in the United States today.

Certain conclusions bear emphasis. First, the Labor Utilization Framework (LUF), and the conventional measure of underemployment it gave rise to, is clearly a superior alternative to unemployment alone as a measure of employment hardship. In keeping with the LUF, it offers a more comprehensive measure that includes other forms of visible underemployment (e.g., involuntary part-time work) and invisible underemployment (e.g., working poverty). Of course, no standardized measure of any important concept will be perfect, and underemployment is not without flaws. Some of these concern problems with the conventional operationalization itself (e.g., using poverty thresholds that ignore cost of living differences), while others have to do with related forms of employment hardship (e.g., job security) which it does not measure. Together, these criticisms are minor; underemployment provides a useful way to plot trends over time as well as inequality between groups in the prevalence of employment hardship. In all years these trends are decidedly countercyclical, recently reflected in the fact that underemployment rose and then fell over the 1990s owing to the recession early in the decade and subsequent economic expansion. Inequality between groups in the risk of underemployment are often striking, and should be an issue of great policy concern. Women, minorities, the young, and those with low educational attainment are all especially vulnerable to underemployment. Moreover, these vulnerabilities are often particularly acute among residents of rural areas and central cities. . . .

## References

Barker, K., & Christensen, K. (1998). *Contingent work: American employment relations in transition*. Ithaca, NY: Cornell University Press.

Citro, C. F., & Michael, R. T. (1995). *Measuring poverty: A new approach*. Washington, DC: National Academy Press.

Clogg, C. C. (1979). *Measuring underemployment: Demographic indicators for the United States*. New York: Academic Press.

De Anda, R. M. (1991). Inequality at work: A comparison of underemployment and stratification between Mexican-origin and White workers. Unpublished doctoral dissertation, The University of Arizona, Tucson, AZ.

——. (1994). Unemployment and underemployment among Mexican-origin workers. *Hispanic Journal of Behavioral Sciences*, 16 (2), 163–175.

——. (1996). Falling back: Mexican-origin men and women in the U.S. economy. In R. M. De Anda (Ed.), *Chicanas and Chicanos in contemporary society* (pp. 41–49). Needham Heights, MA: Simon and Schuster.

De Jong, G. F., & Madamba, A. (2001). A double disadvantage? Minority group, immigrant status, and underemployment in the United States. *Social Science Quarterly*, 82, 117–130.

Hauser, P. M. (1974). The measurement of labor utilization. *The Malayan Economic Review*, 19, 1–17.

Hippie, S. F. (1997, December). Worker displacement in an expanding economy. *Monthly Labor Review*, pp. 26–39.

Jensen, L., Findeis, J. L., Hsu, W., & Schachter, J. P. (1999). Slipping into and out of underemployment: Another disadvantage for nonmetropolitan workers? *Rural Sociology*, 64, 417–438.

Jensen, L., & Slack, T. (2000). Marginal employment. In E. F. Borgatta & R. J. V. Montgomery (Eds.), *The encyclopedia of sociology* (pp. 1719–1725). New York: MacMillan.

Levitan, S. A., Mangum, G. L., & Mangum, S. L. (1998). *Programs in aid of the poor* (7th ed.). Baltimore: Johns Hopkins Press.

Lichter, D. T., & Jensen, L. (2001). Rural poverty and welfare before and after PRWORA. *Rural America*, 16, 28–35.

Mutchler, J. E. (1985). Underemployment and gender: Demographic and structural indicators. Doctoral dissertation. The University of Texas, Austin.

Nelson, M. K., & Smith, J. (1999). *Working hard and making do: Surviving in small town America*. Berkeley, CA: University of California Press.

Slack, T., & Jensen, L. (2002). Race, ethnicity and underemployment in nonmetropolitan America: A thirty-year profile. *Rural Sociology*, 67 (2), 208–233.

Soltero, J. M. (1996). *Inequality in the workplace: Underemployment among Mexicans, African Americans, and Whites*. New York: Garland.

Sullivan, T. A. (1978). *Marginal workers, marginal jobs: Underutilization of the U.S. work force*. Austin: University of Texas Press.

Sullivan, T. A., & Hauser, P. M. (1978). The Labor Utilization Framework: Assumptions, data and policy implications. National Commission on Employment and Unemployment Statistics. Background Paper No. 18. Washington, DC: USGPO.

## Review

1. What is meant by underemployment?

2. Among which groups is underemployment the highest?

3. Compare underemployment in nonmetropolitan with metropolitan areas.

## Application

Check unemployment and underemployment on the web. What differences do you find in the sheer number of hits? Read some of the materials on underemployment. What kind of information did you gather that could add to this article? Write a letter to the editor of a local paper, pointing out the importance of underemployment and suggesting that some action is needed for the federal government to be more aware of the problem and to take it into account in creating labor-related policies and programs.

## Related Web Sites

1. *http://www.ironminds.com/ironminds/ issues/001121/workplace.shtml.* A personal story of dealing with underemployment.

2. *http://www.oise.utoronto.ca/~dliving stone/beyondhc/.* An article about underemployment in Canada.

---

# Part Four

## *Education*

Education is the institution involved in socializing people to function in their society. In the United States, education enables people to be effective citizens, to prepare for upward mobility, and to engage in personal development. The value that Americans place on education is reflected in the following data on attainment. From 1960 to 2000, the proportion of Americans completing four or more years of high school rose from 41.1 percent to 84.1 percent and the proportion completing four or more years of college rose from 7.7 percent to 25.6 percent.

The two selections in this part illustrate that education in the United States has many problems. The first selection examines the plight of ghetto schools. The second looks at a common problem in schools today—a culture that fosters cruelty and violence. ✦

# 32
# Savage Inequalities

*Jonathan Kozol*

*In theory, social institutions operate for the well-being of people. The government protects citizens and provides essential services for them. The economy allows people to fulfill their basic needs and aspirations. Education provides people with the skills necessary to function in the economy and with the necessary information and understanding to pursue meaningful lives. And so on.*

*However, the fact that inequality pervades every society suggests that institutions do not benefit everyone equally. We have already presented selections about the unequal division of labor in the family and inequalities in the economy. In this selection, we encounter a graphic picture of inequality in education, inequality that exists among schools in the same district.*

*Americans value education. We tout it as a necessary resource for social mobility and as essential to the pursuit of a fulfilling life. Indeed, education functions this way for some people. But not for all. Kozol, the author of this selection, has taught in ghetto schools where students face severe hurdles to an adequate education. Those hurdles include inadequate resources such as supplies and well-trained teachers; a climate of fear engendered by gangs and weapons; a student culture of contempt for learning; and homes that may offer little in the way of preparation and support. In sum, the students are in a situation of **ritualized deprivation**—a school atmosphere in which the rituals of teaching and learning go on while the students focus more on surviving than on learning.*

In order to find Public School 261 in District 10, a visitor is told to look for a mortician's office. The funeral home, which faces Jerome Avenue in the North Bronx, is easy to identify by its green awning. The school is next door, in a former roller-skating rink. No sign identifies the building as a school. A metal awning frame without an awning supports a flagpole, but there is no flag.

In the street in front of the school there is an elevated public transit line. Heavy traffic fills the street. The existence of the school is virtually concealed within this crowded city block.

In a vestibule between the outer and inner glass doors of the school there is a sign with these words: "All children are capable of learning."

Beyond the inner doors a guard is seated. The lobby is long and narrow. The ceiling is low. There are no windows. All the teachers that I see at first are middle-aged white women. The principal, who is also a white woman, tells me that the school's "capacity" is 900 but that there are 1,300 children here. The size of classes for fifth and sixth grade children in New York, she says, is "capped" at 32, but she says that class size in the school goes "up to 34." (I later see classes, however, as large as 37.) Classes for younger children, she goes on, are "capped at 25," but a school can go above this limit if it puts an extra adult in the room. Lack of space, she says, prevents the school from operating a prekindergarten program.

I ask the principal where her children go to school. They are enrolled in private school, she says.

"Lunchtime is a challenge for us," she explains. "Limited space obliges us to do it in three shifts, 450 children at a time."

Textbooks are scarce and children have to share their social studies books. The principal says there is one full-time pupil counselor and another who is here two days a week: a ratio of 930 children to one counselor. The carpets are patched and sometimes taped together to conceal an open space. "I could use some new rugs," she observes.

To make up for the building's lack of windows and the crowded feeling that results, the staff puts plants and fish tanks in the corridors. Some of the plants are flourishing. Two boys, released from class, are in a corridor beside a tank, their noses pressed against the glass. A school of pinkish fish inside the tank are darting back and forth. Farther down the corridor a small Hispanic girl is watering the plants.

Two first grade classes share a single room without a window, divided only by a blackboard. Four kindergartens and a sixth grade class of Spanish-speaking children have been packed into a single room in which, again, there is no window. A second grade bilingual class of 37 children has its own room but again there is no window.

By eleven o'clock, the lunchroom is already packed with appetite and life. The kids line up to get their meals, then eat them in ten minutes. After that, with no place they can go to play, they sit and wait until it's time to line up and go back to class.

On the second floor I visit four classes taking place within another undivided space. The room has a low ceiling. File cabinets and movable blackboards give a small degree of isolation to each class. Again, there are no windows.

The library is a tiny, windowless and claustrophobic room. I count approximately 700 books. Seeing no reference books, I ask a teacher if encyclopedias and other reference books are kept in classrooms.

"We don't have encyclopedias in classrooms," she replies. "That is for the suburbs."

The school, I am told, has 26 computers for its 1,300 children. There is one small gym and children get one period, and sometimes two, each week. Recess, however, is not possible because there is no playground. "Head Start," the principal says, "scarcely exists in District 10. We have no space." The school, I am told, is 90 percent black and Hispanic; the other 10 percent are Asian, white or Middle Eastern.

In a sixth grade social studies class the walls are bare of words or decorations. There seems to be no ventilation system, or, if one exists, it isn't working.

The class discusses the Nile River and the Fertile Crescent.

The teacher, in a droning voice: "How is it useful that these civilizations developed close to rivers?"

A child, in a good loud voice: "What kind of question is that?"

In my notes I find these words: "An uncomfortable feeling—being in a building with no windows. There are metal ducts across the room. Do they give air? I feel asphyxiated . . ."

On the top floor of the school, a sixth grade of 30 children shares a room with 29 bilingual second graders. Because of the high class size there is an assistant with each teacher. This means that 59 children and four grown-ups—63 in all—must share a room that, in a suburban school, would hold no more than 20 children and one teacher. There are, at least, some outside windows in this room—it is the only room with windows in the school—and the room has a high ceiling. It is a relief to see some daylight.

I return to see the kindergarten classes on the ground floor and feel stifled once again by lack of air and the low ceiling. Nearly 120 children and adults are doing what they can to make the best of things: 80 children in four kindergarten classes, 30 children in the sixth grade class, and about eight grown-ups who are aides and teachers. The kindergarten children sitting on the worn rug, which is patched with tape, look up at me and turn their heads to follow me as I walk past them.

As I leave the school, a sixth grade teacher stops to talk. I ask her, "Is there air conditioning in warmer weather?"

Teachers, while inside the building, are reluctant to give answers to this kind of question. Outside, on the sidewalk, she is less constrained: "I had an awful room last year. In the winter it was 56 degrees. In the summer it was up to 90. It was sweltering."

I ask her, "Do the children ever comment on the building?"

"They don't say," she answers, "but they know."

I ask her if they see it as a racial message.

"All these children see TV," she says. "They know what suburban schools are like. Then they look around them at their school. This was a roller-rink, you know. . . . They don't comment on it but you see it in their eyes. They understand."

On the following morning I visit P.S. 79, another elementary school in the same district. "We work under difficult circumstances," says the principal, James Carter, who is black. "The school was built to hold one thousand students. We have 1,550. We are badly overcrowded. We need smaller classes but, to do this, we would need more space. I can't add five teachers. I would have no place to put them."

Some experts, I observe, believe that class size isn't a real issue. He dismisses this abruptly. "It doesn't take a genius to discover that you learn more in a smaller class. I have to bus some 60 kindergarten children elsewhere, since I have no space for them. When they return next year, where do I put them?

"I can't set up a computer lab. I have no room. I had to put a class into the library. I have no librarian. There are two gymnasiums upstairs but they cannot be used for sports. We hold more classes there. It's unfair to measure us against the suburbs. They have 17 to 20 children in a class. Average class size in this school is 30.

"The school is 29 percent black, 70 percent Hispanic. Few of these kids get Head Start. There is no space in the district. Of 200 kindergarten children, 50 maybe get some kind of preschool."

I ask him how much difference preschool makes.

"Those who get it do appreciably better. I can't overestimate its impact but, as I have said, we have no space."

The school tracks children by ability, he says. "There are five to seven levels in each grade. The highest level is equivalent to 'gifted' but it's not a full-scale gifted program. We don't have the funds. We have no science room. The science teachers carry their equipment with them."

We sit and talk within the nurse's room. The window is broken. There are two holes in the ceiling. About a quarter of the ceiling has been patched and covered with a plastic garbage bag.

"Ideal class size for these kids would be 15 to 20. Will these children ever get what white kids in the suburbs take for granted? I don't think so. If you ask me why, I'd have to speak of race and social class. I don't think the powers that be in New York City understand, or want to understand, that if they do not give

these children a sufficient education to lead healthy and productive lives, we will be their victims later on. We'll pay the price someday—in violence, in economic costs. I despair of making this appeal in any terms but these. You cannot issue an appeal to conscience in New York today. The fair-play argument won't be accepted. So you speak of violence and hope that it will scare the city into action."

While we talk, three children who look six or seven years old come to the door and ask to see the nurse, who isn't in the school today. One of the children, a Puerto Rican girl, looks haggard. "I have a pain in my tooth," she says. The principal says, "The nurse is out. Why don't you call your mother?" The child says, "My mother doesn't have a phone." The principal sighs. "Then go back to your class." When she leaves, the principal is angry. "It's amazing to me that these children ever make it with the obstacles they face. Many do care and they do try, but there's a feeling of despair. The parents of these children want the same things for their children that the parents in the suburbs want. Drugs are not the cause of this. They are the symptom. Nonetheless, they're used by people in the suburbs and rich people in Manhattan as another reason to keep children of poor people at a distance."

I ask him, "Will white children and black children ever go to school together in New York?"

"I don't see it," he replies. "I just don't think it's going to happen. It's a dream. I simply do not see white folks in Riverdale agreeing to cross-bus with kids like these. A few, maybe. Very few. I don't think I'll live to see it happen."

I ask him whether race is the decisive factor. Many experts, I observe, believe that wealth is more important in determining these inequalities.

"This," he says—and sweeps his hand around him at the room, the garbage bag, the ceiling—"would not happen to white children."

In a kindergarten class the children sit cross-legged on a carpet in a space between two walls of books. Their 26 faces are turned up to watch their teacher, an elderly black woman. A little boy who sits beside me is involved in trying to tie bows in his shoelaces. The children sing a song: "Lift Every Voice." On the wall are these handwritten words: "Beautiful, also, are the souls of my people."

In a very small room on the fourth floor, 52 people in two classes do their best to teach and learn. Both are first grade classes. One, I am informed, is "low ability." The other is bilingual.

"The room is barely large enough for one class," says the principal.

The room is 25 by 50 feet. There are 26 first graders and two adults on the left, 22 others and two adults on the right. On the wall there is the picture of a small white child, circled by a Valentine, and a Gainsborough painting of a child in a formal dress.

"We are handicapped by scarcity," one of the teachers says. "One fifth of these children may be at grade level by the year's end."

A boy who may be seven years old climbs on my lap without an invitation and removes my glasses. He studies my face and runs his fingers through my hair. "You have nice hair," he says. I ask him where he lives and he replies, "Times Square Hotel," which is a homeless shelter in Manhattan.

I ask him how he gets here.

"With my father. On the train," he says.

"How long does it take?"

"It takes an hour and a half."

I ask him when he leaves his home.

"My mother wakes me up at five o'clock."

"When do you leave?"

"Six-thirty."

I ask him how he gets back to Times Square.

"My father comes to get me after school."

From my notes: "He rides the train three hours every day in order to attend this segregated school. It would be a shorter ride to Riverdale. There are rapid shuttle-vans that make that trip in only 20 minutes. Why not let him go to school right in Manhattan, for that matter?"

At three o'clock the nurse arrives to do her recordkeeping. She tells me she is here three days a week. "The public hospital we use for an emergency is called North Central. It's not a hospital that I will use if I am given any choice. Clinics in the private hospitals are far more likely to be staffed by an experienced physician."

She hesitates a bit as I take out my pen, but then goes on: "I'll give you an example. A little girl I saw last week in school was trembling and shaking and could not control the motions of her arms. I was concerned and called her home. Her mother came right up to school and took her to North Central. The intern concluded that the child was upset by 'family matters'—nothing more—that there was nothing wrong with her. The mother was offended by the diagnosis. She did not appreciate his words or his assumptions. The truth is, there was nothing wrong at home. She brought the child back to school. I thought that she was ill. I told her mother, 'Go to Montefiore.' It's a private hospital, and well respected. She took my advice, thank God. It turned out that the child had a neurological disorder. She is now in treatment.

"This is the kind of thing our children face. Am I saying that the city underserves this population? You can draw your own conclusions."

Out on the street, it takes a full half hour to flag down a cab. Taxi drivers in New York are sometimes disconcertingly direct in what they say. When they are contemptuous of poor black people, their contempt is unadorned. When they're sympathetic and compassionate, their observations often go right to the heart of things. "Oh . . . they neglect these children," says the driver. "They leave them in the streets and slums to live and die." We stop at a light. Outside the window of the taxi, aimless men are standing in a semicircle while another man is working on his car. Old four-story buildings with their windows boarded, cracked or missing are on every side.

I ask the driver where he's from. He says Afghanistan. Turning in his seat, he gestures at the street and shrugs. "If you don't, as an American, begin to give these kids the kind of education that you give the kids of Donald Trump, you're asking for disaster."

Two months later, on a day in May, I visit an elementary school in Riverdale. The dogwoods and magnolias on the lawn in front of P.S. 24 are in full blossom on the day I visit.

There is a well-tended park across the street, another larger park three blocks away. To the left of the school is a playground for small children, with an innovative jungle gym, a slide and several climbing toys. Behind the school there are two playing fields for older kids. The grass around the school is neatly trimmed.

The neighborhood around the school, by no means the richest part of Riverdale, is nonetheless expensive and quite beautiful. Residences in the area—some of which are large, free-standing houses, others condominiums in solid redbrick buildings—sell for prices in the region of $400,000; but some of the larger Tudor houses on the winding and tree-shaded streets close to the school can cost up to $1 million. The excellence of P.S. 24, according to the principal, adds to the value of these homes. Advertisements in the *New York Times* will frequently inform prospective buyers that a house is "in the neighborhood of P.S. 24."

The school serves 825 children in the kindergarten through sixth grade. This is approximately half the student population crowded into P.S. 79, where 1,550 children fill a space intended for 1,000, and a great deal smaller than the 1,300 children packed into the former skating rink; but the principal of P.S. 24, a capable and energetic man named David Rothstein, still regards it as excessive for an elementary school.

The school is integrated in the strict sense that the middle- and upper-middle-class white children here do occupy a building that contains some Asian and Hispanic and black children; but there is little integration in the classrooms since the vast majority of the Hispanic and black children are assigned to "special" classes on the basis of evaluations that have classified them "EMR"—"educable mentally retarded"—or else, in the worst of cases, "TMR"—"trainable mentally retarded."

I ask the principal if any of his students qualify for free-lunch programs. "About 130 do," he says. "Perhaps another 35 receive their lunches at reduced price. Most of these kids are in the special classes. They do not come from this neighborhood."

The very few nonwhite children that one sees in mainstream classes tend to be Japanese or else of other Asian origins. Riverdale, I learn, has been the residence of choice for many years to members of the diplomatic corps.

The school therefore contains effectively two separate schools: one of about 130 children, most of whom are poor, Hispanic, black, assigned to one of the 12 special classes; the other of some 700 mainstream students, almost all of whom are white or Asian.

There is a third track also—this one for the students who are labeled "talented" or "gifted." This is termed a "pullout" program since the children who are so identified remain in mainstream classrooms but are taken out for certain periods each week to be provided with intensive and, in my opinion, excellent instruction in some areas of reasoning and logic often known as "higher-order skills" in the contemporary jargon of the public schools. Children identified as "gifted" are admitted to this program in first grade and, in most cases, will remain there for six years. Even here, however, there are two tracks of the gifted. The regular gifted classes are provided with only one semester of this specialized instruction yearly. Those very few children, on the other hand, who are identified as showing the most promise are assigned, beginning in the third grade, to a program that receives a full-year regimen.

In one such class, containing ten intensely verbal and impressive fourth grade children, nine are white and one is Asian. The "special" class I enter first, by way of contrast, has twelve children of whom only one is white and none is Asian. These racial breakdowns prove to be predictive of the school-wide pattern.

In a classroom for the gifted on the first floor of the school, I ask a child what the class is doing. "Logic and syllogisms," she replies. The room is fitted with a planetarium. The principal says that all the elementary schools in District 10 were given the same planetariums ten years ago but that certain schools, because of overcrowding, have been forced to give them up. At P.S. 261, according to my notes, there was a domelike space that had been built to hold a planetarium, but the planetarium had been removed to free up space for the small library collection. P.S. 24, in contrast, has a spacious library that holds almost 8,000 books. The windows are decorated with attractive, brightly colored curtains and look out on flowering trees. The principal says that it's inadequate, but it appears spectacular to me after the cubicle that holds a meager 700 books within the former skating rink.

The district can't afford librarians, the principal says, but P.S. 24, unlike the poorer schools of District 10, can draw on educated parent volunteers who staff the room in shifts three days a week. A parent organization also raises independent funds to buy materials, including books, and will soon be running a fund-raiser to enhance the library's collection.

In a large and sunny first grade classroom that I enter next, I see 23 children, all of whom are white or Asian. In another first grade, there are 22 white children and two others who are Japanese. There is a computer in each class. Every classroom also has a modern fitted sink.

In a second grade class of 22 children, there are two black children and three Asian children. Again, there is a sink and a computer. A sixth grade social studies class has only one black child. The children have an in-class research area that holds some up-to-date resources. A set of encyclopedias (World Book, 1985) is in a rack beside a window. The children are doing a Spanish language lesson when I enter. Foreign languages begin in sixth grade at the school, but Spanish is offered also to the kindergarten children. As in every room at P.S. 24, the window shades are clean and new, the floor is neatly tiled in gray and green, and there is not a single light bulb missing.

Walking next into a special class, I see twelve children. One is white. Eleven are black. There are no Asian children. The room is half the size of mainstream classrooms. "Because of overcrowding," says the principal, "we have had to split these rooms in half." There is no computer and no sink.

I enter another special class. Of seven children, five are black, one is Hispanic, one is white. A little black boy with a large head sits in the far corner and is gazing at the ceiling. "Placement of these kids," the principal explains, "can usually be traced to neurological damage."

In my notes: "How could so many of these children be brain-damaged?"

Next door to the special class is a woodworking shop. "This shop is only for the special classes," says the principal. The children learn to punch in time cards at the door, he says, in order to prepare them for employment.

The fourth grade gifted class, in which I spend the last part of the day, is humming with excitement. "I start with these children in the first grade," says the teacher. "We pull them out of mainstream classes on the basis of their test results and other factors such as the opinion of their teachers. Out of this group, beginning in third grade, I pull out the ones who show the most potential, and they enter classes such as this one."

The curriculum they follow, she explains, "emphasizes critical thinking, reasoning and logic." The planetarium, for instance, is employed not simply for the study of the universe as it exists. "Children also are designing their own galaxies," the teacher says.

A little girl sitting around a table with her classmates speaks with perfect poise: "My name is Susan. We are in the fourth grade gifted program."

I ask them what they're doing and a child says, "My name is Laurie and we're doing problem-solving."

A rather tall, good-natured boy who is half-standing at the table tells me that his name is David. "One thing that we do," he says, "is logical thinking. Some problems, we find, have more than one good answer. We need to learn not simply to be logical in our own thinking but to show respect for someone else's logic even when an answer may be technically incorrect."

When I ask him to explain this, he goes on, "A person who gives an answer that is not 'correct' may nonetheless have done some interesting thinking that we should examine. 'Wrong' answers may be more useful to examine than correct ones."

I ask the children if reasoning and logic are innate or if they're things that you can learn.

"You know some things to start with when you enter school," Susan says. "But we also learn some things that other children don't."

I ask her to explain this.

"We know certain things that other kids don't know because we're taught them."

She has braces on her teeth. Her long brown hair falls almost to her waist. Her loose white T-shirt has the word TRI-LOGIC on the front. She tells me that Tri-Logic is her father's firm.

Laurie elaborates on the same point: "Some things you know. Some kinds of logic are inside of you to start with. There are other things that someone needs to teach you."

David expands on what the other two have said: "Everyone can think and speak in logical ways unless they have a mental problem. What this program does is bring us to a higher form of logic."

The class is writing a new "Bill of Rights." The children already know the U.S. Bill of Rights and they explain its first four items to me with precision. What they are examining today, they tell me, is the very *concept* of a "right." Then they will create their own compendium of rights according to their own analysis and definition. Along one wall of the classroom, opposite the planetarium, are seven Apple II computers on which children have developed rather subtle color animations that express the themes—of greed and domination, for example—that they also have described in writing.

"This is an upwardly mobile group," the teacher later says. "They have exposure to whatever New York City has available. Their parents may take them to the theater, to museums. . . ."

In my notes: "Six girls, four boys. Nine white, one Chinese. I am glad they have this class. But what about the others? Aren't there ten black children in the school who could enjoy this also?"

The teacher gives me a newspaper written, edited and computer-printed by her sixth grade gifted class. The children, she

tells me, are provided with a link to kids in Europe for transmission of news stories.

A science story by one student asks if scientists have ever falsified their research. "Gregor Mendel," the sixth grader writes, "the Austrian monk who founded the science of genetics, published papers on his work with peas that some experts say were statistically too good to be true. Isaac Newton, who formulated the law of gravitation, relied on unseemly mathematical sleight of hand in his calculations. . . . Galileo Galilei, founder of modern scientific method, wrote about experiments that were so difficult to duplicate that colleagues doubted he had done them."

Another item in the paper, also by a sixth grade student, is less esoteric: "The Don Cossacks dance company, from Russia, is visiting the United States. The last time it toured America was 1976. . . . The Don Cossacks will be in New York City for two weeks at the Neil Simon Theater. Don't miss it!"

The tone is breezy—and so confident! That phrase—"Don't miss it!"—speaks a volume about life in Riverdale.

"What makes a good school?" asks the principal when we are talking later on. "The building and teachers are part of it, of course. But it isn't just the building and the teachers. Our kids come from good families and the neighborhood is good. In a three-block area we have a public library, a park, a junior high. . . . Our typical sixth grader reads at eighth grade level." In a quieter voice he says, "I see how hard my colleagues work in schools like P.S. 79. You have children in those neighborhoods who live in virtual hell. They enter school five years behind. What do they get?" Then, as he spreads his hands out on his desk, he says: "I have to ask myself why there should be an elementary school in District 10 with fifteen hundred children. Why should there be an elementary school within a skating rink? Why should the Board of Ed allow this? This is not the way that things should be."

Stark as the inequities in District 10 appear, educators say that they are "mild" in comparison to other situations in the city. Some of the most stunning inequality, according to a report by the Community Service Society, derives from allocations granted by state legislators to school districts where they have political allies. The poorest districts in the city get approximately 90 cents per pupil from these legislative grants, while the richest districts have been given $14 for each pupil.

Newspapers in New York City have reported other instances of the misallocation of resources. "The Board of Education," wrote the *New York Post* during July of 1987, "was hit with bombshell charges yesterday that money earmarked for fighting drug abuse and illiteracy in ghetto schools was funneled instead to schools in wealthy areas."

In receipt of extra legislative funds, according to the Post, affluent districts were funded "at a rate 14 times greater than low-income districts." The paper said the city's poorest areas were underfunded "with stunning consistency."

The report by the Community Service Society cites an official of the New York City Board of Education who remarks that there is "no point" in putting further money "into some poor districts" because, in his belief, "new teachers would not stay there." But the report observes that, in an instance where beginning teacher salaries were raised by nearly half, "that problem largely disappeared"—another interesting reminder of the difference money makes when we are willing to invest it. Nonetheless, says the report, "the perceptions that the poorest districts are beyond help still remains. . . ." Perhaps the worst result of such beliefs, says the report, is the message that resources would be "wasted on poor children." This message "trickles down to districts, schools, and classrooms." Children hear and understand this theme—they are poor investments—and behave accordingly. If society's resources would be wasted on their destinies, perhaps their own determination would be wasted too. "Expectations are a powerful force. . . ," the CSS observes.

Despite the evidence, the CSS report leans over backwards not to fuel the flames of racial indignation. "In the present climate," the report says, "suggestions of racism must be made with caution. However, it is ines-

capable that these inequities are being perpetrated on [school] districts which are virtually all black and Hispanic. . . ." While the report says, very carefully, that there is no "evidence" of "deliberate individual discrimination," it nonetheless concludes that "those who allocate resources make decisions over and over again which penalize the poorest districts." Analysis of city policy, the study says, "speaks to systemic bias which constitutes a conspiracy of effect. . . . Whether consciously or not, the system writes off its poorest students."

## Review

1. Compare the poor schools described by Kozol with those of your own experience.

2. What are the major deficiencies in the poor schools described by Kozol?

3. Contrast the resources and programs in the poor schools with those in Riverdale.

4. Why are resources not allocated more equitably to various schools in the district?

## Applications

1. With your instructor's permission, organize a workshop for your class on inequality in education. Among other things, you can

   a. show clips from movies that portray education in a poor neighborhood

   b. have teachers or administrators from poor and wealthy schools describe their resources and programs

   c. have students from poor and wealthy schools describe their experiences

   d. have students find and report on information culled from popular or professional writings

2.  Visit a school in a poor area and one in a wealthy area. Ask for permission to sit in and observe a class for an hour. Tour both schools and note their facilities. Write up a report of your observations.

## Related Web Sites

1.  *http://www.edweek.org/.* Site of a weekly web educational journal that covers all aspects of elementary and secondary education.

2.  *http://www.ed.gov/index.jhtml.* Home page of the U.S. Department of Education with access to numerous publications, speeches, press releases, and data sources.

---

# 33
# At School, a Cruel Culture

*Darcia Harris Bowman*

*The school, in theory, is a place of learning. Every student is encouraged to maximize his or her potential and to discover the joy of gaining a wide range of understanding about the world in which we live. As Kozol showed, a ghetto school may be a place where students must put as much effort into surviving as into learning, a place where learning is severely impeded by ritualized deprivation.*

*What about schools in well-to-do neighborhoods? Do they also have problems? In the 1990s the nation was shocked by a series of shootings at schools, none of which were in ghetto areas. The shootings dramatized the fact that school violence is a serious problem. Recent surveys show that literally millions of high-school students have had physical fights at school at least once during a year's time (including 20 percent of males), have had property stolen or damaged at school, and have admitted to carrying a weapon to school during the 30 days prior to the survey (13 percent of males and 4 percent of females).*

*There is an atmosphere of fear in many of the nation's schools. Students may feel more apprehension about safety than excitement about learning opportunities as they go off to school. The threat of violence comes both from the loner who shows up one day with a gun and the known bullies who can make life miserable for others. Darcia Bowman labels this situation a "cruel culture." She notes that those who resort to shooting their classmates have often been the victims of bullying or scorn. Most bullied students do not go to such lengths, of course. But the experience of being bullied or taunted does detract from students' ability to maximize their learning. In an atmosphere of fear, the school becomes something to endure rather than a place to flourish.*

Elizabeth Catherine Bush's parents hoped her life would improve after they removed her from the reach of bullies in the Jersey Shore Area School District in Pennsylvania last year and placed her in a small private school.

But even at Bishop Neumann High School—a 230-student Roman Catholic institution in nearby Williamsport with a mission to educate "in a climate of love and hope"— the teasing continued. When the distraught 14-year-old shot and injured a popular cheerleader in the school cafeteria on March 7, and then threatened to turn the gun on herself, some believed the treatment she had received at the hands of other students was to blame.

"At Jersey Shore, she had stones thrown at her, she was chased. There was a note left in her locker that said, 'Get out of this school, get out of this town, or we'll harm your parents,'" said the girl's mother, Catherine A. Bush. "[The bullies] just gravitated to her. I think it's anyone who chooses a different path . . . or believes something different from what other kids think."

Teasing, name-calling, and bullying have long been synonymous with adolescence, but the possible consequences of a schoolwide culture of casual cruelty have never been as deadly as they are today.

From Jonesboro, Ark., to Santee, Calif., teenagers allegedly abused by classmates have been fighting back with bullets. In the bloodiest of those vengeful rampages, two teenagers in Jefferson County, Colo., killed 12 of their classmates and a teacher before taking their own lives in April of 1999.

While the incidents have prompted many districts to heighten security and crack down on bullies, some experts argue that not enough attention is being paid to changing the unfeeling or openly hostile way so many students treat one another on a day-to-day basis.

"One of the issues that seems to be surfacing more and more is the need to focus on bullies—anti-bullying rules, zero tolerance, classes on how to deal with bullies," said Nancy Guerra, a professor of psychology at the University of California, Riverside. "My only concern here is that bullies are defined as extreme cases of kids who taunt others, pick on those weaker. [They] are few and far between. What is really happening," she said, "is that there is a more general atmosphere of meanness, where teasing and taunting are the norm among most students, rather than the exception."

Young people seem to agree.

In a nationwide survey of nearly 70,000 students in grades 6–12, only 37 percent of the respondents said students showed respect for one another. Fewer than half considered themselves positive role models for other students. And, while 80 percent of the girls surveyed said it bothered them "when others are insulted or hurt verbally," only 57 percent of the boys expressed a similar attitude.

"The only zero tolerance that happens in schools is the zero tolerance between kids," said Russell J. Quaglia, the director of the National Center for Student Aspirations, located at the University of Maine in Orono. "I think we're worse off now than we were in the 1950s with the race issues. We've got 'people' issues now. It's a lack of sensitivity [among students], but it's also a lack of a sense of responsibility for someone other than themselves."

## Angry Young Men

Elizabeth Bush of Bishop Neumann High, who according to her lawyer was ridiculed for her strong religious beliefs and her tendency to befriend other ostracized teenagers, is a rarity among the school shooters who have grabbed headlines in recent years. Overwhelmingly, the attackers have been boys: Andrew Golden and Mitchell Johnson at Westside Middle School in Jonesboro, Ark.; Kip Kinkel at Thurston High School in Springfield, Ore.; and Eric [Harris] and Dylan Klebold at Columbine High School in Colorado.

The country saw yet another name added to the list of boys angry enough to kill on March 5, [2001,] when 14-year-old Charles Andrew "Andy" Williams, allegedly opened fire in a restroom at Santana High School in Santee, Calif.

Mr. Williams reloaded his father's .22-caliber handgun four times during the course of the shooting, according to a police affidavit

for a search warrant of the boy's home unsealed last week. Two students were killed, and 13 other students or staff members were wounded.

The 9th grader, who faces being prosecuted as an adult, was described by other students as the target of incessant teasing and physical bullying. According to investigators, he said the people in Santee were different from those he had known when he lived in Frederick County, Md., until moving to California with his father last year. And, although he told police he had friends at Santana High, he also said he was disappointed with the school.

What many of the teenagers seem to have in common is a sense of alienation from peers.

In about two-thirds of school shootings that the U.S. Secret Service reviewed for a study last year, the attackers had felt persecuted, bullied, threatened, attacked, or injured by others. The agency found that a number of the teenagers had suffered sustained, severe bullying and harassment. The experience appeared to play a major role in motivating the ensuing violence.

"I think the biggest problem we have is the amount of alienation and rage in our young people," U.S. Secretary of Education Rod Paige said March 11 on the CBS News program "Face the Nation," after the school shootings in Santee and Williamsport.

"We [have] to figure out ways to make sure that a quality adult is in the life of every child, and we hope that quality adult would be a parent," Mr. Paige said. "But if it's not going to be a parent, then the school has to step in and fill the void."

But many researchers contend that some hallmark features of American schools contribute to the isolation of certain students.

Aaron R. Kipnis, the author of the 1999 book *Angry Young Men: How Parents, Teachers, and Counselors Can Help "Bad Boys" Become Good Men*, maintains that schools condone bullying, teasing, and cliques by labeling and dividing students according to their academic and athletic gifts.

"That automatic sorting," he argues, "strengthens cliques and leaves, some students—particularly nonathletic boys—out in the cold."

"The fact that schools issue varsity sweaters with letters to the top athletes, and not the top physics students, underscores this idea that physical prowess and athletic achievement is really what's most important," Mr. Kipnis said in an interview. "Anything else is geeky, nerdy, kooky, or uncool."

Once the lines have been drawn, he said, the groups on top will do what it takes to stay there. "One of the ways cliques reinforce themselves is by putting down whoever isn't in with them with teasing, taunting, and—in the case of some of these boys we've seen—physical abuse," he said.

## Setting an Example

If administrators and teachers hope to prevent violence from erupting in their schools, researchers say, they must reshape not only the attitudes of their students, but their own as well.

"Sometimes, we focus too much on the kids and not enough on the adults who are creating the culture," said Jean A. Baker, the director of the school psychology program at Michigan State University in East Lansing. "Kids see what we choose to show them. Schools that are very effective in preventing this kind of treatment are actively shaping their culture. Modeling the right behavior is a great way to start."

That work in large part falls to teachers and coaches, the adults with whom students have the most contact at school. But whether those authority figures are sending the right messages remains unclear, experts say.

Fewer than half of the students polled by the National Center for Student Aspirations said their teachers valued their opinions, and just 56 percent said teachers respected their thoughts.

"Things aren't going to change because there's a sign on the door that says, 'We care,'" Mr. Quaglia said. "We really need to teach kids respect and tolerance. So how do teachers model this behavior? I'm not sure they do, judging from the data, but I know they can."

Some experts suggest suburban and rural schools, where most of the highly publicized

shooting incidents of recent years have taken place, should look to schools in urban areas for clues on how to foster safer and more tolerant environments. There, where violence is often an everyday part of life, educators must work hard to promote peace and understanding among students from a variety of racial and ethnic backgrounds.

At T. C. Williams High School in Alexandria, Va., a 2,000-student school in a diverse district outside Washington, students are offered a number of avenues for working out their differences, including peer mediation and counseling. But more importantly, Principal John L. Porter said, the adults try to abide by the same code of conduct they want students to follow.

"You don't get on the PA and say 'Hey, we all gotta love one another,'" Mr. Porter said. "You've got to try to promote and show the reasons and the rationale for the behavior and have students understand that we're all different, and we're all people."

In Pennsylvania, Catherine A. Bush has only good things to say about Bishop Neumann High School's efforts and refuses to place the blame for her daughter's actions on students there. But as Elizabeth Bush awaits an uncertain fate in a nearby juvenile jail, her mother can't help but wonder if the cruelty of other students helped put her there.

"I don't know what can be done about this, but we have to do something," Ms. Bush said. "These are children, and we have to help them."

## Review

1. What does the author mean by a "cruel culture" at school, and to what extent do students agree that it exists?

2. Describe the characteristics of and situations faced by young males who are involved in school shootings.

3. What can be done to foster safer and more tolerant environments in schools?

## Application

Summarize this article for a small group of friends or acquaintances. Ask them to share their own experiences of bullying, threats, intolerance, or violence in elementary and high school (either as victims, perpetrators, or observers). What do they see as the causes of such behavior? What did the teachers or administrators do to address the problem? What would they do to change the culture of casual cruelty in schools?

## Related Web Sites

1. *http://serendip.brynmawr.edu/sci_edu/ education/violence.html*. Articles dealing with various aspects of violence in schools.

2. *http://www.lfcc.on.ca/bully.htm*. This site offers information for parents and teachers on all aspects of bullying behavior, including ways to deal with it.

# Part Five

## *Religion*

Religion is the institution that provides meaning for people through beliefs and practices defined as sacred. In symbolic interactionist terms, religion offers a specific kind of meaning to life—transcendent meaning. That is, religion assures people that they are involved in something that goes beyond personal pleasures and pains and has eternal significance.

The great majority of Americans believe in God and practice some kind of religion. At the same time, the extent to which religion is salient to everyday life varies among Americans. The selection in this part describes a group for whom religion is central and pervasive—the Hutterites. ✦

# 34

# A Forgotten People in Our Midst

*Donald W. Huffman*

**P**eople everywhere tend to fall prey to **ethnocentrism,** the view of one's own culture as the right and best way of life. Other cultures are then evaluated in terms of these values and beliefs. The more we learn about human diversity, however, the more we understand how ways different from our own can work quite well for other people.

*Different ways of life are found within as well as between societies. A **subculture** is a group within a society that shares much of the culture of the larger society while maintaining certain distinctive cultural patterns of its own. The distinctive patterns may be primarily religious (Hasidic Jews, Hare Krishna), racial/ethnic (immigrants who maintain the language and ways of the mother country), political (radical student organizations), or others. Subcultures may be viewed by members of the larger society as irrational, backward, undesirable, odd, dangerous, or some combination of those characteristics. In this selection, Donald Huffman discusses the way of life of the Hutterites, a religious subculture found in the United States and Canada.*

*The Hutterites fled to North America from Europe in the 1870s to escape persecution. They live in rural communities and practice Christian communism—working, eating, and worshiping together. Members have no personal possessions. The institution of religion dominates all other institutions and governs every aspect of Hutterite life.*

*There are three main groups, which differ in some ways from each other. The Schmiedeleut branch, to which Huffman refers, is the most progressive of the groups. But all of the groups*

*have a rigidly structured, highly religious, isolated way of life that holds little or no appeal to outsiders. Nevertheless, as Huffman points out, it works well for them.*

## I
## Introduction

**I** remember the day well—having said goodbye to my wife in metropolitan Pennsylvania, I quickly traveled by air to another world. In a brief eight hours I had moved from a modern urban world of possessions and conveniences to a radically different subculture, which one scholar characterized in this way: "Probably no other group in North America is further from mainstream Western values than this one." That group was a Hutterite colony located in the western plains of Minnesota.

But one hour from Hector International Airport in Fargo, North Dakota, I entered a subsociety with a distinctive way of life. From my daily experience of the radio, television, and the newspaper, the automobile, the relatively isolated nuclear family, the once-a-week experience of congregational worship, I was now about to enter a radically different world of insulation and isolation from modern society. It was different in terms of mass media exposure and consumption, a tri-lingual world of Tyrolean, German, and English, a world of work trucks and vans, an everyday experience of extended family relations, a world where religious belief and practice permeate daily existence, from the spoken prayers before and after an afternoon snack and every meal, to a worship service each day from 6:00–6:30 p.m., and a one and a half hour service on Sundays. Truly this was a different social and cultural world, one from whose historical roots and experiences in modern society we can learn a great deal, and one that for years has fascinated me, a professor of sociology keenly interested in cultural diversity and varied religious groups.

It was late in October 1998 that I drove into the Spring Prairie Colony in western Minnesota with the intention to live with the

Hutterites. A sabbatical granted me by my college had given me this rich opportunity. With relative ease I had located a number of rich secondary sources on the Hutterites. Then came the more daunting task, that of gaining entrance into one of the more than 300 colonies located in the Plains states and the western provinces of Canada for the purpose of conducting field research. Given the relative isolation of Hutterite colonies, both social and geographical, this was not an easy task. In the end, however, it was a very rewarding process. . . .

What did I discover, both as a sociologist and person who had been granted this unique opportunity to live with the Hutterites?

## II
## Historical and Religious Background of the Hutterites

Before I elaborate on some of my major findings, it is initially important to place this sect in historical perspective. For, as I quickly learned, to understand the Hutterite way of life one must first understand their roots.

The Hutterites, often referred to as "a forgotten people," have a rich and long history which is well-documented. From their roots in the Protestant Reformation, this Anabaptist group has persevered for well over four centuries as a radical experiment in communal living, what they themselves term "community of goods." In fact, they are the longest surviving experiment in communal living recorded in modern Western history.

Beginning with their roots in the Anabaptist movement in Switzerland in the 1520s, the Hutterites have moved from Moravia (now Czech Republic) to Hungary, Romania, Russia, the United States, and Canada. Their core beliefs—which can be traced to the New and Old Testaments and their beginnings as a distinct Christian sect in the 1530s—include adult baptism, community goods, and the total separation of church and state. This latter belief is attested in the Hutterites' refusal to bear arms or to participate in existing social and political institutions, either

through membership or leadership in such activities. Of signal importance—in keeping with the Apostolic Church, particularly as reported in Acts 2, verses 44–47—is the norm of living in colonies where community of goods, or sharing of all their goods in common, is practiced faithfully in each Hutterite colony. These beliefs and practices are directly linked to their frequent migrations from country to country, with reports that these migrations often occurred under the cloak of darkness and over treacherous mountain passes as they fled for their lives. It is a historical fact that the Hutterites have been threatened and persecuted by civil authorities in both Europe and the United States. Even more startling is the fact that their severest persecutors bore the name Christian. The Catholic Church, The Lutheran Church and Reformed Churches of John Calvin and Ulrich Zwingli frequently charged the Hutterites with heresy. Numerous leaders of the early Hutterite movement, including Jacob Hutter himself, were martyred for their faith. They were tortured on the rack for their beliefs and practices such as adult baptism; they were hanged, beheaded, drowned, and burned at the stake by religious authorities of the day who shared the Christian faith with them.

## III
## Survival and Prosperity: The Significance of Religion and Family in Colony Life

Given the numerous persecutions and hardships the Hutterites have experienced over the past four centuries, the central question I would like to address as a sociologist is: How have they survived and even prospered in the modern world?

I have no doubts that the Hutterite children are key to our understanding here. The 20 to 30 children and teenagers I observed during my week-long stay were, on the surface, like any in wider American society— lively, rambunctious, curious, eager to learn. But they are being molded in a very distinctive way. As children whose lives are lived nearly every moment in a colony largely cut off from the wider world, they are socialized from the day of their birth to become baptized adult members of the colony by the ages of 19 to 21. From early exposure to their deeply religious parents, to other relatives in the community who provide child care while parents engage in tasks assigned to them, to the colony nursery school for three to five year olds, to the colony school for first through ninth grades—children are thoroughly educated in the Hutterian way of life. Their education includes German language training (essential for studying the Bible and understanding the daily worship service conducted in German) in classes which they attend for two hours each school day from the age of six on. The children are early and continuously taught Hutterite history and hymnody and core communal values such as cooperation, shared work, and respect for all elders. In the Spring Prairie Colony a well-equipped print shop publishes a wide range of Hutterite school materials, including history texts, catechisms, workbooks, flash cards, maps, and songbooks, all of which are used in many colony classrooms. The print shop is run by a Hutterite elder (a former school teacher) and his son, with whom I had the privilege of working during my colony stay.

It was startling to me to discover that a group of 130 people, including 55 adults and 75 children, all of whom had unique personalities and talents, could function so well together as a cohesive community. This raised to consciousness a fascinating question: How could such cooperation and obvious unity of purpose exist on a daily basis, given the wide range of tasks that need to be accomplished in order for the colony to survive? One major factor, no doubt, is the division of labor which a number of early socioeconomic theorists, including Adam Smith, Herbert Spencer and Emile Durkheim found to be a powerful form of social cooperation that simultaneously allowed people to greatly increase their production. The labor of each individual, so coordinated, added to the wealth of all. During my stay in the Hutterite colony I observed such well-defined division of labor and community cohesiveness where carpen-

ters, plumbers, field workers, dairymen, hog and turkey managers and workers, meat processors, machinists, feed mill operators, housekeepers, beekeepers, printers, cooks, ministers, teachers, and mechanics all worked in complementary fashion to enable the colony to exist and thrive day by day. But for the Hutterites the key cohesive factor, as I discovered, is not division of labor, as important as that is to them. It is, without doubt, religious belief, religious practice (ritual), and community of goods that holds them together. Again Durkheim's sociological theory is relevant here. As argued in his *Elementary Forms of the Religious Life*, religion is another powerful force bringing about social cohesion amongst a tribe or group of people. In his classic definition of religion, Durkheim speaks of it in terms of "beliefs and practices which unite into one single moral community . . . all those who adhere to them" (1965, p. 62). I observed the powerful, binding force of religion in Spring Prairie Colony. For the Hutterites, religion permeates life. From the first spoken prayer before breakfast at 7:00 a.m., to the prayer following breakfast (and each meal), to the daily religious instruction of the children and youth (particularly the focus in the daily 4–6 p.m. German school with a Hutterite elder as teacher), to the experience of congregational worship each evening, and the frequently heard affirmation in both work and leisure that "if the Lord wills, it will be" religion is the life and breath of the Hutterite colony.

Religion is the key means of social control and is obviously effective because there has been no crime in Spring Prairie Colony in the 20 years of its existence. Admittedly, this is not a utopia. The minister, as leader of the colony, made that quite clear to me on a number of occasions during the long, broad ranging discussions we had each evening. "We are human beings with our frailties. But with God's help, through repentance and confession should there be any infraction of colony ordinances, things [that] can be are made right again." As for shunning, a practice Hutterites share with their Amish cousins, this extreme means of social control has had to be exercised only once in the colony's 20-year history. In this instance, within a week of his isolation (meals and lodging were provided the person separate from the colony dining hall), the young man made confession of his wrongdoing before the congregation and was at once fully re-integrated into colony life.

Religion is so effective amongst the Hutterites, not only because it centers the colony by drawing them together in worship, work and leisure time (as I experienced in the Sunday evening "singing" in which many youth gathered in an apartment for socializing, refreshments, and the singing of spiritual songs), but also because of strong family life which is so evident to the observer.

Large families are prized. The norm in Hutterite colonies today is five to six children per family. Each child is seen as a gift of God. For this reason, the minister spoke passionately about his opposition to abortion, which he considered sacrificing young human lives. The Hutterite family reinforces the importance of cooperation, work, and worship, viewing them as ways to glorify the God who both brought their people into existence and strengthened and maintained them through centuries of dislocation and persecution.

Add to this the daily interaction of children, parents, uncles, aunts, cousins, and grandparents, in a true and rare expression of the classic extended family in today's society—all of whom profess and practice their faith. From this, one can only begin to understand the tremendous reinforcement of communal values and standards which the family brings to the Hutterite experience. From this observational and factual base, it can reliably be concluded that faith, family, the living in true community (in the Apostolic sense of "community of goods"), are the keystones of Hutterian cohesion and strength.

## IV
## Work: Shared Responsibilities and Shared Benefits

Work is another activity which enables Hutterite society to cohere. Here Durkheim's and Smith's division of labor thesis, referred to earlier, is relevant. Max Weber's Protestant Ethic thesis is also instructive, though in a negative way for the Hutterites. For the Hutterite, work is practiced in a complementary, cooperative way. The Hutterite view and practice of work is radically different from the current, largely secularized "work ethic" of individual and corporate competition, a "get as much as you can as quickly as you can" philosophy characteristic of so much of business practice today.

Compared to the Old Order Amish and Mennonites, this Hutterite colony—as with many others, I was told—was extremely modern in terms of utilized technology. Large tractors, modern combines, earthmovers, trucks and vans, modern welding equipment, offset printers, sophisticated milking and feedmixing systems, computers, freezers, and one large microwave oven(!) were found in Spring Prairie Colony. Of course, if you are farming thirty-two hundred acres, raising wheat, barley, soybeans and sunflowers; and if you are raising ten thousand turkeys for market and two hundred hogs for sale each week; and if you are milking one hundred thirty-five cows twice a day, large and efficient equipment and a ready source of labor is required, as one can easily imagine. In Spring Prairie Colony this labor, both skilled and unskilled, is available to accomplish all of these tasks on a day-to-day basis. No hired help from the outside is needed, since all 55 adult members engage in the economic activity of the colony, as their strength and age allows. All of the work is under the leadership of the two ministers, the steward (who holds and expends all colony monies), and the farm manager. The first-tier leadership positions are filled by vote of all adult male members. The ministers are first nominated by elders within the colony, and then by elders representing colonies in the Schmiedeleut group. Adult males receiving at least five votes are then placed in the "lot." The one who selects the Bible with a slip of paper in it is the one selected by God to be minister, according to Hutterite belief. This elder will soon be ordained by the community as their minister, a position he will hold for the rest of his life. He can only be removed if he is found to be in serious violation of the Ordnung, the long established Hutterite charter, which specifically states the rules which govern colony life. The steward and farm manager are nominated and voted into office by adult colony members. After a period of probation, they may hold their positions on a permanent basis until either incompetence, infirmity, or death requires a new election.

Regarding the workday itself, it is an interesting mix of hard, steady work interspersed with meals, a brief break of family time after lunch, and refreshments in mid-afternoon. Except for demanding times of planting, harvesting, and the occasional processing of ducks and chickens (during which time members may work from twelve to fourteen hours a day), the day's work usually ceases by 5 or 5:30 p.m. This enables members to get ready for the evening worship service at 6 p.m., which is followed by dinner at 6:45 p.m. I was surprised and impressed by the rhythm of the everyday routine, finding hard work in the fields, the shops, the barns, the school, and the home to be balanced in healthy manner, with ample time for refreshing social times with friends and family. A nice pace, though for some—including myself, as I discovered—a bit too structured and ritualized, particularly with such little involvement with the outside world. With the nearest town being 12 miles away, and the nearest city of Fargo, North Dakota being 25 miles away—and with no readily available means of transportation made accessible to individuals and families except for the conducting of official colony business or for an occasional visit to relatives in another colony (the closest being 85 miles away)—such selected isolation and off-work activity in the colony is certainly understandable.

There are changes occurring in the traditional world of the Hutterite colony. Most notable for Spring Prairie Colony is the change that has recently been mandated by the state of Minnesota in the area of education. It is the requirement that all Hutterite youth must move beyond their eighth or ninth grade education to achieve their general education diploma (GED). To respect Hutterite insulation from the wider society,

the state has allowed students to do their studies within the colony, with a once-a-week meeting with state qualified teachers in a nearby town. While most colony members that I spoke with think this is a good thing, noting that their youth will be better educated than they are, there appears to be an underlying concern amongst the leadership that higher levels of education may lead more of their youth to cho[o]se the modern world over colony life. As sociologists have long known, this is not an unfounded fear or concern, since it is generally recognized that the more education the individual has, the more likely one is to raise questions about traditional ways of life and to seek work that matches one's developing interests and skills.

Since this requirement of a high school education for Hutterian youth has only been in effect for the last several years, it is no doubt too soon to test the effects of increased educational levels on loyalty to and self-selected membership in a colony, which commitment is expressed in the central ritual of adult baptism between the ages of nineteen and twenty-one. This will surely be a rich field for sociological research in the future.

# V

## Colony Life: Insuring the Future Through Expansion, Hard Work, and 'God's Help'

I explored a final question with the leader of the colony, the senior minister, John Waldner, who has been this colony's spiritual leader for 15 years. I asked him if he expected that Hutterite colonies—over 300 of which are in existence today—will survive in the future.

His response was a thoughtful and candid one. He is quite sure that some existing colonies will die in the future. For what reasons? Some will see the rise of false prophets in their midst, who will preach, "We don't need to be so strict in maintaining communal life" or "We can be making some money out in the outside world, to supplement what we do in the colony." Other colonies will probably fail for reasons of poor management, for as the minister said: "Not everyone can be a manager, it is a gift."

He continued: "But Donald, you can tell your students that colony life does work. It has worked for more than four hundred years. You've experienced community life with us and know that it can and does work. We're not a utopia; we have our problems. But we do strive for perfection, to live as the Lord wills us to live as revealed in Scriptures, with Acts 2 serving as our guide." Expressing deep contentment, the minister added: "What more could a person want? While we have no money as individuals, we have our families, our colony made up of relatives and friends, good shelter, and good food, everything we need to live a good life in Christ."

In a reflective mood one evening, John Waldner told me: "I have no doubts that there will be Hutterite colonies one hundred years from now, perhaps fewer, perhaps more. Given our valued religious heritage, our living faith and daily practice of communal living, I trust, that with God's help, most of the colonies will survive and many will thrive in the next century."

The minister, in his mid-sixties, has lived in four colonies, having moved successively into new colonies as they were established. New colonies are planned and developed when an existing one reaches a "critical mass," so to speak. John Hostetler, the leading authority on the Hutterites in North America, notes that

> The Hutterites manage their expansion so that on the average each colony consists of from ninety to one hundred persons. When colonies are too small they become clannish and dominated by a single family, and when too large they do not provide enough employment for the members. When a colony reaches from 120 to 130 persons, it will seek second location. The "mother" colony will form a new "daughter" colony by the process of "cell division." This planned method of splitting is commonly referred to as branching out (1983, p. 17).

Hostetler later adds an important note to the effect that one of the internal threats to the well-being of a colony—a threat of which most Hutterite leaders are very aware—is encountered when the colony's "population exceeds the positions available in the labor force." In such cases "polarization between family members may become a problem" (1983, p. 39).

The Hutterites, in their experience of colony life over a period of 470 years, appear to have satisfactorily resolved the tensions between the costs associated with their colony size and the benefits which they derive as a small community operating in the context of the larger society which surrounds them. In contrast to the Shaker communal experience in which, according to Metin, Miceli, and Murray, "the initially single group was divided into two or more independent groups" (called "Families") to address the costs of work incentives and coordination, most Hutterite colonies of the size of 100 to 130 members have been effective as "income sharing groups." They have been able through their unique organization to maintain "face-to-face contact and to establish trust relations" (1997, p. 140), qualities which are essential to their maximum socioeconomic functioning in the colony form.

No doubt the success of the Hutterites in this regard can further be attributed to their unity of belief and religious devotion, their "linking of work with religion" (ibid.), and their provision of meaningful work for all adults in the colony, which is complemented by the well-organized apprenticeship of youth in all phases of colony economic life. Additionally the Hutterites have developed a distinctive "centralized distribution mechanism" (1997, p. 133) represented in the office of the steward, who, in consultation with the council of the elders, seeks to achieve equality and justice in the communal sense of "from each according to his ability and to each according to his need."

With regard to a colony's "branching out" when it reaches maximum size, I was indeed fortunate to learn firsthand of the process and plans of the Spring Prairie Colony. John Waldner fully informed me of the colony's intention to purchase a thirty-four hundred acre farm some thirty miles southwest of the home colony, at a price of $1,100 per acre. The colony will purchase the land, then rent it to the former owner for four to five years, with the intent at the end of that time to create a new colony to accommodate the growth of the existing one. This new colony development occurs about every 20 to 25 years in a number of colonies located in the United States and Canada. This results in the growth of the number of colonies to offset those that may, for reasons cited above, go out of existence.

# VI
# What Mainstream American Society Can Learn From the Hutterites

In this last section of my article I want to address the following major question which has been in the back of my mind since conceptualizing this research topic. What can be learned from this intentional religious group of the Hutterites which might well have wider American sociocultural application in terms of values; family stability, community cohesion, and social welfare, with particular interest in their treatment of the elderly and the infirm?

First, the Hutterites remind us of the significance of beliefs—both religious and moral/ethical ones—in preserving a way of life, a culture. For the Hutterites, it is clear that religion is the life-giving energy of their existence. Specific beliefs and practices called them into being as a distinctive people in the early sixteenth century, alongside the better known Lutheran and Reformed churches. And religious beliefs continue to structure the way they live, from the moment of their birth, through daily education and worship experiences, through their baptism as adults, to whom one will marry, and even the desired size of their families.

The Hutterites' ethical or prescriptive beliefs—their values, the way they perceive is the right way to live their lives in relation to one another, and the ultimate goals they want to achieve—are again closely woven from the fabric of their religion. Faith in God, community, love, honesty, cooperation, forgiveness, and helpfulness shown in service to one another are values that they seek to live out in their daily existence.

To be sure, the Hutterites exhibit a number of qualities which are in line with broader American culture. It was clear to this observer that they share a number of values with their neighbors and fellow citizens outside their colonies. Such shared values include honesty, helpfulness, family security, friendship, politeness, and responsibility.

But the Hutterites' value system varies from wider American norms in significant ways. The center of their value system, both individually and corporately viewed, is God. The Hutterite norm of community, defined in terms of community of goods and cooperating with and serving fellow members, is clearly an outgrowth of their belief in and valuing of God and his will for their lives as revealed in Acts 2 and other Biblical passages.

In contrast to wider American life, little emphasis is found in the Hutterite colony on competition, on seeking a comfortable, prosperous life as individuals or nuclear family units, on personal freedom, on ambition, or on independence.

Clearly, as this researcher found, there is a sharp contrast between valuing the individual and valuing the community, indicative of a substantive value conflict between mainstream American culture and the Hutterite subculture. Time after time, in the midst of late hours of stimulating conversation with the minister, this point was impressed upon this "outsider" who had been given entrance to the colony to try to understand their way of life.

What can we learn from the Hutterites that is framed by this substantive value conflict? Imagine, if you will, what we as neighborhoods, as work groups, as towns and cities, and as a nation might become if we were to seek more of a balance of these rich value objects. As difficult as it would be to achieve, might this not be a desired goal, a positive aim worthy of investment and of time and energy—to improve the overall quality of our life together as a people, whether we be young or old, black, Hispanic or white, Catholic, Jew or Protestant?

A renewed emphasis on the value of community in the midst of the dominant individualistic ethos of modern American life could lead us in the direction of a new chapter of what has rightly been called "the American experiment."

A second area from which we as "mainstream" Americans can learn from the Hutterites concerns the subject of family stability. Let me initially share some observations regarding family life in a Hutterite colony.

1. The expectation is that everyone (except in rare cases such as illness, for example) will marry, usually shortly after baptism, which occurs between the ages of 19 and 21.

2. The sexual norm for the youth, which appears to be violated only in rare cases, is sex within marriage. Premarital and extramarital sexual relations are strictly forbidden.

3. Once married, each couple is expected, indeed encouraged by the community, to have children since children are so prized, both in terms of their innocent new lives and as future adult members who will perpetuate the colony way of life.

4. The average number of children per family is between five and six.

5. The Hutterites have a ready-made child care system at hand. This includes the primary care of the "housechildren"—ages birth to two years—by the mother, for whom homemaking is the primary profession. At the same time every mother—as is the case with all members—has specific tasks in the wider colony, from cooking, dishwashing, laundry, and the making of almost all of the clothing her family wears, to the occasional colony-wide slaughter and processing of hundreds of chickens and ducks in marathons of two to four days. Beyond the immediate parents, those engaged in child care and nurturance are older brothers and sisters who "watch" the younger children while the adults eat and worship. Aunts and grandparents are also regularly engaged in child care. I observed all of these relatives tending young children

in my brief stay in Spring Prairie Colony. In fact, one of the most delightful experiences I had was to go with a grandfather to baby-sit his grandchildren several evenings after dinner while the mother and grandmother were completing their work of dishwashing in the community kitchen. Every woman engages in dishwashing every eleventh week, according to one community informant. While child-sitting, the grandfather and I read to and played with the children, who were as lively and curious as are my own grandchildren.

I asked one mother who is 35 years of age with seven children, how she could keep up with and care for so many children. Her response was an interesting one and to the point. She said: "I think it would be harder to raise two or three children alone outside the colony than it is raising seven here. We have all our clothing, meals, and child care provided by the colony. What more could we need?"

6. Further contributing to family stability is the fact that relations between husband and wife are viewed as sacred. This relation has some distinctive features, arising out of Hutterite religious beliefs and community traditions: (a) The husband has the final word; he is the authority figure in all married life. This reflects a classic patriarchal pattern. The wife's power is, however, demonstrated and effective in child-rearing. (b) While one observed no public show of affection between husband and wife, there is obvious devotion, respect and care for one another, evident in the observed informal home environment. (c) No divorce is allowed in Hutterite culture. This prohibition is clearly and forcefully stated in the Ordnung, the rules that have governed community life since the sixteenth century. In relation to this, we might well ask the question: How do couples who are unhappy or dissatisfied with one another maintain lifetime monogamy? Clues to the

answer to this question certainly lie in the fact mentioned earlier, that religion permeates and is at the center of every Hutterite's life. The belief that Christ forbade divorce is for them a major deterrent to separation and divorce. In addition, the very nature of colony life, with its daily enforcement of norms and the provision of support to couples or families facing hardship, works in helping couples maintain their marriage vows throughout their lives, literally "until death do us part." Further, the relatively large number of children born to a couple, children who are prized and cherished as gifts from God, helps to hold husband and wife together even if their relationship may not be all that it could be. As part of this no-divorce ethos, mention must be made again of the classic extended family pattern operative in a Hutterite colony. In nearly every family situation there is daily interaction between at least three generations. They visit in each other's homes; they worship together; and they work side by side in the fields, in shop work, cooking and dishwashing, and in the canning of hundreds of large jars of fruits and vegetables. These tasks require nearly every adult member to be engaged intensely in colony life. One gets a sense of being part of one large extended family of 40 to 50 adults every day, so close is the cooperation and accomplishment of the work at hand.

All of these socio-religious factors, the strength of religious norms, the expectation of marriage and the corollary of a large number of children, the provision of family support through a very effective child care system providing relief for parents who might otherwise be stressed by large numbers living in relatively small quarters (basically a living-dining room and all the rest bedrooms), the clear authority structure, the devotion of husband and wife to each other, the stricture of no divorce, and the religious and social resources made available to insure that family ties are maintained, including an effective extended family network of support—all of these factors assist in the achievement of family stability which I observed and [have] been well documented in respected studies.

This is not to say that the Hutterites are free of problems in their colony and family life. As the head minister told me: "We are human, with human weaknesses and shortcomings. So we must work at it, keeping our colonies and families strong and thriving, day by day. It is an ongoing challenge. But with assurance that God has and will provide for what we need in every way, in terms of personal, social and material need, we trust that our ways will be preserved, if it is his will."

So, what applications to modern American life can be drawn from Hutterite family structure? In what ways can we perhaps be instructed by this social aspect of this distinctive subculture in our midst who have often been called "the forgotten people"?

First, the Hutterites remind us of the importance of extended family ties, of the strength that is derived from regular and meaningful cross-generational relationships. I observed this firsthand and wondered how we as mainstream Americans might recapture more of the richness of at least three generational family ties in the midst of our modern urban, industrial, information age. What new forms of extended family patterns and participation can we create as we move into the twenty-first century?

Secondly, we are reminded by the Hutterites of the importance of putting the needs of dependent children and the welfare of the community ahead of our own personal and often self-centered concerns. Imagine the difference that might make in our relations with our children, our spouses, other relatives, and our neighbors if we were to emulate their behavior in this crucial area of our lives.

Thirdly, the Hutterites clearly demonstrate the significance of religious belief as a unifying factor in family as well as community life. Here Durkheim's thesis in *The Elementary Forms of the Religious Life* is born out to the effect that religion is a constructive and effective unifying force in stabilizing communities. When focusing on families as the key building blocks of community, research has shown that religion often enhances marriages and parent-child relationships, as well as increases concern for one's aged family members.

Religion also assists parents in the moral training of their children; hence it often enables youth to avoid some of the pitfalls that hamper their future development, as well as giving assistance in the form of counseling to marriage partners who are experiencing difficulties.

A third area of Hutterite life and experience which might well have wider American sociocultural application falls in the domain of social welfare, and particularly the treatment of the elderly. . . . The Hutterites, as with other traditional cultures, revere the elderly in their colonies. Always made to feel a part of colony life, no matter how little labor they can contribute or how dependent they are due to illness or infirmity, the elderly clearly have no fear for their future. They know that they will be loved and cared for until the end of their days and that care, in so far as it is humanly possible, will be given them in the familiar surroundings of home and colony life.

One can imagine how the quality of American life and society might be enhanced if we were to regularly express deep respect and genuine care for the elderly in the context of our homes and institutions. With the documented aging of our population, ever larger numbers of the elderly are found in every sphere of the common life—family relations, the economy, politics, and religious life. In many of these areas the wealth of experience and knowledge that the elderly represent in wider American society remains largely untapped, largely because basic and genuine respect for them is lacking. They are often ignored or pushed off to the sidelines by younger family members as "over the hill," often bypassed for jobs that they qualify for if they choose to work in their senior years, and given little serious programmatic attention by most religious organizations. In this respect, it is clear that we can learn much from the Hutterites. Each colony insures that every elderly member is included in meaningful social spheres and activities, taking into account their interests and needs, so that the worth and dignity of their lives is affirmed to the very end.

## References

Allard, William A. (1970). "The Hutterites: Plain People of the West." *National Geographic*, July: 99–125.

Bennett, John W. (1967). *Hutterian Brethren: The Agricultural Economy and Social Organization of a Communal People*. Stanford: Stanford University Press.

Durkheim, Emile (1947). *Division of Labor*. New York: Macmillan Co.

——. (1965). *The Elementary Forms of the Religious Life*. New York: Macmillan Co.

Gross, Leonard (1998). *The Golden Years of the Hutterites*. Kitchener, Ontario: Pandora Press.

Holzach, Michael (1993). *The Forgotten People: A Year Among the Hutterites*. Sioux Falls, SD: Ex Machina Publishing Co.

Hostetler, John A. (1974). *Hutterite Society*. Baltimore: Johns Hopkins University Press.

——. (1983). *Hutterite Life*. Scottdale, PA: Herald Press.

Metin, M. Cosgel, Thomas J. Miceli, and John E. Murray (1997). "Organization and Distributional Equality in a Network of Communes: The Shakers." *The American Journal of Economics and Sociology* 56(2): 129–143.

Peters, Victor (1965). *All Things Common: The Hutterian Way of Life*. University of Minnesota Press.

Rideman, Peter (1970 [1545]). *Confession of Faith: Account of Our Religion, Doctrine and Faith*. Rifton, New York: Plough Publishing House.

Smith, Adam (1976a). *An Inquiry into the Nature and Causes of the Wealth of Nations*. Chicago: University of Chicago Press.

——. (1976b). *The Theory of Moral Sentiments*. Oxford: Clarendon Press.

Spencer, Herbert (1976). *The Evolution of Society*. Chicago: University of Chicago Press.

Weber, Max (1958). *The Protestant Ethic and the Spirit of Capitalism*. New York: Charles Scribner's Sons.

## Review

1. Discuss the role of religion in a Hutterite community.

2. Describe the family life of the Hutterites.

3. How is work organized among the Hutterites?

4. Briefly explain what the author says mainstream American society can learn from the Hutterites.

## Applications

1. Religion is central to Hutterite life. How central is it to mainstream Americans? Find some recent information on the involvement of Americans in religion (from the Internet, a book on religion, a Gallup poll, etc.). How would you compare the role of religion among the Hutterites with its role among the majority of Americans? What, if any, aspects of Hutterite life would you like to incorporate more thoroughly into mainstream American life?

2. Keeping in mind that a subculture is simply a group that shares most of the culture of the larger society while maintaining some distinctive elements of its own, identify as many subcultures as you can that exist in the area where you live. How many people do you know who belong to a subculture? Talk with one of them about how and why they differ from mainstream Americans.

## Related Web Sites

1. *http://www.hutterites.org/*. Home page for the Hutterian Brethren, offering extensive information about the Hutterites.

2. *http://mtprof.msun.edu/Spr1993/TBP.html*. Historical overview of the Hutterites, using both published sources and interviews.

# Part Six

## *Health Care*

Surveys of Americans about the important factors in their life satisfaction show that good health is at, or near, the top of the list. Like people everywhere, Americans place a high value on health. The health-care system, therefore, is a matter of great concern. To what extent do people receive adequate care? To what extent can all Americans afford needed health care? Such questions lead to periodic demands for changes in the nation's health-care system so that all Americans can receive adequate care.

One such change has been the emergence and growth of Health Maintenance Organizations, a topic dealt with in the first selection in this part. The second selection illustrates another aspect of health care—the relationship between physical and mental health. The two are closely interrelated, each affecting the other for good or ill as dramatized by the dying AIDS patients described in selection 36. ✦

# 35

# Unhealthy Partnership

## How Managed Care Wrecks Mental Health for Kids

*Joshua Sharfstein*

Health care is one of the most vexing social policy issues in the United States. Americans are disturbed by the escalating costs and by what some regard as substandard care in the various methods of managed care, including the proliferating health maintenance organizations (HMOs). According to public opinion polls, a majority of Americans believe that the tendency of HMOs to deny some medical procedures to patients is a "very serious" problem. And when asked to give an overall view of the American health-care system, a majority agrees there are some good things about it, but that fundamental changes are needed. At the least, people affirm the need for reform in the health-care system, and some assert the need for a national health-care plan.

The costs of health care have risen dramatically faster than the cost of living generally. By the end of the 1990s, Americans spent more than $1.1 trillion for health care, an increase of 65 percent from 1990 and more than 4.6 times the amount spent in 1980! Moreover, in the face of escalating costs, the proportion of Americans without health insurance rose during the decade of the 1990s; by the end of the decade, around 16 percent were not covered.

While much attention has been given to problems in physical health care, mental health care is equally troublesome. According to the U.S. Public Health Service, about 28 to 30 percent of the population have either a mental or addictive disorder, and about 9 percent of all American adults have a disorder that involves some significant functional impairment. In addition, approximately 20 per-cent of children have mental disorders with at least mild functional impairment.

*In this selection, Joshua Sharfstein examines the impact of managed care on the mental health of children. He shows that managed care is as problematic for mental as for physical health care: profit gets priority over patient well-being.*

Fourteen years old and sullen, he came to the hospital on a Sunday afternoon for evaluation of long-standing abdominal pain. As a first-year pediatric intern, I thought of incredible diagnoses: An intermittent twisting of the bowel? A rare parasite? When the preliminary tests came back negative, I told my patient the good news. He just cried, looked away, and held his stomach.

The next morning, a senior pediatrician remarked that abdominal pain is often the only obvious manifestation of depression in children. Returning to the patient's room, I elicited a story of loneliness, anger at his siblings, and unwillingness to confide in his parents. Then I drew in a slow breath and ventured that some people do not find life to be worth living. Doctor, he replied, at night I stand in the kitchen with a knife to my neck and pray for the courage to kill myself.

The next couple of hours passed quickly. I consulted with the primary care pediatrician and explained the situation to my patient's family. After a quick phone call from the psychiatry service to the insurance company, the patient was approved for treatment in a psychiatric hospital.

While I've changed some identifying details of the story for confidentiality, this part can't be altered: It was the closest I came to saving a life in my first year of training. I imagined that referring troubled children to the mental health care system for timely and effective treatment would continue to be an important part of my job as a pediatrician.

But it was not to be. Over the next three years, I observed from a front-row seat as mental health services for children in Massachusetts deteriorated. During my first night shifts in the emergency department, I often heard psychiatrists argue with managed care reviewers over approval for inpatient stays. Over time the next step—finding an available bed in a psychiatric hospital in New England—became the bigger hurdle. Late one night, I watched a frustrated social worker give up after several hours of calling area hospitals and ask a troubled adolescent's mother whether she could just take him home. The mother reluctantly agreed, but when they woke up the boy, he bolted. A melee ensued; after the child was restrained, another round of dialing began.

Eventually my experiences with suicidal or out-of-control children led me through the looking glass: I wasn't sending patients to the mental health system for care; the mental health system was sending children with acute psychiatric emergencies to me. About once a day, pediatric residents admitted a child to "board" on the pediatric unit of the hospital until a bed in a psychiatric facility became available.

Some boarders waited hours, others days. Nearly all were kept company by a "sitter" or security guard; some patients had to be sedated or physically restrained for their own safety. Psychiatrists would generally come by once a day to assess the boarders' mental status briefly and then continue with the bed search. Early one morning, I described three boarders admitted overnight to the inpatient team of residents. "Not more psych kids," they moaned.

I fantasized that somewhere in Massachusetts, corrupt officials had absconded with money intended for troubled children. But what I discovered is far more shocking: The Massachusetts Behavioral Health Partnership—the state's largest mental health insurance company and the outfit responsible for managing mental health care benefits for tens of thousands of children on Medicaid—has, in fact, met all of its contractual obligations. What's more, the state pays the plan, known as "the Partnership," millions of dollars each year in performance bonuses. Policy experts and state officials have called it a national model. And in June 2000, the largest HMO in the state, the not-for-profit Harvard *Pilgrim* Health Care, made plans to contract with the Partnership to provide mental health benefits, yielding the for-profit company approximately 70 percent of the market for children's services.

In New Mexico, Medicaid officials recently pulled the plug on a for-profit managed care experiment after audits showed that 83 percent of patients in one plan were inappropriately treated. In Tennessee and Arizona, the latest studies indicate that half of all children with serious mental illness did not receive any services in the previous six months. In these and several other states, thousands of children have suffered as private managed care plans have reaped profits by denying care.

The Massachusetts experience has led some observers to give for-profit managed mental health care a second chance. But how can a mental health plan be highly regarded even as the service system for children crumbles around it? The answer becomes obvious only with the realization that the plan's purpose was never to ensure access to care for children in need. Indeed, its true function has been to maintain the appearance of success. The company has earned every penny of its more than $200-million plus Medicaid contract by contributing to the illusion that the system is reasonably intact, thereby allowing the state to dodge pressure for more difficult but necessary reform.

The Partnership illustrates what's really missing in public policy for children with mental illness: not more crafty language for managed care contracts, but a political commitment to guaranteeing basic access to care.

## A Shaky Model

This story began on July 1, 1996, when the Partnership started to manage mental health benefits for nearly 400,000 Massachusetts Medicaid recipients. Although its name suggests a special relationship between the company and the state, this "partnership" was a joint venture of two of the nation's largest for-profit behavioral health care firms, Connecticut-based Value Behavioral Health and FHC of Virginia. It was the second attempt under the Medicaid program in Massachusetts to carve out mental health benefits. From 1992 to 1996, after obtaining the nation's first waiver for managed mental health care, Massachusetts officials watched helplessly as Mental Health Management of America enraged hospitals and providers by bungling their payments.

Across the country, many other state officials learned the same unfortunate lesson. Hiring the managed care companies that had successfully tamed costs under employer-based coverage in the late 1980s and early 1990s was not a recipe for success in the public sector. These companies had conquered the private insurance market in no small part by leaving vulnerable patients on the tab of state governments. But now that they were working for state governments, the plans could deny care only at the cost of leaving patients totally abandoned. When a for-profit contractor nearly destroyed emergency crisis services across the state, furious state legislators in Montana canceled a five-year contract after just the second year. Arkansas lawmakers waited only six weeks to back out. Connecticut sued its for-profit contractor for what the state's attorney general described as a "purposeful and systematic" scheme to deny necessary care and eventually settled for $4 million.

By 1996 Massachusetts officials were eager for the Partnership to prove that for-profit managed mental health care could actually work. A successful carve-out would demonstrate an easy option for other state governments that were straining to serve increasing numbers of troubled children. The setting seemed right for a breakthrough. "The people in Massachusetts have better resources and better external consultation to deal with managed care," says David Fassler, a child psychiatrist at the University of Vermont who is an expert on Medicaid managed care. "They had the experience with [the first contract], so when they did the [Partnership] negotiations, they weren't coming in blind. They have more resources in Massachusetts—treatment resources—than in a lot of other states."

But skeptics saw danger in the state's desire to declare the new venture a success: "If either the state or the Partnership says it's not working, they both look bad," observes Susan Villani, former medical director of the Gaebler Children's Center. (The last public psychiatric hospital for children in Massachusetts, the center closed in 1995.) "So there's a lot of investment [in looking] good."

Massachusetts officials took pride in the state's model contract with the Partnership. Under the terms of the Partnership contract, Massachusetts paid the company a fixed fee per child and then limited to $2 million the amount of profit it could make by underspending the budget for services. The contract also allowed for $4 million in bonuses for meeting administrative targets and performance standards. Harvard Medical School psychiatrist and managed care expert James Sabin and Tufts University ethicist Norman Daniels raved in the journal *Psychiatric Services* that Massachusetts and the Partnership "may have developed a win-win approach" and noted, "A visitor to the offices of the Partnership sees the performance targets posted on virtually every wall."

The company's initial incentives largely centered on the nuts and bolts of administrative efficiency. For example, the plan processed 99.5 percent of claims within 30 days, besting the contract's requirement of 95 percent. And the Partnership submitted 100 percent of certain agreed-upon reports by 5:00 P.M. on the due date. During the first year of the contract, the Partnership earned the maximum of $4 million in bonuses.

In subsequent years, the performance incentives were expanded, mostly to encourage the company to offer training for providers and state officials and funding for patient surveys and other support services. The Partnership continued to excel at hitting the targets, earning $5 million in bonuses out of a possible $6.7 million in fiscal year 1998.

Yet something important was missing. Nothing in the contract held the Partnership accountable for providing basic access to mental health care for all enrolled children. It is true that Medicaid rewarded the Partnership for showing that its network included hospitals "within 60 minutes or 45 miles" of the homes of 85 percent of children enrolled. But such a guarantee provided no consolation to parents when all the beds at these nearby inpatient facilities were filled.

While the Partnership kept processing claims on time—86 percent were filed electronically in fiscal year 1998—the demand for inpatient hospitalization was steadily rising, with emergency departments seeing more and more acute referrals. Several area inpatient psychiatric units for children folded. Most significant, openings for troubled adolescents in residential settings such as halfway houses overseen by the state's Department of Social Services disappeared, leaving dozens of children in state custody stranded inside psychiatric hospitals, ready for discharge but with no place to go. From July 1998 to June 1999, according to records I obtained under the state's freedom-of-information law, these children spent a collective total of 8,194 unnecessary days in locked wards.

Suicidal and violent children who needed treatment in inpatient psychiatric facilities were put on indefinite hold. Some became boarders in pediatric hospitals; others languished for days in community emergency departments; a few waited in jail. Martha Grace, chief justice of the Massachusetts Juvenile Court, told *The Boston Globe* that judges occasionally had to send troubled children into locked detention simply to protect them while they awaited psychiatric hospitalization. "To put a mentally ill child in a delinquent or criminal population is not good for either population," Grace said. "Now they're being punished for being ill."

In the absence of performance standards requiring access to care during mental health crises, the Partnership did not immediately provide funding for such patients. In a study of 10 boarders covered by Medicaid from January to May 1999, I found that after subtracting the cost of salaries for people to watch the children and psychiatric staff to evaluate them on nights and weekends, my hospital received about $60 per day for nursing services, physician fees, food, medications, and other expenses. At the time, the Partnership did not, as a policy, accept financial responsibility for care. Meanwhile, for the children stuck inside psychiatric facilities, ready for discharge but awaiting community placements, the Partnership paid just $140 per day rather than the usual fee of more than $500. At least through the first half of 1999, the company stood to profit from the shortage of inpatient psychiatric beds.

The Partnership's unwillingness to expand available inpatient treatment might have been more understandable if the company had created a network of community providers to prevent at-risk children from reaching a crisis in the first place. But no performance incentives held the Partnership accountable for significant problems involving access to outpatient care—a bad omen for a business that posts its goals on every wall.

Years of pounding from managed care had left many Massachusetts communities lacking in child psychiatrists, day treatment programs, and other resources. Nationally, from 1988 to 1997, employer spending on mental health services fell by 54 percent in constant dollars. The impact of these cuts on children's services—which often lack strict professional standards on length of treatment—was disproportionately high. As private managed care plans reduced their benefits, families increasingly turned to the state government for assistance. But state spending in Massachusetts and elsewhere did not match the need. For example, the number of patients on waiting lists for case managers from the Department of Mental Health stretched past 2,000—leaving a multitude of families unable to obtain key assistance in finding mental health services, coordinating with local school systems, and accessing other state programs.

Under these dire circumstances, the Partnership did not rise to the challenge of expanding services to meet community needs. Clinicians complain that credentialing with the plan can take months. The Partnership also pays lower rates to many therapists than other insurers do, and clinicians report difficulty in obtaining reimbursement for time spent apart from therapy sessions. (Because children's misbehavior often occurs at home or in school and may have consequences for the criminal justice system, therapists must often work for free making contact with parents, teachers, and school and court officials.)

Until very recently, the Partnership did not even track outpatient waiting times across its system. The net result: In many parts of the state, families covered by the Partnership have waited upwards of five months for a first appointment. "In five or six months, a lot of these kids become much more in crisis," says Lisa Lambert, assistant director of the Parent-Professional Advocacy League, which surveys its members on waits for care. "Their behaviors escalate, and [then] they are looking to access acute services." In March 1999, two state agencies asked Christina Crowe of the Judge Baker Children's Center in Boston to examine why parents were reporting such dissatisfaction with mental health services in northeastern Massachusetts. Her report described a decimated system in which "access to adequate and effective treatment is deficient at every level."

These findings, however, had no implications for the Partnership's stellar record of meeting its performance targets. Within another few months, the company stood to earn another $400,000 bonus by holding two optional training workshops on child and adolescent issues for Partnership providers and state employees. Even in July 2000, as the mental health care system's collapse hit the front page of *The Boston Globe*, an internal Partnership memo boasted in boldface: "All FY 2000 Performance Standards on track for success."

## No Accountability

Why can't Massachusetts just hold the Partnership responsible for basic access to care? Partnership CEO Richard Sheola says that such a step would be patently unfair. His reasoning: The Partnership has no control over what's really broken with the mental health care system for children.

This claim enables a for-profit company to escape responsibility for children in distress. But it is also true. Massachusetts state agencies, by leaving dozens of children inappropriately stuck in psychiatric hospitals, are largely responsible for the bed crunch

that has forced children to languish in pediatric units, community emergency departments, and jails. The most recent data indicate that children in the care of state agencies spent 20,811 unnecessary days in psychiatric hospitals from July 1999 to June 2000—the equivalent of 57 years of wasted time. Similarly, while the Partnership has not particularly improved community mental health services, the state's support of key elements of the outpatient system has been sorely lacking. At last count, 2,497 children were waiting for case managers from the Department of Mental Health.

It's a catch-22. The state cannot fairly hold the Partnership responsible for basic access to care without first doing a better job itself. But that's exactly what the state government wants to avoid. A real commitment to the mental health needs of children would involve guaranteeing community placements and case management services for all troubled children who need them, backing support teams for families with troubled children, and dedicating additional spending for recruitment and training of new mental health providers. Pilot programs such as the Mental Health Services Program for Youth have reduced foster care rates and improved care for even the most vulnerable children by combining resources from the mental health, education, and criminal justice budgets and creating accountable community-based treatment teams.

But such an investment statewide would be costly up front. Led by tax-cut-obsessed Republican Governor Paul Cellucci, Massachusetts politicians are unlikely to target significant new resources to help such a politically unempowered group. Beyond funding, the political obstacles to reforming the mental health care system are daunting. These would include battles to create new residential treatment centers across the state and to break down the walls between several entrenched bureaucracies. Massachusetts is not alone in failing to tackle these problems: Advocates have recently sued New York and Maine on behalf of emotionally disturbed children who do not receive adequate care, and more than a dozen states have recently reported crises in access to children's mental health services.

Massachusetts, however, has uniquely been able to minimize political embarrassment by hiring a managed care plan, holding it responsible for a limited array of "performance standards," and declaring it a success. Even patient advocates on the national level have been somewhat fooled. In testimony to the New Mexico state legislature, an official of the Bazelon Center for Mental Health Law in Washington, D.C., advised that state to consider a carve-out arrangement for mental health services, citing Massachusetts as a model. The center's policy director, Chris Koyanagi, says approvingly, "People have seen that Massachusetts is monitoring [the Partnership] closely with many performance standards."

"If something is happening in a social system over time, it's been designed in," says managed care expert James Sabin, who early on had high hopes for the Partnership. One could conclude, he adds, that the Massachusetts mental health care system "appears to be designed to keep spending level . . . at the cost of not doing anything for kids."

Last February the health plan moved to dispel the image that it was profiting at the expense of stranded children. According to Partnership Vice President Angelo McClain, "to address any perceptions that [it] stood to gain financially every time a child was 'boarded' in a pediatric unit," the Partnership (in consultation with Medicaid) authorized $502 in daily payments to pediatric hospitals. The plan even increased its reimbursement to psychiatric hospitals for children stranded waiting for community placements.

At times of crisis, the Partnership has stepped in to take some of the heat off the state. In April 1999, *The Boston Globe* reported on its front page: "Suicidal and violent youngsters are languishing in hospital emergency rooms for hours and in pediatric beds for days—and are sometimes simply sent home with panic-stricken parents—because Massachusetts psychiatric hospitals have no room for them." The story made clear that a major cause of the problem was the gridlock generated by children in psychi-

atric hospitals waiting for community placements from state agencies. In response, the Partnership agreed to pay psychiatric hospitals to open more inpatient beds for children, tacitly accepting responsibility and taking pressure off the state.

At first glance, these actions may seem surprising. But they make perfect sense given how the Partnership really earns its money: not by directly shortchanging children, but by fostering the illusion that the system works and earning rewards from the state. Despite a few small steps, the basic dynamic at work in Massachusetts has yet to change. The state government remains unwilling to invest in a comprehensive system of outpatient care that includes residential placements for children who need them. This leaves the Partnership officials on the hook for the bed crisis, a responsibility they do not fully accept. It's a situation that virtually guarantees worsening care.

Massachusetts' unusual relationship with the Partnership could never be sustained if plan officials pushed the state into tackling the bigger issues in children's mental health care. In fact, the Partnership came close to doing just that in the summer of 1998, when the company's leaders decided to cut off payment for children who were waiting beyond a certain number of days for community placements in psychiatric hospitals. After all, they correctly reasoned, Massachusetts was paying the plan to manage medically necessary care, and hospitalization for these children was no longer medically necessary (by anyone's definition).

It didn't take long for hospitals to catch wind of the proposal and start to kick and scream. As pressure mounted, Governor Cellucci's administration faced the choice of finding appropriate placements for the children or simply demanding that the Partnership knuckle under and pay for medically unnecessary care. The knuckling under happened quickly.

Even a trusted not-for-profit health system probably wouldn't risk its own contract by aggressively confronting the state over fundamental problems in the mental health system for children. According to Susan Fendell of the Mental Health Legal Advisers

Committee, "One reason [the Partnership] may not be publicly lobbying for more money spent on the public system of residential services is that they want to be players with the administration." The Partnership is now owned by ValueOptions (the company that resulted when FHC bought out Value Behavioral Health); too much controversy would not make the principals happy.

## Carving Out Real Care

So what should happen with private managed care for Medicaid mental health services? In round one, companies tried—and failed—to apply private-sector cost-cutting strategies to a complex public system. States are increasingly abandoning these contracts. In round two, the companies cooperated with governments to placate providers with efficient reimbursement and to meet limited performance goals, sidestepping fundamental problems in the system. Children still suffer.

Is round three coming to a state near you? According to Gail Robinson, vice president of the Lewin Group, an international consulting firm with expertise in mental health issues, the next few years will be a "critical time" in terms of the future of for-profit plans in public mental health services. "A number of states are finishing with three- or five-year contracts," she says. "They will need to consider the benefits and the cost [of renewal]." Preferring to contract with public and not-for-profit groups, some states responsible for millions of Medicaid recipients have not yet embraced for-profit managed mental health care. But that may change.

To succeed, state governments will have to do more than tinker with the contract language in their deals with managed care plans. They'll have to treat children's mental health as a continuum that includes insurance for psychiatric services, residential care, school support, social services, and the criminal justice system. They'll have to foot the bill for comprehensive community-based services. And they'll have to demand and monitor basic access to inpatient and outpatient care as well as actual improvement in the lives of troubled children. It's

doubtful that for-profit plans can play anything more than a limited role in such a system.

Even the best managed care plan is only as strong as the political commitment to troubled children that supports it. Legislatures must establish measurable goals for the system and hold agencies responsible for meeting them. Through its oversight of the Medicaid program, Congress can do the same. Virtually all state Medicaid plans have federal waivers to allow managed care for mental health services; Congress should pressure the Department of Health and Human Services to require basic data on access to care before approving renewals. The recent denial of a waiver in New Mexico is a good first step.

In light of the public's interest in avoiding school shootings and youth violence, the political prospects of improved services are not dismal. While laws that mandate parity for mental health benefits can be easily circumvented, their passage indicates that legislators are willing to act to improve children's mental health. Rafael Semansky, a policy research analyst at the Bazelon Center, notes one financial incentive that may push the effort along: When a state uses Medicaid funds to intervene in a troubled child's life, the federal government foots about half the bill, but when that child disrupts school or winds up in jail, it's all on the state's dime.

I have yet to assist another patient as I did the depressed 14-year-old during my internship. Instead, I scramble to coordinate outpatient mental health care, school services, and home supports for troubled children in my primary care practice. Sometimes I help to avert a crisis, but often I fail. When I tell any of the current pediatric trainees of my past hope to detect serious mental illness among children and refer them to the mental health system for effective care, they just laugh. . . .

## Review

1. Describe some of the problems that have occurred in the various states as they have tried to utilize managed care for mental patients.

2. Explain what Sharfstein means by the "shaky model" of mental health care.

3. Why is there no accountability in the Massachusetts system?

4. What does Sharfstein say is needed in order for states to provide adequate mental health care?

## Applications

1. Through the Internet, a library, or contact with a local mental health professional, find out what kind of mental health care is available to children in your state. Look also for suggestions as to how the care can be improved. Compare your findings with those in Sharfstein's article.

2. Sharfstein focuses on problems involving hospitalization. Private therapists also report annoying issues as they try to provide care to patients covered by a managed-care system. Talk to a therapist who has patients in a managed-care system. Ask the therapist to identify advantages and problems of treating such patients.

## Related Web Sites

1. *http://www.mentalhealth.samhsa.gov/ publications/allpubs/SMA00-3424/ SMA00-3424ch8.asp.* An annotated bibliography on managed health care from the U.S. Department of Health and Human Services.

2. *http://www.ffcmh.org/.* Site of the Federation of Families for Children's Mental Health, with reports and other information.

Reprinted from: Joshua Sharfstein, "Unhealthy Partnership: How Managed Care Wrecks Mental Health for Kids." In *The American Prospect* 12 (January 1–15, 2001): 24–28. Reprinted with permission from *The American Prospect* Volume 12, Number 1: January 1–15, 2001. The American Prospect, 5 Broad Street, Boston, MA 02109. All rights reserved. ✦

# 36

# Preserving a Vital and Valued Self in the Face of AIDS

## Kent L. Sandstrom

In American society, illness is usually perceived in biomedical terms. A virus or bacterium has invaded the body, the physiological function of an organ has failed, or an essential biochemical has ceased to be adequately produced in the body. In virtually all societies, including our own, some illnesses are considered to have a social or cultural aspect as well. For example, a disease like asthma is believed to be contracted or its condition worsened when the victim is involved in stressful situations. A disease may be associated with disapproved behavior patterns like cirrhosis of the liver with the heavy consumption of alcohol. Thus, this kind of disease may be stigmatizing, and those inflicted with it are regarded by some segments of a society as moral suspects and potential pollutants.

This is the prevalent attitude toward AIDS among certain groups in contemporary American society. **AIDS** stands for "acquired immune deficiency syndrome," a viral infection that causes the immune system to stop functioning and leads to death. There are those who view AIDS as a punishment from God for the victim's immoral behavior. The stigma of AIDS seems to derive from three perceptions: (1) it is a contagious, incurable illness; (2) it can be transmitted by sexual contact; and (3) it is associated largely with two groups of victims—gay men and intravenous drug users.

AIDS is not stigmatized in all circles. There are those who, in fact, have great sympathy for victims of the disease and even those who see its ennobling potential. In short, the moral perception of AIDS in American society is contested territory. This view is Sandstrom's point

of departure for the study of identity among persons with AIDS. Based on his intensive interviews with a small sample of AIDS victims, Sandstrom describes in this selection the challenges faced in the final phases of the illness. He captures the thoughts and feelings of men who struggle with the meaning of their lives, their deaths, and what lies beyond death.

During the past decade sociologists have focused increased attention on the lived experience of HIV disease. Much of their research has concentrated on how persons with HIV disease cope with and counteract stigma (Sandstrom 1990; Weitz 1991), experience and manage uncertainty (Weitz 1989), negotiate sexual relationships (Sandstrom 1996a), utilize doctors and medical resources (Kayal 1993; Weitz 1991), build support networks (Sandstrom 1996b), and, more generally, reconstruct their lives and selves (Adam 1996; Kotarba and Lang 1986; Sandstrom 1990, 1996a, 1998; Weitz 1991). In addressing these themes, sociologists have insightfully revealed many of the central challenges confronted by persons with HIV disease. However, they have not yet delineated the distinctive challenges to self encountered by people with HIV in the twilight of their moral career—that is, when developing serious AIDS-related complications and facing the prospects of profound debilitation and impending death.

This paper attempts to address this gap in the literature by examining the existential challenges that men with AIDS experience during the final phases of their illness career. These challenges include (1) how to come to terms with debilitating symptoms and a diminishing future; (2) how to offset the threats posed by suffering, dependence, and dying; and (3) how to construct and solidify identities that extend beyond death.

In exploring these issues, this paper extends the sociological literature on illness, death, and dying in a couple of important ways. First, it illustrates some of the most prominent identity dilemmas encountered by men grappling with advanced symptoms of a terminal illness. As Kathy Charmaz

(1994, p. 269) has noted, identity dilemmas "include the knotty problems and hard decisions" that emerge as seriously ill people "experience trials, tribulations, and transitions that affect who they are and who they can become." In accord with Charmaz's emphases, this paper highlights the trials, tribulations, and transitions that shape the self-images and identity constructions of men with AIDS, particularly as they come to grips with dying and death.

In addition to this, the paper reveals how men with AIDS construct postmortal identities and sustain a sense of symbolic immortality (Lifton 1978) as they enter the final period of their lives. Through focusing on this phenomenon, the paper offers insight into how people with terminal illnesses fashion enduring selves and futures and, in this process, gain a sense of control and transcendence over death as an ultimate limit. This is an important aspect of their unfolding, "moral experience" (Goffman 1961).

Along with contributing to the sociological literature in the above ways, this paper illustrates and extends the theoretical insights of symbolic interactionism. Symbolic interactionism provides an especially illuminating framework for examining how men with AIDS define themselves and their illness, because it accentuates the processual, interactive, and interpretive dimensions of human experience and selfhood. Following Mead (1934) and Blumer (1969), interactionists assume that (1) people act toward things, including things like AIDS, based on the meanings that those things have for them; (2) the meanings of things are not inherent but rather derive from processes of social and self-interaction (Denzin 1983, 1989a; Durig 1996); (3) meanings have a fluid and mutable quality; and (4) people construct lines of action not only in terms of the meanings they give to objects or events around them or to their internal experiences but also in terms of the meanings they give to themselves. In fact, in fashioning ongoing social acts, the "self" is often the most central and meaningful social object that they take into account (Blumer 1969; Stryker 1980).

Guided by these assumptions, a symbolic interactionist analysis of the experience of men with AIDS focuses significant attention on how they construct meanings for self in light of the unfolding implications of their illness. In a related vein, it also emphasizes how these men's images of self are affected by their visions of and expectations for the future, and vice versa. As implied in the writings of many interactionists, people construct images of self not only in terms of the past and present, but also in terms of their anticipation of the future (Charmaz 1991; Corbin and Strauss 1987; Mead 1934; Markus and Nurius 1986; Strauss 1993). Building upon this premise, this paper examines and portrays how the self-images and identity constructions of men with AIDS both influence and become influenced by their visions of the future, particularly as their illness enters its latter stages.

Finally, in adopting a symbolic interactionist perspective, this paper accentuates how men with AIDS, like all human beings, are actors rather than reactors; that is, they are active agents who, because of their ability to use symbols and engage in self-interaction, do not merely react to the physical and social ramifications of their illness. Instead, they have the capacity to creatively act toward their health situation, to negotiate and transform the meanings attributed to it, and, correspondingly, to exercise a measure of control over its consequences for self (Sandstrom 1990).

## Methodology

This study draws on interview data from an availability sample of twenty-one men diagnosed with AIDS. These men volunteered to be interviewed after (1) receiving a descriptive flyer and letter of invitation from a case manager at a local HIV clinic; (2) hearing a presentation made by the author to an AIDS related support group; or (3) getting referred by an acquaintance who had already been interviewed or who knew the author through his involvement in community AIDS work.

The men interviewed in this study ranged in age from 20 to 56; six were in their 20s; eight were in their 30s; six were in their 40s; and one was in his 50s. The vast majority were White; the only two non-Whites were African American. Fifteen of the twenty-one men had become infected with HIV through having sex with other men. Thirteen of these men identified themselves as gay, while the other two described themselves as bisexual. Among the remaining six men, three had contracted HIV through injection drug use, two had contracted it through sex with infected women, and one had contracted it through blood products he received as a hemophiliac.

All of the men in this study had developed AIDS-related opportunistic infections, such as Kaposi's sarcoma (KS), pneumocystis carinii pneumonia (PCP), cytomegalovirus (CMV), toxoplasmosis, neuropathy, tuberculosis, or dementia. Eighteen of the twenty-one men were suffering from advanced and disabling AIDS-related symptoms during the time that they were interviewed. The remaining three men were comparatively healthy, but they had experienced debilitating and potentially fatal AIDS symptoms in the past.

Everyone in the study was interviewed on at least two occasions, because the interview process was lengthy (an average of four hours), and illness or fatigue made it difficult to talk for more than a couple of hours at a time. I interviewed most of the men at their homes; however, two were interviewed in a private university office because their homes were not conducive to a confidential conversation. The interviews were guided by roughly seventy open-ended questions, including eighteen which explored themes regarding advanced illness, dying, and death. . . .

## Challenges to Self Encountered in the Twilight of the AIDS Career

In the earlier phases of their illness, men with HIV/AIDS struggle most centrally with issues of stigma and uncertainty (Sandstrom 1990, 1996a; Weitz 1989, 1991). They worry about how, whether, or when to disclose their health status and how to address or counteract the threat of devaluation it poses. They also worry about the unpredictable aspects of their HIV infection, such as when it

will provoke serious symptoms, what specific symptoms will arise, what treatments will be available for these symptoms, and how both the symptoms and treatments will disrupt their everyday lives.

As their illness unfolds and advances to its latter stages, the concerns of men with HIV/AIDS begin to change. Stigma becomes a less salient issue for them as their social contacts become more restricted and they surround themselves with a trusted and supportive network of others. In addition to this, their struggles with uncertainty diminish. In fact, men with AIDS feel as anguished about the certainties that accompany their advancing illness as the uncertainties, particularly certainties such as debilitating symptoms and a rapidly diminishing future.

### Coming to Terms With Debilitation and a Shrinking Future

As they grapple with advanced health complications, men with AIDS find it increasingly difficult to manage their illness and preserve an identity apart from it. They discover that they can no longer contain the disease, as they had in the past, by closely monitoring their health practices and reducing their social involvements. Instead, AIDS becomes a defining feature of their lives—it fills their days and compels them to reorder their priorities, activities, and self-conceptions.

In many cases, AIDS triggers or exacerbates symptoms of unyielding fatigue, pain, indigestion, or diarrhea. These symptoms, in turn, evoke feelings of frustration and demoralization in affected men, as highlighted by one of my informants, Peter, when he remarked: "I'm sick and tired of being sick and tired! I really am. I'm sick and tired all the time, you know. That's the hard part about this damn disease—there's such a constancy to it."

As time passes, men with AIDS no longer experience many good days, or periods of restored health, that offer them respite and renewal. Their lives become a litany of bad days—periods marked by continuous sickness and a profound sense of devitalization. As Neil, who had lived with AIDS for over five years, described: "I just feel kind of dragged out. I have a lot of days like that now . . . I just feel dragged out, tired, and icky. I don't even have those real good days that I used to have in the middle of bad ones. It's just fatigue, fatigue, fatigue all the time!"

In addition to being plagued by debilitating physical symptoms, men with AIDS may suffer from impaired mental functioning, such as disorientation, memory loss, dementia, and a general slowing of cognitive processes (see also Weitz 1989). These manifestations of their illness, of course, also limit their activities and disrupt their images of self and the future.

In light of the bodily changes they experience, men with AIDS often feel as if they have grown old prematurely. They recognize that they must deal with the same types of symptoms, feelings, and challenges as their aging relatives. As Peter observed:

> I feel like it [life with AIDS] is similar to being old! My grandmother and I—we are on the same physical level. She's seventy-nine and I'm thirty-nine but it's like we're dealing with the same kind of problems. You know, I could very, very easily be treated as a geriatric patient and it would be proper care. And when my grandmother complains to me, my final line is "Yeah, look at it, I have all the same problems you do and I'm forty years younger. . . ." I really do feel more related to being old in that sense—more than to having AIDS actually. Because all the symptoms just make you old! And you even look old! . . . Looking at me is the same as looking at my grandmother, but she's seventy-eight years old! And she's got these aches and pains and . . . bad days, just like me.

In a related vein, another of my informants, Greg, emphasized the parallels between the issues he encountered in his daily experiences with AIDS and the existential challenges faced by elderly people:

> I know part of it [living with AIDS] is very similar to dealing with issues of being older—of pacing yourself and so on. . . . One of my friends with AIDS said the same kind of thing today at lunch, too. He said, "I feel like I'm ninety years old." And it is like that! I spoke to a church group lately and I read some poems about my

life and stuff. And during the question-and-answer period, this one older gentleman engaged me in discussion in just that way. He said, "I can really identify with where you're at because being seventy-two, I'm dealing with illness and death myself—with things going wrong." And I agreed with him—that it [AIDS] was just, you know, it was just like that. It was like growing old early.

Generally speaking, as their health worsens, men with AIDS—like many elderly people—struggle to come to terms with the threats posed by their diminishing capacities and futures. In addressing these threats, they find it difficult to rely upon the strategies they had adopted in previous phases of their illness, such as maintaining a positive outlook and accentuating the empowering ramifications of life with HIV (Kayal 1993; Sandstrom 1990; Weitz 1991). Instead, these men develop and utilize other adaptive strategies which help them to sustain a sense of control, vitality, and self-value in their daily bouts with advanced illness. One of these strategies is to stop thinking much about the future, as Neil revealed:

> I don't look into the future very much anymore because even though I know some good things will come along I anticipate that it's going to get harder and worse. I don't know, from what I've been able to see with other people it doesn't get better. Or, it stays the same, which doesn't offer me much to look forward to either.

As they wrestle with severe manifestations of their illness, men with AIDS become absorbed in the present and try to suppress thoughts of their prospective health situation. When asked, "What do you see as you think about your health in the future?" the men I interviewed typically gave a variation of the following response: "I don't really see much. I try not to think about it. I guess I'm probably going to get even more sick and die. . . . So, I just live day to day."

By choosing to "live one day at a time," men with AIDS derive a greater sense of control in the present and find new sources of personal satisfaction and fulfillment. Many start to notice and appreciate the beauty of little things happening around them and vivid feelings arising within them. Most crucially, through anchoring themselves in an *intense present* (Charmaz 1991), these men discover a rejuvenating sense of joy, vitality, and transcendence, as reflected in the following excerpts:

> You know, I just feel blessed for each day, really—for the sun, the trees, everything. I just feel like I have a more intense experience of life. Yeah, there's times for me when it even comes off as feeling high—like a high from drugs or something like that, except it's not from that. It's just from being so immersed in life—there's a high in that for me. . . . When I got really sick and truly realized that I had a limited amount of time left to live, I started to look at things differently. All of a sudden each new day was precious to me—it was a gift that offered special surprises. I started to see and experience each moment as sacred, at least in some respects.

When living in the intense present, men with AIDS experience not only a revitalizing sense of joy and transcendence, but also a heightened sense of urgency—urgency to act, take risks, experience things, build new or stronger relationships, and, in their own words, "make the most of the opportunity each new day presents." In addition to this, these men often feel an urgency to complete unfinished business. Given their health situation, they realize that they have a limited future, and they feel motivated to achieve something meaningful while they still can. For example, when reflecting upon how his ongoing health problems affected the goals he set for self, Greg asserted:

> I have this kind of, like, drive underneath about, you know, accomplishing something I feel like, "Yeah, I should be doing this, I should be doing that." . . . There's still other things, more things I want to accomplish—like, I have a couple of research and writing projects I want to get finished and published. Although I, you know, make sure I do things to build my self-esteem and take care of myself daily, there are still like some big things that I would like to do.

In a similar vein, Lee stressed how his worsening symptoms had prompted him to try to make a significant contribution through pursuing some larger-scale goals. He also emphasized how AIDS compels those affected to come to grips more quickly with what they want out of their lives:

> I want to work on low-income housing, and I want to teach people how to do carpentry and design and energy efficiency. I mean, all those kinds of things where if you do a little bit it makes a big difference. Suddenly I want to be doing that . . . I want to do something more meaningful—the illness has spurred that. When you hear people [with HIV/AIDS] say, you know, "this illness is a blessing"—well, ugh, that drives me nuts! It's a fucking disease, don't tell me that it's a blessing! But I think that's where I can understand what they're saying. It has kicked them in the butt to say, "Maybe I better do something with my life. It's only going to be a limited time. Let me get out of it what I want to get out of it."

Nevertheless, while advancing illness and a heightened sense of finitude give men with AIDS greater incentive to make and pursue plans for their future, this becomes extremely challenging when they suffer from debilitating (and sometimes erratic) symptoms. These symptoms make it virtually impossible for them to formulate and follow through on long-range plans. The plans they do make are usually tentative or short-term in nature and hinge upon how they feel on a given day, as Vic observed when discussing how he plans for the future:

> I kind of wait till the last minute. I'll say, "Well, I don't know if I can handle that or not. We'll see." Like, there's, um, well, someone's doing a campout at the end of May [about four weeks away]. And I think I'm just going to wait till the last minute to decide. I'll see how my energy level is. Maybe I can do that, maybe not. We'll see. So in a sense, in a general sense, my plans for the future are a little more uncertain and . . . a little more immediate.

In an effort to maximize their flexibility in planning, many men with AIDS work out tacit agreements with lovers, friends, or family members which allow them to easily change or cancel any plans that they make.

They rely upon these intimate others to understand that plans or outings depend upon their fluctuating health situation.

Along with limiting the abilities of men with AIDS to plan, seriously debilitating symptoms alter their goals for self. As their health deteriorates and they become more disabled, these men have much greater difficulty imagining themselves pursuing new ambitions, roles, or identities. In light of this, they begin to set more immediate and tangible goals. Through attaining these goals, they can sustain a sense of accomplishment and self-worth. Kirby alluded to this when he reported:

> I try to set goals that I can deal with physically. Right now I'm finishing my basement—putting up some Sheetrock. And I just say, "I'll get a couple of pieces of Sheetrock on the wall today." And then I'll sit back and enjoy that—enjoy having some kind of accomplishment.

Overall, the men who suffer from severe AIDS-related complications orient themselves toward attaining smaller-scale goals, such as exercising regularly, going on outings with friends, attending special parties or events, working on household projects, and, more generally, "taking time to do and appreciate little things." By pursuing and attaining these modest goals, they sustain a sense of mastery and control in their daily battles with debilitating symptoms. In doing so, they experience the self-worth that derives from engaging in efficacious action—action that gives one a sense of being "on top of" rather than merely "up to" the challenges that life poses (Brissett 1972).

## Confronting the Threats of Suffering, Dependence, and Dying

As their illness advances and their symptoms become more ominous, men with AIDS struggle to come to grips with their prospective mortality. Yet the threat of mortality is not usually the source of their greatest concerns. When reflecting upon the future, they commonly stress the pain, suffering, and debilitation they are likely to endure as they near the end of their lives. In fact, the men I interviewed felt far more afraid of the dying process than of death itself. When describing their anxieties regarding the future, they shared comments such as the following:

> I'm not afraid of death and what happens after death, I'm more afraid of the transition—it's going from here to there, dying, that's the scary part. . . . The fears that I have connected with it [the future] are to physical pain. I mean death hasn't and doesn't particularly scare me. It's the pain leading up to death that scares me. . . . I've been fairly close to death, but it just doesn't bother me. . . . I guess if anything bothers me it's having to go back to the hospital and go through all those procedures—like having a lung biopsy without anesthesia. That's not fun. . . . Stuff like that is what I don't want to go through again—the pain and discomfort.

In addition to fearing the prospect of pain and suffering, men with AIDS feel concerned about the possibility of losing many of their mental capacities, especially those capacities that are integral to their sense of self. As Lenny remarked:

> It worries me that I might lose my full faculties—my mental faculties. That is one of my major worries. Because I pride myself in being intelligent and rational—and being in control. Yeah, so that is a scary thing for me. And, um, I know it could happen. I mean, I've gone from having an excellent memory to only having an okay memory and things like that. That's been hard to deal with.

Of course, those men who have already experienced symptoms of disorientation or dementia feel particularly anxious about further deterioration of their mental abilities.

At the same time that they grapple with these fears, men with AIDS worry about the prospect of losing valued physical capacities, such as their ability to walk or move around easily. They also feel troubled about losing their sexual capabilities and dealing with the changes this will evoke in their intimate relationships and identities. As Neil indicated:

> As I've gotten more sick I've wondered about how much longer I'll be able to be sexual, I mean, over the last few months my sexual functioning has just gone downhill. It's hard for me to get excited

and, uh, to have sex, especially with my chronic fatigue. Sex takes a lot of energy—it wipes me out for a couple of days. And that doesn't feel very satisfying! But I know it's still important for [my lover]. I just worry about what's going to happen when I get even more sick. I mean, it's gonna get to the point where I'm not going to be able to have sex with him. So then what will happen? How will I feel about that? And how will he react?

As they come to terms with the decline taking place in their bodies and minds, men with AIDS feel especially concerned about the challenges they will face when they become more dependent on others. On one level, they worry about how they will preserve a sense of autonomy, masculinity, and self when they suffer from serious debilitation and have to give others more control over their lives. As Ron observed:

> I was thinking lately that if I become an invalid and have to be taken care of all the time, uh, I'd rather kill myself. That's part of dealing with getting really sick—dealing with how am I going to be taken care of or take care of myself. I mean, you know, it's like a progression of giving up your independence, which is, uh, an important part of your manhood. I mean, first of all, you deal with the humility about being sick and then the humility of having to depend on other people. . . . And then when you talk about becoming an invalid, it's like a process of giving up control—giving up control of, uh . . . your identity.

On another level, men with AIDS worry about the burdens they will impose upon their caregivers in the last phases of the disease. Some men hope that they can avoid having relatives, particularly older parents, serve as their primary caregivers. For example, when reflecting upon his deteriorating health and future care, Bob asserted:

> I don't want to put them [parents] into that maintenance thing. . . . My dad's old and in pretty crummy health, and my mom's seventy-three. So, I mean, I don't want to put them through that, at least from the standpoint of providing basic medical care assistance, or that kind of thing. . . . You shouldn't burden your relatives with that kind of bed-changing crap, you know.

In an effort to deal with these concerns and gain a greater sense of control over their future, men with AIDS usually make arrangements that specify who will care for them and how they should be cared for if or when they become incapacitated. Some make plans for their lovers, spouses, or close relatives to serve as key caregivers because they are the most likely or willing persons to serve in this role. Other men, however, make arrangements to receive caregiving assistance from a variety of others—friends, partners, parents, siblings, hospice volunteers, visiting nurses, and other medical specialists—so that they will not overly burden any one person. These men hope to delegate the responsibilities of caregiving so that no one will feel overwhelmed by and resentful about the tasks involved. Dennis reflected the sentiments of those adopting this approach when he remarked, "It's a major burden for one person to have to do—to have to go through—being a primary caregiver. So you have to spread the load out a little bit."

Along with planning for their future care, men with AIDS make arrangements which are designed to enhance their control over the process of dying. For instance, Rick planned to end his life when his symptoms progressed to the point where he had no real hope for recovery. He expected to make this choice in the near future because of the dramatic loss of vision and energy he had recently suffered. When reflecting upon the future, he stated:

> I am a firm believer in self-deliverance, or in what some people call voluntary death. . . . You know, there's a time when you've just got to say "good-bye," and when that time comes for me, I'll be ready to do it. Other people might try to hang on and hang on, you know, [through] life support and artificial resuscitation. I think that's ridiculous. . . . I don't want to just hang on and depend on someone else to make decisions for me. I want to have some control over the process. So when the time comes and I've become debilitated and my quality of life has diminished, you know, to an extremely low

point, then I'll be ready to perform self-deliverance.

More commonly, men with AIDS exercise control over their dying process by arranging to die a natural death rather than relying upon doctors to make decisions about their health care. They do this in a variety of ways, including filling out living wills which prevent physicians from taking extraordinary measures to prolong their lives (Weitz 1991) and assigning durable power of attorney to loved ones who agree to let them "die with dignity" if they become incapacitated and lose the ability to make their own decisions.

Finally, another way that men with AIDS gain a greater measure of control over their dying and future is through making advanced funeral and burial arrangements, and indicating what types of rituals, memorials, or celebrations they want friends and family to observe.

While discovering ways to gain control over their dying and death is important for men with AIDS, they also devote their energies to sustaining a sense of hope for the future. Some do this by making plans to fulfill lifelong dreams such as finishing treasured projects or traveling to places they had always wanted to see. Others remain hopeful through focusing on the dramatic resurgences of health that they (or their friends) have experienced in the past. Still others derive ongoing hope from the possibility that a medical cure will arrive on the scene before their health deteriorates further. In support of this possibility, they point to the major advances that have taken place in HIV-related medical knowledge and treatments during the past decade. As Alan suggested when discussing his hopes for ongoing survival:

Well, they have come up with medicines, more helpful medicines, you know. . . . And as they come up with better combinations, maybe they can treat me in time. Because I'm still physically intact, you know—my hearing is good, my eyesight is good, and, um, you know, some of the worst things that happen to people I haven't experienced yet. So it's kind of like if they could arrest the virus right now, I could get back into being a normal, healthy person.

In addition to these strategies, men with AIDS often find hope for the future through prayer and spirituality. As a result of their prayers and spiritual beliefs, they feel better able to cope with their suffering and prospective death. Although their spirituality does not always offer immediate benefits, it helps them to feel more hopeful in coming to terms with the future, as Hal revealed:

My spirituality gives me hope. I don't know if it sustains me all the time. There's times when it doesn't feel like it's doing a damn bit of good. But that's okay, it doesn't have to. I don't think that's what spirituality is about. Um, it's just kind of something that helps me in getting through, you know, getting through the days and what lies ahead.

Yet another strategy that men with AIDS use to sustain hope is focusing on the possibility that they will die a relatively painless and serene death. Usually, they recognize this possibility after seeing a friend or lover have such an experience. For instance, Stuart emphasized how a number of his friends with AIDS had "felt a sense of peace and serenity as their lives drew to a close" and "had come to accept and welcome death." In turn, he anticipated that he could have a similar experience as he underwent the last stages of the dying process.

### Transcending Death: Building a Post-mortal Self

As symbolic interactionist theorists have emphasized, individuals coming to terms with terminal illnesses face the task of making sense of their dying and making sense of themselves as dying persons (Lofland 1978; Marshall 1975, 1980). In doing so, they commonly try to give redemptive meaning to their lives and to sustain a sense of personal continuity, often by "accentuating portions of their personal histories for which they wish to be remembered" (Unruh 1983, p. 342). They also strive to gain a measure of control over the final chapters of their lives and over their post-mortal future. This struggle for control becomes integrally related to their struggle for meaning and continuity. By effectively legitimating or making sense of their unfolding biographies and prospective

**Table 36.1**
*Strategies Used to Construct Valued Postselves*

| Strategies | No. of Interviewees Utilizing |
|---|---|
| Sustaining close personal relationships to be remembered as a caring person | 9* |
| Passing on personal mementos or journals | 6 |
| Highlighting enduring vocational accomplishments | 12 |
| Stressing significant volunteer accomplishments (especially AIDS-related education and advocacy) | 11 |
| Embracing visions of a spiritual afterlife | 16 |
| Linking the AIDS self to enduring social and historical dramas | 4 |

*Many of the men I interviewed used more than one of these strategies in building and sustaining a post-self. As a result, the sum total of the numbers listed in the right column of the table is larger than the sample size of twenty-one men.

deaths, terminally ill individuals can gain an enhanced sense of control (Marshall 1980). In fact, through giving redemptive meaning to their lives and deaths, and through defining death as a positive transition for self rather than as a cessation of self, they can gain mastery over it as an ultimate limit. In essence, they can transcend death, at least symbolically (Becker 1975).

As they become increasingly cognizant of their prospective deaths, people with terminal illnesses often experience an "epiphany" (Denzin 1989b)—an existential crisis that challenges or disrupts their fundamental meaning structures and self-understandings. In turn, they begin to reshape their sense of self, linking and anchoring it to what comes after death (Charmaz 1991). In many cases this involves them in efforts to construct or experience an immortal self, or what some analysts call the "postself" (Lifton 1967; Schmidt and Leonard 1986). Through building and becoming anchored in a viable postself, dying individuals find a way to sustain a sense of hope and vitality in their daily lives. They also solidify and preserve important identities and assure themselves that their lives have had or will have an enduring meaning and purpose.

As they come to terms with their prospective deaths, men with AIDS, like others dealing with terminal illness, engage in efforts to anchor their sense of self in a post-mortal future. Those struggling with life-threatening symptoms, such as the men in this study, are especially inclined to devote themselves to

the construction of a postself. They do this in a number of ways. (See Table 36.1 for a summary.)

In some cases, men with AIDS focus their energies on maintaining close and caring personal relationships in the hope that after dying they will "be remembered as someone who reached out and did little things for other people." They may also dedicate themselves to collecting artifacts or to writing journals that will be passed on to friends, family, or the wider public. They hope that this will allow their experiences or "stories" to live on in the memories of others.

In addition to using these strategies, many of the men I interviewed anchored a postself, or sense of symbolic immortality (Lifton 1978), in the enduring contributions they had made through their work as artists, writers, teachers, carpenters, businesspeople, or medical specialists. Several also stressed the "legacy" they would leave as a result of their efforts as HIV/AIDS educators and volunteers or as leaders of the gay community. For instance, Hal and Lee emphasized the significant impact they had made through combating homophobia and promoting HIV-related education and support programs in the small towns where they had lived. Others, such as Bob, Dave, and Jay, accentuated how they made a lasting difference through speaking publicly about HIV-related issues, as highlighted in the following excerpt:

I get up in front of crowds of people and say, "Hey I'm a human being and I have feelings just like you. And I hope that you never find yourself in the same position that I'm in . . ." I talk about all the things that have happened to me—about getting fired from my job and watching my friends die. And I do it in a way that moves them—that gets them to think more deeply about things and, um, that helps them to focus on their common humanness with me—with us, with people with HIV.

As they come to terms with their finitude, men with AIDS not only construct an enduring self in terms of the legacies they will leave behind, they also anchor a sense of continuity in beliefs that they will live on spiritually after dying. In discussing their future and prospective death, my informants shared remarks that illustrated how their religious beliefs, or spiritual outlooks, provided them with a basis for building and sustaining an immortal self. As Curtis remarked:

I think my spirituality is very tied to that—to giving me a sense of living on. I don't think there would be any religion or spirituality if people didn't die, you know. And personally, yeah, it's important in coming to terms with that, um, with living on and what that means.

Drawing upon religious or spiritual frameworks, the men I interviewed often saw death as a transition to a new realm of being rather than as an ending to their personal existence. Although some accepted traditional Christian views of the afterlife, most espoused alternative views because of the anti-gay, anti-drug, or anti-sex messages conveyed by many variants of Christian theology. Rather than thinking of the afterlife in terms of Heaven and Hell, they typically embraced philosophies that emphasize how one's life force continues on in a never ending spiritual journey.

Overall, belief in an afterlife offers men with AIDS an important basis of hope and continuity regarding their present and future. By drawing upon these beliefs, they can solidify and preserve their sense of "real self" (Turner 1976) and anchor it in a future beyond death. This makes the prospect of death less ominous and frightening. Moreover, rather than viewing death as the ulti-

mate loss of self, they redefine it as an opening to new experiences and, implicitly, to an enhanced or transformed self. This conception of death is reflected in the following remarks shared by Trent:

Death is the very thing that makes it possible to transcend—the means by which we transcend. It just opens up more and more possibilities and opportunities for wholeness and for unity with God or the Godhead, whatever we might identify as that.

Given their sense of being trapped in a devitalizing present, men with AIDS who embrace this view even look forward to death, at least on one level, because of the new life they anticipate having afterward. Although they feel somewhat fearful of the dying process, they also feel, as Dennis noted, "excited to move on to the new adventure and wonderful possibilities offered in the hereafter."

Yet, while belief in an afterlife can foster feelings of hope and anticipation regarding the future, it can also evoke feelings of anxiety and uncertainty. For instance, Matt and Vic, who accepted traditional Christian conceptions of the afterlife, worried about what would happen after they died. As Matt remarked, "I wonder whether I'll be shoveling coal in one place or pushing clouds in the other." In a related vein, those men who believed in reincarnation also wondered whether their future lives would be more or less rewarding than their present ones. As Neil pointed out:

I believe in reincarnation . . . [and] that serves as a source of hope, but it's a source of worry, too (laughs). You know, in the next life I could come back in Bangladesh, in the midst of a typhoon (laughs). I mean, people always like to think that things would be better in the next life, but who knows where you might pop up? It might not be so great there. In fact, if there's any sense of justice, many of us [Americans] might come back in an impoverished state.

As noted above, the men I interviewed rarely embraced or expressed traditional Christian views when it came to their images of the afterlife and of a postmortal self. At times, however, they drew upon variants of Christianity in their efforts to immortalize the self and to give both redemptive meaning and social significance to their experiences as persons living with AIDS. For instance, Jay utilized Catholic imagery in defining people with AIDS as part of a "litany of saints" who, in suffering, embodied Christ. As he explained:

> I believe, like Mother Teresa says, that those who suffer the most—they're like Jesus. The more you suffer, the closer you are to the face of Jesus. She talks about that imagery—how when she reaches to the beggar, the leper, the dying person in the street, that that is Jesus. . . . She says, "That person is Jesus in a distressing disguise." And I believe that people with AIDS, in the quality of suffering they endure, become—like others who suffer—most like Christ.

By defining the experience of people with AIDS (and, implicitly, his own experience) in this way, Jay not only gave it a redemptive and transcendent meaning, he also connected it to an overarching legacy and an unfolding sociohistorical drama. In fact, he suggested that people with AIDS had a prophetic historical role to play. They were being "called or chosen to convey a message to others about what was happening around them." In elaborating, Jay asserted:

> I think that people with AIDS have an amazing role to play in history. There's so many messages that have been conveyed and are yet to be conveyed—about the disease and what it means for the planet and how we live. There's so much we can learn from this, and I think people with AIDS can be like modern-day prophets. That doesn't mean other people can't be prophetic, too. There are many people in other situations who have that ability as well, but I think AIDS is, uh, is prophetic just because of its connection with sexuality and, um, life-giving things. It reflects the whole paradigm of planetary illness and how Mother Earth is hurting— and when any living, breathing organism is hurting, what happens sooner or later is disease results. And AIDS is an example of that.

Most importantly, by connecting the experience of people with AIDS to larger religious themes and social dramas, Jay legitimized his own illness experience and gained a sense that it had a redeeming, significant, and enduring purpose. . . .

## References

Adam, Barry. 1996. *Experiencing HIV.* New York: Columbia University Press.

Becker, Ernest. 1975. *The Denial of Death.* New York: Free Press.

Blumer, Herbert. 1969. *Symbolic Interactionism.* Englewood Cliffs, NJ: Prentice-Hall.

Brissett, Dennis. 1972. "Toward a Clarification of Self-Esteem." *Psychiatry* 35:255–63.

Charmaz, Kathy. 1994. "Identity Dilemmas of Chronically Ill Men." *Sociological Quarterly* 35:269–88.

——. 1991. *Good Days, Bad Days: The Self in Chronic Illness and Time.* New Brunswick, NJ: Rutgers University Press.

——. 1990. "'Discovering' Chronic Illness Using Grounded Theory." *Social Science and Medicine* 30:1161–72.

Corbin, Juliet, and Anselm Strauss. 1987. "Accompaniments of Chronic Illness: Changes in Body, Self, Biography and Biographical Time." Pp. 249–82 in *Research in the Sociology of Health Care*, vol. 6 *(The Experience and Management of Chronic Illness)*, edited by J. Roth and P. Conrad. Greenwich, CT: JAI Press.

Denzin, Norman. 1989a. *Interpretive Interactionism.* Beverly Hills, CA: Sage.

——. 1989b. *Interpretive Biography.* Beverly Hills, CA: Sage.

——. 1983. "A Note on Emotionality, Self, and Interaction." *American Journal of Sociology* 89:402–8.

Durig, Alexander. 1996. *Autism and the Crisis of Meaning.* Saratoga Springs, NY: SUNY Press.

Glaser, Barney, and Anselm Strauss. 1967. *The Discovery of Grounded Theory.* Chicago: Aldine.

Goffman, Erving. 1963. *Stigma.* Englewood Cliffs, NJ: Prentice-Hall.

——. 1961. *Asylums.* Garden City, NY: Anchor Books.

Kayal, Philip. 1993. *Bearing Witness: Gay Men's Health Crisis and the Politics of AIDS.* Boulder, CO: Westview Press.

Kotarba, Joseph, and Norris Lang. 1986. "Gay Lifestyle Change and AIDS Preventive Health Care." Pp. 127–43 in *The Social Dimensions of*

*AIDS: Method and Theory*, edited by D. Feldman and T. Johnson. New York: Praeger.

Lifton, Robert Jay. 1978. *The Broken Connection*. New York: Basic Books.

———. 1967. *Death in Life: Survivors of Hiroshima*. New York: Random House.

Lofland, Lyn. 1978. *The Craft of Dying: The Modern Face of Death*. Beverly Hills, CA: Sage.

Markus, Hazel, and P. Nurius. 1986. "Possible Selves." *American Psychologist* 41:954–69.

Marshall, Victor. 1980. *Last Chapters: A Sociology of Aging and Dying*. Monterey, CA: Brooks/Cole.

———. 1975. "Age and Awareness of Finitude in Developmental Gerontology." *Omega* 6:113–29.

Mead, George Herbert. 1934. *Mind, Self, and Society*. Chicago: University of Chicago Press.

Sandstrom, Kent. 1998. "Coming to Terms with Bodily Losses and Disruptions Evoked by AIDS." *Illness, Crisis, and Loss* 48:17–31.

———. 1996a. "Redefining Sex and Intimacy: The Sexual Self-Images, Outlooks, and Relationships of Gay Men Living with HIV Disease." *Symbolic Interaction* 19:241–62.

———. 1996b. "Searching for Information, Understanding, and Self-Value: The Utilization of Peer Support Groups by Gay Men Living with HIV/AIDS." *Social Work in Health Care* 23:51–74.

———. 1990. "Confronting Deadly Disease: The Drama of Identity Construction among Gay Men with AIDS." *Journal of Contemporary Ethnography* 19:271–94.

Schmidt, Raymond, and W. Leonard II. 1986. "Immortalizing the Self Through Sport." *American Journal of Sociology* 91:1088–111.

Strauss, Anselm. 1993. *Continuing Permutations of Action*. New York: Aldine de Gruyter.

Stryker, Sheldon. 1980. *Symbolic Interactionism: A Social Structural Version*. Menlo Park, CA: Benjamin Publications.

Turner, Ralph. 1976. "The Real Self: From Institution to Impulse." *American Journal of Sociology* 81:989–1016.

Unruh, David. 1983. "Death and Personal History Strategies of Identity Preservation." *Social Problems* 30:341–51.

Weitz, Rose. 1991. *Life with AIDS*. New Brunswick, NJ: Rutgers University Press.

———. 1989. "Uncertainty and the Lives of Persons with AIDS." *Journal of Health and Social Behavior* 30:270–81.

## Review

1. Discuss the challenges to the self faced by those in the advanced stages of AIDS.

2. How do AIDS victims deal with the threats of suffering, dependence, and dying?

3. Describe how the men try to transcend death by building a post-mortal self.

## Applications

1. Find an article or a book that discusses the process of dying. What are the challenges that dying people typically face? What are the emotional stages they go through? How are those dying of AIDS similar to and different from those dying of other causes?

2. Invite someone who works at an AIDS hospice to speak to your class about his or her experiences in being with those dying of the disease. How do his or her experiences compare with Sandstrom's findings?

## Related Web Sites

1. *http://www.aids.org/*. This site offers a great range of information from facts about AIDS to treatment news.

2. *http://www.aidsonline.com*. Official site of AIDS, the journal of the International AIDS Society, with access to most of the articles published in the journal.

# Part Seven

## *Technology and Society*

Karl Marx declared that the windmill gave us society with the feudal lord, while the steam-mill gave us society with the industrial capitalist. His statement dramatizes the centrality of technology for the nature of a society. Indeed, few people would question the crucial role of technology in creating the kind of world in which we live. But does technology simply change the context in which we live, or does it affect the way we relate to each other as well? And do the so-cial arrangements in any society—e.g., the ay the society is divided into social classes— bear upon the way technology is used, or is the technology simply there for the taking by anyone in a society? These two questions are addressed in the selections in this part. The first selection addresses the way technology affects relationships. The second looks at the issue of how social arrangements affect peo-ple's use of technology. ◆

# 37

# Technology and the Initiation of Interpersonal Relationships

*Jeffrey S. McQuillen*

How do you go about finding friends, dates, and romantic partners in an increasingly technological world? Does the technology make it easier or more difficult? In this selection, Jeffrey McQuillen examines various research findings and makes some important observations that bear upon those questions. He points out the ways in which television, chat rooms, e-mail, and bulletin boards affect the nature of interpersonal relationships today.

Among other things, the technology directly affects a fundamental aspect of relating that is stressed by **symbolic interactionists**: how we present ourselves to others. In its original formulation by Erving Goffman, **self-presentation** referred to a performance that was designed to influence others. Social relationships were viewed as a form of theater with the backstage area, the actors, and the audience. For example, if you want to establish a romantic relationship with someone, you are the actor, the object of your desire is the audience, and others such as your close friends are part of the backstage. You can confer with your friends about the best way to put on your performance in order to influence the person you want to like you. Your performance will include all those things you do in order to make yourself more attractive.

But that assumes a face-to-face relationship. What happens when you are trying to do the same sort of thing electronically? As McQuillen notes, it's a different ball game in a technological world.

## Introduction

The world has witnessed a steady increase in the advent, adoption, and widespread use of new and varied technologies. With this proliferation of technology, scholars and lay people alike are beginning to ask the question, "How does advancing technologies impact interpersonal relationships?" This paper explores this concern by examining the following three areas. First, brief consideration is given to technology and its influence on social life. Second, the influence of media on interpersonal relationships is explored. Finally, the implications of computer-mediated interaction for relationship development are reviewed.

## Technology and Social Life

Ever since the discovery of the first tool, people have seen these tools, machines, [and] technological advances as positive and desirable (the wheel, printing press, telephone, airplane, TV, satellite, microwave, and PC, just to name a few). They have helped to bring about what McLuhan (1975) has termed the "Global Village." The world is becoming continually smaller. However, as the distance between cultures and countries shrink[s], the distance between interpersonal interactants appears to be expanding. Paradoxically, the closer we get, the further apart we appear to be. As this paper argues, technology (in many ways a positive influence on quality of life), in part, is responsible for this increasing social/interpersonal distance.

Tools are intended to make one's work easier. However, the increased ease and time saved, afford people the opportunity to become less interdependent and more autonomous and self-reliant. For example, where once women gathered at the water's edge to do the laundry in social groups outside the home; men and women now go to the laundry room and turn on the washing machine, quickly returning to the comfort of the living room, kitchen, or den. The tools that were originally designed to aid in the execution of some activity have come to replace that activity. Human input goes from maximum to almost nonexistent. The telephone permits ordering food to be delivered to our front door, cable access provides the convenience of ordering recent-release movies for home viewing, Internet availability permits shopping for "almost anything" on-line. A consumer can take advantage of all of these services and never leave the comfort and isolation of home.

Furthermore, all of this increased social isolation is encouraged and validated. The AT&T slogan, "Reach out and touch someone," encapsulates the ideology being spread by the Techno Barons like Bell, Microsoft, Apple, Time-Warner, etc. The enthymematic force of this slogan advances the position that mediated contact, virtual interaction, and Computer-Mediated-Communication (CMC) (Walther & Tidwell, 1996) are synonymous to face-to-face communication. That is to say, touching someone in an emotional sense is the same as, or equivalent to, physically touching someone. Hence, the paradox; one can be closer because some form of contact (i.e., CMC) is experienced and further apart because that contact serves to create a less accurate representation of the participants and their messages. The absence of the characteristics associated with face-to-face communication can result in a loss of fidelity and an increase in the psychological distance between interactants.

In addition, the desire for this new technology places a heavier financial burden on the necessary income for the interpersonal unit (i.e., the family). Because of personal or economic reasons, dual income families have become the norm. According to Galvin and Brommel (2000), "[f]rom 1970–1990, the number of working married women with children under age 6 increased from 49 to 58 percent" (p. 14). These authors also report, that in families with children 6 to 17, 73 percent of the women are employed. Though the cause for these dual income families cannot be attributed directly to the acquisition, use, or presence of technology, the dual income family gives rise to the "latchkey children" phenomenon, children returning from school before either parent has return from work. These children's contact with parents is limited (Lawlor, 1998), and they spend a large part of their day with babysitters or day-care workers and with the television and/or personal computer. As exposure to these media increase the potential for influence by these media also increase. Rubin (1985) argued that TV viewing is often used for companionship or to battle loneliness. Consequently, television may have an obvious impact on how people initiate and maintain interpersonal relationship[s].

## Idealized and Parasocial Relationship

Technology, specifically television, can have a strong impact on the development and/or maintenance of interpersonal relationships. In 1941 tele-vision, vision at a distance, was first introduced to the country by engineers and industrialists. In the early 1940's less than 5000 sets were in homes in the United States (Biocca & Levy, 1995). However, in less than 20 years, a TV could be found in the majority of homes. Today, over 90% of the homes have at least two TVs. Accordingly, Gerbner, Gross, Morgan, and Signorielli (1986) see television as the great common experience.

Television causes a culture to become homogenized. This effect is known as cultivation (Gerbner et al., 1986, p. 18). "Television is not a force for change as much as it is a force for stability" (Littlejohn, 1999, p. 345). Television has created the sense of the sixty-second solution, the presentation of a simplistic solution to a complex human problem. According to Bate and Bowker (1997), television contributes to two serious problems in the area of gender stereotyping: (1) under representation of women by the media tend[s] to devalue women, and (2) the media's portrayal of men and women reinforce[s] stereotypic and destructive patterns for both genders. These two problems contribute to females being caught up in the "Beauty Myth" (Wolf, 1991). Females become so concerned with their appearance that the tendency toward problems of lower self-esteem and serious eating disorders become[s] commonplace (Wood, 2000). In contrast, men are encouraged to be strong, successful, and sexual. These gender identities are debilitating and maximize incompatibility between men and women. The likelihood of June Clever and the Marlboro Man developing or maintaining a healthy relationship is highly unlikely.

The misrepresentation of genders is further compounded by the tendency for television programming to misrepresent and idealize gender-matched roles. Bill Cosby (*The Cosby Show*) is seen as the perfect father, or at least the perfect "Black" father. Scully (Gillian Anderson) [*The X-Files*] is the perfect partner. Not only is she devoted, skilled, helpful, and supportive; she's pretty and a subtle love interest. [Fox] Mulder (David Duchovny), Scully's masculine partner, is the perfect gender-matched mirror image to Anderson's Scully. *Dharma & Greg* have the perfect marriage, and if not, then the perfect marriage must be Raymond and wife (*Everybody Loves Raymond*). Finally, Martin Sheen's President Jeb (*The West Wing*) is the most compassionate, fair, and moral politician, ever! All of these characters provide excellent examples of the people anyone and everyone would like in his/her life. This perception of "perfection" is dangerous in two major ways: (1) viewers may expect the "real" individuals in their lives to live up to the standards exhibited by the actors in the roles viewers have come to know, appreciate, and even love; and (2) other viewers may get the need for interpersonal companionship, affection, respect, etc. fulfilled vicariously by watching these characters on television. In fact, viewers may develop a symbolic relationship with these characters. People come to believe their relationship (i.e., parasocial relationship) to be similar in many ways to actual, social relationships (Rubin & McHugh, 1987). For example, heavy viewers of a particular soap opera may mourn the passing of a personally liked/loved character. Other viewers may correspond, via fan mail, with a host(s) of a particular talk show. Others may obsess over a character of a sitcom or weekly drama.

Expecting those around us to act in a similar or equally appealing manner as characters in scripted roles can be unhealthy to one's mental and social well being. No one can compete with a character who lives, on an average, for only 30 to 60 minutes once a week. These people, no matter how desirable, are not real. If an individual sets his/her sights on finding someone "just like Fox," or Fox himself, the fan is in for disappointment. Fox does not exist, not even in David Duchovny. If the fan develops a parasocial relationship with "Fox," the situation is equally problematic. That simulated relationship can have serious debilitating influences on one's likelihood of developing and maintaining a normal, social relationship.

The distancing impact resulting from society's increasing reliance on differing technologies and the distortion of one's expectations of interpersonal relationships that may accompany television viewing are further augmented by the possibility of initiating and maintaining relationships via computer-aided communication. On-line relationships are one of the newest forms of mediated interpersonal communication. The following examines how the use of on-line technologies may influence the development of interpersonal relationships.

## On-Line Relationships

Due to the high volume use of e-mail, chat rooms, and bulletin boards for interpersonal relationship purposes, considerable interest has focused on this medium. America On-line is said to carry over 13 million e-mail messages daily (Lawe, 1997). Parks and Floyd (1996) report that people are using e-mail and bulletin boards to initiate and develop relationships (As in Stafford, Kline, & Dimmick, 1999). Their data suggest that on-line relationships develop in a similar fashion to those formed in face-to-face interaction. However, according to Walther and Tidwell (1996), the most common theoretical argument for the inferiority of CMC holds that on-line systems do not have the nonverbal code that is present in Face-to-Face (FtF) conversations. Given a severely limited nonverbal channel, a sender cannot easily alter the relational level of the message (Kiesler, 1986). Because CMC lacks audio and video cues, the message can be seen as impersonal and lack[ing] soicoemotional content (Rice & Love, 1987). Walther and

Tidwell's (1996) interpretation of the social information-processing model suggests that the rate of social information exchanged will be slower, but that the amount, over time, will not differ from FtF. Accordingly, development of interpersonal effects will be slower, but the depth of the relationship will be equal to its FtF counterpart.

Walther (1995) notes that in a number of instances, CMC appears to surpass the relational communication of FtF. This phenomenon is referred to as hyperpersonal communication—communication which is more socially desirable than communication experienced in FtF interactions (Walther & Tidwell, 1996). Walther and Tidwell (1996) highlight three elements of the communication process: idealized perception, selective self-presentation, and reduced cues that [explain] this phenomenon.

## Idealized Perception

According to Walther (1995), users of CMC may judge their communicative partners on limited information. These participants may not realize the negative attributes of the other; instead, [they] opt to judge the other as the "perfect person." When FtF cues are absent, partners may engage in over-attributing impressions. These impressions are based on meager information, such as, misspelling or excessive punctuation. These impressions are not uniformly positive, nor negative. The valence of the evaluation is based on perceived similarities, in the absence of physical exposure to one another.

## Selective Self-Perception: The Sender

In the process, selective self-perception or preferred self-presentation, each participant can impression manage by presenting only that information believed to be favorable about self. One's ability to conceal some aspect (e.g., negative) of self and accentuate others (e.g., positive) is actually enhanced by CMC because of the lack of nonverbal information. The receiver has no (or very limited) information available to test, validate, discredit, or refine the information presented by the sender.

## Reduced Cues

In CMC user's form impressions based on a restricted number of cues. Because of the absence of one's physical being, meaning relies solely on verbal behavior. Scholars argue that verbal behavior is more subject to conscious editing than is nonverbal behavior (Hayakawa, 1949). "In this way . . . meaning and expression matter over looks, gender, race, and other stereotypical physical features" (Walther & Tidwell, 1996). One can censor the information one is willing to give about self. Finally, the lack of physical cues allows greater focus on "private self-awareness."

## Asynchronous Benefits

FtF interactions take place in real-time conversation. Asynchronous CMC permits the participants time to plan and edit comments more mindfully. In contrast, the spontaneous and simultaneous requirements of FtF communication places greater demands on cognitive resources.

## Interpersonal Communication

In order to more clearly consider the difference between CMC-hyperpersonal communication and FtF communication, interpersonal communication and its connection to relationship development need to be more fully characterized. The majority of interpersonal communication scholars tend to agree that interpersonal communication is a quality of communication and not solely a context. Communication between two individuals in a face-to-face setting is a definition more appropriate for dyadic communication (i.e., communication between two participants), but not precise enough to capture the sophisticated nature of interpersonal communication. According to Miller and Steinberg (1975), interpersonal communication is characterized by communication strategies that are adapted to the individual's psychological make-up, rather than the sociological or cultural assumptions of the other interactant. In addition, in order for interpersonal communication to lead to increased intimacy/relational development, the participants must engage in mutual self-disclosure. Self-disclosure occurs when a sender accepts some risk in order to share significant information in an honest and intentional manner with a receiver (Mader & Mader, 1993). These characteristics can be used to more clearly examine the relationship of hyperpersonal communication to interpersonal communication.

First, the idealized perception of the receiver created by CMC does not make the communication more psychologically personal, nor does it make it more accurate. In fact, CMC permits, or even encourages, true infidelity or inaccuracy (i.e., the message does not validate the self-concept of the sender, it obfuscates it). If the perception of a communication partner is more a function of the other's frame of reference rather than characteristics directly related to or associate[d] with that partner, communication is disconfirming. The partner is not being seen for who he/she is, but possibl[y] for whom the other hopes/wants the partner to be.

Second, self-selection under totally "free" conditions does not resemble interpersonal communication. According to Miller and Steinberg (1976), self-disclosure should be honest and risky. When a speaker reveals only positive characteristics he/she is not being honest (i.e., lying by omission) and she/he is assuming very little risk. How risky is it to show all of one's positive qualities?

Third, at times, limiting relational level messages can control emotional reactions and increase the efficiency of task-oriented decisions. Censorship of everything except one's verbal behavior severely limits how much information is risked or shared. To limit the message in this way retards the receiver's ability to consider the unique psychological characteristic of the sender when tailoring messages. Therefore, this strategy restricts the sender from communicating interpersonally and, further, withholds crucial information the receiver needs in his/her attempts to adapt to the communicative needs of the receiver.

Finally, because a response is not due in real time, asynchronous exchanges allow for a cognitive/interactive "time out" that is not typical of FtF interactions. Unlike normal FtF conversation, this delay can reduce the level of stress associated with the need to respond efficiently and quickly. CMC allows the interactants more freedom to use cognitive resources as deemed necessary. However, as Larson, Backlund, Redmond, and Barbour (1978) argued, communication competence (i.e., functional communication/interpersonal competence) requires, at minimum the ability to meet "the minimum demands of a situation and . . . [exhibit] socially appropriate behavior" (p. 1). Delaying real-time feedback changes the nature of the situation and its demands, and further, conversational contribution appears to redefine the nature of interpersonal interaction.

CMC may serve as a tool to encourage, permit, and assist in the development of interpersonal relationships; however, a relationship based solely on CMC will be significantly different from a relationship developed based on FtF. CMC relationships can be compared to interactions at a costume party. Each person becomes the character represented by the costume, partially because of the highly selective self-presentation, the manipulation of one's perceived self, and the highly restricted nature of one's self-disclosive clues. Therefore, talking to someone on-line is likened to talking to a participant at a costume party. You may not know who you're talking with, but the greater shock may appear when you realize that old tried and true systems were unreliable because the quality of information upon which your perceptions were based [was] obviously less than interpersonal quality.

In sum, the growing dependence on technology is allowing each individual to become more and more "self"-sufficient. This gained autonomy has allowed the individual to become more isolated and reclusive. The need for social contact, in many cases, is being fulfilled by the media—especially television. Answering machines, voice mail, and CMC have started to replace Face-to-Face interaction. Relationships are not being initiated with "real" people, but with the projected, edited, "spun" images the users share online. As Shakespeare noted, "all the world's a stage, and all the men and women merely players" (As You Like It. Act II, Sc. 7). However, unlike the parts that Shakespeare envisioned men and women playing, the computer-aged players may aspire to act out scripts less representative of our humanity. CMC may be more appropriate to creating celebrity than to being friends.

## References

Bates, B., & Bowker, J. (1997). *Communication and the sexes* (2nd Ed.). Prospect Heights, IL: Waveland Press, Inc.

Biocca, F., & Levy, M. R. (1995)(Eds.). *Communication in the age of virtual reality*. Hillsdale, NJ: Lawrence Erlbaum Associates, Publishers.

Galvin, K. M., & Brommel, B. J. (2000). *Family communication: Cohesion and change* (5th Ed.). New York: Addison-Wesley Longman, Inc.

Gerbner G., Gross, L., Morgan, M., & Signorielli, N. (1986). Living with Television. In J. Bryant & D. Zillmann (Eds.), *Perspectives on media effects*. Hillsdale, NJ: Erlbaum.

Hayakawa, S. I. (1949). *Language in thought and action*. New York: Harcourt, Brace & World, Inc.

Kiesler, S. (1986, January–February). "The hidden message in computer networks." *Harvard Business Review*, 46–54, 58–60.

Larson, C., Backlund, P., Redmond, M., & Barbour, A. (1978). *Assessing Functional Communication*. Falls Church, VA: ERIC/RCS and SCA.

Lawe, R. K. (1997, May 29). "Computer services 'warping' their way into common use." *Columbus Dispatch*, pp. 1–2 D.

Lawlor, J. (1998, April 26). For many blue-collar fathers, child care is shift work, too. *New York Times*, p. 111.

Littlejohn, S. W. (1999). *Theories of human communication* (6th Ed.). Belmont, CA: Wadsworth Publishing Co.

Mader, T. F., & Mader, D. C. (1993). *Understanding one another* (2nd Ed.). Madison, WI: Brown & Benchmark Publishers.

McLuhan, M. (1975). "Implications of Cultural Uniformity." In C. E. E. Brigsby (Ed.), *Superculture: American Popular Culture and Europe*. Bowling Green, OH: Bowling Green University Popular Press.

Miller, G. R., & Steinberg, M. (1976). *Between people: A new analysis of interpersonal communication*. Chicago, IL: Science Research Associates, Inc.

Parks, M. R., & Floyd, K. (1996). "Making friends in cyberspace." *Journal of Communication*, 46, 80–97.

Rice, R. E., & Love, G. (1987). "Electronic emotion: Socioemotional content in a computer-mediated network." *Communication Research*, 14, 85–108.

Rubin, A. M. (1985). "Media gratification through the life cycle." In K. E. Rosengren, L. A. Wenner, & P. Palmgreen (Eds.), *Media gratification research: Current perspectives* (pp. 195–208). Beverly Hills, CA: Sage.

Rubin, A. M., & McHugh, M. P. (1987). "Development of parasocial interaction relationships." *Journal of Broadcasting and Electronic Media*, 31, 279–292.

Stafford, L., Kline, S. L., & Dimmick, J. (1999, Fall). "Home e-mail: Relational maintenance and gratification opportunities." *Journal of Broadcasting & Electronic Media*, 43, 4, 659–663.

Walther, J. B. (1995). "Relational aspects of computer-mediated communication: Experimental and longitudinal observations." *Organization Science*, 6, 186–203.

Walther, J. B., & Tidwell, L. (1996). "When is mediated communication not interpersonal?" In K. M. Galvin & P. Cooper (Eds.), *Making connections: Readings in relational communication* (pp. 300–307). Los Angeles: Roxbury Publishing Company.

Wolf, N. (1991). *The Beauty myth: How images of beauty are used against women*. New Jersey: Anchor Books.

Wood, J. T. (2000). *Gender lives: Communication, gender, and culture* (4th Ed.). Belmont, CA: Wadsworth/Thompson Learning.

## Review

1. How does our technology enable us to become less interdependent and more autonomous and self-reliant?

2. How does technology impact influence and parasocial relationships?

3. Discuss the consequences of trying to establish relationships on-line.

## Application

Visit one or more chat rooms on-line. Also, read the notices posted on a few on-line bulletin boards, looking in particular for those that seem to be trying to establish a relationship of some kind (rather than just seeking specific information). Summarize in writing your observations, using as many of the ideas in this selection as are appropriate.

Share your findings with your class; then lead a discussion on the advantages and disadvantages of initiating relationships through personal contact and electronically.

## Related Web Sites

1. *http://chat.yahoo.com.* A gateway to a variety of chat rooms.

2. *http://health.discovery.com/centers/ loverelationships/articles/cyberdating. html.* An article that discusses the risks and rewards of "cyber" relationships.

# 38

# The Impact of Mobile Communications

*James E. Katz*
*Philip Aspden*

Technological advances hold a particular fascination for Americans. This fascination may be seen in the quickness with which Americans adopt new technologies as if they represent unquestioned life improvements. It is not surprising that an American sociologist, William Ogburn, developed a theory of social change that gave technology a central place. Specifically, Ogburn argued that technological change is the dynamic element in culture with values and beliefs lagging behind. Because all cultures tend to be integrated, the changing technology forces modifications in value and beliefs. For example, the value on large families in preindustrial societies gradually changed as industrial technology opened up new opportunities for social mobility and rendered obsolete the need for a large number of workers on the family farm.

While Ogburn's theory doesn't account for all of the interplay between technology and social factors, it does underscore the fact of that interplay. Social factors can affect the development of technology, and new technology always has social consequences. In this selection, Katz and Aspden look at the relationships between social factors and a recent technological development: mobile communications. A few years ago a pager was a **status symbol,** a sign that the owner held an important position such as that of a physician. Is this still true? What about cellular telephones? Are they the tools of the rich and important? These are some of the questions probed in this article.

## Introduction

By 1999 it is expected that there will be more than 120 million cellular phone customers worldwide.[1] In mid-1996, there were already more than 38 million subscribers in the United States alone, or about 14.5% of the entire U.S. population.[2] (This contrasts with about 1% in the mid-1980s.[3]) A cheaper but more limited personal wireless system—the pager—had in 1996 about 8% penetration overall but among older teens it was 17%.[4] Yet this adoption rate is small compared to Singapore, where one out of three adults uses a pager. (There are about 90 million pagers in the Asia-Pacific region.[5]) Paging technology is becoming two way, and predictions are for a five-fold increase in worldwide subscribership by the year 2000.[6]

What has been the impact wrought by this technology in people's personal and business lives? The mass media have presented sundry items ranging from a car-jacked man being rescued from his car trunk to British royalty being eavesdropped. But compared to media attention, the intellectual community has hardly probed the uses and implications of mobile communication.

It appears to us that, from a social analytical viewpoint, wireless personal communication has been overshadowed first by the proliferation of personal computers, then by the Internet. Like its intensively scrutinized, socially transformative cousin, the personal computer, wireless personal communication has experienced a revolution since 1983. And like its socially transformative forebear—the telephone—personal mobile wireless technology has been largely ignored by scholars who claim to study communication modalities and social processes. (For a discussion of the scholarly inattention regarding the telephone, see Reference 7.) . . .

## Research Questions

. . . [T]here are numerous questions about mobile communications technology, regarding both how they affect society and human behavior as well as what use reveals about

360

social theory and policy. Our research has focused on some of these. Specifically, we sought to determine:

- The extent ownership is determined by demographic variables. For example, is ownership affluence-driven, gender-based, or ethnically-based?
- The extent ownership reflects functionality needs. For example, are more mobile people more likely to own the technology?
- Whether the technology relieves or generates stress.

Where possible, we also sought to examine how the observed relationship changed over time.

Demographic issues are important given the concern about the commercial uses of mobile communications. There is much riding on whether they are actually a useful tool for economic success. Assuming for the moment that they are, questions of equitable distribution by social class or race assume a great deal of importance. . . .

Another important question is whether wireless communication technologies are fundamentally liberating or enslaving. While the answer is likely to be some combination of both phenomena, it would be helpful to have data which could actually illuminate the question. For instance, while by no means alone, Giddens[8–10] has spoken of the subtle controls over individual movements that technology might give, and Gary Marx,[11, 12] Gandy,[13] and Katz[14, 15] have spoken of the ways in which these technologies can be abused to remove anonymity and freedom.

## Method

In an attempt to address our research questions, we have conducted national opinion surveys over a three-year span. The analysis that follows presents data that suggest preliminary answers to our research questions.

Our main source of data is a 2500-person telephone survey (identified as Survey 95). These data were taken from an October 1995 national random telephone sample, surveyed by a commercial firm under contract from Bellcore. The survey sample has a close match on socioeconomic variables compared with the U.S. population as a whole. . . .

## Results

### Cell-Only and Pager Plus Cell Phone Usage Growing Faster Than Pager-Only Usage

Our approach has been to divide the sample population into four groups—those [who] report owning or using:

1. Neither a pager nor a cellular telephone (the "neither" group).
2. A pager only (the "pager-only" group).
3. A cellular phone only ("the cell-only" group).
4. Both a pager and a cellular phone (the "both" group).

In our 1995 survey, 63% of respondents reported not owning a pager or a cellular phone, 10% reported owning only a pager, and 16% reported owning a cellular phone, while 11% reported owning both a pager and a cellular phone. On the basis of historical data it would appear that over the past few years when there has been significant growth in both cellular and pager usage, pager-only growth has been slow if not static and certainly much slower than growth in cellular-only usage and combined cellular and pager usage. Across our seven surveys spanning nearly three years, 6% to 10% of respondents report being pager-only owners, while cell-only owners grew from 9% to 16% of respondents, and owners of both grew even more rapidly, from 4% to 11% of respondents. . . .

### Cell-Only Usage—No Gender Difference; Pager Users More Likely to Be Male

In the 1995 survey 17% of male respondents and 16% of female respondents reported being cell-only users. Our earlier surveys suggest a growing convergence of the male and female ownership rates for cell phones only.

The gender ownership pattern of cell phones only contrasts with ownership of pagers only and both cell phones and pagers, where proportionally more men than women reported owning them. . . . In the 1995 survey 13% of male respondents and 8% of female respondents reported owning only a pager. Most of the earlier surveys also indicated that proportionally more men than women owned only pagers.

Similarly in the 1995 survey for the cell phone plus pager group, 13% of males and 9% of females reported owning both a pager and a cell phone. Again, the earlier surveys indicate that proportionally more men than women owned both pagers and cell phones.

Our surveys show that the gender mix of mobile communications users has changed from 1989 when Rakow and Navarro[16] reported that "more than 90 percent of subscribers were men." Indeed our surveys suggest that the gender gap for cell phone-only usage is on the verge of disappearing.

### Declining Age of Cell Phone Users; Pagers Mainly Owned by Young People

In the 1995 survey, respondents who reported only owning a pager were predominantly under 50 years old; moreover, ownership rates were approximately the same for all the five-year age categories below 50. Over 50 years old, ownership rates declined significantly down to 1% for the over 65 category. Earlier surveys had similar patterns. . . .

For those in the 1995 survey who reported owning only a cell phone, the age distribution of ownership was somewhat different from the 1995 pager-only age distribution. . . . Ownership of cell phones was spread fairly evenly over the age range 18 to 64 with ownership rates varying from 15% to 22% per five-year age category. This appears to be a change from the results of our earlier surveys where reported ownership rates tended to be highest in the age range 35–55.

For the group reporting owing both a pager and a cell phone, the 1995 survey results indicate a gradual decline in ownership rates from 16% ownership rate for the youngest age category (18–24) to 9% for the 55–59 category. . . . For the categories 60–64 and 65 and older, the ownership rates are about 3%. The earlier surveys show a slightly different

pattern; the 1993 and 1994 surveys indicate peak ownership rates for ages 35–49.

The results of our surveys provide some proof that cell phones are no longer the preserve of "power elites." Our earlier surveys do indicate highest ownership rates across the age range 35–50; however, the most recent survey shows that the highest ownership rates are spread over the age range 18–64, a much broader age range.

For the pager-only group, our surveys show that over 1993–1995 ownership has continued to be predominantly by younger people, that is people aged less than 45 or 50. There is some suggestion in the results of the 1995 survey that the highest ownership rates are at the younger end of the 18–45 age range.

### More Affluent/Better Educated Respondents More Likely to Own Cell Phones

For the cell phone-only group in the 1995 survey, ownership rates increase as household income increases—from 6% for the under $15,000 group to 38% for the $100,000 or more. . . . Similarly for the group which owns both a pager and a cell phone, ownership rates increase as household income increases—from 4% for the under $15,000 group to 26% for the $100,000 or more. The earlier surveys showed a similar pattern of increasing ownership rates as reported household income increases.

For the pager-only group, however, the results for the 1995 survey are somewhat different. Here we see ownership rates independent of household income at around 12% of respondents. This is a change from earlier surveys which show a slight increase in ownership rates as reported household income increases.

We also examined how ownership rates varied with the respondent's highest achieved educational level. . . . In the 1995 survey, ownership rates for the cell phone-only group increase with higher educational levels—from 10% for the group who left school without gaining a high school diploma (or GED) to 28% for the group who gained a Ph.D. The earlier surveys showed a similar pattern.

In the 1995 survey, for the pager-only and the pager plus cell phone groups the relationship between ownership rates and highest education level achieved was less clear and it could be hypothesized that these data indicate no relationship between ownership and highest achieved educational levels. The earlier surveys do suggest a weak trend for both groups toward higher ownership rates for those reporting higher educational levels.

Our survey results suggest that pager-only ownership has become "classless," because ownership rates are independent of income and highest educational level achieved. On the other hand, higher ownership rates of cell phones, either alone or in conjunction with ownership of pagers, continue to be associated with higher income and educational levels. It is possible there are independent income and educational effects, but because income and highest achieved educational levels are highly correlated, it is also possible we are seeing a purely income effect or a purely education effect. Later analysis will probe these issues.

## Significant Differences in Ownership Rates Across Ethnic Groups

Analyzing ownership rates by reported ethnic group shows significant differences between ethnic groups in the 1995 survey. Blacks, Hispanics, and Asians (with ownership rates in the range 44%–47%) are more likely than whites (ownership rate 36%) to own mobile communications.

For the pager-only usage, blacks (ownership rate 19%) and Hispanics (ownership rate 17%) have much higher ownership rates than whites (ownership rate 9%) and Asians (ownership rate 5%) have. Asian[s] and whites (ownership rates 23% and 17%, respectively) are more likely to own only cell phones than Hispanics and blacks (ownership rates 12% and 11% respectively). Finally, Asians, blacks, and Hispanics (ownership rates 19%, 17%, and 16%, respectively) are more likely to own both cell phones and pagers than whites (ownership rate 9%).

## More Mobile at Work/Socially More Likely to Own Mobile Communications

In the 1995 survey we asked questions about the extent of mobility at work and socially, since a priori highly mobile people should have a disposition to own mobile communications. Respondents were asked the extent they agreed with the statement, "Your job requires you to be frequently away from your place of work." Non-owners of mobile telecommunications systems were less likely to agree with this statement than owners. For the group owning neither a pager nor a cell phone, only 5% strongly agreed and 15% agreed to the statement, whereas for the pager-only group, 13% strongly agreed and 21% agreed, for the cell phone-only group, 10% strongly agreed and 18% agreed, and for the group owning both a pager and a cell phone, 14% strongly agreed and 24% agreed. . . .

Respondents were also asked the extent they agreed with the statement "In your social life you are frequently away from home." Again, non-owners of mobile communications systems were less likely to agree with this statement than owners. . . . For the group owning neither a pager nor a cell phone, 8% strongly agreed and 27% agreed to the statement, whereas for the pager-only group, 12% strongly agreed and 38% agreed; for the cell phone-only group, 12% strongly agreed and 34% agreed, and for the group owning both a pager and a cell phone, 14% strongly agreed and 36% agreed.

We also used the number of children as a proxy measure for daily mobility and examined whether number of children in the household related to reported ownership of mobile communications. In particular, given Rakow and Navarro's work,[16] we might have thought that the need to do parallel social and work activities would result in those individuals whose households contained children [having] a greater need for communications, with the result that they would be heavier wireless communication users. For the 1995 survey the results suggest there may be a weak relationship between number of children and ownership of mobile communications. Households with no children were less likely to own mobile communications system[s] than those with children. For households with no children, 33% reported owning either a pager or a cell phone or both. For households with one child, the ownership proportion was 42%, with two children, 44%, and for those with three or more children, 39%.

The results of our surveys regarding mobility support the idea proposed by Davis,[17] that the use of mobile communications provides "a sense of personal control over space and time." In regard to control over space, it would appear that those with greater mobility at work or in their social life are more likely to own mobile communications.

## Those Needing to Be in Touch More Likely to Own Mobile Communications

In the 1995 survey we asked respondents the extent they agreed with the statement, "There are often times when you urgently need to get through to another person." Nonowners of mobile telecommunications systems were less likely to agree with this statement than owners. For the group owning neither a pager nor a cell phone, 10% strongly agreed and 36% agreed with the statement, whereas for the pager-only group, 13% strongly agreed and 47% agreed, for the cell phone-only group, 9% strongly agreed and 43% agreed, and for the group owning both a pager and a cell phone, 20% strongly agreed and 45% agreed.

In the only other survey where we asked this question, there was a very similar result. In the late 1993 survey, for the group owning neither a pager nor a cell phone, 8% strongly agreed and 36% agreed with the statement, whereas for the pager-only group, 13% strongly agreed and 47% agreed, for the cell phone-only group, 13% strongly agreed and 38% agreed, and for the group owning both a pager and a cell phone, 8% strongly agreed and 53% agreed.

Again in the context of controlling time, our results support the idea proposed by Davis,[17] that the use of mobile communications provides "a sense of personal control over space and time." Our surveys indicate that those with a greater need to keep in touch are more likely to own mobile communications.

## Stressed Respondents Are More Likely to Own a Pager

We mentioned earlier the ongoing debate about whether mobile communications add to or ease the stress of modern living. To see if we could throw light on this debate we asked, in the 1995 survey, the extent respondents agreed with the statement: "You feel that you have more to do than you can comfortably handle." Those owning a pager reported more agreement with this statement—in the pager-only group 17% agreed very strongly and 37% agreed strongly, and in the pager plus cell phone group 22% agreed very strongly and 26% agreed strongly. For the group without mobile communications and the cell phone-only group, the reported response rates were very similar—17% agreed very strongly and 26%–28% agreed strongly. . . .

In three earlier surveys we also asked this question about the extent respondents have more than they can handle. Taking the four surveys together, the pager-only group reported most agreement with the statement. In each of the surveys, 50% or more respondents either agreed or strongly agreed with the statement.

Earlier we reported that the pager-only group was predominantly under 50 years old. Generally, we have found that younger people are more likely to report that they have more than they can handle, so we investigated whether the fact that the pager-only group was the most likely group to report having too much to handle was just an age effect. For the 1995 survey this proved not to be the case. . . . We divided the sample set into those up to 44 years old and those 45 and over. Anxiety levels for the pager-only group did not decrease with age. For the younger half, 17% strongly agreed and 35% agreed with the statement, while for the older half, 19% strongly agreed and 43% agreed with the statement. For the other ownership groups anxiety levels decreased with age.

Similarly for the early 1993 survey, anxiety levels for the pager-only group did not decrease with age, while anxiety levels for the other three ownership groups did decline with age. For the younger half of the pager-only group, 15% strongly agreed and 38%

agreed with the statement, while for the older half, 11% strongly agreed and 43% agreed with the statement. As in the 1995 survey, the anxiety levels decreased with age for the other groups.

Although our surveys did not explore changes in feeling of overload before and after owning mobile communications, our surveys do indicate that the pager-only group is particularly likely to express feelings of overload. Whether this is a group inherently subject to stress or the ownership of pagers generates stress, we are not able to deduce.

### Those Owning Mobile Communications More Likely to Own PCs

In the 1995 survey, those owning a cell phone were more likely to own a PC than those without a pager and a cell phone and those owning only a pager. . . . Sixty-one percent of those only owning a cell phone and 59% of those owning both a pager and a cell phone also owned a PC. The percentage of PC ownership in the other two groups was much less—40% for the group without mobile communications and 43% for the pager-only group.

In our earlier surveys, we observed a somewhat similar pattern with the group without a pager and a cell phone having the lowest PC ownership rates, about 30%. PC ownership rates for the pager-only group were significantly higher than the neither group and were generally in the 40%–55% range. In the 1993 and 1994 surveys, PC ownership rates for the cell phone-only and both groups were significantly higher than the pager-only group. Ownership rates for the cell phone-only group were generally in the 55%–65% range and for the both group in the 60%–80% range. In some cases the ownership rates for the both group were significantly higher than for the cell phone-only group.

There are various plausible explanations for the relationship between mobile communications ownership and PC ownership. A similar relationship exists with the ownership of answering machines.[18] Those owning mobile communications have lifestyles requiring the use of electronic tools such as PCs and answering machines. Alternatively, there are people with a predisposition to want to own new technological devices such as mobile phones, PCs, and answering machines. . . .

## Discussion

Our data suggest many interesting relationships upon which theoretical interpretations could be built. Space limitations preclude a full elaboration of these possibilities but, guided by our discussions at the outset of the article, we can highlight a few intriguing possibilities. In particular, we discuss whether wireless communications are "a rich man's toy," assertions that wireless communications are contributing to a stressful or rushed life, and whether wireless communications are a chain of control around the necks of the mobile proletariat.

### Digital Divide

Considerable policy attention has been devoted to whether certain ethnic or income groups are going to be at a structural disadvantage as a result of the information revolution. While most attention has been devoted to access to computer resources, issues of universal service have also been the focus of significant work.[19, 20] Our analyses indirectly reflect on this debate and [suggest] some ambivalent conclusions. On the one hand, our model of mobile communications ownership suggests that owners of mobile communications are likely to be from higher income brackets. On the other hand, there appears to be a weak education effect and no gender effect at all. Where one would expect a race effect—whites more likely to own mobile communications—our data suggest otherwise. It is blacks and Hispanic[s] who are more likely to own wireless communications.

The importance of income may be weakening. In general, the ratio of ownership rates of those with reported household incomes above $35,000 to those below $35,000 declines during the period of our surveys for all ownership groups. . . . For the pager-only group, this ratio declines from 2.5 (early 1993 survey), through 1.7 (late 1993 and

1994 surveys) to 1.1 (1995 survey). Thus by 1995, the income effect for pager-only ownership had almost disappeared. For the cell phone-only group, the ratio is 2.3 for the 1995 survey, much less than for the earlier surveys—3.6 for the early 1993 survey, 4.2 for the late 1993 surveys, and 4.2 for the 1994 surveys. For the cell phone plus pager group, the value of the ratio in the 1995 survey (3.0) is the lowest of all the surveys, but the ratios in the other surveys do not display a consistent downward pattern—the ratio is 3.3 for the early 1993 survey, 7.5 for the late 1993 surveys, and 4.4 for the 1994 surveys.

## Race/Ethnic Issues

As mentioned earlier, racial/ethnic self-identification was an important predictor variable. In particular, black and Hispanic respondents were much more likely to own either a pager or both a pager and cell phone than were whites. Asians, though, were more likely to have either a cell phone only or both a cell phone and pager than were whites.

For pager-only ownership, we can posit here for discussion an "affordable luxury" hypothesis, which holds that those who do not have status in society will be more likely to buy low-cost items/services that they perceive are associated with high-status individuals. Given this hypothesis, it may be that blacks and Hispanics, if they can afford it, are more likely to buy a pager.

Certainly a competing explanation—that members of these communities might like to be in greater contact or are more outgoing and connected than, say, whites, is equally plausible. In fact, given the reports at the outset of our article about Singapore and the popularity of wireless communication in Hong Kong and throughout Asia, the cultural pattern explanation seems also a good fit. For example, this might account for the high cell phone ownership among Asians.

Rather than putting forward definitive answers, we introduce these ideas as possible explanations for our results. By no means do we purport that we have exhausted the range of possible explanations. Instead, we look forward to future studies which can clarify the social role of wireless communication within various cultural settings and identities as well as by demographic categories.

## Gender Issues

Mobile communications have been held by many to be a male power tool, yet our models do not suggest any statistical gender effect. Our earlier analyses showed that ownership of mobile communications was related to gender. We speculate that ownership of mobile communications is determined more strongly by social location effects, for example, having a highly mobile job or needing to keep in touch, than by gender. . . .

## Rushed Attitudes and Communications Needs

Since "overload" does not have any independent explanatory power in predicting ownership, one might be tempted to say that wireless communication does nothing to relieve such feelings. However, there are competing explanations that cannot be discarded since the data are cross-sectional (as opposed to panel or experimental data). The first possibility is that other variables incorporate its explanatory power. In this case, business and social-related mobility, and "need to keep in touch" attitudes capture whatever statistical power that the feeling of being rushed would have otherwise contributed.

An alternative explanation is that those in our survey who were wireless communication adopters had even higher feelings of overload prior to the technology's adoption. Therefore, the formerly above average feelings of overload have been reduced to those of the average non-adopter. Hence, because we have no prior data, any change in the more overloaded group who adopted the technology line (non-adopters) level would be masked (see Reference 21). Another plausible explanation is that wireless communication users would have even higher levels of overload were it not for wireless communication. Again, without temporally linked data, we cannot disentangle change over time.

Yet another possibility is that the people who feel overloaded do not perceive that pagers and cell phones can help them reduce overload anxieties. By contrast our model supports the view that those who are highly mobile or need to keep in touch perceive pagers and cell phones as useful to them. While far from definitive, the data do suggest that one prediction about wireless communication's impact, namely that it would add to people's feelings of being rushed and overloaded, does not seem to be borne out. Given that there is no difference between users and non-users of wireless communication regarding their feeling of overload, it seems likely that wireless communication does not add to such feelings. (Of course we cannot definitively rule out the possibility that wireless communication adopters were less rushed than non-wireless communication adopters, prior to their adoption decision.) If this lack of impact were borne out, it would seem to refute some of our arguments made elsewhere[22] as well as those of Gergen[23] and other critics of technological culture.

## Age

Usually one of the best predictors of early adoption of technology is age, with younger people being the early adopters. Interestingly, our data suggest that for cell phone usage it is middle-aged people who are the early adopters. This might be because of the cost, but we also believe the nature of one's occupation is probably even more central to the adoption decision. Still our data do not definitively shed light on it, but our background interviews would seem to suggest that occupational category is important in first introducing the user to the technology, and second in creating the environment within which it is adopted.

The one area we do see age making a difference is with pagers. This makes sense, given the relatively low cost of pagers, plus their desirability among youngsters as a prestige symbol.[24]

## Conclusion

Our investigation reveals that while no longer "a rich man's toy," cellular telephone ownership is associated with income, although the income affect appears to be declining. Further, in contrast to some of the more pessimistic speculations about cell phone ownership, including our own, there is as yet little evidence to suggest that cell phone ownership has a pernicious impact on the quality of life. However, as we indicated earlier, we cannot be sure of the antecedent situation in a cross-sectional study, so any claims about impact must be extremely circumscribed.

In general ownership seems guided by what we might call "social location" variables, that is a combination of socioeconomic, demographic, and life-style conditions which influence decisions perhaps more powerfully than individual personality characteristics. People may not personally wish to have wireless communication, but due to conditions of their life—such as job exigencies, work, and personal mobility—they find they need to have wireless communication. Thus while we found no relationship between certain personality measures, such as extroversion or phone liking, perceived "needs" can be an important predictor of service utilization, in this case a perceived need "to keep in touch." This finding is somewhat at odds with an initial analysis of some of the early data reported here, which purported not to find a relationship between needs and telecommunications technology use.[25] Certainly the relationship between needs and gratifications is one that has been explored at length in the mass media literature; that they should be connected in the telecommunications area as well should not come as a surprise. Yet we anticipate that "social location" will eventually become recognized as equal in importance, if not paramount to, the needs-based model.[26]

Interestingly, racial/ethnic self-identification is an important variable. The importance of this variable was somewhat surprising to us. While there are several possible explanations, for example cultural patterns and geographic location of respondents, the importance of this variable also fits with notions we have been working with, which may be characterized as "affordable luxury." This concept means that certain (apparently) high-status items are available for purchase at relatively low cost. Hence groups or individuals who might not have a high status, as defined by the dominant society, might seek to enhance their status in various ways. Certainly the more affordable a luxury is, the easier it would be for people to buy it. Explanations along this path might help us to understand not only wireless communication ownership, but a host of other behaviors as well. Currently we are exploring this area and hope to report on it soon (see Reference 26).

In terms of policy issues, such as information rich–information poor, or the so-called digital divide, some of our findings are troubling. Specifically the income dimension of wireless communication ownership suggests that there is a possibility that those who cannot afford may be shut out of many of society's benefits, with severe personal and political ramifications.[27, 28]

Summing up, we have seen some surprising data shedding light on wireless communication relative to income, age, education, ethnicity/race, household ties, social activity, and job activity mobility and attitudes. These data reflect on important theories of equity, innovation, gender relations, and quality of life issues. While we have only scratched the surface, we believe we have shown that this much-neglected area of wireless communication can have both substantive and theoretical import.

## References

1. Staff. *Common Carrier Week*, June 6, 1994.

2. Staff. "Cellular Telecommunications Industry Association, Wireless Growth Sets New Annual Records," Mimeo. September 19, 1996, Washington.

3. Mayer, William G. "The Rise of the New Media," *Public Opinion Quarterly* 58(1), 124–146 (1994).

4. Miller, Leslie. "New World to Navigate: New Worries for Adults," *USA Today*, August 27, 1996, D-1.

5. Staff. "Singapore Celebrates 1 Millionth Pager Customer." (0179) AP Wire Services, September 6, 1996.

6. Szaniawski, Kris. "Operations Push Low-Cost Advantage," *Financial Times*, November 27, 1995, 5.

7. Dimmick, John W., Sikand, Jaspreet, and Patterson, Scott J. "The Gratifications of the Household Telephone: Sociability, Instrumentality, and Reassurance," *Communication Research* 21(5), 643–663 (1994).

8. Giddens, Anthony. *The Consequences of Modernity*. Polity Press, Cambridge, in association with Basil Blackwell, Oxford, UK, 1990.

9. ——. *Modernity and Self-Identity*. Stanford University Press, Palo Alto, CA, 1991.

10. Bryant, Christopher G. A., and Jary, David, eds. *Giddens' Theory of Structuration: A Critical Appreciation*. Routledge, London, 1991.

11. Marx, Gary T. "The Surveillance Society: The Threat of 1984-Style Techniques," *The Futurist* 19 (June), 21–26 (1985a).

12. ——. "I'll Be Watching You: Reflections on the New Surveillance," *Dissent* 32 (Winter), 26–34 (1985b).

13. Gandy, Oscar H. *The Panoptic Sort: A Political Economy of Personal Information*. Westview, Boulder, CO, 1993.

14. Katz, James E. "Public Policy Origins of Privacy and the Emerging Issues," *Information Age* 10(3), 47–63 (1988).

15. ——. "Social Aspects of Telecommunications Security Policy," *IEEE Technology and Society* 9(2), 16–24 (1990).

16. Rakow, Lana F., and Navarro, Vija. "Remote Mothering and the Parallel Shift: Women Meet the Cellular Telephone," *Critical Studies in Mass Communication* 10(2), 144–157 (1993).

17. Davis, Dineh M. "Social Impact of Cellular Telephone Usage in Hawaii," in Pacific Telecommunications Council Fifteenth Annual Conference Proceedings, Session 3.1.1. to 4.4.1. (January 17–20, 1993), Volume 2. James G. Savage and Dan J. Wedemeyer, eds., Pacific Telecommunications Council, Honolulu, HI, 1993, pp. 641–649.

18. Katz, James E., and Reich, Warren. "Public Attitudes Toward Voice-Based Electronic Messaging Technologies in the United States," *Behavior & Information Technology* 16(3), 125–144 (1997).

19. Firestone, Charles M. *The Emerging World of Wireless Communications*. The Aspen Institute and Institute for Information Studies, Queenstown, MD, 1996.

20. Anderson, Robert H., Bikson, Tora K., Law, Sally Ann, and Mitchell, Bridoer M. *Universal Access to e-mail: Feasibility and Societal Implications*. RAND, Santa Monica, CA, 1995.

21. Campbell, Donald, and Stanley, Julian C. *Experimental and Quasiexperimental Designs for Research*. Rand McNally, Chicago, 1963.

22. Aspden, Philip, and Katz, James. *Mobility and Communications: Analytical Trends and Conceptual Models*. Report for the U.S. Congress, Office of Technology Assessment, OTA N3-16040.0, Washington, D.C. November 1994.

23. Gergen, Kenneth J. *The Saturated Self: Dilemmas of Identity in Contemporary Life*. HarperCollins, New York, 1991.

24. Katz, James, and Wynn, Eleanor. "Teens on the Phone," Technical memorandum number 24350. Bell Communications Research, Morristown, NJ, November 1, 1994.

25. Stienfield, Charles, Dudley, Kathleen, Kraut, Robert, and Katz, James. "Rethinking Household Telecommunications," Paper presented at the International Communications Association Annual Meeting, Miami, FL, 1993.

26. Katz, James, Aspden, Philip, and Fussell, Susan. *Symbolic Aspects of Telecommunications Services: Affordable Luxury and Status Issues*. Bellcore, Morristown, NJ, Mimeo.

27. Aufderheide, Patricia. "Universal Service: Telephone Policy in the Public Interest," *Journal of Communication* 37 (Winter), 81–96 (1987).

28. Sawhney, Harmeet. "Universal Service: Prosaic Motives and Great Ideals," *Journal of Broadcasting & Electronic Media* 38 (Fall), 375–395 (1994).

## Review

1. Describe the growth of mobile communications technology.

2. What age and gender differences exist in the use of mobile communications?

3. What racial/ethnic differences exist in the use of mobile communications?

4. How does social class interact with the use of mobile communications?

## Applications

1. Perform a content analysis of mobile communication ads to determine to whom and for what purposes they are marketed. Marketing agencies do a good job of determining who uses their products and to whom they should market them. With this in mind, are the findings of Katz and Aspden consistent with what you learned by examining the ads? If not, how would you explain the differences?

2. Interview three men and three women who own cellular telephones. Begin by asking them why they purchased the phones. Then ask them about their schedules—see whether their jobs require them to be frequently away from their place of work and/or their homes. Ask whether they often urgently need to get through to others. Finally, inquire about the effects of the phone on their well-being: in what ways has it added to or diminished the stress in their lives?

   How do your results square with those of Katz and Aspden? Did you find any differences between the answers of the males and those of the females? If so, what were they and how would you explain them?

## Related Web Sites

1. *http://www.mercurynews.com/mld/mercurynews/business/technology/personal_technology/5867613.htm?1c*. A newspaper article about the way cell phones are changing our social habits.

2. *http://www.clarity-innovations.com/files/youthandcellphones.pdf*. Report on the use of cell phones by youth.

Reprinted from: James E. Katz and Philip Aspden, "The Impact of Mobile Communications." In "Theories, Data, and Potential Impacts of Mobile Communications: A Longitudinal Analysis of U.S. National Surveys," *Technological Forecasting and Social Change* 57 (1998):133–56. Reprinted by permission from Elsevier Science. ✦

# Unit V

## *Social Processes*

Although social institutions contribute to their stability, societies are characterized by various processes and change. Traditional societies tend to conform to accepted models from the past and change more slowly. However, modern societies are distinguished by diversity and dynamism. They are a breeding ground for variations of all kinds, from technological innovations to fundamental changes in religious and political values.

One important process is **deviance,** which is behavior that violates social norms. In its popular usage, deviance denotes something negative and undesirable, but sociologists use the term in a neutral sense. Certain types of deviance, such as the murder of innocent victims, are universally condemned. Yet it is also true that what is deviant to one group may be normative behavior to another. And what is deviant to one generation may be applauded by later generations. After all, the Founding Fathers engaged in deviance when they rebelled against the established order. Norm violations that are widely defined as serious and unacceptable may provoke reform or other social changes. Selections 39 through 41 deal with various aspects of deviant behavior.

The second process is **social change,** which involves alterations in social phenomena at various levels of human life from the individual to the global. Social change includes population processes. Selection 42 illustrates one type of population shift—immigration and the struggles of immigrants to adapt to their new social setting. Social mobility is also a form of change. Selection 43 looks at a relatively recent kind of mobility, a conscious decision to move down. Finally, people strive to bring about change through social movements; whether movements make any difference is explored in selection 44. ✦

# Part One

## *Deviance*

How much deviance is there in any society? The answer has to be, a great deal. Think of it this way. Everyone violates the mores and folkways at some time. Indeed, everyone does something at some time that violates the law (littering, speeding, and taking office or school supplies home for personal use are among the common violations).

Clearly, however, people regard some kinds of deviance as more serious than others. Prostitution, violence, urban gang activity, and putting children at risk are types of deviance with which the selections in this part deal. ✦

# 39
# Violence and Post-Traumatic Stress Disorder in Prostitutes

*Roberto J. Valera*
*Robin G. Sawyer*
*Glenn R. Schiraldi*

**W**hat do you feel when you see a prostitute? Pity? Sympathy? Scorn? Indifference? Many "respectable" people consider prostitutes as evil, undesirable, and pursuing a deviant way of life that threatens the moral structure of society. They believe that people enter prostitution because of sexual desire, money, or the unwillingness to do "normal" kinds of work to earn their living.

Such ideas raise questions about deviant behavior in general: do people choose it because it is their preference, or can the behavior be understood as the outcome of various kinds of victimization and deprivation? In this selection, the authors examine the lives of inner-city prostitutes and find a considerable amount of violence not only in their present lives but in their past as well. They also examine the extent to which prostitutes suffer from post-traumatic stress disorder (PTSD). PTSD is an anxiety disorder that results from severely traumatic events and involves such symptoms as nightmares, recurring thoughts about the traumatic event, minimal involvement with life, and guilt. After reading this selection, you might ponder the question of why anyone would want or be willing to enter such a life.

The study of health-related issues concerning commercial sex workers has predominately focused on establishing and analyzing rates of sexually transmitted infections (STIs) and human immunodeficiency virus (HIV) in this population (Deisher & Paperry, 1983; Alexander, 1987; Suleiman, Suleiman, & Ayroza, 1989; Modan et al., 1992; Simon, Morse, Osofsky, & Balson, 1994; Weiner, 1996). Although exposure to STIs is a constant danger for prostitutes, numerous other under-researched health risks also pose a threat. Prostitutes in general appear to be at great risk for additional serious health problems related to their profession, such as physical and sexual assault, robbery, murder, physical and mental health problems, and drug and alcohol addiction (Alexander, 1987; Silbert & Pines, 1982). Even though all prostitutes are potentially impacted by these events, some studies suggest that street prostitutes are at a greater risk than those who work in environments off the street, such as brothels (Deren et al., 1996).

The occurrence of assault perpetrated against prostitutes may be the most serious risk to their health. In an exploratory study of San Francisco prostitutes, 82% reported being physically assaulted since entering prostitution, 55% reported being attacked by clients, and 30% reported being attacked by non-client males (Farley & Barkan, 1998). Similar results were obtained in an earlier study of 200 juvenile and adult females who were either former or current prostitutes in the San Francisco Bay area (Silbert & Pines, 1982). Sixty-five percent of the sample reported being physically assaulted by their customers, 66% of the subjects reported being assaulted by a pimp, and 36% reported being beaten on a regular basis (Silbert & Pines, 1982).

Sexual assault, like physical assault, is a frequent event experienced by street prostitutes. The Council for Prostitution has estimated that female prostitutes are raped approximately once a week (Hunter, 1994). Farley and Barkan (1998) reported that 68% of their sample (female, male, and transgender males) had been raped by their customers, and that female and transgender males were more likely to be raped than their male counterparts. Similarly, Silbert and Pines (1982) identified 73% of their female subjects as having been raped. In a related study looking solely at males, adolescent male prostitutes were identified as being vulnerable to rape, torture, slave pornography, and/or dangerous sexual practices (Pierce, 1984).

Individuals who are exposed to violent acts such as rape or physical abuse, even once in their lives, are potentially at risk for experiencing various types of psychological distress. However, street prostitutes who are exposed to violent acts almost every day are at an even greater risk than the general public for psychological distress (El-Basel et al., 1997). One specific psychological outcome related to an individual being exposed to violent acts is Post-Traumatic Stress Disorder (PTSD). Because street prostitutes are clearly at risk for suffering a disproportionate level of violence such as rape, and physical assault (Silbert & Pines, 1982; Hunter, 1994; Farley & Barkan, 1998), they are in turn also at risk for PTSD. This type of stress disorder is typically assessed following a specific traumatic event, not during a series of traumatic experiences, as is the case of studies focusing on street prostitutes. Because of this difference, researchers suggest that the incidence of PTSD may actually be higher than data reported in these studies (Farley & Barkan, 1998).

The purpose of this study was to survey street prostitutes in Washington D.C. to examine existing levels of violence and to assess the population for the existence of PTSD. It was hoped that the findings of this study might add to an extremely limited pool of information about this population and increase the level of understanding of the presence and influence of PTSD in inner-city prostitutes. . . .

## Methodology

The challenge in studying street prostitutes is establishing a trusting relationship with them that would permit collection of valid information (Sullivan, 1996). To optimize levels of cooperation, the first author and volunteer surveyors had established a prior relationship with this community in Washington D.C. through their respective experiences working with the Helping Individual Prostitutes Survive (HIPS), a volunteer service organization. The first author and trained volunteers collected data during the evening and early morning in three locations of Washington D.C. known by HIPS as areas where prostitutes meet their clients for the exchange of sex for money. Individuals approached to participate in this survey were either known prostitutes from previous work through the HIPS program, or were individuals who through their style of dress, location in an area of established prostitution, and obvious solicitation of customers, were identified as being prostitutes. To confirm their status and eligibility to be included in this study, potential respondents were approached and confirmed as prostitutes by being asked directly if they exchanged sex for money or material compensation. Individuals were then asked to participate in this study and were advised by interviewers that any involvement was entirely voluntary and all information would be anonymous. In order to minimize duplication of surveys, a unique eight-digit code was assigned to each participant, and because of a concern about literacy levels, all surveys were answered in an interview format. Following the completion of the questionnaire, participants were given five dollars in cash, and thanked for their time. The surveyor also offered a referral card to all participants for mental health counseling with a mental health professional.

## Instrument

To assess levels of PTSD authors used the PTSD checklist (PCL) (Weathers, Litz, Herman, Huska, & Keane, 1993) which is comprised of 17 items. The PCL consists of three sub-scales related to the 3 symptom clusters of the Diagnostic and Statistical Manual of Mental Disorders 4th edition (DSM IV): sub-scale B (re-experiencing symptoms), sub-scale C (avoidance and psychotic numbing symptoms), and sub-scale D (hyperarousal symptoms) (American Psychiatric Association, 1994). . . . To assess levels of violence and other related issues such as childhood sexual experience, age of entry into prostitution, desire to leave prostitution, gender, ethnicity, sexual orientation, and current age, a series of discrete items was adapted from an existing instrument (Farley & Barkan, 1998).

## Limitations

A limitation of this study is that the sample of female, male, and transgender participants may not be representative of the population of street prostitutes in Washington D.C. since random sampling was not used. Also, the possibility exists that the 40 individuals who refused involvement in this study were in some way different from the subjects who participated.

## Results

One hundred and forty individuals working as street prostitutes were approached during the course of this study. Of those individuals approached, 40 decided not to participate in this study, resulting in a response rate of 71.4%. The 40 individuals who decided not to participate were all female. None of the subjects refusing participation responded negatively to the question establishing their status as prostitutes, and, in fact, the following most common reasons for not participating would seem to reinforce their involvement in commercial sex: lack of time, needing to make more money before they could talk, needing to meet a date (person to have sex with for money), and that their pimp was nearby watching.

The total sample size obtained was 100 participants. Of the 100 participants 42% were female, 32% were male, and 26% were male transgender. Individuals in the male transgender category were biologically male, but dressed as females and represented varying stages of gender transition. With regard to ethnicity, 74% of the sample was African American, 12% White, 3% Hispanic and 11% of respondents described themselves as "other."

The age of participants ranged from 18 to 52 years, with a mean age of 30.61 years with 3% of the participants withholding their age. Caution should be observed in drawing inferences from this age range, because some of the participants who were under the age of 18 may have feared admitting their correct age. Reported age of entry into prostitution ranged from 7 to 35 years with a mean of 18.8 years. A high proportion of prostitutes described working in the business for many years, with half the sample reporting having worked from 11 to more than 20 years. (See Table 39.1.) When asked if they would like to leave prostitution, high proportions of each subgroup responded in the affirmative (females 67%, males 91%, transgender males 73%).

## Childhood Violence

Forty-four percent of the population sampled reported experiencing unwanted sexual touching or sexual contact between themselves and a grown-up as children before entering prostitution, and 1% were unsure. Fifty-three percent of respondents reported that their first sexual experience was with someone their own age, 24% with someone at least five years older, 16% with a family relative, and 7% with an adult family friend. Thirty-nine percent of the population sampled reported that as children they were hit or beaten by a parent or caregiver until they had bruises or were injured in some other way.

## Homelessness

Sixty-six percent of all respondents interviewed reported current or past homelessness (66.7% of female respondents, 78.1% of male respondents, and 50% of transgender male respondents).

## Violence

Sixty-one percent of respondents reported being physically assaulted since they had entered prostitution, with the majority of assaults being perpetrated by customers (75%). Additionally, nearly 80% of respondents reported being threatened by someone with a weapon. Fifty percent of the respon-

### Table 39.1
### Violence in Prostitution

| Item | | Female n = 42 | Male n = 32 | Trans. n = 26 | Sample n = 100 |
|---|---|---|---|---|---|
| Physical assault | | 85.7% | 28.1% | 65.4% | 16% |
| Who assaulted you?* | Customer | 80.6% | 62.5% | 70.6% | 75.4% |
| | Someone else | 13.9% | 37.5% | 29.4% | 21.3% |
| | Pimp | 5.6% | 0% | 0% | 3.3% |
| Threatened | | 90.5% | 84.4% | 88% | 87.9% |
| Threatened with a weapon | | 73.8% | 78.1% | 88% | 78.8% |
| Raped in prostitution | | 73.8% | 12.5% | 34.6% | 44% |
| Times raped in prostitution* Once | | 22.6% | 75% | 66.7% | 36.4% |
| | 2-5 | 61.3% | 25% | 22.2% | 50% |
| | 6-10 | 6.5% | 0% | 11.1% | 6.8% |
| | 11-19 | 3.2% | 0% | 0% | 2.3% |
| | Over 20 | 6.5% | 0% | 0% | 4.5% |
| Who raped you?* | Customer | 71.9% | 0% | 60% | 60% |
| | Someone else | 34.3% | 100% | 40% | 58% |
| | Pimp | 3.1% | 0% | 20% | 4% |
| Upset when asked to do something seen in a pornographic video | | 26.2% | 53.1% | 30.8% | 36% |
| Hurt with words | | 52.4% | 37.5% | 57.7% | 49% |
| Feel that you would be safer if prostitution were legal | | 42.9% | 62.5% | 50% | 50% |

*Percentages are from total subsample meeting original criteria (i.e. raped in prostitution).

dents reported a history of rape, and 44% reported being raped since entering prostitution. Female participants accounted for a majority of these rapes (74%) with half of this subgroup reporting being raped from 2 to 5 times. Similar to physical assault, the majority of rapes (60%) were perpetrated by customers. (See Table 39.1).

## Post-Traumatic Stress Disorder

Scores on the PTSD scale ranged from 17 to 83, with an overall mean score of 41.6 and median of 41.5. Seventy percent of respondents reported one or more Intrusive Re-experiencing symptoms (B symptoms), 52% reported three or more Avoidance and Psychotic Numbing symptoms), and 61% reported two or more Hyperarousal symptoms (D symptoms). Overall, 42% of respondents met the DSM-IV criteria for diagnosis of PTSD. (See Table 39.2).

## Discussion

As expected, street prostitutes in Washington D.C. appear to be frequently exposed to violence. All four areas of violence investigated (physical assault, threats, rape, and being hurt with words) were reported by individuals participating in this study, with women reporting the highest frequency of physical assault and rape. When asked who had physically assaulted them, the most frequent response among all three gender groups was "customers." This speaks to the inherent danger of being a prostitute, with the most violent aspect of the job being the job itself, interacting with the customer. Rates of physical attack (61%) and being threatened with a weapon (80%) in this population were exponentially higher than similar rates of attack (9%) and threats with a weapon (19% men, 7% women) reported in the general population as described in the National Comorbidity Survey (NCS) (Kessler, Sonnega, Bromet, Hughes, & Nelson, 1995). Similarly, approximately half the

### Table 39.2
#### Post-Traumatic Stress Disorder

| Item | Female n = 42 | Male n = 32 | Trans. n = 26 | Sample n = 100 |
|---|---|---|---|---|
| PTSD Severity Score (Means) | 40.2% | 47.9% | 36.0% | 41.6% |
| Percentage meeting DSM-IV diagnosis | 40.5% | 59.4% | 23.1% | 42% |
| Percentage meeting B symptom criteria (Re-experiencing) | 76.2% | 78.1% | 50% | 70% |
| Percentage meeting C symptom criteria (Avoidance) | 52.4% | 65.6% | 34.6% | 52% |
| Percentage meeting D symptom criteria (Hyperarousal) | 59.5% | 68.7% | 53.8% | 61% |

prostitutes surveyed in this study reported having been raped, compared to a lifetime prevalence of rape in the general population of .7% in males and 9.2% in females (Kessler et al., 1995). Clearly, both the threat and reality of violence are common and consistent features of the street prostitute's existence, far outstripping the level of threat experienced by the general population. In relation to rape, females and transgender males responded similarly by reporting that they were more likely to be raped by customers than by anyone else. Males, however, reported that they were never raped by customers. One possible explanation could be customers equating feminine attributes with weakness, potentially leading a male customer to decide at some point in the interaction to have sex without paying, or for him to deliberately seek out women or transgender males exclusively with the pre-conceived notion of raping them. Alternately, the higher levels of PTSD among males could suggest that this group's ability to correctly identify existing threats may have been compromised. Previous research has noted that individuals experiencing PTSD may have difficulties in recognizing or responding to external threats or dangers (Van der Kolk & McFarlane, 1996).

The violence experienced by prostitutes was not exclusive to their work with customers. Many of the participants reported experiencing inappropriate sexual contact as children between themselves and an adult prior to entering prostitution. These data are consistent with other studies suggesting that a high proportion of prostitutes come from homes where abuse and alcoholism are commonplace (Flannery, 1992). Similarly, many prostitutes reported being beaten or hit by caregivers while they were children. An interesting feature of these frequencies is that male prostitutes experienced inappropriate touching by adults, and beatings by caregivers more often as children than either of the other two groups. It is also interesting to note that males showed statistically significantly higher PTSD levels than the transgender group, and that males suffered much higher frequencies of childhood abuses than transgender males. These results are consistent with the NCS study, which also found unwanted sexual contact and physical abuse to be strong predictors of PTSD. In the NCS study, for both sexes, rape was the traumatic event considered most upsetting. For men, rape was the event most likely to be associated with PTSD, while for women it was physical abuse, followed by rape (Kessler et al., 1995).

A large proportion (42%) of study participants met the DSM-IV criteria for PTSD. This percentage is similar to studies of battered women and crime victims reporting PTSD rates ranging from 28% to 45% (Houskamp & Foy, 1991; Kilpatric, Saunders, Veronen, Best, & Von, 1987), and much higher than the reported prevalence (7.8%) in the general population (Kessler et al., 1995). Such substantial rates of PTSD have major implications for programs designed to assist street prostitutes out of the profession. Practitioners in the field must acknowledge the extent and significance of PTSD and the accompanying complications that will impede successful interventions. For example, one of the three general symptoms of PTSD is avoidance. This symptom can lead to an avoidance of emotional ties with other people close to those suffering from the disorder or those trying to get close to them, such as social workers and other practitioners trying to assist street prostitutes. Avoidance can also lead to an existence that makes it difficult to complete activities outside the routine mechanical events of their daily lives, in effect, making it difficult for the street prostitute to change or think of ways of changing his or her present situation. Depression and alcohol/substance abuse share substantial comorbidity with PTSD. Researchers have suggested that these conditions, more often than not, are secondary to PTSD (Kessler et al., 1995), and may in turn interfere with a willingness to cooperate with treatments that can be painful or require effort. Thus, it becomes clear that an understanding and awareness of street prostitutes' psychological health may have a direct bearing on intervention strategies and accompanying efforts at treatment.

Two violent experiences were identified as significantly predicting PTSD within this population: childhood physical abuse and childhood sexual abuse. As mentioned earlier, both factors have also been found to be predictors of PTSD in the general population (Kessler et al., 1995). The fact that these two childhood experiences were more predictive of PTSD than the threat of violence is intriguing and speaks to the need for additional research to examine issues related to childhood experiences that might play some role in subsequent entry into prostitution, in addition to the specific effects of threatened violence on levels of PTSD.

Age of onset into prostitution reported in this research was similar to that reported in other studies (Silbert & Pines, 1983; Farley &

Barkan, 1998; Mackenzie, 1994). However, given that 46% of respondents in this study reported being under 18 when first entering prostitution, it seems likely that at least some portion of survey respondents would have been under the age of 18 at the time of reporting. The likelihood that "underage" prostitutes would lie about their real age to avoid any potential problems with various authorities would seem fairly high.

All three groups of prostitutes evidenced a desire to leave prostitution, with particularly high percentages of males wanting to leave the streets. Although the desire to leave prostitution was common to all groups, intervention efforts that might facilitate this objective should acknowledge that subgroups with different needs and motivations do exist, and more tailored interventions may be necessary to achieve success.

In conclusion, this study confirms the existence of disproportionately high levels of PTSD in a population of inner city prostitutes. Organizations responsible for facilitating programming and assistance that have traditionally focused on the seemingly more obvious problems of substance addiction, HIV infection, and homelessness, clearly need to acknowledge the prevalence of PTSD and its accompanying deleterious effects, that may ultimately compromise the likelihood of successful interventions.

## References

Alexander, P. (1987). Prostitution: A difficult issue for feminists. In F. Delacoste & P. Alexander (Eds.), *Sex work: Writings by women in the sex industry* (pp. 184–214). San Francisco, CA: Cleis Press.

American Psychiatric Association (1994). *Diagnostic and statistical manual of mental disorders* (4th ed.). Washington, DC: American Psychiatric Press.

Deisher, R. W., & Paperry, D. M. (1983). Variations in sexual behavior of adolescents. In V. C. Kell, (Ed.), *Practice of pediatrics*. Philadelphia, PA: Harper & Row.

Deren, S., Sanchez, J., Shedlinn, M., Davis, W. R., Beardsley, M., Jarlais, D. D., & Miller, K. (1996). HIV risk behavior among Dominican brothel and street prostitutes in New York City. *AIDS Education and Prevention*, 8 (5), 444–456.

El-Basel, N., Schilling, R. F. F., Irwin, K. L., Faruque, S., Gilbert, L., Yon Bargen, J., Serrano, Y., & Edlin, B. R. (1997). Sex trading and psychological distress among women recruited from the streets of Harlem. *American Journal of Public Health*, 87, 66–70.

Farley, M., & Barkan, H. (1998). Prostitution, violence, and Posttraumatic Stress Disorder. *Women and Health*, 27 (3), 37–49.

Flannery, R. B., Jr. (1992) *Post-traumatic stress disorder: The victim's guide to healing and recovery.* New York: Crossroad.

Houskamp, B. M., & Foy, D. W. (1991). The assessment of posttraumatic stress disorder in battered women. *Journal of Interpersonal Violence*, 6, 367–375.

Hunter, S. K. (1994). Prostitution is cruelty and abuse to woman and children. *Michigan Journal of Gender and Law*, 1, 1–14.

Kessler, R. C., Sonnega, A., Bromet, E., Hughes, M., & Nelson, C. B. (1995). Posttraumatic stress disorder in the National Comorbidity Survey. *Archives of General Psychiatry*, 54, 1048–1060.

Kilpatric, D., Saunders, B., Veronen, L., Best, C., & Von, J. (1987). "Criminal victimization: Lifetime prevalence, reporting to police, and psychological impact. *Crime and Delinquency*, 33 (4), 479–489.

Mackenzie, G. O. (1994). *Transgender nation.* Bowling Green, OH: Bowling Green State University Popular Press.

Modan, B., Goldschmidt, R., Rubbinstein, E., Vonsover, A., Zinn, M., Golan, R., Chetrit, A., & Gottlieb-Stematzky, T. (1992). Prevalence of HIV antibodies in transsexual and female prostitutes. *American Journal of Public Health*, 82, 590–592.

Pierce, R. L. (1984). Child pornography: A hidden dimension of child abuse. *Child Abuse and Neglect*, 8, 438–493.

Silbert, M. H., & Pines, A. M. (1982). Victimization of street prostitutes. *Victimology: An International Journal*, 7 (1), 122–133.

——. (1983). Early exploitation as an influence in prostitution. *Social Work*, 28, 285–289.

Simon, P. M., Morse, E. V., Osofsky, H. J., & Balson, P. M. (1994). HIV and young male prostitutes: A brief report. *Journal of Adolescence*, 17, 193–197.

Suleiman, J., Suleiman, G., & Ayroza, G. (1989, June). Seroprevalance of HIV among transvestites in the City of Sao Paulo. Paper presented at the Fifth International Conference on AIDS, Montreal.

Sullivan, T. R. (1996). The challenge of HIV prevention among high risk adolescents. *Health and Social Work*, 21 (1), 58–65.

Van Der Kolk, B. A., & McFarlane, A. C. (1996) The black hole of trauma. In B. A. Van Der Kolk & A. C. McFarlane (Eds.), *Traumatic stress: The effects of overwhelming experience on mind, body, and society* (pp. 3–23). New York: The Guilford Press.

Weathers, F. W., Litz, B. T., Herman, D. S., Huska, J. A., & Keane, T. M. (1993, October 24–27). The PTSD checklist (PCL): Reliability, validity, and diagnostic utility. Presented at the 9th Annual Meeting of the International Society for Traumatic Stress Studies, San Antonio, Texas.

Weiner, A. (1996). Understanding the social needs of streetwalking prostitutes. *Social Work*, 41, 97–105.

## Review

1. Discuss the kinds and amount of violence encountered by street prostitutes.

2. In what ways is the violence the same and in which ways does it differ among female, male, and transgender prostitutes?

3. What is meant by post-traumatic stress disorder and how does it manifest itself in the lives of street prostitutes?

## Application

Locate magazine articles or Web sites that deal with prostitution. This selection deals only with street prostitutes. Find information about call girls and brothel workers. Also check on prostitution in other countries. What are the differences and the similarities between the different kinds of prostitutes? How does prostitution vary from nation to nation? How much child prostitution is there in the world? Based on your findings, what steps, if any, would you recommend to deal with prostitution?

## Related Web Sites

1. *www.prostitutionresearch.com/*. A site maintained by a clinical psychologist that includes numerous resources and links on various aspects of prostitution, including violence.

2. *www.bayswan.org/penet.html.* A prostitute's advocacy site that presents information from a prostitutes' rights perspective including trafficking, police abuse, and the decriminalization of prostitution.

Reprinted from: Roberto J. Valera, Robin G. Sawyer, and Glenn R. Schiraldi, "Violence and Post Traumatic Stress Disorder in a Sample of Inner City Street Prostitutes." In *American Journal of Health Studies* 16 (2000): 149–55. Copyright © by American Journal of Health Studies. Reprinted with permission. ✦

# 40
# Islands in the Street

## Urban Gangs as Economic Organizations

*Martin Sánchez Jankowski*

*A persistent question in the study of deviant behavior is why people who violate legal and moral rules behave so differently from those in the mainstream of society. Some of the research has proceeded from the assumption that those who engage in deviance are different kinds of people in some sense, and the research has attempted to identify the differences.*

*An alternate view, however, takes note of the similarities as well as the differences of those who engage in deviant behavior. Virtually everyone, for example, breaks rules at one time or another. Moreover, there are many gradations or degrees of "evil" between the actions of those who are seriously deviant and those who conform. Every society has areas where normal and deviant phenomena overlap.*

*This overlap is the subject of the following selection. During 10 years of research, Jankowski acted as both an observer and a participant in 37 gangs in Boston, New York, and Los Angeles, including Irish-, Latin-, and African-American gangs. (Entry into Asian- and Italian-American gangs was not possible.) In this selection he focuses on how gangs harness the individualism, self-reliance, and competitiveness of members and mold them into a viable organization. In some respects, this task is not that different from the one faced by such non-deviant groups as athletic teams and industrial corporations.*

If there is one theme that dominates most studies of gangs, it is that gangs are collectives of individuals who are social parasites, and that they are parasitic not only because they lack the skills to be productive members of society but, more important, because they lack the values, particularly the work ethic, that would guide them to be productive members of society.[1] However, one of the most striking factors I observed was how much the entrepreneurial spirit, which most Americans believe is the core of their productive culture, was a driving force in the worldview and behavior of gang members.[2] If entrepreneurial spirit denotes the desire to organize and manage business interests toward some end that results in the accumulation of capital, broadly defined, nearly all the gang members that I studied possessed, in varying degrees, five attributes that are either entrepreneurial in character or that reinforce entrepreneurial behavior.

The first of these entrepreneurial attitudes is competitiveness. Most gang members I spoke with expressed a strong sense of self-competence and a drive to compete with others. They believed in themselves as capable of achieving some level of economic success and saw competition as part of human nature and an opportunity to improve one's self-worth. This belief in oneself often took on a dogmatic character, especially for those individuals who had lost in some form of economic competition. The losers always had ready excuses that placed the blame on something other than their own personal inadequacy, thereby artificially reinforcing their feelings of competence in the face of defeat.[3]

Gang members' sense of competitiveness also reflected their general worldview that life operates under Social Darwinist principles. In the economic realm, they believed there is no ethical code that regulates business ventures, and this attitude exempted them from moral constraints on individual economic-oriented action.[4] The views of Danny, Arrow, and Lobo provide three good examples of this Social Darwinist outlook. Danny was a twenty-year-old Irish gang member from Boston:

I don't worry about whether something is fair or not when I'm making a business deal. There is nothing fair or unfair, you just go about your business of trying to make a buck, and if someone feels you took advantage of him, he has only himself to blame. If someone took advantage of me, I wouldn't sit around bellyaching about it, I'd just go and try to get some of my money back. One just has to ask around here [the neighborhood] and you'll find that nobody expects that every time you're going to make a business deal, that it will be fair—you know, that the other guy is not going to be fair, hell, he is trying to make money, not trying to be fair. This is the way those big business assholes operate too! The whole thing [the system] operates this way.

Arrow was an eighteen-year-old African-American gang member from New York:

Hey, man, what do you mean by ethics? Ethics don't pay bills, money pays bills, and I'm hustling to get money. There ain't nobody interested in ethics, morality, and all that shit—the basic line is, did you make money or not? Fuck those guys who lose and then complain, everybody knows that if they won and I or somebody else lost they wouldn't be saying nothing. Hey, it's dog eat dog, and if you ain't up to it, you get eaten, simple as that! And look at corporate businesses, they ain't moral or ethical, they never have been and they ain't about to be either, 'cause they only know that they want money. Since nobody complains about them, nobody will complain about us.

Lobo was a twenty-year-old Chicano gang member from Los Angeles:

I act like they do in the big time, no different. There ain't no corporation that acts with morals and that ethics shit and I ain't about to either. As they say, if it's good for General Motors, it's good enough for me. . . . It boils down to who is smarter, you either take somebody or get taken, and General Motors, General Dynamics, all those big cats know that shit. They take the government's money— that's really mine and yours—for some type of ride. Check this man, they sell a two cent bolt to the government for thirty dollars and don't blink an eye. They get

caught, but they ain't sorry, they're just sorry they got caught. Who talks ethics and morality to them? They keep doing it because that's the rules, so when I do my business, I just do it and if somebody gets hurt, then they get hurt 'cause that's just the way it is.

The second entrepreneurial attribute I observed is the desire and drive to accumulate money and material possessions. Karl Marx, of course, described this desire as the "profit motive" and attributed it primarily to the bourgeoisie.[5] There is a profit-motive element to the entrepreneurial values of gang members, but it differs significantly from Marx's analysis of the desire to accumulate material and capital for their own sake, largely divorced from the desire to improve one's own material condition. Nor is gang members' ambition to accumulate material possessions related to a need for achievement, which the psychologist David McClelland identifies as more central to entrepreneurial behavior in certain individuals than the profit motive per se.[6] Rather, the entrepreneurial activity of gang members is predicated on their more basic understanding of what money can buy.[7] The ambition to accumulate capital and material possessions is related, in its initial stages (which can last for a considerable number of years), to the desire to improve the comfort of everyday living and the quality of leisure time.

This desire, of course, is shared by most people who live in low-income neighborhoods. Some of them resign themselves to the belief that they will never be able to secure their desires. Others attempt to improve their life situation by using various "incremental approaches," such as working in those jobs that are made available to them and saving their money, or attempting to learn higher-level occupational skills. In contrast, the entrepreneurs of low-income neighborhoods, especially those in gangs, attempt to improve their lives by becoming involved in a business venture, or a series of ventures that has the potential to create large changes in their own or their family's socioeconomic condition.

The third attribute of entrepreneurial behavior prevalent in gangs is status-seeking.

Mirroring the dominant values of the larger society, most gang members attempt to achieve some form of status with the acquisition of possessions. However, most of them cannot attain a high degree of status by accumulation alone. To merit high status among peers and in the community, gang members must try, although most will be unsuccessful, to accumulate a large number of possessions and be willing to share them. Once gang members have accumulated sufficient material possessions to provide themselves with a relative level of comfort or leisure above the minimal, they begin to seek the increase in status that generosity affords. (For philanthropic purposes, accumulating cash is preferable to accumulating possessions, because the more money one has, the more flexibility one has in giving away possessions.)

The fourth entrepreneurial attribute one finds among gang members is the ability to plan. Gang members spend an impressive amount of time planning activities that will bring them fortune and fame, or, at least, plenty of spending money in the short term. At their grandest, these plans have the character of dreams, but as the accounts of renowned business tycoons show, having big dreams has always been a hallmark of entrepreneurial endeavors.[8] At the other end of the spectrum are short-range plans (also called small scams) that members try to pull on one another, usually to secure a loan. One member will say, "Can I borrow a few bucks until I get paid?" What he is really saying, however, is, "Can I have so-and-so-many dollars, or any amount to that figure, and if you need some money later yourself, and if I have some, I might give it to you." Once a member has been scammed by another in this way, future requests for "loans" usually elicit some type of respectful refusal.[9] Another common small scam begins with one gang member collecting money from several others for the purpose of obtaining drugs, usually cocaine. Later he returns and claims that he gave the money to the drug dealer, who then ran off with it. Everyone suspects that the gang member used all the dope himself or pocketed the money, and they usually greet the tale with a great deal of hostility,

but punishment is seldom administered. The vast majority of small scams within the gang (among members) are tolerated because all the members recognize that they are all continually running scams, and scams, therefore, are considered within the realm of acceptable behavior. But nine of the gangs I studied (14 percent) viewed running a scam on another member to be unacceptable, because it destroyed a sense of group commitment, and severe punishment was administered to those found guilty of being involved in the scam.

Gang members also engage in intermediary and long-range planning. A typical intermediary plan might concern modest efforts to steal some type of merchandise from warehouses, homes, or businesses. Because most of the sites they select are equipped with security systems, a more elaborate plan involving more time is needed than is the case for those internal gang scams just described. Long-range planning and organization, sometimes quite elaborate, are, as other studies have reported, at times executed with remarkable precision.[10]

Finally, the fifth entrepreneurial attribute common among gang members is the ability to undertake risks. Generally, young gang members (nine to fifteen years of age) do not understand risk as part of a risk-reward calculus, and for this age group, risk-taking is nearly always pursued for itself, as an element of what Thrasher calls the "sport motive,"[11] the desire to test oneself. As gang members get older, they gradually develop a more sophisticated understanding of risk-taking, realizing that a certain amount of risk is necessary to secure desired goals. Now they attempt to calculate the risk factors involved for nearly every venture, measuring the risk to their physical well-being, money, and freedom. Just like mainstream businessmen, they discover that risk tends to increase proportionally to the level of innovation undertaken to secure a particular financial objective. Most of these older gang members are willing to assume risks commensurate with the subjective "value" of their designated target, but they will not assume risks just for the sake of risk-taking.

## The Source of
## Entrepreneurial Attitudes

Gang members' entrepreneurial attitudes and behavior can be traced to four distinct sources. First, there are those psychological traits associated with the defiant individualist character into which nearly all gang members have been socialized. Two aspects of defiant individualism that directly relate to entrepreneurial attitudes are: (1) the lack of trust that gang members have of people in general, and (2) the more general acceptance of the Social Darwinist position that only the fit survive. Their lack of trust in people leads them to become self-reliant and confident that they can and must do things for themselves. An example is Circus, a seventeen-year-old African-American gang member from New York:

> Dig, I don't know if you can trust people, but there ain't no way that you should trust them. I mean, I trust myself, I defend and depend on myself, then I got nobody but myself to hold me back or fuck me up . . . what's more, I can do things better on my own than with other dudes who ain't as talented as me. You dig?

The belief that only the fit survive, in turn, lays the foundation for the proposition that one should exploit those opportunities that present themselves, even if in doing so one hurts other people. The ethic of survival at any cost is somewhat tempered by feelings of attachment (in a number of cases) to family, community, or neighborhood, and some other gang members. Nonetheless, despite some exceptions, gang members generally consider most people as competitors. Take Sweet Cakes, a fifteen-year-old African-American gang member in New York:

> Look, everybody gets certain chances in life and you got to take advantage of them. Those who get ahead are just more better than those that don't. If you mess somebody up by taking advantage of your opportunities, that's just the way it is. You can't worry about it because you were the best this time and you know that if you don't stay competitive, you're done forever. . . . no, I wouldn't mess with my community that way, but the rest of the folks is all fair game.

A second source of entrepreneurial attitudes arises from the tensions between mainstream American consumer culture and the scarcity of resources in low-income neighborhoods. In all social classes, we have seen in the post-war period a gradual but consistent increase in the degree to which young Americans believe money to be a necessary tool for social interaction. After decades of being courted by American businesses, which correctly saw the potential for vast profits in the youth market, children, teenagers, and young adults have come to accept the premise that having cash is necessary to purchase the goods and services that make life worth living. Activities that do not require cash, the consumerist message reads, are not satisfying. As a result, kids of all ages, especially teenagers, feel the need to have at least some pocket money available at all times.[12] This need becomes a sense of urgency for those kids from low-income areas where there is a scarcity of financial resources. The reality for these kids is the need to struggle for the resources that are available and this acts to stimulate creativity. Without creativity, a youth from a low-income or working-class neighborhood would not be able to secure the money that American culture has established as a high priority. It is the need to be creative in order to secure money that has been one of the underlying elements in building the "entrepreneurial spirit" among gang members. The comments of Mano, a fifteen-year-old Puerto Rican gang member in New York, are representative:

> Let me put it like this. There ain't a lot you can do without some green stuff [money] so if you want to have some good times, you got to get it. . . . hell, yes, it's tough out there, that's why you got to be creative in how you go about raising your cash. Those who ain't creative will be paupers, man! Can you digest that? I sure couldn't.

Another credo of American business culture has also stimulated gang members to think like entrepreneurs: the belief that one can improve oneself with one good idea. In talking to gang members, I repeatedly heard the refrain that all one needs is one good idea, and that what separates successful people from failures is that the former are able to cultivate the necessary contacts to operationalize their big idea. In their search for the big idea that will produce the desired wealth, gang members often generate what in effect are a number of small ideas that take on the character of "conning." Understood in this context, "conning behavior," which has often been misunderstood as the effort of weak-minded and/or parasitic hucksters, is an idiosyncratic variant of the general entrepreneurial spirit. Stake, a twenty-year-old African-American man in a New York gang:

> Yeah, man, what you need in life, no matter who you are, is one, not two, not three, but one good idea that you can get working. You do that and you got yourself some easy life, dig it, man. . . . well, yeah, sometimes you be running some deal down on a dude, but sometimes you get ideas and you got to try out to see how good they are. You know like some experiments that people do. And dig, some experiments they be a job on people [take advantage of people], but that's just the way it is. Hell, medical experiments are just researchers doing a job on some poor sucker, and then they tell him it made a difference to society. What do you call that, science, or a con? It's all the same. It's just some people don't want to see it; or they too stupid to see it.

Finally, gang members' entrepreneurial spirit is both stimulated and reinforced by the desire to resist what they perceive to be their parents' resignation to poverty and failure. As small boys, many gang members were keenly disappointed that their parents had not been successful at becoming self-made people who lifted the family out of poverty. Instead, what they observed was their parents' hopeless inability to do anything that would improve the family's material conditions. What stuck in their minds most vividly was their parents' vulnerability: their objective vulnerability in selling their labor on the market and their feelings of being vulnerable. Here are two representative comments.

Dark, an eighteen-year-old member of an Irish gang:

> A few years ago I would be pissed at my old man 'cause he didn't do things like save his money and move from the projects. He just seemed to be unwilling to have a desire to improve himself so that my mother and us kids were better, you know? . . . Later I could see that he didn't have much of a chance, given that he was just a worker. I resented that, not him, but the situation. But you know, after I talked to him, I was more pissed at the way he felt than anything else. He felt like he had no control over the situation; and I said to myself, I'll do everything I can not to let the fuckers make me feel like that. And I hustle all the time trying to develop projects to get money.

Face-Man, a sixteen-year-old Puerto Rican gang member:

> No, my pop didn't have a chance to make it, 'cause if you're a laborer you don't have any power on the job market. What can he offer that's different than seventy thousand other laborers? Get my point? So he couldn't get out of this hole that we live in or help the rest of us too much. . . . He always was feeling nervous about keeping work or getting it. You could always see him worrying about it. This was a lesson to me, and I said I ain't going to lay down and feel vulnerable to these motherfuckers! So I work hard on my various deals.

## Winners and Losers in Entrepreneurial Activity

Most members of gangs, then, have a fairly strong entrepreneurial spirit and engage in a variety of economic activities. Of all the entrepreneurial traits discussed, the one most crucial to an individual gang member's economic success or failure is his pattern of risk-taking. The prevailing view among the public is that nearly all gang activity involves a high degree of risk, but in truth gang members are like other economic actors, making choices among low-risk, moderate-risk, and high-risk ventures. Risk can be defined as the level of jeopardy in the potential loss of material assets, personal freedom, or physical well-being. While the economic environment in which gang members act is a dangerous one, some activities are far more or less risky than others. My observations indicate that gang members who were not successful economically were those whose risk-taking profile fell at either extreme of the spectrum. To be sure, some low and high risk-takers had some successes, but their cumulative efforts were unsuccessful. A good example is the story of Jumbo, an eighteen-year-old member of an ethnically mixed New York gang. Jumbo was always trying to come up with and sell his ideas for making a fortune. He would constantly propose new ideas that had the potential to deliver great profits to himself, those that would help him, and the entire gang, if he could persuade the leadership to commit resources and manpower. During the five years that I studied Jumbo and his particular gang, he had been able to secure gang participation only three times: twice during the first year of his involvement and once only recently for a rather small project. Of Jumbo's numerous entrepreneurial projects involving non-gang members, only a small fraction were successful.

Although each of Jumbo's successful efforts had yielded him several thousand dollars, most had involved high risks. Many of the participants were caught by law enforcement authorities, physically injured, or both. On six occasions, Jumbo had been arrested by the police; he had gone to jail twice. He had also been shot three times and beaten severely four times. Take one episode as an example. Jumbo had decided that a great deal of money could be made distributing cocaine. He was able to get the gang's support in the initial stage, which was to carry on some form of negotiation with the branch of the Mafia in charge of wholesale drug supplies for his area. He made contact, and the Mafia was in principle interested in his offer to have the gang act as the local dispensing agent. In listening to Jumbo's sales pitch, I was struck by how organized and professional it was, but I was also struck by the risks that he took in negotiating with the Mafia, which clearly had more bargaining power. Once the agreement in principle had

been made, Jumbo raised the ante by asking for a commission that was so high that everybody (both the syndicate's men and his own) laughed, though the members of his own gang did so in a somewhat uneasy manner. Once it became clear that he was serious, the syndicate made a counterproposal that cut his opening figure by seven-eighths. Jumbo balked at the figure and said he would not make the deal.

After the meeting, he told the leadership of the gang, who were quite angry with him, that he wanted to skip the Mafia as a source and open a drug mill (drug factory) himself. The gang leaders admitted that his idea had the potential to earn big profits, but they were not interested because too many risks were involved. At this juncture, Jumbo said he would do it on his own. In the following weeks, he was able to solicit eighteen people to help him, only three of whom were from the gang. They started to make "treated marijuana" (marijuana spiked with other drugs) and some synthetic LSD. The operation lasted about three weeks, until three of the workers were shot at (no one was actually hit) and the place of business was fire-bombed. Jumbo and another participant escaped with second-degree burns. The money and time that Jumbo had invested in this project were considerable and the potential return was great, but the risks proved too high and the project ended in failure. Yet although his losses repeatedly outran his gains by an overwhelming margin, Jumbo persisted in undertaking high-risk projects, judging the prospects of high returns worth the dangers. However, for Jumbo, as well as others, such ventures generally end in bodily injury and/or loss of time and money.

At the other end of the risk-taking spectrum is Toga, a twenty-year-old member of an Irish gang. On one occasion, he had the idea that he could make good money by stealing car radios and selling them. He found a person who would buy the radios from him and then proceeded to look for radios he could steal. After one week he had become proficient enough to have stolen ten radios. As he became more efficient, he was making several hundred dollars a month from this project. Because the word had spread that he had been relatively success-ful, he was able to persuade a number of peo-ple that a larger operation would be ex-tremely profitable, and they agreed to join him. Before the new group was to start, how-ever, Toga said that they needed to get some equipment that would help them break into cars that had sophisticated alarm systems. All of the new members of the group agreed to invest in the new equipment, which cost several hundred dollars. Having secured this new equipment, the larger group went to work, and within a month they had accumu-lated more than one hundred radios. The man Toga had been selling the radios to now declined to buy them, saying that the opera-tion had gotten too big, and that he would not be able to move that many radios fast enough. Toga then asked if he knew of any-one who would buy in quantity, and the buyer agreed to check around and get back to him. Toga described this conversation to his group, telling them not to worry, that they would start making money as soon as he and the new buyer were able to make a deal.

By now the place where the group was storing the radios was so crowded that they had to rent a small space in an adjoining building. This required still more capital. Toga received a message from his first buyer that he had found a buyer who could handle the volume. But when Toga was told that the new buyer was part of the syndicate, he be-came uneasy. He could not decide whether to go ahead and meet with this new buyer or to try to find another one. He told his group that working with the syndicate would pre-sent some risks to all of them and their oper-ations. Maybe they were being set up by the syndicate, he said, and maybe the syndicate would take all their radios or expect them from now on to work for it. While Toga was trying to decide what to do, the number of ra-dios was rapidly increasing—there were now over eight hundred in storage. Toga finally made a date to meet the syndicate's represen-tative, but then decided not to go, believing, as he told me, that there were too many risks. So he contacted his old buyer and asked him whether he knew of someone else. His old buyer told him that he had blown it: there

was no one else who could deal in such vol-ume.

Needless to say, the other members of Toga's group were frustrated and angry. They had endured personal risks and invested money and time, and all they had to show for it was several rooms filled with stolen radios they could not peddle. Toga's reluctance to take a chance resulted in the failure of the enterprise, and he was given a generous amount of time to return some of their money to his confederates. Though Toga generated more ideas, he found it difficult to get other gang members to participate, and the gang as an organization would not do so. Over the eight years that I observed Toga, he continued to exercise a caution that consis-tently resulted in missed opportunities and failures.

In contrast, the successful gang entrepre-neur tends to assume a moderate risk pro-file. He is likely to pursue a strategy where risk is present, but has been reduced to a moderate level through careful planning: se-lection of the type of activity, location, strat-egy for executing the task, protection from being apprehended. Like a mainstream busi-nessman, the successful gang entrepreneur calculates risk factors, the probability of the venture failing, and the odds of misfortune of various sorts. A good example of this type of gang entrepreneur is Grisly, a nineteen-year-old gang member from New York.

Grisly decided that he would steal stereos and televisions from apartments and then resell them. Before he began his venture, he made contact with two people who bought stolen objects and he entered into an agree-ment to sell to both of them. As he said to me: "The smart thing to do is find more than one buyer, in case one of them is picked up by the police, or if one of them can't buy what you have 'cause they just don't have the money or they can't move them. If you do that, you keep moving your stuff." Then he talked to a number of people in the gang to see if they were interested. He offered a percentage of the amount obtained from the buyer. He then had each of them look at buildings that might have easy access. They also checked out what kinds of locks the apartments had and avoided all those with police locks. They discussed various techniques for ascertaining if people were home before they burglarized a place. They also worked out a warning system to minimize the risk of being caught. Eventually, Grisly decided not to become involved in the burglaries himself, but to buy the stolen objects from those who did and then sell them to his contacts. After accumulating a significant amount of money from this, he moved on to more extensive projects. Because Grisly was well organized and attentive to details, his plans were successful, and most of the gang members wanted to be involved in his projects. In Grisly, then, we see the successful gang entrepreneur who selects enterprises that require some risk but takes steps to ensure that he does not lose everything if the business fails. Because he also works to minimize the risks for his associates, he has little difficulty in recruiting accomplices.

## Economic Activity: Accumulating

With a few exceptions, nearly all the literature on gangs focuses on their economic delinquency.[13] This is a very misleading picture, however, for although gangs operate principally in illegal markets, they also are involved in legal markets. Of the thirty-seven gangs observed in the present study, twenty-seven generated some percentage of their revenues through legitimate business activity. It is true that gangs do more of their business activity in illegal markets, but none of them wants to be exclusively active in these markets.[14]

In the illegal market, gangs concentrate their economic activities primarily in goods, services, and recreation. In the area of goods, gangs have been heavily involved in accumulating and selling drugs, liquor, and various stolen products such as guns, auto parts, and assorted electronic equipment. These goods are sometimes bought and sold with the gang acting as wholesaler and/or retailer. At other times, the gang actually produces the goods it sells. For example, while most gangs buy drugs or alcohol and retail them, a few gangs manufacture and market homemade drugs and moonshine liquor. Two gangs (one African-American and one Irish) in this study had purchased stills and sold their moonshine to people on the street, most of whom were derelicts, and to high school kids too young to buy liquor legally.[15] Three other gangs (two Puerto Rican and one Dominican) made a moonshine liquor from fermented fruit and sold it almost exclusively to teenagers. Both types of moonshine were very high in alcohol, always above one hundred proof. While sales of this liquor were not of a magnitude to create fortunes, these projects were quite surprisingly capable of generating substantial amounts of revenue.

The biggest money-maker and the one product nearly every gang tries to market is illegal drugs.[16] The position of the gang within the illegal drug market varies among gangs and between cities. In New York, the size of the gang and how long it has been in existence have a great deal to do with whether it will have access to drug suppliers. The older and larger gangs are able to buy drugs from suppliers and act as wholesalers to pushers. They shun acting as pushers (the lowest level of drug sales) themselves because there are greater risks and little, if any, commensurate increase in profit. In addition, because heroin use is forbidden within most gangs, the gang leaders prefer to establish attitudes oriented to the sale rather than the consumption of drugs within the organization. In the past, when the supply was controlled by the Italian Mafia, it was difficult for gangs to gain access to the quantity of drug supplies necessary to make a profit marketing them. In the past ten years, though, the Mafia has given way (in terms of drug supply) to African-American, Puerto Rican, and Mexican syndicates.[17] In addition, with the increased popularity of cocaine in New York, the African-American, Puerto Rican, and Dominican syndicates' connections to Latin American sources of cocaine supply rival, and in many cases surpass, those of Mafia figures.[18] With better access to supplies, gangs in New York have been able to establish a business attitude toward drugs and to capitalize on the opportunities that drugs now afford them.

Some gangs have developed alternative sources of supply. They do so in two ways.

Some, particularly the Chicano gangs, have sought out pharmacies where an employee can be paid off to steal pills for the gang to sell on the street.[19] Other gangs, particularly in New York, but also some in Los Angeles, have established "drug mills" to produce synthetic drugs such as LSD (or more recently crack cocaine) for sale on the street. The more sophisticated drug mills, which are controlled by various organized crime families, manufacture a whole line of drugs for sale, including cut heroin, but gangs are almost never involved in them. Those gangs that have established a production facility for generating drugs, no matter how crude it may be, generate sizable sums of money. Whether a gang is able to establish a sophisticated production and distribution system for drugs depends on the sophistication of the gang organization and the amount of capital available for start-up purposes.

Stolen guns are another popular and profitable product. Gangs sometimes steal guns and then redistribute them, but most often they buy them from wholesale gun peddlers and then resell them. Sometimes the gang will buy up a small number of shotguns and then cut the barrel and stock down to about 13 to 15 inches in length and then sell them as "easily concealable." A prospective buyer can get whatever he wants if he is willing to pay the going price. In the present study, the Irish gangs have been, commercially speaking, the most involved with guns, often moving relatively large shipments, ranging from sawed-off shotguns to fully automatic rifles and pistols of the most sophisticated types.[20] It was reported that these guns were being moved, with the help of Irish social clubs, to the Catholics of Northern Ireland for their struggle with the Protestants there. No matter what the destination, rather large sums of money were paid to the Irish gangs for their efforts in acquiring the weapons or helping move them. Although all the gangs studied were involved in the sale of illegal guns, illegal gun sales constituted a larger proportion of the economic activities of Irish gangs than they did for the others.

Gangs in all three cities were also involved in the selling of car parts. All the parts sold were stolen, some stolen to fill special orders from customers and others stolen and reworked in members' home garages into customized parts for resale. Business was briskest in Los Angeles, where there is a large market, especially among the low-rider clientele, for customized auto parts.[21] The amount of money made from stolen auto parts varies according to the area, whether or not the gang has an agent to whom to sell the parts, and the types of parts sold. On the whole, revenues from stolen auto parts were not nearly as high as those from selling illegal drugs, guns, or liquor, and so less time is devoted by gangs to this activity.

Gangs' business activities also include a number of services, the three most common being protection, demolition (usually arson), and indirect participation in prostitution. Protection is the most common service, both because there is a demand for it in the low-income areas in which gangs operate and because the gangs find it the easiest service to deliver, since it requires little in the way of resources or training. Gangs offer both personal and business protection. Nearly all the gangs had developed a fee schedule according to the type of protection desired. Most, but certainly not all, of the protection services offered by gangs in this study involved extortion. Usually the gang would go into a store and ask the owner if he felt he needed protection from being robbed. Since it was clear what was being suggested, the owner usually said yes and asked how much it would cost him. When dealing with naive owners, those who did not speak English very well or did not know American ghetto customs, or with owners who flatly resisted their services, the gang would take time to educate or persuade them to retain its services. In the case of the immigrants (most of whom were Asian or Near Eastern), the gang members would begin by explaining the situation, but usually such owners did not understand, and so the gang would demonstrate its point by sending members into the store to steal. Another tactic was to pay a dope addict to go in and rob the store. After such an incident occurred, the gang would return and ask the owner if he now needed protection. If he refused, the tactics were repeated, and almost all owners were finally convinced. However, for those owners who understood and resisted from the start, more aggressive tactics were used, such as destruction of their premises or harassment of patrons. More often than not, continued pressure brought the desired result. However, it should be noted that in the vast majority of cases, no coercion was needed, because owners in high-crime areas were, more often than not, happy to receive protection. As one owner said to me: "I would need to hire a protection company anyway, and frankly the gang provides me much more protection than they could ever do."

Gangs also offer their services as enforcers to clients who need punishment administered to a third party. Small-time hustlers or loan sharks, for example, hired some gangs to administer physical coercion to borrowers delinquent in their repayments. More recently one gang offered and apparently was hired by a foreign government to undertake terrorist acts against the government and people of the United States.[22] Although that was an extreme case, nearly all gangs seek enforcement contracts because the fee is usually high, few resources have to be committed, and relatively little in the way of planning (compared to other projects) is needed.

The permanent elimination of or damage to property is another service gangs offer. This more often than not involves arson, and the buildings hit are commonly dilapidated. The gang's clients are either landlords who want to torch the building to get insurance money or residents who are so frustrated by the landlord's unwillingness to provide the most basic services that they ask the gang to retaliate. In both cases there is usually much discussion of the project within the gang. These service jobs require a good deal of discussion and planning because there is the potential to hurt someone living in the building or to create enormous hardship if people have no alternative place to live, and the gang will do almost anything to avoid injuring people in its community. The gangs of New York have the most business along these lines, particularly in the South Bronx, but arson is a service offered in Detroit, Chicago, and Philadelphia as well. As one gang leader from the Bronx said:

You just don't bomb or torch any building that someone wants down. You got to find out who lives there, if they got another place to go, if they would be for takin' out the building and if they'd be OK with the folks [law enforcement authorities]. Then you got to get organized to get everybody out and sometimes that ain't many people and sometimes it is. If there is lots of people in the building, we'd just pass [refuse] on the job. . . . [N]ow if we can work all these things out, we take the job and we deliver either a skeleton [outer walls are standing, but nothing else] or a cremation [just ashes].

Many potential clients know that a gang will refuse to burn down a building in its neighborhood if some type of harm will come to residents of its community, and so they contract with a gang from another area to do the job. Such incidents always ignite a war not only between the affected gangs but also between the communities. Take the example of the Hornets, a gang from one borough in New York that had contracted to set on fire a building in another borough. Although no one was killed in the fire, a few people were slightly burned, and of course everyone who lived in the building became homeless. At the request of a number of residents, the Vandals, a gang from the affected area, began to investigate and found out who had contracted to torch the building and who had been responsible. Then, at the request of an overwhelming majority of the community, the Vandals retaliated by burning down a building in the culprit gang's community. Hipper, a twenty-year-old member of the Vandals, said:

We got to protect our community, they depend on us and they want us to do something so this [the burning of an apartment building in the neighborhood] don't happen again. . . . we be torchin' one of their buildings. I hope this don't hurt anybody, but if we don't do this, they be back hurting the people in our community and we definitely don't be letting that happen!

This is an excellent example of the bond that exists between the community and the gang. There is the understanding, then, among the community that the gang is a resource that can be counted on, particularly in situations where some form of force is necessary. Likewise, the gang knows that its legitimacy and existence are tied to being integrated in and responsible to community needs.

Prostitution is one illegal service in which gangs do not, for the most part, become directly involved. Gangs will accept only the job of protecting pimps and their women for a fee (fifteen, or 40 percent, of the gangs in this study had), and in this way they become indirectly associated with the prostitution business. Yet they generally avoid direct involvement because they feel protective of the females in their communities, and their organizations are wary of being accused by neighborhood residents of exposing female members of the community to the dangers associated with prostitution.

The last type of economic activity in which all the gangs in the present study were involved has to do with providing recreation. Some gangs established numbers games in their neighborhoods.

One New York gang had rented what had been a small Chinese food take-out place and was running numbers from the back where the kitchen had once been. (When I first observed the place, I thought it was a Chinese take-out and even proposed we get some quick food from it, which met with much laughter from the members of the gang I was with.) This gang became so successful that it opened up two other numbers establishments.

One had been a pizza place (and was made to look as though it still served pizza slices); the other was a small variety store, which still functioned in that capacity, but also housed the numbers game in the back rooms.

Setting up gambling rooms is another aspect of the recreation business. Eleven of the gangs (or 30 percent) rented small storefronts, bought tables and chairs, and ran poker and/or domino games. The gang would assume the role of the "house," receiving a commission for each game played. Some of the gangs bought slot machines and placed them in their gambling rooms. Five (or 14 percent) of the gangs had as many as fifteen machines available for use.

Finally, ten gangs (27 percent), primarily those with Latino members, rented old buildings and converted them to accommodate cockfights. The gang would charge each cock owner a fee for entering his bird and an entrance fee for each patron. All of these ventures could, at various times, generate significant amounts of capital. The exact amount would depend on how often they were closed by the police and how well the gang managed the competition in its marketplace.

Turning to the legal economic activities undertaken by gangs, I observed that two ran "mom and pop" stores that sold groceries, candy, and soft drinks. Three gangs had taken over abandoned apartment buildings, renovated them, and rented them very cheaply— not simply because the accommodations were rather stark, but also because the gang wanted to help the less fortunate members of its community. The gangs also used these buildings to house members who had nowhere else to live. Undertaken and governed by social as much as economic concerns, these apartment ventures did not generate much income.

Interestingly, the finances of these legal activities were quite tenuous. The gangs that operated small grocery stores experienced periodic failures during which the stores had to be closed until enough money could be acquired (from other sources) to either pay the increased rent, rebuild shelf stock, or make necessary repairs. For those gangs who operated apartment buildings, in every case observed, the absence of a deed to the building or the land forced the gang to relinquish its holdings to either the city or a new landlord who wanted to build some new structure. Though there was a plentiful supply of abandoned buildings, most gangs lost interest in the renovation-and-rental business because such projects always created a crisis in their capital flow, which in turn precipitated internal bickering and conflict.

Other legal economic activities undertaken by the gangs I studied were automobile and motorcycle repair shops, car parts (quasi junk yards), fruit stands, and hair shops (both barber and styling). However, most of these ventures contributed only very modest revenues to the gangs' treasuries. Furthermore, the gang leadership had difficulty keeping most of the legal economic activities functioning because the rank and file were, by and large, not terribly enthusiastic about such activities. Rank-and-file resistance to most of these activities was of three sorts: members did not want to commit regularly scheduled time to any specific ongoing operation; members felt that legal activities involved considerable overhead costs that lowered the profit rate; and members calculated that the time required to realize a large profit was far too long when compared to illegal economic activity. Thus, when such projects were promoted by the gang leadership and undertaken by the rank-and-file, they were done under the rubric of community service aid projects. The comments of Pin, a nineteen-year-old African-American gang member from New York, are representative of this general position on legal economic activity:

> No, I don't go for those deals where we [the gang] run some kind of hotel out of an old building or run some repair shop or something like that. When you do that you can't make no money, or if you do make something it so small and takes so long to get it that it's just a waste of our [the gang's] money. But when the leadership brings it up as a possibility, well, sometimes I vote for it because I figure you got to help the community, many of them [people in the community] say they sort of depend on our help in one way or another, so I always say this is one way to help the community and me and the brothers go along with it. But everybody knows you can't make no money on shit like this.

## Economic Activity: Consuming

Nearly all economic activity that gangs undertake is for the purpose of financing consumption, which takes three forms: goods/commodities, recreation, and basic resources (material and psychological). In the first category, drugs and alcohol are the items most often purchased by gangs, and they try to provide quantities that will satisfy their membership. Some gangs, like Chicano gangs, purchase and use heroin, cocaine, marijuana, and various chemical drugs like barbiturates, amphetamines, and angel dust. Other gangs, like those in New York, forbid the use of heroin, but buy pure cocaine and crack cocaine. Alcohol is used by nearly all the gangs, but I found that the Irish used it most, not so much because they have a tradition of drinking as because the supply of drugs was controlled by nonwhites and they did not want to do business with nonwhites. However, most gangs do not dispense drugs or alcohol free of charge to their members. Rather they sell the drugs or alcohol at cost or provide a limited free supply to members at gang-organized parties. For example, some of the gangs had rather sophisticated clubhouses whose bars sold drinks and small sandwiches (warmed in the microwave) at cost. In addition, at their parties they would have a limited amount of cocaine available to "help people get in the party mood." Furthermore, some of the gangs in all three cities purchased equipment for the members' use: pinball machines, table soccer machines, table tennis, pool tables, and slot machines. They also purchased some athletic equipment: baseball gloves, bats, balls, bases, some basketballs, and handballs. One gang went so far as to purchase a motorcycle for recreational use.

Parties and group recreational activities are an important aspect of gang life, just as they are for other social organizations like the Elks and Moose lodges. A good deal of money is spent on items that will be consumed at their parties, picnics, and outings (barbecues); at times some gangs will rent a hall for a party.

Lastly, gangs allocate money or resources on hand to assist those members and their families who are having difficulty procuring food, clothing, and shelter. A gang's emergency fund serves to reassure members that temporary relief will be available if times are bad for themselves or their families.[23]

### Endnotes

1. Nearly all studies of gangs incorporate this theme into their analysis. One of the exceptions is Cloward and Ohlin, *Delinquency and Opportunity*, which argues that many delinquents have the same values as other members of American society. However, even Cloward and Ohlin incorporate some of the conventional argument by accepting the premise that gang members' skills to compete with the larger society have been retarded by a lack of opportunity.

2. See Charles Sabel, *Work and Politics* (Cambridge: Cambridge University Press, 1987), pp. 1–30, on the importance of worldviews in affecting the behavior of individuals in industrial organizations and politics.

3. David Matza mentions a comparable tendency among delinquents to deny guilt associated with wrongdoing when he discusses the delinquent's belief that he is nearly always the victim of a "bum rap" (see Matza, *Delinquency and Drift* [New Brunswick, N.J.: Transaction Books], pp. 108–10).

4. I use the term *economic-oriented action* the way Weber does: "Action will be said to be 'economical oriented' so far as, according to its subjective meaning, it is concerned with the satisfaction of a desire for 'utilities' (*Nutzleistung*)" (Weber, *Economy and Society*, I:63).

5. See Karl Marx, *The Economic and Philosophical Manuscripts of 1844*, 4th rev. ed. (Moscow: Progress Publishers, 1974), p. 38.

6. See David C. McClelland, *The Achieving Society* (New York: Free Press, 1961), pp. 233–37.

7. See Lee Rainwater, *What Money Buys: Inequality and the Social Meanings of Income* (New York: Basic Books, 1974). Also see Richard P. Coleman and Lee Rainwater, *Social Standing in America: New Dimensions of Class* (New York: Basic Books, 1978), pp. 29–45.

8. See the accounts of successful entrepreneurs from poor families who dreamed of grandeur and became America's most renowned business tycoons in Matthew Josephson, *The Robber Barons: The Great American Capitalists 1861–1901* (New York: Harcourt, Brace & World, 1962), especially [the] chapter entitled "What Young Men Dream," pp. 32–49.

9. Being respectful maintains the social etiquette established in the gang and acts to deter physical confrontations between members. For an example similar to that reported here, see Kaiser, *Vice Lords*, pp. 41–42.

10. See Thrasher, *The Gang*, pp. 198–200.

11. Ibid., p. 86.

12. In comparing the interviews of older men who had been in gangs during the 1930s, 1940s, 1950s, and 1960s with those who are in gangs today, I found a clear and significant difference in the role that money plays in the everyday lives of these individuals from different generations. Simply stated, the interviews indicate that the importance of money for "normal everyday activity" increases from the 1930s generation to that of today.

13. Both the theoretical and empirical literature focus on the gang's criminal activity. For theoretical discussions, see Kornhauser, *Social Sources of Delinquency*, pp. 51–61. For empirical studies, see nearly all of the classic and contemporary work on gangs. A sample of this literature would include Thrasher, *The Gang;* Herman Schwendinger and Julia Schwendinger, *Adolescent Subcultures and Delinquency* (New York: Praeger, 1985); Cloward and Ohlin, *Delinquency and Opportunity;* Cohen, *Delinquent Boys*. Two exceptions are Horowitz, *Honor and the American Dream*, and Vigil, *Barrio Gangs*.

14. There are two factors that have encouraged gangs to be more active in illegal markets. First, gangs, like organized crime syndicates, attempt to become active in many economic activities that are legal. However, because so much of the legal market is controlled by groups that have established themselves in strategic positions (because they entered that market a considerable time in the past), gangs have found it difficult at best to successfully penetrate legal markets. Further, there are financial incentives that have encouraged gangs to operate in the illegal market. These include the fact that costs are relatively low, and while personal risk (in terms of being incarcerated and/or physically hurt) is rather high, high demand along with high risk can produce greater profit margins. Despite the fact that these two factors have encouraged gangs to be more active in the illegal market it is important to emphasize that nearly all the gangs studied attempted to, and many did, conduct business in the legal market as well.

15. The Schwendingers indicate that "youthful tastes regulate the flow of goods and services in the [adolescent] market" and gangs do take advantage of these tastes. See Schwendinger and Schwendinger, *Adolescent Subcultures and Delinquency*, p. 286.

16. See Fagan, "Social Organization of Drug Use and Drug Dealing Among Urban Gangs," pp. 633–67; and Jerome H. Skolnick, *Forum: The Social Structure of Street Drug Dealing* (Sacramento: Bureau of Criminal Statistics/Office of the Attorney General, 1989).

17. See Francis A. J. Ianni, *Black Mafia: Ethnic Succession in Organized Crime* (New York: Simon & Schuster, 1974). Also see Moore, *Homeboys*, pp. 86–92, 114–16.

18. See Peter Lupsha and K. Schlegel, "The Political Economy of Drug Trafficking: The Herrera Organization (Mexico and the United States)"

(Paper presented at the Latin American Studies Association, Philadelphia, 1979).

19. This paying off of employees for drug supplies began, according to Joan Moore, in Los Angeles in the 1940s and 1950s (see Moore, *Homeboys*, pp. 78–82).

20. These gangs can procure fully automatic M-16s, Ingrams, and Uzis.

21. Low riders are people, nearly all of whom are of Mexican descent, who drive customized older automobiles (1950s and 1960s models are preferred), one of the characteristics being that the springs for each wheel are cut away so that the car rides very low to the ground. Some of these cars have hydraulic systems that can be inflated at the flip of a switch so that the car can ride low to the ground at one moment and at the normal level the next. For a discussion of the importance of customized automobiles in Los Angeles, especially among Chicano youth, see Schwendinger and Schwendinger, *Adolescent Subcultures and Delinquency*, pp. 234–45.

22. The El Rukn gang in Chicago was recently indicted and convicted of contracting with the Libyan government to carry out terrorist acts within the United States. See *Chicago Tribune*, 3, 4, 6, 7 November 1987.

23. The gangs give many of their members, and sometimes the community as a whole, the same psychological comfort that the political machine provided urban ethnic groups in the late nineteenth and early twentieth centuries. See Raymond Wolfinger, "Why Political Machines Have Not Withered Away and Other Revisionist Thoughts," *Journal of Politics* 34 (May 1972): 365–98.

## Review

1. In his research, Jankowski found that nearly all the gang members studied possessed five attributes that were entrepreneurial in character or that reinforce entrepreneurial behavior. What were these attributes?

2. What are four sources of gang members' entrepreneurial attitudes and behavior?

3. What impact do the risk-taking patterns of individual gang members have on their degree of economic success or failure?

4. The gangs discussed in this article concentrated their illegal economic activities primarily in goods, services, and recreation. In what specific types of goods, services, and recreational activities are gangs most commonly involved?

## Application

A juvenile gang is an excellent example of a deviant subculture. It has its own way of life and is separated from the mainstream of society. The purpose of this assignment is to examine how popular movies portray this aspect of gangs. Arrange to rent two or three recent movies that depict gang life. For each movie, make notes about the following features of the gang:

a. norms or rules

b. distinct language

c. values and beliefs

d. rituals

e. division of labor

f. nicknames used by members

Summarize your findings about gang culture and compare its features to the culture of the larger society.

## Related Web Sites

1. *http://www.iir.com/nygc/*. Site of the National Youth Gang Center, offering publications and links to other sites.

2. *http://abstractsdb.ncjrs.org/content/AbstractsDB_search.asp*. The National Criminal Justice Reference Service offers about 50 government publications dealing with juvenile gangs.

# 41

# The Razor Blade in the Apple

## The Social Construction of Urban Legends

*Joel Best*
*Gerald T. Horiuchi*

*The legends and myths of traditional societies usually relate heroic exploits and high ideals. Although these stories also have a role in modern society, folktales of a more contemporary nature, sometimes referred to as urban legends, have evolved alongside them. Characteristically, urban legends focus on the hazards of modern life and the threat they present to the innocent or ignorant. They often have some basis in fact, and their usual protagonist is not a supernatural being or heroic figure but an ordinary person. The familiar stories of rats found in soft-drink bottles and pets exploded in microwave ovens are typical urban legends that began with actual incidents and evolved through countless tellings and retellings. In some cases, the legends may be pure fiction. Recently, for instance, millions of Americans received e-mail messages warning them against downloading any document containing a certain word in the title. The word varied somewhat, but the message was the same—this document contains a virus that will wipe out your hard disk if you download it. The problem of viruses is a real one, but so far as we know there was no basis for the warnings and no such documents were ever sent or received.*

*In this selection, Best and Horiuchi examine the frightening urban legend of Halloween sadists who give children dangerous, adulterated treats. They show a typical way in which urban legends can arise and spread. Their detailed analysis of the origin and development of this particular legend is complemented by a*

*thoughtful discussion of its sociological implications.*

The 1970s witnessed the discovery of a frightening new deviant—the Halloween sadist, who gave dangerous, adulterated treats to children. Each year, Halloween's approach brought warnings to parents:

> . . . that plump red apple that Junior gets from a kindly old woman down the block . . . may have a razor blade hidden inside (*New York Times*, 1970).

> If this year's Halloween follows form, a few children will return home with something more than an upset tummy: in recent years, several children have died and hundreds have narrowly escaped injury from razor blades, sewing needles and shards of glass purposefully placed into their goodies by adults (*Newsweek*, 1975).

> It's Halloween again and time to remind you that . . . somebody's child will become violently ill or die after eating poisoned candy or an apple containing a razor blade (Van Buren, 1983).

Various authorities responded to the threat: legislatures in California (1971) and New Jersey (1982) passed laws against Halloween sadism; schools trained children to inspect their treats for signs of tampering; and some communities tried to ban trick-or-treating. According to press reports, many parents restricted their children's trick-or-treating, examined their treats, or arranged parties or other indoor celebrations. By 1984, the threat of Halloween sadists was apparently taken for granted. Doubts about the threat's reality rarely appeared in print. Several Oregon third graders wrote letters to a newspaper: "I wish people wouldn't put poison in our Halloween treats" (*Times*, 1984). Adults questioned for an Illinois newspaper's "Sidewalk Interview" column (*DeKalb Daily Chronicle*, 1984) expressed concern: ". . . part of it is checking to make sure you know your neighbors and checking the candy. I think it's terrible that people are doing this and I guess people's morals have to be examined." "Dear Abby" printed a letter describing a North Carolina hospital's program to X-ray treats (Van Buren, 1984); radiologists at a Hanford, California, hospital checked 500 bags of treats (*Fresno Bee*, 1984).

Halloween sadism is thought to involve random, vicious, unprovoked attacks against small children. The attacks seem irrational, and the attackers are routinely described as disturbed or insane. These "child-haters" are theorized to "have had a really deprived childhood"; having been "abused as children," they are now "frustrated and filled with resentment against the world in general" (Isaacs and Royeton, 1982:69). Law enforcement officials and the media reaffirm that the threat is real, urging parents to protect their children against sadistic attacks.

Although Halloween sadism is widely regarded as a serious threat, it has received little scholarly attention. In this paper, we examine the phenomenon from a sociological perspective, addressing three issues. First, we try to assess the incidence of Halloween sadism in order to demonstrate that the threat has been greatly exaggerated. Second, we draw upon a concept from folklore studies to argue that the belief in Halloween sadism is best viewed as an "urban legend." Finally, we suggest that urban legends are a product of social strain and of the social organization of the response to that strain.

## A Holiday for Sadists?

There are no reliable official statistics on Halloween sadism. Minor incidents, particularly those that do not involve injuries, may never be reported to the police. Cases that are reported may be classified under a wide range of offenses, and there is no centralized effort to compile cases from different jurisdictions. Moreover, the circumstances of the crime—the young victim, the unfamiliar assailant, the difficulty in remembering which treats came from which houses—make it unlikely that offenders will be arrested.

While the true incidence of Halloween sadism cannot be measured, newspaper reports reveal changes in public reaction to the threat. Therefore, we examined the coverage of Halloween sadism in four daily newspa-

pers between [1958] and 1984. For *The New York Times*, we checked all entries under "Halloween" in the paper's annual indexes for information about Halloween sadism. *The New York Times Index* proved to be unusually complete, listing even short items of a sentence or two. The published indexes for two other major regional newspapers, the *Chicago Tribune* and the *Los Angeles Times*, were less thorough, so for each year, we read both papers' issues for the first three days in November. Finally, we examined all Halloween stories in the files of the *Fresno Bee*. Our search found stories about 76 alleged incidents of Halloween sadism, which included at least the community where the incident occurred and the nature of the attack. Table 41.1 shows the number of incidents reported in each year.

### Table 41.1
*Reported Incidents of Halloween Sadism, 1958–84*

| Year | Number of Incidents | Year | Number of Incidents |
|------|---------------------|------|---------------------|
| 1958 | 0 | 1972 | 1 |
| 1959 | 1 | 1973 | 4 |
| 1960 | 0 | 1974 | 1 |
| 1961 | 0 | 1975 | 2 |
| 1962 | 1 | 1976 | 2 |
| 1963 | 1 | 1977 | 0 |
| 1964 | 3 | 1978 | 0 |
| 1965 | 1 | 1979 | 3 |
| 1966 | 5 | 1980 | 0 |
| 1967 | 4 | 1981 | 0 |
| 1968 | 3 | 1982 | 12 |
| 1969 | 7 | 1983 | 1 |
| 1970 | 10 | 1984 | 0 |
| 1971 | 14 | | |

Obviously, the 76 incidents identified through this procedure do not form a complete list of cases of Halloween sadism. However, there are several reasons why it is unlikely that many serious incidents—involving deaths or serious injuries—were overlooked. First, the papers' coverage was national. The 76 reported incidents came from 13 states and two Canadian provinces; while each of the four newspapers concentrated on incidents in its own region, all reported cases from other regions. All four included at least one case from the South—the only major region without a newspaper in the sample. Second, the 76 reported cases were generally not serious. Injuries were reported in only 20 cases, and only two of these involved deaths. It seems unlikely that newspapers would choose to print accounts of minor incidents, while ignoring more serious crimes. This impression is bolstered further by the frequent appearance of stories— often from different states—about other Halloween tragedies: children struck by cars and other accidental deaths; people murdered when they opened their doors, expecting trick-or-treaters; racial disturbances; vandalism; and so on. At least two of the newspapers carried reports on each of the two deaths attributed to Halloween sadists. It is therefore unlikely that the list of 76 incidents excludes any fatal instances of Halloween sadism. Table 41.1 reveals two peaks in the pattern of reporting. Thirty-one of the 76 incidents occurred in the three years from 1969 to 1971. This wave of reports encouraged recognition of Halloween sadism as a threat. As a holiday when millions of children venture out at night, Halloween has a long history of tragic accidents. Routinely, newspapers and magazines print lists of safety tips, warning parents against flammable costumes, masks that obscure the wearer's vision, and the like. A systematic review of such lists found no mention of the danger posed by sadists before 1972; but, from that year on, lists of safety tips almost invariably warned parents to inspect their children's treats for signs of tampering. At the same time that these warnings spread, reports of Halloween sadism fell to a few per year until 1982, when there was a dramatic increase. Of course, this reflected the fear caused by the Tylenol murders. A month before Halloween, seven people died after swallowing poisoned Extra-Strength Tylenol capsules. In the weeks that followed, there were hundreds of reports of "copycats" adulterating food, over-the-counter medications, and other household products. As Halloween approached, the media repeatedly warned parents that trick-or-treaters would

be in danger. After raising the specter of Halloween sadism, the press naturally covered the incidents that were reported. A year later, however, coverage fell to pre-Tylenol levels.

Examining the reports of the 76 incidents leads to three conclusions. First, the threat of Halloween sadism has been greatly exaggerated. There is simply no basis for *Newsweek's* (1975) claim that "several children have died." The newspapers attributed only two deaths to Halloween sadists, and neither case fit the image of a maniacal killer randomly attacking children. In 1970, five-year-old Kevin Toston died after eating heroin supposedly hidden in his Halloween candy. While this story received considerable publicity, newspapers gave less coverage to the follow-up report that Kevin had found the heroin in his uncle's home, not his treats (*San Francisco Chronicle*, 1970). The second death is more notorious. In 1974, eight-year-old Timothy O'Bryan died after eating Halloween candy contaminated with cyanide. Investigators concluded that his father had contaminated the treat (Grider, 1982). Thus, both boys' deaths were caused by family members, rather than by anonymous sadists. Similarly, while the newspaper reports rarely gave detailed information about the remaining 18 cases in which injuries were reported, most of the victims were not seriously hurt. Several incidents involved minor cuts and puncture wounds; what was apparently the most serious wound required 11 stitches. In short, there were no reports where an anonymous sadist caused death or a life-threatening injury; there is no justification for the claim that Halloween sadism stands as a major threat to U.S. children.[1]

A second conclusion is that many, if not most, reports of Halloween sadism are of questionable authenticity. Children who go trick-or-treating know about Halloween sadism; they have been warned by their parents, teachers, and friends. A child who "discovers" an adulterated treat stands to be rewarded with the concerned attention of parents and, perhaps, police officers and reporters. Such a hoax is consistent with Halloween traditions of trickery, just as the fear of sadists resembles the more traditional dread of ghosts and witches. The 76 reported incidents included two cases that were identified as hoaxes at the time, and it seems likely that other cases involved undiscovered fraud. After all, it is remarkable that three-quarters of the children who reported receiving contaminated treats had no injuries. Efforts to systematically follow up reports of Halloween sadism have concluded that the vast majority were fabrications. After Halloween of 1972, *Editor and Publisher* (1973)—the trade magazine of the newspaper industry—examined several papers' efforts to trace all local reports of Halloween sadism; it concluded that virtually all the reports were hoaxes. Ten years later, in the wake of the Tylenol scare, the confectionary industry tried to reassure potential customers in a "white paper" on Halloween candy tampering in 1982 (National Confectioners Association et al., n.d.). The report noted that "more than 95 percent of the 270 potential Halloween 1982 candy adulterations analyzed by the Food and Drug Administration have shown no tampering, which has led one FDA official to characterize the period as one of 'psychosomatic mass hysteria.'" Further, a confectionary industry survey of police departments in "24 of the nation's largest cities, as well as smaller towns in which highly-publicized incidents were alleged to have occurred, found two reports of injuries—neither requiring medical treatment—from among the hundreds of claims of candy tampering." Thus, not only does a survey of press coverage reveal fewer reports of Halloween sadism than might be expected, but there is good reason to suspect that many of the reports are unfounded.

Third, the press should not be held responsible for the widespread belief that Halloween sadism poses a serious threat. While the news media can manufacture "crime waves" by suddenly focusing on previously ignored offenses, the press has given Halloween sadism relatively little publicity. Many of the 76 reported incidents received minimal coverage, in news stories of only two or three sentences. Often the reports were embedded in larger stories, such as a wire service summary of Halloween news from around the country. Nor did popular magazines highlight Halloween sadism; before 1982, only two short articles focused on the problem. The absence of authentic cases of serious injuries caused by Halloween sadism undoubtedly explains this limited coverage. While the publication of annual warnings to parents to inspect their children's treats, as well as occasional short items reporting minor incidents, may help keep the fear of Halloween sadism alive, the media do not seem to be the principal channel by which people learn of the danger. Rather, knowledge of Halloween sadism apparently spreads by word of mouth.

## Roots of an Urban Legend

The belief in Halloween sadism as a serious threat can be understood using a concept developed by folklorists: Halloween sadism is an *urban legend*. Urban legends are contemporary, orally transmitted tales that "often depict a clash between modern conditions and some aspect of a traditional lifestyle" (Brunvand, 1981:189). Whereas traditional legends often feature supernatural themes, most urban legends "are grounded in human baseness. . . ." (Fine, 1980:227). They describe criminal attacks, contaminated consumer goods, and other risks of modern life. Halloween sadism combines two themes found in several other urban legends: danger to children (e.g., the babysitter who cooks an infant in a microwave oven; the child kidnapped from a department store or an amusement park); and contamination of food (e.g., the mouse in the soft-drink bottle; the Kentucky Fried Rat). These legends, like that of the Halloween sadist, are typically told as true stories. They "gratify our desire to know about and to try to understand bizarre, frightening, and potentially dangerous or embarrassing events that *may* have happened" (Brunvand, 1981:12). Urban legends may even have a factual basis; soft-drink manufacturers have been sued by people claiming to have found mice in their drinks. Whether a legend begins with a real incident or as a fictional tale, it is told and retold, often evolving as it spreads. On occasion, urban legends appear in newspaper stories, reinforcing the tale's credibility

(Brunvand, 1981). The belief in Halloween sadism is maintained through orally transmitted warnings about the dangers contemporary society poses for the traditional custom of trick-or-treating. These warnings, which greatly exaggerate the threat, are an urban legend. That some incidents of Halloween sadism have occurred, and that the media have reported such incidents, does not disqualify the warnings as legends.

Viewing Halloween sadism as an urban legend helps explain why the belief became widespread when it did. News reports of Halloween sadism are not new. But the general perception that Halloween sadism is a serious threat can be dated to the early 1970s. This was the period when the press began reporting more incidents and warning parents to inspect treats, and legislatures began passing laws against Halloween sadism. In general, urban legends are products of social tension or strain. They express fears that the complexities of modern society threaten the traditional social order. Urban life requires contact with strangers who—the legends suggest—may be homicidal maniacs, unscrupulous merchants, voyeurs, or otherwise threatening. By repeating urban legends, people can respond to social strain, expressing their doubts about the modern world.

While it is obviously impossible to establish a causal link between particular social tensions and the spread of a particular urban legend, folklorists typically examine a legend's element[s] for clues about its roots. Some legends feature a transparent message, but others are more difficult to interpret. In the case of Halloween sadism, a plausible argument can be made that the legend's flowering in the early 1970s was tied to the heightened social strains of that period. The late 1960s and early 1970s were years of unparalleled divisiveness in post–World War II America. The media exposed several serious crises to the public, including an increasingly unpopular war, ghetto riots, student demonstrations, and increased drug use. It was a period of intense social strain. Three forms of strain that emerged or grew during these years seem related to the growing fear of Halloween sadism.

### Threats to Children

The form of strain that seems most clearly linked to a belief in Halloween sadism was the growing sense that children were no longer safe in the United States. During the 1960s and early 1970s, physicians and social workers promoted child abuse as a major social problem; the popular press responded with dozens of dramatic stories about children who had been cruelly treated by their parents. The rhetoric of this campaign emphasized that all children were potential victims, that child abuse occurred in all sectors of society. But even parents who remained confident that their children would never be abused could worry about losing their children to other threats. Older children adopted radical political views and experimented with illegal drugs. Other parents found their grown children facing a less symbolic threat—death in Vietnam. The social conflicts that marked America during these years must have left many parents wondering if their hopes for the next generation would be fulfilled.

Since the emergence of the belief in Halloween sadism, the generation gap seems to have narrowed, but threats to children remain visible. The movement against child abuse continues to spread, receiving still more publicity. And, during the late 1970s and early 1980s, emerging campaigns against incest, child pornography, child molesting, and abortion may have contributed to a larger sense of children in jeopardy. Perhaps the clearest link between threats to children and the fear of Halloween sadism appeared during the series of murders of Atlanta schoolchildren. In 1980, STOP, an organization of the victims' parents, argued that "the city should organize Halloween night events that will minimize dangers to the children" (*New York Times*, 1980).

### Fear of Crime

Other forms of strain involved more general threats. Survey data reveal that the fear of crime grew substantially between the mid-1960s and the early 1970s (Erskine, 1974; Stinchcombe et al., 1980). Although violent crimes often involve offenders and victims who are acquainted, the fear of crime focuses on the threat of an anonymous attacker. The threat of an unpredictable, unprovoked criminal attack parallels the Halloween sadist menace.

## Mistrust of Others

Survey data also reveal rising expressions of general mistrust during the early 1970s. The proportion of Americans who agreed that ". . . you can't be too careful in dealing with people" rose from 45.6 percent in 1966, to 50.0 percent in 1971, to 54.3 percent in 1973 (Converse et al., 1980:28). Studies of urban dwellers in the 1970s found high levels of mistrust for strangers (Fischer, 1982). While warnings about the collapse of the neighborhood in the anonymous modern city have proven exaggerated, the belief that people now live in greater isolation remains widespread. The social conflicts of the 1960s and early 1970s may have encouraged doubts about the trustworthiness of other people. Such doubts provided another form of strain during the period when the belief in Halloween sadism spread.

These sources of strain—threats to children, fear of crime, and mistrust of others—provided a context within which the concern about Halloween sadism could flourish. The Halloween sadist emerged as a symbolic expression of this strain: the sadist, like other dangers, attacks children—society's most vulnerable members; the sadist, like the stereotypical criminal, is an anonymous, unprovoked assailant; and the sadist, like other strangers, must be met by doubt, rather than trust. Placed in the context of the late 1960s and early 1970s, the spread of Halloween sadism is easily understood.

If these sources of strain account for the belief's spread, what explains its persistence? The extraordinary social conflicts of the early 1970s have moderated, yet the belief in Halloween sadism remains. Why? First, some of the same sources of strain continue to exist: the media still publicize threats to children (e.g., child abuse), and the fear of crime and strangers remains high. Second, and more important, Halloween sadism is an established urban legend; it can remain as a taken-for-granted, if dormant, part of American culture. The survey of

newspaper stories found only five reports of Halloween sadism from 1976 to 1981—less than one per year. However, warnings about sadists continued to appear during these years and, of course, the Tylenol poisonings in 1982 led to both predictions and reports of Halloween sadism.

Third, folklorists have traced the evolution of some legends over centuries. Legends seem most likely to persist when they have a general, underlying message (for instance, warnings about trusting outsiders) which can be tailored to fit new situations. Thus, the dangers of eating commercially prepared food were detailed in nineteenth-century stories about cat meat in baked pies and, more recently, in tales about rats sold at fried-chicken franchises. Like other urban legends about homicidal maniacs, the Halloween sadist legend expresses fears about criminal attacks. Given the general nature of this threat, the legend may persist as long as the custom of trick-or-treating.

Where do urban legends fit within the broader framework of sociological theory? At first glance, the fear of Halloween sadists resembles some of the instances of collective hysteria in the collective behavior literature. The Halloween sadist can stand beside the "phantom anesthetist" of Mattoon (Johnson, 1945), Taipei's "phantom slasher" (Jacobs, 1965), the "June bug epidemic" in a Southern textile plant (Kerckhoff and Back, 1968), and the windshield pitting in Seattle (Medalia and Larsen, 1985) as a focus of exaggerated fears. Studies of collective hysteria usually account for the emergence of hysterical beliefs as a response to social strain: the Mattoon episode occurred during wartime; the workers in the textile plant were putting in heavy overtime, and so on. In response to this strain, there emerged a belief in some threat, "an ambiguous element in the environment with a generalized power to threaten or destroy" (Smelser, 1962:82). This threat is credible, frightening, and difficult to protect oneself against:

> Instead of simply having a feeling that something is awry, the belief in a tangible threat makes it possible to *explain* and *justify* one's sense of discomfort—instead of anxiety, one experiences fear, and it is

then possible to act in some meaningful way with respect to this tangible threat rather than just feeling frustrated and anxious. (Kerckhoff and Back, 1968:160–61—emphasis in original.)

However, some of this model's key features do not fit the emergence of the belief in Halloween sadism and other urban legends. Collective hysteria is bounded in time and space. Hysterical beliefs are short-lived; they typically emerge, spread, and die within the space of a few days or weeks. Further, they are typically confined to a restricted locality—a single region, town, or facility. In contrast, the belief in Halloween sadists appears to have spread more slowly, over a period of years, and to have become an established, taken-for-granted part of the culture. Nor has the belief observed the normal geographic limits of collective hysteria—reports of Halloween sadism have come from throughout the country, suggesting that the belief is nationwide. If the Halloween sadist resembles the threats identified in instances of collective hysteria, the dynamics of the beliefs spread do not fit the hysterical pattern.

## Implications: 'Halloween and the Mass Child' Revisited

Holiday celebrations reflect the larger culture. The events celebrated, as well as the customary ways of celebrating, reveal the society's values and structure. And, as society changes, its holidays often take on new meanings, consistent with the altered culture. Where earlier American celebrations were communal, ceremonial, and often religious or patriotic, contemporary observances tend to be individualistic, materialistic, secular occasions, marked largely by unstructured leisure time.

Gregory P. Stone's (1959) "Halloween and the Mass Child" developed this thesis. Stone traced the evolution of Halloween activities in his lifetime, from the elaborate pranks of adolescents in the 1930s, to the playful trick-or-treating of young children in the 1950s. He found the 1950s children did not understand the extortionate premise of "trick or treat"; for them, Halloween was merely an occasion to receive candy. Stone interpreted

this shift as consistent with the changes in American values described in Riesman's (1950) *The Lonely Crowd:*

> ... Riesman's character type of "other-direction" may, indeed, be a *prototype* of American character and not some strange mutation in the northeast. Consumption, tolerance, and conformity were recognizable in the Halloween masquerade of a near-southern town. Production, indignation, and autonomy were not. (Stone, 1959:378—emphasis in original.)

Twenty-five years after Stone's analysis, the fear of Halloween sadism has further altered the meaning of Halloween. While Stone saw trick-or-treating as a part of the emerging culture of consumption, folklorists view Halloween as among the least commercialized of modern holidays. But this informality has been labeled dangerous by those who warn against Halloween sadists. Children are urged to refuse homemade treats and accept only coupons or mass-produced candy with intact wrappings, as though commercialism offers protection. Long celebrated through vandalism and extortion, Halloween has been a symbolic expression of disorder. Today, the Halloween sadist has become an annual reminder of the fragility of the social bond—an expression of growing doubts about the safety of children, the trustworthiness of strangers, and the strength of the modern urban community.

### Endnote

1. Certainly other elements of everyday life, while not receiving as much attention, are far more hazardous. In 1980–81, according to the U.S. Consumer Product Safety Commission (1982), 60 children under age five died in product associated deaths involving nursery equipment and supplies; another 13 deaths involved toys.

### References

Brunvand, Jan Harold, *The Vanishing Hitchhiker* (New York: Norton, 1981).

Converse, Philip E., Jean D. Dotson, Wendy J. Hoag, and William H. McGee III, *American Social Attitudes Data Sourcebook* (Cambridge: Harvard University Press, 1980).

*DeKalb Daily Chronicle*, "Sidewalk Interview," 1984, October 28:10.

*Editor and Publisher*, "Press Finds Halloween Sadism Rare but Warns of Danger," 1973, 106 (March 3):22.

Erskine, Hazel, "The Polls: Fear of Crime and Violence," *Public Opinion Quarterly*, 1974, 38:131–45.

Fine, Gary Alan, "The Kentucky Fried Rat," *Journal of the Folklore Institute*, 1980, 17:222–43.

Fischer, Claude S., *To Dwell Among Friends* (Chicago: University of Chicago Press, 1982).

*Fresno Bee*, "No Tricks Found in Fresno Treats," 1984, November 1:B1.

Grider, Sylvia, "The Razor Blades in the Apples Syndrome," unpublished paper, 1982.

Isaacs, Susan, and Robert Royeton, "Witches, Goblins, Ghosts," *Parents Magazine*, 57, 1982, October: 66–9.

Jacobs, Norman, "The Phantom Slasher of Taipei," *Social Problems*, 1965, 12:318–28.

Johnson, Donald M., "The 'Phantom Anesthetist' of Mattoon," *Journal of Abnormal and Social Psychology*, 1945, 40:175–86.

Kerckhoff, Alan C., and Kurt W. Back, *The June Bug* (New York: Appleton-Century-Crofts, 1968).

Medalia, Nahum Z., and Otto N. Larsen, "Diffusion and Belief in a Collective Delusion," *American Sociological Review*, 1985, 23:180–86.

National Confectioners Association, Chocolate Manufacturers Association, and National Candy Wholesalers Association, "Halloween/1982: An Overview," unpublished paper, n.d.

*New York Times*, "Those Treats May Be Tricks," 1970, October 28:56.

——, "Atlanta and Miami Curbing Halloween," 1980, October 31:A14.

*Newsweek*, "The Goblins Will Getcha. . . ," 1975, 86 November 3:28.

Riesman, David, *The Lonely Crowd* (Yale University Press, 1950).

*San Francisco Chronicle*, "Capsule Caused Halloween Death," 1970, November 10:3.

Smelser, Neil J., *Theory of Collective Behavior* (New Free Press, 1962).

Stinchcombe, Arthur L., Rebecca Adams, Carol A. Heimer, Kim Lane Scheppele, Tom W. Smith, and D. Garth Taylor, *Crime and Punishment* (San Francisco: Jossey-Bass, 1980).

Stone, Gregory P., "Halloween and the Mass Child," *American Quarterly*, 1959, 11:372–79.

*Times* (Beaverton, OR), "Letters," 1984, October 25:36.

U.S. Consumer Product Safety Commission, *Annual Report*, 1982. (Washington: U.S. Government Printing Office).

Van Buren, Abigail, "Dear Abby," *Fresno Bee*, 1983, October 31:D2.

——, "Dear Abby," *Fresno Bee*, 1984, September 30:C4.

## Review

1. What are the three issues addressed in this article?

2. What three conclusions were formed by the authors after examining newspaper reports of 76 incidents of Halloween sadism?

3. What forms of strain seem most clearly linked to a belief in Halloween sadism?

4. How does the fear of Halloween sadism fit in with instances of collective hysteria described in the collective behavior literature?

## Application

At a library or newspaper office, examine the coverage of Halloween sadism in your local newspaper. Read over specific references and articles for mention of alleged incidents of sadism. Prepare a summary of your findings and contrast them with those of Best and Horiuchi.

## Related Web Sites

1. *http://www.snopes.com/*. This site has a multitude of urban legends, organized into various categories.

2. *http://www.scambusters.org/legends.html*. Many urban legends now are associated with computers and the internet; this site has a long list of them.

Reprinted from: Joel Best and Gerald T. Horiuchi, "The Razor Blade in the Apple: The Social Construction of Urban Legends." Edited from the version originally appearing in *Social Problems*, Vol. 32, No. 5, June, 1985, pp. 488–499. Copyright © 1985 by the Society for the Study of Social Problems. Reprinted with permission. ✦

# Part Two

## *Social Change*

Social change, as conflict theory asserts, is both normal and pervasive. Fueled by such things as technology, population processes, economic shifts, conflict, and new ideas, every society is in a process of ongoing change. The change is more rapid in some than in others, but none escapes the change.

Social change always has consequences for individuals. Some kinds of change are welcomed, while others are resisted. Some change enhances people's well-being, while other kinds of change threatens well-being. This interaction between change in the larger society and the struggles of individuals and groups to defend and enhance their well-being is a theme that runs through each of the selections in this part. ✦

# 42

# Life in Big Red

## Struggles and Accommodations in a Chicago Polyethnic Tenement

### Dwight Conquergood

Beyond birth and death rates, immigration is the social process which most affects a nation's demographic profile. Immigration, which has been an important consideration throughout the nation's history, continues to affect society. Every year a large number of people legally immigrate to the United States (970,000 in 2000), most of them from Latin America and Asia. And although it is difficult to determine accurate figures, a substantial number enter illegally every year.

Many legal immigrants have come either under certain categories of preference (e.g., relatives of current citizens, desirable occupations, etc.) or as political refugees. Certain economic and political problems greet these immigrants when they arrive in the United States. For example, they are more likely to resettle in urban areas where deindustrialization deprives them of jobs that might have been a first step toward upward mobility. In addition to employment problems, their housing might be owned by absentee landlords who care less about the condition of their property than about maximizing their profits. At the same time, poor housing often becomes a focal point for political and business elites who want to "redevelop" the residences of immigrants into something more acceptable to the middle-class indigenous population.

In this selection, Conquergood addresses these problems from the point of view of the residents of an "urban slum"—the Albany Park neighborhood in Chicago. While Albany Park had been predominantly Jewish, by the 1980s its Latino population had grown to one third and its Asian population to one fourth. A section known as "Little Beirut" dramatizes the demographic shifts in Albany Park, with more tenements and a higher proportion of non-whites and residents on public assistance than in other vicinities. Outsiders regard Little Beirut as a "war zone" in which crime, drugs, and gangs are rampant. In the process of conducting this study, Conquergood himself lived in "Big Red," a three-story, red-brick tenement building in Little Beirut.

When Albany Park developed signs of decline in the 1960s, established residents and community institutions formed the North River Commission to slow or reverse the process. By the middle of the 1980s, the NRC began to have some success with new commercial and residential developments in the area. Since Little Beirut stood out as the sore thumb of Albany Park, it eventually became a primary target of NRC redevelopment efforts.

> Everyday life invents itself by poaching in countless ways on the property of others.
> —Michel De Certeau,
> *The Practice of Everyday Life* (1984)

I moved into Big Red in December 1987 in order to begin research for the Changing Relations Ford Foundation project.[1] At the time I moved in to the A2R apartment, previously occupied by an Assyrian family, I was the second white resident. An elderly Jewish man lived in C2L. The ethnic breakdown for the other 35 units was 11 Hmong, 10 Mexican, 10 Assyrian, 2 Sino-Cambodian, 1 Puerto Rican, and 1 Puerto Rican-Mexican mixed. During the twenty months I lived in Big Red, the ethnic mix was enriched by African Americans, Appalachian whites, more Puerto Ricans, and new immigrant Poles (see Figure 42.1). I lived in Big Red until the end of August 1989, when along with all my A stairwell neighbors I was displaced and that wing of Big Red was boarded up. I rented an apartment just one block north of Big Red and continue to live in Little Beirut and interact with my Big Red networks at the time of this writing.[2]

Initial inquiries about renting an apartment pulled me immediately into interactions with other tenants. Beyond the "Apartment for Rent" sign, there was no formal assistance for prospective tenants: no rental office, telephone number, or agency address. Yet every vestibule and stairwell was un-locked, open, and filled with friendly people.

### Figure 42.1

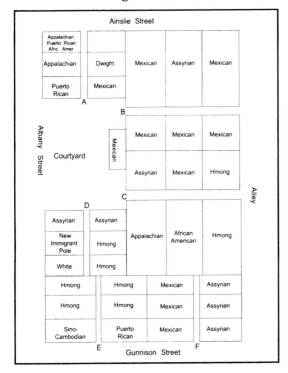

All the business of renting the apartment was conducted informally, through face-to-face interactions with other residents. In twenty months, I never signed or saw a lease. It was a few months before I actually saw the absentee owner. The word-of-mouth way of getting information brought me into contact with a number of neighbors who graciously shared with me what they knew and ven-tured outside in the bitter chill of Chicago December nights to track down the janitor. Sometimes we would find the janitor, some-times we would not: he held down another full-time job in order to make ends meet. Sometimes when we found him he would not have the keys.

From one perspective, the rental manage-ment of Big Red was highly inefficient and required unnecessary trips, long waits, and

delays. On the other hand, the absence of a managing authority made all the residents interdependent. By the time I was ready to move in, I was on friendly terms with several neighbors and had received offers of help with the move, including the loan of a car.

The physical dilapidation of Big Red is even more apparent from the inside than the outside, but it is mitigated by the warmth and friendliness of the people. Indeed, the chronic state of disrepair, breakdowns, and emergencies requires for survival a neigh-borly interdependence unheard-of in effi-ciently managed middle-class properties. Crises create community, but this is particu-larly true when the crisis relates to physical space that people share over time. When the plumbing on the third floor leaks through the second floor ceiling with every toilet flush, the residents of those two floors get to know one another in intimate ways.

It is the human quality of life in Big Red that eludes outsiders. The following NRC memo (1989) captures coldly the physical state of disrepair in Big Red. Even though it notes that "the building is currently fully oc-cupied by low-income families," it discur-sively evacuates the human element, forget-ting that people transform a tenement into a home:

> Due to neglect by the previous owners over the past 15 years, the property has declined into a critical state of deteriora-tion. The building has suffered severely from a lack of any capital improvements. The mechanical systems are only par-tially operative or not performing at all. Prior attempts at building security have been feeble so that the apartments and common areas are open to abuse by any-one willing to gain access. The major apartment components are functionally obsolete and that, coupled with cosmetic neglect, greatly limits the marketability of the apartments and presents potential health and safety hazards. A few recent examples include a total lack of hot water, the collapsing of a back porch, rats and roach infestation, and small arson fires in the vestibules.

From the inside, one gets a more detailed experience of the building's deterioration, but that is complemented with a complex understanding of how people maintain human dignity within difficult structures. A casual inspection would reveal scores of housing-ordinance violations but might not capture their meaning in the day-to-day lives of the urban working class and under- and unemployed. The children complain of mice in their beds. Housewives trade stories of "roaches in my refrigerator." They make stoic jokes about this indignity, dubbing them "Eskimo roaches." They say that the roaches move more slowly but can survive in the cold, "just like Eskimos." One day I opened my refrigerator and discovered a mouse scurrying around inside. The refrigerator was decrepit, and the door did not always stay shut. There were jokes about "super-rats" so big that the traps would have to be "anchored." These and other vermin stories about aggressive mice and flying cockroaches resemble "fish stories." Through exaggeration and shared laughter they made the situation more bearable.

To limit the story of Big Red to appalling physical conditions would be misleading. Michel de Certeau in *The Practice of Everyday Life* investigates the creative and manifold "tactics" ordinary people use to resist the "strategies" of the strong—the hegemonic forces of governments, armies, institutions, and landlords. He illuminates the myriad ways vulnerable people "operate" within dominant structures and constraints, what he calls "the art of making do." To illustrate his intellectual project, he uses the metaphor of "dwelling":

> Thus a North African living in Paris or Roubaix [France] insinuates *into* the system imposed on him by the construction of a low-income housing development or of the French language the ways of "dwelling" (in a house or a language) peculiar to his native Kabylia. He superimposes them and, by that combination, creates for himself a space in which he can find *ways of using* the constraining order of the place or of the language. Without leaving the place where he has no choice but to live and which lays down its law for him, he establishes within it a degree of *plurality* and creativity. By an art of being in between, he draws unex-

pected results from his situation. (de Certeau 1984:30)

Even highly vulnerable people are not simply contained by the structures, both physical and socioeconomic, within which they find themselves. Through imagination and human energy they contest and create "dwelling spaces" inside even forbidding structures.

The tenants of Big Red exploited the marginality, illegalities, and transgressive nature of Big Red in manifold ways. They turned the owner's negligence, which bordered on the criminal, to their advantage. While they suffered, to be sure, from the owner's neglect and lack of building maintenance, they also used his irresponsibility to circumvent typical middle-class restrictions, rules, and "tastes" pertaining to residential life, such as in the use of stairwells, courtyards, and alleys. Hmong women roped off a section of the front courtyard and planted a vegetable garden during the summer of 1988. The rest of the courtyard was an intensively used social space: the center was a playground for a group I will call the Courtyard Kids, while the fence between sidewalk and courtyard served as a volleyball net for teenage girls. The back area bordering on the alley was converted into an unofficial parking lot and open-air garage for working on old cars that were always in need of repair. Some back stairwells were used to sell drugs during the summer of 1989, when dealers set up operations in two Big Red apartments.

The back area also was used for weekend *bracero* alley parties. Whereas the courtyard and front sidewalk of Big Red were informally designated spaces for the evening sociability of women and children, the back alley, at night and on weekends, was a masculine space, so marked by one section of the back wall used as a urinal. This was the time when *braceros* shared the price of a case of beer, with a sensitively enforced code that those who were unemployed or newly arrived would be graciously exempted from any pressure to contribute. For those holding jobs, it was a source of esteem to assume a greater responsibility for financing these parties. This was a time for dramatizing the hardy manliness of their jobs by complaining about sore backs, tight muscles, blisters, and cut hands. Friendship networks of exchange and sharing developed at these alley parties. It was a sign of my acceptance when I first was invited to join these parties and then allowed, after initial protest, to contribute to the cost of a case of beer. Soon afterward, the three neighbors who worked at the Easy Spuds potato-chip factory began offering me free sacks of potatoes that they brought from work. Both the tools and the labor that helped me mount the steel security gate across my back door came from contacts made at the *bracero* parties. The front stairwells and lobbies were prime sites for display of gang graffiti, and during the winter the stairwells were used as spillover rooms for social drinking, talk, and smoking. In some respects, the residents had more autonomy and scope for use of Big Red than would have been possible within a better maintained, middle-class building.

## The Art of Making Do: On Kinship, Kindness, and Caring

Tenants stretched scant resources by "doubling up," a common practice enabled by the irregular management of Big Red. In order to save money on rent, two or three families shared a single apartment. The one-bedroom apartment directly above me was home to a Hmong family with three small children, and another newlywed couple with an infant, plus the grandmother. Nine people (five adults and four children) shared this one-bedroom apartment. The one-bedroom basement apartment sheltered two Mexican sisters. One sister slept with her four children (ranging in age from seven to sixteen years old) in the single bedroom, while the other slept with her three small children in the living room. The Assyrian family of twelve lived in a three-bedroom apartment. A Mexican family with six children shared a one-bedroom apartment. These "doubling up" arrangements probably would not be permitted in middle-class-managed buildings.

Perhaps the most vivid example of this practice is the large heteroglot household that lived above me during the summer of

1989. Grace, an Appalachian mother of six children with a Puerto Rican husband, lived with Angel, her Puerto Rican "business" partner, who brought along his girlfriend, his younger brother just released from prison, the brother's girlfriend, and his African-American friend (who before the summer was over went to prison), as well as a single pregnant mother and her best girlfriend—fifteen people in one three-bedroom apartment. The household was anchored by Grace's Public Aid check and Angel's street hustling activities. Two years earlier, Grace had been homeless, living on the streets with her six children; the girls had panhandled and the boys had stolen food and cigarettes from stores. She had a network with street people, and Angel was plugged into the prison culture, so three to five extra people would "crash" at the apartment at any given time. This household was the most multicultural one in Big Red, embracing whites and African Americans who cohabited with several Latinos and one Filipino. The illicit lifestyle of street hustling and drugs brought together these several ethnic groups in strikingly intimate ways. Their unruly household had many problems, but racism and prejudice never surfaced.

The gathering together of extended families and the creation of "fictive kin" (Rapp 1987:232) are primary tactics for "making do" within Big Red. A twelve-year-old Assyrian Courtyard Kid articulated this conventional wisdom: "It's good to have friends and relatives nearby so you can borrow money when you need it." Indeed, the culture of Big Red was characterized by an intimacy of interactions across apartments, expressing in part the kinship networks that laced together these households. When I surveyed the apartments at the end of my first year of residence, I discovered that every household but two (one of those being mine) was tied by kinship to at least one other apartment in Big Red. The young Mexican family with three small children directly below me in A1R, for example, had strong ties to the B stairwell. The husband's widowed mother lived in B1L, along with his sister, thirty-year-old single brother, and three cousins. His older brother lived across the hall from the mother in B1R, with his five children. Their cousins lived in B3R. Further, the three brothers and half-brothers all worked at the same place: the Easy Spuds potato-chip factory in Evanston. The families all ran back and forth from one another's back porches. Raul in A1R had three children, Salvatore in B1R had five, and two or three children always stayed with the single adults and grand-mother in B1L, so there were many cousins to play with, circulate outgrown clothing among, share transportation, and collec-tively receive parenting from multiple care-givers. The grandmother in B1R had high blood pressure (one of the first things I was told when introduced) and was always sur-rounded by caring relatives. Maria, the daughter-in-law from A1R, spent so much time with her frail mother-in-law in B1L that it took me some time before I figured out in which apartment Maria actually lived.

The functional importance of this propin-quity with immediate relatives became clear when Maria told me about her husband Raul's being laid off from work for seven months. One can get through such a crunch with immediate family close by. This sup-portive net of family is extended by several friendships with other Latino families in Big Red, as well as more friends and family in or near Albany Park. A more financially suc-cessful older brother who is a delivery-truck driver regularly visited from near Hoffman Estates. He had purchased a shiny new Ford truck with a camper cover that was shared with the Big Red kin for shopping trips.

Aurelio (Mexican), who lived across the hall from me in A2L, had a sister with a large family who lived in B2R. Over the summer, two of his younger brothers arrived from Mexico without papers, and they lived with his sister. Aurelio had eight sisters and seven brothers; all but the youngest lived in or near Albany Park. Three brothers and their fami-lies lived on Whipple Street around the cor-ner; they and their children visited back and forth all the time. They pooled resources for major family celebrations. For example, Alfredo, Aurelio's baby boy, was baptized with four other cousins; a huge party and feast in the church basement followed for all the extended family and friends. All the

working brothers and sisters co-financed the *quinceanera* debutante celebration for Aurelio's niece; Aurelio bought the flowers. Thanksgiving 1989 was celebrated jointly with six turkeys. My first week in Big Red I could not find anyone with the key to get my mailbox unlocked. Gabriel, one of Aurelio's brothers from Whipple, passed by, pulled out a knife from his pocket, and forced it open for me. That incident represented the quality of life in Big Red, the back-and-forth visiting between households and the spontaneous offering of assistance.

Aurelio's family was also tied strongly to the financially strapped family (two sisters rearing their seven children together with-out husbands) in the basement of B. I think they were cousins, or maybe just good friends, but everyone in A2L looked out for the extended family in the basement because there was no father. The older sister did not speak English.

Alberto, the kid from C2R, practically lived with Aurelio. At first he told me that they were cousins, then later that they really were not blood cousins, but like adopted family because they had lived close together for so long. They had been at Whipple to-gether and then had both moved to Big Red. The same is true for Raul and Hilda, directly below me, and their relatives in B stairwell: they had come from Whipple along with Aurelio. The president of the Whipple block club, a white woman, remembered Aurelio and his relatives; she had had an altercation with them that led to a court hearing and the breaking of all the windows on two sides of her house. She described the entire group negatively as "clannish."

Another example of a kin network in Big Red was the Assyrian family with ten chil-dren in D1R. They were on Public Aid with monthly rent of $450. Unable to afford a tele-phone or transportation, they were among the most needy, even by Big Red standards. In this case it was the wife who articulated the kinship lines. Her sister and husband lived two floors above them in D3R. The sis-ter drove them to church, which was the hub of their social and economic sustenance (they obtained free meals there and clothes for the kids). The mother lived with the sister on the third floor, but every time I visited the family in D1R, the mother was there helping with caring and cooking for the ten kids, the oldest of whom was sixteen. The wife's brother lived just around the corner on the Gunnison side, in E1R. The brother's apartment was one of the more nicely furnished in Big Red. The D1R family depended on the brother for telephone use. The Assyrian family directly across the hall from them were cousins. The first time I was invited to this family's home for Sunday dinner, the children had picked leaves from trees in River Park; the mother stuffed the leaves with rice and served them with yogurt made from the powdered milk that is distributed once a month at the Albany Park Community Center.

The two ethnic Chinese families from Cambodia were intimately connected. The wife in E1L was the eldest daughter of the family in C1R, and both families helped manage the sewing shop in the basement.

The Hmong are noted for their kinship solidarity. Because they lived on the top floors, by and large, they could leave their doors open. Related families faced one another and shared back and forth, one apartment becoming an extension of the other. The kids ran from one apartment to the other, ate together, and blurred the household boundaries. The Hmong in the United States have not assimilated to the model of the nuclear family. My observations of the Latino and Assyrian families suggest the same, but the extended-family pattern was strongest among the Hmong. The Hmong neighbors directly above me had an apartment the same size as mine, one bedroom. It housed five adults—two brothers, their wives, and a grandmother—as well as the four small children of the older brother (the oldest child is eight) and the baby of the younger brother. They got along handsomely in this one-bedroom apartment. The kids skipped down to my apartment frequently for cookies. They were extremely happy children, polite and very well-behaved.

This same Hmong family in A3R, the Yangs, demonstrated remarkably the importance of having kinfolk nearby. In December, when their Hmong neighbors across the hall moved to an apartment just across the street because they had suffered for a month with a waterless toilet, the Yangs could not bear to be alone on the top floor of our stairwell. Within two weeks they moved just across the courtyard to the D3L apartment in order to be close to their cousins living one floor below them in D2L. The mother explained that they had moved because she needed kin nearby to help with child care. This was the family's third move within Big Red in order to achieve close communal ties with relatives. Their understanding of "closeness" differed from that of white established residents. First, the Yangs' departing friends from A3L had only moved across the street, still in the 4800 block of Albany, within sight and shouting distance. Further, their cousins in D2L were in the same building, just across the courtyard. The Yangs, however, wanted a degree of intimacy that required side-by-side proximity to relatives or friends.

Even families from different ethnic groups expressed their friendship in "the idiom of kinship" (Stack 1974). The Mexican family in C2R told me that their new downstairs neighbors (Appalachian) in C1R were their "cousins." They claimed knowledge of a family tree that traced the Appalachians' family roots back to Spain, where the connection was made with the Mexicans' forebears. When I pressed the Mexican teenager who told me this, he did not know the specifics. But that did not seem to matter; he was delighted to have "relatives" living directly below him. He informed me that his neighbors—he calls them "hillbillies"—had told his family that they were also related to me, tracing their Irish side to my Scots background.

This interconnectedness with intimate others is highly functional for the people of Big Red. Carol Stack notes: "The poor adopt a variety of tactics in order to survive. They immerse themselves in a domestic circle of kinfolk who will help them. . . . Friends may be incorporated into one's domestic circle" (1974:29). Notwithstanding the unpleasant physical conditions, Big Red was an extraordinarily pleasant and human place to live because of the densely interlaced kin and friendship networks. My neighbors were not self-sufficient; therefore, they did not privilege self-reliance in the same way that the white middle class does. Sometimes they had difficulty making it from one paycheck to the next. They worked at connecting themselves to one another with reciprocal ties of gift-giving and the exchange of goods and services, as well as the less tangible but extremely important mutual offerings of respect and esteem. What Jane Addams observed almost a century ago still applies to Big Red: "I became permanently impressed with the kindness of the poor to each other; the woman who lives upstairs will willingly share her breakfast with the family below because she knows they 'are hard up'; the man who boarded with them last winter will give a month's rent because he knows the father of the family is out of work" (Addams 1910:123–24).

This ethic of care and concern for one another cuts across ethnic groups. The older sister of the Cambodian-Chinese family in C1R cut the hair of Latino neighbors, and the Latino youths in turn "looked out for" her family. I was amazed when the sixteen-year-old Mexican from the basement apartment walked through the courtyard on her way to the high school prom. She was beautifully dressed, with all the accessories. I knew that this household of nine sharing a one-bedroom apartment did not have the resources to finance such an outfit. I learned later that the dress had been borrowed from an aunt, the shoes from a neighbor, the purse from a cousin, and the hair-bow from another neighbor, and that her hair had been styled by the Cambodian neighbor.

This ethos of solidarity was expressed in the common greeting—used by Latino, Hmong, Assyrian—"Where are you going?" "Where have you been?" "I haven't seen you for a while." They expected answers and explanations. They were interested in one another's business. It was from the Mexicans that I learned the Hmong paid $20 a month for their garden plots in the vacant lot down the street. An Assyrian man I had not yet met knocked on my door one day and asked me whether I could help him patent an invention. He explained, "I look through your window and see all the books and thought you must have a book on this."

Taking my cue from neighbors, I started a back-porch "garden" in June 1988. Within the first week of setting out the pots, I had gifts of seeds and cuttings from four of my immediate neighbors.

One of the poignant examples of interethnic sharing deserves a full transcription. Ching, a small eight-year-old Hmong boy from E3R, approached me one day in the courtyard:

**Ching:** Mr. Dwight, do you know Julio [twenty-year-old Mexican resident of Big Red]?

**DC:** Yes.

**Ching:** [obviously troubled] Is he gang? [In order not to violate street ethics, I deflected Ching's question.]

**DC:** Why are you worried about that, Ching?

**Ching:** [staring at ground, voice sad] Because he's my friend.

**DC:** He's my friend too. How is he your friend, Ching?

**Ching:** Because he's nice to me. He always gives me lots of toys, the toys he used to play with when he was a kid.

**DC:** Why do you think he's in a gang?

**Ching:** Because people say he's gang.

As the example of Ching makes clear, people value the intangibles of friendship and caring as much as the tangibles of money, food, or toys that change hands. That is not to depreciate the real need for material support. Julio's hand-me-down toys are the only ones Ching has. Ching's family moved into Big Red because they had lost their savings on a house they bought. The house had been burglarized twice, and they had lost everything. The father told me that they had moved into Big Red to recoup, to start over again.

The Big Red ethos of familiarity and reciprocity continues, for even though many of us have been displaced from the building, we still live in the area. In early July 1990, two teenagers (Assyrian and Mexican) hailed me as I carried a bag of groceries down one of the streets of Little Beirut. Consistent with local custom, they examined what was in my bag and said, "Thanks, Dwight," as they reached for two yogurts. There was no need to ask for the food. The nature and history of our relationship enabled them to assume this familiarity. Two days later, as they were riding around the neighborhood, they spotted me again and pulled the car over; the Assyrian fellow leaned out the window and offered me some of his food: "Hey Dwight, you want some of this shake?" These two incidents capture the quality of life in the Big Red area. At a micro-level, every day is filled with a host of significant kindnesses and richly nuanced reciprocities. To use a term from the streets, people are "tight" in Little Beirut (meaning tightly connected, not "tight" with their money). These micro-level courtesies provide a buffer against the macro-structures of exclusion and oppression. They enable people to experience dignity and joy in structures like Big Red, refashioning them into "dwelling places."

The fine-grained texture of the daily acknowledgments and courtesies that characterize life in Big Red provides a counterpoint to the blunter treatment the residents sometimes receive when they enter the system controlled by established residents and bureaucracies. Teenagers expelled from school have asked me to accompany their mothers to the principal's office for reinstatement because when the mother went alone, as one student put it, "they did not see her." In a communication system that required a different style of assertiveness, she was invisible. When I accompanied Mexican and Guatemalan mothers to school offices or police stations, all the attention and eye contact would be directed toward me, the white male. One time, after the high school principal had been persuaded to give one of my young neighbors a second chance, the mother gratefully extended her hand to thank him. But the principal reached right past her to shake my hand. Quite literally, he did not see her. A short, dark-complexioned Mexican woman, she had three factors that contributed to her invisibility: race, gender, and class.

Sometimes the erasure is not so subtle. While standing in line at the Perry Drugstore checkout line, one of my Assyrian neighbors gave me an updated report on her finger, which had been bitten by a rat as she slept in Big Red. Although the bandage had been removed, the finger still looked as if it had been slammed in a car door. The cashier, a white woman in her late fifties, treated my neighbors very curtly at the checkout. Before the Assyrian woman was out of earshot, and as the cashier was ringing up my purchases, she began talking to the neighboring cashier, also an older white woman. Here is what the two of them said, in full hearing of the Assyrian woman, her husband, her granddaughter, and me:

**Cashier 1**: Can you believe it? If my father were alive to see what's happened to the neighborhood!

**Cashier 2**: I know. Don't get upset.

**Cashier 1**: I hate getting upset first thing in the morning.

**Cashier 2**: They're not worth it.

**Cashier 1**: I know I shouldn't let them upset me.

**Cashier 2**: They're not worth it. They're trash.

## Tactics of Resistance

The residents of Big Red coped with their oppressive circumstances typically through circumventions, survival tactics, and seizing opportunities. They did not have the power and clout to confront the system head-on. They survived via connections, evasions, street-smart maneuvers, making end-runs around authority. De Certeau describes the "tactical" thinking of people everywhere who must find space for themselves within oppressive structures:

The space of a tactic is the space of the other. Thus it must play on and with a terrain imposed on it and organized by the law of a foreign power. . . . It does not, therefore, have the options of planning general strategy and viewing the adversary as a whole within a distinct, visible, and objectifiable space. . . . It must vigilantly make use of the cracks that particular conjunctions open in the surveillance of the proprietary powers. It poaches in them. It creates surprises in them. It can be where it is least expected. It is a guileful ruse. (1984:37)

The Big Red tenants turned the "absenteeism" of the landlord to their advantage to enact spatial practices and temporal rhythms that would not have been tolerated in well-managed buildings. They had their tactics for dealing with the landlord. Mrs. Gutierrez from time to time would unleash a blistering tongue-lashing on him. She always announced to neighbors, days in advance, that she was going to "really shout at him this time." She would gather more complaints from the neighbors, gradually building up steam for one of her anticipated confrontations, and then, at the opportune moment, she would "really let him have it." Though none could match the explosive force of Mrs. Gutierrez, I overheard many women as they stood on back porches and denounced him.

Perhaps the best example of tactical resistance unfolded when the city shut off the water supply to Big Red because the landlord was $26,000 in arrears for payment. This action was taken at the end of June 1988, during a summer in which Chicago broke its previous record for days in which the temperature rose above 100 degrees Fahrenheit. During the three days of the water shutoff, temperatures soared to 105 degrees.

Attempts to work within the system were ineffectual. I contacted NRC, the powerful community organization, but it could do nothing to remedy the immediate crisis. I personally called several agencies and officials in the city, including the Water Department. It is legal, within the City of Chicago, to shut off [the] water supply for a large building as a method of collecting debt payments. The only result my flurry of telephone calls produced was that a city inspector did visit Big Red during the time we were without water, wrote a report, sympathized with us, then drove away. We never heard from him again. If we had depended on his official intervention, Big Red would still be without water. What all the city bureaucrats told us was that they did not have the authority to turn the water back on until the debt was cleared, or at least a partial payment was deposited. The owner, of course, was unaffected by the city's action. Never easy to reach, insulated in his lakefront condominium, he did not even know that the water had been shut off.

By the third day without water, the situation was intolerable. The gross inconvenience, the outrage of having no water for drink, bathing, or flushing the toilet, intensified by the 105-degree heat, incited radical action. It is hard to say whose idea the final solution was, because I think we came to it collectively. I remember that we were all standing in the courtyard, quite bedraggled and exhausted. Mrs. Yang, the Hmong mother from C3L, kept insisting, "We have to do something!" Spontaneously, we decided to take action into our own hands, dig down to the water main, and turn the water back on ourselves. This action was not only unauthorized, it was illegal.

This plan required several steps of coordinated action across lines of ethnicity, gender, and age. The hue and cry raised during the first day of the water shutoff drew in the white Democratic precinct captain, who lived one block north of Big Red. He became involved in the day-to-day drama of the water crisis as it unfolded. He donated his tools and garage workshop for the Hmong smiths to fashion a custom wrench to turn on the water valve. Mexican, Hmong, and Assyrian residents of Big Red all took turns with the digging. This activity attracted several "sidewalk supervisors," many of whom were homeowners from across the street, others just passersby, including African Americans and whites. The diggers reached the water main only to find the valve sheathed in an eighteen-inch sleeve filled with dirt. A Puerto Rican woman volunteered her vacuum-cleaner hose, and extension cords were plugged into the nearest apartment outlet, which happened to be Assyrian. The Hmong ran back and forth with the white precinct captain to fashion the wrench that would turn the valve. This took several attempts. Once they got it to fit, the next problem to be solved was determining what manipulation turned the water on. A full turn? Half turn? To the right or left? The water company does not make it easy for unauthorized people to take control of their water supply. An elderly Assyrian woman was stationed in the window to check her sink and report the results of each trial turn: "Nothing yet—yes, a trickle, do that again—no, nothing—O.K., that's it."

It was close to midnight by the time the water flowed. Everyone was exhilarated. Several of the men went to the Mexican *bracero* bar down the street on Lawrence to celebrate. No one bought his own beer. Everyone crossed over and spent his money buying someone else's beer, although in the end there was an equal distribution of monies. There was much camaraderie, backslapping, handshaking, and clicking of bottles.

The audience of this drama was enlarged by a front-page story in the *Chicago Tribune*, "In Crisis, Immigrants Learn Who Their True Friends Are." Several follow-up stories and editorials appeared in the Lerner neighborhood newspapers, all supporting the pluck of the Big Red residents and condemning the conditions that allowed a building full of vulnerable people to go for a prolonged time without water during the worst of Chicago's summer heat wave. Spokespersons for the Water Department went on record to say that no legal action would be taken against the Big Red residents who circumvented the law to regain control of their water supply.

This crisis tightened the community. In a crisis, boundaries are suspended or become porous. The sixth month into the project, I had made headway in meeting my Big Red neighbors, but most of the meaningful interaction had been with neighbors sharing my stairwell. By the time the water was turned back on, I had been inside thirty-five of the thirty-seven apartments. The shared hardship of going without water during one of Chicago's most notorious heat waves threw Big Red into a "communitas of crisis," a heightened sense of "we-feeling" (Turner 1977:154). It was easy to approach anybody sharing that experience. Residents who had not previously met were greeting one another with warm familiarity by the end of the second day. This crisis transformed my position in the building from semi-outsider to an informal advocate of sorts. It accelerated trust and rapport with neighbors by a great leap.

\*\*\*

On August 1, 1989, the president of Oakwood Development Company, who was also president of the Albany Park Landlords' Association, took control of Big Red. The absentee owner had failed to make his mortgage payments, and the building was being cited in criminal housing court because of building-code violations and physical deterioration due to his negligence. Notices had gone up warning of another water shutoff because of the owner's failure to pay the water bill. The court appointed Superior Bank as receiver. With NRC urging, the bank appointed Oakwood Development Company as manager of Big Red. Empowered by the state and allied with community organizations, an Oakwood Development crew used sledgehammers to break into the basement of Big Red to take charge of the utility meters and other facilities.

Almost immediately after the takeover, Oakwood and staff interviewed various residents and quickly pinpointed two drug-dealing apartments, the busiest one being the apartment above me that Bao Xiong and her family had formerly occupied. Oakwood used the crisis of drug trafficking as an excuse to evacuate the entire stairwell. With hindsight, I believe the drug dealers, who were real, became the lever Oakwood deployed to start emptying Big Red as quickly as possible.

When Oakwood took control in August, Big Red was fully occupied and still had a vital building culture and ethos of solidarity. Within four months, half of the Big Red households were displaced. One year later, thirty-one of the thirty-seven apartments were vacant. Empty and boarded up, Big Red looms like a ghost building. The wrenching violence of this intervention was muted in the euphemisms that Oakwood and NRC used to describe their actions:

"turning the building around," "turning the neighborhood around."

Oakwood, a multimillion-dollar company that specializes in managing low-income rental properties, works closely with NRC. The NRC director of housing development lives in an Oakwood building. Oakwood and NRC estimate that it will require a $1.5-million loan to purchase and rehabilitate Big Red. NRC Housing Development is working on getting a low-interest loan package through Chicago Equity Fund[3] and Community Investment Incorporation. The NRC Housing Development director explained the plans for Big Red: "We want to make it a community project—bring together Oakwood experience and profitmaking know-how with NRC philosophy and provide quality rehab for poor people. Make it a good solid community, *but integrated with the rest of the community*" (emphasis mine). The partnership of Oakwood's "profit-making know-how with NRC philosophy," united against the market individualism of "slumlords" as much as the transgressive tenants, is a classic example of the complex way investment property mirrors "the internal tensions within the capitalist order" and anchors a coalition between private investment and the public sector in advanced capitalist societies (Harvey 1985:61). The absentee landlord of Big Red was displaced along with the residents: his locks were smashed with Oakwood sledgehammers on the day of takeover. The competitive tensions and profit-making dictates of capitalism are softened, elided, and simultaneously enabled by the moral rhetoric (NRC's "philosophy") of community organizations concerned with the public good. Community organizations like NRC produce strategic definitions of "the public good," "quality of life," and "good solid community" that are advantageous to capital development.

The NRC phrase "but integrated with the rest of the community" codes the middle-class anxiety about Big Red. Big Red transgressed the system by remaining outside it. With an unresponsive absentee landlord and an array of mostly new-immigrant working-class tenants, Big Red eluded middle-class strategies of containment and control. The plurality, fluidity, and openness that made Big Red accessible and accommodating to new-immigrant and working-class tenants were among the very qualities that the middle class finds forbidding. Situated in the center of Little Beirut, Big Red focused and displayed middle-class fears and ambivalences about difference, density, deterioration, and demographic change.

## Endnotes

1. The Northwestern colleagues with whom I worked on the Ford Foundation Changing Relations Project were Paul Fiesema, Jane Mansbridge, and Al Hunter, assisted by graduate students Mary Erdmans, Jeremy Hein, Yvonne Newsome, and Yung-Sun Park. I wish to acknowledge support from the Ford Foundation, which funded the Changing Relations project through the Research Foundation of the State University of New York, Grant 240-1117. The Center for Urban Affairs and Policy Research (CUAPR) at Northwestern University facilitated the work of the Chicago team of the Changing Relations project. I thank the staff of CUAPR for their expertise and cheerful support. I am particularly grateful to my colleague Jane Mansbridge, who carefully read earlier drafts of this chapter and offered many helpful criticisms and suggestions.

2. The conditions and people of Big Red can be seen in segments of two documentaries: *America Becoming*, produced by Dai-Sil Kim-Gibson for the Ford Foundation, and *The Heart Broken in Half*, produced and directed by Taggart Siegel and Dwight Conquergood.

3. Chicago Equity Fund is a not-for-profit loan company for low-income housing funded by a group of Chicago millionaires, who get a special tax break in exchange for the entailment that money go toward housing that will be designated low-income for fifteen years.

## References

Addams, Jane. 1960 [1910]. *Twenty Years at Hull-House*. New York: Penguin.

De Certeau, Michel. 1984. *The Practice of Everyday Life*. Translated by Steven Rendall. Berkeley: University of California Press.

Harvey, David. 1985. *Consciousness and the Urban Experience: Studies in the History and Theory of Capitalist Urbanization*. Baltimore: Johns Hopkins University Press.

Rapp, Rayna. 1987. "Urban Kinship in Contemporary America: Families, Classes, and Ideology." In *Cities of the United States: Studies in Urban Anthropology*, edited by Leith Mullings. New York: Columbia University Press.

Stack, Carol B. 1974. *All Our Kin: Strategies for Survival in a Black Community*. New York: Harper and Row.

Turner, Victor. 1977 [1969]. *The Ritual Process: Structure and Anti-structure*. Ithaca, NY: Cornell University Press.

## Review

1. What were the patterns Conquergood found that residents utilized while they were trying to "make do"?

2. How did the crisis of having their water shut off affect the residents of Big Red?

3. What were the factors in the "middle-class anxiety" that led to the demise of Big Red?

## Application

Extended familial ties are of major importance to some ethnic groups. Divide your class into sections. Assign each group a different ethnic/immigrant group that came to the United States earlier in the country's history. Using the library to locate historical sources, try to discover the nature of the experience of each ethnic group. Were norms of cooperation and "making do" apparent for these other groups? How important was the extended family in their experiences?

## Related Web Sites

1. *http://www.mcauley.org/health%20and%20housing%20w%20sr%20eduts%20final.pdf*. A review of literature investigating the relationship between housing quality and health.

2. *http://www.iss.co.za/Pubs/Monographs/No78/Chap5.html*. Report of tenement life in South Africa, useful for comparison purposes.

# 43

# Plain Living

## Deciding to Move Down

*Trudy Bush*

*Almost every generation in the United States has expected to do better than its predecessor. It has been assumed that in the "land of opportunity" everyone would—and would want to—attain a higher position on the occupational ladder than their parents. Thus, not to move up has been a cause for embarrassment for many Americans. Worse yet, those who have experienced* **downward mobility** *often have found the experience extremely traumatic. Strained and broken marriages, tension in the family, and personal emotional problems have been associated with people who struggle with downward mobility.*

*Ironically, during the 1990s, a period of dramatic economic growth and opportunity for upward mobility, some Americans began to question the value of moving up. In particular, they questioned the personal and relational costs of reaching and maintaining the lifestyle to which most people were aspiring. Books, videos, and seminars told Americans how they could simplify their lives. Simplicity Circles emerged—small groups of four to eight people who met regularly to explore ways to simplify their lives. Life simplification does not mean moving down to the poverty level; at the same time, it is a firm rejection of the notion of attaining the highest standard of living you can. Those who participate in the voluntary simplicity movement try to cut back on demands for their time and energy and to devote themselves to matters they deem essential—family, friends, personal passions, and so forth.*

*In this selection, Trudy Bush gives some background to the quest for life simplification and relates the stories of a number of Americans who have opted for it. Some of the people she discusses are motivated to simplify their*

*lives for religious reasons. But the motivations vary among those who have chosen to simplify. In many cases, it is simply a matter of weariness with the "rat race" and a yearning for less tension and more fulfillment in life.*

"The Jones' are surrendering!" a TV news reporter proclaims. "The family with whom we've tried to keep up is throwing in the towel!" The camera pans to four desperate looking people standing in front of a large house. "We've had it," the wife says. "We're exhausted. We never see each other. And we have so much debt that we can't keep up anymore. It's just not worth it."

So begins Beyond Affluenza, a recent public television special made in Seattle. The one-hour program and its prequel, Affluenza, document the current expression of an ideal that recurs throughout American history—simplicity. The Puritans and Quakers emigrated here to live out an austere and simple ethic. The founding fathers believed that civic virtue is accompanied by material restraint. In the 1840s, Henry Thoreau sought to live deliberately at Walden Pond, and Ralph Waldo Emerson and Bronson Alcott experimented in simple rural living. That experiment was repeated in the back-to-nature communes of the 1960s and '70s, which were inspired in part by people like Scott and Helen Nearing, who had pioneered the simple life of rural homesteading decades earlier.

Many people today are again willing to trade relentless consumption for a more intellectually and spiritually rich life. For most of these people, the pursuit of simplicity means gaining control of their money and their time so that both can be used more intentionally. By downsizing their expectations of material affluence, people are able to discover and invest in what really matters to them, whether that is family, relationships, community involvement, environmental responsibility or a new, more satisfying kind of work.

Who is pursuing the simple life? Among those trying to live more deliberately is a young man who leaves a lucrative position at Microsoft in order to do what he has always wanted—be an actor and help others by volunteering, especially as a Big Brother. A family opts to live on less money after the husband refuses to accept a job transfer that would have him designing weapons and the wife decides she wants to stay at home with their children; to act on these values, the family renovates an old house, relies on bicycles instead of a car, and grows some of its own food. A 50-year-old corporate attorney retires from his practice in order to run an environmental organization; he and his wife recycle and compost so effectively that they fill only one garbage can a month. And a couple who keeps a large home in the suburbs decides to rent out part of it to graduate students from other countries. The rental income frees them to devote fewer hours to paid employment, and they are enriched by their friendship with their tenants.

The idea of living more simply has spawned hundreds of books, videos and seminars. While some of the recent books can be classified with pseudotherapeutic self-help literature, many are both useful and philosophically serious.

What is making this ideal so appealing to people in a time of such conspicuous affluence? The search for a simpler life is usually a response to a crisis like war or economic depression, according to historian David Shi, author of *The Simple Life*. But Shi thinks there is a "psychological malaise" at work in our culture. "We've never before had such high levels of anxiety and depression among affluent people. Though people are materially well off, they're discovering that their lives seem hollow and meaningless. They're searching for meaning and, in many cases, they're also looking for alternatives to the frenetic pace of their lives."

Shi, president of Furman University, points out that during the '90s the work week actually increased for the first time in more than a century. "Even our leisure time has become scheduled, has lost its spontaneity. And among all the hoopla about our prosperity is the disturbing fact that the three most commonly prescribed drugs are an ulcer medication, an antidepressant and a pain reliever. Underneath the surface of success and material splendor, many Americans are struggling to cope."

If the voluntary simplicity movement has a geographical center, it is the Pacific Northwest, particularly Seattle. That's the home of three of the most dedicated practitioners and eloquent advocates of the simple life— Vicki Robin, Cecile Andrews and Janet Luhrs. Seattle is also the home of Earth Ministry, "a Christian, ecumenical, environmental, nonprofit organization" which has just published *Simpler Living, Compassionate Life: A Christian Perspective*, an anthology of essays and a curriculum intended to be used by churches. The people in Seattle are, Shi says, developing an infrastructure that the simplicity movement has seldom had.

On the day I visited Robin at her home near the university, the scene was bustling with people who were carrying around furniture and setting up a picnic table in the garden. "A team is here working on something called the 'ecological footprint,'" Robin explained. The ecological footprint is a concept developed by Mathis Wackernagel of the University of British Columbia to measure humans' impact on the environment. "He worked out a way to translate objects into the number of acres it would take to produce the material for them," Robin said. "This morning the team weighed the futon on which you're sitting to see how many pounds of cotton it contains. They're now working on a bedroom, and they'll do the kitchen next."

By translating everything into acres, Wackernagel (who, with William Rees, published *Our Ecological Footprint: Reducing Human Impact on the Earth* in 1995) has measured the ecological footprints of people in different countries. The average American has a more than ten-square-acre footprint, while the global average is under three. "If you divide all the arable land on the planet by the world's population, you find that we're already overpopulated and overconsuming. We're going into debt globally," Robin says.

The ecological footprint project meshes nicely with Robin's own work—to provide a method for mastering personal finances, as the first step in finding new road maps for living. With the late Joe Dominguez, she coauthored *Your Money or Your Life,* one of the bibles of the voluntary simplicity movement. Still selling briskly, the book (first published in 1992) spent more than a year on *Business Week's* best-seller list. It details nine rigorous steps for gaining financial independence.

Robin, a thoughtful, reserved woman in her 50s, lives frugally, co-owning her house with three other women, driving a well-maintained old car, and buying many of her clothes in thrift stores. She plows the income from her book into the charitable foundation she established with Dominguez. The New Road Map Foundation, staffed by volunteers, provides grants to other nonprofit organizations. "One of my favorites is the Northwest Earth Institute," Robin says. "It was created by a man who had been a partner in a major law firm in Portland, Oregon. He and his wife were concerned about environmental degradation and set out to teach people the basic principles of living in a way that cares for the earth. They and their small staff developed four courses that people take at their workplace during their lunch hours. More than 250 businesses have offered these study groups in ecology and voluntary simplicity."

When I asked her if environmental concerns were the main impetus for her work, she said, "That's a very strong motivator for me—that we're taking God's creation and treating it as though it were ours to use up. But I've always had many layers of passion motivating my decision to live more simply. To me, this movement is spiritual, ecological, social and cultural. Though many of the people I know are deeply engaged in a spiritual quest of one kind or another, it's getting less and less fashionable for Americans to frame their lives around their values and beliefs.

"We need to be more deeply rooted in our values, and more devoted to loving and caring for one another. We need to live in a way that fosters community and that doesn't destroy other cultures. We're losing cultures—that whole web of intelligence that tells us how to survive and live well in a particular environment. It's not just the environmental wall that we'll soon hit; there are many walls.

We're relinquishing species after species, habitat after habitat, social structure after social structure. We have no idea how essential the things we're destroying may be to our own well-being."

These crises give the present interest in simplicity a new urgency, Robin believes. She cites studies that indicate a large cohort of Americans hold values inconsistent with those of the dominant culture, even though many of them are still living as part of that culture. She wonders if the voluntary simplicity movement is like "a change in the geography of the ocean floor that's creating a swell on the surface but won't impact the shore. Or are we seeing such an intense and rapid shift in people's thinking that, like a huge wave hitting the shore, it will really bring about changes?"

Robin wonders if there might be some way to speed up the process, to increase people's awareness of their feelings of discomfort and dissonance so that they become willing to endorse social policies—consumption and energy taxes, for instance—that will change the direction of our culture. Given what we're up against, she asks, "Can we afford to be evolutionary, or do we need to be revolutionary? What form would such a revolution take? And how big is the constituency that would back major changes in our public policies? How much of their lives are people willing to put on the line for their ideals?" She has no answers for these questions, but, she says, "I keep my nose pressed against them."

Cecile Andrews, author of the widely used book *The Circle of Simplicity,* radiates energy and enthusiasm for her ideas and for her region. "People really care about the environment here. The Pacific Northwest is a kind of frontier. Lots of people move here seeking a better life."

As the home of Microsoft, Seattle also is full of people familiar with high-tech industry and the hi-tech lifestyle. But, says Andrews, "People still remember when their lives were more relaxed. Simplicity is kind of a double response—both to the environmental crisis and to the feeling that life has become chaotic and out of control. We're all working so hard that we've almost lost the ability to enjoy ourselves. The high point of people's lives seems to be crossing something off of their to-do list. That's as good as it gets!"

For Andrews, the simple life is the examined life. In its present manifestation, voluntary simplicity is a middle-class movement of well-educated people "who like to think and read, who look thoughtfully at every aspect of their lives and consider the consequences of their decisions." It doesn't necessarily entail a log cabin or pinched frugality. "I hate people to think of simplicity as only frugality," Andrews said. "Rather than frugality, I prefer the term 'morally responsible consumerism.' Paring back is part of simplicity, but an even bigger part is dealing with the inner emptiness that makes people so obsessed with consumerism—the lack of spiritual concerns, of community, of a sense of meaning. Simplicity means being inwardly rich, being joyful, and feeling a sense of connectedness."

Like Robin, Andrews believes that our economy has become so environmentally destructive that we will eventually be forced to change our way of life. But she doesn't see that change coming soon. Though voluntary simplicity is growing, so is consumerism. At this point, the movement is still about individual, not social, change. But eventually the individual movement will affect corporate structures and public policy. Simplicity, she says, is a Trojan horse. "We look so benign that nobody's afraid of us. Then we pop out and change society."

Andrews's favored tool for helping people to examine their lives and to resist consumer culture is the study circle. A former community college administrator, she wants to find a noncompetitive way to bring people together and help them think for themselves. "Simplicity circles are built around people's personal stories," she explained. These small groups usually meet in people's homes once a week for a ten-week period, discussing such topics as how to change consumption habits, build community and transform work.

"During the session on community, we begin by talking about times during our lives when each of us has experienced community. There's no leader—we just go around the circle, and people tell wonderful stories. After we've examined what's happened in our own lives, we go on to critique society. The third step is to brainstorm ways in which we can take action. We plan small, specific things each of us will do that week. If people focus only on what they can do to change the larger society, they begin to feel helpless. But each of us can do something in our own neighborhood, our own community. The following week we report back and compare our experiences. I wanted these study circles to be something people could do without needing training, without relying on experts, without paying any dues. It's something a group can do on its own." Simplicity circles are now meeting throughout the English-speaking world, she said.

Janet Luhrs is a single mother raising an 11-year-old son and a 13-year-old daughter. She said her parents taught her to live below her means and to choose her work according to what she loved to do. Luhrs spent her 20s living frugally so that she could devote herself to writing.

"Then, when I was 30, I thought I was missing out on something, and I went to law school. That's when my life became complicated. I graduated, got my first credit cards and bought expensive, corporate kinds of clothes. We had our first child and decided we would hire a nanny to raise her, while I went out to work as a lawyer. But that lasted only a few weeks, before I asked myself, 'Why am I doing this?' I fired the nanny, stayed home and had another child."

Luhrs's concerns became focused when she took a class on simplicity taught by Andrews. "It was like finding home," she says. Seven years ago she began publishing a quarterly newsletter, *Simple Living: The Journal of Voluntary Simplicity*. "I really started it to teach myself," she explains. "I had known how to live simply as a single woman in my 20s. But I didn't know how to do it, with kids and a mortgage and credit cards."

Four years later, Bantam Doubleday Dell asked her to do a book on simplicity. *The Simple Living Guide: A Sourcebook for Less Stressful, More Joyful Living* (1997) is an encyclopedia of information about everything from the pleasures of simple dating and romance to creative real-estate financing.

Luhrs sees herself as the practical generalist of the simplicity movement, the person who tells people how to do it. All three women think of their work as interrelated and complementary. "Vicki began by focusing more on people's concerns about money, while I was interested in time," Andrews noted. "Janet attracted a lot of people who were fascinated with the ingenuity part—50 ways to have a good time without spending money, or isn't it fun to plant your own garden and cook your own food. My group is probably more the cafe society, who like to talk about the philosophical aspects and the policy implications."

All three bear out Shi's assertion that "the people who have succeeded in maintaining a commitment to simplicity over time are disproportionately people with a powerful spiritual foundation—that is, some sort of transcendent element in their outlook that gives them the fortitude and the tenacity to maintain this mode of living in the face of all of the conflicting tendencies and temptations around us." Robin talks a great deal about God and about the relationship between simpler living and spiritual development. Evy McDonald, who runs the New Road Map Foundation with Robin, has written a "Group Study Guide for Contemporary Christians" to be used with *Your Money or Your Life*. The curriculum has been tested by church groups in a variety of denominations. McDonald is now studying to become a United Methodist pastor. Indeed, Robin and McDonald's work reminds one of the dictum that summarizes John Wesley's economic advice: "Earn all you can, save all you can, give all you can."

Andrews has been a Quaker and is now a Unitarian. She was raised as a Methodist. "My church taught me both to think things through and to be concerned with social justice," she said. "I see simplicity as a core social-issue. People worry about how our way of life, our consumption patterns, are affecting people around the world. They're taking seriously that quote from Gandhi, 'Live simply so that others may simply live.'"

"For years now I've gone back and forth between the Quakers and the Unitarians," Andrews said. "I love the Quaker philosophy, and the silence. But Quakers are quiet people, and I'm not. Unitarians are loud and talkative, like I am. My church voted that morally responsible consumerism should be the main issue Unitarians study and discuss this year. Because they provide both spiritual nurture and community, churches are going to have a central role in the simplicity movement—and the movement may help to revitalize the church."

Luhrs was raised as a Catholic but doesn't belong to a church. "I'm still probably a Catholic at heart," she said. "But I've opened up to a much more eclectic spirituality. I've done a lot of meditation and exploring of different kinds of spiritual traditions. I consider simplicity as a spiritual way of life—if you stop working around the clock or worrying about being in debt or shopping compulsively, then you have time to try to be a better person rather than just an accumulator. Spending time cultivating your virtues rather than your closet is a wonderful way to live."

Robin, Andrews and Luhrs each have projects under way that build on their previous work. Robin is gathering material for a book about how people define and use the freedom that *Your Money or Your Life* is designed to help them find. "Though the book is extremely effective, taking all nine of the steps it advocates is quite challenging because we tend to be uneasy with that degree of freedom. People wonder, 'What will I do with myself if my teacher, my boss, my society aren't telling me what to do? How do I give of myself? What is myself?' We've handed people a solution, but we're also handing them another problem. I've been interviewing people from all kinds of backgrounds and cultures. The variability in the way people define freedom is fascinating. God gave us free will. It's what distinguishes us from other creatures. So not to know how to use our freedom well is misusing our greatest gift."

Andrews is addressing the social-justice implications of simplicity. "I'm trying to figure out how we can talk about this with poor people," she said. "I would never use the word 'simplicity' with people who are struggling to meet their basic needs. Our emphasis on consumption, and the growing gap between the rich and poor, presents a self-esteem issue for poor people and a threat to our democracy. The expense of political campaigns gives the poor less and less of a voice in government and society. A lot of us grew up in families that wouldn't seem at all affluent now. But people felt OK about themselves. Now poor people are learning to judge themselves as losers. They see luxuries on TV and think, 'I should have that, I'd be happy if I had that.' But very few will ever have those luxuries."

"I'm trying out a new idea for how I can talk about values with poor people without coming across as Lady Bountiful. I'm working with a newspaper for the homeless on movie reviews from a poor person's perspective. It's also a way of educating the middle class about the viewpoints of the poor, since middle-class folks buy these newspapers and like to read reviews. And I'm facilitating a writing project for poor people."

Luhrs is working on a book on the effect of simple living on intimate relationships. "I find that the people interested in simplicity live together more consciously, with more awareness," she said. "They really put a lot of time, effort and thought into their relationships. Simple living means a lot of different things for them. Some think of it as a sort of inner simplicity that consists of being more honest about who they are. For some, it's simplifying their outer lives so they're not spending their time fighting about money or worrying about debt. Working together on these lifestyle issues makes people feel closer to each other."

It is significant that these three leaders of the simplicity movement are women, and that women are disproportionately represented throughout the current movement. In holding full time jobs and fighting their way up the corporate ladder while raising children and trying to maintain homes and families, women have perhaps been more conscious of the frenetic demands of life and more inclined to change priorities. (In the past, men like Alcott and Emerson were the public spokesmen for the simplicity ideal, but of course women did much of the work that made simple living possible.)

Though Shi contends that simplicity movements go through cycles and rarely manage to build a long lasting structure, Robin, Andrews and Luhrs think that the movement has become so mainstream that it won't go away. Their own opportunities to speak are increasing, and they see their audiences growing. The call for a simpler and more intentional, sustainable and meaningful way of life continues to find a deep resonance.

## Review

1. Is the voluntary simplicity movement a recent phenomenon or does it have historical roots? Explain your answer.

2. Discuss the philosophy of the voluntary simplicity movement.

3. What, according to the advocates, are the implications of simplicity for social justice and intimate relationships?

## Applications

1. Interview five students. Ask them about their aspirations for their lives—what kind of work they want to do and what kind of lifestyle they hope to maintain. Also ask them how the lifestyle they hope to achieve compares with that of their parents. Do any of them indicate a desire for simplicity? Or do they aspire to replicate or surpass their parents' lifestyle?

2. Do you agree or disagree with the philosophy of the voluntary simplicity movement? Write an essay explaining your position. Point out how your position will affect your life decisions.

## Related Web Sites

1. *http://portland.indymedia.org/en/2004/ 01/278231.shtml*. News article about

the extent of involuntary downward mobility in the United States.

2. *http://www.webster.edu/~corbetre/philosophy/simple/downward.html.* One man's thoughts about the value and rewards of adopting a simpler lifestyle.

# 44

# Do Social Movements Make Any Difference?

*David S. Meyer*

**W***hat are your options if you are concerned about the environment, peace, racial and gender equality, or other social issues? An often-heard saying is, if you don't like the way things are going, register your opposition at the ballot box. Some Americans are convinced that the best way to bring about desired change is through their votes.*

*Others, however, come together in various organizations that constitute a **social movement**. Social movements are organized efforts to promote or resist some kind of change. They illustrate well the approach of **conflict theorists**, who stress the inherent conflict of interests between various groups in society and the need for social action in order to pursue those interests. There are, however, various ways to pursue interests.*

*Some individuals, who are a part of a movement, lobby politicians. Some engage in vigorous educational campaigns. Others resort to tactics like disruption of social life, civil disobedience, and even violence. The question raised in this selection is: Whatever the specific tactics employed, do social movements bring about the desired change? And even if not all the aims are realized, how many of the gains made by environmentalists, women, racial/ethnic minorities, peace activists, and others can be attributed to the efforts of the movements and how much would have occurred anyway? Such questions are addressed in this selection as David Meyer examines a variety of social movements and their impact on social change.*

**S**ocial movement activists, such as those who protested the Iraq War often become discouraged when their immediate goals are not attained. But research shows that such movements can have deep and long-lasting consequences for politics, society and the activists themselves.

In January 2003, tens if not hundreds of thousands of people assembled in Washington, D.C. to try to stop the impending invasion of Iraq. It did not look good for the demonstrators. Months earlier, Congress authorized President Bush to use force to disarm Iraq, and Bush repeatedly said that he would not let the lack of international support influence his decision about when—or whether—to use military force. Opposition to military action grew in the intervening months; the Washington demonstration coincided with sister events in San Francisco, Portland, Tampa, Tokyo, Paris, Cairo, and Moscow. Protests, albeit smaller and less frequent, continued after the war began. Did any of them change anything? Could they have? How? And how would we know if they did?

Such questions are not specific to this latest peace mobilization, but are endemic to protest movements more generally. Social movements are organized challenges to authorities that use a broad range of tactics, both inside and outside of conventional politics, in an effort to promote social and political change. Opponents of the Iraq War wrote letters to elected officials and editors of newspapers, called talk radio shows and contributed money to antiwar groups. Many also invited arrest by civil disobedience; some protesters, for example, blocked entrances to government offices and military bases. A group of 50 "Unreasonable Women of West Marin" lay naked on a northern California beach, spelling out "Peace" with their bodies for a photographer flying overhead. Besides using diverse methods of protest, opponents of the war also held diverse political views. Some opposed all war, some opposed all U.S. military intervention, while others were skeptical only about this particular military intervention. This is a familiar social movement story: broad coalitions stage social movements, and differences within a movement coalition are often nearly as broad as those between the movement and the authorities it challenges.

Political activists and their targets act as if social movements matter, and sociologists have been trying, for the better part of at least four decades, to figure out why, when and how. It is too easy—and not very helpful—to paint activists as heroes or, alternatively, as cranks. It is similarly too easy to credit them for social change or, alternatively, to dismiss their efforts by saying that changes, such as advances in civil rights or environmental protections, would have happened anyway. What we have learned is that social movements are less a departure from conventional institutional politics than an extension of them—a "politics by other means." In the end, we find that movements crest and wane, often failing to attain their immediate goals, but they can lastingly change political debates, governmental institutions and the wider culture.

It is often difficult to tell whether activism makes a difference because the forces that propel people to mobilize are often the same forces responsible for social change. For example, it is difficult to decide whether the feminist movement opened new opportunities to women or whether economic changes fostered both the jobs and feminism. Also, authorities challenged by movements deny that activism influenced their decisions. What politicians want to admit that their judgments can be affected by "mobs"? Why risk encouraging protesters in the future? Finally, movements virtually never achieve all that their partisans demand, and so activists are quick to question their own influence. As a result, proving that movements influence politics and policy involves difficult detective work.

But research shows that social movements can affect government policy, as well as how it is made. And movement influence extends further. Activism often profoundly changes the activists, and through them, the organizations in which they participate, as well as the broader culture. The ways that movements make a difference are complex, veiled, and take far longer to manifest themselves than the news cycle that covers a single demonstration, or even a whole protest campaign.

## When Movements Emerge

Activists protest when they think it might help them achieve their goals—goals they might not accomplish otherwise. Organizers successfully mobilize movements when they convince people that the issue at hand is urgent, that positive outcomes are possible and that their efforts could make a difference. In the case of the war on Iraq, for example, President Bush set the agenda for a broad range of activists by explicitly committing the country to military intervention. More conventional politics—elections, campaign contributions and letter-writing—had already played out and it became clear that none of these activities were sufficient, in and of themselves, to stop the war. In addition, the President's failure to build broad international or domestic support led activists to believe that direct pressure might prevent war. The rapid worldwide growth of the movement itself encouraged activism, assuring participants that they were part of something larger than themselves, something that might matter. In effect, President Bush's actions encouraged anti-war activism to spread beyond a small group of perpetual peace activists to a broader public.

With peace movements, it is clear that threat of war helps organizers mobilize people. Threats generally help political opposition grow beyond conventional politics. Movements against nuclear armaments, for example, emerge strongly when governments announce they are building more weapons. Similarly, environmental movements expand when government policies toward forests, pesticides, or toxic wastes become visibly negligent. In the case of abortion politics, each side has kept the other mobilized for more than 30 years by periodically threatening to take control of the issue. In each of these cases, those who lose in traditional political contests such as elections or lobbying campaigns often take to the streets.

Other sorts of movements grow when the promise of success arises. American civil rights activists, for example, were able to mobilize most broadly when they saw signals that substantial change was possible. Rosa Parks knew about Jackie Robinson and *Brown v. Board of Education*—as well as Gandhian civil disobedience—before deciding not to move to the back of the bus in Montgomery, Alabama. Government responsiveness to earlier activism—such as President Truman's desegregation of the armed forces and calling for an anti-lynching law—though limited, fitful, and often strategic, for a time encouraged others in their efforts. And the success of African American activists encouraged other ethnic groups, as well as women, to pursue social change through movement politics.

As social movements grow, they incorporate more groups with a broader range of goals and more diverse tactics. Absent a focus like an imminent war, activists inside and political figures outside compete with one another to define movement goals and objectives. Political authorities often respond with policy concessions designed to diminish the breadth and depth of a movement. While such tactics can divide a movement, they are also one way of measuring a movement's success.

## How Movements Matter: Public Policy

By uniting, however loosely, a broad range of groups and individuals, and taking action, social movements can influence public policy, at least by bringing attention to their issues. Newspaper stories about a demonstration pique political, journalistic and public interest in the demonstrators' concerns. By bringing scrutiny to a contested policy, activists can promote alternative thinking. By displaying a large and engaged constituency, social movements provide political support for leaders sympathetic to their concerns. Large demonstrations show that there are passionate citizens who might also donate money, work in campaigns, and vote for candidates who will speak for them. Citizen mobilization against abortion, taxes, and immigra-

tion, for example, has encouraged ambitious politicians to cater to those constituencies. In these ways, social movement activism spurs and supports more conventional political action.

Activism outside of government can also strengthen advocates of minority positions within government. Social movements—just like presidential administrations and congressional majorities—are coalitions. Antiwar activists in the streets may have strengthened the bargaining position of the more internationalist factions in the Bush administration, most notably Colin Powell, and led, at least temporarily, to diplomatic action in the United Nations. Mobilized opposition also, for a time, seemed to embolden Congressional critics, and encouraged lesser-known candidates for the Democratic presidential nomination to vocally oppose the war.

Social movements, by the popularity of their arguments, or more frequently, the strength of their support, can convince authorities to re-examine and possibly change their policy preferences. Movements can demand a litmus test for their support. Thus, George H. W. Bush, seeking the Republican nomination for president in 1980, revised his prior support for abortion rights. A few years later, Jesse Jackson likewise reconsidered his opposition to abortion. Movements raised the profile of the issue, forcing politicians not only to address their concerns, but to accede to their demands.

Although movement activists promote specific policies—a nuclear freeze, an equal rights amendment, an end to legal abortion, or, more recently, a cap on malpractice awards—their demands are usually so absolute that they do not translate well into policy. (Placards and bumper stickers offer little space for nuanced debate.) Indeed, the clearest message that activists can generally send is absolute rejection: no to nuclear weapons, abortion, pesticides or taxes. These admonitions rarely become policy, but by promoting their programs in stark moral terms, activists place the onus on others to offer alternative policies that are, depending on one's perspective, more moderate or complex. At the same time, politicians often use such alternatives to capture, or at least defuse, social movements. The anti-nuclear weapons movement of the late 1950s and early 1960s did not end the arms race or all nuclear testing. It did, however, lead to the Limited Test Ban Treaty, which ended atmospheric testing. First Eisenhower, then Kennedy, offered arms control proposals and talks with the Soviet Union, at least in part as a response to the movement. This peace movement established the framework for arms control in superpower relations, which subsequently spread to the entire international community.

In these ways, activists shape events—even if they do not necessarily get credit for their efforts or achieve everything they want. The movement against the Vietnam War, for instance, generated a great deal of attention which, in turn, changed the conduct of that war and much else in domestic politics. President Johnson chose bombing targets with attention to minimizing political opposition; President Nixon, elected at least partly as a result of the backlash against the antiwar movement nonetheless tailored his military strategy to respond to some of its concerns. In later years, he suggested that the anti-war movement made it unthinkable for him to threaten nuclear escalation in Vietnam—even as a bluff. In addition, the movement helped end the draft, institutionalizing all-volunteer armed forces. And, according to Colin Powell, the Vietnam dissenters provoked a new military approach for the United States, one that emphasized the use of overwhelming force to minimize American casualties. Thus, the military execution of the 1991 Persian Gulf War was influenced by an anti-war movement that peaked more than three [*sic*] decades earlier. This is significant, if not the effect most anti-war activists envisioned.

## Political Institutions

Social movements can alter not only the substance of policy, but also how policy is made. It is not uncommon for governments to create new institutions, such as departments and agencies, in response to activists' demands. For example, President Kennedy responded to the nuclear freeze movement by establishing the Arms Control and Disarmament Agency, which became a permanent voice and venue in the federal bureaucracy for arms control. A glance at any organizational chart of federal offices turns up numerous departments, boards, and commissions that trace their origins to popular mobilization. These include the Department of Labor, the Department of Housing and Urban Development, the National Labor Relations Board, the Environmental Protection Agency, the National Council on Disability, the Consumer Product Safety Commission and the Equal Employment Opportunity Commission. Although these offices do not always support activist goals, their very existence represents a permanent institutional concern and a venue for making demands. If, as environmentalists argue, the current Environmental Protection Agency is often more interested in facilitating exploitation of the environment than in preventing it, this does not negate the fact that the environmental movement established a set of procedures through which environmental concerns can be addressed.

Government responses to movement demands also include ensuring that diverse voices are heard in decision-making. In local zoning decisions, for example, environmental impact statements are a now a routine part of getting a permit for construction. Congress passed legislation establishing this requirement in 1970 in response to the growing environmental movement. Indeed, movement groups, including Greenpeace and the Sierra Club, negotiated directly with congressional sponsors. Similarly, juries and judges now routinely hear victim impact statements before pronouncing sentences in criminal cases, the product of the victims' rights movement. Both public and private organizations have created new departments to manage and, perhaps more importantly, document personnel practices, such as hiring and firing, to avoid being sued for discrimination on the basis of gender, ethnicity or disability. Workshops on diversity, tolerance, and sexual harassment are commonplace in American universities and corporations, a change [in] just two decades that would have been impossible to imagine without the activism of the 1960s and 1970s. In such now well-established bureaucratic routines, we can see how social movements change practices, and through them, beliefs.

Social movements also spawn dedicated organizations that generally survive long after a movement's moment has passed. The environmental movement, for example, firmly established a "big ten" group of national organizations, such as the Wildlife Defense Fund, which survives primarily by raising money from self-defined environmentalists. It cultivates donors by monitoring and publicizing government actions and environmental conditions, lobbying elected officials and administrators, and occasionally mobilizing supporters to do something more than mail in their annual membership renewals. Here, too, the seemingly permanent establishment of "movement organizations" in Washington, D.C. and in state capitals across the United States has—even if these groups often lose—fundamentally changed policymaking. Salaried officers of the organizations routinely screen high-level appointees to the judiciary and government bureaucracy and testify before legislatures. Mindful of this process, policymakers seek to preempt their arguments by modifying policy—or at least their rhetoric.

## Political Activists

Social movements also change the people who participate in them, educating as well as mobilizing activists, and thereby promoting ongoing awareness and action that extends beyond the boundaries of one movement or campaign. Those who turn out at anti-war demonstrations today have often cut their activist teeth mobilizing against globalization, on behalf of labor, for animal rights or against welfare reform. By politicizing communities, connecting people, and promoting personal loyalties, social movements build the infrastructure not only of subsequent movements, but of a democratic society more generally.

Importantly, these consequences are often indirect and difficult to document. When hundreds of thousands of activists

march to the Supreme Court to demonstrate their support for legal abortion, their efforts might persuade a justice. More likely, the march signals commitment and passion to other activists and inspires them to return home and advocate for abortion rights in their communities across the country, thereby affecting the shape of politics and culture more broadly.

The 2003 anti-Iraq War movement mobilized faster, with better organizational ties in the United States and transnationally, than, for example, the movement against the 1991 Persian Gulf War. But how are we to assess its influence? Many activists no doubt see their efforts as having been wasted, or at least as unsuccessful. Moreover, supporters of the war point to the rapid seizure of Baghdad and ouster of Saddam Hussein's regime as evidence of the peace movement's naiveté. But a movement's legacy extends through a range of outcomes beyond a government's decision of the moment. It includes consequences for process, institutional practices, organizations and individuals. This anti-war movement changed the rhetoric and international politics of the United States' preparation for war, leading to a detour through the United Nations that delayed the start of war. The activists who marched in Washington, San Francisco and Los Angeles may retreat for a while, but they are likely to be engaged in politics more intensively in the future. This may not be much consolation to people who marched to stop a war, but it is true. To paraphrase a famous scholar: activists make history, but they do not make it just as they please. In fighting one political battle, they shape the conditions of the next one.

## Recommended Resources

Arkin, William M. "The Dividends of Delay." *Los Angeles Times*, February 23, 2003. Arkin details the influence of the peace movement on U.S. military strategy in the Iraq War.

Giugni, Marco, Doug McAdam, and Charles Tilly. *How Social Movements Matter.* Minneapolis, MN: University of Minnesota Press, 1999. This collection employs diverse approaches in examining the outcomes of social movements across a range of cases.

Klatch, Rebecca. *A Generation Divided: The New Left, The New Right, and the 1960s.* Berkeley,

CA: University of California Press, 1999. Klatch traces individual life stories of activists on both ends of the political spectrum during a turbulent period and beyond.

McAdam, Doug, and Yang Su. "The War at Home: Antiwar Protests and Congressional Voting, 1965 to 1973." *American Sociological Review* 67 (2002): 696–721. Antiwar protests set an agenda for Congress, forcing resolutions about the war, but could not influence the outcomes of those votes.

Meyer, David S. "Protest Cycles and Political Process: American Peace Movements in the Nuclear Age." *Political Research Quarterly* 46 (1993): 451–79. This article details how government responses to peace movements affect policy and subsequent political mobilization.

Meyer, David S., Nancy Whittier, and Belinda Robnett, eds. *Social Movements: Identity, Culture, and the State.* New York: Oxford University Press, 2002. A collection that addresses the link between protesters and context across different settings and times.

Rochon, Thomas. *Culture Moves: Ideas, Activism, and Changing Values.* Princeton, NJ: Princeton University Press, 1998. Rochon looks at social movements as a primary way to promote new ideas and alter culture.

Tarrow, Sidney. *Power in Movement.* New York: Cambridge University Press, [1994] 1998. A broad and comprehensive review of scholarship on movements, synthesized in a useful framework.

## Review

1. Why is it difficult to determine whether various changes occur because of the efforts of a social movement?

2. Discuss some of the conditions that give rise to a social movement.

3. How do social movements affect public policy? Give some examples.

4. Discuss the effects of social movements on political institutions and on the people who participate in the movements.

## Application

Select one of the social movements mentioned in this selection that is of interest to you. Using an Internet search engine or library resources, see if you can find any information about change that can be attributed to the movement. Also note whether the movement failed to bring about specific kinds of change it advocated. What tactics were involved? What finally seemed to bring about the change? Do you think the participants in the movement were satisfied with the outcome? On the basis of your findings, what would you recommend to people who want to successfully pursue some kind of change (or resist some kind of change) through a social movement?

## Related Web Sites

1. *www.wsu.edu/~amerstu/smc/smcframe. html.* This site provides numerous articles and links for a wide variety of social movements.

2. *womhist.binghamton.edu/.* More than a thousand documents and numerous links to other sites that deal with women and social movements.

---

# Subject Index

CPSIA information can be obtained at www.ICGtesting.com
Printed in the USA
BVOW07s0211280514

354512BV00003B/8/P